You Must Set Forth at Dawn

Wole Soyinka

You Must Set Forth at Dawn

A Memoir

METHUEN

in association with

Published in 2007 by Methuen in association with Bookcraft

Methuen Publishing Ltd, 11–12 Buckingham Gate, London SW1E 6LB

www.methuen.co.uk

Bookcraft Ltd, 23 Adebajo Street, Kongi Layout, New Bodija Estate, Ibadan, Nigeria

www.bookcraftafrica.com

ISBN: 978-0-413-77628-0

A CIP catalogue record for this book is available from the British Library

Photo credits: every effort has been made to identify copyright holders. In case of oversight, and upon notification to the publishers, corrections will be made in subsequent printings. Unless otherwise noted, all photos are from the author's collection: 3, 4, 6 and 8, Hope Photo Studio; 5, Babs Photo Service; 9, Martin Banham; 10, Nicholas Treatt (Paris); 11, Felix Adenaike; 14 and 15, *Daily Times*; 16, *Tell Magazine*; 17, Michel Claude (UNESCO); 18 and 19, *The Guardian*; 23, United Nations (UN); 26, *The News*; 28, the White House; 30, Kole Omotoso; 33, Fatai Adiyeloja. Photo inserts researched, edited, and designed by Bankole Olayebi, with the assistance of Ify Anyanwu, Ayo Olofintuade, Mercy Roberts and Gbenga Sogbetun.

Maps on pages xi–xiii created by David Garner. Map on page xiv created by Sherifat Oladokun.

Book Design: Bankole Olayebi, Ify Anyanwu and Mercy Roberts.

Printed and bound in Great Britain by Biddles Ltd, King's Lynn, Norfolk

To all the fallen in our common cause,

and to the surviving, scars and all, clamorous or hidden.

....

To all my stoically resigned children.

....

And to my wife, Adefolake, who,

during the season of a deadly dictatorship, demoted me

from the designation of Visiting Professor to that of

Visiting Spouse, but was still left with only an

Invisible Spouse as I was swallowed by

my study even during visiting hours.

Contents

Acknowledgements

FIRST ACKNOWLEDGMENT GOES TO MY RELAY OF editors, Ann Godoff, Ileene Smith, and Will Murphy. To this heroic triad, I extend, additionally, one hand in sympathy, and the other as a sign of exoneration for any flaws in this tract, since I am quite certain that these are the result of my own decisions.

For data checks, I am deeply indebted to Kunle Ajibade, Tunde Awosanmi, Laolu Akande, Etienne Galle my French translator, and Bankole Olayebi my Nigerian publisher. They have had to compensate for the diary I have never kept and for a kaleidoscopic mental gadget that sometimes pretends to the function of memory, not to mention the loss of useful documentation, the result of raids on my home during the Nigerian season of dictatorship insanity or, simply of a peripatetic existence.

My gratitude also goes to the W. E. B. Du Bois Institute, Harvard University, and the International Institute of Modern Letters, University of Nevada, for conditions of attachment that enabled me to devote some time in between global crisscrossing to another biographical undertaking, one which, in my more rational moments, I had sworn I would not extend beyond "the age of innocence", as delimited in *Aké: The Years of Childhood*.

Lastly, it would be churlish not to acknowledge the industry of those assiduous scribblers whose monographs, conference papers etc., on the life of this subject finally goaded me into abandoning a rational decision: not to pursue the task of recollection and reflection beyond the age of innocence calculated at roughly eleven and a bit. While, unlike those authoritative voices, I still hesitate to claim definitive knowledge of the subject, I can at least flaunt the advantage of having lived with him all his life, without even a day off, which is far longer than has any other being on the literary planet.

The States of Nigeria, 1955-1995

Three Regions, 1955

Four Regions, 1963

Twelve States, 1967

Nineteen States, 1976

Twenty-one States, 1987

Thirty States, 1991

Thirty-six States, 1995

Chronology

POLITICAL MILESTONES IN NIGERIA SINCE 1960

1960
1 October   Independence from Britain

1962
May   State of emergency declared in Western Region;
                abortive census exercise

1963
August   MidWest Region created
1 October   Nigeria becomes a republic
November   Census shows a population of 55.67 million

1964
December   Election crisis

1965
Oct–Dec   Political crisis deepens after Western Regional elections

1966
15 January   First military coup: overthrow of First Republic and
                establishment of Ironsi regime
29 July   Second military coup: establishment of Gowon regime
Sept–Oct   Ad Hoc constitutional conference

1967

January	Aburi meeting to forestall imminent civil war
27 May	Creation of twelve states to replace four regions
30 May	Military governor Odumegwu Ojukwu announces secession of Eastern Region and declares Republic of Biafra
6 July	Start of Civil War

1970

12 January	End of Civil War

1973

November	Provisional census finds population of 79.76 million; later annulled

1975

29 July	Third military coup: establishment of Murtala Mohammed regime

1976

3 February	Twelve states replaced by nineteen states
13 February	Fourth military coup (abortive); Murtala Mohammed assassinated. General Olusegun Obasanjo becomes Head of State

1978

21 September	1979 Constitution promulgated, ban on politics lifted

1979

1 October	Inauguration of Alhaji Shehu Shagari as civilian president and establishment of Second Republic

1980

December	Fundamentalist Muslim uprising in Kano (Maitatsine riots)

1981

22 June	Governor Balarabe Musa of Kaduna State impeached

1983

13 Aug–3 Sept	Federal and state elections
31 December	Fifth military coup: establishment of Buhari regime

1985

27 August	Sixth military coup: establishment of Babangida regime
20 December	Seventh military coup (abortive) announced; coup plotters, including Gen. Maman Vatsa, executed

1986

January	Return to civilian rule by 1 October announced; Political Bureau appointed.
February	Nigeria joins the Organisation of the Islamic Conference (OIC)

1987

March	Christian-Muslim clashes in Kafanchan, Kaduna, Zaria, Katsina
11 July	White paper on Political Bureau Report; timetable for return to civilian rule on 1 October 1992 announced
September	Two more states (Akwa Ibom and Katsina) created

1989

May	Constitution promulgated; two-party system adopted
5 October	Nigerian Electoral Commission recommends six out of thirteen political associations
7 October	Armed Forces Ruling Council (AFRC) dissolves all thirteen political associations and 'manufactures' two parties: National Republican Convention (NRC) and Social Democratic Party (SDP). Opposition calls for a national conference.

1990

22 April	Eighth military coup, led by Major Gideon Orkah (abortive)
August	ECOMOG moved to Liberia

1991

April	Muslim-Christian conflicts in Bauchi
27 August	States increased to thirty
12 December	Federal capital moved from Lagos to Abuja
14 December	Federal, state assembly, and gubernatorial elections

1992

2 January	Presidential election shifted to 5 December 1992
19 March	Census returns announced: 88.5 million

Aug–Sept	Party presidential primaries
October	AFRC annuls presidential primaries, dissolves NRC and SDP executive committees
November	Presidential election postponed to 12 June 1993, and date of hand-over to civilians to 27 August
5 December	National Assembly inaugurated

1993

2 January	Transitional Council headed by Ernest Shonekan appointed; National Defence and Security Council replaces AFRC. Calls resume for a Sovereign National Conference research.
29 March	Presidential candidates nominated: Bashir Tofa for NRC, M.K.O. Abiola for SDP
10 June	Abuja High Court grants Association for a Better Nigeria (ABN) an injunction to stop presidential election
12 June	Presidential election still held
16 June	ABN secures another injunction to stop further release of election results by NEC
23 June	Presidential election annulled; NEC and transition programme suspended
27 August	Dictator Ibrahim Badamasi Babangida 'steps aside'; Interim National Government (ING) named, with Ernest Shonekan as Head of State
10 September	19 February 1994 announced as date for new presidential election
24 September	Abiola returns from self-exile
10 November	Lagos High Court declares ING illegal
17 November	Ninth military coup: establishment of Abacha regime. All democratic and transition structures dissolved.

1994

14 January	Commission for Constitutional Conference appointed
May	National Democratic Coalition (NADECO) issues ultimatum to the Abacha regime to relinquish power by 31 May
June–July	Abiola proclaims himself president, paralysing anti-government restoration of 12 June presidential election. Strikes and demonstrations by oil workers and other civil society constituents.

July	Constitutional Conference begins
December	'First Phase' of Transition to Civil Rule programme which stipulated 17 January 1995 as date of lifting of ban on politics, announced

1995

March	Coup plot involving former Head of State, General Olusegun Obasanjo and forty-four others 'uncovered'. Obasanjo goes on trial with others. Death sentence later commuted to life imprisonment.
27 July	Report of Constitutional Conference submitted
1 October	'Comprehensive' timetable for return to civil rule on 1 October 1998 announced
10 November	Ken Saro-Wiwa and eight other Ogoni minority rights activists executed; worldwide condemnation
11 November	Nigeria expelled from Commonwealth

1996

30 September	Five new political parties announced
1 October	Six more states and 138 local government areas created

1998

June	Sani Abacha dies. Abubaker Abdulsalami takes over and immediately begins to release political detainees including former Head of State, Olusegun Obasanjo.
July	M.K.O. Abiola dies suddenly. Renewed calls for a Sovereign National Conference.

1999

May	Olusegun Obasanjo is sworn in as civilian president after disputed election. Calls for a Sovereign National Conference continue.

2000

December	Oputa Panel for Human Rights inaugurated

2001

December 23	The nation's attorney general, Bola Ige, is assassinated in his house

2003

May — Obasanjo re-elected amidst accusation of massive rigging. Public calls for a Sovereign National Conference remain unabated; Obasanjo refuses.

2004

Acquittal of Bola Ige's accused murders, including prime suspect, former Osun State Deputy Governor, Iyiola Omisore.

2005

February — To stifle calls for a Sovereign National Conference, Obasanjo sets up National Political Reform Conference. Its composition and terms of reference rejected by civil movements and some states who insist on a genuinely representative Sovereign National Conference.

June — South-South delegates to the conference walk out over dispute on how much oil revenue should go to oil producing areas

July — Obasanjo receives report of the conference and declares it a success. Opposition pronounce it a fraud, and proceed with plans for their own National Conference.

1 October — People's National Conference inaugurated in Lagos

ÌBÀ -
For Those Who Went Before

ÌBÀ-
For Those Who
Went Before

Outside myself at moments like this, heading home, I hesitate a moment to check if it is truly a living me. Perhaps I am just a disembodied self usurping my body, strapped into a business-class seat in the plane, being borne to my designated burial ground – the cactus patch in the grounds of my home in Abẹ̀òkúta, a mere hour's escape by road from the raucous heart of Lagos. Perhaps I am not really within the cabin of the plane at all, but lying in a coffin with the luggage, disguised as an innocent box to fool the superstitious, while my ghost persists in occupying a seat whose contours have grown familiar through five years of a restless exile that began in 1994. For my mind chooses this moment to travel twelve years backwards when, drained of all emotion, I accompanied the body of my friend Femi Johnson from Wiesbaden in Germany, bringing him home in defiance of the unfathomable conspiracy to leave him in that foreign land like a stray without ties of family and friends. And the pangs that assail me briefly stem from the renewed consciousness of the absence of this friend, whose thunderoll laughter and infectious joy of life would have overwhelmed those welcoming voices that I know await me at destination. Despite the eternal moment of farewell by his open coffin in the funeral parlour in Wiesbaden, it was difficult then, and remained continuously so to reconcile that self with the absence of a vitality that we had all taken so long for granted, his big but compact frame in a box, immaculately dressed as though simply from habit – be it in a double-breasted suit with a carnation freshly cut by his chauffeur from the frontage garden, then laid ritualistically beside his breakfast set, or else in his casual outfit, its components no less carefully matched for all its seeming casualness, or his hunting attire that appeared selected for a genteel English countryside ramble instead of a *rumble in the jungle*. Difficult to accept the closed eyes which would bulge under some inspired business idea, the prospect of a gastronomic spread at the sight of a passing, generously endowed female or simply charged with a newly thought up mischief – but always lighting up the space around him. Still, I could not rest until I had brought him home, exhuming him from the graveyard in Wiesbaden, and the clinicality of my motions at the time made me wonder if I had left my soul in that alien graveyard in his stead.

It must be of course the coincidence of the airline that triggers off such a sombre recollection, in the main – that final homecoming for Femi was also on a Lufthansa flight. And it was a coming home for me also, since my moment to moment existence from the time of his death, until his re-burial, was only in some ethereal zone, peopled by eyes of the restless dead, from distances of silent rebuke. I came back down to earth only when he was himself within the earth of his choice, earth that he had made his own – Ìbàdàn. And it is this that now reinforces the unthinkable and irrational, that this same Femi – OBJ to numerous friends, business partners and acquaintances – is not in Ìbàdàn at this moment awaiting my return, his sweaty face, black as the cooking pot, supervising the kitchen in a frenzy of anticipation, and an array of wines lined up to celebrate a long anticipated reunion! Femi should be alive for this moment. If any being deserves and could contain in himself the entirety of the emotions that belong to this return, it is none other than OBJ, and he is gone.

It is a long craved homecoming, my personalised seal on the end of the nightmare that was signalled by the death of a tyrant, Sani Abacha, yet here I am, trying to find reasons for my lack of feeling, trying to ensure that it is not just a mask, a perverse exercise in control, this absence of the sheerest quickening of the pulse. It is that other homeward journey of twelve years past that stubbornly sticks to the mind, that of a friend, forever still in a casket in the belly of the plane. I, seated among the living, but stone cold to the world, conscious of this fact but only in a detached way, and wondering why I was still so devoid of the sensation of loss. It could be, I acknowledge, the aftermath of the battle to bring home his remains – plainly it had left me drained of all feeling. This return has not, so it must be that I have carried that home so obsessively in my head these past five years that I am unable to experience the journey as one towards the recovery of a zone of deprivation. The absence of Femi, who persists in looming large, a territory of dulled bereavement, is only a part of it. The adrenalin had been secreted over time, stored up and then – *pfft* – evaporated in an instant, there being no further use for it.

One seeks these explanations somewhat desultorily, since I already acknowledge that this is not quite the homecoming I had anticipated, not quite the way my return had been planned, not this legitimate arrival, swooping towards Lagos on a normal flight as if Lagos were Frankfurt, New York or Dakar. Surely it is not the same white-haired monster, that same WANTED man with a price on his head, hunted the world over, who is headed home, steadily lubricated from the aircraft's generous bar. I continue to interrogate the featureless flatness of my mind – compared to it, the pastel evenness of the Sahara desert over which we appear to be eternally suspended seems a craggy-wild, untamable and exotic piece of landscape.

I acknowledge that I am not much given to sentiment but after all, I am not normally averse to being welcomed home! Indeed, I often wonder if, for others similarly embattled, homecoming does not gradually become a central *motif* of their active existence. For instance, I find I dislike airport farewells – the exceptions have usually been preceded by some kind of tug-of-war to which I eventually yielded, often through emotional blackmail. By contrast, I am somewhat more accommodating with the motions of being welcomed back though, even here, I am just as likely to be found sneaking in through the back door. Generally, my inclination is simply – *to have returned. To find myself back where I never should have left.* Or where returning is no different from having never left, a routine recovery of a space of normal being, temporarily fractured, restoration of which has no significance whatsoever and requires no special recognition. In any case, each homecoming differs wildly from the last, and this goes back to my very earliest awareness of such an event – the end of a physical separation – that was when I first returned home from studying overseas – on New Year's Day, 1960, the year of Nigeria's Independence. Then, feeling already long-in-the-tooth at twenty-five, I had contrived to sneak home, to the discomfiture of parents, family and relations. Normally, such a return should have been an occasion for celebration, varying from modest and restricted to festive and all-embracing, the latter gathering in distant clans and even total strangers, with that ringing invocation that must have been adopted by the first-line beneficiaries of European education: *Our Argonaut has returned from over the seas after a long, perilous voyage in his quest for the Golden Fleece!* – or any of its hundred variations.

It is perhaps the sedateness of this return that continues to sit awkwardly on me, an abrupt usurpation of the other furtive homecoming that nearly was! Not that I regret the change, oh no, not for a moment! *T'ágbà bá ńdé, à á yé ogun jà* – thus goes the Yoruba wisdom – as one approaches an elder's status, one ceases to indulge in battles. Some hope! When that piece of wisdom was first voiced, a certain entity called Nigeria was not yet thought of. In any case, I appear to have failed in my ambition to 'grow old gracefully' – no more strife, no more susceptibilities to beauty's provocation, etc. – a process I had once confidently set to begin at the magic figure of 49, seven times seven, the sacred number of my companion deity, Úgún. But at least, I accept that there comes a moment when age dictates the avoidance of certain forms of engagement. That makes sense, and is also just. Indeed, to be thankful for this form of homecoming, I have only to recall one turbulent entry into Lagos – that of June 28th, 1993, in the violent aftermath of the cancellation of that year's presidential elections by the dictator, Ibrahim Babangida – now that was easily the most physical and foolhardy return of my existence, yet not so dangerous as the planned alternative to the present return may have proved, had it materialised. I should feel grateful that I have been saved the quieter, secretive and certainly most risk-laden mode of re-entry that was moving towards execution before Babangida's successor, General Sani Abacha, the 'Butcher of Abuja', kindly took his leave of the world. There comes a point in one's life when one should no longer be obliged to sneak into one's homeland through mangrove creeks and smugglers' haunts, and in ludicrous disguises!

I worry, therefore, about the absence of feeling, the absence of even a grateful nod to Providence, seek some reassurance that my senses are not fully dead, that the emotional province of the mind is still functioning. I obtain a measure of relief however, indeed I begin to worry now that the senses may be roaming out of control when, even within the recycled air of the plane's interior, overflying nothing but Sahara dunes and dust, I could swear, suddenly, that I already smell the humid air of Lagos, the fetid dungheaps, the raucous marketways and overcrowded streets. I am certain that I can hear, dominating even the steady purr of the jet engines, the noisy street vendors with their dubious bargains, the sly conspiratorial grins of some as they offer contraband of the most dangerous kind – and this had become routine even before I fled into exile in November 1994 – banned publications that they would slide out from under the pile of other journals, like pornography in other places – *psst!* They sidle up to motorists at traffic junctions and hold-ups, with the mainstream journals on conspicuous display. Then, indifferent to the risk that the prospective customer might turn out to be a secret service agent or one of Abacha's ubiquitous informers, they flash the sensational cover of *Tempo, The News, The Concord, Tell* or some other hit-and-run *samizdat* – SANI ABACHA BARES HIS FANGS! WHOM THE GODS WILL DESTROY! ABACHA'S AGENTS ON RAMPAGE: MOTHER KILLED, ELEVEN YEAR-OLD HELD HOSTAGE IN POLICE CELL! SCANDAL ROCKS ASO ROCK! WHO KILLED BAGAUDA KALTHO? Then, the cat-and-mouse games, the mandatory raids – some days, weeks, even months in police cells for these stubborn vendors, some of them no older than ten or eleven. And no sooner are they released than they are back on the streets. Even the police grew weary of the charade. Such sights filled one's blood stream with a political rush; the truth was however, that I would rather be miles distant from the obligations they imposed, 'taking my gun for a walk' in the bush, far from the stressful streets.

I cannot wait to repossess the bush, or maybe it is the other way round, let the bush re-possess me. The bush and its furtive breath. Refuge and solace. The mere thought brings in its train the *smells*, and soon my seat is isolated and wreathed in nothing but the very smells of the bush! The thought of resuming my forays into those silent growths finally quickens my pulse, hesitant, just perceptibly, sobered by the thought that Femi, whom I also taught to hunt, will no longer be a part of it. And yet, there perhaps is where I would most painlessly recover his presence – in those swathes of isolation, that terrain of so many sensory ambiguities. Enfolded within the tropical bush, the effect is tranquilising – until, of course, the moment of the approach of a quarry – not that the pulse quickens all that noticeably even then. It does not matter whether it is the Harmattan season of dry air with its parched or burnt vegetation – except in the early morning when the foliage is misted over and even the earth is deceptively damp – or the rainy season that leaves one tangling with moist thickets, fording swollen gorges, sliding on treacherous rocks and being sucked into mud gullies, day or night – at night – with nothing but a few stars seen through branches, or fireflies to test one's patience and judgment as you wonder whether they are the eyes of a wild cat, a tree cyrax or twin rain drops caught in the light of your night lamp.

All that matters is the escape into timelessness, interrupted by furtive pads of a four-footed quarry or the sudden burst of the brown bush-fowl or grey-streaked guinea-fowl soaring and screaming over trees. An instant only to decide whether or not the latter is worth the try – even if you downed it, how much time would it demand to plunge into the hostile fastness to retrieve your booty? In the process you become insensitive to the rank presence of a far larger quarry, the prized *egbin*,[1] or *ìgalà*,[2] or a patriarch or matriarch of the *ẹtù*[3] family, the arch-survivor of the species – *àdìmú* – whose heavy meat could feed a fair-sized company of guerrillas long lost in the bush... definitely it is the bush, the bush alone – smells, muted sounds, textures, and its often impenetrable silence that finally bathe me in a glow of warm anticipation. It is that, that alone, not any other resumption of relationships or recovery of suspended voices. Is this some form of misanthropy?

Or perhaps it is the suppressed fear that my house is gone anyway, that I am returning to a conspicuous gap in the landscape at which I had hacked and quarried, years before my departure, to give expression to my appetite for space. News of the invasion had reached me, but the dimension of the destruction had been vague and guarded, as if the kind couriers had agreed to hold back the worst. In truth, regarding the building itself, I had not planned to encase so much space within walls, just a small cottage, after my retirement from university service, but with as much grounds as I could afford. Still, hovel or mansion, the soldiers' violation hung over it, as it hung over many other homes that were owned by perceived enemies of the dictator, Sani Abacha. The house had been built almost entirely from the windfall of the Nobel Prize. I expanded it from its original design only because I wanted to create a space for the periodic retreat for writers and artistes – typical of fantasies of those who are suddenly bombarded with more money than family generations before them ever laid eyes on! Thus was born the notion of *Essay Foundation*, named after my father, whose initials S.A. had coalesced in my childhood mind as one word – *Essay*.[4]

The human landscape that I left behind has altered, irreversibly, deeply pockmarked with craters of loss. It was already near unbearably depleted with the loss of 'OBJ', the irrepressible Femi Johnson, but that a familiar feature both on the personal and national terrain, Ojetunji Aboyade, should vanish within a mere

---

[1] Quadruped of the deer/antelope family.
[2] Same as above.
[3] Large specimen of the rodent family.
[4] See *Aké, the Years of Childhood*.

three, four weeks of my departure seemed a perverse act of some vengeful deities – but, to what end? To impart an already conceded lesson on mortality? And the timing, so soon after my escape, seemed cruel.

My escape became known only when I had resurfaced at a press conference in UNESCO, towards the end of November. Two weeks later, I was back next door to Nigeria, in Cotonou, Benin Republic, a place largely populated by Nigerian nationals, especially the Yoruba. My family had been smuggled out to join me for a christmas/New Year reunion that might be the last for – who could tell how long? Our mainstay in Cotonou, Akin Fatoyinbo, himself once a prison actor in a Kafkaesque scenario under the regimen of an earlier dictatorship – that of Generals Buhari and Idiagbon – chose to break the news to me without any preliminaries. I was working at my improvised desk in our bungalow, rented for the season, when he drove in from Lagos. His face was stone as he placed the newspapers before me, wordlessly. A thick black banner across the front page seared my sight as it encountered the definitive pronouncement: PROFESSOR OJETUNJI ABOYADE DEAD! I swept the bunch of papers off the table, leapt up and walked away into the bedroom.

It was an indelible warning. By the end of this exile, the human landmarks to which I had grown accustomed would vanish, just like this, irremediably. Oje – hardly anyone ever called him by his full name – Oje had been my vice-chancellor at the University of Ifẹ̀ – later renamed Obáfẹ́mi Awólówò University after the death of that politician and sage, Obafemi Awolowo, a first-generation nationalist of Yoruba stock who never lost his political fire until his death in 1987. I never really knew how the attachment with Oje developed and deepened, but it was perhaps inevitable. He was one of that breed of tireless intellectual sparring partners, cunning at fashioning theoretical propositions that were guaranteed to provoke you and keep you in animated debate until lunch dissolved into dinner and then, late supper.

The news of his death left me with an irrational suspicion of a conspiracy of progressive abandonment by friends and colleagues, a sinister plan of deprivation of a valued landscape.

"No, thank you. I already feel superfluous."

"But that budgetary provision you're so concerned about – the IMF relief package – we could discuss it some more on the way to the airport."

At that point, I came clean. "No way", I said. "I saw Femi off at the airport and he never made it back. I am not accompanying you."

"I don't believe this" he shouted. "Look at you! All your *ṣákárà*[8] – beneath it all, soft. You're scared stiff. No, worse, you're superstitious."

I shrugged, unmoved. My mind was already made up. Into the earth-hugging ambulance, yes, but to follow and watch him being loaded into the winged counterpart, taking off into the same ozone that had swallowed Femi forever – out of the question! "Call me what you like", I shrugged. "I am not coming with you." I accompanied Femi virtually into the plane, and he vanished forever. This time, 'No'. This way, I know you'll be back in no time."

"Coward! I will never let you live this down."

"I'll survive that. Femi is not around to help you make a perpetual feast of it, so, once again – journey safely. I may visit you there, I may not. The beer is very good in Germany, by the way. Tell the doctors to pin the placard 'One Man, One Beer' by your bedside where you can see it. It will get you up and about in no time."

My fingers felt considerably lightened, and I began to tap out his graveside tribute, invoking his earlier match that ended in his favour...

Oje Aboyade had a close brush with death about four years before. Even the specialists at the German hospital who performed the life-saving operation on him marvelled at his survival. He became, in effect, a side-show for the students at the teaching hospital; they all came to examine his case-notes and gawk at the miracle man. His recovery was total, and it most certainly was not that ailment which finally took him away. After that 'refurbishment', and coming as he did from a long-

---

[8] Bravado.

*lived family, I most confidently expected him to outlive the rest of us,
and would often say so. That was careless; I should have remembered
the Nigerian killer factor. Simply defined, it is the stressful bane of the
mere act of critical thought within a society where power and control
remain the playthings of imbeciles, psychopaths and predators.*

Oje's close-cropped head, grudgingly pocked with a few white
tufts, rose before me, the deceptively mild roundness of his face
lightly lined with cicatrices of his Àwẹ origin. His name was an
instant giveaway – to the knowledgeable – as scion and heir of
the family ancestral masquerade, the *ọ̀jè*. So proud was he of this
legacy – deemed 'heathen' by the disciples of christianity and islam
– that he ensured that the names of his two male children bore the
prefix, *ọ̀jè*. Yet he was an unfailing Sunday worshipper at his church
in Bodija Housing Estate, Ìbàdàn, and even some kind of deacon.

Aboyade was deeply immersed in a project in Ìbàdàn – the
Development Policy Centre – long before I fled into exile. The seed
of the idea had been sown as far back as 1978, under the military
regime headed by General Olusegun Obasanjo – who would later
resurface as a civilian head of state in 1999. That original idea for
a civilian think tank had ended up as yet another military
appropriation, becoming the National Institute of Policy and
Strategic Studies located in the far North, in Kuru. General
Obasanjo blithely assumed that Oje would still agree to direct the
new institution, but no. It was not what he had envisioned. Not
only had his idea been purloined, it had become militarised.
Stubbornly but patiently, he persisted with his original vision,
finally began to see it take material form twenty years later. During
that earlier inception, I frequently accompanied Oje in the search
for a suitable location, and we settled on an estate being developed
near the Aṣèjìrẹ́ dam, just outside Ìbàdàn. I sat with him through
several brain-storming sessions with Obasanjo in Dodan Barracks,
Lagos, then the seat of government, poring over blueprints before
the military ruler appropriated it for his constituency. Finally, a
year before Oje's death, the original idea was back within Ìbàdàn,
on a more modest scale, but a fully civilian institution, and
independent of any government dictation.

Encumbered by other preoccupations, I drifted in and out of

the resurrected project. About four years before his death, Oje took me to the site where the offices were in quite an advanced state of construction. He had already recruited his team and earmarked my own office space – typically informing me of this with the utmost casualness, no prior consultation.

I wandered around – it seemed a logical retirement home for this ageing author and itinerant lecturer who, I had long acknowledged about myself, would remain creatively restless, right across the border of senility. The environment was finely balanced – within, but fully shielded from the sprawling city of Ìbàdàn. Already, the site seemed charged and vibrant, pulsating with intellectual energy – but then, I admit I am biased. Construction sites often affect me as inspiring spaces, potent with inchoate forms, and knowing that this one had materialised out of sheer persistence, and aspired to become a warehouse of cross-fertilizing minds, it was inevitable that I would imbue even the slurry caked cement mixer, temporarily silenced, with an intellectual fecundity. Sometimes it seemed a pity that a polished, elegant edifice should ever replace the chaotic terrain of the architectural Muse in labour – but of course one is ultimately consoled by beauty of a different kind – hopefully! An addict, I wandered over mounds of sand and gravel, stepping over uprooted stumps and negotiating reinforced concrete pillars. Pools of water from recent rains stagnated on the concrete flooring.

There were some smashed rocks, mostly flat slabs, scattered over the grounds, dug up during the laying of the foundation. Oje's collaborator and architect, Alhaji Adetunji, voiced a plaint about how or where to dispose of them – they did not fit into his landscaping scheme. Oje only pretended to mull over the problem, he was already nodding his head mischievously in my direction. The look on his face said clearly – *there's your godsend; you couldn't ask for a more accommodating scavenger.* My house in Abéòkúta – which to him was the structural expression of all unregistered idiosyncracies – was then approaching completion. I also pretended to think it over. A few days later, a lorry load of shale slabs and stones was dumped on my grounds, with a message that if I wanted any more, I would have to organise their transportation myself. That was typical of the Alhaji, a self-effacing persona who would say very little but act spontaneously and generously. The slabs and rocks went into the paving of the frontage of my Abẹ́òkúta home – and far more restricted 'Essay Foundation for the Humanities'.

The circumstances of Oje's departure resurrected twinges of that far more ancient, far closer bereavement, a leave-taking by my father, 'Essay', one that also took place *in absentia*, owing yet again to the exigencies of my political choices. My prison memoirs, *The Man Died*, published not long before his death, had not endeared me to the regime in power, and was unofficially banned from circulation. The dictatorship under which I underwent that prison spell – that of General Yakubu Gowon – still ruled our lives in 1972. It was nowhere near the viciousness of Abacha's, but not so benign that I dared fail to concede to my mother – the 'Wild Christian' of my childhood memoirs, *Aké* – the reasonableness of her warning, when she learnt of my plans to risk a return home. Her message to me was in character – *by all means, come home. I'll even send you a first class ticket. Understand however that you'll be coming for two funerals, the other one guaranteed by such folly.* I remained in London. Wild Christian survived her life companion several more years, and then was kind enough to transmit to me, in her own way, the moment of her passing away. Booked to fly to Ghana for a meeting on the fated day, indeed, already standing at the checking-in counter, my feet turned leaden. I refused to take the final, routine step for my boarding pass. Instead, I turned round, drove back to Ifẹ̀ to await – I did not know what. Doors and windows locked to give the illusion of absence, I awaited whatever it was that had made me turn back. It was there that the news found me.

Just as they had both done at my father's death, ignoring the fact that I was home and, with my siblings, had begun to immerse myself in the tasks that fall on the children, Oje and Femi still took charge of much of my own share of the arrangements, aided by Yemi Ogunbiyi, a former student who had become a colleague at Ifẹ̀. Wild Christian's funeral also took place in our second hometown, Ìṣarà, and she was buried next to her husband. I was

able to perform my ritual functions as ọmọ olókù, one of the
'children of bereavement', unlike my father's funeral when Oje
and OBJ stood surrogate. Their functions at his funeral were
anything but ritual. They smuggled in a tape on which I had
recorded my farewell, including lines from Dylan Thomas' poem
to his dying father, and ensured that it was played at the funeral
service. With both friends and accomplices gone, it was just as
well that I had no more parents to lose!

My mother's warning over Essay's funeral had not been
misplaced. Secret service agents – my eternal chaperons! –
swarmed the routes leading to the town, convinced that I would
indeed attempt to sneak into the country. They converged on the
church and, on hearing my voice over the loudspeakers, concluded
that I had eluded their net and was delivering the funeral tribute
in person. Soon enough, they discovered the mechanical source
of the voice and, once the service was over, swooped down on the
church in an effort to seize the tape – but why? To reassure their
bosses that I had not shown my face after all, that it was only my
disembodied voice that had evaded their roadblocks? Or to
interrogate the tape and find out by what agency it had landed in
the church? No matter, my two collaborators took charge, even
succeeded in hiding the recording machine itself – a bulky Grundig
– from the police agents and ensuring that the tape remained
where it belonged – with the family. Under Abacha, those agents
would not have waited until the funeral service was over. They
would have stormed the place of worship, arrested the tape
recorder and carted off the officiating prelates for interrogation!

On my political landscape, easily the most accusing void, created
by one who had been central to my mission in exile these past five
years – is that of the industrialist, Bashorun Moshood Kashimawo
Abiola. Abiola was the elected president of a nation who never
did preside over more than his home, his vast network of businesses
and, finally, his place of detention. It is a pointless habit, one knows,
to label what is clearly the crime of others as a failure in one's self,
but that irrational speculation sometimes lays claim to such a place
in our reverses. Ken Saro-Wiwa's death, on that dark Friday of

November 10, 1995, hanged together with eight of his companions in Port Harcourt prison, was another, a brutal, universally condemned act of judicial murder whose recollection, even now, chills one to the marrow. Abiola's was however, one of unmatchable, lingering cruelty. Robbed of victory, imprisoned and isolated from human contact for nearly four years and then, on the eve of his second victory, a victory that was signalled by the death of his gaoler and usurper of his mandate, Sani Abacha – to end up – wasted!

What the democratic aspirations of the nation had anticipated, following the sudden death of Abacha in June 1998, was a search for a negotiated future in which, logically, Abiola, the imprisoned president-elect, would play a central role, in all likelihood as the head of an interim government of national unity. No one of any note still denied that he had won the 1993 elections for the presidency. Then, one month after the death of Sani Abacha, in the presence of a delegation of United States officials – Thomas Pickering, a former ambassador to Nigeria, Susan Rice, a member of President Clinton's administration, etc., Abiola was served the cup of tea that has now attained legendary status in the nation. Abiola suffered a seizure minutes after that cup, collapsed and died. I try to recall if ever there was a Tantalus in Nigerian history or mythology but none seems adequate. Only D.O. Fagunwa's Ọgbójú Ọdẹ, the hero buried up to his neck in captivity, victim of a vicious palace conspiracy, comes close, but that was a tale that at least offered its readers the moral reward of a rescue, and a happy ending.

The truth, I know, will come out some day. Four years to effect his murder, but murder him they did in the end, and I cannot but feel that it was due to some insufficiency on our part, on mine, though I do not really know what I, or anyone in the democratic struggle, could have done to prevent it. It continues to strike me as grossly unfair that, a few days to his death, I should have been caught up in Vienna by a faxed message warning of his imminent murder. Because of that warning, and despite its futility both with regard to time and means, I tend to drag with me a nagging element of blame. It was small comfort that I would discover later that I was not the only recipient of the message whose text so clearly verged on the hysterical. Even at its most level, matter-of-fact register, this was a source we had learnt not to take lightly. In this instance, the frame of mind of this specific writer – we named our key information sources collectively *Longa Throat,* after Richard Nixon's Nemesis, *Deep Throat* – appeared to have affected his switches between upper and lower cases:

> *The only addendum the new regime and its collaborators has is to: ENSURE THAT CHIEF M.K.O. ABIOLA DOES NOT BECOME THE PRESIDENT OF NIGERIA IN WHATEVER FORM... Let me state here categorically that this is not a prediction at all. It is a pre-conceived plan of the new regime, exposed by an insider...*

> *THE IMPORTANT REPORT SENT TO ME TODAY: A NOTORIOUS GANG IN THE NIGERIAN ARMY has completed their plan to assassinate Chief Moshood Abiola as a final settlement of the ABACHA/ABIOLA war in a 'no victor, no vanquished way'. Believe it or not, if the report given to me is anything to go by, Chief Abiola's death could come within few days or before the end of September. This may look ridiculous, unthinkable or like an outright fabrication, but believe it or not, it is true. Tell Prof. and other pro-democracy groups both abroad and at home to mount a very intensive pressure on Abdulsalami to release Chief M.K.O. Abiola now!*

> *The new regime would fail to protect Chief Abiola from his assassins because it has not been able to persuade them to rethink the Nigerian National question. They might even seize power from Abubakar in order to achieve their destructive plan. These people are hell bent on destroying the corporate existence of Nigeria than see Abiola become the president.*

The last leg in the relay through which the message had travelled was none other than my son, Ilemakin, who had long thrown himself into the struggle on his own, slipped out of the country and begun to carry out some missions for the democracy movement. The desperate appeal finally reached its destination on my last day in Vienna, but only after the departure of Kofi Annan, Secretary-General of the United Nations. A day earlier, I had been locked in a tête-à-tête with him for nearly an hour and a half. He seemed quite relaxed, the human rights conference that had brought us both to Austria appeared to have fulfilled all the aims of the UN, and Kofi Annan was now looking forward to his next mission – travel to Nigeria the next morning where he would visit the new – decidedly interim – Head of State, Abubakar Abdulsalami, and of course see Moshood Abiola in prison. Neither of us required any urging to accept that we had to meet and talk before his departure.

My patience was severely tested with his 'reasonableness'... *yes, yes, Wole, an opportunity has opened up now with Abacha's death, and we musn't waste it. A lot can be achieved, the crisis can now be resolved but, you know, you must tell your people also to be reasonable. The opposition simply has to be reasonable.*

Reasonable? Were we being unreasonable? After nearly thirty years of military rule, the last five under the most repellent of the species, we were asking for the immediate release of the elected president – and all remaining political prisoners – and the setting up of an interim government headed by Abiola, the legitimate president. An interim government that would last a year, maybe two. In tandem, the nation's representatives would meet at a Sovereign National Conference to ascertain what was the real will of the people, lay the grounds for the next elections while reviewing the terms of association of the constituent parts of the nation. Then general elections – what was unreasonable about such proposals? Indeed, what alternative was there? I had the sinking feeling that Kofi was travelling with a prepared script, a script already agreed between the UN and a caucus of Western governments. The programme of our democratic coalition was not to be part of that script.

Warning of the death threat to Abiola was delivered into my hands only after Kofi Annan had left for Nigeria and had even held his meeting with the prisoner! If I had received it earlier, I would have submerged all political discussion under the urgency of bringing Abiola out of prison immediately! Certainly I would have served formal notice on the UNO, insisting – for whatever it was worth – that its secretary-general refuse to meet Abiola except at liberty, in his own home, surrounded by his family and political associates. We had learnt from experience to trust any warning from *Longa Throat*. It was all too late however, Abiola was already dying, his organs weakened by a devilish regimen of slow poisoning. It will all come out in its full Byzantine details – of that, I live in total confidence.

So, our discussion – and my principal concerns – were taken up mostly with Nigeria's future, not with any thoughts of danger to the man at the centre of it all. By the end of that meeting, so convinced was I that that future was already decided by others that I sent messages home immediately, urging that all pressure should be mounted on the visitor to make him *listen* to our programme and press it on the new landlord of Aso Rock, General Abdulsalami. Yet I warned in the same breath that it would be futile anyway. Such were the frequent contradictions that defined many moments of that democratic undertaking. Futility stared one in the face, but inaction was far more intolerable.

Wryly and incongruously, at such moments would float to the surface of my mind one of my mother's favourite aphorisms, with her comic Yorubisation of the key English word 'trying': *itirayi ní gbogbo nkàn* - the trying is all. Wild Christian applied it to a full gamut of incompatible situations – from the shrug of resignation that followed a failed attempt to charge exorbitantly for her goods, to falling with full relish on the dubious results of an exotic recipe that she was attempting for the first time. Abiola was – like the French socialist President Francois Mitterrand, which is where the similarity ends – a dogged disciple of the doctrine of *itirayi*. It was not his first attempt to become the president of Nigeria. A Yoruba from the South, his first, over-confident foray was ridiculed and scuttled by a feudal cabal who found it laughable that anyone outside their privileged caucus should even dream of ruling the nation. They took his money – lots of it – but derided his ambitions, openly. Abiola made a strategic withdrawal, bade his time, launched himself on a philanthropic crusade, broadened and reinforced his political base. At the second outing, he succeeded. And for that, Abiola was killed.

Instinctively, I turn towards the window when the captain announces that we have entered the Nigerian air-space. The plane's shadow dances over a few minarets and walled cities of the North. We are still some distance to destination, the full length of the Nigerian land mass has yet to be crossed. For a moment I think I caught a glimpse of an oasis, but it is only the sun's glint on a flat, corrugated iron roofing, undoubtedly a factory. My mind returns to the fate of my own house, the modest Essay Foundation dream. Now *that* I had effectively abandoned, perhaps in self-defence – brick by red brick and beam by beam, including its wild, ample grounds where I had experimented and succeeded – against all odds, I was told – in cultivating the wild, now rarely seen berry – àgbáyùn[9]. The lore, backed by generations of frustrated farmers, was that it never fructified in captivity. Through trial and error, varying the combination of sunshine and soil, moisture, shade and whatever else I could recall from my amateur flirtation with viniculture, I produced a freak success, a feat of which I was inordinately proud, since I am no farmer. The oldest and the youngest in the family – Tinuola and Folabo, are the family's green fingers. Femi, next to me in age – Jamani, to distinguish him by his childhood nickname from his namesake, OBJ – is the fisherman. I took to hunting. Cultivating the àgbáyùn, that stubborn berry that coats every morsel of food for hours afterwards with a natural sweetness, was also an irony, as I do not like sweets and only gave the berries away.

There was my mini field of wild mints also. When I retired from the Nigerian university system in 1985, thinking of various occupations for survival, I considered a project for freezing or drying my wild mint for sale, especially to bars and tea-houses around the world. Fantasising as a small-scale trading maverick, one who identified, produced and marketed a select item or two in demand, virtually from my doorstep, making a living out of it

---

[9] A berry that remains as sweetener on the tongue, hours after it is eaten.

to sustain a retirement into purely creative pursuits – this has long been a favourite pastime of mine. I suppose it was my fascination with the world of Wild Christian, that modest trader in a medley of commodities, that promoted such fantasies. I knew it would come to nothing, but it provided moments of unmatched bliss to sit in those ample verandahs, survey my lordly domain and weave my magic carpet of a life of inter-dependency between the arts and the farm. The mini grove of wild mints, and the àgbáyùn, were doomed to remain contemplative vistas, nothing more. I enjoyed watching them grow, sniffing the air around them and accompanying their flights to myriad cities in air-sealed bags. But all I did was lace the occasional drink with the mint leaves and distribute the àgbáyùn berries to friends. Once, a few hundreds of the latter were forgotten in my freezer, where they duly rotted when the infamous electrical supply took even its feeble charge away for prolonged periods that coincided with my absences from home.

Perhaps the memory of its one dedication still hovers around the estate – at the first anniversary of Femi Johnson's death – or, more accurately, of his re-internment – the Foundation received its first guest, an absentee guest and permanent resident. Then the grounds had come alive, peopled, that one time, by the very creative tribe it was meant to serve. I try to recollect the animated faces and voices… Odia Ofeimun, the poet and journalist; the critic Biodun Jeyifo; poet and playwright, Femi Osofisan; Tunji Oyelana, Jimi Solanke, musicians and actors; Francesca Emanuel, singer and lifelong collaborator; Bola Ige, a lawyer and politician but a friend of the arts, and occasional poet…then we formally named a wing for our late friend, slaughtered a goat and consumed gourdfuls of palm wine, and cases of its bottled and labelled expatriate siblings. Celebrating Femi Johnson's life? Or assuaging our loss yet again? No matter, he was one of us, actor and singer, even though a businessman, and we were sealing his present memory into those walls…

The memories – yes – but the physical casing of the idea? Mentally abandoned – at least, so I continue to hope – flushed into the thin stream that I had widened into an artificial pond,

past the catchment groves of repose along the watercourse – now
certainly silted up, or covered in an oily slick that oozed lazily
from that strange soil. I remind myself that I once abandoned even
the cactus patch, a bristling phalanx of thorned markers among
which I had assigned the role of covering my remains – yes, that
was the ultimate proof of my detachment. It was due especially to
the dismissal of that last attachment that, faced with the real
possibility that I might be killed in exile, I seized greedily on a
chance encounter, a revelation, on the island of Jamaica. I imbued
the event with a fated dimension, read it as a solemn
pronouncement and offering from predecessors to the ancestral
realms. Alas, even that substitute would prove treacherous,
impressing on me all over again the lesson I thought I had mastered
– never to call deeply to anything as mine, never becoming
attached, not even to a prospective burial ground.

In 1990 – in my mental calendar, the Year of Mandela's Release –
when he made Jamaica one of his first stopping points for his
reunion with the living world, I made a startling discovery on
that same island. If Mandela was retrieving the space of freedom
on a global scale, I was also discovering a micro-world that was
founded in freedom. Thus did I embark on a pilgrimage that would
begin as sentimental, and evolve into a morbid attachment.

The timing of my presence in Kingston, Jamaica, with
Mandela's – even though we never did meet on that soil – imbued
my discovery with an indefinable sense of augury. But then, let it
be recalled that, like a large portion of the world, I had carried the
calvary of Nelson Mandela and the struggle against Apartheid
South Africa on my shoulders for longer than its continental
replacement, the horror of an Abacharised Nigerian nation. Apart
from participating in the mandatory FREE MANDELA marches,
disinvestment campaigns, lecture sessions, a UN anti-sanction-
busting commission, etc. etc., I had presented an early student
play at the London Royal Court Theatre - *The Invention* - on the
insanities of the Apartheid system. Decades after that production,
I titled a collection of my poems *Mandela's Earth and Other Poems*
and, it seemed the most appropriate gesture, as I prepared for
Stockholm in 1986, to dedicate my Nobel acceptance speech to

him. (That was the speech in which, to my eternal chagrin, I listed Montesquieu among the contributors to European racist thinking – may the shade of Montesquieu find it in his ancestral heart to forgive that libel!)

To find myself again in Kingston on a lecture engagement in 1990, for the first time in nearly fifteen years, just as the entire city was emptying itself out for Mandela, was already more than sufficient. It was a symbolic gift that I regarded as personal, not shared with the millions of ecstatic hordes that had laboured for, and now celebrated his freedom. To discover a portion of my own homeland in that far-off place *at the same time* – now, that was a miracle that could only be wrought by a Mandelan avatar!

For it was only on this visit, my second ever to that island, that I was made aware of a slave settlement called Bekuta, a name that immediately resonated in my head as none other than the name of my hometown, Abẹ́òkúta. This centuries-wide reunion with my own history sent a tingle down my vertebrae – an encounter with descendants from my own hometown, Abẹ́òkúta, on a far-flung Caribbean island, in the hills of a once slave settlement called Jamaica?

The group of slave descendants who founded the settlement, in flight from the lowland plantations, had sought out a hilly terrain that would prove near impenetrable for their pursuing owners, but one that would also remind them of home. They found it in the county of Westmoreland and settled among its rockhills, naming it Abẹ́òkúta. Ade Adefuye, the Nigerian High Commissioner in the West Indies had already become acquainted with this history and could not wait to arrange a visit. What was only an academic, though exciting, discovery for him and others was, in my case, a most affecting experience. I found it strange indeed that, during my first visit to Jamaica in 1976, for CARIFESTA – the Caribbean Festival of the Arts – no one had thought to mention the existence of this settlement, or propose that we pay it a visit!

A famous Nigerian, now also deceased, had preceded me on this voyage of a private discovery, I was informed. This was Fela Sowande, a composer, but a totally different spirit from his younger and more famous namesake, the 'afro-beat king' and iconoclast, Fela Anikulapo Kuti. Sowande had been completely overwhelmed – he broke down in tears. This older cousin would exact his emotional revenge on me some years later, unintentionally, for it was his symphony – *Ọbángíjí,* based on melodies from our common birthplace – which, unexpectedly swarming out of violin and cello strings of the Swedish orchestra on the Stockholm stage, as I moved forward to receive the Nobel award – nearly succeeded in making me a victim of the shamelessness of tear ducts. It was a brief, but tense struggle! The rockhills of origin stood me in good stead but, it could have gone the other way. (The horror of it – the immaculately pressed, ribboned and sashed master of ceremonies, the Swedish Prince Consort himself, compelled to lend me his handkerchief!) Really, the Stockholm ceremonials should not spring such surprises on middle-aged susceptibilities!

As the island slowly recovered from the hangover of Mandela's visit, I could not wait to answer the call of Bekuta. There, I encountered one of my yet living ancestors, the oldest inhabitant of the settlement, frail, as one would expect a being of over a hundred years to be. Now, let no one dare tell me I do not know an Ẹgbá face when I see one! The parchment tautness of her face, the unmistakable features of the Ẹgbá death-mask, captured so immutably in Demas Nwoko's [10] painting *Ogboni,* attested her origins distinctly against any skeptical voices. Not much motion was left in her body, else her body rhythm, I was certain, would have reinforced what her face pronounced. As she became bedridden, she ordered her bed moved to the window that overlooked the rockhills. Now, all she sought was that her eyes would open and close on those rocks, dawn and dusk, until her final moment.

She was the sole survivor of the original settlers. Her voice was still remarkably strong. Did I imagine the unmistakable Ẹgbá twang in her Jamaican patois? Of course I did, but what a conceit to let linger in the resounding chambers of one's head! *Oh yes, the real name is A-be-o-ku-ta* - never did music sound so tanned, so ancestral in authority - *but it gradually became corrupted to Bekuta. I tell them all the time - the name is A-be-o-ku-ta, but how many of*

---

[10] Nigerian painter and sculptor.

them can remember that! They don't even remember what it means, not less I remind them. I was a child when we came here. When our people dance for you and cook you fùfú, ewédú, jógí and other foods from home, no one come tell you that we descendants of slaves from A-be-o-kuta. But yes, much has been lost. The government help a little, they come here sometimes, bring visitors, and the local council preserve our history by staging shows every year. We observe the seasons of the gods... Ṣàngó, Obátàlá, Úgún[11]...*we used to have a* babaláwo,[12] *but I don't think anyone remember how to read Ifá* [13] *anymore... some of the children go away and never return... in fact, the best dancers are the older ones, they the ones who keep our traditions alive. They teach their children, but the children not very interested. They only do these things when there are important visitors, so I don't know what going happen when the older ones die off...*

They danced for us, sedate, ceremonial steps of the Ègbá, fed us dishes whose recipes had been carefully preserved from the vanished home. These were the life exiles, generation exiles, those who had died to a faraway homeland and awakened to a new earth, exiles to whom the call of origin had thinned over time and dissipated into the winds of passage, drifting with mists from the cascading waters of Bekuta rockhills and evaporated the same way. It vanished wistfully into the territory of legends, of the deities of mountains and valleys, was fleshed out in purely performance modes that increasingly underscored its now vestigial status. Recollection stepped gingerly into temporary recovery spaces of town halls or school fields, ever submissive to the present. The exigencies of that present – careers, economic survival, politics, etc. – reinforced their supremacy over memory or sentiment. After each emergence, the adaptive masks and costumes of origin re-entered their normal abode of camphor saturated boxes and shelves – until the next festive or commemorative occasion.

Not the sheerest thought of that vivid state of suspended animation, exile, had I entertained on my encounter with that settlement in the Year of Mandela's Release. I was paying a call on family, preferred not to see the sparse population of Bekuta as

---

[11] Yoruba deities.

[12] Diviner, priest of divination.

[13] The Divination Corpus.

exiles, but simply as one of the many branches of the Ẹgbá, a clan of wanderers who vanished into the forests one day and could not readily find their way back. Regarding my own future, exile was simply not on the divination board.

Three years later, all had changed. A new dictator, Sani Abacha, an identical agenda – the perpetuation of military rule – but a different cast of mind, and with an increasingly ruthless, ever widening network to act it out. The thought of real death – not the remediable conceit now of exile as a mimic death – became an insistent, strident companion. As I set out on one mission after another, in pursuit of what, surely, simply had to be the vital key to repossession of one's real space, my mind took refuge in Bekuta. It was not a morbid condition, just a matter-of-fact possibility that stared one in the face. Agitated by the thought that some misguided friends or family would take my remains to Nigeria, I announced publicly that, if the worst happened, I did not want Abacha's triumphant feet galumphing over my body, and would settle for the surrogate earth of Jamaica. And I began to make preparations to buy a piece of land in Bekuta.

Fate, I concluded, lured me back to Jamaica for the next determining visit in 1995, barely two years into the exile that followed the ascendancy of Sani Abacha. The vehicle was *The Beatification of Area Boy*, a play that was originally intended for Lagos, but was now headed for production in the land of the Rastas. Bekuta beckoned. My first free weekend in Kingston found me motoring through the hairpin bends of the mountain road towards Westmoreland, the county where Bekuta was situated. I could not wait to transfer the deeds to my cactus patch to Bekuta.

Motoring with me was Gerry Feil, my American friend and film-maker, whose bulk belied his restless energy, with permanently irritated features that grumpily matured with age into a passable double for the patriarch of the Flintstone family. He arrived in Kingston with his daughter, Anna, titled my wine-daughter, a special relationship that came from her ceremonial induction into wine from childhood, a rite of passage that is *de riguer* in my own household where the mother has a choice of being a voluntary accomplice, she is herself immobilised by a generous dosage, or else locked in the toilet until it's all over. Such sustained devotion to the cause of wine must have been mystically transmitted to the oenophile nobility of France, and resulted in my most treasured recognition, to which even the Nobel takes second place. During a lecture visit to the University of Tours, the vice chancellor and I were dragged off to a deep underground *cave*, a veritable multi-chambered grotto. There, over feeble protests at my unworthiness, I was inducted into the *Commanderie de la Dive Bouteille*, a centuries old order that boasts membership of Rabelais, Voltaire, among other illustrious humanists. That was definitely the highlight of my career.

Gerry had visited me in Nigeria several times – Ìbàdàn, Ifẹ̀, Abẹ́òkúta - the first time as a member of the exploratory team of British director Joan Littlewood who was seeking to film my play, *The Lion and the Jewel*. Each of Gerry's visits was marked by one memorable event or another, but perhaps none more unsettling than his stay in Abẹ́òkúta while I was still living in a rented house, supervising the building of the first ever home – modestly conceived at the time – that I could call my own. Gerry, to whom the combination of heat and humidity remained a potentially fatal threat, spent all night in my motor car, engine running, to guarantee an air-conditioned environment. My home, alas, lacked such a basic amenity. This meant, quite simply, that I obtained no sleep that night, since a stubborn spectre stuck to the inner membrane of my eyelids – Gerry's corpse in the morning, gas fumes having seeped into the interior of the car. Earlier efforts to make him seek remedy in a bathtub filled with cold water – where drowning in his sleep was less likely than carbon monoxide poisoning – had proved futile. My guest insisted that he entertained no fear of death by water but argued that submersion in water all night would only aggravate his condition. I came downstairs every half hour to seek a clear patch in the misted over windows through which I could check if he was still breathing. The following night, after intense persuasion, I induced him to transfer to a negotiated air-conditioned room not far from me, just for the nights, while he returned to spend waking time with a host who otherwise would have turned a nervous wreck.

The invitation to Westmoreland was mainly for Anna. She was then looking for a subject for her thesis in Social Anthropology and it occurred to me that the story of Bekuta was a ready-made subject – a violent dispersal, exile, enslavement, liberation, the search for a substitute homeland and – resettlement. It was a research subject for which I made no attempt to disguise my own vested interests. What was left of the cultures of the original homeland? How had the descendants adjusted? Had polygamy survived? – that last was inspired by more than a cursory interest in a return-to-roots. It could produce, maybe, objective criteria for evaluating a domestic arrangement that contrasted so profoundly with serial polygamy, as practiced in the Western – especially American – world. Was there any syncretism in the new micro-culture of the *aráa Bekuta*[14] with the cultures of other Jamaican settlers or indigenes – and so on? Anna came armed with a tape recorder and video-camera, seeking preliminary material with which to persuade her supervisors that this was a worthwhile subject for a thesis. I was prepared to accompany her project statement with a recommendation of such enticing prospects – even in blank verse if that would help – that it would make her supervisors salivate and even attempt to take over the project to boost their CVs.

It took a while to find the village on this decisive encounter, far longer even than the journey from Kingston, where the driver had done his best on those treacherous, sometimes vertiginous roads, to ensure that we prematurely gained my dream patch of the after-life. On the way back to Kingston however, I had cause to regret that he had not succeeded, had not ended the dream in the most brutal way that he appeared mindlessly capable of doing, so complete was the collapse of my anticipations. Only five years had passed since my 'Mandela' visit and yet, not many people in neigbouring, virtually next door villages appeared to have heard that exotic word – *Bekuta*! Those whose eyes lit up at the sound were no longer sure if it still existed. *Bekuta? Sure, me once know the place. But is it you going find anyone still living there?*

---

14 People of Bekuta.

he search on our own, seeking, unlike
, not roots. It was an extended holiday
ite weekends, so there were no officials
needed them, I boasted – Ègbá blood
mind that I routinely refer to myself,
a marriage of Ìjèbú and Ègbá, the two
:entage. As for any local descendants
hance upon, they had long substituted
e and *kola* nut, the calypso and reggae
inately, such was my impatience that,
rival, late as it was, I decided that we
tring before dark. Thus we would
s, leaving only a handful of blind alleys
for the following day.

kuta with only a little extra agony the
ld lady was dead, but that was expected,
called home. Something far larger had
died however, and that was Bekuta itself. It was the old lady who
had kept up the settlement and its traditions through sheer will-
power – we knew that already, but had not guessed how solitary
a task it was, how her spirit had been the very existential force of
the village. Now the homestead had died with her. The younger
generation immediately pulled up stakes and departed. Her
granddaughter, who was settled a modest walking distance away
from Bekuta, found my pilgrimage amusing ...*but no one pay much
time for that Africa foolishness. She only one keep all that in she head,
so when she gone, no one pay any mind to such things.* If only she
knew what rusty daggers she was using to slash at my entrails!

Yet some stubborn retention was in evidence, as we found
when we visited the original site with its few surviving relics. We
put questions to them one after the other, Anna ran her
miniaturised camera on the miniaturised village and took notes,
but it was clear – this was no treasure trove for the would-be
researcher, and there seemed to be even less substance to my quest.
It was some consolation – as if the spirit of the dead matriarch still
ruled in odd corners of a few hearts – that the granddaughter,

---

[15] Yoruba traditional social music.

that same dismissive granddaughter was still unable to tear herself away completely from the terrain. She had stayed behind, and her grandmother's grave was in her small orchard, neat, carefully tended, and overlooked by the rockhills upon which, I could only hope, the matriarch's eyes had closed at the end.

But the times had been unkind to Bekuta. Piece by piece, the story of the death of a village was elicited through indifferent voices. Some years earlier, a flash flood had sent torrents cascading down from the mountains and swept away much of the hillside settlement, washed away their crops and even taken a toll in lives. The survivors relocated in a few terraced plots scooped into the hills, protected by overhanging rocks, but mostly in the plains below. A year later, Nature struck yet another blow – a renewed flooding – and the spirit of Bekuta was broken. The village was now in the throes of death, and the old lady's passing simply sealed its fate. Three, four years after her death, the last of the small community – with any shred of vitality – had vanished. The jungle had reclaimed its space.

Dispirited, we returned to our hotel. And then, while lying in bed and licking my wounds, from across the oceans, thousands of miles away, another Ègbá spirit flew away. The news came on my portable radio and it sounded so strange, a floating contradiction that was at once detached from, yet infused with the world from which I had myself just earned a lover's rebuff. My young cousin, the *abàmì èdá*[16] that the world knew as Fela, was dead. He had not yet attained his sixtieth year.

A naked torso over spangled pants, over which a saxophone or microphone would oscillate on stage, receiving guests or journalists in underpants while running down a tune from his head, in the open courtyard at rehearsals or in any space where he held court – all constituted the trademark of his unyielding non-conformism. Far more revealing than such skimpy attire however was his skin-taut skull and bulging eyes, permanently bloodshot from an indifferent sleeping routine and a dense marijuana diffusion. His singing voice was raspy, not intended to

---

[16] Weird, unique being.

entice but arrest with trenchant messages. Sparse and lithe, Fela leapt about the stage like a brown, scalded cat, whose *miaaow* was a rustle of riffs eased from a saxophone that often seemed better maintained than his own body. Fela loved to buck the system. His music, to many, was both salvation and echo of anguish, frustrations and suppressed aggression. The black race was the beginning and end of knowledge and wisdom, his life mission, to effect a mental and physical liberation of the race. It struck me as a kind of portent – that it was while visiting this distant outpost of my home, Abẹ̀òkúta, in Westmoreland, propelled – but quite soberly, objectively – by thoughts of death, that I would receive news of the death of that other musician member of my family – the irrepressible maverick, Fela Anikulapo-Kuti.

How would one summarise Fela? Merely as a populist would be inadequate. Radical he certainly was, and often simplistically so. Lean as a runner bean, a head that sometimes struck me as a death-mask that came to life only on stage or in an argument – more accurately described as a serial peroration, since he was incapable of a sustained exchange of viewpoints, especially in politics. Only Fela would wax a record jointly according heroic virtues to such an incompatible trio as Kwame Nkrumah of Ghana, Sekou Toure of Guinea and – oh yes, indeed – Idi Amin Dada the terror of Uganda. It was however sufficient for my cousin that, at one time or the other, they challenged, defied or ridiculed an imperial power – any voice raised in denunciation of the murders by Idi Amin, or the torture cages of Sekou Toure, was the voice of a western stooge, CIA agent and imperialist lackey. There were no greys in Fela's politics of black and white.

Memories flitted across the night – such as one of my least treasured experiences – the feeling of being designated as dog food! It was 1984, and I had travelled to Paris in order to campaign for Fela's freedom at a mammoth music concert when yet another dictatorship, that of General Buhari's government which had flung him in prison on spurious charges of a currency offence. Under the general anti-racism and human rights slogan – *Touche pas à mon pote* – Don't touch my mate! - the organisers of the concert planned to devote a special spot to publicise Fela's unjust imprisonment and mobilise world opinion on his behalf. I had accepted their invitation at extremely short notice, had never before attended a pop music concert, having no inclination towards high-decibel events and mass excitation.

The trouble came from my efforts to approach the sacred arena where the artistes, handlers, etc., were tented – I shot to the venue straight from dumping my bags at the hotel and without the dozen or more passes required to open up the succession of barriers – someone had omitted to provide them. My lasting image from that concert was that of me about to be eaten at each barrier by teams of obviously starved Alsatians, launched – it appeared – by their handlers, even while they pretended to restrain them. Nobody will ever persuade me that those dogs are ever fed, or that they are not trained to identify innocent humanity as their next meal! I had seen footage of white police officers unleashing their kindred monsters on black protesters in Apartheid South Africa – at no time did the thought ever cross my mind that I would some day come close to taking over those victims' role, in Paris, especially as an honoured guest. My mission, I assumed, was to deliver a message to the world, thereafter escaping into the sanity of the furthest cafe from the raucous, drug-stoned environment within which millions of presumably sane people actually find hours of ecstasy. Still, once within the protective barriers, I carried off my mission with all due dignity as became an ambassador of the *Black President* – one of Fela's many unofficial titles – and delivered my message against the background of his blown-up image even as his music was blared over the Paris night.

For nearly the last five years of his life, Fela was fully convinced, not only that he was a reincarnated Egyptian god, but that he had actually begun to reverse the aging process, that is, was growing younger and would again revert to childhood and infancy. By that token, my àbúrò would have watched his own funeral, unobserved by mere mortals. Wreathed in a marijuana induced serenity – for I have no doubt that there would be gardens of vintage *ganja* in Fela's heaven – he would have enjoyed the irony of his funeral, the magnitude of which was an unintended gift to us exiles of Abacha's misrule. He was laid in state at the huge Únikan Race Course in the heart of Lagos, a now degraded monument to vainglory that an earlier dictator, Yakubu Gowon, had built for himself. It was designed as a parade ground that would show off the might and splendour of the military regime, and the first visiting dignitary to grace those grounds would have been Queen Elizabeth II of England. Alas, while attending a meeting with other African heads of state in East Africa in 1976, Yakubu Gowon learnt that he had been overthrown in a coup that was mounted by his own palace guard. The royal visit was cancelled. I found it altogether fitting that Fela should lie in state on those very grounds as nearly a million of his countrymen and women came to pay him tribute.

On the day of Fela's funeral, the whole of Lagos stood still, all businesses were suspended and any governmental presence banished. The mammoth crowd at the funeral of this most vocal and unrelenting dissident being was, firstly, a tribute to his person. Following this however, it was also a statement of defiance to the regime of Sani Abacha. Despite his quixotic outbursts, near blasphemous, since they appeared to support the rule of Sani Abacha, the fundamental message of Fela's art and lifestyle was anathema to any military or dictatorial regime, and thus he remained a persona non grata even to Sani Abacha, whose persecution of Beko, his brother, was a warning to the maverick tunesmith that not even he was untouchable. Fela's funeral was thus an occasion that the people exploited to the full, pouring out in a way that defied the regime's ban on public gatherings, making the *Black President* the mouthpiece of their repressed feelings, even in his lifeless form. Neither the police nor the military dared show its face on that day, and the uniformed exceptions only came to pay tribute. Quite openly, with no attempt whatsoever at disguising their identities, they stopped by his bier, saluted the stilled scourge of corrupt power, mimic culture and militarism. It was a much needed act of solidarity for us.

Outside public adulation however, my mind remained retentive of a decades old image of Fela, a private one, not the familiar stage torso swivelling above sequined trousers, leaping about on stage with inimitable verve, a leaner version of James

Brown. It was a fleeting moment of revelation, glimpsed during one of my infrequent visits to him, a trapped moment of repose when his inner thoughts appeared to overcome his darting eyes and they remained in place, deep windows into a wistful, deeply dissatisfied being. There was no audience, no need for role-playing. His familiar, loose wrapped marijuana stick of almost mid-size cigar proportions smouldered over his lower lip, diffusing sufficient smoke to intoxicate an audience of a hundred or more. He had a faraway look, filled with discontent, and I thought I read in those eyes a longing that they could will the pungent fumigation that emerged between his lips into a transforming agent for a nation's putrefactions, yet acknowledging that he was powerless to effect this dream, that the mocking immensity of the task would for ever render him tormented, inconsolable.

I found a private symmetry about his passing, mostly in the way it chose to touch me in a remote space of separated, yet close kinship, as if this public death had been sent across radio waves to re-attach me to that distant, but progressively depleted landscape. Despite the weight of a double bereavement, I accepted, quite factually, that I was not destined to be buried in Bekuta, but remained cautious about whether or not I should read the loss of Fela-Bekuta as an omen that I was not meant to perish in exile.

Bekuta is dead; long live Bekuta? Or wherever tugs at one, inexplicably, like the power of Úgún's magnet directed at one of his metallic vessels. That hope/prayer/doubt, shadowed by the soaring rockhills and their presiding deity, ògún, or whatever emanations remained within those granite veins, had the effect of simplifying – and intensifying – my mission in exile. Back in Kingston, I seized the first occasion to make it known that I had changed my last will and testament! Burying me in Bekuta, I announced, would be the same as burying me in some prinstine jungle which had bartered away its soul. Since hoping to find another Bekuta outside Nigeria was stretching the laws of probability beyond limits, my mission in exile became even more personalised – to exploit every second towards the retrieval of my cactus patch, but purged definitively of a tyrant's triumphalist tread.

PART 1

Òṣún and I

Early Intimations

The suggestion that I was possessed quite early in life by the creative-combative deity, Úgún, is a familiar commentary of some literary critics who stretch my creative fascination with that deity, undeniable in my works, beyond its literary purlieu. If I was persuaded of that, I would have headed long ago for the nearest *babaláwo*[1] for the rites of exorcism! I am, contrary to all legitimately cited evidence – and none more damning than this accused's own history – actually a closet glutton for tranquility. An oft quoted remark of mine – *justice is the first condition of humanity* – does however act constantly against the fulfilment of that craving for peace, an insertion into my mental template that can be regarded as a 'categorical imperative'. There is nothing mystical about it, nothing beyond an over-acute, remedial sense of right and wrong, of what is just and unjust.

A casual involvement – at a most impressionable age – with the Abẹ̀òkúta women's movement, narrated in *AKÉ*, may have prepared the soil. That began in the late nineteen-thirties when the women, led by my aunt, the formidable Funmilayo Ransome-Kuti, rose against unjust taxes and chased the feudal lord, the Aláké of Abẹ̀òkúta, from his throne. So might also the induction,

---

[1] Priest of divination.

from schooldays, into the propensities of the class bully, merging
onto a broader canvas of the arrogant ways of colonial domination.
That last, in turn, formed a continuum of visceral identification
with the victims of Apartheid South Africa, a condition that
ironically honed itself to an insurgent pitch only when I arrived in
the United Kingdom in 1954, into the homeland of a colonial power
that ruled with violence in parts of Asia and Africa, Kenya most
notoriously on the latter continent.

Studying in England in mid nineteen-fifties, vacations found
most of us, African students, headed for London from all over
the British isles to earn some extra money – mostly as porters in
railway stations, post offices, bars and chain restaurants. We
would then gather at the Overseas Students Club in Earls Court,
the University of London Students' Union, or the West African
Students Union in Porchester Terrace, Bayswater. There, virtually
only one topic dominated all conversation – colonisation and how/
when to end it! The West African colonies appeared to be on their
way to negotiated independence, so our agitated sights were set
in other directions. Kenya was embroiled in the *Mau Mau* revolt, a
truly indigenous, internally generated struggle, in which the forests
favoured the liberation fighters. South Africa however occupied
a special place of bafflement, rage and despair. Awareness of that
degraded zone of existence, on the soil of our own continent, that
apprehension of a world that assigned to one's race a condition of
subhumanity was all-consuming. We began to prepare ourselves
against the day when we would reclaim that humanity – by force
of arms, if needed.

This obsession with the humiliation of racist entrenchment
in Southern Africa was not one of bloodless empathy – we did,
after all, savour mild dosages of that condition in our encounters
with the white natives in their own territory. Even as a student,
occupying a mostly sheltered environment, I did not escape my
share of pointed acts of contempt or rejection. My over-
anthologised poem, *Telephone Conversation*, the record of an
exchange with a landlady, was only one of the many trite
encounters with British racism. On public transport, for instance
– admittedly I *enjoyed* having a seat to myself in a filled up double-

decker bus, it made turning over the abnormally broad pages of
The Yorkshire Post much easier but – could I really pretend not to
notice, or fail to be stung by the fact that a boarding passenger
had traversed the length of the bus, seen the one empty seat next
to me but had chosen to retrace his or her steps and climb upstairs
to search for a vacant seat? That the same passenger came down
again – no standing allowed upstairs – and chose to attach his or
her arm to a strap-hanger sooner than take that empty seat? Or
even more blatantly – as you were about to take the nearest vacant
seat on a two-seater bench, the occupant next to the window shot
up, quickly extricated his or her body and moved to another seat,
or remained standing. Incidents like these, even in the mid-fifties,
were mind-numbingly commonplace.

In shops, you turned invisible. The shopkeeper ostentatiously
pretended not to see you and turned to attend to someone who
entered the shop long after you. He was quick on the apology and
excuses, of course, the moment you shouted a belligerent – *Excuse
me!* Then followed the predictable – *Oh, so sorry, were you next?*
The oiled, hypocritical voice, the worse for being in a thick, regional
accent, when – irrationally – one somehow expected the country
yokels to be more human than their cosmopolitan sophisticates.

How did one cope? Sometimes by invoking the inner
confidence of one's mental superiority – that was easy enough,
many of the natives were ignorant of much that was routine
knowledge to any student. For a start, they did not even know
where on the globe Africa was to be found. More to the point, in
our own colonised territories, a white man was always associated
with lordly positions of authority, yet here they were, finally
exposed in all grime and sweat, workers and peasants like our
own mortal beings, often more wretched and impoverished than
the poorest menial at home! Corporeally, all our student nostrils
were in complete agreement that white people – almost uniformly
– stank! They gave off a most upsetting odour, only slightly less
upsetting than the belated discovery that they actually thought
that we also stank! On balance, it was impossible to make an
issue of racial slights all the time and, the more politicised of us,
faced with a racial affront, simply switched our minds to that

distant bastion of racism itself – Apartheid South Africa – *you wait!* – an inward, vengeful mutter – *you are not remotely close to the league of your Apartheid kin. When we have wiped out that main reservoir of racial disdain, these poisoned outposts of the same affliction will simply wither away, atrophied from lack of further nourishment from the ultimate exemplar.*

Writing poems such as *Telephone Conversation* – together with the satisfaction of reading it over *their* own radio station, the BBC, also helped. So did attempts to write for theatre. A full-length play over which I laboured for months had a Boer family trapped in their farmstead where they were slowly eaten by black soldier ants – I rode the horses of vengeful symbolism to their knees! The play was long on purple passages, commented my lecturer. I was encountering such a phrase for the first time but instantly understood what he meant, and promptly added it to my vocabulary of self-censorship. More importantly however, I found that it owed far too much to Eugene O'Neill, whose works I was studying at the time, so after reams of sheets trying and failing to expunge all further borrowings, I committed the first *auto-da-fé* of my career and lit a fire to consume the play.

A shorter play – *The Invention* – was produced as one of the Royal Court Theatre's Sunday night experiments in December 1959. It climaxed in an explosion that wiped out a group of white scientists who had been brought together to research, scientifically, the accurate determination of racial types in South Africa – so much for wish-fulfilment by the theatrical route! To make matters worse – a cautionary portent for our future plans perhaps? – the explosion refused to come on cue!

Off-stage, we followed the descent of South Africa into a solidifying black negation. By 1955, the final stages of cementing that nation's Apartheid structure by the Nationalist government had been reached, with the black population uprooted from proximity to white estates – except under licence as daytime servants and menials – and resettled in the so-called townships, but more accurately described by its other name – shanty-towns. In our projections, this pointed to only one conclusion: at the first sign of uprising by the black population, those shanty-towns would be surgically taken out, bombed out of existence with no danger whatever to the white population! It was that stark, that logical. An internal war of liberation, in the manner of Kenya's *Mau Mau*, appeared to have been rendered impracticable, literally overnight. This was our youthful analysis as we fumed impotently from a distance. As a counter-insurgency action in the preventive mode, the Boers' move was a master-stroke.

We knew our history however. The Spanish Civil War had given birth to a volunteer international force, of which the Writers and Artists units, such as the Abraham Lincoln Brigade played courageous but mostly tragic roles. As we argued and constructed possible scenarios at the student clubs, buoyed by tea and biscuits, lager-and-lime and cider, sandwiches and sausage rolls, warmed by the glow of the fireplace after a hard day's work delivering christmas parcels or lugging railway baggage, our conclusions pointed us in a similar direction – to prepare ourselves for the liberation war in South Africa. We saw that ill-used tip of the continent being restored to the black race by a Continental Brigade of volunteers converging on the south from every corner of the black land mass. It was the most obvious solution. That future was so clear to us – our generation could not escape the destiny of marching south to terminate the racial insult that rebuked our very being as black peoples. Whenever I had cause to think of that prospect, I confess that I felt nothing but a warm glow of anticipation. It made it easy to ignore, even lift one's ego above personal encounters with racial prejudice – I *knew* something that my local tormentors did not!

We knew, beyond all doubt, our place within the evolving organism of new nations. We, the young generation of that independence phase, a renaissance people who would transform the strange bequest into a world marvel. The only way to grasp this confidence, this self-assurance is to treat it as *pure knowledge*. Not intuition, not revelation, not blind faith, not ambition, not deductive reasoning or a conscious sense of mission – no, simply as *knowledge* in its purest, unassailable form! We *were* the renaissance people! And we were working in our various fields – quite indifferent to any special designation – to bring about this renaissance.

If there was a 'plan of action', that took place within continental leadership, it took substance, bearing, from the merging of nationalist forces at the leadership apex. Beginning with two mutually antagonistic blocs, the 'Casablanca' and the 'Monrovia' groups, a collective effort was progressing in the direction of the formation of an Organisation of African Unity. Even more significant for us was the struggle at the grassroots, the commencing wars of liberation from settler colonialism in Kenya, and from the Portuguese 'assimilationist' deception in Angola and Cape Verde. Defined by these efforts, we would be the transforming auxiliaries of an inchoate substance, a yet undefined entity, of spaces that just happened to be called Nigeria, Gold Coast, the Rhodesias, Ivory Coast, Senegal, Cameroon, etc. The future spread itself before us, a vision of the reassemblage of a much abused, much violated people on whose heads the ultimate insult had been heaped – broken in pieces and then glued together like the shell of the tortoise in folk mythology. We were unstoppable.

But first, we had to liberate our kinsfolk to the South!

I enrolled in the officer training corps of my university in 1955, opting for infantry. Alas, my membership of that unit was fated to be extremely brief. In 1956, the Suez war broke out and I received my call-up letter. I now learnt for the first time that, as a colonial, I was liable to be called up anytime to serve Her Royal Majesty. I had imagined that I was conveniently exploiting Her Majesty's training facilities to prepare myself for a liberation war, but it appeared that Her Majesty's government had other plans for me. At the time of the call-up, I was only required to present myself for training with other reserves, but all I saw was my over-clever self being loaded onto a landing craft, heading away from South Africa, fighting on the side of the French and British against Abdel Nasser over a canal that was situated on his own soil! This ill-disguised attempt to re-colonise Egypt all over again, to compromise her sovereignty, did not appear to be a logical progression from the Continental Brigade that we had conjured up by the fireplace of Porchester Terrace. I sent in a letter declining my call-up. I was summoned to the recruitment office and reminded that I had taken an oath of loyalty to the Queen, and that my enrolment in the officer training corps meant, in effect, that I had enlisted. The refusal of an order, I was quietly informed, could earn me a court martial.

It was quite true about the oath of loyalty. There was an anteroom in which we all, new volunteers, were assembled, and from which we were summoned one by one. An officer sat behind the desk while beside him stood another, a card in his hand. That card contained the oath. Yes, the words were unambiguous... *to be ready to serve and protect Her Majesty at all times...* words to that effect. I was thoroughly unprepared and frankly, shocked. I was a citizen of an upcoming nation called Nigeria – not yet fully independent, admittedly, but I carried a passport that declared me a citizen of Nigeria which, in turn, was defined as a British protectorate. That Nigeria was a hotbed of nationalism – Herbert Macaulay, Nnamdi Azikiwe, Nwafor Orizu, Bode Thomas, Obafemi Awolowo, Mbonu Ojike of the *Boycott the Boycottables* fame – meaning, boycott all foreign products – these were names that we conjured with, and their joint endeavour was towards the separation of that nation called Nigeria from the control of that same Majesty the Queen. How then was I supposed to swear an oath of loyalty to her and her dominion?

I never thought of backing out at that point. I had come this far, I had decided on the training, and in any case, the juggernaut was rolling and I was trapped within it. To the two officers conducting the proceedings, this was pure routine. There were several more of us to be put through the same ritual, and I guessed that neither was really listening to whatever response the recruits were uttering. So I put on my thickest Yoruba accent, ensuring that nothing intelligible emerged from my throat. The administrator of the royal oath assumed, naturally, that this African could not really cope with the Queen's English – that is, if he was listening at all. As if it mattered in the slightest! My signature in the register was an affirmation of the oath I had taken – legal and binding! Still, I clung to the crumb of consolation that the oath had not truly passed over my tongue which, as soon as I left the induction room, I proceeded to rinse – with others – in the bar with a glass of celebratory sherry – cost threepence, subsidised mess price.

Now came payment time, premature and politically unthinkable! I packed up my supply kit, tucked it in the furthest corner of the neglected attic of my lodging in Ash Grove – where, for all I know, it may still be gathering dust till today – and vanished! One thing I was sure of – there was bound to be further correspondence before I was either press-ganged and sent to camp, formally arrested and court-martialled, and/or deported. I sent off a letter saying that a mistake had been made. I am a citizen of Nigeria, I explained, not of Great Britain. There was silence from wherever the menace had emerged. Later on, I discovered that the deployment office may have had a legal question on its hands. If I had been a native of Lagos, it would have been a different matter. Lagos was a colony, and its citizens were thus colonial subjects. They carried a kind of quasi-British citizen passport which made them colonial citizens of Britain. I, on the other hand, being from the interior, belonged to the second-class citizenship of the extended British Empire. I was a 'protected' being, a member of the 'British Empire', not a colonial subject. It was the only time I felt grateful to be classed a second-class citizen.

The war soon ended, mercifully, and Her Majesty's army lost all interest in me. I would not smell any form of training until some months later when the Soviet Union, taking advantage of the West's misadventure in the Suez, invaded Hungary, and a volunteer student training camp was opened in Nottingham, North of England. There was no hesitation. I signed up. This was indeed closer to the kind of training I needed. I must state this quite clearly – I did not intend to go into Hungary to fight, but there were supportive functions that I felt I could perform for the cause of those nationalists in return for my training. My imagination declared that a black face would be far too conspicuous in the midst of such a war and, fully sympathetic though I was to the Hungarian national cause, and the right to take up arms to repel a bully – even an ideologically progressive one – I had my priorities, and could not really see how a black face could be justified slinging molotov cocktails in the streets of

Budapest. The prospect of getting killed in such a strange land that I only knew from history books, and for its robust red wine, the *Egri Bikaver*, cheaply suited to my student means, struck me as grotesque – a black festering corpse alone in a snow-clad street, all other casualties vanishing into the protective colouring of their natural environment? On the other hand, that prospect was balanced by the lure of acquiring the experience of urban warfare which, from the news bulletins, was largely what was being waged by the Hungarian nationalists against superior forces - molotov cocktails against tanks, and street-to-street fighting. It looked like a perfect rehearsal opportunity for what we had conjured up for – *Destination, Johannesburg!*

The uncertainty of my position, given the unpredictable situation in Hungary, resulted in my taking the trouble to write one of my rare letters to Essay – my father – taking him into confidence. It seemed only fair, just in case I was wounded, taken prisoner or worse. Only years later did I find it curious that I should ever have imagined that his response would be at least sympathetic, albeit disapproving. Instead, it was scathingly dismissive. I could picture him seated at his desk, his pen moving swiftly and noisily over the lined sheets: *You were sent over there to study. In any case, charity begins at home, so if you feel inclined to jeopardise your studies by succumbing to some warlike urge, kindly return home and make this your battlefield.* It was such an infuriatingly rational response that I refused to write him another letter for even longer than usual. And the abrupt end of the conflict appeared to have taken his side. The Hungarian resistance collapsed and any further discussion became academic, with him having won the argument by default. I felt intensely annoyed and held him personally responsible for the defeat of the Hungarian nationalists.

Essay was right, though he did not know it at the time, although prescient would be a more accurate expression for his proposed amendment to my battle plans. Indeed, I often wondered if, from time to time, once I had become embroiled within my own borders, he had not wished that he had encouraged me to go and take my chances on the Hungarian front! By then, of course, he no longer had a say in the matter because, in the meantime, in company with my University of London/Porchester Terrace master-planners, I had made a startling discovery!

The nationalists, the first generation elected leaders and legislators of our semi-independent nation had begun to visit Great Britain in droves. We watched their self-preening, their ostentatious spending, their cultivated condescension, even disdain towards the people they were supposed to represent. There were exceptions but, in the main, they did not appear to have emerged from the land and people we left behind when we journeyed out to acquire some skills and learning. While we dreamt of marching south to liberate Southern Africa, they saw the nation as a prostrate victim to be ravished. We accepted invitations to their public talks, informal meetings, even partook of their lavish receptions. Some were stark illiterates, though full of bombast. This strange breed was a complete contrast to the nationalist stalwarts in whose hands we had imagined that the country could be safely consigned while we went on our romantic liberation march to Southern Africa. The exceptions engaged us in serious discussions, outlined their vision not only for the nation but for the continent, pleaded earnestly that we hurry home and join hands in building the future. Most of the time however, as we ran eagerly to welcome the protagonists of the African Renaissance, we were bombarded by utterances that identified only flamboyant replacements of the old colonial order, not transforming agents, not even empathising participants in a process of liberation.

Some turned students into pimps, either for immediate rewards, or in return for influence in obtaining or extending scholarships. Visiting politicians financed lavish parties for one sole purpose – to bring on the girls! They appeared to have only one ambition on the brain – to sleep with a white woman. For that privilege, in addition to discarding the dignity of their position, they would pay more than the equivalent of our monthly student allowances. We watched them heap unbelievable gifts on virtual prostitutes, among whom both British and continental students could be counted. It was lucrative time for willing 'escorts'. We were not prudish, we drank and danced with them till cockcrow, took women off them between their first drink and last boast but, we asked ourselves, were these men, who routinely conducted themselves with such gracelessness, the true representatives of a national mandate? And their version of the message of the committed minority that also urged our early return home was – *come back quickly and stake your claims. The earlier you position yourselves, the bigger your slice of the national cake.*

I recall one publicly humiliating instance: a national figure, a truly revered name in a highly sensitive political position. He got so carried away with his date that he paid for a one-night stand with a cheque, beneath which, just in case his scrawl was indecipherable, he had written his name, complete with official position. The girl, a brilliant student from an upper-class British family, but a notorious nymphomaniac, known to everyone, flounced to our table at the students cafeteria, flaunted the cheque in our faces, asking in a loud voice what kind of a would-be independent nation would produce a political leader who could act so stupidly. *I could so easily blackmail him with this*, she boasted. We succeeded in coaxing the cheque out of her – a medical student promised to introduce her to a new 'virile' boy friend if she surrendered the cheque. She agreed, and we destroyed it. She was completely indifferent to the money – it was sufficient that she had our 'national figure' in her power.

One scandal after another was hushed up by the British Home Office, which was the main sponsor for many of these 'study' or 'familiarisation' tours – familiarisation, that is, with British-style democracy, its institutions and bureaucracy. The Crown Agents, the main purchasing and forwarding agents for the colonial governments and visitors, continued to ship home luxury items for our overnight Croesuses, reams of indents – the order forms – and payment demands flowing between Nigeria and the United Kingdom as the august visitors blithely took possession of goods and ignored the payment half of the transaction. Often, the Home Office stood indemnity.

Conduct on home territory, from the news that reached us, appeared to be of the same nature. The pan-African project was becoming farcical. The alienation of many of the first-generation leaders was total and, for the first time, we began to wonder if the power relationship between the political elite and their people was not paralleled by that between the Boers and the black South African majority – a master-servant relationship, the monopoly of privilege by a minority, with its complement – the denial of rights or human respect to the people. We read in this a double betrayal, an act of treachery from within. In those student caucuses – sometimes shared with Hull, Liverpool or Manchester or wherever the vacation labour market took us – we compared notes and came to only one conclusion: the Writers and Artists' Brigade could wait – first, it was essential to secure our rear. The weapons of confrontation need not be the lethal kind – we could join forces with the progressives, make a trenchant use of the pen, the stage, propagate progressive ideas, mobilise the people and expose their betrayers. The contested arena would be strewn with words, with polemics, not soaked in gore. My adopted Muse would remain Úgún, but only he of the biting lyric.

Alas, that wilful deity would refuse to bow to mortal preferences within his dual nature!

Reunion With Òsún

It would be a waste of time to deny that a special bond, a very personal communion with the road has remained an essential part of my relation with the physical world, right from childhood, so early that it is no longer possible to recall how I came to embrace, almost in an osmotic manner, the road as the fusing agency of human preoccupations. This went beyond the merely physical – the road's linkage of Ìṣárà, my father's birthplace, and Abẹ́òkúta my maternal origin, where I was also born and mostly raised. The forest paths and lanes that laced the thatch and rust-roof farmsteads and lush farms fed the rudimentary roads between villages and towns, providing a seamless weave of mystery and discovery. The women traders from Ìṣárà, heads pressed down with bales and baskets, whose feet covered those roads and pathways every market day, laden with merchandise, perfumed the household in Aké, the rockbound parsonage of childhood. They were caravans from distant lands, their indigo dyed feet covered in red laterite as they filed into our backyard, bringing the exotic, animistic world of Ìṣárà into the christian aura of Aké. Then, right from my first journey between those two axes of my then total existence, in a wood-panelled lorry, jammed against basketloads of vegetables, yams, dried fish, beads and trinkets, bales of *adìrẹ kíjìpá, aṣọ-òkè,*[1] the still vegetal passages opened up into a succession of way stations before final destination, the road was a magic lantern whose projections, by some potent hand hidden in those dense forests, unwound as a sash of multiple designs on which we rode from marvel to marvel.

This revelation of the road's infinite resources endured for a while, competing with the railway which also had an ambiance all of its own, its rhythmic raucousness subdued, turned even mesmerising between stations by a pristine awesomeness of nature through which it snaked, leaving the viscera suspended between a pastoral innocence and the chants of commerce that began with an echo and invocation of the names of the market outposts – Olókèméjì, Ọ̀tà, Wásìmi, Láfẹnwá,... The women were my first mystics of the road, but they were no less palpable, powerful and political. It was the same women, or their market companions, who formed the vanguard of the assault on the feudal bastion of a repressive monarch, the Aláké of Abẹ̀òkúta. Despite the support of the colonial district officer, they routed him, sent him into a prolonged exile.

With the years, the magic of the road would begin to dissipate, but not so completely that, by the year of my first homecoming, the end of my study stint in England in 1960, I could not recover, or maybe simply stubbornly imbue this ageless sibling with something of its childhood retentions, whenever I motored along the highways. The five-year interruption in England and Europe by the road's pure functionality, its transformation on the landscape into just an efficient conveyor belt did sober me down somewhat, but not in entirety. A special responsiveness remained, even patches of its mystic rapport.

Is it necessary to emphasise that I felt little of that 'mystic rapport' with the highways of Europe? Maybe there were once gods in Europe but they are all dead or migrated elsewhere – except perhaps in the isolated crags and music of Wales, the poetry and drama of the Irish, the extant rituals of the Celts and the Fjords of Scandinavia. Greece has kept her gods – the peaks and gorges of Delphi remain eternally god-suffused. Also, grudgingly perhaps,

---

[1] Tie-dyed (*adìrẹ kíjìpá*) and woven textile (*aṣọ òkè*).

the Carpathian mountains of Bulgaria. The new gods and goddesses of Europe, alas, were to be found only on the cinema screen and on the pop stage – confronted with their iconic eruptions, I was able to understand, at last, the true meaning of pagan adulation.

It was good fortune that I could return home – where the gods were still only in a state of hibernation – under conditions of personal independence. I arrived on the wheels of a Rockefeller Fellowship on New Year's day, 1960, to research traditional dramatic forms. Most essential of my equipment was a Land Rover, and that vehicle became an extension of myself through which I negotiated my relationships with the overall society. I penetrated east, north, south at will, toured the entire West African coast on the trail of festivals and performing companies, keeping touch with gods and goddesses everywhere and celebrating their seasons, encountering and savouring exotic names like Dorma Ahenkro, Koton Karfi, Maiduguri, Ouagadougou, constantly at war with self-installed lords of remote inland borders who held the keys to the gates of some invisible, paradisial independencies that presumably floated above the artificially divided peoples of West Africa.

My forays outside Nigeria were infrequent, but they triggered off a habit of marvelling at a meaningless separation – Ghanaians, Togolese, etc. – just what did they mean to those who were so described? Culture and language differed within each nation as frequently and as profoundly as they found identities across the borders of such nation spaces; the arbitrariness and illogicality of their groupings hit any traveller in the face – and remain meaningless to a huge majority of those whom the borders enclose or separate. It was true of the pre-independence entities, and it is still mostly true today.

The road and I thus became partners in the quest for an extended self-discovery. Early morning departure was my favourite hour, you caught the road's exhalation as it rose from the tarmac with the sun's heated awakening, piercing the early mists in a proprietorial mood – you owned the road and all that lay revealed along its rises and plunges, its contortions and its arrow directness on both flatland and crests that sometimes appeared aimed at a horizon shimmering at the very edge of the world. Even the rarest encounter with another vehicle in that sublime hour was an act of generous concession on your part – it is only your early morning kindness that permitted it to trundle past, another wraith from the bowels of the earth.

I would throw a few clothes into what I called the 'Mungo Park' trunk that remained permanently screwed down into the back of the jeep. Nothing, absolutely nothing could substitute for setting out at that hour of the gods' retreat. Then, over the next days and weeks – Àkúré, Ìdànrè, the mountain retreat of Úgún; Kaura Namoda – a landscape of baobab sentinels ushering the traveller into Sokoto and the sonorities of the muezzin; the return track, hugging the Dahomean border – Kishi, cornfields into the horizon; Ìséyìn, weavers' looms under lean-tos; Abéòkúta balanced on rock boulders and – Lagos. I camped down in villages, in the truck, sometimes gratefully enjoyed the courtesy of rest houses built for the colonial district officers where the uniformed waiter, immaculate in standard attire, service conditioned from colonial days would pad in gently in the morning with a tea tray...

But I did not ask for tea! Yes, master – he (old enough to be my father or even grandfather) – replies, setting down the tray and pulling back the curtains... *No! Leave that alone, I'm not awake... Yes, master,* he replies, pulling the curtain open all the way... *Will master like me to make fried or scrambled eggs with the toast?* Oh, you house-trained antiquated robot, master would like to scramble Papa's head for breakfast! It was surreal! But for those stubborn early morning rituals, such interludes of luxury were only too welcome. I suppose the UNIVERSITY OF ÌBÀDÀN logo on the Land Rover had much to do with such undeserved courtesies - the university counted for something in the early sixties, and nowhere was reverence for any symbol of learning more solemnly manifested than in the hinterland. I sometimes arrived in the midst of a festival, the turbanning of a village head or a wedding, where I became an instant honoured guest. I was confronted with deep dishes of pounded yam, steaming stews and venison, gallons of fresh tapped palm wine or the most exotic bottled brands that had no business in such rural, isolated corners of the world!

Another trajectory took me through Ọ̀yọ́, city of the fiery god, Ṣàngó, leather craft and decorated gourds; Úshogbo, watched by her river goddess Ọ̀ṣun; Ilorin, Bida of glass beads and hennaed women; then Minna, scattering hordes of monkeys and baboons, plump, mouth-watering guinea fowl all the way to Kaduna, Kano, and Maiduguri of dry dust, turbaned horsemen and minarets, from where the obvious route back was to hug the Cameroon border to the east – Yola, Markurdi and confluence of the great rivers, Gboko, Abakaliki – pounded yam and roadside venison – Awka of furnaces and open smitheries, then a plunge southwards into the riverine areas... Ikot-Ekpene and outsize *ekpe* masks, Calabar of fiery *ogogoro* [2] and light-toned pulchritude, the sweep of the Niger through Port Harcourt, gathering towards its assignation with the sea, sleepy Sapele, pontoons and potfuls of *pito,*[3] then historic Benin and her outsize coral bangles, bronzes and women's landscaped coiffures...

In some mountainous areas – Obudu, Ìdànrè, Enugu, Jos Plateau – in moments of utter sublimity, the road winds like a cummerbund around the sagging waists of clouds, slicing off the peaks, dipping vertiginously into bottomless basins, a trampoline strung across tree-tops on which, you *know*, the gods take their night repose. Reluctantly I take my leave of them, head back into Ìbàdàn or Lagos where the muck, dust and grit of weeks were dissolved in beer and High Life bands in the night clubs – Victor Olaiya, Roy Chicago, Eddie Okonta, Bobby Benson, and the more intimate air of the juju bands – Orlando Owoh, Dele Ojo, Denge, or the appropriately named one with the high-pitched voice – Tunde Nightingale.

It was dust, laterite dust for the most part, or narrow ribbons of macadam, but reasonably well maintained, some no smoother than quiltwork. Pontoons, not bridges – there was no Lokoja bridge, no Asaba-Onitsha bridge, none between Warri and Sapele, only pontoons. The few bridges that interrupted the stretches of highway were single-lane bridges that could only take one vehicle at a time, and some were even shared by the railway line. It was

---

[2] Locally distilled gin.
[3] A drink from Millet.

while waiting for a pontoon at Lokoja that the doyen of the indigenous language novel – D.O. Fagunwa – would vanish in the most mysterious manner, as mysterious as his novels that formed our fictional sensibilities from childhood and peopled that accommodating world with its strange characters – *Ùgbójú Ọdẹ nínú Igbó Irúnmalẹ̀, Igbó Ìrìnkèrindò, etc.* I translated the first into English as *The Forest of a Thousand Daemons,* thereafter wisely gave up my ambitious project to translate *all* his works, so taxing did I find the density of his Yoruba usage!

So many versions of Fagunwa's death – or disappearance – but all are agreed that he was standing by the River Niger in broad daylight, waiting for the pontoon, like others, to take his motor car across the river. Perhaps he strolled along the embankment and slipped – here the versions diverge – but he was never seen again, nor was his body ever recovered. It was as if he had been claimed by one of those very creatures that crowded his imagination and were vividly brought to life in his works, as if one of them had emerged from that naked sunlight, visible to him alone, taken his arm and led him off into the unfathomable habitations of the mind.

It was not all idyllic, nor was death always mysterious, even awe-inspiring in the manner of Fagunwa's disappearance. Like the many faces of Úgún, god of the road, the road was also a violent host. I stared into the many faces of death, but most often, death just taking its leave, its back indifferently turned on heartbreak and destruction. In those early sixties, just after independence, the bridges that were inherited from the departing British were not only narrow and rickety, some were suspended, it seemed, between earth and sky, between the world of the living and the ancestor, attached to some mysterious anchor that was invisible to all but its original engineers. They appeared to lie in wait for unconscious participants in some infernal lottery. These – in addition to the still, neatly broken forests – mostly formed the backdrops to the scenes of death that were enacted before me so often in the West African interior, as if the ritual audience they awaited had to be a stranger...

By the side of the road, a small cluster of men and women, mute, isolated still forms, their faces partly hooded. Strewn around them, the shattered contents of what were once tall jute bags. Now the kolanuts are strung around their feet, outsize chromatic beads under the early sun. Only when one sees a row of corpses, neatly laid side by side does one grasp the inexorable loneliness of mortality. The stillness confers on the senses a replete, understated solitude that the frenetic realms of community, service, friendship, love and other relationships routinely obscure. A vehicle or two upended, torn, mangled, wrapped around a tree or simply neatly chipped, a fatal slice taken off its corner, or else nothing but a tell-tale swathe through the forest, and the camouflage of shrubs and trees that the errant vehicle had pulled around itself like a resentful shroud. A jagged opening through the railings on one side of the bridge might narrate the beginning of a trajectory that ended on the distant rocks below, waters swirling around a few scattered pieces of metal and wooden body frame, all unearthly still. Such tableaux instigate the reconstructing functions of the mind, instantly at work to fashion out the progression of events, stringing the vanished sequences together. Without that, the laid-out forms could well be outer space-forms in suspended animation, awaiting revival on arrival at destination, or else wrapped-up exotic tubers, levitated from within the deepest recesses of the earth.

Those early scenes of death had a solemnity about them, a graceful pronouncement of leave-taking where the precedent violence is gently absorbed by, indeed sublimated beneath that shawl of multiple existences that the Yoruba wrap around their consciousness as a testament of continuity: the world of the living, the ancestor and the unborn. Then, and only then – in those early sixties when death on the road was an isolated, discrete event, was it possible to sustain one's early mystic rapport, however tenuously, with the road. The road was old, and it was young, ageless as the peoples through whose lives it threaded, young as the same peoples who were being collectively transformed, and perhaps I assumed the function of the wanderer whose occupation was to bear witness to the road's many phases that mirrored not merely human fate but, more directly and effectively, an immediate entity in formation.

The newly demarcated space had been christened Nigeria by the spouse of a colonial officer, but it was one whose ancestral exhalations stubbornly overwhelmed its merely convenient administrative identity. I wandered through those arteries with mixed feelings, bounced not only up and down the seat of the Land Rover but – as the sun came up – between the delineation of the physical world and the misty trails of unseen presences. Undoubtedly something of this consciousness went into my encounters with those scenes of death in the early days, robbing them of the reality of violent rupture and leaving in their place the mere rites of passage, insinuating a pervasive aura of the invisible world of ancestors. The simplest way to put this therefore is perhaps that death, in those early days, had a sense of proportion – death knew its place.

My soul has grown deep like the rivers...

If Langston Hughes, the black American poet, had driven through Nigeria in a Land Rover at the beginning of the sixties, he would have written, I am certain – *My soul has grown deep, like the road.* He did visit eventually, but I doubt if he ever took up that general invitation that I issued soon after my reunion with Úgún:

> *Traveller, you must set forth*
> *At dawn*
> *I promise marvels of the holy hour...*

In the road's later decay, rather like the sustained conceit of *The Picture of Dorian Gray,* is recorded a nation's retreat from a humanism that I had imbibed, quite unconsciously, from childhood. I was fated to watch the nation turn both carrion and scavenger as it killed and consumed its kind, the road remaining an obliging stream in which a nation's fall from grace was duly reflected. To the scenes of violence and contempt for kind that would later become commonplace, a strange encounter from those idyllic days underscores the flight of marvels and the end of the holy hour. It was recorded by a journalist, and I had myself witnessed variants of such enlightenment from 'dumb beasts' on the road – I have a distinct recollection of this solemn choreography, once, not far from Àkúrẹ́, and then further north, between Jebba and Kaura Namoda:

A crow had been killed by a motor vehicle and then, in what seemed like a practised ritual, the corpse was surrounded by other crows. One after the other, they landed, then began to circle the stricken bird in deliberate formation. After a while, they stopped, moved nearer the lifeless form in what appeared to be a tightening of the circle, closing the gap between them and the corpse. Then they began a series of cawing, moving their beaks up and down in unison – it was a kind of ordered ululating, and the eerie scene looked strangely like some kind of service being held over their slain companion. Shortly after, they lifted the corpse with their beaks, taking little hops, until the entire gathering had disappeared with the corpse over the verge.

A journalist had narrated that encounter in the newspapers at the time, awed by the scene. I recollect my instant reaction to the journalist's story – it was gratitude that I had not narrated my own experience of that nature. As a known writer, tarred with the brush of a profession remarked for poetic liberties, no one would have believed me. Still, there it was, even the crows appeared to accord some dignity to their dead. And the humans did no less at that stage when I still boasted a visceral companionship with the road. Death was constant companion, but its victims were not mere carrion on the road. Each scene of death was – after the initial disorientation – almost a haven of tranquility. The survivors, even the injured awaiting help formed a serene community – transfigured, it seemed, by a surreal wind that blew across them briefly, and altered their lives for ever. Enfolding such scenes in an immense, invisible cloak was a palpable presence of time in its absolute stillness.

There was a practical reward to my preoccupation with the road – it was a talisman against alienation, that altering phenomenon that separates the individual from community being. This condition had begun to disfigure the social landscape of the nation not long after Independence, especially in the cities. Out in the hinterland, one could still wallow in a mystic bond with the land, and thus with a people's eternal, collective being. If I was an initiate in this process of the coming-in-being of a nation, the road was my personal mentor, conspirator and – in the growing face of alienation – an unassuming safeguard. Alas, its revelations also plunged me into the parallel politics of its violent being.

First Skirmishes

I returned to Nigeria on New Year's day, 1960; it was to a nation that was wound up to a fever pitch of social expectations – and self-confidence – as her date for independence from British rule drew close. Its future was already mapped out however, for the eve-of-Independence elections had already taken place the previous year, and all that was left was for the British government to hand over power to the victorious party and take its leave.

I was not pessimistic about the future, but extremely cautious, having come into contact with the first generation leaders in my student days in England. The enemy, as I had identified it, was power and its pitfalls, a cautionary *motif* that dominated my would-be Independence play, *A Dance of the Forests*. The view was not shared by the cultural bureaucrats, quick to smell out subversion. They cautioned that the play contained a subversive message. It had won the contest for the official theatre presentation for the occasion but was now deemed a damper, unsuitable for a festive occasion. I staged it anyway, in an alternative venue, using the prize money, and forming a theatre company – the *1960 Masks* – in the process.

On the much anticipated Independence Day, October 1, 1960, the 'subversives' presented their shoe-string world-view on the stage of the University Theatre, Ìbàdàn, while the nation celebrated its formal liberation from colonial bondage in a series of sumptuous events and ceremonials in the capital, Lagos. The nation space known as Nigeria had come of age, a federation made up of three semi-autonomous regions – the Eastern, the Western, and the Northern Regions – the last occupying a landmass larger in size than the other two combined. Each had its own legislature in its regional capital, while a Federal house sat in Lagos, the nation's capital. Those regional legislatures – or Houses of Assembly – had been in place since 1952, and functioning. However, the results from the preparatory federal elections of 1959 that decided who held power at the centre, conducted by the departing British officials, had been most bitterly disputed, and it was already a divided nation that ritually lowered the British Union Jack that October, folded it away, and hoisted the green-white-green of Nigeria – surely the most uninspiring national flag on the surface of the earth! The white was said to symbolise peace, green stood for agriculture; combined they misrepresented the sum of a nation's imagination.

Recent memoirs[1] by former colonial officers have revealed how crooked that beginning was. The elections that placed a government in power at the centre were rigged – by the British! John Bull was not about to leave an independent Nigeria under the control of any uppity radicals – as the southern nationalists – the East and the West – were perceived. Thus, on instructions from the British Home Office, even the Nigerian census was falsified, giving an artificial majority to a North that was largely feudalist by tradition and conservative in political outlook. The census was actually based on sample head counts – random or selective, no one knew – which were then roughly multiplied by the acreage of the land mass, irrespective of actual population densities!

In its resolve to ensure that the nation was handed over to a conservative power, the British did not rely on a concocted numerical strength alone. After all, the North did harbour radical

---

[1] In 1992, the memoirs of a former colonial officer, Harold Smith, were ready for publication but suppressed by the British government. The author sent me the   manuscript, in which he revealed that he was ordered by the Home Office to take part in the rigging of the 1959 elections.. In his own words – 'it was the British who taught Nigerians the art of rigging'.

or rebellious elements in quite sizeable numbers – the Tivs, in what is still known as the Middle Belt, or the Northern Elements Progressive Union. And so, to make absolutely certain that power did not fall into the wrong hands, specific instructions were issued by the British Home Office to its civil servants – the final results of elections to the federal legislature must be manipulated, where necessary, in favour of the political conservatives. Archival material, now free of the time constraints of the Official Secrets' Act, testify to this. An admission, and even statement of regret was wrung out of a serving British minister during the Abacha years. The precedent had however been set, and rigging now answered the name of democracy.

Not surprisingly, the nation's flag began to unravel rather quickly after Independence. To begin with, each of the three regions, West, East and North, had its own restless minorities. A low-intensity armed warfare, largely unpublicised, accompanied the nation into Independence in the Tiv region of the North. Elections merely modified the geography of hostilities.

On Independence Day, October 1, 1960, my own West was ruled by the Action Group party, led by the dour, ascetic Yoruba, Obafemi Awolowo, affectionately known as 'Awo'. However, his party lost the fight for federal control at the centre to the Northern Peoples Congress (NPC), the North-based party, which was headed by Sir Ahmadu Bello, a feudal Fulani scion. Ahmadu Bello claimed descent from the legendary Othman dan Fodio, the jihadist who once swore that he would dip the Koran in the Atlantic.

The NPC also controlled the Northern Region. In the East, the party that held power was the National Council of Nigeria and the Cameroons (NCNC), led by the charismatic, US-educated Nnamdi Azikiwe, an Igbo, a self-described Fabian whose oratory at public rallies drew shouts of 'Ze-ee-eek' from delirious crowds. That party also lost to the NPC at the centre, but teamed up with the winner to form a ruling coalition at the federal level. The position of the nation's prime minister fell, naturally, to the senior partner, the NPC.

The leader of the NCNC, Nnamdi Azikiwe, having failed to capture power at the centre, announced his retirement from politics, waxed biblical in a valedictory speech that declared that, with national Independence, 'my task is done'. He was compensated with the ceremonial position of Governor-General of Nigeria, representing the Queen of England – Nigeria had chosen to remain within an arrangement that was still called the British Commonwealth, headed by the Queen. Sir Ahmadu Bello, leader of the victorious party, chose to remain at the head of the regional northern government, nominating his lieutenant, Tafawa Balewa, a former school teacher, as the first Prime Minister of the newly independent nation – regional heads of government were designated 'premiers'. The Action Group of the West thus remained the minority opposition party in the federal legislature. Unlike his Northern counterpart however, the leader of the Action Group, Awolowo chose to lead the opposition at the federal level, leaving his second-in-command – Ladoke Akintola, a nationally acknowledged master of Yoruba oratory and a shrewd political strategist – as premier of the West.

The developing fissures, nation-wide, were perhaps inevitable, given the artificial grafting of the British parliamentary system on a patchwork nation with different pre-colonial histories and systems of self-governance. The West was the first to manifest the contradictions. An open rift developed between the party leader Awolowo – and Akintola, his lieutenant in the West, a region whose politics had always been as volatile as its people were politically advanced. The rift intensified, and the party broke in two, with a little help from the recruiting ambitions of the ruling party, the NPC. The breakaway group in the West, transformed into the Nigerian National Democratic Party, the NNDP, was led by the erstwhile lieutenant, Ladoke Akintola. It became increasingly perceived as an ally of the ruling party, the NPC; certainly its political ideology became more conservative, more openly impatient with the 'radical' tendencies of the parent party. Defections, intrigues, ideological polarisation, political blackmail, greed for a 'slice of the national cake'... finally all the ingredients were in place for a new political experience, an arbitrary order of governance. In 1962, the elected government of the West – and with it, democracy – was suspended, and the region placed under emergency rule.

The immediate justifying episode for taking over the West, one that fulfilled the condition of 'a breakdown of law and order, was provided when the Western House of Assembly converted its chambers into a boxing-cum-wrestling arena. This well laid plan to destabilise that region was activated by a pre-set signal in the shout *"Iná l'órí òkè!"* – Fire on the mountain! A legislator vaulted benches and desks, seized the speaker's mace and attempted to make off with it. It ended up in two pieces, but only after first drawing blood from the head of a fellow law-giver. A famous image, captured by an alert photographer in the press gallery, showed my favourite political maverick, Tony Enahoro, escaping the mêlée through a window.

Tony Enahoro would again take to flight, this time clandestinely through the borders, but that was yet some months away. For now, the organisers of this legislative rout had achieved their purpose, and the nation – the Western Region at least – embarked on a novel adventure. The region was placed under an administrator, a medical doctor then in government service and, we would learn later, personal physician to the Prime Minister, Tafawa Balewa. He had powers to rule by decree, detain citizens without trial. The nation had heard of such things in other places but never imagined that we would actually taste of it in Nigeria – little did most imagine that this was merely a rehearsal for worse. The administrator wasted no time in placing political leaders under his sanction, including my friend from student days, Bola Ige, a lawyer and rising leader within the Action Group.

Bola Ige's final, and most prolonged place of detention was an isolated Rest House on the outskirts of Ubiaja, the divisional headquarters of Ishan in the then Benin Province – about 600 kilometres from Ìbàdàn. His party, the Action Group, was undisguisedly the real target of Federal intervention. A few token politicians from the breakaway branch of the Action Group – the NNDP – were also detained, but mostly in cosy circumstances. Government catering rest houses were their favoured choice, where they continued to conduct party affairs and even receive connubial visits. A quite substantial proportion of Nigerians – among whom I was – read in the move of the Federal Government the beginning of an attempt to strangle the democratic infant in its crib and turn the nation, gradually, into a one-party state. So soon – I could be forgiven for thinking – the actualisation of warnings from *A Dance of the Forests?*

A more adaptable, more pugnacious theatre company than the professionally competent but top-heavy 1960 Masks was clearly required. Enter *Orísun Theatre,* primed for instant, improvised sketches on the political situation. The administrator's dictatorial conduct in the West, his uneven apportionment of sanctions, hard suspicions of a 'secret agenda' provoked my lampoon on his office and governance style. It took the form of a song adapted from 'The Vicar of Bray' and was published in the media. Nothing untoward resulted from this foray beyond a friendly warning passed through 'official channels' of Ìbàdàn University where I was serving my stint as a Rockefeller Fellow in Drama. The administrator was not pleased. He was prepared to tolerate the exercise of my freedom of expression, but wanted me to know that he was in the West, after all, to carry out a repair job, to stop the West from descending into utter chaos. This, he urged us to appreciate, was a delicate task of healing – for which, presumably, his medical training especially fitted him. He expected the academic community to cooperate with him in the achievement of his mission. I assured my interlocutors that I was indeed engaged on an important contribution to his objectives as I proceeded to prepare a series of political satires, the first of which would appear on stage as *Before the Blackout.* It included a dramatised version of the adaptation from 'The Vicar of Bray'.

And then, as if the political scene was not sufficiently heated or complicated for such a young democracy, the nation was riveted by news of a far grimmer dimension than a mere rough–and–tumble among lawmakers – a conspiracy had been unearthed that sought to execute what would have amounted to a civilian coup d'état. The nest of conspirators was located in the Action Group. There was talk of proscribing the party altogether. Its leading figures were rounded up, some were placed under house arrest, others taken straight to prison – it all left the nation, but especially the Western Region in shock. Gradually, the net contracted, closing in on the real target. No one was especially surprised when the party leader himself, Chief Obafemi Awolowo, was arrested.

The trials followed lengthy, drawn out investigations, during which the name of an Irish police officer, Mr. John Lynn, pioneered the conflation, in Nigerian modern history, of an individual name with torture. When trials began, a number of the accused protested that their statements had been made under duress, their confessions extracted under torture. The statements were nonetheless admitted in evidence. Not surprisingly virtually all the accused, including Obafemi Awolowo, were found 'guilty as charged' and sentenced to long terms of imprisonment. The judge then committed the astonishing indiscretion of proceeding to recuperate from his marathon hearing as a vacation guest of the head of the ruling (and 'persecuting') party, directly after convicting and sentencing the accused. Never was a well known Yoruba saying more eagerly seized upon: *The witch cried one night, and the child died the morning after; who still disputes that it was the witch who killed and consumed the child?* It contributed in no small measure to the interpretative twist given to the judge's words when, before delivering judgement, he declared, 'my hands are tied'. Even while considering his verdict deeply flawed, I believe till today that his words were completely innocuous, being no more than the standard observation by any judge that, no matter his personal inclinations or public expectations, he was duty bound by the law. For the majority of government adversaries however, the judge had admitted that he was carrying out orders!

With those trials, the Nigerian political atmosphere was drastically transformed. The hunt continued for the fugitives, including Tony Enahoro, nearly all of whom had taken refuge in Ghana, then enjoying the reputation of a radical nation under the leadership of Kwame Nkrumah.

I remained one of the skeptics. I believed there was never any weighty matter to the treason attempt, and hold till today that Awolowo, in particular, was a victim of political intrigue, largely fomented by the NPC, but with the full collaboration of elements from within the breakaway party, the NNDP. This, perhaps, was because I was aware that, in pursuit of its increasingly socialist objectives, the Action Group leadership had decided to send some cadres to be trained at the Winneba Ideological Institute in Ghana. A number of young African revolutionaries in the anti-colonial struggle also attended the course, some of whom returned home to take up armed struggle against colonial domination – Angola, Guinea Bissau, Mozambique. Additionally however, clobbered by the strong-arm tactics employed by the governing parties, as well as the extra-legal deployment of the local constabularies under the control of the governing parties – thugs and local government police were becoming indistinguishable – the Action Group engaged in some soul-searching and concluded that it had been negligent in its physical department. The party thereupon assigned a number of its youths to specialised training – self-defence and general toughening-up sessions – in a camp said to have been set up in Northern Ghana. I had a good rapport with some of the inner circle of the Action Group and its allied opposition groups. In addition to Bola Ige, who was never arrested or charged, I had become quite close to Dr. Chike Obi, a wiry, eccentric mathematician who was reputed to have come close to uncovering the proof of the elusive 'Fermat's theorem' – nobody knew exactly what 'Fermat's theorem' was about, or who Fermat was, but academic folklore had placed this theorem at the pinnacle of mathematical pursuit, and the media had enshrined the name in public consciousness. It was a surprise to me to learn that Chike Obi had launched a political party in Eastern Nigeria, the Dynamic Party, but no surprise that it was a radical leaning party that preached revolution – and even dictatorship! – as the only recipe for the nation's ills. The latter remained our main point of disagreement. It was typical of the mathematician to have driven one of the suspects – Tony Enahoro himself? – to safety across the border, for which he was arrested, but later released. Between Bola Ige and Chike Obi, I obtained quite reliable information on the thinking within the party.

That some elements within the Winneba trainees from the Action Group may have been converted by the actual

revolutionaries in waiting at that school and organised themselves
into an insurgent unit, bent on overthrowing a government that
was considered reactionary, a stooge of the British government,
etc., was a distinct possibility, and probably closer to the truth.
That Obafemi Awolowo was involved in such an attempt was a
charge that I found incompatible with the man's nature – his entire
nature was legalist-constitutionalist to a fault. Chike Obi was an
astute reader of politics, quite close to Awolowo, and he was
contemptuous of those charges. I visited him at Kirikiri prison a
few times, taking, naively, a bottle of cognac to keep him company.
The bottle was taken in charge by the prison officer who promised
that it would be kept among his other possessions until his release.
That was my first intimation that such indulgences were not
permitted on the prison menu.

Tony Enahoro became Nigeria's 'Most Wanted', accused of
being one of the masterminds of the plot – now that, I felt, was
likely to contain more than a grain of truth. In the anti-colonial
struggle, Enahoro's record was one of direct, confrontational
activism, while Awolowo was a convinced, indeed punctilious
legalist. Alerted in good time of his impending arrest, Enahoro
fled to Ghana, then to the United Kingdom, convinced of his safety
in a thriving democracy. At the request of the Nigerian
government, he was arrested and detained in London. A
determined attempt to extradite him back to Nigeria to stand trial
with others turned into a *cause celebre*. It wound its way through
the British courts, the Houses of Parliament, and the Privy Council
– then the final Court of Appeal. Whether Enahoro was guilty or
not, I found it intolerable that all the progressives were being netted
and incapacitated, and decided to contribute to the effort to prevent
his extradition. In any case, there was the issue of equity: any
means to recover what has been unfairly or illegally acquired
cannot be unfair or illegal. Electoral robbery, rather than equitable
contest, was already the rule in the nation.

Enahoro's case now took centre stage in the British Houses
of Parliament – to sustain the time-honoured claims of political
asylum, or butter up the ego of democratic neophytes in apprentice
nation states? I became restless with the knowledge that I was

fortuitously placed to lend a hand, thanks to relationships I had developed with one or two figures in the British establishment while undergoing my apprenticeship at the Royal Court Theatre, London. An interventionist tendency had begun to manifest itself in my temperament, though I was yet to become fully conscious of it. I scraped together what money I could find, borrowed the rest, bought a ticket and flew into London to add my own quota to the lobby against his extradition, profiting from my friendship with Tom Driberg, an *enfant terrible* of the British Labour Party, and Lord Kenneth of the House of Lords, whom I had known in his plebeian days as Wayland Young.

To my astonishment, the battle was lost. The space of political sanctuary had always seemed a universal given, now it appeared that there were huge gaps in my history education. Tony Enahoro was flown home to stand his trial, like the others, on the charge of treasonable felony. He was found guilty and joined his leader, Awolowo, and other party leaders, for a long sojourn in prison.

The field for the consolidation of one-party rule was now wide open. The ruling party and its allies could afford to throw all democratic restraint to the wind, the opposition having been demonised and discredited. The government was now well placed to lay claim to the mantle of democratic defenders even as it engaged in undemocratic conduct. Alas, it had completely misread the mood of the West!

Long before the convictions, the emergency had ended, the worthy doctor retired to his clinic, but not without first restoring order – that is, overseeing the emergence of the breakaway party, the NNDP, as masters of the West, with its leader, Ladoke Akintola as Premier. In the federal chamber, the NCNC, having served its purpose, found itself increasingly marginalised, fed only crumbs from the 'national cake'. The honeymoon was over and it filed its divorce papers – citing spousal abuse and public humiliation. It was promptly replaced by the bride-in-waiting, the NNDP.

The power of incumbency now decided electoral results. The Action Group, leaderless, lost direction. It would boycott elections, reverse itself, box itself into strategic corners, retreat, lick its wounds, re-organise, and await the next elections. From his prison cell, Obafemi Awolowo gradually acquired the image of a victim of political intrigue and injustice, a martyred visionary and leader, thanks to the NNDP misgovernment and repressive measures. There was no ambiguity about it – the NNDP was unpopular. The West seethed with resentment.

The next regional elections of 1965 approached. Virtually every woman and child, aged and ailing, donned their battle gear in readiness for a desperate fight. For that contest, the Action Group teamed up with the former partner of the ruling party – the NCNC – to form a new coalition – the United Progressive Grand Alliance (UPGA). The alliance boosted the morale of both the Action Group and the Western electorate. Tacticians were exchanged. Badly needed resources flowed into the strangulated coffers of the AG. The region simmered as even the normally apolitical prepared for what they embraced as a revenge match, where scores would be settled definitively, and the world would know just who enjoyed the people's support. It was to prove a contest between terror and resistance into which I would be drawn for my first taste of political blood.

My life of sponsored and footloose research – and private theatrical activities – ended at the University of Ìbàdàn in 1962. After a few months of unemployment, I transferred to the University of Ifẹ to earn an honest living as lecturer in the English department – Ifẹ's temporary campus was then still located in Ìbàdàn, the seat of government for the Western Region. The NNDP government, which now ruled the West, was proprietor of the university – and this was where the problem began!

In preparation for an electoral blitzkrieg throughout the region for the 1965 fight, the university was designated a den of opposition that had to be either bought over or crushed. Thus, one unexpected day, the Deputy Vice-Chancellor, standing in for his boss, summoned a special congregation. Its sole purpose, conducted with all pomp and due solemnity, was to annunciate a new university credo – the word was actually used in the address: *the credo of the university is that it must support the government of the day!* It was that crude, an inglorious performance whose shame, or thought of potential consequences must have overwhelmed the messenger himself since he did not even wait for the usual comments or debate but fled the hall immediately afterwards, and the campus. He did not return until a week later, after the government had virtually taken over the campus. He could hardly be blamed – the Vice-Chancellor had himself earlier transferred to Lagos, leaving the unsavoury task to his deputy.

Five or six resignations followed immediately. Among them was the taciturn – except in political matters – Professor Victor Oyenuga, biologist and diehard card-carrying member of the Action Group; Sam Aluko, economist, another Action Group strategist, myself; two or three expatriate lecturers, notably Robin Horton the anthropologist, who would move East and settle down with a Nigerian wife. We gave the university the required three months notice. Obedient to instructions from the Ministry of Education however, the university responded by accepting the resignations – but with immediate effect. All resigning lecturers would be paid three months salary in lieu of notice, and were ordered to vacate their university residences within forty-eight hours!

The arena of polemics outside campus had already degenerated into the physical. Even theatre – especially political satire of our kind – to promote which I had extracted a group of young actors from the 1960 Masks into a separate unit, the (Orísun Theatre), reinforced with new recruits – had become fraught with such violence that the actors had to be trained in basic self-defence – my favourite innovation being an unorthodox use of fire extinguishers in enclosed spaces. We learnt quickly to adjust, since those performances, to reach their audiences, required spaces where the actors were exposed to instant reprisals. Now the ivory tower itself was about to be physically assailed by the crudity of political intolerance.

Sam Aluko was a smallish lecturer with slightly bulging eyes that blinked furiously above a permanently truculent posture, while he launched his rapid delivery tirades in a heavy accent that was easily recognisable as that of the Èkìtì people. An Action Group economic adviser, he was away in Lagos attending a political meeting when the strong arm of the NNDP government descended. To leave no doubt whatever in the minds of the anti-credo group that the government's intent was understood, the Permanent Secretary of the Ministry of Education filled his white Mercedes Benz car with thugs, invaded Sam Aluko's house, terrorised his wife and children, flung their furniture and luggage all over and out of windows and smashed a few household items. They left, warning that they would return after twenty-four hours. They tried also to find the residences of the other lecturers but failed – in any case, they were not eager to remain too long on campus, and two of us actually lived off-campus.

We heard the news, mobilised what forces we could, and rushed to protect Aluko's family. Legally, the resigning lecturers were entitled to remain in their residences until the end of the three-month notice, so we prepared to keep a roster of guards over Aluko's home until the three months had expired. Joyce, Sam's wife, and the children were however much too traumatised – all they wanted to do was quit campus as fast as possible. I could hardly insist, since I lived off-campus, and my quarters were well secured. We had to content ourselves with guarding the premises until she and her family could leave in an orderly and dignified manner, then occupied the house for a week or so afterwards in the hope that the Permanent Secretary's goons would return, expecting to find a defenceless family.

The 'refuseniks' had learnt their lesson however. What was a hastily improvised group of a 'volunteer defence force' – actors, academics, the odd poet and writer, a few civil servants, a handful of fiercely politicised patrons of the *Mbari Club* who badly wanted to 'do something!' etc. – was whittled down, streamlined into a close-knit group to develop tactics for confronting the incipient fascism. At the time, it did not even bother to give itself a name.

The mobilisation was timely. It meant that we were not too ill-prepared when the 1965 regional elections began and a people's electoral will was openly ridiculed by the incumbent government. Before all-out violence finally replaced further pretensions to legality, the opposition had circumvented the government controlled public radio with its steady announcements of falsified results. The true results from both urban centres and far-flung villages, straight from the desks and trestles of the counting rooms, certified by the contending candidates and returning officers, were telephoned to the broadcasting studios of the Eastern Region, from where they were broadcast to the nation, and to the outside world. A team of radio journalists from the alliance partner, the NCNC-controlled East, also arrived in the West to cover the elections. Led by a seasoned broadcaster, Mazi Ukonu, also a comic performer on radio, the team arrived with a transmitter that was installed – I discovered to my horror – in the home of the imprisoned leader of the Action Group, Awolowo!

Too late for relocation, we could only monitor what knowledge of, or plans the government had for the transmitter, then make contingency plans for its evacuation, if necessary. The field team from Enugu, pointed in the direction of key areas by our opposition group, and sometimes escorted for their safety, recorded and transmitted comments on the ongoing electoral charade, reported graphic incidents of violence. Hunted by NNDP police and 'stalwarts', denounced by the government as foreign infiltrators sent to rig the elections, their operation was meant to last only two or three days, but we managed to persuade them to remain until the very last result from the remotest hamlet had been recorded and broadcast. Ukonu and his team were held 'prisoners' till their task was completed, but never were prisoners more willing and obliging, even while somewhat apprehensive for their safety.

On the last but one night of the presence of the Eastern broadcasters, we were finally alerted that the location of the transmitter had been discovered by the police who would raid Awolowo's house the following day. The information came too late to dismantle and transfer the equipment, so we quickly improvised a defence of the transmitter, awaiting the police assault. Some set up a diversionary ambush around a school across the road from Awolowo's home. We kept armed vigil. My favoured couch was the carpeted floor beneath a massive oak desk of the imprisoned leader. The assault did take place – but only after the final broadcast by Ukonu's team. When the police forces arrived on the planned dawn raid, Awolowo's house had been emptied, and Ukonu and gang were well on their way back to safety. The band of volunteers had had their induction into the new requirements for the political arena; they slipped out before dawn, returned to their homes with relief and awaited the next developments. The region hung on edge. An election had been stolen – would the robbers insist on clinging to stolen goods?

The answer was provided in time tested ways. More opposition leaders were arrested, their homes and businesses vandalised and, in some cases, thugs were sent to rape their women, at times with the husband forcibly held down to witness the violation. The people, at first on the retreat, began to respond in kind. The homes and offices of government loyalists were torched, agents killed – sometimes in broad daylight, openly, and in urban centres, ambushes were laid for the marauding police squads. A new expression entered the vocabulary of politics – *weti è!* – literally, douse it (with petrol), then set it on fire! The police had their tear gas canisters, Mark IV rifles, pistols, and even the occasional sub-machine guns; the resisters had in the main just the locally fabricated 'Dane' guns, some shotguns, machetes, and – improvisation. The recipe for a concoction, invented by the farmers and used to deadly effect remains largely elusive till today – when the police arrived on their raids in rural areas, the seats and back rests of their unguarded trucks were smeared – or sprayed – with this substance. Minutes after the raiders returned and regained their seats, the effect began – presumably by then the mystery unguent had percolated through their clothing, the process being accelerated, we learnt, by the amount of sweat on their shirts. They leapt up, began to tear off their clothing, convulsed in pain. It was nothing I ever witnessed personally, nobody seemed to have died from its effect, but it was narrated by the victims themselves, who described the effect as one of intense, sticky burning. An African prototype of the napalm perhaps? I called it the 'Medea Effect.'

Finally, seeing that the campaign of intimidation had failed at voting time, the final 'voter returns' were simply plucked out of thin air and announced on radio and television, fulfilling the blasphemous boast of the then Deputy Premier of the region on state television that launched the doomed elections: *whether you vote for us or not, we don't give a damn, since we're going to win anyway. The angels will descend from the heavens to cast their votes on our side...*

Spells of Sanity

The 'roaring sixties' were not, however, an unbroken period of political outrage and response, of impositions, of a bleak intensity that sometimes appeared to have dominated, even defined the life of a young man of thirty. It was not without periods of enlivening relief, both within and outside the nation. Teaching remained a constant respite, a mental undercurrent that restored a sense of proportion and highlighted the absurdity of much of the political reality. It was however a rather difficult time for my head of department, a pleasant Scottish lady whose real specialisation was bibliography. She could not understand why the departmental timetable was never good enough for me, so that I had to make independent arrangements with my students, and my classes took place at any time of the day, night or weekends, and sometimes simply occupied a continuous weekend before another vanishing act! Once, she happened to read an essay submitted by a student, who had taken to heart my proposition that for Emily Brontë's 'Heathcliff' – yes, Emily Brontë did fall in my lap! – an apposite metaphor would be the vampire. With the same intensity as the student had pursued the theme, the Scottish lady tried to contest the notion, without the slightest trace of humour, thereby provoking me to improvise a sturdy correlative of clues from which I refused to budge. Finally, she sighed, shook her head and looked out of the window at a huge tree on whose branches bats clustered in their thousands. Instantly, her face lit up and she pointed to the leathery blobs, 'When you teach *Wuthering Heights* at night to the background of those squeaky little things, I suppose you're bound to see vampires.'

The Mbari Club remained a place for shedding political

tensions – even while introducing some of its own. Workshops, exhibitions, plays, music recitals, a well-stocked bar where both the locals and the expatriate community would stay up till the early hours... eccentric individuals whose interests and activities provided periods of escape – like the artistic projects of a truly talented artist nicknamed Mr. G., for his unfailing regularity in picking up the common social disease in brothels, to the exasperation of his doctor, a Nigerian, who did not believe in patient confidentiality. A totally different kettle of fish, who also drank as one, was Mitholfer, of an impressive but well packaged girth. An officer of indeterminate functions in the American Information Service, Mitholfer lived near Femi Johnson in his first home at Onírèké, so we often met there. Mitholfer showed such fervid interest in my take on the political goings on that Femi and I challenged him to deny that he was a CIA agent, specially assigned to me. He would only respond with his Bhudda smile, then go to sleep in his chair. Always good for the latest rumours, for 'complots and stratagems' behind enemy lines – the corridors of power – Mitholfer always thoughtfully visited with his cold bag holding ten or twelve bottles of beer. He was the only being I knew who, after downing six 75 litre bottles of Star Beer, could still hold an impeccable conversation. Even more impressive was the fact that he could balance a frothing mugful of the seventh in one hand, holding the mug against his chest or with his arm extended across the arm-rest, fall asleep, stentorous snores issuing from ample caverns, then wake up with a jerk as his head threatened to snap off the edge of the back rest but – not a drop spilling from the mug! He seamlessly resumed the upward journey of the mug, took a swig, resumed the conversation exactly at the point where he slept off, then went into the same routine over and over again. At first, we thought it was an act, faking sleep so that he could pick up unguarded tid-bits, but we tested his condition in several ways and there was no doubt about it – after the fourth bottle, Mitholfer was on his way to Star spangled dreamland. So we nicknamed him 'Lanke Omu', after the adventurer of Amos Tutuola's *The Palm Wine Drinkard*.

'Carlo Mancini', a chubby, unflappable Italian, also a Femi

Johnson neighbour, came to Nigeria through Ghana, where he worked for a construction firm, going through his monthly salary with a steadfastness that sustained Ghanaian nightclubs and their habituees. After nearly two decades in Anglophone West Africa, Mancini yet retained his own stimulating vocabulary and syntax of the English language. Certain words, sometimes of the simplest and commonest usage, stubbornly eluded him. For instance, he could never recall the word 'erazer' or 'rubber'. Instead, after scratching his head for a long time, he would hit on a substitute that exploded with relief and clarity – give me a *write-and-cancel!*

In Accra – so went his own life account – a favourite night-club habituee took him in hand and pleaded, 'Carlo, you strike me as a very bright person. I know you're good with your hands. So why do you dissipate your money and life this way? I want you to try handing me your salary every month. You can drink all you want in the house, far more cheaply, and we'll put something aside every month so you can start your own business. I want you to be your own boss!' Carlo at first found the idea outlandish, but not too unwelcome, so he decided to give it a try. Before long, they had moved in together and entered into a *write-no-cancel* marital bond that netted three children and a thriving business. They transferred to Nigeria – not that it stopped Carlo making the occasional forays into Nigerian fleshspots but then, the sixties' nightclubs were the true melting pots of all classes and nationalities, genial, music saturated joints with exotic names, or simply intriguing – *Risikat, Agoji Mayor, Seven Sisters, Black Morocco* or *Caban Bamboo* – the last being a Lagos favourite where the erratic band leader and proprietor, Bobby Benson, presided over a motley crew of barmen and stewards and his own band, among whom he rotated his bouts of fisticuffs as if on principle or from boredom. His complaints covered the full range – from his musicians selling his musical instruments or their services to others, thus missing engagements, to stewards making off with the takings, drinking his beer, watering his whisky or drunk asleep on the job, rifling the till or shortchanging customers. He punched them out of doors, yet a week later, they are back on duty. Bobby Benson arranged my adaptation of the traditional song *Mà á fę́ę*, and never missed his mischievous ritual of attribution, always introducing the number as 'Wole's song – don't blame me' – before its rendition.

On the night waves rode also the other class of musicians, deeply indigenous *jùjú, ṣákárà, àpàlà, agídìgbo* bands that played till the early hours of the morning, where rival political thugs exercised a choice of declaring a truce, or busting up the joint the moment they set eyes on one another. *Kongi's Harvest* took its life from the night habituees, variations on the theme of power, its obsessions, pretensions and sensualities. Fittingly, we used Bobby Benson's place as a daytime rehearsal venue during preparations for the staging of that play at Black Arts Festival in Dakar, 1966. Erratic even in friendship, Bobby would lock us out in a sudden fit of pique, provoked perhaps by abandonment by his latest paramour, or frustrated at a debtor who had again given him the slip. He would lock himself in his permanently pitch-black living quarters that seemed to have been quarried out of Caban Bamboo's underground warrens. I knew the back door into the interior, so now he had to open up when I beat on that door. He appeared in his velvet, ankle-length dressing gown with a boyish, apologetic grin, baldly lie that he had not known that we were coming to rehearse and, in any case, when were we going to pay for the hire of the rehearsal space? Hours later, freshly bathed and wreathed in his favourite perfume – it was Paco Rabanne – he would stroll out, his neat goatee leading, a three-piece striped immaculately pressed suit, a gold waistcoat chain across a mere suspicion of a paunch, a silver-topped black walking stick, a fedora set at his 'rascal' angle. Followed by a steward with plates of fried rice and chunks of peppered chicken, he regally gestured him to set it down, tipped his hat towards us and sauntered out for the day. We had not ordered it, yet there it was, and with a bill attached – Bobby never joked with his accounts.

Headed for Ọ̀ṣun, north-east of Ìbàdàn, home of Suzanne Wenger the Austrian artist, and a greater contrast could hardly be imagined. With her husband, Ulli Beier, an assignment roulette in Europe had brought them into Nigeria and both promptly 'went native', Suzanne not just culturally but viscerally and spiritually, holding nothing back in herself. She had, in effect, found that self.

She was inducted into the priesthood of the goddess of Ọṣun river whose mystic grove she proceeded to adorn with startling – sometimes controversial – sculptures, aided by a circle of local artistic initiates that she progressively gathered around her. Together they turned the grove into one of the strangest, yet most meditative spots in the nation. Wiry and sprightly, large green eyes and a remarkable sense of self-deprecation, Suzanne always declared herself insulated from politics, yet remained intensely political. One hand fought off the indiscriminate loggers who had no care for the pristine serenity of the grove, a tranquility that she had absorbed and carried around with her everywhere, yet uncoiling its serpentine energy at will. These were desperate men who even once sent assassins to deal with the 'interfering white witch'– if only they knew that this was a woman who had risked the Nazi concentration camps for her role in hiding potential victims of the gas chambers! Her other hand she kept for fending off the over enthusiastic tourist entrepreneurs – both private and governmental - who also saw the grove as a money-making enterprise, to be enhanced by tinselly, exotic events. That left just her body and spirit to paint and sculpt with!

Ọṣun grove, paradoxically, must have been created by the gods specifically for the 'Wild, Wild, West', a region that needed a spring of healing or at least, escape, a periodic immersion in the quiescent depths of the pacific deities. To escape into Ọṣun grove was always a journey into timelessness, a most dangerous indulgence, since the question on leaving was always – do I really have to leave? Why need I leave? To achieve what, exactly? This temptation to take Ọṣun with one, inside one, was the strongest internal battle that had to be fought – Ọṣun tugging at the end of a long, frayed rope, Úgún at the other...

And sometimes it was outward bound – there, I was more fortunate than most. Unemployed twice in the first five years of my return home, and for stress inducing lengths of time - it was not for a total lack of opportunities but for a lack of the ideal position that would cater to both body and spirit - flexible, and stimulating. During such slack phases, I would take out my slim conferences/lectures file and, with a new regard - of longing and of necessity! – reconsider those overseas invitations that I had shunted aside for some time, being too preoccupied with unequal dialogues with sole administrators, political (and academic) vampires and allied modes of ungainful employment. It was not that I had never busied myself evolving lucrative schemes for keeping Orísun Theatre – my most immediate responsibility and political vehicle – afloat and active, envisioning its self-sustaining future as a formidable enterprise that would be quoted on the stock market – no – there was no failure of ideas in that direction. Art could be made to pay its way, I contended, and I was the mogul especially destined to prove it. All schemes alas, collapsed on the drawing board. Then my economic health prescribed, without further consultation, a spell on the lecture and conference circuit of the United States and Europe. Even the batteries of conflict require periodic charging.

The Transcription Centre in London, managed by the art historian Dennis Duerden with the Albert Einstein head of hair, was the central magnet, a dependable refuge for many impoverished or simply displaced writers and artistes, especially from South Africa – Ezekiel Mphahlele, Lewis Nkosi, Mazizi Kunene etc. – reminding one that there was still a world out there with even more intractable problems, both political and artistic. Even the campaigns against the atom bomb, the Aldermaston marches in which I participated after my return to Nigeria, provided spaces of political recuperation, since the problems of nuclear destruction did not reach down into my personal core of identification, but was widespread as a diffuse, generalised concern with millions of unknown others – òrun má a wó, òrun má a wó, kì ńṣe òrò ẹnìkan.[2] By contrast, the affairs of the Western Region of Nigeria seemed to have possessed me in a very personal, obsessive way.

After my 1960 return to Nigeria, fortuitous timing enabled me to participate in the Aldermaston march twice. It was both as an act of solidarity with former colleagues on the march, and a chance to renew a rather specialised sphere of acquaintance – among them the pipe smoking British philosopher with a wilful

---

[2] 'The heaven is falling, the heaven is falling' – is hardly a one-man preoccupation.

shock of white hair, Bertrand Russell. My encounters with him remained largely tantalising, but I remained impressed by his contempt for American racism and British colonial policies in Kenya. Outside the marches, we met in a soggy British café or two with other admirers and disputants, but also in his own home, thanks to my friendship with his secretary, Ralph Schoenman. Ralph was a white American fugitive from South of Mississippi who once spirited a black youth away from near lynching in Little Mo, Alabama and barely escaped evisceration as a 'nigger lover'. The youth was a budding blues writer and singer who had watched his father lynched, and it was thanks to a fragment of one of his compositions, retained by Ralph, that I came to experience, vicariously, the fatalism and despair in victims of Jim Crow culture –

Sometimes, I feel I could kill a man
Just for being good lordy, just for being good...
Little black mother with my heavy child
Take that child out of here.
Take him out and leave him there
Before he find he's black

Ralph appeared to devote every free weekend to perorating in the Speakers' Corner in London's Hyde Park. His interest lay in two topics only – the atom bomb, and American racism. I wandered to his spot from time to time, fascinated by his ability to repeat the same two speeches over and over again, without the slightest variation, not even in tempo, or inflection.

Joan Littlewood's theatre of sheer lunatic genius at Stratford, London – sometimes an entire day or more would be passed moving from rehearsals to bar, then a restaurant and back again. Even though she knew you would be long gone before performance, if the spirit mounted Joan, she assigned one a role on stage – or urged you to create your own. The problem began when, struck with the possibilities of that moment's intervention, it became glued to her conception and she could no longer imagine the play without it. Worse, no one else would do, and then she turned on the spigot to hose you down with her most elegant persuasive spiel – *damn you fuck-face, you can take off for your fuck'n country, be back in time for performance can't you? What's keeping you in that fuck'n place anyway? They're all fuck'd up, I hope you know that, they don't have room for fuck'n poets there, anyone can tell that. Gerry, you tell him the fuck'n truth. Tom Driberg knows the fuck'n lot, he's a friend of Nkrumah you know, and he says he's the only one worth a shit...!*

But it's off to a literary conference in Italy hosted by a San Giorgio Foundation in Venice. I had never been to Venice and so, not even Joan's persuasive skills would keep me from going there. Just as well, it turns out to be one of those bashes tailored for an unemployed dramatist, on the run from polite creditors! The organisers at St. Giorgio thought nothing of making available six different brands of wine during coffee breaks. And where else would I have run into W.H. Auden? – Stephen Spender I had already met. Feeling always unsure – not exactly insecure but lacking absolute self-assurance – in my relationships with older, established writers – some of whom had provided the subjects of one's student essays! – it was a relief to find myself adopted – indeed appropriated, fusslessly monopolised by the two icons of British poetry. W.H. Auden's face – I have read at least a dozen descriptions of that phenomenon, so I'll add mine – struck me instantly as a compressed lump of volcanic lava in controlled convulsion.

They took me in tow, unveiling the surprises of the local culture, including the glass factory where I bought a delicate, spiral lined decorative flask that has miraculously survived all displacements till today! For an operatic performance, the duo proceeded to commandeer the subscribers' box of a Venice domiciled Guggenheim heiress, where the audience, instead of keeping their eyes on the stage, swiveled them at every opportunity at THE box. I assumed that the two doyens of poetry were the objects of attention – wrong! Stephen Spender had planted a rumour that I was an African prince on a world tour, and a special guest of Peggy Guggenheim – my habitual, plain Yoruba smock, nothing flowing or trailing, nothing at all exotic, was sufficient to lend minimal credence – and the opera habituees could not have their fill of gawking! The Guggenheim heiress owned her own palazzo – palazzos came in different sizes, and hers was certainly above medium range – and was befittingly stocked with art works from the classical antiquity to the modernists. Sculptures – open air and gallery cloistered – jostled for attention with priceless paintings – she threw her collection open to public viewing at set hours.

Stephen Spender's concoction, it turned out, was only one half the story – for the heiress, he and W.H. Auden had planted a slight variation: an African prince, with a large entourage, a collector and patron of the arts, was on a world tour. Happily, she surrendered her opera box to the prince and his entourage – which of course ended up as just the two English poets. Later, they explained the thinness of bodies in the box to her by claiming that they only learnt, at the last moment, that the 'entourage' was not allowed to sit with His Highness, so they had been allocated seats elsewhere in the circle. I was somewhat puzzled – they were her friends anyway and could borrow or share her box any time they were in Venice – so I asked them, why the fib? Spender nodded gravely as he explained in his gentle, reasonable voice – the poor girl has more money than she knows what to do with, so she should have something money can't buy – royalty.

They, of course, owned up to the convoluted deceptions afterwards. The heiress was sending her private gondola to bring us to lunch, and the continuing absence of an entourage had become impossible to explain. W.H. Auden persisted in distracting me from feasting my eyes on her collection – *don't miss it when she turns her arse, dear boy. She had it sliced off, surgically you know, flattened it, so she could wear those Charleston dresses of the Swinging Twenties.* Poetry, literature and cultural issues were not neglected – the Foundation's agenda occupied the conference hours but – neither was mischief by that deadpan duo, a wildly differing image from what one had built up from reading – and studying – their poetry.

Not a note of mischief, by contrast, did I ever detect in their Paris counterpart, Pierre Manuel, but an abundance of good humour and a warm urbanity. In addition to his poetry, Pierre was both a historian and social philosopher. He completed the small circle of the expatriate company of which I greedily availed myself as respite from tilting at windmills on one's local landscape. A member of the board for the Congress for Cultural Freedom, he also occupied some kind of position in the French government. Ironically, usually in a fit of frustration, I would experience intense bouts of resentment against them all, on both sides of the English Channel – but only for my inability to conjure up their presence at will within Nigeria, including their roosting spaces – living room, bar, restaurant, concert or seminar setting – vanish into their uncomplicated (so it struck me), simply creative, apolitical environments, if only for an hour or two, a day or so, from time to time. Quite early in our encounters, perhaps fresh from a contestation with some of my francophone colleagues – the Mauritian poet, Edouard Maunick, the Congolese Tchicaya U Tam'si, some of whose uncritical advocacy of *la civilisation francaise* – triggered off my periodic bouts of mild francophobia – I would accuse Pierre Manuel of his nation's brainwashing of its colonial subjects into becoming mimic French. Pierre's indulgent response was to reward me with that uniquely French *moue* of the lips, accompanied by a hand gesture of modest negation, unknown to any other nationality of my knowledge, and a prolonged post-prandial afternoon was taken up with his defence of French colonial history.

My enduring education by Pierre Manuel however took a different form – I was inducted into the secret for controlling garlic breath – a few coffee beans, chewed slowly – *so, next time, you won't have to turn down the escargots on account of the garlic.* Pierre had accurately guessed why I turned down his recommendation of that national specialty, observed my reaction as the waiter described the making of the sauce and then, the flinching of my nostrils when his order arrived! I warned him however that not all the coffee beans in Columbia, Kenya and Jamaica could meet the requirements of a friend of mine named Femi Johnson, who ate garlic as if he wanted to drown in its juice. *Well, bring him over if he is ever in Paris, and we'll try a few garlic recipes together.* I did, sooner than either thought likely. Femi traveled to Paris with a Nigerian drama troupe to the Nancy Festival, while I attended to an engagement at the Sorbonne. I half-heartedly participated in their garlic saturated lunch in Pierre Manuel's apartment, as we continued the former discourse of the comparative merits and demerits of French and British colonial policies, the simmering cauldron of Nigerian politics totally banished, or at least relegated to a niche within the larger context of world politics, colonialism and its consequences. It was one of the unmatchable luxuries of this period, entangling one's mind in every issue except what was being spun in the political looms of my Western Nigeria.

The Congress for Cultural Freedom, founded to promote freedom of speech and cultural expression, was always a generous host. It occupied offices in Boulevard Haussman and operated like a more formalised Transcription Centre in London – that dependable haven to passing African writers. It also had a far more efficient machinery and clout for mobilising international outcry when such writers were endangered. Funds from the CCF went into projects of our own Mbari Club in Adamasingba, that cultural roosting place that doubled for artistic manifestations and political intrigues. The literary and intellectual European journal, *Encounter*, edited in London by an American expatriate, Melvin Lasky, his neatly bearded face a passable – but fleshier – copy of Lenin – was the British window on artistic trends in a post-World War II era, and a voice that did aspire to some objectivity during the ongoing Cold War.

Like so many other writers and artists from the African continent, I always looked forward to meeting Melvin, a wide-ranging mind, full of cultural schemes. In turn he had toured the continent, spending several days in Nigeria. As I drove him back to his hotel in my Land Rover one evening, close by Ìbàdàn's pioneer television station – *WNTV: First in Africa* – I swerved suddenly to ensure that I did not miss a large, shiny snake attempting to cross the road. I appeared to have succeeded. I reversed the car, and there it was, stopped in its tracks but still writhing in the light of the headlamps. I ran over it two more times to make sure it was quite dead, still it continued to writhe. So I reached for the engine crank behind me and descended, ready to apply the *coup de grâce*, Melvin wisely declining my invitation to join in the fray. It turned out to be no snake at all, but a discarded film strip – very likely thrown out by the television station! Melvin used the incident to end the narrative of his African excursion, published in *Encounter* – his concluding words continued to ring in my head for some time afterwards: *in Africa, you confront a serpent, and it turns out to be a film strip!* How I often longed for his *mot juste* to be uniformly true!

Soon enough, we would discover that we had been dining, and with relish, with the original of that serpentine incarnation, the Devil himself, romping in our post-colonial Garden of Eden and gorging on the fruits of the Tree of Knowledge! Nothing, virtually no project, no cultural initiative was left unbrushed by the CIA reptilian coils. The first Congress of African Writers and Intellectuals in Makarere, Uganda, after the wind of independence blew across the continent, had been sponsored by the Congress for Cultural Freedom and *Encounter*. The same source infiltrated *Transition* magazine, the pioneering journal of ideas in post-colonial Africa, that was created and edited by the East African Indian of Brahmin extraction, Rajat Neogy. Not one of us had the slightest suspicion that a Farfield Foundation of America, which so lavishly expended its resources on the continent's post-colonial intellectual thought and creativity, was a front for the American CIA! When the scandal blew open, Melvin Lasky did not deny direct knowledge. My mind flew immediately to Pierre Manuel who was on the board of the congress, hoped fervently that he was as ignorant of the origin of these resources, as was most certainly Stephen Spender, who attempted to rescue that truly stimulating journal, *Encounter*, from its tainted origins. He took over the editorship and sought fresh resources for its continuation.

The struggle for a continent's ideological adhesion was not however strictly bi-polar, a contest between east and west, between KGB and CIA, or whatever names by which their cultural surrogates operated. It raged between one European country and another in varying degrees of subtlety and seduction – sometimes simply as a rivalry for spheres of influence between colonial powers. What mattered to us was that it provided numerous platforms for the cultural vanguard of the contested continent. With a somewhat less disinterested drive than, for instance,

Sweden and other Scandinavian countries, there was also Germany, a former colonial power, wooing Africa's immediate post-Independence writers and artists, opening up venues in Berlin, Erlangen, Tegel, Munich to francophone, anglophone and lusophone writers. Perhaps because the Scandinavian countries had no colonies, they appeared to be less inhibited, and perhaps less calculating, in pursuing a collaboration with the African liberation struggle – beyond their mostly forgotten participation in the slaving enterprise, and in a comparatively minor key, they had no excess baggage from the past. Thus, they could seek to channel that continent's creative and intellectual surge towards a close association with their peninsula. Black American jazz musicians, some fleeing from recruitment for the Vietnam war, had found refuge in Sweden, enlivening the night life of her major cities. Perhaps this also triggered off a special interest in the continent of origin itself – it was difficult to tell. All that mattered was the evident and open-minded reach of that region into African arts and literature, leading to encounters between the two cultures, in which we were more than ready to participate. As for Germany, she had lost her African colonies, but some cultural links remained, and her cultural front, the Goethe Institute, was determined to reinforce those links, giving both the Alliance Francaise and the British Council a good run for their money. The rivalries guaranteed days of greedily imbibed camaraderie on neutral grounds among African products of the colonial adventure, nurturing – without any conscious intent – a *renaissance* hankering for the generation's creative energies. Kindred spirits, different levels and contexts of embattlement, engaged in a moving feast of cultural and political narratives of comparative fortunes: Tamsir Niane of the Republic of Guinea, refugee in Leopold Sedar Senghor's Senegal, safe from the increasing paranoia of Sekou Toure, the revolutionary-turned dictator of the Republic of Guinea who was quietly assuming proprietorship of infamous torture cages that would not be exposed until years later; Ama Ata Aidoo, her playwright career just beginning, and Kofi Awoonor, her Ghanaian colleague, poet and novelist, basking in the progressive limelight of their Ghana under Kwame Nkrumah; Okot p'Bitek –

Song of Lawino – who would later drink himself to death in Idi Amin's Uganda; David Rubadiri the soft-spoken but steel-willed Malawian poet, cautioning his listeners about the increasing authoritarianism of the Malawi ruler, Hastings Banda; the South Africans – Ezekiel Mphahlele, Lewis Nkosi, Mazisi Kunene, etc. – in their own unique capsule of the displaced, gradually reconciling themselves to an inevitable armed struggle; Taban lo Liyong, solidly entrenched poet in his Africanity, unlike Tchicaya U Tam'si, the Congolese poet with the game leg who remained incorrigibly French, yet passionately black, reading his moving poem to the lynched American boy, Emmett Till; Camara Laye, author of the elegiac childhood reminiscences, *The Dark Child,* seated in the café exterior in Erlangen, his eyes turned towards the mercury skies as he sighed: *Regardez! Ici, ce n'est pas un pays. En Afrique, il y a le soleil, il y a du riz, il y a du piment, mais ici* – and again a dolorous sigh – *non, ce n'est pas un pays* – (Take a look at that! This is not a country. In Africa, you have the sun, there is rice, and there is hot pepper sauce, but here – no, this is not a country...)

We did not require much urging – few, if any at all, passed up the opportunity for such encounters. Some were already domiciled, by choice or by circumstances, in the home of their colonial patrons. For others, each invitation was a respite, a banquet to be savoured, sometimes greedily devoured. We met, debated, wined and dined, pursued amorous prospects and felt recharged... all too soon, it was time for each to return to a different clime and terrain, and confront his or her own serpents.

I fulfilled a long held craving in 1963 – to visit post-revolution Cuba for the first time. An invitation arrived from Casa de las Americans and found me more than ready. An invigorating respite, not unexpectedly, debating the purpose of art and ideology with the Cuban intellectual vanguard of the revolution. My former Royal Court colleague, the working class playwright, Arnold Wesker, somewhat self-conscious in his custom-built Maoist suit, was at least well suited for a photo call when news came unexpectedly that he had won a prestigious prize. All ideological tussle was forgotten as we suspended the agenda and moved into the celebration mode at the Casa, continuing late into the night.

Edward Albee's *Who is Afraid of Virginia Woolf?* found unexpected popularity among working class revolutionaries – it seemed a paradox, this rite of exorcism between a middle-class American couple, totally divorced from the ideological concerns of a world in turmoil. Then a four to five hour harangue by Fidel Castro at the Conference of Socialist Architects, and a fear building up in me that I was watching a personality cult in the making, one that might breed a nation of revolutionary sycophants. A tour of the island, visiting the high water landmarks of the revolution, starved for wine from the rationing policy in Havana the capital, we found the countryside more accommodating. In a modest seaside restaurant where we stopped for lunch, a cask of robust red wine, allegedly 'washed up' from a Spanish smuggling vessel was unstoppered in our honour by the straight-faced restaurateur, who appeared unfazed by the presence of the revolutionary watchdogs. We did not get to Santiago de Cuba until late that night, blissfully drunk.

I fell in love with a dancer in Havana, came close to eloping with a widow in Santiago de Cuba, ate frog's legs in a restaurant for the first time and marveled at Cuban technical ingenuity in keeping ancient Yankee Cadillacs purring smoothly with improvised spare parts. From time to time, the question of Albee's play would come up, a paradox to some of our fellow conferrers who remained amazed that such a play should find a place in revolutionary environment. Ritual, I offered, ritual. Ritual is largely classless – and a flagging debate erupted, as stridently as when I had offered that proletarian art – like the arts of indigenous peoples – had its secure place, but should not be permitted to tyrannise over individual departures that offer insights outside the blinkers of the party line. What was remarkable was that the Cuban revolutionaries, in the main, agreed, but the European socialists – in the main – deplored the notion as bourgeois.

'Bourgeois' was also enemy territory in the United States of the sixties, and sometimes passed interchangeably with 'white', 'racist', segregationist – against all of which the black writers were producing a powerful body of revolutionary work. My visit to the States in 1964 was a lavish concourse, openly sponsored by the

US State Department, its intent being to bring virtually all of Africa to dialogue with the United States. No expense had been spared. All disciplines – from the Arts and Sciences, economics, philosophy and possibly even religion – were in attendance, making it look as if Africa had been emptied of all analytic, creative, or political structures for this grandiose effort to capture minds in the open contest between the ideological blocs. Africa was the much sought-after prize and one side at least – the West – was prepared to spare no expense to grab and keep it within its orbit. Lodged in the largest hotel suites I had ever been in my life – a Hilton – three or four had been allocated the four-bedroom suite, including Dennis Duerden of the Transcription Centre, I said to my colleagues: *listen, we had better indulge to the fullest* – we did! – *because it will never happen again* – it never has!

Finding myself in the States a second time not long after, invited by the International Institute of Education to visit the nation's cultural institutions – both structures and human – was a chance to pursue a personal agenda – seeking out radical spirits in the combat zones of the black nation within the American embrace. The black liberation movement had begun. The Spirit House of Leroi Jones – later Imamu Baraka – hovered between a monastery and a revolutionary training school, both joined in a regimen of rigorous discipline and leader worship that was nearly cultic in character. It was wildly different in style and mood from the more democratic setting of Theatre Lafayette in mid-Manhattan, definitely also a revolutionary den for black liberation and equality, where Ernie McLintock, Ed Bullins, Ben Caldwell and others held sway through their plays, smoked marijuana, needled the white establishment, and warned, just like Leroi Jones and others of that movement, of the Apocalypse to come, unless...

Into other battle zones or cultural oases, the visits were deeply restorative furloughs, interjections of comparative sanity, since even the insanities of others, as long as one remained sufficiently detached, inject a sense of proportion into one's own. Every escape, planned or fortuitous, was however guaranteed to be curtailed and thus, ultimately, I felt constantly shortchanged afterwards. Still, they were valued interruptions in what was fast becoming an existence dominated by politics of the immediate, demanding instant response. Sometimes the curtailment of the duration of such external reliefs was of my own ordering, not of any urgent summons from home that stemmed from an unexpected and menacing development. Sooner or later came that moment when the mind revolted. I looked round, listened to the conversation around me – a pretentious note perhaps, some posturing, a preposterous proposition, an artificial ardour, a comfortable liberalism or the intrusion of a vicarious revolutionary warrior – and the wine would turn flat on my tongue, my mind go blank, leaving only the rebuke: *what are you still doing in this place?* The following day found me at the airport, headed back to that region of the world that would come to be dubbed the 'Wild Wild West' by a young military officer who, undergoing his Sandhurst training during the Western Regional elections, had no inkling of the political destiny that awaited him.

WANTED!!!

The most extended break from the gathering fire-storm of Western Nigeria came from the Commonwealth Arts Festival of 1965, then it was back to base to have one's face rubbed in the muck of the Western regime, aided and abetted by the Federal Government - increasingly arbitrary, vindictive and desperate. My series of socio-political sketches, *Before the Blackout, The New Republican,* etc., had served to calm the rioting conscience for a while, and the urge to intervene in a more direct way would have been stilled – perhaps – but for one afternoon of sheer serendipity!

Saturday was the weekly concession to a full-bodied Nigerian menu in the Femi Johnson home – otherwise, my friend Femi, then married to an English wife, would dine on steak and gravy, lamb chops and mashed potatoes, fish and chips, shepherd's pie and all other delicacies that could be found at any English table. My presence in the Femi Johnson household, whenever I found myself in Ìbàdàn on a Saturday afternoon, had thus become routine – I went there to be overfed! The warm reception of my play, *The Road,* most especially through a much quoted review by Penelope Gilliat of *The Observer,* had been gratifying, but that was no solace for nearly two weeks of barely tolerable to execrable restaurant fare that one could afford in 1965 London. I was now teaching in the University of Lagos but was poised to resume a position in the University of Ìbàdàn Theatre Department. Returning from the Festival, a huge craving for some solid Nigerian cooking had been stored up and, as the first Saturday came round, I could hardly wait to head for Ìbàdàn and Femi's gourmandising company. In truth, I was suffering from a double starvation. I needed to catch up with the news, explore the ongoing politics of the West that had taken the gloss off my theatre debut at any international festival.

In attendance as usual on that day was a mutual friend, Michael Olumide, then controller of the broadcasting station in Ìbàdàn. The announced election results dominated all discussion, and it was not long before a pall of depression hung over an afternoon that was normally devoted to pure, unabashed gluttony. The West, to which we all three belonged, was being stolen right under our noses.

And then, quite casually, and in all innocence, Michael Olumide dropped his bombshell and it instantly launched a turmoil in my head. I lost any further interest in the Saturday feast. What Michael had said, so casually, was that he had been summoned by the Premier to record his victory speech. There was also the possibility that the Premier would come into the studio and make his broadcast, live. The recording was intended as a back-up, in case he could not leave what had become his prime-ministerial fortress – and prison. Whatever the final decision, the victory broadcast of the NNDP, and Akintola's re-election as Prime Minister of the West – our West – would be made that night!

The broadcast had to be stopped! Ukonu and his radio crew were long departed, so a counter broadcast, relayed through the Eastern transmitters as the election results had been, was impossible. The Premier held all the cards. A fait accompli, consecrated on radio waves, would demoralise the opposition, and that broadcast, from a position of incumbency strength, would have commenced the process of legitimising a detested regime, with the resultant danger of resignation and apathy from a cowed populace. Another four years under the NNDP could easily become a life sentence for a struggling democracy – there was the very real danger that the now barely hidden agenda to formalise a one-party dictatorship by the victorious alliance would become irresistible. Opposition would be crushed. There would be money or contract-induced defections. Some would succumb to blackmail. Others would be squeezed into submission with assaults on their means of livelihood. Some of the NPC, NNDP politicians had already begun to raise the chant for a 'one-party democracy'. The continent was filled with such models of power consolidation masquerading as democracies. Their would-be imitators in the nation virtually drooled in envy as they cast glances at such bastions of the crudity of power. The formal capture of the West was bound to reinforce the proponents of an iron hand.

I had wrestled intermittently with the problem of violence. To be caught up in a violent situation, compelled to respond to it, presents no agonising choice, to initiate it is another matter. I had never seen myself as a pacifist, never persuaded myself that the liberation of any tyranised space can always be achieved by non-violent means. I tried to caution myself however about the dangers of unstructured violence, violence that comes to exist for itself, as a glorified end, loses all focus, control, and no longer discriminates between its two principal clients positioned at either end of a living axis – Power and Freedom. The most principled of struggles has its share of psychopaths – and I was fortunate to have received early education from encounters with a few of these almost from the start of my political involvement. I was equally lucky to find myself within a close-knit group whose members believed that violence was a stage to be avoided for as long as, and wherever possible, insisting however that self-defence constitutes its own justification. This includes defence against violation, such as acts of robbery or extortion. Rape. Against any form of dehumanisation. Even to be robbed is to be diminished, and to be robbed of the seemingly intangible – such as a civic voice – is to be diminished as a citizen. To resist such a diminution meant, in my view, a simple act of self-defence, of self-preservation.

The elections had thrown up many instances where the most diffident individual found himself compelled to write his own limited rules of engagement, in response to real violation. My favourite recollection was that of a young politician, Soji Odunjo, a few years younger than I. He was probably the youngest of the Action Group candidates, a wispy, normally mild-mannered youth, rather self-retiring in demeanour. I had known him long before he entered politics only as the junior brother of a colleague from the old University of Ìbàdàn. Perhaps politics did course secretly through Soji's veins – he was, after all, the son of one of the founding members of *Ẹgbẹ́ Ọmọ Ûdùduwà*, the Yoruba cultural organisation that later metamorphosed into the Action Group. Nevertheless I was quite surprised to discover that Soji so much as considered entering the wild world of politics of the mid-sixties.

After voting had ended and the votes were tallied, Soji found himself faced with a crooked returning officer who refused to release the results in his electoral ward. He had campaigned hard and fair, against all odds, displaying unsuspected political instincts, and now all he wanted was that the results, already announced to the waiting crowd, should be set down so that he and his opponent could sign the returns as required by electoral law. The officer however insisted that the results would only be released at the state capital, Ìbàdàn, there to be broadcast over the radio station. Since Soji knew by then – as did the entire region, indeed nation – what happened to the returns en route, he dashed home, returned with a loaded shotgun whose muzzle he now pressed against the head of the returning officer. I remain convinced that Soji would have been incapable of pulling the trigger even if the officer had persisted, still, by the count of three, the man had handed over the card. His mission accomplished, Soji drove to the collating office in Ìbàdàn where he lodged the results, then went home to sleep the sleep of the just.

Thinking of the course I was about to embark upon, I found my position no different from Soji's – except that I was not even a candidate but was acting as one of the electorate who felt bound to protect his rights. In consonance with the majority of the populace of the Western Region, I was being robbed of a voice. A series of false results had already been announced, of increasingly cynical attributions. We had countered this by our own broadcasts but now, this act of robbery was about to be made official by the head of the robbery consortium, the Premier, also principal receiver/beneficiary of the stolen goods, all rolled in one. Picking somewhat distractedly at my plate in Femi's dining-room, I found it only slightly incongruous that I should be considering, and with complete equanimity, whether or not I should arm myself before going to recover – or at least prevent the formal acquisition of – this stolen property. I would have preferred that we took over the broadcasting station entirely and occupied it for some days, stoking up the now inevitable uprising with the usual messages of resistance and solidarity, but what forces we could muster were hopelessly inadequate for such an undertaking. We had no precedent to follow, not even the time to stock up for a prolonged siege. A well-directed police action would flush us out in no time!

That afternoon, with its lack of alternatives, informed me with a quiet certitude that I was finally tired of dramatic sketches which, however scabrous, only drew symbolic blood from the veins of Power. Suddenly, that language of intervention – despite the occasional physical assaults on the actors and threats of disruption – became inadequate, even self-indulgent. Fast receded was that homecoming projection of my role as being no more than that of a truth-crier, of weapons no more lethal than my portable typewriter and paper.

The next few hours flashed before me in that instance – both as already defined motions, as well as logistical options – but not the likely consequences; that section was blanked out. Looking back, I appeared to have been focussed entirely on practical matters, details. I knew at once that I had to obtain a good tape recorder, and recollected, in that same instance, just who possessed such high-fidelity equipment – a serving US Peace Corper doing some field research at the University of Ìbàdàn. Now all I saw, detachedly, was my *doppelgänger* walking through the back stairs of the broadcasting station where I had been a frequent contributor, onto the corridor where the director's office was located, past his office, past the cubicle of Amos Tutuola, author of *The Palm-wine Drinkard*, then up a short flight of steps to the left, before a right turn at the landing. The crucial door was on the right. It led into the control room through which one had to pass in order to enter the studio where I had done dozens of broadcasts. I would not be going into the studio however. The control room from which the tapes and records were played was the target. I wondered who would be on duty, knowing however that I could rely on the commitment of the majority of the staff in that station.

Would the Premier come in person? The political situation was unravelling fast, and the Premier was a shrewd calculator who instinctively homed on survivalist tactics – it was therefore quite possible that he would decide to make a live broadcast. Between recording and broadcast, much could happen and Akintola, a master of improvisation, would want to enter any last-minute development into his speech, and manipulate it to his advantage. This complicated my thinking, since the Premier would then travel in a motorcade, and the studio would be swarming with police escorts and perhaps a truckload of his party's 'irregulars'. Obviously, I would have to arrive early, just before nightfall. A curfew was in force, which was good, since we were masters of the curfew. We needed the dark. I chose the record library as the most strategic position in which to place myself – one had to walk past it to reach the studio. If the Premier came in person however, what would we do?

We? No, in my mind's eye, everything was reduced to one person. I am always amused – or irritated, depending on mood – by much that has been written on my so-called 'loner' mentality. As if in a mountain climb, the one individual who plants the flag on the summit and beats a quick retreat before a snowstorm obliterates all landmarks, was not backed up or preceded every step of the way by the rest of the team! On any of them could have fallen the task of making that final sprint to summit. Of course, I entered the studio alone. There were armed police swarming all over the outer premises. If I took others with me, detection would likely have occurred before we even breached the perimeter of the building – unless of course the intention was that others should expose themselves to detection and so create a distraction for my entry. That option was unnecessary. It was much easier for one person, obviously one familiar with the building, to slip in and out of store space, record library, offices and corridors all the way to the studio. If we had had one more day, we could have found an excuse to bring others into the building in broad daylight, given them the opportunity to memorise the geography of stairwells and landings. There simply was not the time.

The recording of my counter-message settled, it was easier to concentrate on peripheral but crucial details, such as – who would drive me to the Broadcasting House? Next thought – guns – to go armed or unarmed? That did not generate much agonising; the unpleasant but unavoidable word was – *coercion*. I was not going into the studio to preach to the studio engineer and the continuity officer that their moral duty lay in removing the Premier's tape and substituting my own. I had no idea who would be on duty, and even if I did, and their sympathies were with the opposition, they were entitled to their overt neutrality. If they were militantly with us, then they would enjoy the charade of submitting – like the broadcaster, Ukonu – to *force majeure*. If they were not... well, then they could wallow in the indignation of having been made to act under duress. If things went wrong and the police were somehow alerted – there was no time to think of consequences beyond knowing that, unless I was shot at or about to be shot at, I would calmly surrender myself for arrest – *once the tape was running*. I was in no two minds about that.

And so, finally, there still persisted one critical question: suppose the man came himself, surrounded by his entourage? There was only one answer to that: prevent him entering the Broadcasting House in the first place, scare off his motorcade en route. Again, the niggardly collaboration of time! There was not enough of that commodity to mobilise the entirety of our small band. Still, I knew the normal haunts of the marginal ones, including the faithful Kodak, a former thug and mercenary who had chosen to throw his lot with us. In turn, he could rouse another four or five from whichever dens they had thought to pass an uneventful or predatory weekend. Hidden in the dark among the buildings, behind vending kiosks or trees – trees had not yet been eaten on Ìbàdàn roads, or in other urban centres for that matter, to assuage the hunger for development – they would man the immediate approach to the Premier's destination and pepper the motorcade with a few shots. Knowing the high state of alert in which the town was seized, it was certain that the immediate reaction of his security outriders would be to accelerate and tear past the broadcasting house without pausing. Unable to determine how large a force was firing at them from the darkness and the ominous emptiness of streets under curfew, that was only common sense.

At last I could feel inwardly at peace. I rejoined the conversation, putting a few innocent questions to Michael, and abandoned the rest of the Saturday feast.

It all proceeded according to plan. The duty officers responded as any sensible persons would under the gun, removed the Premier's tape and replaced it with mine. It ran long enough for the message to the government to be clearly transmitted – *drop your stolen mandate, leave town and take your reprobates with you etc. etc.* Then a disbelieving senior operator in another control room roused himself from his paralysis, rushed into the studio and cut off the transmission. By that time, I had slipped away. My retreat was unhindered.

Before dawn, I was in flight to the Eastern Region, later to confront the weird experience of seeing my face pasted on the pages of newspapers as a Wanted Man. One of the studio staff, A.O., had sworn to the identity of the intruder! Indeed, he recounted in detail a conversation that, he claimed, took place as he carried out the intruder's instructions – under a gun pointed directly at him, he repeated *ad nauseam* – to remove the Premier's tape and substitute it with his. The evening of the raid, A.O. had indeed proved an unstoppable conversationalist – perhaps he did need to babble in order to steady the hands that quivered so badly that, in the end, it was a junior assistant, Friday Ifode, who completed the task of threading the tape.

Once the police investigations began, A.O. continued to supply details of the one-sided exchange, a virtual monologue, how he had expressed astonishment at seeing me in Ìbàdàn since I was supposed to be in London, etc. The others swore they heard nothing of the kind, or else had caught only snatches of the exchange, not sufficient to identify the gunman. We thought the intruder was his friend, they shrugged, since A.O. appeared to know everything about the stranger's movements, even while he was in London.

I was already underground even before I was declared 'Wanted' – that was all part of the decision of the small band of 'irregulars' that went under different aliases for the purpose of a public but elusive voice – including, at one stage – CWIL, Committee of Writers for Individual Liberty – a most misleading title, since only the poet Christopher Okigbo and I thought of ourselves as writers. There were however two or three lecturers from Ifẹ̀ and Ìbàdàn University. Other members, like Kodak, belonged on the fringes of mainstream society. Members of my itinerant performing group, the Orísun Theatre, had slipped, imperceptibly, into the role of an informal Intelligence gathering unit, a productive network that co-opted friends, families, lovers and former schoolmates working in junior positions within the establishment. The Pyrates – that campus fraternity that meant so many contrary things to bemused or terrified Nigerians – refused to be left out of any direct action, though their participation was limited to a hard core of three or four at any time. Doig Simmonds, a British medical illustrator, was the sole expatriate member – mostly on the periphery. A designer and printer of most of our leaflets, he was not involved in any of the public activities. Doig did however surrender his fowling piece to me, a skeletal gauge that could just about pluck the feathers off a bush fowl at a ten yard distance, but made an impressive amount of noise, especially in an enclosed space. It earned its keep in some of the encounters that took place as we monitored the electoral process in remote areas, where violence had replaced even a semblance of an electoral choice.

By the time the police felt sure of the identity of the intruder, I had left Ìbàdàn town and indeed the borders of the Western Region. I resurfaced in Enugu, Eastern Nigeria whose Premier, Dr. Michael Okpara, was in active alliance – United Progressive Grand Alliance – with the opposition Action Group of the West. I told him of our plans to muster a sustained resistance against the NNDP government and he gave me the run of his state, requesting only that I keep out of sight of the police which was under a central command – that is, mostly took orders from Lagos. Just to be on the safe side however, he invited in the commissioner of police in Enugu and introduced us to each other. Nothing more was said.

My host in Enugu was the same Dr. Sam Aluko, the economist crudely ejected from the campus of Ifẹ University. Through some strange workings of his mind, he would find himself, a quarter of a century later, quite comfortable in the position of economic adviser to the nation's most notorious despot, General Sani Abacha, who looted the nation's monetary reserves with as much abandon as he tortured, imprisoned and killed her citizens. It was however, the familiar face of my activist colleague that welcomed me without a thought while the police pursued my imaginary trail to equally phantom sightings all over the country.

It did not take long before the police tracked me down to Enugu. My telephone calls to Femi Johnson had been monitored and their originating station easily traced. If Enugu, it also stood to reason, thought the NNDP police, that an obvious point of contact for the fugitive would be his erstwhile colleague, Sam Aluko. Within two days of my arrival, the East Regional police command received a signal from Ìbàdàn that Aluko's house should be searched. Sure enough, Sam received an advance notice from the Enugu police that they would arrive the following morning on their hunt for the fugitive.

They arrived as promised, armed with copies of the WANTED notice that was now home to my photograph. A charade ensued. Sam accompanied them as they looked through the rooms one after the other, passed through the living room where I was seated, looked right through me as through a window pane. Content with the futility of their mission, they sat down with the Aluko family in the same living room. With a straight face, they enquired of Sam Aluko if he had had any news of me. Sam shook his head in the negative. Well, be sure you keep us informed if he makes contact – we'll leave this WANTED notice with you in case you lay eyes on anyone resembling him – again looking straight through me as I sat sipping my coffee. Sam took the poster, scrutinised the photograph, nodded and assured them that he would definitely get in touch, then accompanied them out of the house.

Some days later, the same police advised Sam that I should move to a new place. A fresh group of detectives was being sent directly from Ìbàdàn to ferret me out. Sam Aluko, they sensed, held the key to my whereabouts. The new squad would be paying him a visit and would likely remain in Enugu to monitor his movements, convinced that he would eventually lead them to my hiding-place. By then however, the situation in the Western Region – the breakout of insurrection, and the disintegration of the NNDP regime – had created the right conditions for my return to Ìbàdàn and the certainty of a trial. Dr. Okpara provided a nondescript Volkswagen car that took me straight to Lagos and to the safe house of a colleague, Dapo Fatogun, a journalist and Marxist with ties to Red China.

Dapo was a saturnine intriguer, virtually expressionless, with a complexion that appeared to shroud him in perpetual darkness. I had a hat on, no other disguise, except that I had shaved my wisp of a goatee. Dapo took over and drove me round the newspaper offices where the shock on the faces of the editors and staff was worth the sometimes uncomfortable manoeuvres Dapo took me through to ensure that we escaped police detection. At each newspaper office, I followed the prepared script: high on indignation, how shocking it had been for me to discover, after my return from a habitual creative retreat, that I had been declared 'Wanted' by the police! I took the strongest exception to such criminalisation tactics. If the police wanted me, I protested, all they had to do was to look seriously. The friendly press, as usual, hammed it all up in full accord with a favourite subject, set to work to prepare their sensationalist copy for the following day.

We drove to Ìbàdàn. I had to decide on a place where I would spend my last night of freedom – my own home being out of the question. I had been briefed regularly about the police enquiries, interrogations etc., information supplied even by some of the police who had been sent after me. I knew in detail those who had volunteered information, even unasked, some (especially two expatriate colleagues) who had been terrorised into collaborating, revealing some of my movements that could invalidate an alibi. Others, however, Femi Johnson among them, refused to oblige the police in any particular.

All I knew of Femi's politics was his outrage at the electoral fraud. He was not a member of 'CWIL', I had never subjected him to any test of solidarity nor asked him to participate, even marginally, in our activities. Yet Femi had taken extra pains to frustrate the police every way. Indeed, so eager was he to confuse the investigators that he deliberately distorted the time and content of our telephone conversation, little realising that the distortions would prove useful to the prosecution! That very *gaffe,* its touching motivation, contributed to my choice of his home for my last evening at liberty. It was an intuitive feeling – I knew I could feel as safe and secure with him as I did in the professional hideout of my Marxist colleague, Dapo Fatogun, with its elaborate network of communication and warning systems.

The drama now shifted to the court. My lawyers – with the exception of their senior counsel, volunteers who never asked a penny – joined me in secret later that night – Tayo Onalaja, Kayode Somolu, Jide Olatawura, Dele Ige – the first three would become High Court judges years on, while Dele turned to business. His brother Bola Ige, also a lawyer, however stayed on the sidelines, contributing legal advice from his chambers. As a noted politician in opposition, it was not considered advisable that he participate openly in my defence. Together we worked out the strategy for my surrender.

By morning, the papers would be filled with news that I had resurfaced, and would submit myself for arrest some time that same day. My lawyers would contact the police, lay a false trail by inviting them to come to my own house in Fẹ́lẹ̀lẹ̀ at ten in the morning to pick me up. I would however remain in Femi's house and report directly to the Ìyágànkú police station at the same hour. That would prevent any act of bad faith on their part, such as storming my house and pretending that they found me in hiding and had conducted a difficult arrest. Those moments were bread and meat to Femi. His eyes shone in the sheer enjoyment of scheming and counter-plotting. That light dimmed only when the terms of my indictment were announced, framed to ensure the maximum penalty possible, short of capital forfeit – robbery with violence, carrying a life sentence. The stolen item: one magnetic tape. Cost, two pounds, seven shillings.

We had indeed underestimated the regime in that one respect – its choice of the charges under which I would be tried. We were more than prepared for a political trial, indeed, I looked forward to it. But not armed robbery! The possibility of such a vindictive interpretation of a purely political act had escaped both my small band and the lawyers altogether – if it had occurred to me, I would most certainly have dug deeper underground, burrowing away from both East and West as far as possible!

It was, when all is fairly considered, a most uncharitable way to respond to what, in essence, amounted to no more than borrowing some air time on a public facility. True, I had made away with the tape of the Premier of the Western Region – and there was the unavoidable introduction of a firearm in the process – but I did leave my own tape in its place. And if it was a question of content, well, the comparative value of both messages was something that could have been settled amicably in a court of arbitration. I would be the first to admit that, in wit, wordplay and verbal resonance, my humourless message – and in strident accents of the English language to boot – was no match for Oladoke Akintola's adroit Yoruba. Still the cost of both tapes was the same, and the labour I had put into ours certainly equalled that of the Premier who had all the resources of the state at his disposal for a recording in his living room. Such basic principles of equity not withstanding, forgetting our people's own wisdom that is expressed in the sentiment – *Exchange is no robbery* – Akintola's government still insisted that I be charged with robbery, and of the armed variety.

That context of criminality was the only sinister element in what would otherwise have proved a period of welcome rest and enforced immobility. I could catch up on neglected reading and calmly observe the world of petty criminals, their hunters, accomplices and relations as they milled around the police yard and passed by my makeshift cell. Despair, desperation, a world of deceits and opportunism and the occasional, impulsive acts of kindness. Interrogations sometimes took place in my presence, or else I sat in the corridor within earshot of threats, cajolery, whining, denials and the most odious lies, delivered with a stolid, inflexible countenance. Most memorable perhaps of the many revelations of this world of crime and detection was an encounter between a known kingpin of the underworld and his interrogator, the latter clearly terrified of a prisoner who openly relished his reputation as a most violent specimen. That underworld figure was short, jet-black in complexion, and with a square set face, but was built like the concrete cylinder that served as the wheel of a primitive tarmac compressor. He gave off a thick air of menace that percolated through even to me.

The poor 'E' branch officer to whom fell the task of interrogating him tried to carry out his preliminary task, which was to physically secure his charge. In the most diffident manner, virtually plaintive, he asked permission to clamp him with leg-cuffs. The lord of the underworld gave him such a look of dare and disdain that the officer fell to whining and pleading. The cuffs were left alone and a dialogue – supposedly an interrogation – ensued between cat and mouse, with the prescribed roles reversed. Another officer happened to walk by – maybe on a casual inspection – and quickly demonstrated that confident authority often achieves what physical force could not. It was then the turn of the gangster to fall to whining, swearing that he never at any time objected to being restrained with the cuffs. The officer said nothing further, merely fixed him with a telling look and pointed to the abandoned cuffs. King Kong took the cuffs in his own hands and aided his earlier captive of terror in securing his ankles. It was easily the most abrupt, most dramatic change of attitude that I had ever witnessed in any human being.

Formal security around me had grown quite slack as the case wore on. For instance, a famous picture – it appeared also in foreign newspapers – showed me being escorted across the road from my police cell by one policeman only, unarmed. Before then, earlier pictures had shown me with apparently no escort – in reality, I was constantly under the far more efficient guard of three plain-clothes officers. Infuriated that the prisoner was photographed walking – to all appearances – without guards, the government ordered that I must never again be seen without the visible company of a uniformed officer – *he's a common criminal, accused of a serious crime, and should be presented as such!* So the plainclothes detail was removed, and only the somewhat tubby uniformed police remained to ensure my security. During any of those walks across the road to the court and back, I could have been rescued by any single member of our group if I so wished, rushed into a car conveniently parked or cruising along the road, before that solitary officer could raise an alarm.

The NNDP government found itself in the unexpected situation of a growing international interest in the prisoner, was unsure how to respond to it and yet continue to depict itself as a legitimately elected democratic body, deeply wronged by the disruptive act of one individual. Questions were raised in the British House of Commons. Was the writer being unjustly persecuted? Was a fair trial possible in a situation of political chaos? Was the prisoner being kept in humane conditions? Had democracy failed in its largest ex-colony, etc. etc.? In its desperation to respond to these and other hue and cry from outside, the government fell into one self-contradiction after another. Its predicament was not helped by an untoward incident that resulted from a non-cooperation campaign I had embarked upon, a quite unscripted event that no one, certainly not I, could have foreseen.

Fed up with delays over bringing me to trial, I went on a hunger strike, demanded to be moved from my makeshift detention place in the police office to a proper cell with other criminals. An interlude of tranquility had been welcome at the beginning – I had, after all prepared for it when I agreed to the decision over my return – but, after two, now approaching three months of 'ongoing investigation', the wait was becoming oppressive. My outward composure and resignation were fast becoming lies, increasingly difficult to sustain. From a mere suspicion, I became convinced that the government was deliberately stalling my trial.

The longer I could be shown off to the world as being accorded VIP treatment – detained not in prison, not in a cell but in a police office – the longer the government could afford to delay my trial and thus place me indefinitely out of circulation. The West was boiling and, frankly, I felt deprived of my rightful share of action. My demand was granted and I was taken to the regular police station cells and locked up.

I made one immediate discovery - those cells were far filthier from the inside than their evident griminess when one merely looked in from the outside! The smears against the wall established a definition – it could only be human excrement! – that made the body shrink from touching them. Still, I had asked for it, and all that was left was to look forward to a clean bath when this was all over.

That same night, I received unexpected visitors, a development which, considering my yet unpublicised transfer to a new residence, could not have come about as the result of a chance visit, as later claimed in court by my police assailant. A deputy commissioner of police, Loremikan, escorted by a detachment, stormed the station and demanded access to my cell. The duty officer had no choice but to comply. My door creaked opened. Before me stood this stranger, staring at me with indescribable venom. He was dripping with tear-gas cannisters, grenades, side-arms and drunken saliva. Before I could begin to assess the nature of the invasion – beyond the clue that his slobbering face offered as it accused me of causing problems for the government – this apparition had baton-charged me repeatedly at the base of my rib-cage and I was left gasping for breath.

Taken to hospital the following day, the x-rays revealed contusions but, luckily, no broken ribs. My lawyers took a complaint to the judge a few days later. The judge – Justice Kayode Eso – was infuriated, summoned Loremikan to court, turned him into a mop and scrubbed the floor with him, leaving him dribbling yet again, this time in sheer terror. The courts, at that time, did command authority! Justice Eso sent for the police inspector in charge of the station, ordered him to take me back to my former place of detention – his office – and charged him personally with responsibility for my body. The inspector was to consider himself answerable to the court for my safety.

The press, both local and international, covered the episode with vengeful glee. From then on, the atmosphere around me changed completely. The police insisted that I return to the University Teaching Hospital periodically for treatment where, as the gods who oversee these matters had evidently decreed, a nurse with whom I was having an affair also resided. Since orders had been given that I was to have minimal contact with the public outside the police station, I was given appointments at odd hours – again at the insistence of the police – mostly in the evenings outside the regular out-patient hours. It became routine. After examination and treatment, my obliging police escort – now back to mufti – took the route to a particular block of apartments in the hospital complex. He stayed downstairs nursing a cold beer while I went up to be nursed. A baton charge by a drunken officer was something that I – and most prisoners, I am certain – would consider a small price to pay for such conditions of restraint.

Such reliefs, to tell the truth, were relished far more for their context of defiance, as a statement of some personal control over my environment, than necessity or desperation. Of far greater value to me was an event of touching revelation, one that occurred on the night before the verdict. This was when I first experienced, with sheer wonder, the potential depths of human friendship. Firstly, Femi Johnson had hardly missed one day of visit during my detention and trial, turning up sometimes even twice or thrice – on his way to the office, returning home from office or setting out from home for no other purpose than to keep me company, remaining as late as the police would permit him. Only one other person came close to the consistency of his visits – that was the poet, Christopher Okigbo, then representing Cambridge University Press in Nigeria, and an informal member of CWIL. He brought his latest verses in typescript, scribbled over in his neat, tiny handwriting, read them aloud to me, sometimes with Femi as his only other audience. Armed with a hamper of food and drinks, we might even have lunch or dinner together in that office turned residence. A young German journalist, Gerd Meuer, then married to an Indonesian, would also drop by occasionally, with an Indonesian spread prepared by his wife. On this night however, the last before my sentencing, it was Femi who appeared with his now familiar basket.

I was reading. I looked up suddenly with that feeling that someone was watching me – there he was at the window, just looking in.

"How long have you been standing there?"

"Ages!" he sighed. He shook his head in a gesture of disbelief, his shoulders unusually slouched as he came round to the door. My guards were chuckling – he had signalled them to keep silent, not reveal his presence, while he simply waited until I looked up or he got tired of waiting. His entire manner was uncharacteristically down at the mouth. I waited for him to throw off the mask, to detonate the joke behind it. But there was no hidden mirth lurking in Femi's throat.

"What's the matter?"

"I don't understand" he said. "I've been standing there, watching you for at least thirty minutes."

"Don't exaggerate."

"But... how can you? Tomorrow is the day, isn't it?"

"You mean, the verdict?

"What else is there tomorrow? You know, you're not normal. *Wole, èdá ni e o. Èdá ni e.*[3] You are not normal at all. How can anyone normal just sit there reading as if nothing is happening?" He put down the hamper. I must have been truly absorbed to have failed to respond much earlier to the aroma, but then I had developed a fussless capacity for obliterating my environment. I lifted a corner of the cloth, drew in a lungful of delights.

"Hmm. Last supper."

"It's not a joking matter," he protested.

I lifted the cloth aside to inspect the dishes. "I am not yet condemned, you know. And if I were, even the condemned man is allowed his last breakfast – and of his own choice."

"You're not normal."

We ate, but it was all I could do to eat as heartily as I felt, since Femi's mood could not be breached. For once, his famous

---

[3] You are a weird being, a weird being.

appetite appeared to have deserted him. "You're ruining my dinner," I complained.

"Look, suppose the judge hands you the full life sentence?"

"Femi," I assured him, "there is nothing like life imprisonment in what I see of my future."

"What makes you so sure?"

"Just take it from me – no life-time in prison. In fact, no prison stay at all."

"So what are you doing here?"

"Resting. In police detention."

"You can afford to be flippant," he complained.

"That's a good one coming from you."

For the umpteenth time, he cast his eyes around the prison cell, took in my camp-bed which was folded against the corner, as usual, until it was time for me to turn in. Femi shook his head, as if he was seeing it for the first time.

"You may not get that in prison, you know."

Again, I assured him I had no intention of rotting away in prison. "It does not matter in the least if the verdict goes against me. I promise you, I am not going to prison."

"You think he'll give you a suspended sentence? You think he can?"

"I have no idea what sentence he's going to pass. He can give me the full life sentence. I'm simply assuring you that I am not going anywhere near the prison."

There seemed no other way to handle his dolefulness. It hung over him like wet smoke, blotting out the sheerest vestige of his normal ebullience. In a way, it was quite comic since it ill-fitted an irrepressible prankster and raconteur who could tell the same story a hundred times to the same audience, yet drag a laugh out of them. He drank, and that appeared to give him a little appetite. I tried to fill the space with conversation but his responses were desultory.

Finally, it was time to go. A huge sigh came from somewhere in his bowels and he dragged himself up, heavily. I watched him walk to the door, step onto the corridor as if he was taking in the air. His purpose, however, was to cast a rapid glance right and left, to ensure that no one was within earshot. He then dashed back into the room and spoke rapidly.

"Look, just listen. I am not a brave man. I am not crazy like you are. I couldn't stand even this condition, being cooped up like this. I would simply break. My driver over there, Mufu, he's different. More like you. And you can't imagine what a fanatic of yours he is. He's ready to do anything for you, you have no idea. So, he's all yours. I don't know what your plans are but I know you're planning something. You're so secretive. Just as well, because I don't want to know. If I don't know anything, then I can't give anything away. I can't imagine torture, I tell you. I'll break before a hand is even laid on me, so it's better for me not to know."

I tried to stem the rush of words. I assured him that I had no sinister plans but he bore me down with his intensity and sense of urgency. "You can abandon the car anywhere you want or take it with you wherever. When I leave you, I'll send Mufu to pack up the plates and things, then you can give him any instructions you want. If you want him to park at a spot near the court premises, or somewhere else, go and wait somewhere, at the border or wherever, just tell him. I have to make some contribution to what is happening. After all, those who are taking on the government's murder squads, they're human beings too. And they are fighting for us all, same as you. Well, that's all there is to it."

I succeeded in interrupting him at last. "All right, all right. I accept your offer. You're being unduly alarmist, I tell you. But, if it will make you happy, send in Mufu. When you've said your goodnight, send him in."

I lay awake for a long time after his departure, marvelling at this man who had said of himself, "I am not a brave man", wondering what his definition of bravery might be. Recollected the many hours he had spent with me in my police cell, the arguments we had, the many points of agreement, his total passion for the cause that had landed me in a predicament whose gravity I resolutely refused to confront, but one that oppressed him so heavily. Now it was time to begin to wonder when next we would meet – in the more natural condition of liberty? Or in the formal visiting room of a walled prison? For now, only one thing was certain – I knew that I was going to have a sounder sleep on that eve of judgement than this friend was likely to have.

I could school myself to appear as indifferent as I wished; the truth was, the trial had not been without tension, even for me. Indeed there were days of testimonies and cross-examinations when the mood swung from euphoria to despair. The prosecution would secure an unexpected piece of evidence or testimony. A surprise witness had seen me somewhere or the other on the crucial day, when I was supposed to have been elsewhere. Evidence was given that I had attended a university senate meeting on the day in question, and the prosecution – to all appearances – had turned this to its advantage. I had indeed attended the meeting, and deliberately, to establish an alibi. From the corner of my eye, I watched the sympathetic security agents share the crowd's anguish when hostile witnesses took the stand, providing evidence that sounded damning, since they seemed to puncture the alibi on which my lawyers had built part of the defence structure. On such days, one would sense the spectators droop, while the prosecutor's team adjusted their wigs at a cocky angle that signalled vindication and triumph, cast challenging looks in the direction of the defence team and departed to the congratulating smirks of the sprinkling of individuals who came to see the government win its case. And thus it proceeded, roller-coaster fashion, day after day, until the day of the verdict.

All we knew of this Judge was that he had remained impervious to numerous attempts by the government to pressure him into delivering a 'Guilty' verdict. Eso advised such extra-judicial lobbyists for the regime – including the Deputy Premier [4] – that their time would be more wisely spent assigning a competent prosecutor to their case. All through the resistance to the regime of the NNDP, the telephone operators – then situated at Oníyanrìn, Ìbàdàn – voluntarily tapped into all calls to and from highly placed government and party officials – indeed, all telephone conversations from Government House routinely passed through the ears of one member of the opposition or the other. In several of those calls, every effort was made to 'bend' Justice Eso, but he

---

[4] See Kayode Eso: *The Mystery Gunman.*

would only respond with a calm assurance that – yes – he fully intended to uphold the law.

I meant it when I said to Femi that I saw no life imprisonment in my future, but this went beyond our confidence in the integrity of the presiding Judge. The political charge throughout the West was such that change, in one form or another, was imminent. The issues that cried for resolution were already beyond the jurisdiction of the courts. Femi was quite right. I was indifferent to the verdict, except insofar as it could be used – if it went against us – in intensifying the insurrection. Looked at in any way, I was confident that I would not remain a prisoner for long. The government was being brought down, and the trial of one 'armed robber' was only a small part of the process.

Came judgement day and – what a sense of drama this judge had! As he reviewed the evidence with a granite scowl on his face, most people in court, Femi most agonisingly, had broken out in rashes, perspired blood or else were intoning last-minute intercessory prayers, expecting the worst. Justice Eso assessed the case for the prosecution at length, upholding most of their arguments, then spent just a fraction of the time in outlining the holes the defence had punched in the prosecution's case and, suddenly, there it was – Eso upheld the submission of our defence – no prima facie case to answer. The prosecution had undone itself. We had secured a verdict through a pure technicality that came from a crucial contradiction within the prosecution's elaborately presented case. The defence strategy had worked and I had not even been placed on the witness stand.

The court exploded, earning the stern, unsmiling rebuke of Justice Eso. 'This court is still in session,' he spat. 'Any unseemly conduct and I shall not hesitate to cite the offender for contempt.' His pebbled lenses raked the interior of his domain, daring any contradiction. The spectators fell silent, restrained themselves until the figure of doom had retreated into his chambers and the door was closed behind him. Then the explosion resumed, engulfing even the policemen and the judicial staff – registrar, court orderly, recorder, everyone. These took advantage of their proximity to the dock in which the accused stood and were first to dash over and shake hands. Our squad – Kodak and company – postponed any indulgence in jubilation – they positioned themselves in a different mode, allowed a few moments intermingling with the crowd, then formed a protective sheath and swept me through.

Mufu, Femi's driver, parked at a distance, but deprived, of his own volition, of the moment of victory had heard the roar, was elated and – a little disappointed. He was already primed for the role his employer had fantasised in case of a 'Guilty' verdict but now, all that was left was to sense his adrenalin evaporate. Still, he made the most of the situation, drove his car right at us and screeched to a halt. The next moment I was in, alone, and he took off like the wind, headed towards Lagos in a deliberate feint, slowing down only when he had assured himself that he had shaken off any likely pursuit of supporters or press, then doubled back to the Johnson home, the only place where I wanted to release all hidden tension, and ease myself gradually into legalised liberty.

We did not deceive ourselves that it was all over. The government had lost face and would begin, we knew, to seek an extra-judicial solution to the predicament in which it had placed itself. For now, there was only one duty to fulfil, and this was to myself: I *luxuriated* in this welcome home by a man who, even while denying it to himself, had tailored the concept of bravery to a unique definition of his own...

PART II

Òṣún,
Less Benign

Uncivil Wars - The Third Force and the MidWest Incursion

It was to be expected that the military coup d'état of January 15, 1966 – the first in the 'stable, moderate, democratic exemplar, the giant of Africa' – would divide the Nigerian nation more sharply than any other event in its six years of full Independence. Up till 1914, the British had ruled present-day Nigeria as two distinct protectorates – the North and the South. In the march towards Independence however, the South was split in two – the East and the West. After Independence, the Western government allowed the MidWest people their own region, thus turning the South into three regions – East, West and MidWest. The North, a mostly moslem region, remained intact, culturally distinct – quite apart from religion – from the South. It was this North, with a largely feudal and conservative outlook, that had held political power since Independence in 1960. The coup changed all of that, effectively pitting the North against the South.

The coup had taken a bloody toll on the North, which lost several of its senior military officers and political leaders. The Sardauna of Sokoto, Premier of the Northern Region, a public enigma behind the facial seclusion of his Arabian turban, was shot dead in his palace. Some of his wives were also casualties. The first prime minister of the independent nation, Tafawa Balewa, also from the North, was abducted and executed. So was the

Minister of Finance, the flamboyant Chief Festus Okotie-Eboh, albeit from the MidWest. Several killings, objectively considered, were not remotely essential to the success of the coup.

In the West however, the 'Wild Wild West' where the people had inhaled nothing but flames at close quarters for most of the preceding years, the coup was a hand of salvation, and they did not especially care by what means it was extended, or how blood-stained it was. Mostly, there were jubilations to the South – East and West and MidWest – while the North was plunged into mourning, and into a deep, visceral distrust and resentment of the South. The Eastern Region earned the greatest loathing from the stricken North, since it soon became noticeable that the leadership of the coup was mostly Igbo, the dominant population of the East. In addition, the Eastern political leadership had been left untouched.

There were some days of a stand-off between the rebels and the military command structure, headed by General Aguiyi-Ironsi, himself an Igbo. The rebel leaders – mostly mid-ranking officers – eventually surrendered to his authority, and Aguiyi-Ironsi emerged as Nigeria's first military Head of State. Once he felt confidently installed, he imprisoned the leaders but prevaricated over what to do with them – bring them to trial, simply dismiss them from the army or – set them free? To many Nigerians – mostly in the South – they were heroes. To the Northerners, they were murderous villains.

Eventually, the North rose up in reprisals – in May the same year – killed several Igbo and other southern residents in their midst and torched their homes and businesses. The Igbo fled to their homeland in the East but, as the wave of killings subsided, were persuaded to return and resume normal life in their adopted homeland. This uprising did not involve a military coup however, and General Aguiyi-Ironsi remained in power.

The counter-coup of July that same year was the bloodiest yet. The Commander-in-Chief, Aguiyi Ironsi, was abducted from the state house during an official visit to the West and killed, together with his host the military governor, Lt. Col. Adekunle Fajuyi. Many other Igbo officers lost their lives, often in a gruesome manner, some of them – suspected participants in the January coup – were dragged from prison detention and butchered in the streets.

Fajuyi had been appointed first Military Governor of the Western Region following the January 66 coup. I had struck up a rapport with him in his first months in office. Our first meeting was at his request – perhaps he was curious to meet the man who was alleged to have held up a radio station. This encounter led to others. He attended my premiere production of *Kongi's Harvest* in the Arts Theatre of the University of Ìbàdàn and was full of schemes for the development of the region so unexpectedly placed under his charge. It was quite in the character of this officer whom I came to know so well in such a short time that, when the coup-makers broke into his residence to arrest his Commander-in-Chief and guest, he refused to hand him over and insisted on accompanying him. For his gallantry, he underwent the same fate as his superior. They were both taken to a forest outside Ìbàdàn, cruelly tortured and executed. His end would later wring a poetic tribute out of me.

When the killings were more or less over, power reverted to the hands of Northern officers, their Igbo colleagues being thoroughly routed and decimated. This was when the name of an officer named Murtala Mohammed first came into Nigerian lore; he was widely rumoured to have master-minded the counter-coup and was expected to take over power. However, a young officer from a minority christian group in the North, Yakubu Gowon, ended up as Nigeria's new Head of State.

And there, with the shift of power, the nation hoped that the blood-letting would cease but – no. A progressive pogrom of the Igbo erupted in October the same year, a hunt for Easterners of all ages who were unfortunate enough to have heeded the call of the new regime to return to their places of work and residence in the North, reassured that all was well. They were gruesomely mistaken. Not merely from the North, but from every corner of the nation, the Igbo fled homewards, wheeled contraptions of every kind bearing their dismal remains and possessions into Igboland. The train loads of refugees from the north bore pitiable cargoes, several survivors with physical mutilations, some women in such a state of shock that they clung to the severed heads of their spouses or sons, cradling them on their laps. Even within Lagos, the hunt for the Igbo continued unabated, either in their homes or at roadblocks. The depletion of my wife's wardrobe during the months of October and November was only one of many private testimonies to the desperation of one's Igbo male acquaintances – not all of them soldiers – who resorted to female disguises to escape detection as they fled eastwards. Images of death and mutilation in Eastern journals, and the television coverage of a savaged humanity erased the final sense of belonging in a people who saw themselves isolated within the nation, and cataylsed their resolve to secede.

The discovery of oil in huge reserves in the East, largely in the Niger estuary, played a role, unquestionably, in the propulsion of the Biafran leaders towards secession, but it would be a distortion of history, and an attempt to trivialise the trauma that the Igbo had undergone, to suggest – as some commentators have tried to do – that it was the lure of the oil wealth that drove the Igbo to seek a separate existence. When a people have been subjected to a degree of inhuman violation for which there is no other word but genocide, they have the right to seek an identity apart from their aggressors.

I was not alone in writing embittered articles on the massacres, especially denouncing the lackadaisical attitude of Gowon's government towards the killings. We accused the government of condoning genocide and urged our own people in the West to distance themselves from any act that might suggest an approval of such insensate slaughter. In addition however, the suspicion developed from a Northern domination agenda, this time through the agency of the military.

It was, expectedly, a period of great tension and mutual suspicion. Violence hung in the air, threatening to break out at any provocation and consume the nation. The various forces in the West that had resisted the NNDP reign of repression regrouped and resumed their meetings, watchful and suspicious of the new military government. When the young Head of State summoned a meeting of 'leaders of thought' - selected prominent citizens in various fields - to Lagos to decide the future of the nation, we worked on the sidelines, contributing to the position of the West through my friend, Bola Ige, a stalwart of the Action Group and close lieutenant of that party's leader, Obafemi Awolowo. Awolowo was of course regarded as a hero and the political voice of the West, and his release from prison, shortly after Yakubu Gowon was installed in power, was easily one of the shrewdest political moves of the new regime.

Most of these meetings took place in Femi's house, then at Oníréké, Ìbàdàn. They were fertile exploratory grounds for Bola Ige, the only party politician of the brainstorming group and a member of the Western Region's delegation to the 'leaders of thought' assemblage. Little did this colleague dream - or perhaps he did already? - that he would one day become an elected governor of the same region, after it became known as Ọ̀yọ́ State. For now, he was still only a junior member of the Western delegation of 'leaders of thought' whose meetings took place in Lagos, closely monitored, we would later find out, by the British High Commission.

I would occasionally accompany him - but only to those preliminary, informal meetings - where the various regional groups tested one another's positions and traded tactical moves. It all took place in an atmosphere of indescribable tension. Delegations stayed in fortified apartments, went about under the protection of armed police and army squads. Lt. Col. Odumegwu Ojukwu, the Military Governor of the Eastern Region, used the alibi of this insecure environment to stay put in Enugu and refuse to participate in any of the meetings, not even symbolically, by sending observers. It was a ploy, Ojukwu was already making plans to secede, but I had personal cause to agree with his dismissal of any notion of a secure environment.

Once, Bola Ige nearly got us both killed in the sedate, residential part of Ìkòyí, where we had gone to consult with the leader of the Tiv delegation, J.S. Tarka. The Tiv are a people who live within what is known as the middle belt of Nigeria - hence the name of their political movement – the Middle Belt Alliance. Politically merged with the Northern Region, they chafed under domination by its ruling oligarchy and commenced armed resistance long before the nation's full independence, continuing, albeit under-reported, even for some years afterwards. In later years, one of the officers who commanded the pacifying forces of the Tiv uprising publicly lamented his contribution to their subjugation.

The politician we had set out to visit, J.S. Tarka, a figure of unquestioned charisma, led the United Middle Belt Congress, a traditional ally of the Action Group of the West. Tarka and I were not close but we appeared to respond to each other through some hidden waves. On my way to my assignation with the radio station in 1965, I made a brief stop at Bola Ige's house to let Bola know that I might be away for a while, although I did not tell him why. It was there that J.S. Tarka and I met for the first time. I was instantly drawn to this man of very gentle bearing, sensing instantly that behind a face that smiled so readily was a cast-iron will, and a radar mind that constantly scanned his environment and its occupants. We spoke briefly in the living room while I waited for Bola to emerge.

Tarka's demeanour changed – it was quite sudden and startling. He looked at me very strangely, broke off in mid-sentence, and did what, to me, was even stranger. He thrust his hand into his pocket and brought out a slim wad of currency notes that he offered to me. I looked at him, questioning, but he insisted that I must take the money. I was naturally taken aback, but finally accepted a pound note. It was a spontaneous gesture, lacking any explanation, except that he seemed to obey an inner impulse. We had only spoken briefly of the political situation, nothing in our exchanges had suggested my being in need of money or on the verge of plunging into some dangerous straits. But he had looked at me as if he knew that he was supposed to help me in some way, was not sure what form the help should take, and could only think of the money in his pocket. Now, a year and a half later, I looked forward to seeing him again, smiling to myself at the thought of his reaction when I solemnly handed back his pound note. I had no thought that I would nearly get killed before I settled my unsought indebtedness.

Bola was at the wheel. At the end of a long driveway into the block of Lagos apartments where Tarka was staying, off Glover Road, Ìkòyí, soldiers suddenly emerged from behind the shrubbery. One of them barked out some orders, gesticulating in a manner that was open to myriad interpretations. Bola thought that he was being ordered to go back. Ramming the gear in reverse, he began to tear off at full speed. His neck twisted round to manoeuvre through the driveway, he failed to see the rage distorted face of the foremost soldier, but I saw him. He slipped off the safety catch of his gun and levelled it at the car, screaming and swearing at us to stop or else! I did not understand the words but the language of all his body parts was most eloquent! The more this soldier screamed, the faster Bola drove, and my re-transmission of what I understood as the soldier's wishes appeared to confuse Bola even more. All this took place in seconds but they were sufficient to instruct me in the often understated measure of eternity. In desperation I hit him on the chest, screamed at him to stop and this finally gained his attention. He stepped on the brakes, perhaps just in time. The soldier caught up with us, his body convulsed in violence, coiled up for a release that could only be obtained by pulling his trigger. And then, Bola remembered that he spoke fluent Hausa and plunged into a torrent of explanation in that language. It calmed the man somewhat, and only then was Bola able to state our business. It was a very relieved Tarka who opened the door to us, having watched the scene, horrified, from the balcony of his third-floor apartment.

Such scenes were being enacted all over Lagos, indeed, all over the country, many of them ending tragically. The cheapest recruit held the power of life and death – and not merely as a result of accidents or misunderstandings as in our case, but as cold-blooded executions, carried out in confidence of impunity. The nation teetered on the edge of disintegration. I continued to write in the media, debate in private. At campus encounters, open-air bars and other informal gatherings, at which the secret service made no pretence at disguising their presence, we railed at the government's lukewarm concern for the plight of the Igbo. The meetings of the 'leaders of thought' continued, but it was clear that any national gathering was incomplete without Igbo participation.

Within my own caucus, our suspicions of Gowon's ultimate goal also continued to deepen. The underlying agenda had begun to emerge, the signals had become more overt - the military was digging in, and would remain in power indefinitely. It was being encouraged to do so by the North, but also by a handful of Western politicians - the remnants of the NNDP faction who had now lost out in the politics of the West - and even groupings of Western professionals and intellectuals, such as 'the committee of ten', who for reasons of their own, began to work for Yakubu Gowon's continued stay in office. The British government, acting through its High Commissioner, had long committed itself to a military dominated agenda, as long as it was led from the North.

After the first military coup - January 15, '66 - the North had raised the shout of *araba* - secession. Indeed, at the first leaders of thought meeting in Lagos, the Northern delegation's position paper was based on its right to secede from the nation. However, a significant development now took place - the North was beginning to lose its secessionist craving. As for the half-way house of a loose federation, or confederation, that was also nixed - governance was to remain under centralised control. Actively prodded by the British government, the North gradually abandoned its secessionist agenda - *you have the whole cake in your hands* - the High Commissioner admonished Gowon. *Why do you wish to settle for half?*

It did not take long for me to regain my place on the security list. Our friends within Intelligence soon let me know that I had been classified as hostile to the government, someone to be closely monitored. Nothing of this however deterred Femi Johnson from remaining openly identified with me. That his brother, a staunch military loyalist had been retained by the new regime as military administrator of Lagos - Lagos was not yet a full state, so it did not merit a governor - meant little to him. Femi was uninterested in ideologies but, we shared a common political principle - justice as the basis of society. The Igbo, he felt, had been cruelly and unjustly treated.

The prospect of war between the East and the Federation loomed larger every day. A last-minute effort to avert it took place in Aburi, Ghana. Since Igbo leadership remained adamant in their refusal to participate in any meetings outside its Eastern enclave, persisting in its plaint of a lack of security for their people, the avuncular military dictator of Ghana, Lieutenant General Ankrah – military dictatorship was now in vogue everywhere! – stepped in and offered the disputants the facilities of its famous retreat at Aburi.

They met over several days in this soothing arena, away from the volatile atmosphere of Nigerian coups, counter-coups and massacres, away from the intrigues and self-serving counsels of still active colonial powers and other behind-the-scene interests, especially of the business world. In Aburi, enemies within Nigeria embraced without, saluted, and held dialogue in a reportedly constructive and pragmatic manner. They exchanged notes on resources, boundaries, military rankings and pecking order, they even yielded up the locations of missing bodies – the hasty burial grounds of assassinated national leaders, military officers and other casualties of the various coups – including former heads of state. When their re-interments took place some weeks later, many in the nation clung to the belief that the remains were not truly those of the victims, that a symbolic farce, with a laudable goal – reconciliation – had been staged. All parties agreed to a solemn undertaking not to resort to violence in the resolution of yet outstanding disputes. It was an undertaking as empty of substance as some of the caskets that were solemnly interred after Aburi.

There was a marked difference of approach for the Aburi encounter, one that already signalled the certain repudiation of whatever agreements were made. The Federal side, led by Yakubu Gowon, attended the meeting with an open book, a laissez-faire state of mind. By contrast, Odumegwu Ojukwu, still Governor of the Eastern Region, and *de facto* leader of the Igbo, had arrived meticulously prepared. Not surprisingly, he largely had his way. The protocols and agreements were signed to fanfare and popped champagnes, and they all returned home with the map of the nation superficially intact but visibly shredded.

On his return, Yakubu Gowon was assailed by his people for
having given away far too much to the Igbo, who continued to
press for the implementation of all agreements to the letter,
screaming bad faith at any seeming delay. By now, the victims of
both the January and June coups had received their ceremonial
burials. That ritual appeared to douse political passions for a while,
but it was clear that this was only the lull before the storm. Soon
enough, Nigeria experienced its first aerial hijacking as a Federal-
owned plane was seized in flight between Lagos and Benin and
piloted to Enugu, capital of the Eastern Region. Gowon retaliated
by freezing a number of assets that belonged to the rebellious
region. A Nigerian Navy vessel went the way of the purloined
plane – a mere sharing of joint assets, the Easterners crowed. The
drums of secession were beating loud and clear. A mass exodus of
Easterners began from all parts of the nation. Once again the roads
were clogged with laden vehicles, but this time in all directions –
the regional leader, Odumegwu Ojukwu had announced that he
could no longer guarantee the safety of non-Easterners in the region
under his control. Some weeks later, he formally ordered all
'foreigners' to leave.

It was obvious – the secession of the East was only weeks
away. Yakubu Gowon had terminated the meetings of the civilian
'leaders of thought', told the bigwigs to remain in their
constituencies until further notice – which would never arrive.
All talk of a return to democratic rule, on which the 'leaders of
thought' had spent so much time in sterile debate, was formally
abrogated. The military was now free to act as it pleased, without
any pandering to the civilian constituency. With every act or public
pronouncement, the breach between the Federal government and
the East widened. A delegation of public figures – politicians,
crowned heads, prelates, etc. – made a last-ditch effort to head off
what now appeared inevitable – declaration of independence by
the Eastern Region. They were courteously received by the
leadership, but returned empty-handed. The position of Yakubu
Gowon's Federal government hardened.

Consolidation of military power would be inescapable once
war was declared. In the thinking of many of us, a military

dictatorship with no foreseeable end appeared to be the worst of all possible evils, including even the 'evil' of secession. The West, untainted by any coup initiative and blameless of any genocidal participation, still held the few potential checks on the slide towards the precipice of war, but that potential was fast diminishing.

With the dissolution of the 'leaders of thought' groupings, my friend the politician, Bola Ige, now spent even more time with our ad-hoc group. This was an eerie period when nothing seemed to be happening, the heart of the nation appeared to have stopped beating, while its body remained suspended in a void. In grim reality however, military leadership was extremely busy – vetting names for a civilian-military cabinet and consulting with the nation's former colonial masters, the British High Commission. It was during this seeming suspension of reality and intense speculation that we decided that the state of mind of Obafemi Awolowo had to be ascertained, and urgently. As an 'outsider' – that is, non-member of any official grouping or political party – that task was given to me. Bola set up the appointment with the leader of the former Action Group, now bestowed with the superfluous and unenviable title of 'Leader of the Yoruba' by the Governor of the Western Region, Colonel Adebayo.

The question on our minds was straightforward: how would Awolowo respond to the looming offer of a position in Yakubu Gowon's government? It was clear that if Awolowo became a part of that government, the last restraints on its policy towards the East would be removed, with the predictable consequence of a civil war. There was however a subsidiary question, one that arose from the first – we were deeply apprehensive for his safety, perhaps no one more deeply than I. Had a swaggering officer, a Major, and of the same Yoruba stock, not boasted to my face that he would personally take Awolowo to the nearest crossroads, tie him to a stake and shoot him as an example because *'we know what he's up to, he has not yet given up his tribal games.* The officer's definition of Awolowo's 'tribal games' was so simplistic that it frightened one, being none other than the Old Man's reported reluctance to serve under Gowon's government if it was bent on war, and his insistence that the West of the Yoruba should not become a war zone, if that prospect did materialise.

That Major B.M. should have spoken to me in such a manner was in itself revealing – he could not conceive, even for a moment that, as a 'social critic', and one with supposedly progressive credentials, I could be anything but the loudest voice in the unreflective chorus of 'One Nigeria!' Both concepts – progressive politics and national unity – were so thoroughly conflated in his mind that, to be progressive or radical was to reject the possibility of perceiving any flaws in the very basis of nation being, or question the structural arrangements that held it together, however precariously. The same officer, like many others, has since repudiated such mindless adherence to the unqualified mantra of 'one nation, right or wrong'. At the time however, he was totally ensnared in such rhetoric, and with a blissful indifference to whatever political ideology such a 'unified entity' espoused.

Awolowo received me in his office, dominated by a massive desk. It seemed even more substantial than it was two years before, when I had slept under it, keeping vigil with others over the radio transmitter as we anticipated a police attack and prepared to repulse it. I could not resist a sneak caress of the desk like a long missed comrade, then succumbed to the temptation of regaling the Old Man with an account of the episode.

Awolowo's eyes lit up with childlike mischief, eager for details. At the mention of the name of Mazi Ukonu, the leader of the broadcasting team and a well known radio comic, he burst out excitedly – *Ukonu? In this study? You mean, in my study? And you under this desk? This very desk? Both of you in here? The election broadcasts were transmitted from here? And by Ukonu himself? I used to listen to his shows over the radio in Calabar (prison). He has a great sense of humour!*

I satisfied his curiosity in all the juicy details, then we settled down to the substance of my mission. I restrained myself from telling him that I knew that the letter from General Gowon, inviting him to serve, was already in his possession, that in fact I knew its contents. It was a secret I felt bound to respect – I had kept it even from Bola Ige, as a close lieutenant of Awolowo, but not a member of CWIL. On the way to the Old Man's home in Ikenne, the courier, a highly placed police officer, had stopped at the chambers of his lawyer friend from Abẹ̀òkúta but whose chambers were in mainland Yaba, Lagos. Together, they had opened the letter – yes, the old-fashioned way – steamed it open, read and copied it. The lawyer, S.S. – a member of a volunteer 'committee of ten' that was formed to drum up support for Gowon's regime, and who had fanatically assigned himself the mission of my own conversion – revealed the contents to me shortly afterwards, perhaps in an endeavour to make me believe in Gowon's goodwill towards the 'Leader of the Yoruba', and thus to the Yoruba. Many years, coups and revelations would pass before the same lawyer found himself renouncing every act that he had undertaken to win support for the regime, advocating nothing less than a separate, independent existence for his own Yoruba portion of the nation. His mantra, which no one could have believed possible in those nationalist sixties had become – *K'ólúkálúkù ma lọ n'tí ẹ̀.*[1]

Seated across the famous desk in Awolowo's study however, my mind was not on my 'elder brother' from my home town, but very much on the encounter with the young Major who had threatened summary execution for the politician – among several other ominous signs. I asked Awolowo:

"Sir, I think you'll agree that Gowon is bound to offer you a cabinet position. Suppose you decide to decline the offer, you realise that your life may be in danger?"

Awolowo looked at me, paused thoughtfully and nodded. "Yes, I suppose I could find myself in that situation.'

My next statement to him was made with great hesitation, since I could not be certain that he would not begin to have doubts about my sanity. "If you decide to refuse," I stammered, "have you thought of going underground? I'm sorry sir, I know that after such a long spell in prison, it is a hard prospect to even consider, asking you to resign yourself to another kind of prison, but I still have to ask it."

Awolowo sat bolt upright at this, then relapsed, again thoughtfully. "Well, I have never thought of that. But I've always insisted to myself that my first duty is to the Yoruba nation. We

---

[1] Let everyone go his own way.

are a nation, you know. And I put that nation first, then the one called Nigeria. If the moment comes when I firmly believe that it is in our interest for me to disappear, of course I will not hesitate. But, you young radical people! What could have moved your mind in such an extreme direction?"

I shrugged. As I sat facing him, I became painfully conscious of his personal history, his travails, a Job of a politician who had been deprived of a merited electoral leadership of the nation, spent several years in gaol for alleged treason, lost his first-born, Segun, in a motor accident, a promising young mind, even as he measured out his days in prison. I wondered if it was even right of me to have suggested such a possible course of action to a man with such a history, but it was too late to back out.

"We like to look at the so-called worst-case scenarios", I explained. "If you stay out of Gowon's government, you will hold a very strong card. For a start, the war – if it comes to that – will lose much of its moral backing and international support. You wear the hat of leader of the Yoruba people – that's nearly one third of the national population. It's a powerful card. To take that card away from you, there are desperate soldiers who will stop at nothing. Sir, if you are killed, I leave you to imagine the consequences. I merely want you to know that we have the means of making you totally inaccessible for weeks, months, and even smuggle you out of the country."

I was conscious of exaggerating our underground facilities, but what I claimed was not very far from the truth. Since the abrupt end to the 'leaders of thought' conferences that were designed to establish the basis for a continued democratic co-existence, we had begun to prepare for every kind of eventuality.

Out of the blue, Awolowo said to me, "One thing I have made up my mind about – I have not led the Yoruba people so far as to have our land turned into a battleground."

I had no idea where his thoughts had taken him, but he continued to speak in that vein for some moments, as if his mind was elsewhere, pondering some decision. Then he leant back in his chair, fixed his gaze on me through his wire-rimmed 'grandpa' lenses that had become, like his cap, his distinctive public symbol.

Speaking almost softly, wistfully, he revealed the little known story of his nocturnal encounter with Ojukwu just a week before.

The 1967 eve of secession, delegation of national public figures, authorised by Yakubu Gowon, to dialogue with Eastern leadership, had been led by Obafemi Awolowo, and the formal, well publicised meeting between the two sides lasted nearly all day. The Easterners listed their grievances and demands, spoke with all apparent seriousness, and saw their guests off to their chalets. Late that same night however, Awolowo was disturbed by a knock on the door.

It was the Eastern leader, Ojukwu, himself. He admitted that he had waited till late into the night so as to be able to speak to Awolowo in strictest privacy. Sure, said Awolowo, but he also insisted that at least one or two persons join him. That was agreed, and Awolowo called up the adjoining chalet, woke up the Police Commissioner for the Western Region, Olufunwa, and a close political aide.

Accompanying Ojukwu was a small team that included a professor of History from the University of Ìbàdàn who had fled, like other Easterners, to their beleaguered state. Years afterwards, during the struggle against the Abacha dictatorship, the same don introduced himself to me at a meeting in the United States in 1996 and revealed his participation at the nocturnal meeting of thirty years earlier. His account was a consistent and detailed confirmation of what Awolowo confided in me that afternoon.

Odumegwu Ojukwu's mission was unambiguous, Awolowo said to me. "The young man had come to inform me that the East had decided on secession, and that there was no going back. All that was left was the announcement of a date. He said, 'Sir, I have not come to argue, but to inform you. It has been decided."

"It was clear that any discussion was futile," Awolowo continued. "After all, we had done nothing but talk all day. Ojukwu confessed that he had agreed to meet the delegation at all only out of respect for my person. Biafra had already taken a decision."

"I was not surprised," the Chief admitted. "I did one thing, though, I made one request of him - in fact, I insisted on it. I said to Ojukwu - at least, let us in the West - I, specifically - have a minimum of two weeks notice before you announce the decision. And he promised. Yes, he promised me that much."

I hesitated, but could not resist asking. "Why two weeks? You told him you needed two weeks – to do what?"

Awolowo gave one of his enigmatic smiles. "You know Olufunwa, the Police Commissioner?"

I nodded Yes.

"Well, apart from me, he is the only one who knows the answer to that question. And he's not likely to tell you either."

I did not press him.

Hardly had Awolowo's delegation settled back into Federal territory than Ojukwu declared an Independent State of Biafra. The date was May 30, 1967. A short while after, Chief Awolowo accepted to serve as Commissioner of Finance under Yakubu Gowon.

The Federal Government had however made a pre-emptive move. On May 27, Gowon abolished all four regions and split the nation into twelve new states. This achieved the goal of dangling before the entities that were newly carved out from the East, the attraction of their own autonomous governance, with all the resources of the oil soaked Niger delta. Between the two strokes, loyalties in the former Eastern Region were split. War appeared inevitable.

As the rumble of the drums of war became truly deafening, I found myself in Stockholm. That outing was the first conference of African and Scandinavian writers in the serene setting of Hässelby Schloss, initiated by Swedish PEN. It was bliss to get away from the newly over-heated nation space of Nigeria and interact with others of one's professionally acquired tribe – other writers. It was on that occasion that we met – most of us for the first time – Per Wastberg, the Swedish novelist who was actively involved with African liberation movements – Mozambique, Angola, South Africa etc.- though we did not suspect it at the time. Per was a close associate of several of Africa's liberation warriors, and especially Eduardo Mondlane of Mozambique – even till today he remains one of the most consistent rescue stations for beleaguered African writers and dissidents. On a personal note, it was Per who introduced my work to Swedish readership.

Within Nigeria, our writers and artistes clan had been scattered by the coups and counter-coups, massacres and consequent insecurity, and now, it was flung to the four winds by the secessionist move. Chinua Achebe, Christopher Okigbo, the poet of *Heavensgate, Labyrinths*, and a volunteer from the Western imbroglio, Cyprian Ekwensi, Gabriel Okara, etc., were holed up in the breakaway state. JP Clark, Mabel Segun, Amos Tutuola and others – all founders and animators of the Mbari Creative Arts movement of Ìbàdàn, were stuck on the Federal side. It had never been much of a close family – we all tended to do our work independently, meeting occasionally, mostly for planning creative workshops, exhibitions, readings and other special events. However, poet and playwright JP Clark and I had been quite close to Christopher Okigbo – all three having been based in Ìbàdàn in those early sixties – and now, I experienced something close to the sadness of a family breakup. I had hoped that Chinua, Christopher and others would come to Stockholm. In that tranquil atmosphere, we could attempt to form, across the belligerent regions, a common front against the looming war. I was against the secession – but only for practical considerations – I doubted Biafra's ability to survive the inevitable onslaught from the Federal side. Not for one moment did I consider the secessionist move itself an act of moral or political felony – it was simply politically, and militarily unwise.

No one turned up from the Biafran side. If someone had, I never would have needed to embark on my fateful mission to Biafra. Far more likely, I would have taken up the invitation of an attractive young lady whom I met in Stockholm, an air hostess, to go hunting reindeer with her father, then travelled to Greece for that nation's autumn wine festival, a cultural indulgence of many dimensions that I had promised myself ever since I first recognised in the Greek deity, Dionysos, a long lost sibling of my personal demiurge, Úgún.

Úgún had other plans for me however. War was declared – no, not in such terms – at the beginning it was simply 'police action'. Very few people in the nation were fooled.

After Stockholm, frustrated by the absence of our Biafrian colleagues, I travelled to London, this time to carry out a series of recorded 'conversations' at the Transcription Centre for African Arts and Culture, a centre of activities – and respite – for a relay of African writers and artists. It was run by the Art historian, critic and broadcaster, Dennis Duerden. The centre was funded mainly from an American foundation, the Farfield, that was later proven to be affiliated with the CIA, though none of us knew it then. Dennis, a loose-limbed Englishman with untamable hair, whose appearance, even in a new suit, somehow succeeded in looking permanently rumpled, enjoyed the unpredictable assistance of one of my associates at the time, Aminu Abdullahi.

Urbane, seemingly unflappable, Abdullahi, a stocky Hausa with a conspicuous single cicatrix on the side of his head, was easily the most passionate and knowledgable African lover of modern jazz that I ever knew. He could tell apart a riff of improvisation by Dizzie Gillespie from that of Miles Davis after only a few notes, and his collection of LPs – long-playing records, now dinosaurs – overflowed his guest room in Dennis Duerden's home into the passageway. It would be much, much later before I would discover that Aminu was the cousin of M.D. Yusuf, then head of Nigeria's Secret Service, the 'E' branch, and even worked for him – if not at the time, then certainly later. That did not diminish the genuineness of his concern about Nigeria's lurch towards an all-out war.

A few sleepless nights brainstorming in Dennis Duerden's apartment resulted in a decision: someone had to go to the East and have a talk with Ojukwu, head of the secessionist state, meet with Chinua Achebe and other leading writers and intellectuals in Biafra. What was required, we concluded, was a revocation of the declaration of secession, and the calling off of all hostilities. Then, using our international connections, invoking the aid of neutral countries such as Sweden with her sound credentials of assistance to African liberation, we would facilitate a return to the conference table. Aminu declared himself ready to make the journey but, there was an insurmountable obstacle: Aminu was not only a Northerner, he looked it, and his accent was a straightforward giveaway. It was difficult enough for even a Southerner, a non-Biafran, to enter the now xenophobic entity called Biafra. A Northerner who entered that breakaway enclave was unlikely to survive his first step. I volunteered to go in his place.

Finally, I could return to Nigeria, unburdened by a sense of impotence. The very night of my re-entry, I was ensconced at my favourite place for both innocent and dubious undertakings – Femi Johnson's house. I gathered my usual group together and outlined what I had brought back, quite fortuitously, from London. The discussion was not complicated – every voice stressed the need to find a language that would convince Ojukwu that the Igbo were not abandoned. That sense of rejection, of isolation, was what stood between any form of *rapprochement* between the Federal Government and the breakaway Biafra. It went beyond politics, moved beyond the implacable Biafran hostility towards Yakubu Gowon's government. The orbit of guilt, as assigned by Biafra, had now expanded to include the Yoruba West, whose people, the Biafrans felt, had betrayed them. Such a Biafran position was rationally untenable. One had only to recall the coups and counter-coups that had resulted in a West that was thoroughly invested by the military, mostly of Northern and Middle Belt origin, thus leaving the West bereft of any military clout or bargaining power. The perception of the West's indifference or leaning towards the Federal cause had taken root however, and it was not subject to reasoning.

There and then, in Femi Johnson's house – and all other accounts of this origination can be authoritatively disregarded![2] – was coined the expression that would later feature in many commentaries, achieving its maximum notoriety in the military incursion of Biafran-led forces into the MidWest Region – the Third Force. In the confrontation between the Federal side and the Biafran, a Third Force, opposed to the Civil War and prepared to mobilise against it, had become a necessity. If Nigeria was the thesis, Biafra the antithesis, then the Third Force resulted from

---

[2] These include my own in *The Man Died* where a number of individuals still needed to be protected.

the synthesis – all impeccable dialectics, lacking only an organised movement and the necessary force to back it up!

Back from his insurance brokerage office, and settled down to dinner, when I told Femi I was going to Biafra, he lost his appetite mid-morsel. Madness, madness, nothing but madness! You'll get shot for nothing. Crossing the firing lines meant, for Femi, crossing the boundaries of sanity. It was not much of an argument, as I had already taken my decision. In the end he offered a well reasoned bit of advice – I should at least speak with someone from the Federal side before venturing across.

The Rev. Father Martins was the chaplain for the Federal army, a blunt speaking soldier, compact in build and rock solid. He had the reputation of not permitting his priestly duties to interfere with his lover's ardour. Once, a totally reliable source informed me, his fellow prelates went to remonstrate with him over an affair which, they warned, was causing embarrassment for the church. They also picked an unfortunate moment when Father Martins was ministering to the young parishioner in question, and they entered without knocking – or perhaps Father Martins had simply not heard them. Finally becoming aware of their presence, Martins snatched his priestly garb from the floor, flung it over the heads of the intruders and, while they were still entangled in the robes, pummeled the muffled mass, kicked it down the stairs and went back to his interrupted offices.

This was the soldiering prelate whom we decided upon as a logical intermediary with the Federal government for my visit to Biafra. We met again thirty-five years after the Civil War, at a social reception, when the Rev. Father was eighty. I thought of asking him what the truth was about the story that we had all enjoyed for upwards of thirty years. Fortunately, I first made the mistake of offering him my seat when he came round to say hallo. He sat me down with such indignant force, truly unbelievable even in a sixty-year old, that I decided that it would be wiser to let him take his secrets to the grave.

As expected, Father Martins was delighted to learn that not everyone had given up, gave his blessing on the effort for a last-minute appeal to Ojukwu. He promised to speak to General Gowon, brought out his best, non-communion brandy, poured us both generous shots, and wished me luck.

Even so, it was with great reluctance that Femi reconciled himself to my going – the very thought of guns going off was something to which he was allergic, little did he imagine that, as the war endured, he would himself visit some of the towns liberated by the Federal troops, drawn by the demands and opportunities of his insurance profession, and sometimes within earshot of bombardments across the firing lines. In 1967, the battlefront still signalled for him the nearest that any mortal could conceive of the promised end of the world – a point over which not many people would disagree.

I set out from his house, with the doleful face of a normally ebullient friend staring at me across the table. He was especially troubled by the latest rumours that attempts by the Federal troops to infiltrate Biafra had moved the skirmishing to Auchi, a border town in the MidWest State, next to my destination. The MidWest, separated from the seceded state by the River Niger, served as a buffer state between breakaway Biafra and our Western Region. Nothing would dispel Femi's forebodings until I returned a week later, in one piece, but in far greater danger than I ever was while close to the firing lines.

The Igbo are the predominant ethnic group in the seceded region that became Biafra, but they also shared the MidWest State with other ethnic groups such as the Itshekiri, the Urhobo, Ijaw and others. This Igbo link across the River Niger made it logical that the MidWest remain neutral, not be forced to take arms against their kin in Biafra. I spent the night in Asaba, the riverside border town of the MidWest and an Igbo stronghold, as guest of Professor Edozien, once master of Tedder Hall at the University of Ìbàdàn. We spoke late into the night, a discussion that brought in his friends and neighbours, eager to learn the news from Lagos and the West. The atmosphere in that Igbo town, Asaba, was predictably one of apprehension. This anxiety, so evident in my host and his companions, did make me feel that perhaps, after all, I had not embarked on a pointless journey. That sense of futility had begun to gnaw into my setting-out confidence as I drove further and further from the comparative stability of Ìbàdàn, and deeper into that territory of tensions.

Although Biafra was supposed to be under a blockade, and Asaba Bridge – the link across the southward flowing River Niger - was blocked on both the MidWest and secessionist sides, traffic – both human and goods – flowed both ways through bush tracks to the river banks, both north and south of the Asaba Bridge. From Asaba, paddle canoes ferried virtually every commodity to the town of Onitsha on the Biafran side, and returned just as heavy laden. These tracks were patrolled by Federal soldiers based in Asaba, ostensibly to enforce the blockade. I ran into the patrols from time to time and was stopped only once, but the soldier only wished to be absolutely certain that his eyes did not deceive him, marvelling what WS could be doing in the bush so far from Ìbàdàn or Lagos.

Onitsha, a market town on Biafran soil, can be described as the twin city to Asaba, situated directly across the River Niger from the latter. From the moment of my disembarkation from the canoe, it was clear that secession was not just a word to the Igbo, but a total alteration of existence, even down to a collective psychology. Any stranger was spotted immediately and either followed, reported, or accosted. In the end he would be arrested and interrogated. Crossing the effervescent market in Onitsha as I walked to find a taxi park, I was mostly recognised and stopped for news. However, the inevitable confrontation was only a matter of time, including some roughing-up – quite mild – by young Biafran vigilantes who were on constant and often manic prowl for *sabos* – saboteurs – a word that translated as all strangers. I was arrested – at the point of wooden guns, pointed at me in all earnestness! – but generally well treated, especially once I was handed over to the local uniformed officer who found me a seat in his office. I had taken the precaution of bringing my passport with me, to make all understand that I accepted that I was visiting a sovereign territory. Transferred for interrogation to Enugu, now elevated from a regional to a national capital, I was routinely locked up in a police cell, treated as a regular suspect – all possessions confiscated, belt, shoes and underpants taken away. Then the senior police officer in charge returned, ordered that the latest batch of *sabos* be brought before him. The moment I appeared, he underwent a moment of utter disbelief, then leapt out of his chair and released me to a torrent of abuse on his subordinates.

It was while waiting for my transfer to a hotel that Christopher Okigbo drove in, kitted for war – albeit in casual civilian clothing, but complete with rifle and ammunition belt – screeched to a halt in front of the station. He was coming from the front, the excitation of battle still fresh in his eyes. For one brief, nostalgic moment, I believe I envied this friend and colleague who would rather be a poet, but had thrown himself fully into a self-defining cause. But he was alone, not within a column of Writers' and Artists' Brigade of our student dreams, heading south to demolish the Apartheid kingdom. Was there really much difference? How is one craving for liberation to be faulted, but not the other?

Chris Okigbo had come for promised reinforcements, both of men and weapons. The Police Commissioner let him into the office, having first made me hide behind the door. When the door was shut and I stood revealed, Christopher let out a screech that brought everyone out of their offices. He broke into a mad jig in front of the astonished officers and wanted to drag me off to wherever. Finally, he had to content himself with accepting that the head of his new state exercised priority over my presence in Biafra. We promised to meet later in the evening, when I would have fulfilled my immediate mission. I watched him load some guns and ammunition into his car, waved to him as he drove off in a small cloud of dust. That was the last time I would see my excitable friend and poet Christopher Okigbo alive. He perished on the Okigwe front, we learnt, with that chant from the Spanish Civil War issuing from his throat: *Non passaran!* [3] One person at least, had given his life to the dreams of youth, but how sad that it should have been on a fratricidal field.

---

[3] They shall not pass.

The Hotel Presidential, where I was lodged as a guest of the government, said it all. Sanctions and a blockade to enforce them had taken their toll, and this once splendid lodging with a commanding view of the city had nothing left that was remotely presidential – except perhaps the size of its rats! Since I was the sole occupant of that vast, derelict space, perhaps they looked to me for company and even sustenance. They accompanied me everywhere – from the dining room to my bedroom suite – with its discoloured ceiling – and formed guards of honour along the corridors of mouldy carpets and peeling paint. If I sought a pessimistic portent for the future of Biafra, the Presidential offered itself most assertively. I tried my best to dismiss this pessimistic image however, eyeballed the rats while I awaited my summons to the leader of the secessionist state.

We met the following morning, in an ornate office, a kind of converted hall, its spaciousness a marked contrast with the cluttered office of his predecessor in office, Dr. Michael Okpara, who had shielded me in that city after the radio hold-up. The irony was striking. On that visit, I had discussed the logistics of popular insurrection with the civil leader, now I was cast in the role of a mediator between professionals at war making, a role in which I felt distinctly ill-fitted. Preaching pacifism – even of a limited, tactical kind – in the midst of evident wrongs, has always struck me as a task specially designed to separate saints from mere mortals, and I have never succeeded in finding my proper size in haloes. It became possible to actually exercise conviction in the mission only when I reminded myself that I had really come to call for restraint, even a temporary one, while accompanying moves were made to reassure the Biafrans of the recognition of their just cause.

Meeting Ojukwu face to face, I tried unsuccessfully to remind myself that I was now facing His Excellency Lieutenant-Colonel Odumegwu Ojukwu, head of an independent state, not the young Emeka whom I had known in Yaba, Lagos, in the early fifties. Then I was laying siege to the heart of the younger sister of his own object of attention, envying the jazzy sports car that brought him to his tryst while I pedalled to battle on my bicycle. Heavily bearded and already balding from the forehead, self-conscious of his new status to the point of unintended self-parody, especially when taken with his exaggerated upper-class British accent, his delight at my visit was genuine enough.

I outlined my mission: I was there to persuade him to call a halt to the firing from his side while one more effort was made to resolve the conflict between the Federal Government and his now seceded state. The sticky point however was that this would require placing a hold on the secession.

Ojukwu reiterated his charges against the Federal side and painted for me the mood of his people – it was the people themselves, not he, who had pressed for secession. No one, he insisted, could have withstood the tide of that resentful outpouring. It was a plausible case, but one that I found difficult to swallow entire. Ojukwu himself had played a role in manipulating emotions.

I joined in his mid-morning snack, watched him daintily pick his *àkàrà* balls from a silver salver served by a waiter in immaculate white uniform complete with white gloves. It all seemed rather incongruous, impossible not to feel that one was watching an act. The exchange was anything but staged however; we were, after all, engaged in an exchange of life and death – not merely of human beings but of his dream of Biafra.

He would not commit himself. Instead, he insisted that I speak first to a few civilian leaders, some of whom I did meet later on. In turn, I requested to speak with Major Ademoyega, an officer from the West who had been imprisoned for his role in the January 15th coup and transferred to Enugu prisons. That transfer had saved his life. When the counter-coup took place in July that year, the plotters invaded prisons under Federal control, abducted the officers and subjected them to cruel forms of death. Ademoyega however lived to write of his role in the January 15th coup with the explanatory title – *Why We Struck*.

Most fateful of all my meetings in the seceded enclave was that of Victor Banjo, a Yoruba officer. Following some form of convoluted chain of incidents, Victor Banjo had been accused of menacing the former Head of State, General Aguiyi-Ironsi – and had ended up in Enugu prisons. After the declaration of Biafran Independence, he was released by Ojukwu, as were other Yoruba officers and soldiers from the Western Region, some of whom had certainly been involved in the original January '66 coup.

Loose-limbed, slightly bandy-legged, Victor Banjo reminded me very strongly of a browsing *igalà*, that rangy, powerful deer, when it is totally unconscious of any intruder. He exuded a quiet, commanding presence, one who would be at ease in any environment, looking as if he was in a studious contemplation of a world devoid of strife. A total contrast to Ojukwu, his bearing still struck me as a contradiction to the frenzy of war, as if the outer reality had nothing to do with him, personally. Yet the war map on the wall, the guns, even the Spartan nature of his office, and the stiff, attentive poise of his batman told a different story. I noticed the lenses of his glasses at once – very thick – and from the way his eyes appeared to adjust to distance, I guessed that he was short-sighted. Impeccably groomed even in his khaki uniform, this stranger soon revealed himself as an idealist whose politics were quite close to ours in the 'Third Force'. He made no attempt to disguise the fact that he was subjecting me to some deep scrutiny – or perhaps that was simply the effect of his thick lenses – then abruptly appeared to have made up his mind.

A stream of indignation followed as he castigated the failure of Western leaders to condemn the massacres of the Igbo, ridiculed the visit of traditional rulers who had come to the East to commiserate with widows and orphans – too little, too late, and short on sincerity, was his verdict. As for the leader of the Biafran secession, Odumegwu Ojukwu, he had even harsher words for him. If Ojukwu had displayed true leadership, the secession, he insisted, would never have taken place.

Then, again abruptly, he shrugged it all off, dismissed the past with a wave of his hand. He had relieved himself of a long pent-up resentment, and now he had no further use for it. A slim, light-complexioned, quite good looking man in uniform joined us and was introduced as Phillip Alale. He was a complete contrast, restless and excitable. Alale spoke agitatedly and volubly of the lack of ideological grounding in the conflict, slashed the air right and left as he outlined the cleansing that was needed for the diseased polity called Nigeria. For him also, Ojukwu was not the answer to the threat of Northern domination in Nigerian politics. What was desperately needed was a Third Force – he did not actually use the expression – still, his prescription was for a new entrant that would neutralise the two combatants. It was Phillip Alale however who was fated to be neutralised at the firing stake in Biafra, convicted of treason against Ojukwu's government, together with Victor Banjo and two others.

Victor Banjo let him run for some time, then interrupted with a gesture that was nearly imperceptible – he appeared used to commanding effortlessly and economically, like one who needed to conserve his energy. My appearance in Enugu, he pronounced, could not have been more fortuitous. The face of the war was about to change, dramatically, and I was the only one who could transmit some crucial messages to the other side, that is, to the leaders of the West, both military and civilian, but especially to a certain Lieutenant-Colonel Olusegun Obasanjo. It was there, right in Victor Banjo's command room, that I heard that name for the first time, and was informed that Obasanjo had only recently been appointed Commanding Officer in charge of the Western Area Command, with his headquarters in Ìbàdàn. Obasanjo had once served in a subordinate capacity to him. His response to the message I would take, Banjo stressed, would be crucial to the changes that were being contemplated on the Biafran side.

I became a marked man on account of my visit to Biafra. Delivering the messages that I brought back with me however turned me once again into a 'Wanted Man' but, this time, that designation had turned sinister, and all the more deadly for it being unannounced.

On the third night after my departure from Enugu, Victor Banjo broke the Federal stranglehold on Biafra and led the breakout military unit that had been in secret training. The obstacles that blocked both the Biafran and MidWest ends of Asaba bridge were flung aside and Banjo's army crossed the bridge in a rapid move, took over the MidWest state on the other side of the River Niger. It could be rightly considered a politically fatal move for the Biafrans, even militarily self-defeating – unless of course such a move proceeded strictly according to plan, which was to plunge straight through to Lagos in an all-night advance and swarm over the seat of government without a loss of momentum. That invading force did not, and the result was that the rebel forces were soon spread too thin for any effectiveness. The move also played straight into the hands of the Federal Government both militarily and politically. What was formerly a limited war, in which one of the states still retained sufficient autonomy to insist on its neutrality – *no shooting on MidWest soil, declared the governor, David Ejoor* – that war now expanded to involve the entire nation. It changed the terms of conflict, enabled the Federal Government to mobilise the nation against the allegedly expansionist agenda of the Biafrans. It altered the scale and tempo of the war from a desultory 'police action' to one of 'total war', leaving no room for further neutrality.

If I had earlier hesitations about delivering the messages from the architect and leader of that MidWest incursion, they vanished completely and even took on an urgency once Victor Banjo's troops had made their move, although not fully according to script. The crux of his message was this: *Let them understand in the West that I am not leading a Biafran army but an army of liberation, made up not only of Biafrans but of other ethnic groups. Make the governor of the West and other Western leaders understand this. Urge them not to be taken in by any propaganda by the Federal Government about a Biafran plan to subjugate the rest of the nation, and especially the West.*

Moving as rapidly as I dared, since it was clear that I had come under heavy surveillance, I carried out my mission to the civilian leaders, with one exception – Chief Obafemi Awolowo. Even before I left Enugu, I refused to accede to Banjo's insistence that I speak to 'Awo'. After my meeting with that politician, I simply felt, intuitively, that the approaching conflict was not one in which he should be involved.

A Moment of Truth – And the Lies of History

I was left only one individual on Victor Banjo's call list, and the most critical – Olusegun Obasanjo, Officer Commanding, Western Zone. It was the moment of truth, the hardest, most risk-laden decision of all. Obasanjo's junior officers, with whom I had maintained steady contact since my return, warned me to beware. In the same breath, they clearly wished – well – maybe if... I weighed the risks. They were difficult days for objective, rational choices. While I hesitated, Victor Banjo had broken through to the MidWest, but now paused to secure the MidWest militarily and politically, making inflammatory broadcasts. The West became confused, and awaited direction from its leaders. I chose.

I called Olusegun Obasanjo over a secret telephone in his bedroom, of whose existence he had not known. In his memoirs – *My Command* [1] – Obasanjo tells the story of how he had to search for the source of the mysterious ringing that he eventually traced to a wardrobe in his bedroom, one of the few details in that narrative that can stand the test of veracity in the midst of so many half-truths, outright lies and coy adumbrations. A few more calls later, and we agreed to meet 'unaccompanied and unarmed' – another truthful detail from his memoirs – at a petrol station on

---

[1] *My Command:* Heinemann, Ibadan 1980.

the road between non-commercial Jericho and Mọ́kọ́lá sections of Ìbàdàn. Now I had truly burnt my bridges, I told myself. There was no turning back.

Even before the fateful meeting with Obasanjo, Femi's brother, Brigadier 'Bolus' had cautioned him about his association with me. I still recall the exact words that Femi said his brother had used: '*Ṣọ́ra l'ọ́dò ẹ̀ o, ẹnu ńfẹ́ si lá'ra. Mi ò tii mọ kíni ń'lọn gan, ṣùgbọ́n, ṣọ́ra l'ọ́dọ̀ ẹ̀.*' – 'watch yourself with him, tongues are fanning the wind in his direction. I don't know exactly what is going on but – watch yourself'. His brother was right. What he did not know was how far committed Femi was – not to the Biafrian side as such but - to the liberation of the Western Region from the domination of the North.

With the incursion of Victor Banjo's troops into the MidWest, all subterfuge, all fence sitting came to an end, affecting both soldiers and civilian leaders alike. Obafemi Awolowo surrendered his bargaining powers. The MidWest, formerly a part of the West, a self-declared neutral until now, had been invaded and occupied. That region now threw its weight formally behind the Federal Government where Awolowo was now Minister of Finance under Gowon's Federal Government, and it put an end to all his options. Nnamdi Azikiwe, an Igbo, former President of the Nigerian federation, had already taken his place on the side of his fellow Biafrans. Not that he had much choice. At the time of the January '66 coup that was led by a preponderance of Igbo officers, Azikiwe had been on a seemingly endless 'health cruise' in the Caribbean, and news of the coup caught him, incongruously, on the isle of Haiti, then groaning under the misrule of 'Papa Doc' Duvalier. The timing of the cruise had been too pat, and the Northern proponents of the counter-coup that brought Yakubu Gowon to power in July did not believe for one moment that Azikiwe had not been taken into confidence over a coup that oversaw the decimation of Northern leadership. Azikiwe wisely kept beyond reach of the new regime, became a roving ambassador for the breakaway region, a powerful voice, internationally, in the Biafran cause.

Azikiwe's counterweight on the Nigerian side was Anthony Enahoro. Chief Anthony Enahoro was a most effective minister in Yakubu Gowon's government. Indeed, his advocacy contributed much to the international acceptance of the Federal cause. Enahoro exuded an easy charm and was gifted with intelligent eloquence, a persuasive Edo nobility in the midst of so many fakes. He was one of the early youthful nationalists, a political model from our schooldays. Enahoro had learnt his ropes at the feet of Nnamdi Azikiwe, 'Zik of Africa', who would however denounce him during that anti-colonial struggle as an intemperate agitator, when the younger man stood trial for sedition against the colonial government. Anthony Enahoro never forgave Azikiwe for that act of repudiation, and later switched his allegiance to Obafemi Awolowo and his party, the Action Group, joining his leader in prison as one of the casualties of the treasonable felony trials. He was among those who were freed by Yakubu Gowon in the shrewd political move to gain support among southerners in the conflict with the breakaway Biafrans. Enahoro was a diehard Federalist – at least, then. Together with Obafemi Awolowo, they outweighed the influence of Nnamdi Azikiwe in mobilising international support.

In his position as Commissioner for Information, Tony Enahoro was the government spokesman who would read out to the international press, after my arrest and detention, an infamous confessional statement that had me admitting that I had been negotiating the purchase of war planes for Biafra! It was of course intended to silence any further hue-and-cry over my continuing detention without trial. I found it rather ironic – and a little depressing at the time – that the 'fugitive offender', not quite many months out of gaol, would be the one to read such a damnable fabrication and wave the 'confessional statement' in the face of the international press! Perhaps the most easily disproved of the charges – next to the ridiculous claim that I was purchasing arms, including planes, for Biafra! – was my alleged admission that I had held a meeting *in Benin* with Victor Banjo, the leader of the invasion, on the very night that his troops took over the MidWest state. A few weeks after Tony Enahoro's press conference, an indignant Femi Johnson encountered the Commissioner on the Ìbàdàn golf course and refused to let that chance meeting go to waste.

"That can't be true!" he challenged the Commissioner. "I was with Wole in Ìbàdàn throughout that day – you can check from my wife and a number of other people whose names I will provide you – all day, including dinner. He could not have been at that meeting as alleged. That confession must be a forgery. It's a frame-up."

Enahoro was taken aback. He asked Femi how sure he was of his facts. Femi swore that he was ready to back up his statement anywhere. The Commissioner asked him to write a formal letter to that effect, which Femi did the following day, making sure that Tony had it in his hands before he returned to Lagos. To further engage his interest, Femi reminded Enahoro of his own past predicament as a 'fugitive offender'– the title of Enahoro's account of that experience – and of the voluntary role I had played in the efforts to prevent his extradition.

Tony Enahoro replied, "Oh, that was then. This is war, you know. The rules are different."

Curiously, I found myself in agreement with Tony Enahoro – it *was* war - and I never held his indifference against him, which was just as well, since we were destined to join forces two decades later against a far more detestable foe, the dictator Sani Abacha. Even so, I must confess that I was rather nettled at the baldness of the dismissal. I suppose one always nurses a secret expectation of some kind of reciprocity, even if it exists on a purely rhetorical level. As for the statement that Femi handed to him the following day, that was the last that he ever heard from Tony.

Femi had cause to be a hundred percent certain of my alibi. Not only was I with him most of that crucial day, I had again involved him in my course of action, imposed a chore on him – which was to find me a new hiding place. It had become necessary to 'go under', even while remaining active. His house was now 'hot' and I had no wish to implicate him any further in this latest entanglement. Tongues from the police and military Intelligence were indeed 'fanning the wind' towards my person, and I still had some urgent tasks ahead, tasks that required total seclusion. I also needed a secure place for the two or three final meetings that were left – with members of my group for instance, even with Bola Ige, and indeed, one or two military contacts. I could no longer go to people, but could get them to come to me if I succeeded in finding a secure venue. Obasanjo remained the exception – we had agreed to meet at Jericho.

Femi went away to make enquiries, returned with information about an expatriate civil servant who had gone on leave. His house was unoccupied, not even the servants' quarters were tenanted. Femi obtained the number and address of the bungalow – in the Ìyágànkú government quarters, virtually under the nose of the police – and drove me casually past the house in daytime while I looked it over. Close to the police though it was, it was most obligingly secluded – the expatriate owner was a kindred spirit, he believed in a surround of lush vegetation. Best of all, it had a functioning telephone.

Later that night, he dropped me by the fence, armed with a torch, and the now regulation hamper of food and drinks. Gaining entrance through a window was easy. Once assured of entry, I told him to get lost. *Don't come near me again. From now on, you don't know me, never saw me in your life. If I am absolutely desperate for some item, I'll telephone or get a message to you somehow. You can bring it at night time, drop it at the point where you've just let me off and keep going. You've done enough, you've done more than you should have done. Now, get out and look after yourself.* The shocked look on his face was a marvel to see, but he saw at once that I was in deadly earnest, sensed at once that this bout of conflict with a military government, and in war time, was far more serious than my earlier political skirmishes.

I underestimated Femi yet again, forgot that he did not willingly let go of some space of collaboration. The many instances when I denied him participation, he succeeded in inflicting on me a sense of betrayal, as if I had deprived him of a natural entitlement that was well within his conspiratorial competence. He insisted on driving me to the rendezvous. In vain I impressed on him the fact that I had my arrangements well in hand, that one of my own group was far better equipped to handle any untoward situation but, most important of all, he would be exposing himself to unnecessary risks. He flared up – *Why shouldn't I? If I get arrested, well, what exactly would they charge me with? That you had dinner in my house, told me to drop you at the petrol station and return for you after an hour – since when did that add up to a crime? You're going to meet the man in charge of zonal security on some crucial national matter, leaving from my house – everybody knows you stay here after all. So I drop you and pick you up again, what's wrong with that?* And then, the clinching argument – *in any case, we know each other. I've done insurance for him and his colleagues – we get on quite well. In fact, I'll say hallo to him as I drop you...*

I drew the line there, surrendered the others. Just drop me at the petrol station and take off, I insisted. As it happened, the rendezvous was close to Femi's home. He would pick me up at my hide-out after dark, take me to the encounter, I would satisfy his burning curiosity over a late dinner, and then my man – not him – would return me to my base.

I got busy on the telephone, even as I continued to ask myself, *do I really want to meet this man?* More meetings with his junior officers followed where we debated that issue.

I had already delivered the core of Victor Banjo's message over the telephone, but Obasanjo wanted very much to discuss it in some detail. I knew what the truth was – he needed to ask questions. Questions to help him decide which side to support? Or questions that might yield snippets of intelligence for securing his own base in aiding the Federal cause? It was all very suspicious and, to make matters worse, character references from his own officers were not especially reassuring – the kindest word that summarised their assessment of their commanding officer was – cagey. The situation in the MidWest remained fluid, indeed, there was a lull for several weeks, as if both the Federal and Biafran sides were weighing up each other or else – which was more likely – waiting to see which way the West would respond to the new situation. Fighting had not yet flared up on the next obvious front – the border between the West and MidWest. The West itself was undergoing its final moments of fence-sitting, never mind the stout declarations of allegiance to the slogan of 'One Nigeria'!

The British High Commission Intelligence network, for once,

had been caught on the hop, though we were to learn later that it had not failed completely – the High Commissioner did report the likelihood of the MidWest crossing to Yakubu Gowon's government, but could not pinpoint the date. Much, so much now depended on the decision of the Western Command. It was a military situation, and not even the governor of the West could take that decision - he had no forces under his command. Banjo was holed up in Benin. The bulk of Federal troops, weapons and logistical resources were bottled up in the Northern sector, since the MidWest had earlier refused to allow any fighting on its soil – a position that was no longer tenable. The Federal Government desperately depended on the West holding firm to the Federal cause - in short, one man now held the key, and that was the officer in charge of the Western Command, Olusegun Obasanjo.

Several of Obasanjo's officers had no sympathy whatsoever for the Federal cause. It was not that they were against a unified nation, no, they simply felt that the internal arrangements of the existing nation entity were lop-sided, weighed in favour of Northern privilege. Even within the army, they knew what it was to be second class citizens – given the chance, they would be Biafrans! Again the question remained suspended - *should I really meet this man or not?* It all boiled down to the fact that, in the view of his own officers, Obasanjo could not be trusted. He could set a trap, have me arrested for 'consorting with the enemy' or whatever. And so they insisted on leaving such a risky decision to me even while stressing that a voice like mine might just do the trick. There was not much time. Finally, I abandoned all further hesitation – I called him once more. Obasanjo remained more than eager to meet.

The venue remained Jericho, at the petrol station, in a quiet part of Ìbàdàn. Again we set the conditions – *both to come alone, unarmed and unaccompanied.* Even then, I continued to battle with unresolved doubts – going underground and operating from there seemed a far more rational option. In the end, it was probably those frenzied four, five days of intense cloak-and-dagger meetings with Western leaders – politicians, labour leaders, even senior police officers of whose existence Femi would be kept completely oblivious – that tilted the scales. Time was running out for Victor Banjo and his version of the 'Third Force' continued to await a sign from the West. I had no further contribution to make, no more unfulfilled chores. I was drained. It was time for a decisive act. I agreed to deliver yet again - but this time face to face – the message I had brought back from Biafra, one that was given to me in Enugu - *not* Benin!

Femi picked me up as agreed. I had already organised a driver, one of our group, to wait for me by Christopher Okigbo's now abandoned and locked up domain, Cambridge House, a mere walking distance from Femi's house. I tried a last minute variation – was it not simpler, I suggested, for him to drop me by the waiting car, go home and I would join him for dinner and the eagerly awaited de-briefing? OBJ would not hear of it. Well, would he at least drive past the road junction by Cambridge House where my man was waiting, pause long enough for me to change his instructions? Was it all right if I told the fellow to tag along, follow us to the rendezvous but continue straight on, just checking that we were safe? My friend, addict of intrigues, ignored my sarcastic tone and generously gave his consent.

Neither Obasanjo nor I, it turned out, kept strictly to the agreed conditions of our meeting – *to meet alone, unarmed and unaccompanied.* In my own case however, the failure was unintended. Femi at the wheel, we stopped by the desolate Cambridge House to brief the waiting driver of the slight change of plans. He was to follow us the short distance to the petrol station, drive past, and park his car at a distance from where he could ensure, however, that the other side kept to the bargain, then return to Cambridge House to await my return.

At the petrol station, Femi drew up in the shadow cast by the street lighting off the low enclosure wall. A few moments later, Olusegun Obasanjo's Volkswagen Beetle drew up, stopped at the other side of the pumps. A Yoruba cap, an *ikòrí*, firmly pulled over my forehead, I walked across from where we had parked, jumped into the seat beside him. From the shadow of the wall, Femi turned round to go home immediately – keeping at least to the terms of our agreement. Obasanjo took off just as fast in the direction of nowhere, followed however by a car that – he would later admit – was his security detail. That uninvited guest was however spotted by my own 'Third Force' (TF) driver who promptly threw out all instructions and followed the intruder. The agreement had been broken, and he considered his original instructions no longer valid.

And my good friend, O.B. Johnson? As he recounted it to me later that night, he was indeed headed home when he observed through his rear mirror that Obasanjo's vehicle had acquired two tails. Trust my friend, he turned around and followed the convoy of three vehicles, sensing foul play! Spotting the anomaly was not difficult. The sight of any vehicle on the streets at night was sufficient to generate attention at such a time – a partial, largely self-imposed curfew was being observed on Ìbàdàn streets and, in any case, Onírèké was a very quiet part of Ìbàdàn at that hour. Thus began the only comic relief that would come my way since my return from Biafra.

When our TF driver found that Obasanjo's car was followed, he also decided to follow, resulting in Femi's decision to also make a turnaround. And so – to adapt one of Fela Anikulapo's anti-establishment songs –'*wetin follow be say Follow-follow follow Follow-follow*'[2] through the twists and turns of Ìbàdàn roads for several minutes, before Obasanjo somehow succeeded in losing everyone, including his own security detail. I turned in my seat and looked back quite openly and saw what was going on. Obasanjo drove in a way that could suggest that he was merely taking precaution, attempting to throw off any incidental tail, and I pretended to *swallow-swallow* the deception. I have sometimes wondered how an aerial shot of those minutes of the pursuit would have looked, with cutbacks to vehicle interiors and the bewildered faces - and thoughts - of the various occupants! The soldier wore a loose *agbádá*. I took the opportunity of the first lurch to lean into him - of course he was armed, as he would cheerfully admit years later, in the home of Aboyade, our perennial peace-broker, when we reviewed the events of that night – *Me? I am supposed to be a soldier, do you*

---

[2] What then developed was that the follower found himself followed by another follower, etc.

think I would agree to meet someone just from Biafra, in the dead of night, on a deserted street, without protection? I would deserve to be court-martialled!

In the flickering lights of the street lamps, each tried openly to assess the other. Even beneath his *agbádá,* I could discern the beginnings of a paunch, while his face bore the recognisable tribal marks that read Owú stock, one of the branches of the Yoruba. The Owú are reputed to be pugnacious by nature, there was however nothing remotely soldierly about his bearing. His expression remained inscrutable, but his voice sounded relaxed, even self-confident, and he asked his questions as if the answers carried no import that extended beyond the two occupants of the car. Nothing whatsoever to indicate which way he felt about the war, no sense of his awareness of the critical position in which he found himself. He sounded more like a village headmaster who was awaiting the visit of a schools inspector and wanted to know all about the likely areas of interest of the visitor. His face became animated, taking on a queasy slyness, only when he asked how I came to know about the telephone in his wardrobe.

Again, I tried to justify the physical encounter to myself. The core of Banjo's message had been delivered. The man's insistence on our meeting therefore had to be his need for a direct 'character reference' – in short, to see the messenger in person, assess his genuineness, and hopefully believe in the truthfulness of his message: *in breaching the neutrality of the MidWest, Banjo was not acting for Biafra, but planned instead to bring the war to an end.* Again and again Banjo had urged me – as if I needed any urging! – to emphasise this to Obasanjo – *this is not a Biafran army, and this is not a Biafran agenda.* I was to detail how he had persuaded Ojukwu to let him train an independent force *ostensibly* to promote that leader's ambitions. The training had gone on secretly in the MidWest, right under the nose of David Ejoor, the Military Governor, who had however remained genuinely oblivious to such activities. To obtain both men and weaponry, Banjo had to agree to train and move an independent force through the MidWest, sack the centre and install a regime that would endorse Biafra's secession. However, there Victor Banjo's and Ojukwu's interests were supposed to part company. Victor was solidly against the secession.

However, Nigerians are weaned on the caution that goes – *cunny man die, cunny man bury am.*[3] Victor Banjo understood clearly – as I also did even from my one encounter with Ojukwu – that the warlord meant to take over the nation. It was a view that has since been confirmed by some of the historians from the Biafran side. On Victor Banjo's part, it was equally clear that he meant to ignore Ojukwu's ambitions once he had seized Lagos and was guaranteed the support of the Western command. He intended to take over the nation, including Biafra. I do not believe for a moment that he meant to terminate that secession by force of arms, indeed, that would have been a near impossible attempt, considering the fact that his liberation force was made up largely of Biafran soldiers.

Guaranteed the support of the Western Region in overwhelming numbers however, Banjo could have ensured that any ambitions of Ojukwu in the larger national context were successfully thwarted. Banjo's immediate constituency was the West, and he needed, at the very least, some form of assurance from the Western leaders. This was why he was desperate that his message to Obasanjo should be couched in unambiguous terms: *tell Obasanjo that the liberation forces at my command do not wish to fight on Western soil. All we seek is unimpeded passage to Lagos through the Western Region.*

This was the message I reiterated to Obasanjo that night as we drove through the deserted streets of Ìbàdàn warrens.

But now a necessary digression – on the minor but instructive theme of revisionism in purported historical narratives – using as an intimate example the notorious fictionalising of my telephone exchanges and eventual meeting with Olusegun Obasanjo during those crucial nights when the fate of a nation hung in the balance, and one man held the key to its future – at least its immediate future. That man of fluctuating destinies, Olusegun Obasanjo, would later become a military Head of State, a prisoner of another military dictator and occupant of the Death Row, and then a civilian President – albeit elected under extremely dubious circumstances

---

[3] The con-man fakes death, but another con-man will bury him.

– in 1999, and under even more discredited circumstances in 2003 *(see Supreme Court judgement, Buhari vs. Obasanjo, 2004)*. Obasanjo has earned himself a reputation as an assiduous chronicler of the immediate past, but one most prone, alas, to the extreme latitudes of creative licence.

The mission that I had undertaken, just before, during and immediately after the MidWest invasion was to transmit Victor Banjo's objectives to Obasanjo. I was to tell him in very bald terms that Victor wanted an unimpeded passage to Lagos, that he wished to avoid a battle in Western Nigeria – *finis!* This was the exact message I delivered. What I did or said outside that meeting was a different matter, and this included how my future activities were influenced by Obasanjo's response to the message I had delivered to him.

The decision to meet him at all had been a most difficult one, fraught with warnings. The most forceful had come from the young officer in Military Intelligence who had revealed to me the existence of the secret telephone in Obasanjo's bedroom, and its number, to facilitate direct contact. Yet even he could not bring himself to wholeheartedly endorse the final meeting. His distrust of his superior officer was unambiguous. Such warnings were responsible for my writing down, then *memorising* the precise words in which I proposed to deliver Victor Banjo's message. If I was arrested and brought to trial, I wanted to ensure that my words would not be distorted, or taken out of context.

I had crammed my lines so efficiently that I still remembered them years afterwards when Obasanjo published his account of the war in *My Command.* There, among other lies, he claimed that I had asked him to name his price for letting Victor Banjo's troops through the West! Even combatants who have done their best to disembowel one another in wartime do embrace and carry on with life afterwards and so, although Obasanjo's betrayal of the very event of our meeting was certainly the most crucial factor that led to my incarceration, I found – to my pleasant surprise, I think – that I could meet him afterwards without rancour. I experienced no obstacle to resuming our brief and untoward relationship on a new footing, and was able to collaborate on a number of national schemes when he became Head of State.

What I found impossible to stomach however were his constant attempts to re-write – and tendentiously to boot! – a history of which I had been a part, in no matter how minor a role. And so, both privately and publicly, I was drawn into the repetitive, excruciatingly boring and frustrating imposition of setting him right whenever – in order to secure a temporary advantage, often petty but distracting – he resorted to twisting the true narrative of events. Following the publication of his book – and after the ensuing bout of public exchanges – we met in the home of Ojetunji Aboyade, then Vice-Chancellor at the University of Ifẹ, who sometimes complained that he felt that his life mission was to act as referee and conciliator during our frequent wranglings.

It was virtually – no contest! I began by reciting from memory my opening statement to him on the occasion of our *Follow-follow* meeting, word for word. Then, not nearly so precisely but as close to exactitude as made no difference, even on his own admission, I repeated his comments, questions, my responses, and his final statement. Even the unscripted exchanges were still fresh in my mind – one passes much time in total recall in the quiet of prison solitary confinement! The recalled exchanges were so logical in their content and sequence that Obasanjo could only stare, dumbfounded. I accused him of coming armed to our meeting, contrary to our agreement – he laughed and admitted it. I repeated yet again that I had offered no opinion, no comment on the message I had brought, had said nothing that could be remotely construed as an attempt to sway him one way or the other. Obasanjo remained mute for several moments, then gave his familiar schoolboy-caught-in-the-act mischievous smile and – *apologised!* Aboyade gave his verdict, exhorted me to accept his apology as gracefully as he had proffered it.

And that should have ended this matter but – Olusegun Aremu Obasanjo, 'conqueror of Biafra', would not act his true self if he did not seize the next event of a public disagreement in the media to repeat, and in the very language that he had himself repudiated, the falsehood he had tried to implant in public perception. One of the occasions for this was his failure to obtain election – or nomination – as the Secretary-General of the United Nations, a failure that he attributed to me, with some justification. In common with a number of civic organisations, we warned that he was not fit to be placed in charge of such a body on account of proven human rights violations that continued even on his private (militarised) farm after his tenure of office. Nettled, Obasanjo exhumed a discredited account of our encounter during the Civil War and commenced a new round of doctored narratives.

Public lies should never be allowed to lie. I seized the next anniversary of Victor Banjo's MidWest invasion – September, 1980 – to organise a public lecture at the International Institute of Public Affairs, Lagos, simply to denounce once again, and authoritatively, the man's compulsive need to consolidate a private invention, demanding why it is never sufficient that one accept responsibility solely for one's deeds, for better or worse, without being compelled to deal with the emendations of others who are mostly impelled by concerns for their career, their image, or psychological needs.

It is necessary to make a distinction: this is not to deny that I would have preferred that Obasanjo accede to Banjo's request. It is simply that I had set out with the resolution *not* to attempt any persuasion or – to use Obasanjo's own favourite word – apply any 'pressure' on him. I stuck scrupulously to my brief, delivered a 'plain, unvarnished tale', consciously avoiding any further expansion of the danger I had already incurred by meeting with an unreliable factor in the developing scenario. I could not rule out recording installed in his car – after all, a telephone had preceded him, the commandant of the vast Western domain, into his bedroom – and he knew nothing of it! Far too many details in personal memoirs are not even slips of memory but self-serving fiction. Obasanjo wanted to ingratiate himself with his superiors in Lagos, even to the extent of claiming I had asked him to name a price for his 'treason'– against which temptation he had of course presented an armour of loyalty that could not be dented by filthy lucre! Not once, in my entire involvement in this saga, did I encounter any situation in which 'ten pieces of silver' ever featured. Ojukwu neither discussed nor offered any, nor did Victor Banjo. Then who was financially placed to ask our man to name his price? This courier, who hardly ever balanced his monthly salary?

Just as unprincipled was the so-called 'confessional statement' read out by the then Commissioner for Information, Anthony Enahoro, on behalf of the government – my alleged meeting with Banjo in Benin, the attempted purchase of arms etc. - all baseless, cynical concoctions by the government, concerned that the provable extent of my activities might not provide sufficient grounds for holding me in prison indefinitely, or for convicting me of some heinous offence in a court of law. Still, it was wartime and, on balance, my activities could easily have resulted in a kangaroo trial and execution, or other extra-judicial solutions of a terminal kind. None of these consolations reduces the intensity of one's violent dislike to being lied against. Watch even a notorious Nigerian thief defending himself in a court of law - *Your Worship, why do they keep accusing me of stealing a chicken? As God is my witness, all I stole was a goat!*

It must be admitted that many coup-makers on the continent - and Nigerian career officers are no exception – sell their allegiances, indeed put themselves out for hire by businessmen for instigating a coup. This was a real development that came years later, definitely long after the Civil War, and even after the coup d'état that ousted the regime of Yakubu Gowon, a coup that no one could possibly accuse of being prodded by moneyed interests. We simply were not in the buying and selling business, and in any case, we had no funds whatsoever to throw around. Even if we had, we would not have spent such funds on dubious allegiances. I owe it to the memory of Victor Banjo to contest such dishonourable, even unsoldierly distortions of his motives and conduct, to testify, above all, that Banjo did *not* act to promote Biafran secession or aid an Ojukwu takeover of power in Lagos. If anything, Banjo felt that he should take over power and, confronted with the two discredited combatants who were propelling the nation towards a bloodbath, those of us that were self-described as the 'Third Force' had no doubt whatsoever that Banjo represented the most viable corrective.

Obasanjo's response at the end of our nocturnal ride through the sleeping streets of Ìbàdàn, a response that I would later transmit to Victor Banjo from my hideout, nearly word for word, was this:

"Well, tell him I have taken an oath of loyalty to Lagos. There are other routes to Lagos – by water through Úkìtìpupa for instance. If he makes it to Lagos and takes over, well, my oath of loyalty is to Lagos, and I'll stand by that. But to let him pass through my Western Command, that would be betraying my oath of loyalty. Whoever is in power in Lagos - that's the person to whom I owe my allegiance."

Words to that effect, not nearly as close to the original today, I am sure, as my recollection of them in 1980 in the Aboyade home, with both husband and wife as audience, but close enough.

My fateful meeting with Obasanjo concluded, I took up permanent residence in the hidden bungalow where I dared not switch on the lights at night. It was from this bungalow that I telephoned Obasanjo's reply to Banjo in Benin, *verbatim*. I kept up communication with him, acting as intermediary between him and his increasingly impatient collaborators in the West – our faithful colleagues at Oníyanrìn telephone exchange ensured that no one was tapping into the lines. I would phone and exchange notes also with Banjo's sister, Mrs. Ogunseye, then lecturer, Institute of Librarianship at the University of Ìbàdàn, in an attempt to assess this warrior's likely, real, immediate and/or long-term intentions, to understand why he remained in Benin playing governor or administrator or kingmaker, why he took the irrational step of proclaiming yet another secessionist state – the MidWest – instead of moving straight to Lagos and dislodging Yakubu Gowon's government.

Haba! The people of the MidWest had not requested their own independent state *à la Biafra*, so what was the point? On the contrary, they were seething – at least in the non-Igbo parts of the state – seething under what they read as a Biafran force of occupation. In any case, why should Banjo, an outsider, attempt to donate independence to a people whose neutrality had been breached and who were now drawn into a widening conflict? Each night I issued the same plaint, with ever increasing desperation – what was keeping him in Benin? We spoke in coded language – *Grandfather is gravely ill. The doctors say they must operate tomorrow; any further delay and it will be too late - do you understand that? Can you make it to his bedside in time? The theatre is fully equipped but the clinic itself may shut down any day ...there is problem with the expatriate staff; the nurses are threatening to walk off the job... etc. etc.* And Banjo would reply - yes, definitely he would be at the clinic in the morning. Most definitely. And again his supporters in the West would prepare to facilitate his passage.

Then he was recalled to Enugu by Ojukwu, who had become suspicious of his procrastinations, only to be sent back again to his Benin Command. Time seeped away, the initiative and all its advantages shifting day by day to Lagos. Banjo no longer appeared to be the independent operator who had set out from Biafra at the head of a force that was motivated, at least, by some ideological pretensions. His public pronouncements became more and more erratic and contradictory, while our position underground turned increasingly precarious. The uprising that was planned to accompany his entry and provide a popular base for his incursion began to lose momentum. Whatever public support he enjoyed in the West was gradually eroded as the Federal Government, thoroughly panicked and poised for flight at the earlier stages, uncertain which officers and commands it could count upon, recovered from its fright, rallied wavering support, mobilised and moved against the invaders. The role played by the British mission at this critical time in shoring up the confidence of the regime has yet to be fully narrated – it certainly was not a negligible factor. The result was all that mattered; Victor Banjo's dawdling in Benin had closed down one possible chapter in the direction of Nigerian history - with whatever consequences, good or ill.

The moment came when everyone, even the most ardent optimist, knew that Victor Banjo would never make that crossing to Lagos. He had left it till too late, and now the Federal Government had re-positioned its forces and was moving in to recapture the MidWest Region. It was time to disband.

I had become worried for the safety of many of those with whom Banjo had also made direct contact, his sister, Mrs. Ogunseye most especially. Banjo telephoned her constantly, sometimes passing messages to me through her – especially if he had missed a call from me. Otherwise, Banjo appeared to dispense with caution – depending on the state of his mood – brimming with confidence or desperate and frustrated. Then he would speak unguardedly, mentioning by name politicians and even military officers from whom he expected support, complaining of their lack of action.

What he had expected these people to do exactly, I never really understood. Of course, plans for a popular uprising in his favour, the moment he moved into Lagos had been agreed upon but – that the people should mount such demonstrations *ahead* of his arrival? Or perhaps invite him in to come and declare an independent Western State as he did in the MidWest? The West was submerged under Federal guns! But Banjo's telephone calls to many individuals – politicians, labour leaders, intellectuals and others – in the West and Lagos merely grew wilder. He telephoned even Obafemi Awolowo, harangued Yakubu Gowon, spoke to Adebayo, the Governor of Western State, rebuked several of his military colleagues – both diehard federalists and sympathetic ears. Telephone lines were constantly tapped – after all, we did some tapping ourselves – and I feared that Victor's careless conversations with her sister would get her into trouble – and over nothing. It fell to me, finally, to tell her to cut off all communication with her brother, and begin to act to protect herself. She agreed to take no more calls from Banjo.

The breeze that tongues were fanning in the direction of my person had turned into a powerful wind! By now, we had ample proof that Obasanjo had disclosed our conversation to his bosses in Lagos, passing it over the telephone, with his own deadly slants, to Gowon. The young officer from Military Intelligence was the first to alert me, offering to spirit me to a safe place. Several others urged flight, insisted that I disappear altogether. I did not require too much persuasion, and began to prepare. Bayo Oduneye, a young colleague at Ìbàdàn University Theatre Arts Department, became one of the many peripheral – but quite innocent bit players in the escalating drama. He offered me his Volkswagen Beetle, in a kindred spirit to Femi Johnson - *Take it. If you find some means of sending it back, do so. If not, whenever you're settled, send word where I can go and pick it up.* He had friends in the military and had also learnt that there was an unannounced dragnet for me – indeed, who did not know it by then?

My arrest, in fact, needed not have happened. Halfway to safety, going by habit through a mental check-list, I pulled up with a shock. There was a base – one of a handful - used by the veterans of confrontations with problematic governments. Seasoned over the years from neophyte volunteers in the Western electoral struggle of 1964/65 into organised cadres by the time of the Civil War, their commitment had transferred to the cause of what now called itself the 'Third Force'. Now they were standing by, ready to ignite popular demonstrations in support of Victor Banjo – once he crossed over into Lagos. More alarming still was the fact that they had links with other groups all over the West and Lagos – even I did not know, by this time, how widespread they had become, since some of these links were run by politicians - but they had turned most restive since the West began its protests against Federal military presence in the West, decrying it as 'an army of occupation', and demanding its removal.

I realised suddenly that my final instructions to disband were extremely likely to have missed this very special base. It was tucked away in Abadina village - the site of the University of Ìbàdàn - close to the farms of the Agriculture Department. It was a most convenient place, the humble quarters of a junior university employee, situated virtually at the very edge of campus. Additionally, a motorable swathe, the handiwork of an agricultural tractor, by-passed the main entrance to the university and led directly onto the road to Ọ̀yọ́, and from there to a number of safe houses in any direction, including back to Ìbàdàn or Lagos, or in the direction of Ṣhakí, in extremity, and a choice of smugglers' routes to the border with the Republic of Benin. There were no telephones in that part of Abadina, so it could only be reached through a human courier. Its very security meant, however, that it had received no news from me of the changes in events.

I became worried that the members, still congregating around that post, might proceed on some hare-brained action of their own.

Failing to hear anything, they might act impetuously, endanger themselves and decimate the remnants of the organised civilian opposition to the regime. Agitated, I turned back, drove undetected for the hundred kilometers to Ìbàdàn. On the way I stopped at the Mbari Club at Adamasingba to pick up any idle member of my acting company, the Orísun Theatre, to act as courier. It was only the tall, statuesque Betty Okotie, an early member of that company, who was available.

She too had learnt of the manhunt. She entered the car and we arrived on campus – again, sticking to the back routes, joining up with the road that led to the College of Technology. My intention was to remain in the car some distance from the Abadina post while she went in and brought out whoever she found in place - there was always the possibility that the police had tracked it down and now had it under surveillance. That final base scuttled, I would wait for the dark, then head for one of the unofficial border-crossing points to a 'safe house', or even, if the situation demanded it, into the neigbouring country.

At the barrier that separated the College of Technology from the University of Ìbàdàn however, a policeman was waiting, armed with a rifle. He looked in the car, blinked, and sighed. That was the first and only sign I would obtain that the manhunt had extended to the peripheries of the university campus. Crestfallen at what he had to do, the policeman pulled me aside and - as if he knew what had brought me back – quickly whispered that he would escort me wherever I wanted to go before turning me in - "in case" – his whisper went even lower - "in case there are urgent things you wish to take care of – sensitive documents and things like that. They will come and search your house, you know. It's the least I can do for you, Mr. Soyinka."

Not one shred of misgiving did I entertain. I had learnt to read faces and voices – with varying degrees of accuracy, admittedly. In this case, I was over a hundred per cent certain of the man's sincerity - it was not a trap. We dropped off Betty Okotie, whom I sent off to Femi with news of my arrest. I visited our last operational base, closed it down and dispersed the lingering faithfuls. Then, with my policeman still in charge, I stopped at my university quarters on Ebrohimie Road, informed my family that I might be away for a while, enjoyed a light but tasty meal, shared by my police captor – I did not know when next such tastes would be afforded me – and set off on the route to prison detention.

A tussle then began for my body. The Governor of the Western Region, Colonel Adebayo, anxiously discussed my situation with some of his commissioners, knowing that one of them, Bola Ige, would convey his assessment of my predicament to me. Adebayo stood his ground for some time and stalled my repatriation to Lagos. Any interrogation, he insisted, should take place in Ìbàdàn where I had been arrested. Indeed, he later sent me assurances in my place of detention that I would not be removed from Ìbàdàn, only to send the same emissary, some days later, to tell me that it had been agreed that I should proceed to Lagos, but that he had received personal assurance from Yakubu Gowon that it was he who personally wanted to see me, and merely to ask me some direct questions about my visit to Biafra. I would leave in the morning, the governor said, escorted by his own people, and would be back in Ìbàdàn that same day.

I had to smile at that! The truth of course was that the West, most of the West including the governor and his cabinet were against the Federal regime but lacked the means to enforce its will. That time had passed when the Western Region government, backed by its 'leaders of thought', could demand that all non-Western troops, bluntly described as an army of occupation, be removed from the West. With Banjo's military incursion into the MidWest State however, Gowon had further consolidated his authority all over the nation. The slogan – *To keep Nigeria one/ Is a task that must be done* – meant that there could be no fence-sitting. Centralisation – was anyone surprised? – had made a dramatic comeback. You bowed to the central authority in totality or were considered to have ranged yourself with the rebels – spelt d-e-v-i-l-s! You were an agent of destabilisation. Fifth columnist. Neo-colonial agent – never mind that it was the former colonial master, the British, who stood solidly behind the regime. Gowon rode on a high crest of nationalist fervour, and nationalism meant – no Balkanisation. The very name 'Gowon' was turned into a quite clever 'oral' acronym – *Go On With One Nigeria.* Civil servants 'voluntarily' donated a percentage of their salaries to the war effort, to a special fund called 'Troops Comfort Fund'.

Regarding that 'patriotic' exercise, there was one exception, one of a virtual handful, who defied that hysterical phase of patriotism – this was my elder sister Tinu, then deputy principal of the Nursing School of the University Teaching Hospital, Lagos. She had nothing against keeping Nigeria one, offered no opinion regarding how one went about it, but as long as her brother was in prison detention without trial, nobody had better touch her take-home pay! She refused to sign the 'voluntary donation' form and declared her lack of interest in comforting any troops. Throughout the entire period of national jingoism, indeed, throughout the war with Biafra, no one dared touch Tinu's salary.

My last telephone call, made from my home where I shared a meal with my police captor, was to Femi. He was still in his office. I told him that there was a message – concerning rehearsal schedules - on its way to him through one of the Orísun company. To this I added tersely: *this is just for information. You are NOT, repeat NOT required to be at these rehearsals. I have no idea how long they might take. This is a different play altogether and – I already warned you - there is no longer any role in it for you. So, take a sabbatical, will you? Understand?*

His voice was heavy with sadness and foreboding, but it did say that he understood.

The Conquest of
Civilian Pride

Two years and four months later – a year and ten months in solitary confinement – I emerged from Kaduna prison,[1] armed with a rehearsed slogan. It was my chosen antidote to the national jingle that continued to set my teeth on edge – *To keep Nigeria One/Is a Task that Must be Done.* I had nothing against the oneness of the nation called Nigeria – indeed, as I once remarked, why should I wish to add yet other consulates to my rounds of visa applications? The travails of my passport, sometimes three stuck together, the hostile frowns of immigration officers searching, not only for their nation's visa but for space on which to place their stamps, are sufficient to warrant a subjective opposition to the infestation of the global map with new national entities! What I do contest is the basis on which a nation calls itself one, a crucial debate that is easily obscured by cheap, meaningless slogans. I had long resolved that this basis could be one thing only: equity between the constituting parts. In short – political parity, also known as political justice for the parts within the whole. And so, as I descended from the plane at Ìbàdàn airport in January 1969, and found myself confronted by the press, I had only one statement for them – *To keep Nigeria one/ Justice must be done.*

---

[1] See *The Man Died* – Prison Memoirs

Then came the shock. The then Chief Justice of the Federation, a scion of Ègbá royal stock – that is, from my own birthplace – felt compelled to respond to my slogan. Without an immediate relevance to the purpose of his next public outing, the worthy judge could not wait to declare that justice not only existed in the nation but was well and thriving! The media were on to me immediately, eager to offer a platform for me to take the battle to him. I declined the bait, yet I was deeply troubled. Unknown to him, the judge had set me the first puzzle in my re-integration progress into society. I needed time to digest what struck me as a most unnecessary self-interposing between a government, with which I was undoubtedly at war, and myself, this being an intervention by the symbol of an institution that I had not assailed in any way. It was such a gratuitous intrusion that I feared that it had a deeper meaning that was yet hidden from me, something that my long absence from society had made me miss. Why – I asked myself – why should a supposedly independent judiciary concern itself with the grouch of a known dissident? Was that institution now a mouthpiece of the state?

I was thrown into a mental quandary. I had not, after all, addressed nor assailed the formal structure of justice, and I assumed that this was obvious. Alas, my prison existence in a circumscribed world, with its limited but coherent relationships of objects and events, that internal logic that defines the very nature of routine, had totally unfitted me for such an arbitrary, adversarial interjection. It was my first test on returning into the real world, and I was thrown off balance. I recovered an emotion that I had long forgotten – *fright*! Was this what was in store for me even after such a brief confinement – a mere two years and four months, no matter how endless it had appeared at the time. What had become of the nation? Its civic institutions? How deeply had the militarised state eroded their foundations? Suppose the state had chosen to bring me to trial after all – where was the impartial arbiter into whose hands my fate would have been thrust? Only at that moment, when indeed there was no longer likelihood of being brought to trial for any crimes, did I first experience fright!

Was the statement of the Chief Justice intended as an official affirmation of the *justice* of the war? The definitive word on the tragedy? What was the view of his peers on the Supreme Bench, those who were Igbo or sympathisers, or perhaps had lost friends and relations in the war? He was, after all, only a first among equals.

I proceeded to review the immediate actuality of our nation being, given the costly, devastating war that was now, thankfully, drawing to a close. War, after all, must be considered an abnormal event in any nation's life. To start with, by the very nature of war, all norms of justice are surely set aside. You do not invoke some code of jurisprudence to decide whether mercenaries should fight your war or foreign pilots be brought into a conflict to bomb one side or the other into submission. Once the shooting has begun, attempting to obtain a court order for the restoration of the *status quo ante* or whatever between the combatants is an absurdity – the deciding role has been conceded to *force majeure,* with or without the restraining hand of national or international realpolitik or the Geneva Convention. Thus, somewhere, within the nation called Nigeria, some feeling of a suspension – at the very least – of the expectations of justice had to exist, some plaint of unmerited affliction, of deep-rooted suffering. Any thinking being must surely concede that elementary probability! There had to be innocent victims, individual and community. The Biafrans, major actors in this war, assuredly nursed a feeling of injustice. The MidWest Igbo, firstly compromised by their kin from across the Niger, then 'liberated' by Federal forces and slaughtered in batches for 'collaboration' with the Biafrans, must feel engulfed in bloodfounts of injustice. The minorities of the Delta region, forced into an unwanted entity called Biafra, brutalised, had surely undergone at the hands of Biafrans a passage of monumental injustice. The very process of their liberation must have caused some undeserved suffering, thus breeding a sense of double injustice. Justice denied, injustice unmerited, even as expressions of the barest possibilities, surely existed beyond dispute – what then, I continued to demand of my captive audiences – close friends and comrades – what problem could the Chief Justice possibly have with that?

Mentally, I began looking over my shoulders, a burgeoning paranoid – it was not quite how I had envisaged my induction into normal existence. I was made more acutely aware how deeply that commodity called justice, however qualified, was central to my ordering of self-apprehension, and of the human community, and it was not a healthy feeling. The world, I felt, was out of tune, if the pinnacle of the structure of justice considered it necessary to assume the responsibility of responding to a man who had just emerged from confinement where he had been consigned without trial, most of it in solitary confinement, lied against without a means of defending himself. If only in his own right, for no other cause beside his own, this emerging recluse surely had a right to proclaim a prima facie case of injustice, since he had never been brought to trial for any crime. The legitimacy of a Chief Justice was non-existent outside the basis of Nigerian ground rule – *deemed innocent until proven guilty*! But the main shock for me was the fact that anyone at all, apart from a recognised government mouthpiece or a political adversary, should assume the responsibility of attempting to counter what, at best, would be considered no more than the rhetoric of defiance!

I was truly obsessed with the need to find a meaning – so compulsive must have been my need for clarity after my prison sojourn. Everything had to make sense. I had to find a logical process, a credible *sequitur* to what went before, a rational cause in any situation that aspired to produce an effect. I worried about this statement as a dog does an unraveling ball of wool, little realising that I was taking it so *personally*! The Chief Justice had not, after all, sentenced me to prison. I wore out the patience of my handful of listeners – did the man interpret justice in the titular sense – that is, justice as Chief Justice of the Federation? Did he imagine that I had cast doubts on his existential definition or indicted his functional reality? What had happened to the national edifice, its pillars, in my absence?

It was an unsettled period of intense speculation. Perhaps it was a continued variation of that phase in prison when I created totally theoretical problems and sought to solve them mathematically – a subject I had hated in school – just to pass the time. Prison in solitary is a state in which one creates a microcosmic but coherent world, albeit a world of the lowest hierarchy. The prisoner's condition depends firstly on the will of his principal gaolers, far removed from his predicament, and next, on their immediate agents who regulate his day to day existence. Below those levels however, the prisoner is a complete master of his universe, and that universe is regulated – if only for sanity – on strict, objective lines. Mine was certainly a world that was populated by trivia, by the mundane, but its very ordinariness was ordered and predictable. An improvised pen remained exactly where you chose to hide it, day after day and week after week. If by chance it was discovered, that probability had long been built into reality, and thus became a logical development. My ink – *soyink*, I called it – developed experimentally but, once perfected, it followed the laws of supply – and quality – precisely as anticipated. The trusty left your food tray on the same spot day after day and you reciprocated in like manner when you were done. Toilet paper was supplied – one roll for so many days. So were cigarettes. If there was a change – a rare occurrence – in the routine, then there was a reason for it. When the superintendent paid a surprise visit, that also slid into a niche of normality – a surprise visit was exactly as it should be, a surprise. And so on and on. Any unpredictable or irrational element was banished from that universe as a phenomenon that belonged to other hierarchies where one was not in control. By contrast, the environment from which I had been forcibly removed two years earlier, one into which I was now re-entering, I began to discover, was a more palpably humanised terrain, yet it was one that refused to answer to the name of logic and coherence. It did not guarantee the security of the predictable, nor rational explications of the unexpected.

My re-education was gradual, and of course it began with recollection of what daily existence had been like before my detention. The Chief Justice had unknowingly administered a salutary shock. I now learnt to recognise that I had been released from prison into a paradox – a nation that wallowed in triumphalism, yet was under subjugation. It was a society that fed contentedly from a common trough of humiliation but paraded itself as the People of Victory. Paradox did not exist in my prison environment, hence my disorientation by the quite commonplace response of a Chief Justice. I did not immediately recognise the nation I had left behind, yet my absence had not really amounted to much in a nation's life. Perhaps if nearly two years of those twenty eight months had not been spent in solitary confinement, if for instance, I had had steady contact with visitors, newspapers, radio, I might have been inducted into the altered psyche of the nation, would have been better prepared for the norm of citizen sycophancy and self-abasement that had replaced the self-esteem on which we earlier rode, as the rightful place for a people who had no history of internal subjugation. A new social culture had however emerged in civil society – allegiance to the military and a need to promulgate the righteousness of a war, now in its final days. I had done nothing more than provide Justice with its own opportunity – there was, apparently, more than one means of contributing to the Troops Comfort Fund!

With victory go the spoils of war. Civil society lay at the feet of the conquerors, and within that civil society were many who had genuinely cheered, even sacrificed for the war of oneness. For others, the military had become enthroned as the new elite, and the level of fawning and jockeying to be merely noticed and smiled upon by any pretender in uniform already spoke of a nation that was loudly pleading to be crushed underfoot. The army was only too willing to oblige, the message ground into public consciousness – young and old, bigman and nonentity – that there was a new overlordship sprung to life in full formation, that the ragged boot of the lowest corporal rested permanently on that rung of the ladder where the hands of the civil engineer, the business tycoon, the university professor, the crowned head and even cleric competed for a hold that might eventually haul up the rest of the body one more conceded step. And as each military boot scraped itself onto the head of the civic worthy below, that head turned upwards with a most ingratiating smile and received the full dollop of the scrapings in its wide open mouth.

With the entrenchment of the military, the season of unsolicited Curriculum Vitae begun – *please sir, I am available for a parastatal board membership, diplomatic posting, one-man management board, administrator, commission of enquiry, tenders board, etc. etc.* There were of course uplifting exceptions, individuals who turned down lucrative temptations and chose to stick to their professions, or hundreds of unknowns who simply refused to accept any act of humiliation by a soldier, even fought them physically at the risk, sometimes at the cost of their lives. Such was the lady radiographer, Dupe Oke, who was slapped by a soldier at a roadblock at Ìdí-Ayùnré, some miles from Ìbàdàn. Her crime had been no more than failing to understand what exactly the soldier demanded of her. She had opened the boot of her car for inspection, opened her glove-compartment but the soldier kept jabbering some more instructions. "I'm sorry I don't understand what you want" she finally said, and was rewarded with a slap across the face. "You no understand, you no understand what? You think I come here waste time for grammar people like you?"

He did not get much further. Dupe flew at him and sank her teeth into his face. It took nearly the entire crowd of motorists awaiting their turn to be searched, to prise open her teeth and release the soldier. It was one of the lucky cases – she could easily have been shot. The people rallied round however. One of the travellers raced to the nearest cantonment in Ìbàdàn and returned with a superior officer and some military police in tow. The soldier, raw flesh dangling from his cheek, was arrested and taken away. His pathetic sight did not save him. He was given the 'guardroom' treatment for more than three months, we learnt, while Dupe received apologies and an escort to her destination.

Not so fortunate was Ola Rotimi, playwright and director, the recollection of whose ordeal, which he himself narrated to me on my return from prison, would sometimes jerk me awake, right in the middle of the night, covered in sweat. In vain I admonished myself – why do you give yourself this vicarious agony? But it was a scene that persisted in my head for a long while, and at all hours. I would recall it right in the middle of my work and stop. A long time would pass before I realised that I had been staring at the wall, my heart beating rapidly as I put myself irrationally through a bout of anxiety, one that would sometimes trigger a slight trembling in my hands. *In Ola Rotimi's position, what would I have done? What was the right decision at such a moment? Why should anyone be subjected to such a dilemma?*

Ola, close to Ikòròdú town, on the 'old Ikòròdú road' as it became later known, after the dual carriageway that now linked Ìbàdàn to Lagos was built. There was the usual succession of road-blocks, each roadblock hardly knowing or caring what the dictator of the last - sometimes within sight of each other - had done. Ola Rotimi, a short being with broad shoulders and a boulder of a head, was lecturer and dramatist at the University of Ifẹ̀. He had his family with him, his foreign wife and children. Sometimes when the line of vehicles was long - which was often – the soldiers would go up and down the line, scrutinising the passengers, pounce on a random choice and wave the others on. This was what happened to Ola. A soldier came alongside, looked in the car – it was a station-wagon without a closed luggage section – asked to see his papers and then waved him on. Ola pulled out of the line, like others who had been similarly cleared, and moved. Suddenly a soldier stepped out at the head of the queue, stopped him, and ordered him to pull aside. Ola Rotimi obeyed.

"Come outside!" he ordered.

Again, Ola did not argue.

"Everybody, come out. Yes, all of you, come out!"

Ola opened the door of the car and helped out his family.

"Stand there. Stand over there."

Ola began to protest. "But what's the matter...?"

"Shut up! You no know wetin you do? You jump queue." Ola Rotimi began to explain that he had been cleared to move but the soldier again shut him up. "You jump queue, you tink say I no see you? You tink you be big man so you no fit wait like everybody?"

Ola pointed in the direction he had just come from. "Your companion over there passed us. You can ask him, he'll tell you..."

The man snarled. "Oh, you telling me what to do? You still dey talk grammar? I show you pepper today. Come on, turn your back."

"What?"

"I say turn your back!" The soldier had slung his gun over one shoulder, and Rotimi now saw that he had replaced it with a horsewhip. "You getting twelve lashes to teach you lesson – turn your back."

For what must have seemed an eternity, said Ola Rotimi, he merely stared at him, unable to believe his ears. Another soldier had moved up, with his gun pointing at his trapped man. The first one screamed at him again, unslinging his gun. "You deaf or what? If I count three and you no yet turn your back, I fire you on the spot!" And Ola both heard, and saw him remove the safety catch on his gun.

"One...!"

In between *One* and *Two*, Ola Rotimi said to me, I reviewed my life in a flash. His intense eyes must have enveloped his wife, his three children, through his thick-rimmed glasses, aimed another look at the unprepossessing figure, towering over Ola's five foot three frame, and now virtually frothing at the mouth with insane rage. In that brief moment, his entire world was wrapped up in one thought: "Am I about to make my wife a widow, and these ones fatherless?"

"Two...!"

Again a flash of his lifeless body on the road, his wife and children kneeling and wailing, but helpless beside it. He presented his back to the soldier.

"Put your both hands on the car!"

Ola obeyed. As the lash tore into his back again and again. Ola, who was anything but pro-Biafrian, swore that his wish at that moment was that a rogue Biafran plane would penetrate through to Lagos and unleash a barrage of bombs on the very spot where he stood, pulverising everyone including himself, equalising torturer and victim with its deadlier weaponry of arbitrary terror.

For a long time after Ola had poured out his bitter heart to me, I continued to sweat out that lethal question: *what would I have done?*

Such dehumanisation of the populace did not take place only at checkpoints that were formally manned, but these were the most public places, and their audiences were guaranteed to cover the entire gamut of civil life. Day by day civil society endured, witnessed, and passed on the message. The uncertainty with which the traveller set out in the morning, deprived of the authority of office or security of the home was a constant, debilitating companion. It preyed on innocence itself, instilling an irrational fear because of the irrationality of the lords of existence to whom an unintended slur, a gesture adjudged to be lacking in the respect that was due to the wielders of guns and horsewhips could result in instant, public humiliation, or worse. The most favoured school of domination by the occupying force was thus the public arena, or the nearest to it, sometimes improvised or converted, as might be a private occasion such as a wedding, a child naming ceremony or a funeral. It could be one of those ostentatious parties – the ubiquitous ówambè parties – that routinely spilled over into streets sealed off to traffic to accommodate the over-affluent of civil society or relatives and cronies of the military. There, any act deemed lèse majesté, would result in the open 'drilling' of the offender, or his kidnapping on orders from the unofficial chairman of the occasion, bloated already from commandeered authority, doubly bloated from ample food, XO cognacs, Veuve Cliquot champagne – nothing less would do for khaki – and triply bloated from the obsequious attention of his hosts. And if the erratic Electricity Power Authority chose that moment to inflict a routine blackout on the arena of pleasure, what better sport than to send a military jeep for the local station manager, haul him out of bed, order him to shed power from other sources and restore electricity to the hallowed spot! Then, to impress on the locals the lesson that such acts of gross disrespect would never be tolerated, he would order his underlings to strip him half-naked and frogmarch him around the dance arena, then send him to the guardroom where his head was shaved with a piece of broken bottle, his body lashed with the infamous twisted cable and subjected to further indignities for days until friends, relations, local and distant dignitaries of the town came to plead for mercy – *sorry sah, the slight was*

*unintended, he didn't know that Your Excellency would be attending
the party or he would have suspended the power-shedding schedule
until the party was over.* And oh, no question about it, civil society
constantly collaborated in its own humiliation. A private quarrel
was no longer arbitrated by any of the traditional routes of
community intervention or even by the local courts. It sufficed
that one knew someone in uniform, however low in rank. Come
Judgement Day and the man of khaki connection descended on
the offending party with a bunch of his pals. They smashed their
way into the household, slapping, kicking, vandalising and often
making off with the miscreant – or hostage – until the terms of
settlement, as dictated by the complainant, were accepted by the
accused.

And it spread, and spread, and the culture was imbibed by a
prostrate society, one governor and petty administrator striving
to outdo the next in sadism. From major and petty contractors to
teachers, students, to all seekers after essential documents – title
deeds, certificates of occupancy, certified true copies of this and
that – to unpaid pensioners, to hoteliers, to local government
councillors and more, more and more – sooner or later all strata of
society find themselves knocking at the door of some government
office, usually located at the secretariat. Thus the secretariats
guaranteed regular captive spectators, as these were turned into
stadia of blood sports masquerading as 'discipline'. And of course
to ensure that the lessons there were driven home, literally, state
television and other media would be summoned in advance to
capture and disseminate the images - the spruced-up, tick-tock,
no-nonsense administrator, enforcing public discipline in set-up
scenarios.

Brigadier, captain or colonel administrator arrives at his office
five minutes before the official opening hour. On the dot of half
past seven, he orders the gates to the secretariat closed while his
soldiers take up position by the main gate and seal off all other
entry points. Then, any worker arriving late, no matter his or her
rank, age, or physical condition, is made to do the 'frog hop'. A
frog hop? Literally hop, or jump like a frog! The culprit attaches
his fingers to his ears, lowers himself on his haunches and hops

on one spot, circles a tree or parked vehicles or, up and down the
road. Laggards are assisted to improve their performance with
the application of the *koboko,* the infamous rawhide whips, across
their backs or knees. The real horror however, is not this act of
public torture, but the ingratiating 'Uncle Tom' smile on the faces
of some of the victims. It is as if, knowing there is no other purpose
to this spectacle, no other intent than to destroy their dignity, they
try to draw the sting from their abasement and pass it off as a
joke. Don't show resentment, pass it off as merely humouring the
strange ways of this unwanted breed and behold, the shame
evaporates. It is all a staged performance in which symbolic roles
have been assigned - and without prejudice.

Úgún be praised, there were always those few who hissed
their contempt at their would-be disciplinarians, turned their backs
on the scene, got into their cars or simply walked away, went
home to write out their resignation letters. Some got away with it,
others were still forcefully compelled to comply or else were
arrested and taken away, where they received their augmented
dosage in the military guardroom. A number of deaths occurred –
from heart attack – from this unaccustomed exercise, but it made
no difference. Dis'pline was dis'pline, and the civil servant was
required to submit to its irrationalities. It did not matter in the
least - to come down to administrative realities - that the nature
of the employee's duty sometimes required that he or she visit
some other offices, do some rounds in a relevant professional
constituency, resume his routine of inspections of some critical
installations before resorting to his desk - no - such explanations
were dismissed with full military aplomb. Be at your desk on the
dot of 7.30 a.m or else - prepare to be *dis'plined!*

Humiliation filled the streets, the highways, in competition
with violence. It entered the homes on camera cables and infested
the media with tales of horror. Freedom had begun to compare
most unfavourably with prison existence, yet the mood around
me appeared to be one of celebration - of victory over a great evil
called secession. I now began to feel like a stranger, though
surrounded by familiar landmarks - it was rather like going to
sleep in a familiar room, yet waking up each morning in the wrong

neighbourhood, a feeling that was undoubtedly aggravated by recollection of those months in prison solitary, difficult as they sometimes proved, in which one constituted the entirety of his world, undisturbed. Resumption of my friendship with Femi provided some solace, but nothing really helped to resolve the question that obsessed me: *what would I have done in Ola's place?* – that is, what would I have done in place of the many Olas that I knew, some of them old enough to be the grandfathers and mothers of the agents of their humiliation? The only certitude in my mind was a negative one – I had not thought that prison regimen could ever lay claim to leaving the inmate with more dignity than victims of the *dis'pline* in which civil society daily acquiesced.

My sense of estrangement was compounded by the lingering effects of a loss that had taken place in my absence – that of my private den. All animals need a hole into which they can crawl from time to time. With every passing day, I acknowledged that while in prison, I had looked forward to retreating into mine, once I was released. Indeed, solitary confinement appeared to have deepened what had once been mere habit into a visceral need.

The den was gone. Its shell remained – a converted motor garage – but only as another space of estrangement. A visitation – or a series of visitations – had turned the den into just another warehouse. I had not thought that so much empathy could be lodged, over time, within a mere array of man-made objects, creating an aura of near inviolability. Without that den of escape, I turned increasingly irritable, impatient and restless – even I could sense that, without the aid of surprised stares and protests. A physical distancing from an alienating environment was only a matter of time.

I was discovering much about myself. I had thought that the state of imprisonment, where the environment is not of one's choosing, would inoculate an inmate with resistant germs against any future sense of privation, make one indifferent to possessions. I gradually learnt that the state of freedom also breeds desires and expectations, including the craving for an accustomed space, a sanctuary, a physical, palpable, intimate space, not unlike solitary confinement in a prison cell, but of course, a space of one's own choice and designation. Already alienated from the public environment, I was now deprived of an intimacy that I once relished, one within which I could take refuge from the outside world, and also regain a sense of fluidity in the creative process.

Perhaps if my marriage – briefly resuscitated by shared tribulations and the emotions of reunion – had held out, the throb of alienation would have been muted. However, the differences that had turned that marriage into mere effort before my imprisonment resurfaced in no time at all, increasing a daily, prolonged craving for a handy escape, a familiar, welcoming lair. I still entered the converted garage from time to time, but it had lost its deep, self-absorbent aura.

I threw myself into the filming of *Kongi's Harvest,* under the direction of Ossie Davis, the black American actor, with the possessed cineaste, Francis Oladele, as the producer. Day after day, the designated lead, Gaius Anoka, expected from the Biafran territory, failed to turn up – we found out later that he had been denied a clean bill of health by the de-briefing team of the victorious Federal side, and thus not permitted to leave the subdued enclave. Ossie Davis filmed around and around his absence but, in the end, there was not one scene left that could be shot without the figure of the dictator, Kongi.

All eyes turned on me – till then, I had contented myself with adjusting the script and tackling Ossie's queries, but mostly working with the music. Now – enter the star! – I stepped into the role of the dictator for one of my least memorable performances. Still, the frenzied and intense pace of that preoccupation helped. Being on location most of the time, a shifting environment, succeeded in blunting the need of the animal for his lair. In between shoots however, on returning home, there was no congenial space into which I could withdraw. Not until I had lost this sanctuary did I discover how deep dyed I was in that 'deadly sin' from which I had so blithely excepted myself – attachment! It was a surprise – and something of a discomfiture – to find that I did own something that I deeply valued. It did not help matters that the blow that routed my assumptions had been struck from within my family.

Ironically, the transgressor, nay junior brother – who narrowly escaped decapitation or worse at my hands – would provide, for me as for both family and acquaintances, proof of the redemptive potential of any human being. Kayoos – his favourite nickname - became a christian born-again – yes, the real thing, I testify to that! – as authentic a born-again christian and evangelist as you would hope to meet on this side of sin. Kayoos was transformed into an actively caring asset to the whole family with all its extensions, and to friends. At the time however...!

As I emerged from prison and was re-installed in my campus home, it was not difficult to observe that among the endless tumult – family, colleagues, friends and even total strangers – who invaded the house, one face, with its wide, guileless smile, a booming baritone voice, was conspicuous by its absence. This absence was made all the more noticable by the fact that the face had made a very brief early appearance on my arrival at Ìbàdàn airport, when its owner had held me in a powerful and emotional embrace. And then it disappeared altogether!

That was strange. Kayoos' natural place was at the heart of celebrations, and this was an occasion especially tailored for his expansive, adventurous and outgoing nature. Kayoos was very affectionate. I knew that he remained fond of me even when I had totally given up on him, having taken my turn fully at the rehabilitation roulette in which he engaged the rest of the family, and got thoroughly burnt for my pains. I had indeed begun to remark openly that only a prison spell would make him confront the realities of life – thus the ironic fact that my mother and I did have a meeting point – in prayer. I prayed that his prison experience would not scar him for life, but would be very short, sharp and painful, thus achieving what all our efforts in the family had failed to do. Wild Christian, needless to say, harboured no such thoughts. She simply importuned God to change him, in His own good time of course – she hastened to reassure Him – but really tomorrow, preferably.

Even before my prison detention, I was undoubtedly the most severe on him. I forbade him not only my home and office, but my presence. That did not stop him occupying one of the rooms in the tiny annexe to the official residence, intended for the house

-help, but often converted into colourful student pads. I knew that my wife – another of the rehabilitation team – had let him stay there, but I pretended not to know. He kept out of my way and never entered the main house while I was around. Once I was out of the way however, Kayoos came in and helped himself to whatever he needed, ran errands for my wife and played with his nephews, nieces and cousins – in short, everyone behaved like a true Yoruba, or indeed the average African. You snarl at the stray sheep but pretend that you never noticed that the side door has been left open for it to sneak in at night.

The garage was home to my modest collection of – mostly traditional – artworks. I lavished all my spare resources in acquiring them, and they were indeed a main source of marital friction. It had become my habit to turn the motor garage – in whatever house I occupied – into a gallery-cum-study, and this was where I spent most of my time, working among the ancestral masks, the gods, their caryatids, shrine posts and vessels, basking in their aura. It provided a working ambiance that suited my temperament, rather like being within a web of emanations from multiple existences. But the gallery also served a less exalted purpose. Along its backyard, separated by a heavy copse that was home – we would discover much later – to a nest of pythons, ran one half of the dual carriageway that led into the university campus. This meant that a car could stop or be parked behind the house while its passenger walked through the copse directly to the garage without disturbing the household. As my marriage disintegrated, this *sanctum sanatorium* would serve as a venue for desperate assignations, usually in the dead of night. The snakes, fortunately, did not appear to have been unduly disturbed by these nocturnal intrusions.

Nor were the gods under whose watchful eyes they took place. It was my very private world. Within it, I experienced no sense of betrayal, guilt did not obtrude, did not exist. Marriage, now a mere formality, remained equally protected in its own continually expansive world of responsibilities, emotional impositions and domestic bargaining, but this arena of deities and ancestors remained impervious to its moralities. Heavy wood sculptures, bronzes, caryatids and votive vessels, ceremonial drums and metallic gongs – they provided a relief for the mind when inspiration flagged and my fingers fluttered aimlessly over the typewriter. Most times however, they proved an additional impetus for those stretches when the fingers tapped a productive rhythm on the keys. While I was locked away in prison, family and visitors found it most touching to see Kayoos turning up from time to time to dust my collection, take out the cobwebs and spruce up the appearance of big brother's prized sanctum.

And then, one day, my wife visited a colleague of hers. A friend from the United States had been staying with that lady and now he was getting ready to leave. Strewn all over the floor, in various stages of wrapping and packing, were souvenirs he was taking with him. Quite innocently, she sensed a familiarity in some of the artifacts, and observed that her friend's visitor appeared to have similar tastes to mine. Then she picked up another piece. Interesting, that also looked familiar... and then another, even more familiar. Suddenly, she felt dead certain. The coincidence was too much. There could not be such a consistency, the pieces were not merely familiar, they looked identical, and there were far too many of them. One piece in particular belonged in the living-room, so she had grown accustomed to it. She excused herself and returned home. Yes, it was gone, so were a number of other pieces within the house, and a lot more from the garage-museum.

The collector had no misgivings whatsoever. He had bought them, and he had bought them legitimately. He knew to whom they belonged, but had been made to believe that Kayoos had been given the authority to dispose of them – this was easy enough to believe, as Kayoos was well known in expatriate circles as a dealer in traditional items, though not necessarily antiquities. And what was more logical than to assume that the family of an imprisoned man, *incommunicado*, might need to dispose of some personal items to take care of immediate financial needs!

What items that could be retrieved from the hapless visitor were taken back, but of course he was not the only buyer from Kayoos' limitless source. A number of coveted objects had disappeared forever.

While I sojourned in prison, oblivious to my bereavement, a series of family meetings and consultations with friends began. Bola Ige, lawyer and combative politician, undertook the task of extricating Kayoos from the criminal consequences of his enterprise, since the effort to recover other items had necessarily involved the police. Femi Johnson was at hand to give advice and exert his influence in other vital directions. As the day approached for my release, the meetings were resumed with one agenda: how to break the news to me, and what to do about this near unhealable breach. The first decision was predictable, being based on what even those outside the immediate family had instinctively grasped, or had been told, about my attachment to these works of art – Kayoos was ordered to keep his distance from me. He could come and join in the welcome on the very first day, but that was all. And so he seized the earliest chance to break out from the crowd and give me that most expressive hug, disappeared into the crowd, and swiftly left town.

The moment I could escape the throng of visitors, my first visit was to this private den. I had been twenty-eight months absent, but I had a total recall of my collection – how they were stored, how one related to the other across the room or jostled for shelf space with another. I knew in which direction I turned at my desk to rest tired or questing eyes on an Úgún here, an Èṣù there, I knew which corner Úsanyìn reposed with his skeletal birds, cowrie beads and train of leather thongs, where the divination tray was propped against the bamboo support, or where, I would joke, a field of force was generated between a phallus-burdened monkey and a caryatid with a split vulva. And there were the bronze miniatures whose patina I caressed as I strolled between the bamboo shelves that I had constructed myself, the uprights festooned with ancestral masks or elaborately carved hunter's fly-whisks. Now, all I saw were gaps, clamorous absences.

I asked questions, obtained vague answers from my wife... oh, some of the items had been sent for restoration and then kept for their own safety... anyway, Professor This or That would speak to me about them later. Something was wrong, I knew, but I chose to be patient. There were, in any case, more pressing concerns that had been created by my absence.

They came like a mournful delegation to break the news of a family bereavement – an uncle, a cousin-in-law, a mother-in-law, an elderly family dependant, and of course, lurking in the background, ready to interject some balm or whisk me away to some place of recovery was – OBJ. They judged that the moment was right, having allowed me a few days to settle back into domesticity, be reabsorbed into a living community, but also to recover from the overpowering waves of well-wishers. Now there was this family matter to be settled, a breach to be healed. I listened to voices of entreaty, numbed... *You have to remember, whatever it takes, he is still your brother. The important thing is that we are able to give thanks to God for your safe return. Add this to the list of the trials that you underwent, even though you did not know it at the time, this loss is part of those trials nonetheless. Only God knows what he has in store as compensation, but certainly he means to make restitution a hundredfold. You have your family, your children, your standing in the world is a thing of envy in the minds of thousands you've never heard of... family is family, no matter what...* and on and on and on... The case was still with the police. They were waiting for me to return before they could close the files. As the owner of the stolen or missing goods, only I could give them instructions to do so. If I could find my way to doing this as soon as possible, then we could all get over the nightmare and put it all behind us.

They had done their duty. I thanked them. I replied that I had listened carefully to what they had to say and assured them that I had taken the disaster stoically. I had no interest whatever in exacting the appropriate penalty from the scoundrel. As far as I was concerned, there was no case, there was to be no criminal pursuit, and the case should simply be allowed to lapse. None of them should however expect that I would take myself to the police station or write a letter asking that the case be discontinued. Just let it lapse. If they wanted me to get over this blow as quickly as possible, it would be the only way – that it be dropped like a stone into a pond. *Finis!*

They remained worried. It seemed to them a kind of closure but one that lacked an impermeable casing. Yes, they were in full agreement. It would be asking too much from me to take the active step of approaching the police. But suppose they brought the officer in charge of the case to me and I gave him instructions? I considered this, then thought up an even better idea for my peace of mind – I wanted so desperately to be alone – look, I proposed, why don't you write the letter? Make it short and to the point – *I, Wole Soyinka, complainant in the matter of the stolen antiquities, hereby declare that I do not wish to pursue any criminal charges and hereby authorise you to close the case.* Something along those lines. Just write it and I'll sign it. I don't even wish to read it. Write it now, right now, I want the matter closed.

They all turned to my friend, Femi Johnson. He had been part of the conspiracy from the beginning, though he had said nothing so far, since this was basically a family ritual. Quickly, he wrote the short one-paragraph letter. I signed it. Then came some hemming and hawing. I looked around the faces; obviously they were not done... well, *there is still the family matter.* Family matter? What family? *Well, your brother... when can he come to see you? He has to know that you've forgiven him.*

I was puzzled. What were they talking about? Had they really failed to fasten on the one conclusion that occupied my mind? Yes of course, there was the sense of betrayal, but it went further. The collection was my life, so I felt as if I had been murdered. It was quite simple – anyone who was capable of doing this could only have done it out of a conviction: that I would not emerge from prison alive. I looked at their faces, surprised that this obvious awareness had eluded them – *he wished me dead, he assumed me dead, he was stealing from a dead man!* Could they not see this as clearly as I did? I heard one of them say, we've told him to stay away for now. *No, no, you tell him to stay away for good. For good! It's no longer a family matter because I no longer consider him family. So tell him to keep away. I don't wish to see him ever. I don't wish to know him. In fact, I do not know him.*

That evening, after they had left, I went into the garage and packed my books and papers. I did not bestow so much as a glance of regret at my silent companions, feeling only an expanse of deep violation, of betrayal and deep distrust - not focussed on any being, since I had truly wiped out my assailant's existence from my mind.

All I had left was a void, the loss of a vital organ. But it also triggered off a process of self-chastisement... *See? That's what comes of becoming attached to material things. Now see how devastated you are. Were these really anything but props? Crutches! Deprived of your crutches, you are crushed! Yes, crushed! So much for those phases of self-dissolution in which you indulged in prison confinement, when even your physical self vanished and you found peace in the abode of nothingness. So much for your claims of companionship with the hermit priest Malarepa: 'I need nothing. I seek nothing. I desire nothing'. Does it require the barrenness of a prison cell to induce such wisdom in the mind, and is such wisdom so soon dissipated on emerging from confinement?*

Still, no one could deny that it was right to remain attached to my books and papers, or at least, to need them for my living, so I piled them into the car and drove to my office behind the theatre. I tumbled them in a corner and, in that deadened state of mind, chloroformed by loss and repudiation, proceeded to set up a new work space. The gods remained in their own abode, abandoned, but this was a condition to which they had been accustomed for the past two years anyway, and even since eternity. They were free to seek their own remedies, all I asked for was my peace of mind. My re-installation in this neutral space completed, I drove furiously to Femi's house, late as it was. He was expecting me. We drank late into the night.

It took years before I would again acknowledge the right of this rump collection to a place in my existence, or move to replenish it. The healing came gradually, Kayoos underwent a virtual transfiguration, becoming almost one with the playful, even sometimes watchful presences in one's inner sanctuary. At the time however, the void in my private space only augmented the hollowness that beset me whenever I was thrust into the public arena, from which I had become even more viscerally alienated. It left me craving distance, a tactile and sensory severance. I slipped out fusslessly and, into my first – and only – spell of voluntary exile.

PART III

Interlude to a Friendship

Interlude to a Friendship

*L*ooking back, it strikes me with some astonishment that, until his death in 1987, one constant, a large presence in the 'extra-curricular' undertakings of my adult existence has been Olufemi Babington Johnson. Just who was this being?

I have often wondered what he would have made of Sani Abacha. What role would he have played in our struggle? I know that he would not have hesitated one moment to place resources at my disposal, most especially for *Radio Kudirat*, the opposition radio that drove Sani Abacha to distraction. He once paid me an unusual compliment, an invaluable gift, if only he knew it! He confided it in his second wife, Folake, who passed it to mine, her namesake. This man said of me: *You can leave your heart with Wole and travel to Hong Kong. When you come back, it would still be beating.* I must confess that I have never ceased to ponder, and be moved by this tribute. The views of women with whom I have had disastrous relationships will probably differ but – best to stay away from that literal track!

This, of course, was a tribute that was infinitely appropriate for him, and I wondered if he ever thought about himself that way, or made it a guiding principle of his existence. I only know that his words hovered around my head like a talisman long after his death, as if in silent exhortation. To a degree, we do aspire to

live up to a view of others, no matter how stoutly we deny it.
During the fight against Sani Abacha's tyranny, I could hardly
deny to myself the echo of Femi's words in urging on me that
obsessive mission – to keep the heart of a nation, of a people beating,
even after a demented dictator had ripped it out and squeezed its
lifeblood down his throat.

Femi's generosity was not limited to tributes to a friend. As
one frustrated year succeeded the last, I would imagine scenes of
clandestine meetings – London, Kampala, Paris, Lisbon, Dakar,
Vineroz, etc. – where his first question would most certainly be:
how can I contribute? Then would follow a self-deprecating
catechism of his lack of physical courage. The cloak-and-dagger
arrangements that would precede such a meeting – for his own
protection – would have set his eyes dancing with relish. We would
meet for lunch or dinner. Straight from the first course, I would
spring the surprise, letting him realise for the first time that I knew,
and had been moved by his tribute... *Femi, you want the heart of
that nation of ours to continue beating, not so? Well, help me fund a
clandestine opposition radio.* A double take, the inimitable laughter
boom, a threat to 'hammer that woman's head' – his wife's, for
betraying his confidence – and his next question would be – what
do you need, and how soon?

Difficult now to imagine that once, we did not speak to each
other for nearly seven months and I pronounced our friendship
at an end. It was absurd, a falling out that made little sense but, it
did happen. I declared it all dead – the years of intense bonding,
of arguments, risks, of political and other – far more delectable –
exploits, both the casual encounters and others that demanded
elaborate organisational skills, and complex logistics, covering up
for each other as needed. Or the theatre and other performance
ventures, the hunting expeditions and of course – the hours at his
generous table, or at my skimpier one that gave up, very early, all
attempts to rival his sybaritic largeness. A sonorous baritone singing
voice and a compulsive performer, Femi, with his artistic
sensibilities, could have shaped his life in a different direction, in
a different environment, but he chose to become an insurance
broker and entrepreneur, and an immensely successful one.

Perhaps what drew me to him was part recognition of that road not taken, the repressed artist within the nattily suited business man, a keen political animal that yet fled politics, one who did not hesitate to take the hearts of others into his hands for safe-keeping, or resuscitation.

The Kenyan writer, Ngugi wa Thiong'o never met Femi Johnson in his lifetime, but his wife did. So did Ngugi's comrade-in-arms, Micere Mugo, one of the dissidents of Kenya's intelligentsia, resolutely opposed to the corrupt and repressive government of Arap Moi. At the height of Arap Moi's paranoia and draconian rule of the nineteen-eighties, I became desperate to make contact with Ngugi, about whose condition in prison we were receiving only disquieting news. I had not yet developed any of the multiple identities that I was later obliged to adopt, and owned only one passport. A personal appearance in Nairobi would have been short-lived – a press conference perhaps, and I would be back on the next plane under police escort – assuming that I was even allowed into Kenya in the first place. In any case, Ngugi's associates – Micere Mugo and others – had advised against a personal visit by me.

As if by a miracle, the African Association of Insurance Brokers decided to hold their annual conference in Nairobi. I had letters and money to deliver to Ngugi's wife – I was then Secretary-General of the Union of Writers of the African Peoples, an organisation that I initiated in Ghana in 1972, and was formally inaugurated in Dakar the following year under Leopold Sedar Senghor's patronage. I had squeezed a little money together from our members' contributions and this was to go to Ngugi's aid. Even more important than the immediate monetary relief was the need to establish contact, to get a message to Ngugi that we were not simply sitting on our hands, indifferent to his predicament. Never – I am certain – has a meeting of insurance brokers been so conveniently timed in the cause of the Arts – but it would happen for Femi and me! My friend readily agreed to carry out the mission.

"If they catch you," I joked, "you're on your own. Only if I learn that you are actually about to be executed will I come for you personally."

"Don't worry. Before anyone lays a hand on me, I'll spill the beans."

"Good. That's exactly what I want you to promise. No heroics. Begin with Micere – she'll either be at the university or someone will know where she is. Micere will bring you to Ngugi's wife – it may require a long journey by road."

"I'll find her."

"That's most important. We want to know what she wants us to do, how she wants us to react to what is going on. Who else needs help. Be sure to have a long conversation with her. I want news about Ngugi – when she saw him last, how he is, how he's being treated, etc. etc."

He gave a mock salute. "Yes, commandant!"

"And don't forget to insure yourself. I volunteer to be your beneficiary."

Femi's trepidation at such assignments was genuine. Equally genuine however was his relish of them! He revelled in the business of flattening letters and cash into false compartments of his suitcase, making clandestine phone calls from the public box in the lobby of his hotel rather than from his room, trying out different verbal codes to disclose his identity and that of the person whose intermediary he was. Our insurance broker carried out his mission to the letter, and then some! He undertook a long, roundabout journey by road to meet Ngugi's wife, delivered the funds – to which, needless to say, he had added his own generous contribution, unasked. Instead of joining on the organised safari tours with his colleagues, Femi spent two days in Kenya awaiting the contact that had been sent to penetrate through to Ngugi in prison. He met other contacts, wrapped up his mission and landed in Lagos still wreathed in the high state of euphoria that only commenced – on his admission – once his plane had left Kenyan airspace. Then he eased himself into his accustomed role as the life and soul of the returning delegation for the rest of the journey, they little suspecting what their extrovert colleague had been up to while they were indulging in the fleshpots of Nairobi. Micere wrote a long, glowing report of his performance. They continued to correspond for a while after his return.

Orlando Martins, a famous Nigerian film actor who could boast of Paul Robeson and Ronald Reagan as his screen companions in the fifties, had retired home to Nigéria. Now he was old, alone, and incontinent. Femi moved him to his sumptuous home in Ìyágànkú, the setting for many gourmandising soirées, set him up permanently in his guest chalet, paid all his medical bills and ministered to every want, whim and caprice – and Pa Orlando, as he was fondly known, was more than a trial for Job and all the saints. There Pa Orlando stayed, bullied the cooks if his food was too salty or under-salted or ...*take it away, I've told you I don't want it swimming in oil...and this time don't forget the ow-nions!* There he remained, Femi's terminal guest, and Femi paid all the funeral expenses...

...Or the children of the villagers where we sometimes went to hunt, victims of all kinds of diseases that defied treatment. Femi arranged for them to come into town and be examined by doctors. Sometimes he would assign a car and a driver to ensure that they came regularly for treatment until cured...

Àjoje l'ódùn - the joy is in the sharing – was his favourite refrain. And he lived it! Many experienced this only in those summative occasions that he particularly relished, such as his christmas parties. Even now, nearly two decades later, at christmas time, the city of Ìbàdàn still undergoes the pangs of bereavement – and this extends beyond the middle-class to which he belonged, since his festive hand extended to stewards, drivers, his acquired hunting families who were mostly farmers or working class. No, he did not invite Ìbàdàn's ten million population to his home, but to listen to complete strangers speak in awe of the famed parties, they must have believed he did. Both for those who shared his bounty, and for thousands of Ìbàdàn's inhabitants who never ate from his board, Femi Johnson was synonymous with the transformation of christmas/New Year into one huge feast that could only have been dreamt up in pagan Rome. It became a recognised institution – no one gave a party on the last Saturday before christmas – that was OBJ's day. You did not give a party because you expected to be

invited and, if you were not on his guest-list, some of your likely
guests might be and, between the two, you did not stand a chance
with a rival party. All likely guests were headed for THE party at
Ìyágànkú, where two or three live bands played till early morning,
a film might be screened, and at least three roasts, over which the
host had personally sweated all day, were now ready for their
piecemeal internment.

Literally, the table groaned under the weight and variety.
The Lebanese section was standard. He had visited Lebanon quite
early in his career – then as employee in the insurance business –
when Lebanon was still Lebanon and the business centre of the
East. He never tired of narrating the experience, and it was mostly
– food! A whole roast sheep, and, as a special mark of honour, he
had been served the eyes. Then the creamy dips – *houmus, tahini,
taramosalata, labneh,* and on to the spiced, scented pinenut rice,
grilled aubergines and – oh yes, what constituted for him the most
hilarious delicacy when he discovered what they were –
sweetbread! He had many Lebanese friends in Ìbàdàn, and there
was the Lebanese restaurant that later became his Sunday dinner
haunt. It was owned by the Haddad family and there Femi would
be found religiously with his family, armed with a couple of bottles
of wine. It was this restaurant that mostly catered for his christmas
parties.

Long before the array of food dazzled his guests however,
Femi had already entered the festive mode. He supervised every
aspect of preparation – except the autonomous Lebanese
department which had become adept at ignoring his constant
emendations, once his main list had been accepted. And so – apart
from his own assignment, which was to turn the pink cadaver of
a pig or ram into a work of art, pleasing to the eye and glorious on
the palate – Femi busied himself with supervising - that is,
choreographing the field of consumption. He was especially
delighted with the traditional food department – the women and
their young assistants (usually their children) among huge clay
pots and pans, plucking, stoking, kneading, pounding, turning
various farina, boiled yam and cassava flour into *èbà, iyán, àmàlà,
fùfú,* Femi among the bubbling vats of seafood, venison, beef,

mutton, vegetable stews, the cracking noises of giant snails being separated from their shells, and the numerous browning chickens-on-the-spit.

"*Awọn ìyá ńdi àrò*"[1] – and his eyes would sparkle, surveying the field of the busy women – "just the sight of them all over the compound, bent over the fires and cooking pots, vegetables being washed and sliced, meats being cut up and slapped into the huge *bàsíà* [2] of oil, all day long – yes, that's the best part of it. The festive atmosphere of preparation, even more than the result."

But this was not always any part of him, not at the start of the sixties when we first became really acquainted. It was not part of him, and he wanted no part of it. Later, he would become quite candid – but perhaps only with me – and mock himself over that phase of his choice of a life-style, when, in his own words, he must have cut the appearance of a displaced Englishman. I did not really set out to change him. I accepted him as he was. But then, I was not about to change either, or accommodate him where my temperament revolted profoundly against his inclinations. Certainly I was not about to join him at lunch or dinner eating boiled carrots, potatoes, tasteless fish fillet or steak, lamb chops and soggy cabbage – all of which I rejected after a first full year in England, 1954/55, when I dutifully ate anything that was put before me. It was my health strategy for that strange, cold and dismal land that existed, surely, solely to ensure my death from a thousand cold related diseases!

My reasoning went thus: British weather was unfit for human habitation, yet the Britishers, including their young, vulnerable children, somehow survived it – the evidence was apparent in the many geriatrics who littered the landscape. The explanation could only be found in the kind of food they ate. Thus, for a stranger to survive, he had better submit to their diet, right down to the last revolting speck of mashed potato and the disgusting lick of brown gravy that covered the tasteless slab of undecipherable meat. I ate it all. Some items were less unbearable than others, certainly their breakfasts – oats or corn flakes, kippers, eggs fried or scrambled,

---

[1] Women at the festive hearth.
[2] Wide-mouthed metal cooking pot.

bacon and sausages, slabs of bread with butter and marmalade, mugs of tea or synthetic coffee with milk and sugar – I was yet to lose my sweet tooth! British breakfast was quite enjoyable, but the rest – ! Well, I ate it all, dutifully, as one swallows medicine. On the dot of twelve months from my first day in England however, I deemed my body to have built up sufficient resistance to survive any winter, fog, smog, clammy rains and darkness at noon. I began to pick and choose, discovered the hideouts of Indian restaurants and the one or two Italian whose choices were limited to spaghetti bolognese or neapolitana.

It was therefore quite a shock to find, in the heart of Ìbàdàn, any human being, and a Nigerian Yoruba to boot, who actually served, of his own volition, British cuisine. I would sit with Femi and his family at dinner table, nursing a mug of beer, but I reserved my stomach space for dinner at home, or in one of Ìbàdàn's 'sharp corners'.

Saturday afternoon at OBJ's was however a different matter. Then the table went totally native: èbà, àmàlà, iyán, with half a dozen stews to choose from – this was where I first knew that food was more than simply getting something down in the stomach as fusslessly as possible, that eating actually involved a self-surrender that rendered homage to Òpápálà, the deity of hunger. The family – and this included his British wife, Barbara – ate! They consumed with a gusto that bordered on celebration – yes, the celebration of food. Michael Olumide, the involuntary instigator of the broadcasting hold-up, was a regular at the Saturday afternoon phenomenon. He matched Femi morsel for morsel but Femi, his napkin always tucked into his shirt-collar like a bib, had the edge on him. Lunch began at about one o'clock but rarely was the table cleared before four or five. It was true that in 1960 when I first witnessed Femi's weekend splurge, I had been away for four years, and perhaps I had forgotten that that was how people ate at home. But no, there was my own father as contrast, his picky style of eating. Even my mother, Wild Christian, who was a far more conscientious trencher lady – neither of them, and certainly none of the grown-ups around me, ate with such single-minded quantification. I watched the Johnson family in fascination – nothing in my childhood, adulthood or foreign sojourn had prepared me for such an elemental performance!

It became a challenge. I could not accept that even mere children – the oldest was then no more than twelve – should consume more than I did. I went without food for a full day before joining them, then two days, after which I refused to push that particular remedy any further. Would stomach exercises help? How did one expand one's stomach capacity – I had no idea. It always ended with my gasping for breath while Femi and others carried on as if the world of food was on the verge of extinction.

Next to the joy of eating however, was perhaps Femi's love of the city of Ìbàdàn and conversely, our shared, visceral recoil from the overgrown city of Lagos.

Lagos, opening up to a motorist from the interior like the fetid tail of a rooster on heat, was a city from which we both instinctively recoiled – quite unlike hundreds of thousands of Lagosians who swear that they cannot bear the provincialism of other towns – even of the large, beehive city of Ìbàdàn. For them, there is no life outside, or after Lagos!

The day that Femi formally repudiated Lagos and established himself as a *de facto* citizen of Ìbàdàn, the modern heartland of the Yoruba commercial world, was not too long after the end of the Civil War and my release from prison under Gowon's military rule. That he should take the precaution of entering in his will a wish to be buried in Ìbàdàn was a shock only to his family, not to those who truly knew him. I did not know the contents of his will, nor had he ever thought to mention any of its provisions to me, yet, an alternative to Ìbàdàn as his resting place was a possibility that my mind could not remotely contemplate when Femi collapsed in that city, but drew his last breath in a hospital in distant Frankfurt.

The end of the Nigerian Civil War in 1969 brought with it a false economic optimism that swelled the population of Lagos, the national and business capital, beyond rational management. What was already a city under stress had become a clear case of swarming, warring, multiple personalities, lacking all coherence or identity. If there was any character left to Lagos by the end of the sixties, it was that of a khaki and camouflage ubiquitousness, with the civilian *agbádá* and *babanriga*,[3] or a three-piece suited mendicancy that fawned on the former. Together, they squeezed Lagos until it choked on its own vomit, then stomped on the writhing corpse of a city whose human vitality was rivalled by none in all of black Africa.

Femi was still an employee of a brokerage firm – Law, Union and Rock – in charge of the branch office at Ìbàdàn. Then one day, he received a letter that would have set many Lagosian – or indeed provincial – minds aglow – he was not only promoted to a high executive position in the business, he was to take up this new position at the headquarters of the firm in Lagos. Uncertainly, with a visage that belied an elevation in status, and spoke more of a prison life sentence, Femi asked me to go house hunting with him. The quietude of Kaduna's prison solitary still dominated my response to crowded places and I had avoided Lagos since my release. The mere thought of that raucous, overwrought space set off alarms in my nervous system and I demurred. I found a hundred excuses – lectures, rehearsals, family impositions, unexpected overseas engagements etc. It soon became clear that my friend would keep putting off his search until I was free to go with him. There could be no more evasion – I got ready for my first visit to Lagos since my release from Kaduna.

It was, as I feared, a descent into imagined hell. All semblance of community had vanished. The noise, the frenzy, the disorder! This was a mere labyrinth of clogged alleys and overburdened streets, dark mounds of indeterminate sludge, tinsel imports on sales racks or in pedestrian motion, festering carrion, abused and abusive humanity that called itself a city. We inspected four or five houses, and I noticed that Femi's inspection grew more and more perfunctory, more fault-finding and downright dismissive. What went on in his mind, he did not tell but, for me, I was being driven through a built-up habitation of gaudiness and stench. Gutters were packed with garbage, and rivulets of gelatinous fluids overran

---

[3] The northern version of the agbada, usually made of stiffer material.

the streets. Motorised traffic meant a series of hiccups, a fractional circulation of the wheel each quarter hour, no more. The famous Broad Street, then renamed Yakubu Gowon Street, swarmed with a humanity that raced, lemming-like, to some destination of guaranteed perdition. Soldiers were in command everywhere, sheathed in khaki, more often than not a camouflage of ignorance and illiteracy, yet with the assumed carriage of a superior race, conquerors from an alien planet, masters of arbitrary humiliation. Ìta Fájì cemetery, a green area where multitudes once took shelter during their work break, or students read under the trees in daytime and under street-lighting all night, had vanished, made way for a monstrosity called the Lagos Secretariat.

Of course it did not all happen overnight, or begin with the military. The signs were already present at Independence time, when the famous Supreme Court, a masterpiece of tropical architecture, solidly constructed, with airy corridors, wide wooden-louvre windows and a warren of staggered rooms that allowed for the blissful circulation of air and people – was torn down limb by limb and erased from Tinubu Square. In its place was constructed a sterile fountain of cantilevered concrete pancakes – a gift, it was said, of the Lebanese community.

I was close to weeping in the year of Independence, 1960, as the metallic ball swung again and again against the stubborn walls that refused to yield without a fight. We had fought for the preservation of that building, pleaded that it be turned into a museum – if indeed a completely new Supreme Court building was required – but no, some purblind urban planner prevailed on his minister to decree that it make way for the Lebanese fountain whose brief span of gushing glory, its ascension day on the wings of a thousand doves – or pigeons – would diminish to a trickle, dry up altogether, then turn into just another garbage bin for shopkeepers and foodsellers. As for the pigeons that were let off to celebrate its opening, all had vanished in twos and threes. They were trapped by the locals and turned into pigeon kebabs. Reading their fates at the wheels of motorcars in Lagos rush-hour, and the makeshift weekend fires around Tinubu fountains, the rest took off to unknown spaces – probably back to the peace of the cedar groves of Lebanon.

The rot of Lagos had begun long before I vanished behind prison walls, but in the two years of my absence, plus a year after my release when I studiously avoided entering that city, Lagos had accelerated deep down into that pit of decay that is the complementary face of unplanned, greed-motivated development. A greed for unoccupied real estate produced the violation of virtually every available green space. The lush swathes of land in Ìkòyí, the residential retreat of the colonial elite, now enjoyed by the new black colonial aristocrats and lucky civil servants, were being torn up to raise more residences for the equally rapacious military elite who were steadily consolidating their grip on the nation. The famous, royal palm-tree lined 'Love Gardens' of Únìkan had lost nearly four-fifths of their territory. Lagos was choking with mimic high-rise buildings. The city no longer breathed, it coughed, sputtered and spat phlegm. Even the beach-front, the Marina, had been encroached upon all along its length. The oil boom had not been formally inaugurated, but it was clear that some people knew something that others did not, because it was simply illogical that so soon after a costly, inhuman war, there could have been such an accelerated pace of costly, quiltwork development of the capital city.

The canals that threaded Ìkòyí, Únìkan, bringing fishermen and even passengers to the markets of Sand Grouse at Úké Suna, flowed at a somnolent pace behind the police headquarters at Ọbálendé, opened into the lagoon behind the Broadcasting House and lapped the shores of the University of Lagos, were being sanded in, 'reclaimed'. Nothing but stubbornly retentive memory and nostalgia came to the rescue to serve as tenuous backcloth to my radio play, *A Scourge of Hyacinths* and its stage version – *From Zia with Love*, set in a prison overlooking a Lagos canal. A network of fly-overs was under frantic construction, its necessity justifiable perhaps, yet nothing but land greed demanded that the canals themselves should be sacrificed. This concrete burden slung across contracting land summarised the condition of the city – Lagos was collapsing on itself, suffocating the expanded road network that had to service a swollen administration, business and incessant building projects. Traffic circulation, guaranteed to crawl at any time of day throughout Lagos and its environs was the ultimate comment on the general stagnation.

At the time of the radio station 'escapade' in 1965, I was teaching at the University of Lagos, heading the Department of English. Always on the lookout for a residence that discouraged casual access by callers, I waited stubbornly until I could obtain a house on the outskirts even of Yaba, itself a surburb of Lagos. I found it in Igbòbí, a university-leased house that was tucked into a hidden green preserve. It was a place of utter tranquility, yet not very distant from the cacophony of Lagos. There were quiet back streets from Igbòbí to Akọ́kà, the lagoonside village that was home to the university, so I did not have to confront even the comparatively mild traffic of Yaba, and would be in my lecture rooms within a mere ten minutes of leaving home. A palm tree grew thoughtfully just outside my office window, serviced by a dutiful tapper. All I had to do was to hang a jar outside my window. The palm-wine tapper on his way down from the crown of the palm would tip his gourd into my container – undiluted, frothing fresh. I hung an object with a sinister appearance – leather, cowrie shells around a metallic lump – outside my window and warned him that if he dared dilute the palm wine that he dispensed for me with water, or spike it with saccharine, he would fall and break his neck – that is, if the ṣìgìdì [4] of the palm tree did not follow him home and suffocate him at night. He tried to laugh it off, but he believed me.

The university itself was a water-lapped oasis despite the choice of a ponderous boat-house architecture for its main buildings. The design itself was not at fault; it simply puzzled untutored minds like mine why anyone would wish to build huge sampans from concrete rather than from a wide choice of alternative light material, better suited to the tropics and the specific locality. Even if the cement had been donated free or dug directly from the shore, such an extravagant dominance of concrete was an oppressive waste, a contradiction also of the maritime environment. It gave the institution the character of an open fortress. Still, it appeared to perch convincingly, almost

---

[4] A succubus.

gracefully, on its water-bed, and one could hardly cavil at the overall houseboat motif of the central block. The surrounds were still wild enough to attract migrating birds, which made the vast wetlands behind the university a favourite stopover to wherever, and a private repose, a mere minute's walk from my office, the campus obliterated from sight and mind.

But the lagoon, regularly fished by the scantily clad fishermen with their flashing nets, was the answer to the suffocation of the rest of the two sections that made up Lagos - the mainland and the island. Whenever I found myself obliged to go into Lagos on any week day, I drove to campus, entered a canoe with an outboard engine, and would be at the Broadcasting House in Ìkòyí some ten minutes later. There, I commandeered a car from any one of my friends, conducted my business, returned the car and was back in the canoe and into the sanity of Aków̄à, then Igbòbí, all within one, two, or three hours. To make that same journey through the Yaba, then Lagos traffic, as I was obliged to do a few times, was the ultimate torture – it could last half the day.

Remorselessly, to the rhythm of pile drivers, the lagoon vanished, 'reclaimed', and traffic only succeeded in hiccupping through the streets. Lagos, after all, is essentially an island. Even the mainland part of it, Yábà, is still bordered by water, so it remained a mystery why even the rudimentary water transportation that existed from colonial times should have been gradually choked off. The regular ferry between Apapa and Lagos, which discharged workers and traders by the hundreds at fixed hours of the day, had been allowed to sink into decrepitude, operating in fits and starts, sometimes breaking down in the midst of the lagoon, endangering and even taking the lives of its passengers. Perhaps the military rulers had a phobia of water, certainly it would take years after the first military rule – under the civilian governorship of 1979 – before an attempt was made to resuscitate the obvious, generous and effective form of moving humanity and goods.

Femi's car inched and coughed our way through a virtually motionless traffic, as we attempted to view as many as possible on a list of available properties obtained from an estate agent. He was like a man being dragged to his execution. As we approached each prospective house, his shoulders sagged. They would lift only when he saw, or persuaded himself that he had seen some feature or the other that made the house unsuitable - then he became really jaunty. The environment was unfriendly, the ceiling was too low, the elevation of the stairs was for kangaroos, not humans, the interior finish was sloppy, it was too far from the offices, etc. etc. I followed him, totally indifferent to these masterpieces of Lagosian fortress architecture. Already, when you looked a house over, you began with its fortifications – armed robbery was yet to attain its full season of rage, but its tentative reaches were already felt by many. The coarsening of human sensibilities that accompanied the Civil War, both on the battlefront and behind the lines, was being foisted onto the general populace. Violence was palpable in the streets, hung over the bars across the windows, the chains and heavy padlocks from Hong Kong, a predatoriness that embraced the self-advertising rabble and 'area boys' who hung around the motor parks, and the oily business types who stepped out of the luxurious interiors of the latest car models.

It's no good turning to me for an opinion, I kept insisting – *I'm not the one who's going to live here. The bush is where I'm at home, so don't bother to ask me.* Finally Femi gave up, refused to tackle the remaining offers on his list. *You know, I think I'll let Barbara come and take a look at these others.*

Driving out of Lagos, I felt I had been released from prison a second time.

It was late into the night when my telephone rang. Femi of course. He could not sleep. "I've been talking to Barbara", were the first words I could make out, "and you know, she seems to agree with me."

"Agrees with you over what? And what bloody time of the night is this supposed to be anyway?"

"Since when did time matter to you? I thought you ascetic professors don't sleep."

"All right, all right, just tell me what you've woken me up for!"

"I don't want to go to Lagos."

"All right. Don't go."

"No, you haven't heard anything I've said. I'm thinking of leaving the company. You know, resign. Set up my own firm."

Now I was wide awake. "Leave Law, Union and Rock?"

"Yes. What do you think? Hey, ascetic professor, have you fallen asleep again?"

"I'm thinking, dammit"

"So. What d'you think?"

"Listen Femi, if I had a choice at all, I would never work for anybody. So I'm the wrong person to ask for an opinion. I am biased."

"So you agree I should leave Law Union?"

"I already know you're leaving." And I put down the telephone and went back to sleep.

Thus was the impulsive beginning of Femi Johnson and Company, the brokerage firm that would, less than ten years later, blaze skywards in panels of bronze tinted mirrors to attain consummation in the 'Golden Pillar'. That day in 1983, OBJ altered the landscape of Ìbàdàn for ever. It was not that it was the first 'skyscraper' – that privilege belonged to Cocoa House, raised as the cooperative headquarters of the Western Nigerian farmers. Both the Cocoa House and the new skyscraper were separated by less than four hundred yards and virtually stared each other in the face, waiting to see which would blink first. Cocoa House was of the old architectural style, concrete blocks and traditional windows. Femi's achievement was a pillar of gold, all thin steel and blind glass. It reflected the slums through whose intestines it had thrust itself, rising high above them in its dissociated glory. The Golden Pillar became an instant controversy – did such a statement of opulence belong in such a distressed environment? No matter, Broking House, as it was christened by its owner, had transformed the face of Ìbàdàn's commercial centre.

Rightly suspecting that I would disapprove of the scale of the project itself and the compromises that he had had to make with the Ìbàdàn politicians and city councillors to obtain approval

– not to mention the garish architectural style – he kept me deliberately in the dark. On his travels he had encountered this new trend in the urban, commercial landscape, and had dreamt of bringing the city of Ìbàdàn into the late twentieth century in one single, iconic gesture. He was however motivated by much more. The lament at the decay of public services was a constant refrain in most of our exchanges – the curse of Lagos had spread inland and affected vital commercial cities like Ìbàdàn. The oil boom, now in full rampage had meant, ironically, a deterioration in, and even total abandonment of the most elementary standards in the provision of, or maintenance of public amenities. Electricity was at best, epileptic. For water, even government offices relied on delivery by motorised tanks. Often those tankers' hoses were too short to reach the auxiliary tanks mounted on the tops of buildings, so the staff would come down and collect water in buckets which they then carried up flights of stairs – the lifts hardly ever worked – to be left in toilets for flushing. Femi's business required that he visit government secretariats, commercial centres, hospitals, universities, airports, harbours, etc.etc., assessing insurance claims or facilities that sought coverage. After such a visit of inspection he returned dispirited, appalled by the decay in infrastructures. A new building sprang up, was declared open amidst glitz and fanfare by the latest dignitaries and with increasingly extravagant social rituals. For about a month it remained a shining star in a mottled firmament and then gradually, inevitably, it became a slum. The walls acquired grime overnight, the pipes leaked and formed rust patterns everywhere and a familiar smell began to percolate the environment - the smell of humanity dying on its feet.

For my friend, this failure was an affront! Annually, he attended conferences of insurance brokers – London, Cairo, Nairobi, Rome, Cannes – somehow it came to settle in Cannes, year after year. Returning home to an economy that swam in oil revenue, generated vaster resources than its overseas counterparts, OBJ could not accept that a fraction of this resource was not pumped back into the physical structures to make them as efficient as the businesses they conducted. Privately, he resolved to demonstrate

that the run of this malaise could be interrupted. He would create
a model that countered the stereotype, but he revealed nothing to
me.

I watched his ventures grow. The world of business has
always been for me an exotic planet, and I was fascinated by his
meticulousness, his capacity for following up claims. I
accompanied him a few times, even while he worked with Law
Union and Rock, to inspect scenes of disaster that had resulted in
claims. Once it was a school in the remote outskirts of Ìbàdàn – a
village I had never heard of. It had been demolished in a
thunderstorm but, fortunately, the enlightened headmaster had
insured it some ten years before. We asked our way and lost it
again and again. Finally, we came to the final stretch that had
become impassable, thanks to rain floods. We could see the school
at a distance, perhaps only a wall still standing. The corrugated
iron sheets were stretched crazily over debris that looked more
like wooden crates and mud excavations. Immaculate in his white
shirt, tie and black brogues, the insurance-broker agent-inspector
all combined rolled up his trousers and waded through mud and
torrent. I followed, wondering why he had to make a jungle voyage
dressed in such inappropriate clothing. Until then, I had never
imagined the insurance business as extending beyond sitting
behind a desk of papers and negotiating claims.

Like a vicarious achievement of my own, I followed the expansion
of Femi's business from its modest, living-and-dining-room
beginnings, watched his credit soar among the banks and clientèle
through his meticulous handling of their claims, and his knack
for sniffing out shady propositions. Once, he trapped a Lebanese
businessman into admitting that he had driven his car onto the
Lagos-Ìbàdàn road and deliberately set fire to it. Another time, it
was a police commissioner who, forever after, would be referred
to as 'Mà á grateful sí ẹ'[5] or 'Úgún rè é!'[6] During the Western
uprising, his houses had been targetted and razed to the ground.
L-n quickly rushed to a crooked insurance broker, obtained a back-

---

[5] I shall show appropriate 'gratitude'.
[6] Ogun is my witness!

dated policy. Femi easily detected the forgery. He asked the police commissioner to drop by his office. A very civilised encounter followed; in the end L-n was forced – with all cordiality – to admit that the policy was issued after the event. Even so, the lawkeeper failed to accept that this created any problem. Only Femi stood between his application and approval by headquarters, and of course, if Femi played his part... the man removed his pistol from his holster, took the barrel between his teeth – no, not pointing down his throat, simply across his mouth – bit into it and called on the god of iron and oaths to witness an unbreakable pact, if Femi chose to play ball.

   "*Úgún rè é! Mà á grateful sí e.*
Poor man, he had only supplied the incorrigible raconteur yet another musical box, to be wound up – with exaggerated gestures and mimic variations – in both appropriate and only remotely relevant situations. Those who already knew the story were convulsed in laughter, but strangers to the story sometimes took fright. For, given the slightest excuse – perhaps in order to buttress a promise, in affirmation of some declaration, or simply illustrate a story – Femi would dive, virtually dive at a convenient metallic object and seize it between his teeth. It could be a letter opener, a piece of piping, a fork, knife, even a lamp stand – and this among the most staid of gathering, from Venezuela to Campostella – suddenly my friend leapt up, sank his teeth into the metallic juror as if he was suffering from a brainstorm and shouted – *Úgún rè é! Mà á grateful sí e!*

Mi ò rí ikú l'ojú e.[7] No, I did not. Not until that overcast day on the tarmac in Lagos, in 1987. Only then, as he was laid out on the stretcher, awaiting his transfer into the ambulance plane, was I suddenly seized with a premonition that Femi was taking his final leave of a world that often appeared to take its very vitality from his existence.

---

[7] I read no death in his eyes.

PART IV

Dining With the Devil... And an Avatar

Olórikunkun and
Orí Olókun

A Preamble on Menu, Service and Table Manners at the
Devil's Dinner Table

Dining with this breed of hybrid humanity – the military, in its earthly manifestation – is not without its problems, but not any that is insurmountable for those who are not truly hungry, unless of course one takes the view that experiencing acutely, albeit vicariously, the hunger of others can be considered a self-serving rationalisation. It is the easiest leap for those who believe, in any case, that there is a bit of the devil in most of us – *there but for the grace of God, go I* etc. Given half the chance, in a nation like Nigeria, I sometimes feel I would betray, with guaranteed provocation over critical choices, the dictatorial devil in me! One's social and moral responsibility, however, is to curb such a propensity – especially its abuses – not only in oneself, but in others. Ultimately, there is the question of motivation, and goals. I have had many good reasons to work up a good appetite for that diabolical repast, though I dare not deny that a number of such meals have left me with acute indigestion, symptoms of which persist till today!

A public cause, a clamorous need, sometimes imposes choices that appear, on the surface, to contradict one's democratic convictions and indeed, lifelong pursuit. The dilemma of dining with the devil, of cooperation, interaction, even of the most limited kind, with an unelected regime, will always remain a cross upon which committed democrats, reformers, radicals, etc., in any authoritarian corner of the globe, and especially the African continent, occasionally find themselves impaled. It is one that I have confronted quite openly, but resolved effortlessly and unapologetically – even arrogantly, as I was once accused by a television interviewer. What had nettled him was that I insisted that I did not owe him or any other mortal an explanation for my choice, since I considered all justifications superfluous when collaboration is clearly undertaken on behalf of – life, and even, occasionally, progressive politics, policies or creativity.

Or could he also have taken umbrage at my response when, accused of having 'sold out' to the military, I retorted, quite truthfully, that not even the entire Nigerian nation, with all its oil wealth, could afford me? That was one of the burdens that came with the Nobel – plain, matter-of-fact, commonplace declarations that did not raise an eyebrow during one's pre-Nobel existence, suddenly became problematic after that event - *oh, are you saying that because of... you are now bigger than the nation?* At such moments, one longs to tell the nation where to stuff its colonial pride-of-being. Mercifully, a rational commentator took time out to explain the obvious – WS meant simply that his convictions were not for sale.

That particular confrontation occurred over my role in creating a Road Safety Corps under a military regime, to stem the notorious haemorrhage on Nigerian roads, especially on the Ìbàdàn-Ifẹ̀ road. I named it the Slaughter Slab, since it was mostly on this macadam altar that I habitually scooped up my student's brains after filling them with knowledge. Issues of life and death constantly strike me as deserving of more than a genuine or merely rhetorical purism. Certainly I have never undergone any *angst* in this respect. I concede legitimacy to the uncompromising, no-contact position, whose validity may be equally argued, but it is a position that often strikes me as an unaffordable luxury on a continent like ours where the culture of militarised government appears to have developed a remarkable resilience.

Even in late 2002, the once democratic constant, Ivory Coast, underwent the once unthinkable – a military coup! Unthinkable? Ivory Coast's long sustained policy of exclusionism – *ivoirité*, the elegant word for the disenfranchisement of even fifth generation 'foreigners' – was a purulent boil that finally burst open, providing one military section a righteous cause for self-ingratiation into civic acceptance, albeit of a sectarian nature. Nigeria, with its recent exhilarating experience of exorcising the military incubus in 1999 has already undergone two scares. Still, the same Nigeria went on to play Big Brother, wielded a big cudgel in 2004 to terminate a military adventurism in Sao Tome. Not to be outdone, Guinea Bissau followed Sao Tome only a month or two later, while Togo, in the same West African region, attempted an original variant in 2005 – the military made a crude effort to install a son of the deceased dictator, Eyadema, in office, against the provisions of the constitution, simply to entrench surrogate military rule.

It boils down, ultimately, to one's personal confidence in determining the length of spoon with which one dines with the devil, and the ability to keep a firm hold on it. This involves deriving no advantages, no gains, no recompense in the process, if anything, expending oneself both materially and mentally for the attainment of a fixed and limited goal, retaining one's independence of action. Most delicious of all, the ability to walk away from the dinner table, flinging a coin on the table as a tip for the host.

There is a further consideration. In far too numerous African nations, the comparative index of brutality, contempt for the rule of law and abuse of human rights between some so-called democracies and military dictatorships leaves dubious space for absolutes. One has only to consider Kenyan 'democracy' under Arap Moi, or the stale tobacco ash-end of the Hitlerite Robert Mugabe of Zimbabwe, masquerading as a passion for land restitution. Within Nigeria, the lesson is served in the contrast between the 1975 military regime of a Murtala Mohammed on the one hand, and the 79/83 fascistic and wastrel 'democracy' of Shagari's NPN – and so on throughout the continent. Those who insist on inhabiting the real world find themselves subjected to the clamour of what can, and deserves to be extracted from usurped authority on behalf of a nation, on behalf of the non-statistical, palpable humanity that constitutes one's vital environment. For a temperament such as mine, it has never been possible to shunt aside – not for any prolonged period – a sense of rebuke of how much is lost daily, wasted or degraded, how much proves irretrievable, damaged beyond repair, through a position that confers the self-righteous comfort of a purist, non-negotiable distancing.

A line must be drawn however; across from mine will be found the murdering regimes – an Idi Amin, an Emperor Bokassa, a Sergeant Doe, a Mobutu... and of course, General Sani Abacha. Behind them are ranged those who forbid all planning for, discussion or anticipation of a return to democratic rule, setting the stage for life dictatorship – such as General Buhari. Other categories survive on individual assessment. Notwithstanding such finicky distinctions however, dining with the devil remains undeniably a mined board – prone to misunderstanding, betrayal, public skepticism, getting the fingers nicely toasted, mud all over one's face, etc. Sublime intentions are detonated by a diabolical joke – of which one promptly offers itself in all its madcap, cautionary amplitude – but first, a few paragraphs on the devil in that affair.

Some close associates have suggested that I secretly nurture a death wish. They base this claim on the fact that, despite what would appear single-minded efforts of one General Olusegun Obasanjo to push me beyond the borders of existence, we remain – albeit qualified – friends. I find it difficult to explain this undeniable paradox, except to shift the responsibility somewhere else and insist that, in some unfathomable way, Fate appears unbending in its resolve to throw us together – through events, mutual acquaintances, the frequent opposition and less frequent coincidence of interests, etc. – in and out of office. Of course one is never bereft of choice, but I also have a tendency - I have come to admit – to thumb my nose at the machinations of Fate, daring it to do its worst or else, understand that I also feel equally compelled to turn its interventions in a productive direction. Flirting with Fate and emerging relatively unscathed tends to go to one's head, however, which might partially explain why one appears to travel down the same mined road again and again.

Observing, and even interacting at close quarters, with someone who delights in being completely without scruples is frankly irresistible. One speaks here of a political leader who – to cite a notorious instance – graces the dedication of the new official residence of his senate president one night, dines, puts up a performance as the life and soul of the party, mixing gregariously and clowning with other guests, dances with the senator's wife, yet knowing all the while that he has already perfected the plot for his removal from office, which he executes a day or two after. Poor Chuba Okadigbo – he never quite recovered from that sneak mauling that his president awarded him. He died in 2004, a year and a half later, from pulmonary complications after a police tear-gassing during a rally to protest the rigging of Obasanjo's 2003 're-election', and some declared that this was partly due to a psychological enfeeblement from that earlier shock.

It could be a case of letting a writer's instinct take one too far but, perverse though it may seem, I have remained genuinely fascinated by a complex figure who is convinced that he dominates his environment – and thinks he acts the part – but is, basically, a fortunate recipient of the largesse of Fate. After all, how many soldiers, after the bulk of a civil war has been fought and won by others, find themselves positioned to receive the articles of surrender from the enemy, thus appropriating the mantle of the architect of victory? Not one to leave any loopholes in his claims to that laurel, however, the soldier signals his entry into yet another turbulent profession – that of the writer – by producing one of the fastest war histories ever written – *My Command* – remaining blithely indifferent to some furious rebuttals of details by his comrades-in-arms.

Through a regional balancing in military politics – not from deserving, such as participation in the critical coup – the same minion of Fate becomes the No. 2 in the next military regime. The No. 1 is assassinated after only six months in office, and the war hero becomes head of state by default – and not just of any banana republic, but of the most populous, wealthiest nation on the African continent. He escapes the fate of his predecessor and ends a high casualty career, unscathed, in grateful retirement to his farm, escorted into our shared hometown, Abẹ̀òkúta on a white horse, drums and bugles. All agree that the honour is deserved, since, unlike most African leaders, he voluntarily relinquishes power. The gesture catapults him onto international notice. Thereafter he settles back into civilian life, but not quite, since he begins diligently to lay the ground work - establishes an African Leadership Forum, etc. – for becoming a respected statesman, mixing with the powerful at international fora and hosting them in turn on his Ọ̀tà farm.

The saga has not ended. Fate again intervenes and the hero finds himself arraigned before a brutal dictator, one General Sani Abacha, on treasonable charges, earns a death sentence that would be commuted to a lengthy prison spell. A little more than two years of prison life, and his persecutor is assisted into eternity in a subtle palace conspiracy – never mind any claims of his succumbing to excess sexual ecstasy. All this takes place without his lifting a finger. The military, thoroughly discredited as a ruling class and beset by international ultimatums, realise that their time is up, but have no intention of giving up power. And so our hero – now an accredited civilian – is released from prison, formally pardoned, pressed back into service, but now as an 'elected' civilian president.

I suppose I subconsciously acquired the attitude that, as a writer, I had proprietary rights over such a phenomenon and, since he was already indebted to me by an act of treachery on his part, began to regard him as a private preserve for compensatory study. In any case Obasanjo is quite personable – much of the time – and it was not difficult to respond to his evident desire for cerebral company – like most rulers, he desperately wanted to be accepted as a political and economic strategist, and thinker. Was I evincing a touch of masochism? Or perhaps the death-wish proposition of my colleagues? No matter, our hero represented a model of power of an unusual – and dangerous – kind, most especially as he remains basically insecure, and thus pathologically in need of proving himself – preferably at the expense of others. That is one unambiguous assessment that is pronounced by nearly all Obasanjo's acquaintances – superiors, close friends, military colleagues, mistresses and adversaries. Interacting with him at close quarters thus implicated – again, at a subconscious level – testing one's confidence in one's own invulnerability, somewhat like those traditional charms that warriors swear by as bullet deflectors – they wore the charms, but still ensured that no one was pointing a gun at them.

Also, to my intense chagrin, I have been forced to conclude that even advancing years have failed to eliminate from my system a parental inheritance – a missionary streak. Detecting a productive, even sometime imaginative glint in the compost of the soldier-turned-politician is not difficult – Obasanjo is a man of restless energies – and a waste of human potential is something against which a missionary upbringing revolts. A bullish personality, calculating and devious, yet capable of a disarming spontaneity, affecting an exaggerated country yokel act to cover up the interior actuality of the same, occasionally self-deprecatory yet intolerant of criticism, this general remains a study in the outer limits of compulsive rivalry, even where the fields of competence or striving are miles apart.

A deprived childhood, like Obasanjo's, on his own admission, also makes for some measure of indulgence – at least in explaining his deep-seated sense of insecurity. When the need to prove oneself degenerates to obvious sadism however, one is obliged to compare him with his own town mate – Moshood Abiola. Both had the same deprived background, attended the same school, yet differed drastically in openness and generosity. It is significant that Olusegun Obasanjo, since he became an elected Head of State over the corpse of the popularly elected Abiola – who breathed his last under confinement by the same Abacha – finds himself physically unable to utter the name of his thwarted predecessor, even in official speeches. The ex-General routinely dismisses all proposals to raise a memorial to the politician, and these include the resolution of the Nigerian legislature that the Abuja sports stadium be named after a man who was formally crowned 'Africa's Pillar of Sports', by the Organisation of African Unity.

Perhaps it is this sense of rivalry, the fear of being surpassed, even by ghosts, that thoroughly defines the personality of the

General. While, for instance, the majority of the nation clamoured for, and some states continue to mark, June 12 as Democracy Day– that day in 1993 when a disciplined people went to the polls, united in the resolve to terminate military rule – Olusegun Obasanjo persists in imposing May 29th on the nation, this being the date, in 1999, when he was sworn into office after his emergence from prison. A veteran journalist, Kola Animashawun, writing in *The Vanguard*, summed up the General who came back from the dead in a unique expression: "….his ego is bigger than his head."

The size of the General's ego was not uppermost in my mind however, when *I* invited myself to dinner with this Head of State in 1978. When a prize such as *Orí Olókun*, the long lost bronze head of a principal Yoruba deity, shimmers so alluringly within the sight of an *Olóríkunkun*,[1] one may be forgiven for forgetting the long spoon, even in full knowledge that a swishing tail may be hidden beneath the khaki uniform.

Teaching at Yale University some years after this misadventure, I found myself neighbour to the *àṣẹ* [2]-driven scholar, Robert Farris Thompson. He taught African Art history, and generally did his best to infect his colleagues and students with whatever Yoruba spirit of possession had presided over his birth – possibly even conception. If Robert had his way, a pilgrimage to the land of the Yoruba would be a condition for everyone who wished to become an alumnus of Yale or indeed, any higher institution in the United States. Thompson had the same enthusiasm for certain kinds of music and films – and this was how I came to see what was at the time considered a 'cult' film – *Raiders of the Lost Ark*. Since the attraction of *Raiders of the Lost Ark* had temporarily displaced the shrine of *Òrìṣà* in Thompson's mental habitation, my curiosity was aroused. And thus, one afternoon, I set out to watch the film in the company of my once student, then colleague, Henry-Louis (Skip) Gates, Jnr.

---

[1] Literally, a stubborn head.
[2] The word of mystic potency. The invocatory pronouncement that brings into being.

I regret to say that I did not enjoy the movie. From the opening sequences, I began to squirm. It was as if, albeit on a drastically reduced scale – no competitive spectacle, cliff-hanger risks or lethal pyrotechnics – I was nevertheless watching a souped-up documentary of one of my better forgotten undertakings. My feeling throughout was that I had been deliberately set up to be lampooned by Steven Spielberg in the story-line, without even the consolation of a love angle. I was grateful for the darkness that covered my 'blushes'.

The beginnings were near identical. I was indeed close to the end of a seminar in my office when the departmental secretary entered and announced that some colleagues were waiting to see me, and on an urgent matter. I dismissed my class a few minutes early – no, unlike *Raiders of the Lost Ark*, there was no lubricious student bursting at the boobs who sidled up to leave me with a long caressing look and a lascivious invitation – and ushered in my visitors. There were three of them – Akin Isola, a playwright and professor in Yoruba studies, Wande Abimbola, another professor in Yoruba, an academic as well as practitioner of the mysteries of *Ifá*, the Yoruba system of divination, and Olabiyi Yai of Linguistics, a Yoruba whose nationality of the Republic of Benin served yet again to remind one of the disservice that the European powers did to the African continent in their arbitrary division of that continent into so-called national entities. How could I have failed, by the way, after watching *Raiders of the Lost Ark*, to be struck by the coincidence that it was yet another professor of the Yoruba extended family – Farrell Thompson – who was responsible for my presence in the theatre, or that I was watching this sumptuous take-off on my own escapade in company of yet another scholar, Skip Gates, who was undergoing his own phase of Yorubaphilia in the persona *of Èṣù* the deity of the random factor, of reversals, and quirky messenger of the deities!

Back to 1978 and Ifẹ̀ campus however, it turned out that my visitors had come to solicit my help in an unusual undertaking. Why me? First of all, they were aware that I did have some kind of access to the then military Head of State, Olusegun Obasanjo, and this was a matter that required cooperation at the highest possible level of government. Next, there was the matter of the recently concluded Black and African Arts Festival, the notorious jamboree that had guzzled millions of dollars and earned the nation the ire of at least half of the visitors to that festival for its shoddy preparations. Perhaps the single most significant event of that festival however was one that never did take place. This was the repatriation of the original of the symbol – and logo – of that festival, chosen in the confident belief that it would be released by its keepers and put on display.

The famous ivory mask from Benin, exquisitely carved and detailed, remained safely ensconced in the vast labyrinths of the British Museum. It had been looted in the equally famous sacking of the Benin Kingdom by a British expeditionary force in late nineteenth century, launched in reprisal for an earlier humiliating and fatal encounter between a Captain Phillips and King Ovoramwen, the paramount ruler of the Benin Kingdom whose ancestry, one line of legend insists, was none other than Yoruba! The Phillips expedition had insisted on being received in audience by the king during one of his most sacred retreats, when the oba was not permitted to see any strangers. His Majesty's Britannic servants were not to be denied however, and they forced their way into the city, with gruesome consequences. Such insolence was not to be countenanced! Orders were issued to mount a punitive expedition, and they were carried out with equally gruesome efficiency. Numerous treasures, the spoils of war were shipped back to England – to offset the cost of the war, the British dispatches stated, with admirable candour. Among them was the ivory mask, the alleged head of a Benin princess.

Now, in 1975, the Nigerian Minister of Culture, a scion of the Benin Kingdom – none other than Chief Anthony Enahoro – felt that this was an opportunity to bring back at least one of those treasures. The diplomatic bag was scorched to and fro with dispatches from both sides – at least *lend* us the damned thing for the duration of the festival, pleaded Nigeria! Nothing doing, said the British Museum. The British government was of course 'powerless to intervene' – the autonomy of the British Museum being regretfully but conveniently cited as the insurmountable obstacle. Condescending arguments – such as the Nigerian nation lacked the means, will, or sense of value required to preserve its precious heritage – require no comment.

I had not stinted words, alas, in expressing my umbrage at both sides – against the British government for its hypocritical double-talk, and against our own caretakers, a supposed military regime, for its uncreative approach. From the moment that the Nigerian government requested the return of the mask, all was lost! The British government would never part with it, since it would only set a precedent for demands for a wholesale repatriation of all art treasures plundered by colonial forces, to their rightful homes. Indeed, in a moment of righteous rage at ancient wrongs, I went so far as to offer advice that the government should stop drawing further attention to the mask since it would only place its illegal guardians on the alert. The mask was stolen property, and the aggrieved had a right to reclaim their property by any means. What I proposed instead was that a task force of specialists in such matters – including foreign mercenaries if necessary – be set up to bring back the treasure – and as many others as possible – in one swift, once-for-all-time, coordinated operation.

Since that unheeded advice, in 1984, a live trophy in the shape of a former minister, the infamous Umaru Dikko, has been kidnapped from London, bundled to Stansted airport, crated and loaded into a cargo plane awaiting repatriation to Nigeria. It was an amateurishly planned, clumsily executed operation under the regime of General Buhari, and yet it could have succeeded but for the accident that Dikko's live-in mistress happened to have watched it all from the window. She had the presence of mind to take down both the number and description of the car, even before alerting the police. The ineptness of the kidnappers – who had spent months studying Umaru Dikko's movements – could be summed up in the fact that they failed to notice that his mistress routinely waved him goodbye from an upper window when he left the house in the morning. The police found the drugged minister in his crate, together with an Israeli doctor whose task was to pump him full of sedatives at intervals on the flight back to

Nigeria. The majority of the nation was waiting to welcome him, even more enthusiastically than the military.

Spiriting away the Benin mask for FESTAC – the 1977 Festival of Black and African Arts – in good time for the opening of the festival would have been much easier, cost much less and would have redressed, albeit symbolically, an ancient wrong. I was quite ready to be part of the team. The potential consequences seemed trivial, considering the prize. If we were caught, we would simply fight the case all the way to the International Court of Justice at The Hague, bringing the issue of ownership of objects of colonial plunder to the fore on a global level. I had no idea what the inside of British gaols were like, but I could not imagine them being any worse than the ones in which I had been confined in Kirikiri, Ìbàdàn or Kaduna. That repatriation proposal had stuck in the minds of some of my colleagues, agitated now by the discovery of a missing art treasure that belonged to Ilé-Ifè.

Into my office they filed – Olabiyi Yai, small, dark and wiry, behind heavily rimmed glasses; Wande Abimbola, only slightly taller, soft face and gestures, a facial immobility that would sometimes waver between bewilderment and a cunning watchfulness; and Akin Isola, bearded, outstanding cicatrices carved into his light-complexioned skin, a creative writer in his own right and Yoruba philologist. He would later translate my play, *Death and the King's Horseman*, 'back into the Yoruba' from which, Isola insisted, it had originally taken form in my head. Their aspects were so uniformly solemn that I was prompted to ask whose turn it was among our colleagues, such was the regularity with which the infamous slaughter slab – the road between Ifè and Ìbàdàn ate us up. But no, it was not the road on this occasion. The subject was *Orí Olókun,* the famous bronze head of Ifè whose career had turned rather murky since Leo Frobenius, the German adventurer and archeologist, first dug up this ancestral representation nearly half a century earlier.

Olókun – literally the owner, or the god of the seas – was the consort of *Údùduwà*, the twain thus seen as primogenitors of the Yoruba, the black race, and indeed, of all humanity. If Údùduwà was sent to earth by *Olódùmarè* – the Supreme Deity – to directly create and animate earth, Olókun, his consort, performed a parallel task for the seas and the oceans. And yet, as is common to the nature of numberless deities, Olókun is often mythologised and represented also as male. Their offspring *Ọ̀rànmíyàn* (or *Ọ̀rànyàn*) roamed far and wide from the ancestral home, Ilé-Ifẹ̀, to found a Yoruba kingdom whose numerous branches he handed over to his countless offspring.

Other legends differ wildly – it was the Edo Kingdom of Benin that was founded by Ọ̀rànmíyàn, not just any other Yoruba kingdom. And Olókun was brother to Ọ̀rànmíyàn, not his mother.... and so it goes, as is the world of myth and legend. The famous stone plinth, *Ọpá Ọ̀rànyàn,* still stands in Ilé-Ifẹ̀, and is held to mark the burial place of that warlike brother, or merely a cenotaph, indicating the spot from which he vanished. The ancestral link between the Edo and the Yoruba is undisputed however, and it has remained part of the Benin coronation tradition that any new monarch first travel to Ilé-Ifẹ̀ – or is sent a spiritual emissary from Ifẹ̀ – to secure or transmit blessings from his ancestral fount.

Úgún, my patron deity, is the son of *Ọ̀rànmíyàn*, through his principal consort, *Ìṣẹ̀dálẹ̀*, and is thus the direct grandson of Olókun. Beyond legend and mythology therefore, I had a personal stake in the fate of Olókun whose spiritual descendant – through Úgún – I have long accepted myself to be.

Together with some companion figures, *Orí Olókun* – the head of Olókun – was traditionally buried in the courtyard of Ifẹ̀ palace by the priesthood, brought out only at his annual festival when it was ritualistically washed, honoured, and then returned to its resting-place until the next outing.

Leo Frobenius (*The Voice of Africa*) narrates his moment of rapture when, during an excavation, a pick wielded by one of his assistants struck metal. Work was stopped. Carefully scraping off the soil with his hands, he finally held in his hand a piece that the pick had chipped off the cheek of the bronze. After that, his account is filled with negotiations for the sale of this and other bronze pieces, the news of his find filtering to the British colonial officer in Lagos, a chase by that rival which ended just at the Nigerian side of the border with Dahomey (now Republic of Benin) and finally his summary dispossession of this invaluable piece by that representative of His Majesty's government. Frobenius claimed that the tiny bronze piece that was chipped from Olókun cheek was his sole surviving souvenir of his monumental find.

The question that surfaced, decades later however, was this: just what artifact was it that the British civil servant snatched from Frobenius? The real *Orí Olókun*? Or a substitute by the wily German explorer and collector?

An *Orí Olókun* was on display at the Ifẹ̀ Museum, but any serious art or archeology student knew this to be a travesty. The whereabouts of the real head had long remained the subject of much speculation, with no real agreement on the subject, but its loss continued to rankle in a few knowledgeable minds. As if to place one in a state of permanent aggravation, the image that had been adopted for a national stamp had been taken from the fake head in the Ifẹ̀ Museum. Across the waters from the West African coast, a piece that was either the original, or its identical twin, had been reproduced on postcards which are still on sale at the British Museum.

More intimately galling to the university community at Ilé-Ifẹ̀ – at least, those whose disciplines touched upon such matters – was that it was the Ifẹ̀ Museum simulacrum, a piece of unparalleled ugliness, that was used – just as on the postage stamp – as the icon of the university crest. To this peeved community also belonged the ancients of Ifẹ̀ who had known the real *Orí Olókun*, and were subjected to the indignity of occasionally seeing the fake piece proudly displayed in its glass case in the museum of Ilé-Ifẹ̀. Compared to the classical proportions of the real head – colour plates of which appear in a number of books under speculative, indeed sometimes deliberately obscurantist notes - the museum piece is squat, amateurish and misproportioned. Among our circle, it earned only contempt, captured in the nickname that was bestowed on it in a fit of disgust – *Ìpàkọ́ ẹlẹ́dẹ̀* – the back of a pig's head. And now these three dons – one of whom was the author of that apt nickname – were seated in my office, facing me across the desk, quietly informing me that they not only now knew where the real *Orí Olókun* was hidden, but also who had taken it away!

Brecht, Genet, Cheikh N'dao or whoever it was that had occupied my last hour or two vanished into nothingness or irrelevance. The university itself ceased to exist or perhaps, more accurately, it shed its ivory tower pretensions, and finally justified its existence. The walls of my office dissolved in mists of ancient legend, turning my three interlocutors briefly into three sons of *Ùdùduwà*. From across time, I heard only their plea for the restoration of their being, *my* being, to its original repleteness. I could already see that usurper, *Ọgbẹ́ni Ìpàkọ́ ẹlẹ́dè* being finally thrown on the dung-heap where it belonged and a triumphal procession along the ancient route, accompanied by all the purification rituals, ending with the setting of the authentic representation on the mini-podium of the museum. What a feast would fittingly accompany this return! I was outwardly impassive – an instinctive freeze, I have since learnt, takes over at such moments – so impassive, that my visitors thought that they had failed to arouse my interest. Inwardly however – if only they knew! – I was dancing to some music, a sublime music of the spheres into which their words were absorbed as lyrics even as they were uttered, for what the threesome were actually suggesting was that *Orí Olókun* could, and should be brought home!

"...you see? We recalled that you expressed a very strong opinion about the way the problem of the FESTAC mask was handled." The reminder brought me back to the present. "We were wondering – and the dean of faculty agrees, we discussed it with him and he urged us to speak with you – well, considering your closeness to the Head of State... maybe some way could be found to bring back *Orí Olókun*."

I found my voice somehow. "And where exactly is it now?"

I could not believe our luck! *Orí Olókun*, these colleagues were telling me, was not locked up in a national museum with fortifications, guards, electronic monitoring devices, criss-crossing laser beams, robotic strangler guards, etc., but was displayed in a private gallery, not even a public one but a kind of studio-gallery, owned by a famous artist-cum-architect! They had known this for a year, and they claimed to know who had spirited the bust out of the country. There were some pertinent questions to be asked however, such as:

"If you knew this a year ago, why are you coming out with it only now?"

"Well, we were keeping a kind of watching brief. We didn't quite know what to do after Labiyi brought the news. We thought of confronting Pierre – since he admitted taking it out – but decided that it might result in his alerting the possessor, who is a very close friend of his. And the head would disappear once again, maybe this time for ever – at least in our lifetime. But now, he's leaving the university and that link would be lost..."

Olabiyi had been teaching in an exchange programme at the University of Sao Paulo. Pierre Verger, a reputed ethnologist – indeed perhaps the pioneer of Yoruba ethnological studies in South America – *Dieux d'Afrique,* etc. – had been a visiting scholar in the Congos, in France, Brazil and in West Africa while any of us was still padding towards primary school in bare feet and snotty noses. Yai had met Pierre at a party given by the alleged possessor, the architect Carybe, in Bahia. Let Biyi take up the narrative.

"The party was held in the gallery which is actually at the back of the main house, but detached from it. You gain entrance to it by a separate external staircase, quite high up. The gallery contained not merely Carybe's works, finished or in various stages of completion – canvases, designs as well as sculptures – but art pieces from all over the world. Seated on one of the shelves was – my eyes were simply tugged there, directly – *Orí Olókun!* The *real* thing! You noticed the difference at once. This was nothing like that abortion sitting in Ifè Museum. Beautiful. The proportions were unmistakable. I could only gasp with disbelief – but I said nothing.

"All evening, my mind was in turmoil. How on earth did it get there? We all continued to make small talk, but I had only the one thing on my mind. Who spirited it out? How long had it been stored away on that shelf? Well, as the evening wore on, I found myself seated on the stair landing, just outside the gallery. I was joined there by Baba – Pierre – and then I simply could not keep it to myself any longer. I asked him if he had noticed the bronze head and he said he had. I asked 'Is that not *Orí Olókun?*' and he nodded. So I said, 'What of the head sitting in a glass case in Ifẹ̀?' Pierre snorted, 'But everyone knows that's a fake. What you see on that shelf is the authentic head.' Well, I decided that, since he was so forthcoming, I might as well ask the next question – 'How did Carybe get hold of it?'

"That was when he put his finger to his lips – exactly like this – and said, 'S-sh. Don't tell anyone but – I brought it here' "

I was numbed. Pierre? Yai continued:

"At that moment, I decided that I had already betrayed too much curiosity. So I mumbled something like 'Really?' And he re-affirmed it. I tried my best to look as if it was really no concern of mine, looked for some way to change the subject, and we both continued with our drinks on the landing."

My other two visitors nodded to confirm that the story was as they had heard it already. Abimbola added, "He kept it to himself until he returned to the country, and then he confided in us."

"Over the past year we've kept returning to the subject, tossing around one course of action after the other," Isola said.

"But it could have disappeared from there in the meantime", I interjected, pointing out the obvious.

"Ye-es," conceded Labiyi. "But I don't think so. Carybe struck me as one of those collectors who simply enjoy the thrill of having something like that in their possession. You know, just having it there. Think for how long we've had that *ìpàkọ́ ẹlẹ́dẹ̀* in the museum – that tells you roughly for how long he and Pierre have had the real thing in their custody. If they'd wanted to sell it or dispose of it anyhow, they'd have done so before now."

That made sense. And in any case, what mattered was that we now had a lead. We had a sighting that was less than two years old, we had a physical location, we had a live witness, a confession, and the transporter of stolen goods was right on campus. The trail, in comparison to past chases, could be held to be unseasonably warm.

"It's a delicate situation," I commented. "Pierre has a formidable reputation all over the world – including right here, within our own academia. We are all friends of his."

"It is tricky," Akin admitted.

"And he's a foreign national," Olabiyi Yai added.

"That's why we think it should be handled from the very top. Somehow we must get the Head of State involved."

Here followed a long silence, generated mostly from my side. What was going through my mind was, needless to say, my earlier, hardly edifying encounters with this very Head of State. Against the universal wisdom that cautioned, 'Once bitten, twice shy' were ranged the summons of the ancient head of a mythical ancestor – *Orí Olókun!*

We had mended fences since the Civil War, had achieved a large measure of reconciliation, thanks to our mutual friend, Aboyade and my role in the '77 Festival of the Arts. First, in response to his plea, I had saved the festival from collapse by a successful appeal to President Leopold Senghor to bring his country, Senegal, back into the festival after a difference of opinion – this had to do with the ideological ordering of the central event, the Colloquium, and it resulted in Senegal's withdrawal, and a threatened boycott by the francophone countries. Next, I also withdrew on a different matter of principle – the chairman of the festival, Admiral Fingesi, insisted on overriding decisions of assigned experts, remaining locked within military dictatorial arrogance and cultural ignorance. Finally however, with the two-week long festival having turned into an organisational debacle, I was prevailed upon to return and stage a closing event. It proved successful, fortunately, wiped out some of the sour taste in the mouths of most of the visitors, and sent them to their various homes with a much tempered memory of their overall experience. Obasanjo had been very moved by the finale, and grateful for the unexpected reprieve of the national image – indeed, his childlike appreciation was quite touching, revealing an unexpected aspect of the soldier.

All that did not mean however, that I was prepared to put my life in the hands of this erratic being and, thinking of what – I knew immediately – we had to do, there could be no room for a dubious ally to the rear. The four of us in that room shared the same thought – this was no situation that could go the diplomatic route – the lesson from FESTAC had made that clear – someone had to go over to Brazil and take back what was ours. If anything went wrong, we needed the full weight of a government behind us.

I saw my colleagues to the door, promising to let them know within a day or two what course I had decided upon. The first step did not require much thinking – I called up our intermediary, Aboyade – who was always equipped with his latest secret telephone number – and asked him to arrange an urgent meeting with our awkward friend, stressing that it was nothing I could discuss over the telephone. He obtained a meeting for that weekend. For me, work was over for the day, possibly for the rest of the week. My mind had begun to oversee details of an unorthodox mission, and I knew it would not admit any other thought until every step – with all likely variations – was clearly laid out.

We met in his Dodan Barracks residence. For once, this was a brainstorming dinner that could accommodate only one topic. Obasanjo's Úwu eyes twinkled with mischief and glowed with the ardour of a race warrior. By the following morning, a task force had emerged – his Foreign Minister, Adefowope, and an Ambassador Fagbenle, nicknamed 'Docky'. We agreed that Olabiyi Yai and I should travel to Brazil, locate the quarry if it was still in Bahia and if possible, bring it back. *If* possible? I had already resolved that if *Orí Olókun* would simply do its own part and manifest itself to my eyesight, it would end its exile almost immediately, journey back in the diplomatic bag to its home on that usurped podium of Ifè Museum!

I did not however allow the feast of love with this uncertain ally to smother my instincts. Matters could go awry, and we would find the ruler of a hundred million people losing no sleep over the loss of two citizens. Obasanjo, I knew, was capable of ordering his foreign minister to negotiate with Brazil to keep us in one of its gaols for a few years until the scandal blew over, maybe as a condition for continuing trading relations between the two nations. That knowledge was sufficient safety – it was left to me to negotiate our own insurance policy in advance. I insisted not only that we would travel on diplomatic passports, but that the ministry must issue a letter to our embassy in Brasilia, instructing its diplomats to 'lend all necessary assistance to bearers' who would be arriving there on a confidential mission. I would copy and store those letters before departure. In the meantime, the university should take on the responsibility of 'administratively' delaying Pierre Verger's departure, ensuring that he did not arrive in Brazil while we were there. How that was done, 'Docky' shrugged, was up to us.

Back on campus, I plunged into the surrounding bush for the routine of sorting out my thoughts. It was clear that, over the recovery of *Orí Olókun*, I was prepared to dine with the lord of the satanic kingdom himself, even without the aid of the long spoon. I was more than ready to make a Faustian pact – sell my soul in return for that hollowed but weighty mass, hallowed by my history!

I would have preferred to spend a full weekend in one of my deepest hunting grounds, day and night, but that indulgence had to make way for the urgency of preparations. An afternoon retreat into the campus bushes had to suffice. Calmly, sheltered from all human interruption, I considered what we were about to do. Why was I at forty-four plunging into these melodramatic waters with both feet, and fully clothed? I had never been to Brazil, knew that country only for its large population of Yoruba descendants, mostly mestisised from the slave era, their preservation of the world of the òrìṣà whose faithful looked towards Ilé-Ifẹ̀ as their origin. It was in Brazil that the Yoruba world had most penetratingly captured the soul of the Americas to the South, in addition to the Caribbean islands – Cuba, Haiti, Dominica, Jamaica. The òrìṣà are still alive in Brazil – their rites, their liturgy, their sacral calendar, their suffusion of popular consciousness, how much more in the pristine forests of the continent that originally spawned these deities!

It is not everywhere that one feels the pulse of the òrìṣà, nor are all their pulsations the same. Away from human habitation, for instance, in the moist forests, one experiences their emanations largely in a serene mode, osmotic and intimate; in others, they are far more abrasive, intrusive, even querulous. The micro-climates of the western part of Nigeria often astonish with their quilt work variety of growth. Tropical vegetation, home to pristine groves, sheers abruptly away into savannah. Next, with equal abruptness, savannah becomes brushland where the land is brittle with movement, albeit restrained. There, the slightest breeze is a prelude to raspy motions, and one can almost hear the scurrying of ants, inviting dialogue with the intruder or launching questions – in such terrain, one is almost prepared to see the contumacious deity, Èṣù, metamorphose from an anthill, perch atop its mud spire, full of impish designs against the world. Within tropical lushness, my preferred haven for meandering, time stands still, consciousness is muted. One is enfolded in the amplitude of Nature where the incongruities of existence are dissolved or absorbed into numinous forces of which each deity stands wordless medium. In these close forests, intuition reigns supreme.

No worshipper at any shrine, I do not hesitate to extract from those moments in the forest – after an internal review of events – either an admonishment and urge to desist from a course of action, or an end to all vacillation, buttressed with a pledge of absolution. I feel welcomed by, and integrated with forces that sit in silent contemplation over the acts of men, judging or merely marvelling. In the lair of deities I reminded myself that we were about to embark on a mission of restitution. In the compressed time at my disposal, there was no indulgence in prolonged contemplation, much less meditation – whatever measures we took in good faith had the blessing of all the òrìṣà, and would readily answer the laws of humanity. I had taken the precaution of leaving my night lamp behind, so there was no temptation to spend the night roaming the woods. There was time left only for practical tasks, and these included hours of collective research in the university library, looking into whatever else had been written since Frobenius' encounter with Orí Olókun.

Four days later, Yai and I were on our way to Rio de Janeiro, then straight on to Brasilia. A message had gone ahead of us and we were met by a representative from the embassy. Between Yai and myself I do not recall that we had any cash that amounted to much. I had taken all the foreign currency in Femi Johnson's possession – it was not much, unfortunately. There was my credit card which, thank goodness, was not too severely depleted. Nevertheless, we would have to conserve its credit balance as tightly as possible, leaving as much as we could for emergencies. The embassy in Brasilia paid our hotel bill, but that was all. From then on, we were on our own.

I had barely time to observe what an artificial city Brasilia was, stroll through the authentic 'people's quarters' – the humanised space – for about an hour before our flight was due to leave for Bahia. I was not interested in sight-seeing anyway, my mind being focussed on the distant gallery of an unsuspecting architect, and the squatters on its shelves as described by Labiyi. From one of those shelves, the bust of *Orí Olókun* beckoned, awaiting rescue and a rapturous welcome home. Nothing else had much reality.

We needed as much independence of movement as possible and so, in Bahia, I hired a Volkswagen Beetle, mentally adding up the debit on that card with unaccustomed meticulousness. The story we had decided upon was that we were on an official mission to find a local architect who would collaborate in the re-designing of the Nigerian embassy. I bought a camera, insisting on a bag that was designed more for a large cine-camera than a still version. We would take photos of the buildings that were designed by Carybe – it all lent seriousness and genuineness to the cover of the mission.

With Yai map-reading, I drove into town, marvelling at the interminable stretch of beaches, packed with humanity. It was the first time I had seen such a continuous stretch of sand, every square inch of it populated by a throng of sun-worshippers, a chocolate gradation of skin tones that virtually ate up the white sands. Gradually we discovered that we had arrived on a holiday. It would appear that, at every drop of a work-free hour, the

Brazilians repair like lemmings to the beaches. We drove into Bahia – it was virtually empty.

Rooms had been booked ahead of our arrival by the embassy. The moment we deposited our bags, we headed for Carybe's home to do some reconnoitering. There was no one at home – he had also joined the rest of Brazil in their weekend homes – certainly somewhere along the beaches. The residential area where the house was situated was almost uniformly deserted. We drove up and down, I with my camera, taking pictures of the neighbourhood, for all the world like students of architecture, or selective tourists. The residential part of Carybe's home was a low bungalow, next to the road. Set far back was the gallery, its top floor visible over the wall of the compound. I could see the stairs leading up to it, the upper flight and its landing starkly exposed.

"You're sure that sculpture is up there, beyond that door we're looking at?"

"Oh, yes."

I sighed. It had to be! I thought, if the gallery had been on terra firma, not suspended above the walls between earth and sky, tantalising two criminals from the African continent, we would have returned at night, scaled the wall, broken in and retrieved our property. Labiyi had assured me that there were no burglar alarm systems. It was a quiet, middle-class area, crime free – well, that was about to change. Nevertheless, we returned at night, hoping that maybe, just maybe...

No, there was no maybe. The stairs and landing were floodlit, so brightly that I felt certain that they could be seen all the way from Brasilia. We consoled ourselves with a Brazilian dinner – my first. It was a Saturday. We were obliged to cool our heels all through Sunday, waiting for Carybe to return and open up his house to hostile guests.

It was the longest Sunday I had ever known, but that made me absorb what Bahia had to offer even more intensely, especially our visit to the *candomble,* the òrìṣà place of worship, where the *iyalorixa* – the priestess – took one look at us and concluded right away that we were from the original land of the òrìṣà. Clusters of phrases in the liturgy were familiar, despite some changes here and there in articulation and tonality, and of course there were elisions that had taken place over time. Even so, much of the Yoruba language in the liturgy was still recognisable. Despite time and distance, the chants had remained mostly faithful to the original. Indeed, some scholars go so far as to suggest that the purest forms of these liturgies would be found among the slave descendants of Bahia, not in Yorubaland itself, but that is typical of scholastic controversial conceit. What mattered to us was that these worshippers had no doubts about the authenticity of their beliefs, their dances, their invocations, the jealously guarded usages and values that defined their unique identity as the *anago*, proud descendants of the Yoruba in Brazil, generations that had never abandoned their roots, nor let them wither. They danced. There was a possession. The *iyalorixa* prayed for us. I felt uplifted.

Out in the streets, it felt strange, most unreal, eating *akaraje*, the Brazilian identical twin of our very own *àkàrà*, thousands of miles away from its original home, a delicacy – sometimes heavy, doughy cake – made from the paste of black-eyed beans, fried in huge pans, just as one might encounter in a street corner of Abẹ̀òkúta or Ìléṣà, where *àkàrà* remains the domain of women. We cruised the streets, Labiyi showing me landmarks of interest, especially places that narrated the history of the slaves and their struggle for emancipation. There was a poignancy about that day, made all the more troubling by underlying thoughts of what had brought us to this vibrant outpost of the Yoruba people – a marked contrast to 'Bekuta'. Frankly, I would have given anything to avoid such a day; it tended to make the mind rather mellow, the will flabby from nostalgic thoughts, a tendency to transcend space and history, and merge with long estranged relations. Perhaps it was the Sunday quiet of the streets, but one felt transported to a space of empathy with this living shard of a scattered past, indulging vicariously in the resilience that appeared to be the one consoling extract of a people's displacement. It was all very well for the innocent locals; the nefarious – or soon to be – needed to have both their feet on the ground, focussed and honed to a simple, unambiguous goal that went by just one name – burglary! I still preferred to think of it as a kind of unilateral act of restitution but – burglary by any other name was still burglary.

We left messages for Carybe on his doorstep, and he was not slow to contact us on his return. We met the following morning – an affable, relaxed professional who did not attempt to disguise his pleasure at our visit. We spun him the story of our mission. Was this architect the guilty one? Millionaires are notorious for hiring robbery gangs to break into the best guarded art galleries and snatch a canvas, not just a miniature but the full tapestry sized object of lust. Rolled up and transported in furniture stuffing or a dustbin, the art work arrives at the den of the collector, the bemused felons are paid off, leaving the obsessed recluse to contemplate his captive mistress in solitude for the rest of his life. The fact that he dares not exhibit her to anyone – sometimes not even to close family – merely adds piquancy to his salivation! Was Carybe one of these? He did not appear to belong in the millionaire class but, the collector lust never did discriminate between tycoon and impecunious artist.

Carybe invited us to dinner, just as expected. As we sat in his living room awaiting dinner, I silently swore that before I left Bahia, I would eat more than *akaraje* from his home! I would swallow an entire head, uncooked, yet simmering in his gallery! He served drinks – I sipped, but tasted nothing. Outwardly calm, my inner being was quivering. The evening proceeded as expected. While waiting for dinner, Carybe offered, quite logically, to show us through his gallery. I had unslung my camera bag when we arrived, now I picked it up again as we carried our drinks and climbed the suspended stairs into his lair. The door was habitually locked. With difficulty, I tamped down my anxiety as I watched our host fumble with a bunch of keys. What would we find? An emptied space where once *Orí Olókun* reigned? It had been years, after all, since Labiyi last set eyes on this bronze piece. Suppose Carybe had disposed of it in the meantime?

The moment we entered, I received a shock – but what a most delectable shock this was, taunting yet bracing! There, right across the work desk and canvasses piled against the wall, seated on the topmost shelf among a number of sculptural odds and ends, a magnificent indifference to the history-laden voyage that brought

it to an alien yet native land, was the long-sought masterpiece –
Orí Olókun. The difference between this and the *thing* in the
museum gallery of Ilé-Ifẹ̀ was instantly obvious – in any case, one
had seen photo plates of the authentic piece. This face belonged
to those photographs – longer, refined, and anatomically well
proportioned. It had the seriated lines with which one had become
familiar through illustrations in numerous books – nearly all
commentaries directing the reader to accept that the original had
vanished mysteriously – and for ever.

And then – was it a trick of the light? Or was there really a
dark patch on its right cheek, just where Frobenius had written it
would be, that careless moment of *eureka* when one of the diggers
literally 'struck gold', and a piece came off the bronze head before
the searchers had even caught a glimpse of it? What Frobenius
felt as they proceeded to probe the earth more reverently with
their bare hands, bringing out their treasure trove to light, I tried
my hardest to imagine. More critical however was the need to snatch
my eyes away before a fire of lust lit up my innermost wish. I exchanged
looks with Olabiyi, after which I ensured that those fevered eyes in my
head did not again stray towards that spot of attraction. As for
emotions, I concentrated on bending all shafts of hate – no, not on its
present custodian but – on the usurper faraway in Ilé-Ifẹ̀ Museum,
whose images had lorded it over a national stamp, the university crest
and at least a half dozen other public symbols and logos.

Our host gave us a tour of his canvases, opened up his portfolio
of designs and promised to take us round the physical structures
to which they had given birth – that would be the following day.
My mind was a phillistinic blank. We descended for dinner. My
heart beat more insanely than an erratic water pump. Some
disembodied voice however did emerge from within me. It
announced that I would like to return the following day and
browse among his canvasses at a more leisurely pace. I also wanted
to take photos of some of his sketches – was that all right with our
host? He was agreeable, but regretted that he might have to leave
us for some time, since he had an appointment. That's all right, I
said; just tell your house-help to let us in. Biyi and I again
exchanged quick glances. Would we really carry this off?

Dinner was tasteless. No doubt the cooking was of the best, but I tasted nothing. On the drive back to the hotel, we were silent, each wrapped in his own thoughts, and never could a wider abyss have separated the two preoccupations, both stemming from the same cause. Olabiyi was in a state of suppressed excitement. He had been vindicated, and all that was left was to fulfil the rest of our mission. On my part however, I had begun a process of self-chastisement. Since this adventure began to take shape, I had lost my accustomed sense of humour, of an earthling sense of proportion. The last hour in Carybe's house had been deservedly traumatising. I had taken this mission too seriously, I now realised, the perfect prelude to a punitive deflation. Only a tiny fragment of my corrective sense of mischief came to the rescue at this ponderous moment of absolute negation, grateful when Olabiyi broke the silence, unable to control his excitement any longer.

"Did you see it? Did you recognise it?"

I nodded.

"But could you imagine that anyone could be so brazen? I mean, leaving it on the shelf all these years, so conspicuously. As if he didn't care who might see and recognise it."

"Yes, it's a kind of arrogance, I suppose."

"So, how do you propose to set about it?"

I glanced at him in feigned surprise. "Set about what?"

"Well, what we came for. How are we going to lay our hands on it?"

"Oh, that," I replied, and the smile that I attempted to summon, if it appeared at all, must have been twisted. Nonetheless, it would be the only, painfully brief moment of smugness that came my way in that hare-brained escapade. "That's been taken care of. We've got what we came for."

"We have? What do you mean? Because we've established its presence in the gallery?"

"A little more than that" I replied. "It's in the bag."

And still Biyi thought I was speaking in metaphors. "You mean, tomorrow? You sound confident. You think it's going to be that easy?"

I nodded towards the back seat. "The camera bag. Look inside it." I watched him scramble to lift the bag over his seat. "Be careful" I warned. "It's not bronze. I think it's clay."

"Clay? What do you mean clay? And anyway..." He stopped dead. Felt the bulge in the bag. "When...? I mean, how...?" His eyes then lit up and he gasped. "But you weren't gone long enough!"

It was a moment I should have savoured, but what I tasted in my mouth at a moment that should have trumpeted triumph or at least, satisfaction, was – depressingly not for the first time – ashes. It was this that coated my tongue and subverted all taste in the sumptuous meal served by our host. My throat was lined with the stuff. It had all gone too smoothly. I had set down the camera bag as soon as we entered the gallery. When we were summoned down for dinner, I left the bag behind. Then, moments after we sat down at table, I 'remembered' the bag and set off, politely brushed aside our host who offered to send his steward to look for it. I flew up the stairs, placed a stool that I had marked down for the purpose on the work bench, snatched the prize and – gasped! It nearly flew off my hands! I had expected to lift heavy metal, but whatever I had in my hands chastised my impulsiveness with an incongruous lightness. It was a moment of deflation. Too late for questions or theories however, I brought it down, shoved it into the bag, replaced the step and was down in mere seconds.

"It has to be the real thing!" Biyi persisted. "If it isn't, then what on earth is it?"

"I don't know." I admitted. "We'll find out when we reach the hotel."

"But what do we do now?"

"Research, research. More and more research. Our next stop is Dakar."

That moment of shock, of lifting what should have been a sculpted weight of bronze and was worth more than its weight in gold, but proved lighter than tin foil, was nothing compared to the news, from the backup team at home, that greeted us the following morning – Pierre Verger had been released from his 'administrative detention', and by none other than my good friends, the State

Security Services. Our backup team in the university – headed by the dean – had been assigned the role of ensuring that Pierre's end-of-employment documents were withheld for the few days we would be away, thus keeping him within Nigeria. However, yet another force of intervention had joined in the fray – and from within a state agency. Even more remarkable was the fact that he had been put on a plane, and was now on his way to Brazil!

For hours that morning, we speculated on the significance of this move. Was it the result of intense diplomatic pressure? We were in constant touch with our embassy in Brasilia, and had a right to expect that we would be instantly briefed on any development at home, especially one that might have a bearing on our very welfare. The embassy had no messages for us – nothing.

The day's programme had to be followed however. We endured lunch with Carybe and some friends in a favourite Brazilian-Yoruba restaurant, discussed the manifestations of Yoruba culture in Brazil, the race issue and the comparative merits of those fire-waters *caxaca* and *capinrinha*, all the time deeply conscious of the double faces we wore, wondering what to make of this new complication.

'We must get out of here' I said to Yai – unnecessarily, as soon as we were alone.

We left unceremoniously, leaving notes for our Brazilian hosts about some problems at home that required our immediate return. The gods must have felt some remorse for their unkind treatment of their faithful servitors, since it was virtually by a miracle that we obtained two seats on the very next flight out of Rio and heading for – no destination could be more earnestly desired – Dakar!

Our arrival in Dakar brought unusual excitement to the staid laboratories of Senegal's ethnological institute – IFAN, headed by Cheikh Anta Diop, whose views in *The African Origin of Civilisation* had committed the ultimate sin of faulting the theories of canonised Egyptologists – Champolion especially. Most of the staff were only too familiar with the ancient controversy over *Orí Olókun*. They cast their eyes on this head with the greenish patina, the tell-tale hole in the cheek, and the holes strung around the base of the skull, a feature of bronze sculptures cast through the *cire perdue* technique – and they instantly burst into ululations. They pronounced it, unquestionably, the original.

The problem was the material. If clay, was our find the original clay mould from which the final head was cast? But then who on earth took the trouble to coat the head in verdigris and replicate the very appearance of an antique bronze piece? Had yet another set of raiders stumbled on the original clay mould, then faked its surface appearance to hide its authenticity? This was a piece that was cast to perfection. Measurements were taken to compare them with those recorded by Frobenius, that assiduous recorder of weights and measures. Cheikh Anta Diop, a long embattled scholar was beside himself with excitement – *just think of it, if somehow the original mould from which the bronze was cast had been miraculously preserved – what a find! What a find!*

And what a dismal find it proved when, sitting down with a riot of thoughts while we awaited the return of the archival researchers, my eyes fixated on this troublesome object, I finally noticed a tiny, clearly embossed line at the base of the head, just where it joins the neck. The light from Diop's window had made visible what the artificial light in our hotel room – and our downsized powers of observation in Bahia – had failed to reveal. I looked more carefully and – all was made plain. That impish agent of reversals, *Èṣù,* was clearly not done with us!

This fragmentary line was not by itself but was joined to others. They formed the letter – M! And there, just before M, was yet another faded letter – B. The letters BM stamped into this piece, standing for no other institution than – the British Museum! Of course! What we had in our hands was nothing other than a British Museum copy, available on request for a princely sum of – Fifteen? Twenty pounds? Certainly twenty-five pounds at the most. The deflation could not have been more definitive than of a hot-air balloon spiralling down to earth after an unfortunate encounter with the beak of a migrating stork!

When Cheikh Anta returned to his office, I showed him the stamp. He appeared to take it in his stride, looked only a little disappointed but not in the least crestfallen – which would be a generous description of the condition in which he met us. Then I asked the question:

"Where is the original today, from which this was made?"

The question must have struck him as fatuous, since the stamp indicated quite clearly where the copy had originated. But my mind had resumed the hunt. I persisted:

"If we say that this is a copy of what Frobenius described in his travelogue, the one that he dug up, leaving a hole in its cheek, the same one that was displayed both in the Munich and London expositions before it allegedly disappeared, then from what bronze head was this copied by the museum? And when? I rattled off details of the facts we had unearthed in the preparatory days to our departure. Its last acknowledged appearance was at the London exhibition of 1938 in honour of King George's coronation. After that – the entire ethnographic world insists – *it disappeared altogether*. So, from what bronze piece came this plaster replica?" I produced my dossier, flashed the museum postcard. "Look at it. Even on this card, produced and sold to its visitors by the museum, it says: *Present whereabouts unknown.* So, what phantom original gave birth to this museum copy even while its existence is denied?"

Cheikh Anta took the piece, rolled it lovingly in his hands, walked to his chair and sat in it, shaking his head dolefully. "But you know, our white colleagues in this ethnographic business have always been thieves – we know that. But they also put their scholarship at the service of thieves."

I drafted a telegram for the embassy to send to the ministry in Lagos. It read: "MISSION ACCOMPLISHED, BUT INCONCLUSIVE. STOPOVER IN DAKAR TO PURSUE ENQUIRIES." It was the kindest language – to our bruised *amour-propre* – that I could come up with. I flashed our letter of mission authorisation to the embassy and requested that they check us into a hotel and take care of the bills. This was more than conservation of our remaining finances – more than ever, it became important to ensure that the involvement of the government was established at every stage. Once our flight back into Lagos was arranged, the embassy sent another telegram to the Foreign Ministry providing details of our arrival, requesting that we be met.

We were not. We waited an hour at Ikeja airport, then
concluded that our message had not been received or that
arrangements had gone awry. On our way out of Nigeria, we
had been taken to the airport by ministry officials, accorded full
VIP protocol. Our embassy in Dakar had also been more than
hospitable, placed an official car at our disposal while we remained
there, driven us to the airport and assisted in clearing immigration
formalities – in short, we had no cause to think that we were no
longer on an official mission. Still, the bare fact stared us in the
face - no official was there to meet us - neither from Adefowope's
ministry, nor from Dodan Barracks.

It turned out that we had arrived on a day when nearly all of
Lagos was at a standstill. Nobody who was anybody was to be
found in Lagos – all were headed for Benin, homeland of those
close cousins of the Yoruba from whom, according to legend, they
were descended in the first place. The oba of that famous kingdom,
Oba Akenzua *Iku Akpolopkolo* had died, and his nearly interminable
obsequies were approaching their climax. Successive military
regimes ostentatiously kow-towed to the traditional rulers – unless
of course they stood in the way of military will, in which case, the
oba, obi or *emir* soon learnt just who wielded real power. Otherwise,
the military paid due obeisance to the monarchs, and the Oba of
Benin was certainly among the most venerated.

Traffic around Benin City moved in two directions. The top
brass and cream of Lagosian society and other cities trooped
towards Benin to pay homage, while strangers and beggars trooped
the other way – they could not flee Benin and its environs fast
enough! Traditional lore claimed that a certain number of human
sacrifices must be made on the death of an oba, and such victims
were selected from among strangers. True or false, many preferred
not to find out. In addition, all indigenes of the kingdom, the Edo
people, were required to shave their heads as a sign of respect
and homage. Even my good friend, the democratic litigant, Gani
Fawehinmi, 'Senior Advocate of the Masses', though no native of
Benin, shaved his head clean – a gesture that struck me as dyeing
one's attire a deeper indigo than the weeds of the bereaved. I felt
irritated that Gani should lend his authority to a feudal imposition,

even while I acknowledged a rapport with the traditional institution itself as an essential part of the cultural landscape.

Thus, I lamented a failed mystic linkage between the passing of a descendant of Údùduwà, and the return of the authentic head of Olókun. Instead, all we had was a pale symbol, a plaster cast of his deified sibling, just in time to participate in the funeral rites of one of the branches of the great primogenitor. It occurred to me that maybe Yai and I should also shave our heads, not in homage to the passing of this monarch, but in remorse for a mission from which we returned empty-handed – even worse – returned with a mere shell of the historic weight of the scion of Údùduwà. I tried to console myself that we nonetheless held in secret custody an object that could substitute for the royal death-mask, but was only rewarded with a decided hollow feeling in my stomach, as hollow as the clay head in our possession.

I sensed that something had gone badly wrong. The absence of protocol – the Benin events notwithstanding – was ominous. Still, there was nothing else to do but await the return of the vicarious mourners. We headed for Ìbàdàn. Aboyade, our abetting ex-Vice-Chancellor, was also nowhere to be found, and we assumed that he was part of the official delegation to Benin. Yai proceeded to Ifè while I stopped off at Femi's, both to unwind and to relieve him of his predictable, ravenous hunger for the narrative of our voyage.

In Ifè, news of the safe return of the 'argonauts' had circulated, and jubilations had begun. History Department, African Studies, Languages, Philosophy, Drama, the dean's office, etc. were gearing up to celebrate in grand style. We had the sobering task of stopping them from slaughtering the fatted calf. Not only had the real objective proved elusive, there was now a serious risk that the leakage of our real objective into diplomatic circles would have one guaranteed result: the authentic *Orí Olókun* would now sink deeper and deeper into an impenetrable hiding place. To have propagated its non-existence for so long, and now to have a bunch of skeptics taking melodramatic risks to puncture that myth of a mystic disappearance would send a message to the illegal possessor – *hide it away, dig a hole like its original habitation in Ilé-Ifè, bring it out to gaze upon from time to time, and perhaps exhibit it to a few intimates!*

So much for the speculative fate of *Orí Olókun*. Of more immediate concern to us was our own fate, the two *olórikunkun* who had undertaken this thankless mission. Who was responsible for the departure of our suspected colleague whom we had supposedly left in the guest house of the Vice-Chancellor? The answer was dispiriting.

In its anxiety to ensure that Pierre remained in the country, the Ministry of Foreign Affairs had involved the police. The consequences could not have been more disastrous. The police, on its own, decided to 'carry out investigations'. They visited Ifẹ̀ Museum and found an *Orí Olókun* in its accustomed place, unscathed. They spoke to the curator – had there been a break-in at the museum? No, the curator assured them. Nothing missing from the collection? Not even a bronze head? No, everything was in its place. And what would be his reaction if he were told that the head of *Orí Olókun* was missing? Well, if they would kindly follow him, he would show them the *Orí Olókun* piece on its accustomed podium in the glass case. The harassed man answered their questions in the strictest manner possible. He did not reveal that we had visited the museum at the planning stages and that he was part of the project, though not of the conspiracy. He knew his archeological history and had indeed admitted to us that, each time he passed by the pretender in its glass case, he felt like smashing the case and throwing out the piece. He had unprintable names for Mr. Frobenius.

The police listened, took notes, returned to base and filed their report. It was succinct and damning: no theft had been reported from Ifẹ̀. *Orí Olókun* was in its place, large as life. There had been no disturbance of his peace nor of that of his companions on display at Ifẹ̀ Museum.

Piecing the rest of the story together was easy enough. Pierre Verger was questioned. Did he know anything of a missing *Orí Olókun*? He denied it. Did he make enemies while at Ifẹ̀, colleagues who might be interested in scheming his downfall? A puzzled Pierre told them that he knew of none such among his colleagues. Was he on good relations with Wole Soyinka? Absolutely, said Pierre. And Olabiyi Yai? What did he know of him? Labiyi and he worked closely, said Pierre, and he had played host to Labiyi in Brazil. Their academic areas of interest threw them together quite often. Akin Isola? Wande Abimbola? Any contest for academic preferment between you and them? Pierre replied in the negative. Well, declared our SSS to Pierre, you are clearly the victim of some intrigue. And those first two we have just named are at the centre of it. Right now, they are in Brazil – to do what exactly, we do not know, since it is now clear that they were never after any missing object. Maybe they went over there to further whatever sinister plot your friends at the university had cooked up against you. No matter, we apologise for all the inconvenience, and hope you do not hold us responsible for it. University politics are clearly beyond us and quite frankly, we would rather be kept out of them. There is a flight out to Brazil tonight – would you like to be on it? Pierre was more than willing; he was ready to fly out of Nigeria and never dirty his feet on her soil for the rest of his life! Perhaps only Yai and I, on the entire planet, had felt more eager than Pierre to depart from alien territory during those crucial twenty-four hours.

Our planes did not cross each other over the Atlantic – not quite. Later, as we conducted a detailed post-mortem on the sequence of events, followed up the actions of the police and the departure of Pierre, we discovered that we were actually in Rio de Janeiro – in the departure section of the airport – at the very moment that Pierre was passing through to Immigration and Baggage claims. Fifteen minutes either way, and both gladiatorial groups would have encountered each other, perhaps in the parking lot, or at the frontage of the airport building!

We were about to discover that the devil sometimes takes a sabbatical! That other descendant of the line of Údùduwà, Obasanjo, the Head of State, became suddenly inaccessible, evaporated as the authentic Orí Olókun was alleged to have done. I suggested that perhaps he had travelled to Benin incognito, strayed into the path of the ritualists hunting for sacrificial strangers and was now keeping company with the late Oba of Benin. I called the more than familiar telephone number and a strange voice answered. I announced who I was and asked to speak to the Head of State. I was rewarded with a barked response:

"Do you have an appointment?"

"Do I what-did-you-say?"

"Have an appointment, I said. Do you have an appointment to phone the Head of State?"

I still was not sure I had heard right. I repeated my name and the voice retorted, "Yes, I heard you say who you are. And I asked you if you had an appointment."

"You want me to make an appointment to call your ọ̀gá? Now how exactly does one do that?"

"That is not my business to tell you. Do you think you can call the Head of State just like that? Without an appointment?"

Well now, I thought, it is not only the Edo kingdom that is being turned upside down. The nation itself, Nigeria, appeared to have tumbled into some time warp and was spinning out of control. Maybe some aliens had even taken over Dodan Barracks. Could this possibly be the same Dodan Barracks that I called up any time, the same head of state with whom I brainstormed together with Oje, sometimes over dinner or a weekend lunch, a wine bottle tucked under my armpit to guard against wine poisoning from his indifferent stewards? We had commenced this exercise – could only have begun it! – with his active approval and collaboration. Now here was some strange voice which breezily, even insolently admitted that it recognised the identity of the caller, but required that this same caller somehow make an appointment in order to speak to his boss. I put down the telephone, turned to Akin Isola next to me and sighed.

"We are in trouble. Deep trouble." And I narrated what had been barked at me from the other end of the line.

"What next?" Akin demanded.

In that moment, my mind was made up. "I leave for London. We've wasted far too much time."

"Leave for London? What for?"

"I am heading for the British Museum. I want to find out from which bronze original this plastic copy was made. Certain forces have entered this, forces for which we hadn't bargained. Pressures. Diplomatic, certainly. Just think – why was Pierre released without our being informed? I think we are about to be sold, bargained away. Before that happens, I need to have pushed this search as far as possible. From now on, we ignore that devil in Dodan Barracks. We ignore the ministry and we ignore the police. We are on our own and – so be it."

And so, it was back on the trail, but in a different mode. There would be no more skulduggery. Between the members of the original team, and the recruited arts historian in the Fine Arts Department, Babatunde Lawal, we had already compiled masses of literature. I pored yet again over this material, returned to the library to scrutinise bibliographies, indexes and footnotes even more closely, looking for clues that we might have overlooked or considered unimportant. Now it was desperation for more knowledge, for a closer approximation of the truth, that drove me.

It was strange. Only a few days had passed when nothing mattered in the world but that moment when I would hold a physical object in my hands, restore it to its rightful home and bask in the contentment of a historic closure. Now all I wanted was the truth, the truth of a location, the meaning behind nearly a half century of deception. I felt the pressure of time. Any moment from now, I expected to be warned off in some manner that would be difficult to circumvent, probably summoned and read the riot act, such as – any further action on my part regarding *Orí Olókun* would 'jeopardise the bilateral relations with this or that government and will not be tolerated.' The next casualty would be my passport, then all forms of harassment, such as being summoned for interrogation. Arrest or detention was out of the question, that much at least I was quite sure of. The Obasanjo regime badly craved the reputation of following the rule of law.

Femi's wife, Barbara, was away in England – her location could not have been more fortunate. Femi – he had now joined in the chase – proposed her recruitment for the next stage of enquiries. She would visit the British Museum and find out all she could of the 'missing' original. Obviously the British Museum held the key. I was now certain that news of our escapade would have spread, and the doors battened against any Nigerian looking researcher. Barbara was British however, and she would not arouse suspicion. We fed her all the accumulated information and suggested a few trails for her to follow, the most promising of which was that the head had once been acquired by a British family, then lent – or sold – to the British Museum. We supplied the name of the family.

Barbara was thorough – she succeeded in tracking down the descendants of that family, located not far from London. She spoke to them on the phone and confirmed that the family had surrendered the head to the British Museum. From the latter, Barbara extracted information that the main museum had in turn loaned it to one of its branch institutions. A little more probing revealed that this was none other than the Burlington. I asked her to pay a visit to Burlington Museum without attracting attention to herself.

In my head, alarm bells continued to jangle, warning me that discretion was now belated. What mattered however was to establish the exact whereabouts of the original, now that we knew that the British Museum had made replicas from it. It would be no exaggeration to state that I had now become obsessed. I wanted *Orí Olókun* – badly – even if it was only to set my eyes on it! I wanted it more than I had ever craved any object in my life. In moments of sober reflection, long after it was all over and I analysed my state of mind during this period, I came to understand what the mystique of the Holy Grail was about, or the Golden Fleece, how the *epos* of The Quest came to predominate the mythologies of nearly every culture. If I could not bring *Orí Olókun* back, at least I wanted to be able to say: *an end to all these lies, the great distraction contained in 'whereabouts unknown'*. Rubbish! There were those still alive who knew damned well where *Orí Olókun* was. There was a bronze head, the authentic article, on display somewhere, but the scholars kept pretending that it was not *Orí Olókun*, but its simulacrum, churning out theories to suggest that there was yet another bronze piece, probably an imitation or *sculpture of the head of an Ifẹ̀ king, sometimes mistaken for* Orí Olókun. Regarding this attribution however, there was something else we had observed.

This alleged 'twin' of Olókun was always photographed from the left profile, never from the right where the pick had taken off a piece of the cheek and left a distinctive gash. Was this a coincidence? I had researched tome after tome, and while the 'missing' original – in black and white or in colour – was always photographed frontally, rear, right and left profile – the 'twin' appeared only in its left profile. If there was nothing to hide, why was it always photographed from the undamaged profile? The task force had also debated this 'coincidence' – Akinjogbin of History, Wande Abimbola the *Ifá* expert, Babatunde Lawal of Fine Arts and others. We had examined photos, monograms, ethnographic and art history books, museum catalogues, etc., and were always struck by this discrimination – the twin only appeared in its undamaged profile. Some had developed a strong suspicion that there was no 'twin', that is, there was no bronze head in existence, of that particular identity, that did not have the crucial hole in its cheek. And there could be only one of its kind! Of no other bronze head did any archeologist ever report that a piece was taken off the cheek – and at that exact spot!

Frobenius' journeys through Africa have been remarked, with some justification, as an exercise in Teutonic obsession with measurements and detail. He travelled not only with an artist who produced numerous sketches – with finicky dimensions – of art pieces, architecture and landscape, etc. – but with a mobile smelting and casting factory. He made copies of several objects – including bronzes. When the British District Officer learnt of his excavations in Ilé-Ifè in the early nineteen thirties, he put his paid informers on the alert, and thus learnt of the success of the dig almost at the same time as Frobenius was covering up the ravished hole. The District Officer kept an eye on the adventurer's movements, learnt just in time that he was headed for the border with Dahomey and moved to stop the acquisitive German as he was about to depart with his booty. The story, according to Frobenius, was that he was compelled to part with *Orí Olókun*, and succeeded in keeping for himself only the chip that came off the end of the careless pick.

Our reconstruction however, was this: the District Officer parted with what he *thought* was *Orí Olókun*. It was more likely to have been an imitation – that is, not a direct replica of the original – but a totally separate head, a clumsy handiwork of Frobenius' companion. It is that imitation that has continued, till today, to occupy pride of place in Ilé-Ifẹ. Frobenius' companion had mastered the art of *cire perdue*, but lacked the skills to make a copy with the finesse of the original. When the District Officer demanded that he disburden himself of the precious head, Frobenius had simply given him an *original* imitation, fabricated by his artist.

Well, I wanted badly to see the original – or its mysterious 'twin'.

It was indeed on display in a glass case at Burlington Museum, London, its jagged hole conspicuously on view. I was overcome with an irrational feeling that the normal, viewing world was seeing *Orí Olókun* for the very last time, that this 'twin' or whatever would vanish as the next logical stage in a half-century saga. I threaded my way through the museum visitors, mildly disguised, in case my picture had been secretly circulated through Interpol as an art thief to be watched at all costs. I walked past it only twice or thrice, always making sure that the attention I paid to it was less than the amount of time I spent viewing other items on display.

My fears were soon grounded in factual developments. The moment I arrived in London, I called Barbara and asked her to bring me up to date. Through her deft sleuthing, she found that the director of the Nigerian Museum, Ekpo Eyo, was on his way to London. I phoned Burlington, provisioned with a formal but phony title, and asked directly for the director of the Nigerian Museum of Antiquities – had he arrived? Not yet, but he was expected, the museum had received notice that he was on his way.

Eyo's visit could not be a coincidence. Our meddlesome police had undoubtedly contacted him for an opinion during their clumsy intervention, and he had begun to conduct his own research. It led him unerringly to the Burlington. How many other roads, and taken by whom, I wondered, now led to the Burlington Museum?

That conviction of a multiple convergence on that Piccadilly Street warehouse of treasures bred a renewed urgency and made me throw all caution to the wind. I returned the following day –

to do what, precisely, I was not sure, especially as I did not bother any longer with any form of disguise. I was overwhelmed by the certitude of shrinking time, of an accelerated and definitive resolution, albeit unwanted, of this conundrum. I think I wanted to see the head again, knowing that it might be for the last time. If necessary, I would seek out the Curator, declare my interest in this object, speak frankly but not in great detail of the efforts of Ifẹ University to establish the truth of its identity. Burlington, after all, was a public institution; it admitted paying visitors and should not be shy of answering questions. I would ask him how Burlington had acquired it, ask to see records. I think I had become reconciled to the mere satisfaction of holding it in my hands and letting it speak to me through some secret, ancestral vibrations, just so I could know, and share with others the knowledge of the present existence of *Orí Olókun*.

My craving would be assuaged by no less. With it went a mental restlessness and fitful bouts of sleep, pocked by the strangest dreams. I greeted dawn with great relief, waited impatiently until opening time and set off for the museum, a creature under possession, and by the most confused of impulses. I raced up the steps, excited at the prospect of seeing the head again, and headed straight for the hall.

Orí Olókun had vanished. On that podium where it had stood in proud display less than twenty-four hours before, there was – nothing. Not even a replacement. Not a label. Just – nothing. The case was empty.

For what was probably no longer than a few seconds, but seemed hours, I remained in still confrontation with that glass case, willing its erstwhile occupant to levitate, demonstrate its pristine potency and astonish all viewers. What did levitate instead was a member of staff, a black girl who was simply going about her normal duties. There was no longer need for reticence and I approached her, pointed to the case:

"What happened to this one?"

Speaking quite artlessly, she informed me that it had been 'taken downstairs'. Any particular reason? I asked. None that she knew of, she replied. It was quite normal for the items on display to be changed from time to time. Rotation of themes was quite common in that section of the gallery – not throughout the museum – but in the sections that were dedicated to special exhibitions. Where was she from, I asked, and she replied that she was from Sierra Leone.

I hesitated only a moment. Was it possible that I could see the head, even outside the display? It was obvious to me that if at all there was any conspiracy afoot, this girl was not part of it. Her guilelessness could not have been faked, and when she said, sure, follow me, I nearly catapulted her downstairs, fearful that some superior officer 'in the know' might interrupt this totally unexpected visitation. We descended into the nether world where art pieces were cleaned, catalogued and stored until their next emergence to baffle, frustrate or enlighten the world.

Yes, finally there did come the belated reward, a long moment of rapture. There, on the table with other pieces was the unmistakable head at last – *Orí Olókun!*

I did not wait for it to vanish. Outwardly calm, inwardly I simply leapt on it and lifted this exquisite bronze head in my hands. The weight was just what I had anticipated when I climbed the makeshift ladder in Carybe's studio and lifted its copy off the shelf. The gash in the missing cheek was exactly where it had been on the copy. Reverently, I turned it round and round in my hands, peered short-sightedly into the cavity beneath the neck and sought to guess just how old it was. I laughed out aloud.

The girl looked at me, puzzled. Quickly, I improvised, explained that I was simply thinking of how surprised Frobenius must have been when the British District Officer ambushed him at the border and deprived him of his catch. It was a lie. I had just experienced one of those flashes – WS taking suddenly to his heels, up the stairs, weaving balletically through the display cases, dodging pillars and visitors, out through the door, onto Burlington Arcade and into a long stretch heading nowhere in particular, alarms jangling, pursued by the white-coated museum staff shouting *Stop Thief!* – a scene straight out of *Oliver Twist*, only in this case augmented by the phlegmatic London bobbies on the beat blowing their whistles, motorcycle police, Scotland Yard, the Fire Brigade, Boys Scouts and St. John's Ambulance...

However, the race was over – I knew that! – and I remained rooted to the concrete floor of the chilly semi-basement of this outpost of the British Museum, in my hands the authentic *Orí Olókun*, no matter what the Western pundits say. I sighed, looked around the other treasures looted by the imperial forays of European powers. I think it was in that process that I noticed, for the first time, that the museum worker was quite pretty, indeed more than merely pretty – she had a solicitous charm, just the kind that tended to set off vibrations for a different kind of pursuit. For a few brief moments I wondered – should I make a pass, turn her into an ally and commence a slow, meticulous planning for an inside heist? It seemed worth thinking about. Take her out, cultivate her slowly, gently, wait until the madcap escapade in Bahia was forgotten, the follow-up by the director of Nigerian Antiquities and – certainly – my own visit, which, I did not need to be told, would have raised a few eyebrows. It did not matter if it took an entire year from planning to execution. At the very least, here was a chance to keep an eye on the movements of *Orí Olókun*. No matter where it went, this girl would take note and pass on the news.

I laid down the bronze head, gently, returned the curator's smile. Her charm drew me, in its own right, and I was more than certain that there was a reciprocal tug. Yet, unusually, even that consolation was not one of which I was prepared to avail myself – it carried with it the certain risk that I would draw her into a renewed web of conspiracy. If I felt that a resumption stood any chance of success, I probably would have persisted but – I *knew*. The moment I held that bronze weight in my hands, I knew, with every strand of intuition, that we had reached the end of the trail. Too many cooks now had their ladle in this broth. Best to withdraw, and abandon the lord of the seas to his overseas retreat.

On my return, I called on Oje in his Ìbàdàn home. He had travelled, it turned out, not to Benin but in the other direction – outside the country to escape the hullabaloo generated by the death of the

Edo monarch. His first question was – had I briefed Obasanjo since my return? Negative, and I recounted the efforts I had already made. Right, let's do it now, he proposed. No way, I said to him. As far as I was concerned, his man no longer existed.

Oje could not believe that 'our friend' had blocked his phone against my calls, so I called him again from Oje's house, announced myself, then split the earpiece between us so that he could listen to every word. It was the same voice, and his answer was, if anything, more curt, rudely dismissive. I hung up. Oje said, all right, let's wait fifteen minutes, and then *I* will call. I did not doubt what the result would be and remained indifferent. Oje put his call through and, as soon as he announced himself, received the kind of genial response that I last received before the fateful trip to Bahia. He made an appointment to see Obasanjo. T h e n he turned to me, and never had I seen Oje so woebegone. "Someone has been feeding him lies," he announced.

"And what is that to me?" I replied. "There is only one word for this – treachery! Beginning from him and transmitted all the way down the official ladder. Not only was Pierre released, he was told the entire truth and put on a plane to go there and – confront us. On his own territory! From then on we were dead meat to this Dodan Devil! We were not met on our return and then, for days, there was no contact. Listen Oje, if you haven't worked this out by now, the truth is – we were not meant to return."

Oje protested vehemently. I shouted him down. "I tell you, we were not meant to return! These people were getting rid of a problem. We've worked out movements on both sides, and we found that Pierre nearly caught us flat-footed in Brazil. One more night…! That devilish mind did not expect us back."

Oje was nothing if not persistent. He went for his appointment and had a long heart-to-heart talk with Obasanjo. On his return he announced that he had made an appointment for us both to go and see him. I laughed. No, I did not wish to set foot in Dodan Barracks ever again nor see the face of that Head of State. Oje piled on the pressure – *at least listen to what he has to say.* I remained adamant I had had enough. I wanted nothing but the solitude of my bush, nothing more.

Eventually, he prevailed. He had recruited Femi Johnson to his side but it was not so much the combined pressure that wore me down but – my own curiosity. I wanted to confront the man, study the expression on his Úwu cicatriced face, follow those eyes as he tried to wriggle out of this one, then give him a piece of my mind, and leave. Even so, I nearly backed out at the last moment. I had developed a visceral revulsion towards, not only the seat of government but towards anyone associated with it. Even Oje had not escaped this guilt by association, I realised. It was, after all, several days after my return from London before I could bring myself to stop at his house, and this was only because I was staying in Ìbàdàn that weekend, nursing back my self-esteem, in the congenial setting of Femi's home.

Still, I ended up accompanying him to Lagos and into Dodan Barracks, grim of countenance. As we walked through the deserted complex and passed by the sparse allotment of officers on duty, I scowled at each in turn in case that was the miscreant who had given himself the pleasure of telling me to book an appointment for a telephone call. We entered the familiar space of his private lounge. I braced myself for the diatribe that was coiled at the root of my tongue, untended, but capable, I was certain, of atomising the heads of a dozen heads of state, all dictators. We had hardly settled down before Obasanjo himself entered the room and plunged directly into what must have been a well-rehearsed and difficult text.

"The police messed up" he announced. "But they are my men. The ultimate responsibility rests with me and so – I accept responsibility for their action, and I apologise. I apologise on their behalf." Before I could open my mouth to reply, he added, "Look Wole, if I wanted to get rid of you, I would put you against a wall and shoot you. But I could never send you to a strange country to be killed or injured. I would never send a fellow Nigerian to another country to be killed. I could never do that. It is against my soldierly training."

I had too much piled up within me and was not about to let him off easily. I plunged into a bitter *reprise* of the succession of betrayals Yai and I, as well as the others at Ifè, had undergone. I was particularly galled at the ignorant intervention of the police –

if the police had to be brought into play, was there no police section better qualified for such a role? What happened to the Antiquities Squad, specially created to stem the illegal flow of national treasures overseas? Oje interrupted, imploring me to accept the man's regrets and draw a curtain over the entire episode. And then, suddenly, the devil himself was chuckling. I was taken aback – was it all a joke to him, and did this include his apology?

"Look, I've already said – heap it all on my head. I have accepted full responsibility – *àbí?*" And, his rotund frontage virtually heaving with – in my reckoning – sadistic mirth, he continued, "But you know, it is also your fault. It doesn't matter what you do, the police have a chronic distrust of you. If they see you walking south, they think it must be a trick and that you're really headed north. That's the problem. For them you represent – a permanent headache. Anyway, please, let's forget it. I apologise."

From testimonies among his closest circle, this must constitute one of the half dozen times that Obasanjo ever apologised for any action in his life. I had been a two-time recipient. I wondered, wryly, how soon there would be a third, and if I would have to receive it, like Pierre Verger's from me, posthumously.

Epilogue

Now what was the real story? How did Olabiyi Yai come to believe that the authentic head had somehow landed, after unrecorded vicissitudes, in Carybe's studio?

The clue had to lie in his conversation with Pierre. He believed it because Pierre told him. When it was all over and the misadventure put to rest, I asked Yai to go through the scene at the party at which this 'confession' was made – leave nothing out, consider nothing of no importance, see nothing as lacking in significance. I made him go through Pierre's dialogue and his, their gestures, comportments, states of inebriation – in as full detail as he could recollect.

The exchange, Yai reaffirmed, took place on the top landing of the suspended stairs. Pierre had gone outside for fresh air with a drink in his hand. He sat on a step, and Olabiyi who, all that evening, had had the hidden eyes in his head rivetted on no other object but that bronze piece, finally said to Pierre:

"Baba, is that not the famous head of *Orí Olókun* sitting on that shelf."

"Of course" said Pierre.

"But – what of the one in the museum at Ifẹ̀?"

"Oh that. Everyone knows it's a fake."

"Are you quite sure about that?"

"There isn't any serious scholar who believes in that thing."

"Then how did Carybe get hold of this? When? How did he get it out of Nigeria?

And then Pierre looked warily right and left, as if to make sure that there was no one within earshot. He leant forward, put a finger across his lips and said:

"S-sh. Don't tell anyone. I brought it here myself"

I believe that account of their exchange. What Yai missed was Pierre's boyish sense of mischief, not too different from that of his countryman, Abdias do Nascimento, the artist and playwright, who was also sojourning at Ifẹ̀ at the time. Abdias' intervention at any symposium on identity, culture, race or whatever, was always guaranteed to immobilise his audience in fierce denunciation of Brazilian racist policies, reeling out statistics and calling for world intervention. And then Abdias, ending his diatribe abruptly and resuming his seat, would turn to me and – *wink*!

That evening outside Carybe's studio, Pierre, the scholar, was making a mockery of all efforts – including his, probably – to solve a mystery that had defeated dozens of archeologists, art historians and ethnologists. He was amused, it now seems clear, by Yai's naive belief that this long-sought head was actually sitting among the jumble in some architect's studio gallery in Bahia. Pierre did not consider for a moment that his act was convincing. He forgot that this was a party atmosphere, with plenty of booze, where lurked the possibility of confessions made – *in vino veritas.*

After all the diplomatic hassle had subsided, tempers cooled and even the police acting somewhat chastened, I commenced the process of inviting Pierre back to Ifẹ̀, as a special guest. The university was more than willing to create an occasion to make public amends, offer him an open apology and exonerate him before the university community. The Ministry of Foreign affairs however refused to approve his visa. Indeed, we discovered that he had been placed on a list of prohibited aliens!

There could be only one explanation for this. Many more – undoubtedly vicious – lies that would embarrass officialdom, were they to be revealed, must have been spilled to Pierre by the police. They could not afford to have Pierre back in the country where the episode could be aired at a public *post mortem*, even as we, the principals, and associated conspirators, winced in chagrin and wiped mud off our own faces. The role of the government and its agencies would have garnered the greatest opprobrium however; at worst we would only have to endure some good-natured mockery.

We let another year or more go by, when a civilian regime was back in place. I succeeded in cutting through all obstacles – no one, as usual, could recall how they came to be placed there anyway, or who ordered them – and obtained a visa clearance for Pierre. Using mutual colleagues such as Doig Simmonds, the Welsh medical illustrator, Peggy Harper, the dance instructor from South Africa – Abdias do Nascimento and others, we invited Pierre to one public event after the other. I swore that I would meet him personally at the door of the plane and escort him to Ifẹ with full grandeur. We arranged for a Yoruba traditional title to be added to the one that he already enjoyed.

We should not have been surprised that Pierre declined. At seventy-plus, his rough treatment at the hands of the police, and the conviction of a betrayal by trusted colleagues were simply too much to overcome. The episode was more or less smothered in Brazil at the time but was exhumed by some enterprising journalists when I was awarded the Nobel Prize. They homed in on both Pierre and myself. Pierre was still bitter, but quite generous in saluting my award. On my part, I heaped all the blame on an ignorant and high-handed police, asked the journalists to pass on our invitation to Pierre yet again to return to Nigeria as my personal and university guest, where he would be informed at first-hand what had transpired, and how the misunderstandings had come about. I added, however, that unfortunately, it was Pierre's impish sense of humour that had triggered off a chain of events among us, his humourless colleagues.

Many of our colleagues believed in turn that I would not step into Brazil ever again, but I have done so, more than once, and even while Pierre was still alive. I looked for him but he had travelled out of Bahia, and we never met. (Had an unforgiving Pierre quit Bahia because he heard I was coming?) The media appeared to have decided to draw a veil of discretion over the episode. Not one mention of the 'quest for the Holy Grail' appeared in the press during my entire stay, where I was also received by the president, himself a novelist of note.

Pierre died some years ago. Reconciliation with that misused scholar was one that I truly craved, but appeasement must now be delayed until our reunion under the generous canopy of Ọrùnmílà.

The 'Evil Genius'

General Ibrahim Badamosi Babangida who, for many years of an eight-year dictatorship, begun in 1985, affected a convincing carapace of indifference to public image, eventually revealed his vulnerability. Nettled by a seemingly consensual and persistent view in the media that he was evil at heart and in intent, he finally retorted that if he was indeed evil, he was at least an evil genius. It was inevitable that he would prove to be another devil with whom I would willingly share a dinner table. If anything, he intrigued me far more than Olusegun Obasanjo. Suave, calculating, a persuasive listener, conciliator – but with sheathed claws at the ready – ever ready to cultivate potential allies, he had a reputation for meticulous planning. I was one with most other coup-watchers who knew Babangida only by reputation, as the mastermind behind a number of earlier coups d'état.

But first, how – apart from his affable exterior – did Babangida succeed in enjoying, at least at the beginning, a quite remarkable level of national acceptability? The answer to that was straightforward: he rode to public favour on the brutal, and hypocritical record of his predecessor, one devil for whom, in my calculation, no spoon existed long enough to justify the risk even of an impromptu snack.

With his partner, Tunde Idiagbon, General Buhari blew onto the Nigerian stage, raising a whirlwind of corrective energy. His first port of call was the Ministry of Petroleum which, during the Obasanjo regime, he had headed. During the Shehu Shagari rule that followed, a hue and cry began of a missing sum of 3.4 billion dollars of the nation's petroleum funds, a sum that was later upgraded to 4.1. The scandal was not new. The accusations were public, pursued with vigour by the social critic, the schoolmaster Tai Solarin, and by an activist with an even more volatile temperament, Dr. Awojobi, a professor of engineering at the University of Lagos. Lithe and intense every inch of his six foot four frame, Awojobi was however more fastidious and persuasive than Tai in his acquisition and presentation of facts. The Shagari government was compelled to set up a commission of enquiry. Its findings were negative – Tai Solarin, it decided, was merely whistling in the wind, and no such funds were missing.

Nevertheless it raised not a few eyebrows that General Buhari, who was at the centre of this scandal, should stage a coup d'état against a civilian regime that had enquired into the affair. The eyebrows were raised even higher when, no sooner had he seized control of the nation, than he made a bee-line for the Nigerian National Petroleum Corporation (NNPC), raided its offices and carted away its files, swearing publicly that he would get to the bottom of the missing funds and announce his findings in a matter of months. This was the last that the nation heard of those files, or the missing billions. Buhari sacked the incumbent head of the NNPC, reinstated his right-hand man from his previous ministerial stint in that department and, at the first opportunity, locked up Tai Solarin under an unrelated pretext – for distributing leaflets calling for a return to democracy.

It was a harsh confinement. Tai Solarin was subjected to a life-threatening regimen in an inclement far North prison. He was refused access to his accustomed medication for asthma, one that had been prepared for him for years by a traditional herbalist and had proved a hundred percent effective where western medicine had failed. As for Professor Awojobi, he died soon after Buhari took over. A vigorous personality and brilliant engineer, Awojobi simply passed away conveniently, ostensibly of hypertension.

That beginning established the pattern. The Buhari regime re-defined all concept of a moral scourge, incorruptibility, transparency and even-handedness in the execution of its own codes of justice. It was this regime that presided over the saga of some 53 suitcases that passed through the needle's eye of the customs at the international airport of Kano. As a measure to stabilise the Nigerian currency and terminate the business of illegal speculation, currency trafficking and other dodgy financial dealings, the Buhari regime ordered the production of a new national currency. So comprehensive were the measures undertaken to ensure that not a single forged or obsolete currency note was blown across the borders, either entering or exiting, that all land, air and sea borders were sealed tight, without notice. If migrating birds were not exactly ordered to be shot at sight, it was only because the Nigerian Air Force was too busy ferrying in the new notes. International transactions were suspended. Too bad for those who were trapped outside or inside until the fiscal exercise of several days was over.

Nonetheless, a Northern emir arrived at Kano airport with 53 bulging suitcases and – who would be waiting to clear him through Customs? Buhari's own aide-de-camp, Major Jokolo! He encountered, and tried to brush aside the stolid opposition of the customs officer in charge of the airport – an unknown civil servant by name Alhaji Atiku who would later become the Vice-President of the nation after the return of democracy. The Customs Officer held his ground as long as he could, but was no match for the aide-de-camp, who had flown to Kano from his duty post in Lagos solely to facilitate the passage of the emir's camels through the needle's eye of the Customs. Entry was eventually effected with only one casualty – not long after, the stubborn customs officer was unceremoniously bundled out of Kano and re-deployed to Lagos. Based on the provisions of an allied regulation however, Fela Anikulapo, the Afro-beat musician, would be sentenced to a long term of imprisonment for failing to declare some foreign currency that he had legitimately brought into the country. Fela had kept the funds as immediate living expenses for his band, due to begin an overseas tour shortly after.

After Babangida came to power, the trial judge visited Fela in prison, apologised to him for his role in his conviction, and admitted that he had only acted on orders. The poor judge! Did he really think that my uninhibited cousin would keep quiet after such a confession? *The judge done come beg me o!* screamed Fela to the media, leaving Babangida no choice but to set free the victim of Buhari's reformist zeal, and dismiss the judge.

So implacable in its dubiety was the moral code of the duo – Buhari and Idiagbon – that most Nigerians, involved in routine, legitimate, decades-old monetary arrangements learnt to take self-protective measures. On my part, I ensured that I was thoroughly 'sanitised' at least a dozen times before boarding an airplane in or out of Nigeria. The decree was uncompromising. Even the possession of a worthless coin or two guaranteed several years in gaol. Currency forms had to be filled going in and out, and an inaccurate entry left the voyager at the mercy of the law. My forms always read 'zero' going in and out – a crossed line across the page and my signature, nothing more. After Fela's ongoing ordeal, no one in his senses would take his chance with those reformists who had placed themselves on high moral grounds, tasked themselves with the laudable goal of stemming the nation's financial haemorrage! The decrees extended to foreign accounts. They were to be closed down by all Nigerian citizens and existing funds repatriated to Nigeria. The results were predictable. Anxious not to lose Nigerian business, foreign banks – and without any prompting from their customers – would offer to send their bank statements to proxy addresses, and many Nigerians took up the offer.

Irrationally perhaps, there I drew the line! I had operated an account with Lloyds since my student days in Leeds, and I was not going to close it down for any sanctimonious terror. Royalties earned outside the country had always remained outside, those from within, within, and that was the way it would remain. Not seeking martyrdom however, I instructed my bank not to forward any statements to me or even write me a letter –

I would call whenever I passed through London if I needed to check the health of my balance or withdraw from it!

While Fela Anikulapo-Kuti languished in gaol, a blue-blood scion of the Northern aristocracy, Alhaji Alhaji Alhaji, known as 'Triple A', then Permanent Secretary in the Ministry of Finance, was caught – literally – with his pants down in the Austrian capital, Vienna. He was robbed of a large sum in foreign currency – in cash – well over and above his legitimate entitlement, and by a local 'female escort'. Dalliance over, 'Triple A' fell asleep. When he woke up, his companion was gone, and so was his wallet. Such was his confidence in a personal immunity that the super civil servant made a report to the Austrian police, and the escapade was bruited over the international press, from where it was picked up and near flogged to death by the Nigerian press, calling for equity in the implementation of justice. The media dug deeper, discovered that this civil servant kept, not one, but several foreign accounts. Their screams became deafening and perhaps did succeed in deafening the ears of the corrective duo. They heard nothing, and so maintained a stolid silence, confident that, sooner or later, the media outcry would subside.

Military coups are usually undertaken to terminate the life of a serving government. The Buhari coup set a precedent in Nigerian history by being openly directed against the political opposition. Leaders in opposition were detained without trial, or else sent to military tribunals on charges for which record, unprecedented sentences became mandatory. Some were freed, sent back again for re-trial repeatedly on the same charges, as was the case of a septuagenarian, Pa Adekunle Ajasin, elder statesman of an opposition party and Governor of Úndó State. Even the pliant tribunal found itself unable to convict the old man and so, after several tries, he was simply left in prison detention to rot. Those found guilty received multiple sentences – some, hundreds of years in gaol, to run consecutively. By contrast, members of the ruling party either miraculously escaped capture – like the fifty-three suitcases – were never brought to trial, or else escaped with comparatively light sentences or easeful confinement.

The truth was that General Buhari, with his partner-in-terror, Tunde Idiagbon, struck against the regime in order to preempt a coup by some 'young Turks'. Seeing that the corrupt government of Shehu Shagari was doomed anyway, they moved to prevent a radical wing of the military from taking over.

The media was muzzled by the notorious Decree No. 2 which prescribed mandatory prison sentence for any journalist who published anything at all that 'embarrassed' a government official, irrespective of whether or not the publication was a hundred per cent truth. Two journalists, Tunde Thompson and Nduka Irabor, were the first casualties of this decree – they had published facts, and not even wounding facts, but facts that the regime did not wish to be published, even though borne out in detail.

And yet another journalist and public commentator, Ebenezer Babatope, was gaoled without trial, not for anything he wrote during the incumbency of that despot, but for having called attention, a year or so earlier, to the threat of a coup that Buhari had made before actually carrying it out. *Watch yon general, Babatope had warned, his ambitions run deep.* Unsuspecting – after all, he had said nothing against the regime once it took power, had quietly enrolled as a student in Warwick University, England – Babatope returned home to prepare for his new life. For his prophetic pains, Buhari honoured him with indefinite residency in a maximum security prison. Babatope did not regain his liberty until the fall of Buhari.

Detention without trial, or imprisonment after a mockery of justice ran rampant. Beko Ransome-Kuti, president of the Nigerian Medical Association, in company of some of his lieutenants, took his turn in prison for leading an industrial strike of doctors. Their demand? An end to the neglect of medical services, the deterioration of teaching and government hospitals, and a demand for improvement in their serving conditions. His place of incarceration was set, not within the state where he lived, or close by, but all the way in the far North, quite deliberately, as far as would make family visits and media attention a near impossibility.

The most unconscionable first of General Buhari and his partner, Tunde Idiagbon, however, was the enactment of an anti-drug trafficking law that was made retroactive, so that even drug offences that were committed before the law was passed came under the same forfeit – in this case, life. Three young men were publicly executed by firing squad soon after the law was passed – a deliberate effort to strike terror in the heart of the nation. The degree of public disbelief in the possibility of such unjust killings would not be equalled for many years – and then not until the killing of Ken Saro-Wiwa the Ogoni leader, and his eight companions. Individuals and civic bodies protested the sentence and warned against the executions of the three young men – there was an especially intense campaign by the Quaker Society and by some women's organisations. On the day of the execution itself, it was as if the nation was under a collective paralysis – this was discernible on the faces of people one met on the streets, encountered in offices and hotel lobbies - faces frozen into that one question – would it happen? Would this event really take place? It did.

Nigerians had been brutalised – deliberately – by the new culture of public executions, dubbed, with gallows humour 'The Bar Beach Show', after an open-air television show then current. After the Biafran War of secession, no one should have been surprised that violent crimes – mostly armed robbery – would rise in frequency, and the military government of Yakubu Gowon introduced public executions by firing squad as its ultimate solution to this terrorisation of the nation. Executions took place on the much patronised Bar Beach in Lagos, and the general public – to my personal chagrin – took to it with gusto, turned them into a public fiesta at which refreshments were hawked, the audience danced, jeered at the felons and cheered the execution squad. Children were conspicuously present. Eighteenth century England could not have boasted a more macabre occasion for public roistering.

Not at the execution of these three young men however! The volume of 'Nos' and the wailing rose to a hysterical pitch as the priest moved forward to offer the last prayers and an officer began to apply blindfolds. Then, the subdued retreat of the priest, the officer's crisp march back to the line of the firing squad, the given order, the shots. There were some faintings. A subdued crowd trickled away slowly, numbed with disbelief. Across the nation, a cold cloud appeared to press down on several million roofs, insinuating the unknown. Some years later, I would write *A Scourge of Hyacinths,* for radio, and its stage version, *From Zia with Love,* creative efforts to cauterise the wounds that came from one's impotence.

If the execution of the three young men was the most execrable deed of the Buhari government, designed to cow the nation, and condition its people into an acceptance of unguessable extremes of judicial violence, the actual process of establishing a norm of despotism – in all ramifications – was much simpler. Buhari passed a decree that forbade any discussion of a return to democratic rule. And that was it! Buhari had interrupted a democratic process that had been thoroughly corrupted by Shehu Shagari and his National Party of Nigeria. All this threw into immediate prominence in public discussion the one question: When? When would the military relinquish power? It took only a few months for Buhari to answer that question. A decree was rolled out: the very word 'Democracy' was criminalised.

Not any more, chortled the suave General Ibrahim Babangida, as he served Buhari a taste of his own medicine, overthrew and confined him in a government residential house not far from the new ruler's home state. Babangida promised democracy, but set up structures that ensured that democracy did not proceed 'too hastily'. *We must learn from the lessons of the past, do it properly and enduringly this time, get rid of the 'moneybags', create an environment that favoured the 'newbreed politicians', debate the actual democratic will of the Nigerian people, evolve an unriggable system for the ballot box, construct state-sponsored headquarters of the political parties in every state – which must be two and two only, one 'a little to the left, the other, a little to the right', embark on a 'learning process'...*

Babangida launched one, then two, then three different structures of mass mobilisation. It was clever, and succeeded with many. The people were kept busy. The charade took a while to become transparent.

This dictator made fascinating study. Some time after he came into power, probably a year afterwards, I was invited to participate in a media assessment of his time in office thus far. My contribution took the form of a cautionary tale – a factual, though whimsical anecdote that drew a parallel from his 'fate' at my hands – unknown to him – in the uncertain hours that followed the first announcement of the 1985 coup, when that coup had yet to identify an heir apparent. For someone who prefers to scoff at auguries and other superstitions, it was a revelation – and not the first – of the irrational part of oneself, an authentic component however, that one learns to accept as part of one's make-up.

I was teaching at Ifẹ̀ at the time, and was on my way out of the country for a conference. Stopping, by habit, at my office for a last-minute desk clearance, I observed a group of lecturers clustered around a transistor radio. Some abnormal event had clearly taken place. Surprised by my evident insulation within a shattered normalcy, they waved me over – hadn't I heard? What did I think? Where would it all end?

It was of course another coup d'état. No new head of state had yet emerged, and my colleagues were caught in a fever of guesswork. Various names were tossed about, known players in this game of deadly musical chairs. First question of course – would the coup succeed? Had it already? Where was Buhari? Idiagbon? Was it Dogonyaro's turn this time? – his name had been prominent on radio as John the Baptist of the coup d'état, after which he made way for a greater than he. This time, it was a new town crier. Other names were trotted out one after the other, chewed over, discarded or pushed aside for the moment. The new herald with a high-pitched voice, who identified himself as Sani Abacha, went through the routine incantation – *all soldiers, except those otherwise authorised, were confined to barracks. Military governors to report for redeployment. Offices, airports and borders closed...* I shrugged with indifference, though also with a sense of relief – I had not especially wanted to make this particular journey.

A bonus day in hand, I left my colleagues to their anxieties, drove back home, dumped my luggage, substituted my travelling gear for a rough-and-ready shirt and boots and set off for the agricultural farm where I hoped some bush fowl would still be found browsing on a late breakfast. My intrusion was swift, deadly and productive, unusually so for such a brief spell, well above my average.

The first àpárò – that half-way bird between a quail and a partridge – flew excitedly above my head, flapping untidily. Without any such prior intent, just on the spur of the moment, I shouted – Buhari! – and fired. It came down, plumb-line. I drew a sight-line with my finger and followed its trajectory to the distant crash site.

True, a crucial part of the hunt anywhere is bringing down the quarry. The rest, depending on the terrain, often turns out to be the harder work – finding the bird in what is often tangled thicket. This first offering was most obliging. I nodded with satisfaction – Buhari was definitely gone.

I had hardly secured it to my waist strap when another took off at some distance, offering a very disciplined flight path. It was all unusually smooth reflex – I pulled the trigger, muttering, Idiagbon. Buhari's Number 2 man was away on pilgrimage to Mecca, but that made him even more dangerous to the coup-makers. He could rally loyalists from a distance and try to reverse events. I need not have worried. Down came Idiagbon to join his master.

It was a most auspicious beginning, since this one also proved an easy find. Úgún appeared to be taking a hand, compensating me perhaps for my aborted journey. Next – Dogonyaro! – Smack! Find. Next, Magashi! one of the shadowy ones. I could not believe it – they were all so cooperative, either falling in clearings or staying put where they fell in the bush. As for the actual shooting, there was none of the usual calculating effort, arms moved in unison, on smooth pulleys, guided by invisible hands. But the tempo of flights remained the most astonishing. I had hunted that patch before. At that time of the morning, the àpárò is more difficult to rouse. Having already breakfasted its fill, it tends to dig deep into the bases of thickets, perhaps take a mid-morning snooze, yet here they were offering themselves up as eager sacrifices. I had been in the bush for less than thirty minutes. One more, I thought, and I clumped around, hoping for one parting shot. Up it went and I swung after, then ahead, muttering, Babangida.

No other word for it, this was – smoking! Babangida followed the example of his predecessors – a hit! Eyes glued to landing spot, I plunged into the bush. This time there was a variation. A clump of feathers marked the spot but, search as I would, there was not a sign of Babangida. Not a trace! Greedy now to post a most unaccustomed hundred percent kill, I devoted another fifteen minutes to the search. Not a sign. I gave up. The sun had risen beyond àpárò tolerance level. It was time to return home.

As I drove into campus, using the back route that took me past the faculty, I noticed the group of lecturers still huddled around the radio, talking animatedly.

"Well, any announcement yet?" I asked them.

"No", they replied. "Just a repeat of the same broadcast, plus martial music."

I announced, matter-of-factly: "Babangida is your next Head of State".

I received incredulous stares. How could they have missed the announcement? "Which station was it on?" Someone wanted to know. Another, "Oh, have you been on the phone to someone in Lagos?"

"It's his turn," I repeated. "That one who's been masterminding all the coups, he's behind it, and he's taking over this time, the seasoned escapologist!"

At home, even after a sobering shower and a coffee, I found no reason to examine the premises of my conviction. It was just a factual, inconsequential tug of knowledge, and I turned my attention to other chores. Towards late afternoon, the rest of the nation also learnt that the new despot was indeed IBB.

Babangida's first move was to throw open the prisons – a very deft, calculating stroke. And he opened up every space of public discourse on every subject under the sun – from Democracy to IMF loans – a most masterful distraction, since he could then carry on his own agenda, indifferent, while debates raged all around him.

Quite unlike my encounters with Olusegun Obasanjo when he was Head of State, I never once dined – literally now! - in Babangida's residence, and only once in official circumstances when I attended a banquet for Nelson Mandela. By contrast, he ate at my Abẹ̀òkúta home on two occasions. The first was a hurriedly improvised affair, organised in response to his own suggestion that he stop by while in my state – Úgùn - for some official engagements. I still lived in my rented house at Ìdí-àbà. At the last moment, IBB nearly played his *àpárò* game with me, pleading the difficulty of extricating himself from an official reception by royal command of the Aláké of Abẹ̀òkúta, the traditional monarch of my immediate domain.

Earlier, his advance team had taken up positions in the cul-de-sac whose *cul* was my house, with a frontage of bamboo trellises, covered in creepers. When the wind blew in the right direction, a poultry yard next door stank to the high heavens. I had once threatened to take the owner to court but he pleaded that the ex-Head of State, Olusegun Obasanjo, now a retired farmer, had obtained a monopoly of the importation rights for the chemicals that were required to transform his chicken shit into odoriferous waste. Obasanjo's prices, he said, were prohibitive, that is, when he chose to sell at all. I endured the stench, hopeful of transferring soon to my own house, then under construction.

Babangida's escorts moved back and forth, talking into crackling walkie-talkies and checking on his probable arrival time. Once, they came in and announced yet again that he was on his way, next that he might not turn up after all – the Aláké was a tenacious host, and it was proving difficult for him to free himself from the palace. I sent word back that he would be for ever persona non grata in Abẹ̀òkúta if he failed to turn up for a dinner that he had himself requested. A newly acquired military acquaintance, fast developing into a firm friend, the beanpole Air Vice -Marshal Ibrahim Alfa, and an ace pilot who had cheated death often, was a member of his official entrourage. At the first opportunity he had detached himself from the official train and arrived quite early in the evening. I don't know about Ibrahim, he announced, he's Head of State, so he can't escape his hosts – that is, if he wants to. In my case, my official participation in the tour is finished and I am here to relax and enjoy myself.

Military protocol is a curious affair, however. Ibrahim Alfa and his two army colleagues shied away from digging into the food until their *òġá* turned up. Nine o'clock, then approaching ten. Among the hungry guests were my own hastily assembled terrors of political confrontation who were there to add some mildly astringent spice to the fare. The 'mildly' was specially pleaded by me on behalf of a long-term agenda, the possibility that something similar to the periodic brainstorming sessions that Oje Aboyade and I shared with IBB's predecessor, Obasanjo, would develop from the first encounter. It made sense not to scare him off by a hostile reception at his very first venture.

When Babangida arrived, halfway through the meal, I was treated to quite a display of body languages! One could see that the military group, unlike the civilians, were ill at ease, clearly wishing they had waited for the *òġá*! As for Babangida, it was equally obvious that he was peeved that the company had not waited, though of course he kept mute. Only half-jokingly, he said to Alfa, as conversation became easier – who asked for this dinner anyway? Ibrahim Alfa, I suspected, had agreed to start only because he was convinced that his boss would not turn up at all – *I know Ibrahim,* he kept sighing, as he looked again and again at his watch. Now he looked a little sheepish, quickly pushed his plate aside. I pretended to notice nothing of the discomfiture of the men of arms, even in mufti. Another of his officers attempted to hide his wine-glass. That annoyed me and I fished it out, filled it and went round the table with the bottle.

Babangida soon settled down. From his first taste, he declared an instant love affair with Lebanese food. What was more, he demonstrated a largeness of appetite that was quite unexpected – he ate like a battalion on the move. I was so impressed that I immediately announced that I had to match him against my trencher champion, Femi Johnson. Babangida agreed to take him on any day.

The second visit, at least a year later, was a more elaborate affair, carefully planned, but rich in melodrama. It immediately acquired some mythical status – at least in the town of Abẹ̀òkúta, later spreading out via Lagos circuits. The commencing national honeymoon with the smiling dictator had frayed at the edges and, awaiting him this time was a clutch of some truly disillusioned critics, led by my pugnacious friend, Sesan Dipeolu. Ses – as he was known to close associates – was a retired librarian from the University of Ifẹ school of leftist disputation, but even there, a maverick, ready to associate with progressive groups – but strictly on his own, non-doctrinaire terms. A balding sixtyish, Ses appeared to lend his face to a permanently puzzled look, as if trying to recollect the last resting place of a yet uncatalogued acquisition. He however became a different being, a bull terrier, when engaged in a bout of contumacy, even at moments when he found himself in basic agreement with the premise of the debate. We anticipated a lively afternoon of some unsparing examination of the policies and governing style of the unsuspecting guest, but the manner of IBB getting to my house – yet in a state of incompletion – easily overshadowed the intellectual or political quotient of the afternoon. It acquired, predictably, numerous variations, in Abẹòkúta most especially, taking impetus from the moment when the Aláké of Abẹòkúta, the paramount king of Ègbá was heard to exclaim after the event – *Hare! Wole Soyinka t'iwa ree s'eyi? L'oju gbogbo wa ne e ro gbe Head of State sa lo!*[1]

The Aláké had good cause for his umbrage. It boiled down to this: we 'abducted' the dictator from the state banquet – with his connivance – and whisked him to my uncompleted house in the jungle fastness of Ajébọ. His Chief of Staff, Sani Abacha, holding fort in Lagos during his boss' extended tour, later expressed outrage at the foolhardiness of his superior who actually trusted his safety to a known dissident, allowed himself to be driven to an unknown destination, with only a half dozen or so of his secret service, leaving his mighty armed convoy behind at the venue of the banquet.

What shocked me, however, as we returned our captive to his venue, was that, despite nearly two hours absence, all the guests had remained in their positions! I had not anticipated this. If the guest of honour vanishes, and all eating and speechifying are over,

---

[1] Incredible! Was it our Wole Soyinka that did this to us? You mean he actually snatched the Head of State right from under our noses?

the obvious course of action is – go home! Maybe the soldiers and civil servants – military governor, even ministers and commissioners – were obliged to remain, but what reasons on earth had the private individuals, independent citizens – including the traditional monarch – for hanging on! Protocol, I was later informed, and that was the day I discovered that protocol was also an eight-letter word, brother to the expletive that involuntarily escaped my throat!

Interactions with Babangida were, needless to say, of a qualitatively different character from those of his fellow dictator, Olusegun Obasanjo who, additionally, came from the same part of the country as I – West, Yoruba and Abẹ́òkúta – though I am also part Ìjẹ̀bú. With Obasanjo, I ritually arrived with my own wine bottle or two tucked under the armpit, knowing that my host – and thus, his staff – did not know the difference between *bùrùkùtù* and beaujolais. That weighty problem did not arise with Babangida, since this was one 'devil' with whom I dined only at my own table. With Babangida, my interventions were precisely named – issue specific interventions – though I do recall two exceptions when discussions ranged broadly, as was more common with Obasanjo. Sometimes those sessions with the latter also took place in Aboyade's home, over lunch. Obasanjo appeared to find his thinking aggressively stimulated by our unorthodox approaches to many issues, and, of course he loved to be thought capable of holding his own intellectually. Fights were routine. He did not take kindly to being wrong footed. He *needed,* sometimes pathetically, to be right! Oje once called him an economic illiterate – he was out of office at the time – and it rankled in his mind for years afterwards. I suspect it still does, even with Oje dead. Babangida never seemed to mind being proved wrong; he still carried out his own decisions anyway.

My meetings with Babangida invariably took place in his office. There were exceptions, of course – once, I trapped him in the Nigerian High Commission in London to demand the fulfillment of a pledge to Robert Manley, the progressive Jamaican leader, during his electoral contest with the US- backed candidate,

Edward Seaga. Babangida had offered help, but the money was never sent. I had been involved in that initiative and now found myself being battered by messages from Jamaica. The honour of Nigeria was at stake but that was never under my custody; what I desperately needed was my peace of mind.

Dove-Edwin, the Nigerian High Commissioner and a friend was hosting a reception for his president, and promised to telephone me once the crowd had left. He did, let me into his residence and pointed to a large reception room, cautioning that he would deny any knowledge of how I got in – Babangida had warned that he wished to see no more visitors that day. My entry was muffled by a thick pile carpet and the dictator heard nothing, Slumped in a crested chair at the opposite end of the long reception room was a figure of – there was no other word for it – *pathos*. For minutes, I stood watching this repository of power, lost in thought, bereft of power and panoply, just another human being who had succumbed to common fatigue, sought a few moments' peace, sank into its tantalising solace even as he was already lamenting its looming departure. I felt somewhat remorseful that I had broken in on a moment when, it was plain, he truly needed to be alone – even rulers deserve their moment of rest, after all. Then I recalled that his own negligence or tardiness had disrupted mine, and I coughed to rouse him. He looked up, was visibly startled, then annoyed - snapping "How did you get in?" I replied, "All right, I'll go away", making no such move. Grumpily, he waved me to a chair.

Fifteen minutes later, we had reached agreement on the modalities of the transfer. I monitored its movements over the next week. Only after I was assured that it was in Robert Manley's possession did I consider any lecture invitations that might take me anywhere close to the West Indies.

Far more exhaustive was another closed-door session in his official jet, an unscheduled tête-à-tête that took place on the way back from Egypt where I had once again undergone one of those reunions with Egypt that have set me wondering just what that fascinating nation and I have against each other! That visit however provided one of the three occasions in Babangida's eight-year governance that I obtained a one-on-one meeting with him for truly in-depth, and wide ranging discussions – the Nigerian rumour mill that peddled my access to him on a daily, even hourly basis notwithstanding.

This infrequency of encounters with IBB was not due to indifference on my part. Whenever circumstances urged the possible usefulness of a meeting with this ruler, I picked up the telephone, or contacted my collaborator, Oje Aboyade – on Obasanjo's recommendation, Babangida had secured the services of my friend as his economic adviser. However, while the rest of the nation called this dictator Maradona, my name for him was Artful Dodger, or *the elusive àpárò*. The flight from Egypt was a godsend; a space without distractions. Babangida slid a panel across the middle of the official jet, and the rest of his entourage were shut out. Nothing disturbed a continuous session of about one and a half hours - no telephones, no whisper from a briefed aide tapping his pad to indicate a next fictitious appointment, a waiting dignitary or delegation – there was nowhere to go, except by parachute.

But now - Egypt! Some pristine secret lurks in that nation that makes it a setting for some of my most enduring episodes of pure chagrin! On this occasion, taking my ease in my own environment, along came a frantic message from the Egyptian President through his ambassador and my own government – would I kindly present myself in Cairo for a very special honour? The occasion was the elaborate opening ceremony of the All Africa Games, 1989. The invitation sounded attractive - sharing a podium with Nadine Gordimer and our Egyptian counterpart, Naguib Mafouz whom I would meet for the first time ever!

The notice was short and the timing awkward. The Egyptian Ambassador and IBB however appeared to take turns, independently, to apply pressure on me – some seasoned diplomat from our foreign ministry was definitely latched onto Babangida's ear! There were the usual arguments... the symbolic union of three African Nobelists, three African tribes on show – Arab, African and South African white – promoting a de-racialised African, pan-

African solidarity. Babangida was himself flying in to join Mubarak in presiding as co-chairman of the Games. I finally thought of one way of easing the strain on my interrupted routine – since it mattered so much to the continent and to him, would he kindly find me a seat on his official plane? He was more than willing.

I undertook to join his flight in Abuja, the capital, but a delayed morning flight from Lagos took care of that. Babangida's plane waited as long as protocol arrangements awaiting him at the Cairo end permitted, then took off without Mubarak's one-third continental symbolism. As the regretful phone call came through informing me of the plane's departure, the Egyptian Ambassador, who had come dutifully to see me off, appeared to be seized by an attack of St. Vitus' dance. I sought to calm him, opened my palms towards the heavens to indicate that we must all bow to the inevitable. It had the opposite effect. He immediately threw himself into a fermentation cauldron of solutions. He would get me into Cairo, he swore, even if he had to accompany me on camel back! Finally – the Egyptian national airline was due in Lagos the following morning on an onward flight to Cairo. He would come personally, ticket in hand, and escort me into the plane. A happy ending glowed on his face, nearly infecting me.

The following morning, it was not the airline ticket that called on me however, but the loyal but desperate representative of the Egyptian government, incoherent with apologies. *Your Excellency, please, you have to be there! An administrative hitch, I am sure. It's the preparations for the Games... you know, the officials are all preoccupied with nothing else. And bureaucracy, yes, bureaucracy, that's our problem. The ticket has not been wired but, for the sake of Africa, Your Excellency, you have to travel. Permit me to assure you, Professor Your Excellency – as soon as you land in Cairo, the Egyptian government will refund your travel expenses. The ceremony will more than compensate for this minor inconvenience. Your friend, your colleague, Mafouz is waiting to receive you, it will be a historic moment. Historic! Believe me, Excellency, this is as much as my job is worth, if I do not bring you to Cairo. The faxes and telexes have been coming fast and furious from the Presidency. The ticket is guaranteed. An administrative hitch, nothing else. I've contacted Egyptian airlines but unfortunately the ticket has not arrived. The embassy, ah, alas, we have no immediate funds...*

With not the sheerest thought that I was headed for yet another *contretemps* in the land of the Pharaohs, a masochistic streak disguised as race solidarity, I headed for the airport on the authority of my credit card. I quashed a deep down apprehension as it tried to rise to the surface, those earlier visits that led me to question if I had been an Egyptian in previous life – as Fela Anikulapo appeared to have believed of himself. Did my prior sojourn involve some negative, unfinished business in that Nile estuary? Certainly the consistency with which my entry into Egypt succeeds in resulting in some level of misadventure – from the hilarious to once life-threatening – has begun to alarm me. Perhaps my mummy is lying in one of the catacombs of the pyramids, or more resentfully, a skeleton of one of the slaves slaughtered to accompany the Pharaohs into afterlife.

Egyptian civilisation, persuasively demonstrated by the scholar Cheikh Anta Diop – *The African Origin of Civilisation*, supplemented years later by Martin Bernal – *Black Athena* – had its origins in the black race, so who is to tell if *Úgún*, my demiurge of war and creativity, did not at some distant age leave his mark on that land, some form of antibodies which now distort the intended trajectory of his followers who happen to stray into Egypt. Something is definitely askew somewhere, calling perhaps for rites of exorcism. I fully intend to delve into the mystery on my next visit which, to succeed, must scrupulously avoid all traces of officialdom!

For I never did meet Mafouz. Nadine Gordimer did not appear. No mention was made of any national honours. I was not received at the airport. Hotel rooms were non-existent. A taxi driver, to whom death in a motor accident was obviously no death at all but preparation for his next, elevated reincarnation, maybe as a priest of Isis – all but ended my career on the road between the airport and the hotel, courtesy of the tourist desk at the airport that eventually located some vacant form of habitation. It turned out to be a kind of athletes' transient lodge.

I got busy on the phone and left a message with the embassy

– surely someone must know of my arrival. The message that remained stuck in the desperate larynx of the abandoned VIP was however much richer: *WS speaking, you know, national treasure, special invitee of President Mubarak, yes, it's I, the Akínlatún of Ẹ̀gbá, the Akọgun of Ìṣárà, one third African symbolism at the All-Africa games, Commander of the Order of the Niger, etc. etc., who was to have hitched a ride in the presidential jet but was unpatriotically prevented by some domestic airline – yes, it's me, I made it on my own but don't quite know where I am and what to do. This contretemps is happening all over again – HELP!* For hours afterwards, I awaited rescue. None was forthcoming. History, my cyclic bugbear, appeared to be the presiding Muse at these All Africa Games.

After a few hours pondering this latest round of *dejà vu* on my Egyptian incursions – not least of which was a painful recollection of my truncated participation at the laying of the foundation stone of the Library of Alexandria – I was now ready to depart. It seemed fated. Somewhere in one of those tombs was the unappeased ghost of a wronged ancestor – mine – and my energised physical aura from the land of the Yoruba had once again aroused its millennial resentments, seeking redress or absolution at my hands. I turned for help to the front desk – literally a desk – asked for a copy of flight schedules heading anywhere out of Cairo. Even that motion reeked of a mimicry of the past.

Barely moments before I should have left for the airport however, a car screeched to a halt in front of the dormitory, and a flustered young man, tall and thin in his well tailored but flapping jacket, leapt out and introduced himself as a diplomat from the embassy. He had just picked up my message. In a few more minutes I was re-installed in another hotel, less Spartan, where, it turned out, reservations had indeed been made for me. At the desk, the young man enquired if there was any message from the Egyptian government for his guest – there was none. He then took off to track down his Egyptian counterparts to ensure that I had the necessary passes required to enter the stadium, promised to be back in time to accompany me to my seat – security being rigorously enforced. He returned in no time, crestfallen. He had been unable to find anyone who knew anything of my visit, much less of being a special guest of the Egyptian government, or personally of President Mubarak! I told him to go back to his duties – I was more than content to wander through the streets of Cairo, return to the hotel in time to watch the opening spectacular on television, then catch the first flight out of Egypt the following day.

He would have none of it. This wind-swept young diplomat, whose fragile frame totally belied his energy, took me in tow on one of the wildest drives in my nomadic career. He bullied, raged, forced his way through barriers of security checkpoints, with nothing but his diplomatic credentials and inadequate passes – he had not planned to go near the stadium until this challenge arose. At one stage, while his driver whimpered and cowered, he rode shotgun on the car bumper, screaming and cursing, directing the driver to an alternative checkpoint wherever the resistance proved unbreachable until he delivered me right into the sanctum sanctorum of the VIP sector, just to one side of the presidential box.

The show began and we were treated to a sumptuous display of the glorification of the Egyptian President Mubarak in between snatches of a grand parade of the Pharaohs, the Sphinxes, and passages of Egyptian history and heritage. Where, however, were the black Egyptians? Egypt, after all, did boast a black Pharaoh or two?

Babangida, it turned out, fared no better at the hands of Egyptian protocol. It had been announced in Nigeria that he would launch the games jointly with Mubarak but, the Egyptian organisers appeared to have forgotten that little detail. Mubarak's broad shoulders, sheathed in an impeccably turned suit, undertook the onerous task, while Babangida sat passively in the presidential box, to all purposes just another spectator. I do not think that Nigerian-Egyptian relations were enhanced by the undoubtedly impressive extravaganza of that very Egyptian occasion. The beginning of a Yoruba-Egyptian rapport also suffered yet another setback, as the Akínlatùn of Ẹ̀gbá, Akọgun of Ìṣarà, etc. etc, was left with yet another African solidarity hole in his pocket.

A Pen Coalition

General Vatsa, a heavy-set officer with deep-cut design of a radiating cicatrix that identified him instantly as being from one of the minority ethnic groups in the North, was an unusual soldier, a versifier on social themes and private thoughts. Vatsa courted the Nigerian writers and artists and dearly wished to be counted as one of them. Shortly after my spell in prison, and the publication of my account of that experience in *The Man Died,* he wrote some verses in protest at what he considered an unbalanced attitude in my book. Critical though they were, I was rather touched by this approach from a man of war, very different from the more usual – *What! Is he still talking? He should thank his stars he got off with his life!*

Later, we met, and I was again taken with his apparent thoughtfulness on the problems that confronted the nation. We never became friends, but I found him quite amiable and progressively disposed. During the presidency of Shehu Shagari and his party the NPN, I made the record *Unlimited Liability Company*, dedicated to the ineptness and corruption of that government, and the general decay of society. When it was launched at the Museum Kitchen garden at Únikan, Lagos, I was surprised to find this military man present. He sat quietly at his table, bought thirty copies of the record – for distribution among his military colleagues, he said.

I preferred to keep him at a distance, naturally, though I studied him keenly, from habit. When a high-ranked military officer attends a 'subversive' event, such as the launching of a sarcastic record against the government, and takes such material back to the army mess for distribution, he becomes a subject for some extra attention. It was just as well, because Vatsa would later defend – indeed, as it turned out, actually instigate and direct – a raid on the home of Obafemi Awolowo, the former opposition leader of the Unity Party of Nigeria, when the now inevitable coup took place in 1983 and the civilian dictatorship of Shehu Shagari was overthrown by the reputed man of discipline, General Buhari.

Obafemi Awolowo was not a member of the ousted government, but in opposition. He was rumoured to have in his possession some sensitive documents that related to the 3.8 or 4.1 billion dollar scandal yet unresolved during the previous two regimes. Mamman Vatsa raided Obafemi Awolowo's home in Ikenne, looking for 'classified documents', but never revealing the subject of classification. The writer and 'factionist', Kole Omotoso, interacted closely with Mamman Vatsa, through his functions as President of the Association of Nigerian Authors. During their discussions on Nigerian politics, Mamman Vatsa defended the raid, even threatened that Awolowo would be placed on trial for being in unauthorised possession of restricted documents. It was an empty boast however, but that was Mamman Vatsa.

Still, Vatsa, who had been placed in charge of Abuja capital territory, did his duty by the literary tribe to which he wanted so badly to belong. He allocated some property towards the project for a Writers' Village in Abuja and even supplied a military transport plane to take the writers to their annual conference, landing the Association's executive in hot water among some of the members, for getting too close to, and accepting favours from an unelected regime, even for the benefit of writers. Quite a few writers did take the purist line – no accommodation, in any form, with any military regime. Others believed that a silver lining – as long as it was not pocket lining! – could be mined from the darkest clouds. It all made for lively polemics, sometimes pitting the genuine puritans against the merely rhetorical contenders for the halo of the holier-than-thou.

Now, however, Mamman Vatsa was in deep trouble. Vatsa and Babangida were bosom friends, right from childhood. Their wives were also reported to be equally close. Vatsa may have been merely tolerated in the regime of Buhari and Idiagbon – the story was that he virtually forced himself on those coup-makers and was fobbed off with the then lightweight post of minister of Abuja capital territory. True or not, with the ascendancy of his friend Babangida, Mamman Vatsa came fully into his own. He was retained in his earlier position, but the ministry became as powerful as Mamman chose to make it. Mamman lived the good life. He devised a cape for his attire, referred to himself as Emperor of Abuja capital territory, which he ran with a free hand, apportioning valuable real estate to individuals and corporations according to his private laws.

What went wrong between the two friends, no one could really tell, but it was put down to rivalry between their wives as much as to Mamman Vatsa's own ambitions. A peer of both men in the military, General A. A., remarked that Vatsa's ambitions were not unlike Macbeth's – dormant, until fanned alive by a wife with a stronger will. I never did meet his wife, so I cannot tell. But it has proved impossible to erase from my mind the presence of that soldier who sat watching quietly at the Museum Kitchen, Úníkan, at the launching of my record, *Unlimited Liability Company*, and openly bought copies of the 'subversive' material for his colleagues. His appearance was the furthest imaginable from Caesar's 'lean and hungry', but his sly watchfulness made me think more of his co-emperor's nervous perspective on Cassius, than of Macbeth as putty in the hands of his worthy lady.

No matter, came 1988, and the nation's mildly watchful life under the smooth dictator was suddenly sent awry by the announcement of a coup attempt and, implicated at the highest level was the poet-soldier, General Mamman Vatsa. It was a numbing sight, watching on television the dapper general, Emperor of Abuja territory and friend of Nigerian writers, led in chains into court in company of other accused. Nigeria had become innured to coups, coup attempts and rumours of coups, but this was the strangest yet – the dictator's bosom friend, accused of masterminding his friend's overthrow.

Mamman Vatsa was found guilty – with several others – and sentence was pronounced – death by firing squad. Nigeria's military regimes were not noted for commuting sentences for treason – always a cynical charge, considering the means by which the complainant government had itself come to power. The public braced itself for the usual announcements of executions, went about its business with a sense of *deja vu* – *let them decimate one another; maybe when they've become sated with their own blood they'll return to the barracks and leave the nation in peace.*

One person felt – No! This was John Pepper Clark – now Bekederemo-Clark – poet and dramatist. We had been quite close in the early sixties, in the heydays of the Mbari cultural project when Nigerian writers and artists made a creative home in the slums of Adámásingbà, in Ìbàdàn. Indeed I had the distinction of taking off a corner of his German made Karman Ghia – now an obsolete model – against a palm tree. His coupe, unlike the standard Nigerian vehicle, was a left-hand drive at a time when Nigerians drove on the left side of the road, as bequeathed by British colonisers. JP's car was one of the rare exceptions. He was also prone to accidents at the time, which was why he readily surrendered the car to me whenever we were together. Such was the rate of his encounters with walls, trees and gutters that I once felt compelled to slaughter a sacrificial goat on his behalf, right on the open stage, during the production of his play, *Song of a Goat*. Naturally, I never really considered that it was I who had caused the accident but his car which, under JP's aura, took a yen to the palm tree on the way to my university apartment.

JP Clark had become troubled. Mulling over his drink – as I imagined it – the stocky, pugnacious poet had perhaps run through the reel of casualties in the numerous coups and allied killings, was perhaps even haunted by a sense of vicarious responsibility for the initial coup – JP, I always suspected, did have a first-hand knowledge, albeit vague, of the very first coup d'état of 1966. With Christopher Okigbo, he had accompanied one of the principals – Major Emanuel Ifeajuna – across the border, the latter in female disguise. JP turned back at the border while Christopher crossed over to the Republic of Benin (then Dahomey) taking charge of Ifeajuna who was by then virtually an emotional wreck, haunted – Christopher related – by images of bloodstreams cascading from his dying victims, his superior officers, none of whom was a stranger to him.

JP brought back with him the manuscript of Ifeajuna's account of the coup, hurriedly put together during his period of hiding by that young major and former athlete – he was one of the four who set a joint 6'6 record in high jump at the Commonwealth Games in Vancouver, 1956. Knowledge of the existence of the manuscript set off a wild hunt by Gowon's Military Intelligence, desperate for an authentic, first-hand account of those who had plotted the '66 coup, who had done the killings, what civilians, especially politicians, had prior knowledge or had collaborated in the putsch. For a while JP Clark was deemed a security risk. So were his publishers, Longmans, whose editors at one time or the other held the explosive manuscript in their possession, debating the wisdom of releasing its contents into the market.

I could picture JP tabulating the waste, the losses, and the uncertain returns: the 1966 coup, and attendant deaths; the revenge killings of May, known as the 'minor massacres' – some distinction! – then the counter-coup of July and yet more killings, a truly gory affair where even my serene hometown, Abẹòkúta, was the setting for the flaying of a garrison commander – tied to the back of a Land Rover and dragged round and round till death took pity on him. Hot on the heels of that counter-coup followed the 'major massacres' of September that same year, a further revenge killing but also consolidation of the July counter-coup. Then the bloody attempt of 1976 – known as the Dimka coup – a failure, but it terminated the life of Murtala Mohammed, the charismatic dictator, a once military reprobate himself who, on attaining power, most unusually became a reformed man and a convinced social reformer, earning adulation beyond an objective balance of his detractions and achievements. At some point, JP Clark must have sighed – *Enough.*

I was enjoying one of my periods of total hibernation in Abẹ́òkúta when my peace was crashed by a least expected face, at the sight of which I could only blink in disbelief. I was in fact, returning from a successful foray into the bush. I stepped out of my jeep all grimy and sweaty, retrieved my gun and the brace of birds when I heard a voice I had not heard for a long time, issuing from my house frontage:

"Good God, you mean you actually catch these things when you go in the bush?"

It was indeed John Pepper Bekederemo-Clark, poet and playwright, with whom my relationship had not been lately of the best. He came close, inspected the birds and burst into a loud chuckle. "I'd heard about your hunting but I never knew it was something you actually did."

I did not know what to make of that, but understood that there was awkwardness on both sides. I could not imagine what on earth he wanted.

"JP, how on earth did you find this place?"

"Oh it was tough. But I remembered I knew someone in Abẹ́òkúta who was bound to know where you were." He introduced his companion. "In any case, I was determined not to leave till I found you. If I hadn't found you today, I would have returned tomorrow."

I thought, what is he up to now? Our last reconciliation effort had been short-lived, so what instigated this visitation from my tempestuous colleague?

"Mamman Vatsa," said JP, and the words tumbled out. "We must save him. Not just him but all the others. There is far too much blood-letting. We have to persuade Babangida that he can break the spiral of blood and set the nation on a new course. We have to do something, Wole. After all the killing that followed the Dimka coup, we can't allow this to happen. We have to act. History will not forgive us if we failed."

JP's idea was that three of us, himself, Chinua Achebe and I – often dubbed the 'elder statesmen' of Nigerian contemporary literature – should make a publicised personal appeal to Babangida and the Ruling Council for the lives of the accused, based principally on the plea that the nation had had enough of killings, and all future action should be directed at national healing. Moreover, Vatsa's attempt, as far as we knew, was yet only a plot in the making. We should appeal to Babangida's sense of history and stress that this was an opportunity to map out a different course for his administration from the accustomed pattern of vengeance. There were hawks within the final decision-making body, but there were also the doves, JP declared, including probably Babangida himself, who might be inclined to save the life of his childhood friend. Our position would strengthen his hand. JP paced restlessly, totally consumed by his optimism. He had spoken to the secretary or assistant secretary to the cabinet and that official would facilitate the meeting. It would help of course if I also telephoned ahead. In any case, JP pointed out, bristling with confidence, if we three walked right up to Dodan Barracks, knocked on the gates and demanded to see the President, who was going to deny us entrance? Our combined stature would open any door in the nation.

His enthusiasm was infectious. We would pool resources. JP was already in contact with someone else who would contribute additional weight to our demand. I would call Aboyade, compel him to follow up the case after our visit. Chinua Achebe, he revealed, already awaited us in Lagos.

Our arrival at Dodan Barracks the following day was a much anticipated event, covered by the media corps that was permanently encamped at the Presidency. It was clear that the civil servant who attended us was no hawk. He welcomed the initiative with more than a functionaire's disinterest, took pains to impress on us our chances of success, offered opinions on what arguments would have the greatest effect, how to stand our ground against any counter arguments, etc. Babangida was in a meeting when we arrived but, even as we were ushered into his wing of the sprawling complex, he came to meet us outside, beaming his famous, later notorious tooth-gap smile. Once we were seated, he thanked us profusely for the visit, assured us in advance that he understood that our intervention had been motivated by the highest humane principles.

Chinua Achebe spoke, I followed, and JP added his plea, each using the precious minutes we had extorted from Babangida's schedule as forcefully as we knew how. It was a sombre half-hour, intense, and we were all conscious of – no other way to put it – the near sanctity of our mission. I think both Chinua and I were somewhat startled to hear JP introduce a rather arcane dimension that he had remarked upon briefly during our earlier exchanges – he had traced the blood pattern of such challenges to power backwards, and observed that a cycle of violence appeared to emerge every four years. Babangida was uniquely placed, he argued, to break the four-year jinx. Not for one moment did I imagine that such a basically superstitious argument would impress those hard-headed soldiers but then, one never knew, and soldiers are notorious for their superstitious outlook anyway. Babangida, the consummate listener, gave equal attentiveness to all the arguments, nodding gently.

We were done. Babangida hung his head for a few moments before speaking. "Gentlemen, I wish to thank you, believe me, with all sincerity. I don't know if you're aware that Vatsa and I were very close, very close indeed. His wife and mine – they are like sisters. So you see, for me, this is not just a military affair, it is a heart-rending situation, a family tragedy. And I am sure you can see how sincerely I welcome your intervention. I suspended a meeting the moment I heard you were here – in fact, I was annoyed that I hadn't been informed earlier. Since when has Dodan Barracks been honoured by the presence of the three leading writers of this nation!"

He gave one of his broad smiles, then turned solemn once again. "We need more of this kind of exchange, I mean that seriously. And not just when there is a crisis of this nature. You must feel free to call on me any time. We could do with your advice on affairs of the nation."

The general took a deep breath, raised his head to give emphasis to his next words. "Regarding what brought you here, I wish to give you my word of honour – I shall go into the crucial meeting determined to do everything in my power to save them. I assure you, I shall not be party to their execution. That I can promise you. You have no idea how much your visit here has helped me. Again, I give you my word, I shall do my uttermost to see that the lives of those men are spared."

How we maintained a semblance of dignity, refrained from letting out a loud whoopie, launching into cartwheels or breaking into an *atilogwu*[1] dance, I shall never know, but we all three admitted that our lungs were dying to burst into a victory song as soon as we heard that pledge: *my word of honour*.

The secretary was waiting nervously to debrief us – it was as if he had a personal interest in the result and sure enough, he admitted it. A very close relation of his was among the condemned and, it would appear, he did not believe that there had been as serious an attempt to overthrow the regime as was claimed. When we gave him a quick summary of the meeting, the uplift in his mood could be weighed. He thanked us profusely. We had done a world of good. Now we had given Babangida all the moral support he needed to deal with the hawks and bring the waverers over to his side. The principal hawk, whom he named, would now find himself isolated and, in any case, now that the Commander-in-Chief had set his mind against the executions, that was the end of the matter. The press had picked up news of our visit and were waiting outside. We revealed nothing, gave no interviews, but our presence and purpose at Dodan Barracks were over radio and television within the hour. The nation, equally sick of incessant blood-letting, had already begun to breathe some air of hope.

The secretary saw us to our car. I drove. We managed to hold down the euphoria until we had driven round the first corner and then, burst into yells – JP's being the most manic. I drove off as if on a triumphal lap on a race circuit. Mission accomplished, and with an affirmation that we hardly dared expect. We badly needed to celebrate – so we repaired to Bintu's restaurant. We ordered the worthy proprietress to 'shake up her kitchen double quick' for a special workout, and extract whatever wines she kept in reserve for her brother, my friend OBJ, who came there sometimes to lunch or dine. We kept our secret but made no effort to disguise our euphoric condition, raised glasses to one another

---

[1] An energetic dance of the Eastern Igbo people.

and to bemused customers who must have concluded that the 'elder statesmen' of Nigerian literature had finally gone collectively off their minds. We knew we were also celebrating more than the mere reprieve of our fellow writer and his companions, we were celebrating a reunion – the three of us together – and bound in a common purpose – after nearly two decades!

For JP, it was a personal vindication that brought a very special reward. "My circle of friends," he admitted in Abẹòkúta when he bemoaned our prolonged estrangement, and he made a tight circle with his thumb and forefinger, "my circle of friends has contracted to a mere – dot." I had never known any human being make such a humble confession, nor heard it ever since. We were thus celebrating JP's renewed embrace of a loosely defined community of literary pioneers, and he, the main celebrant, had engineered it himself, and in such style – saving the lives of a footloose member of the wider artistic community. It was a moment to be savoured.

JP wanted us to make a night of it but, I needed my retreat, and it was the thought of Lagos traffic at closing hours that finally prised me from the table and into my car, with the thought that the next Sunday night would definitely be spent at Femi's in Ìbàdàn, since no celebration was complete until Femi and I pronounced it so – through a consummative, summative celebration. He would be waiting anxiously, insisting on a verbatim account – nothing less ever satisfied him – *wait, wait, wait, stop! Oh, you know, you really are very irritating – don't jump, don't jump. You don't know how to 'knack gen'[2], that's your trouble, it's not the same as writing. Go back – so, he came out of his office to meet you. Right. Begin from there. What did he say? All right. Does he go around with bodyguards? What of Chinua Achebe? All right, in what order did you speak? What do you mean – didn't Achebe come to Abẹòkúta? He didn't? You mean JP sought you out alone, all by himself? What! You see, you have to go back. I keep telling you, you gave me the impression that all three of you took the decision in Abẹòkúta. See? See what I keep telling you? Now you have to start all over again. Don't leave anything out. So, JP came to Abẹòkúta,*

---

[2] Nigerian slang – breath life into a good story.

you were coming in from the bush – which reminds me, where is my
share of the àpárò...?

Driving to Abẹ́òkúta, smiling all by myself like a lunatic as I
anticipated my 'debriefing' at Femi's table in Ìbàdàn in another
day or two, I knew that I still needed something to bring me down
from the clouds before I could do any work that night – or maybe
it was best simply to drink some more wine, go to sleep and then
wake up in the middle of the night to work? I was undecided.
There was however a good half-hour of daylight when I arrived,
enough time to go into the walled-in overgrown courtyard just
behind my house where a few àpárò families had made their home.
I hunted that patch of land with extreme parsimoniousness, just
those times when my body needed to be decompressed, or I was
confronted by the spectre of an empty larder and the rare
unexpected – and hungry – visitor.

I rushed upstairs, grabbed my gun, rushed out again and
dashed into the bush. I heard Seyi, my landlady's son hailing me
from the window of their half of the house, but this was no occasion
for one of his hunting lessons. I needed my own exulting company,
not shared with anyone, least of all an eager young pupil. So I
shouted back that I would see him later, feeling a little guilty.
Twenty minutes later, I outwaited a bird and forced it to fly.

Seyi came running in after the shot to assist me in finding the
victim – so I thought. But no, he was merely waiting until he had
heard me fire so he would not alert the quarry, and of course also
make sure that he could safely approach. I heard him coming,
and soon enough he appeared. I stood still as usual, with my eye
affixed to the landing spot, then signalled to him. Normally Seyi
would be leaping and thrashing towards the indicated spot, but
now he remained in a kind of apologetic stance, watching me, I
later surmised, with a kind of pity.

"It's over there," I shouted. "Go where my arm is pointing."

All he said was: "The TV covered your meeting with
Babangida."

"Already? It went quite well. Move." The light was fading
fast. "It's over there by the tree."

"They've shot them" he said.

I heard only the word 'shot', so I nodded and moved forward, not taking my eye from the spot. "Oh yes, it landed over there. Let's go find it."

"Vatsa and the others. It was on the six o'clock news, just as you were driving in."

The world froze before my eyes. "Shot who? What are you talking about?"

"This afternoon. About an hour ago."

I said, stupidly, "But the Council... they were not to meet until late this afternoon. That's when the final appeal would be decided."

"They met earlier. At three-thirty. They confirmed the sentence and the accused were taken straight from their cells and shot."

My mind unwound itself like a clock, timing our activities. We had left Dodan Barracks around a quarter to twelve. The Council was not even supposed to meet until five o'clock – the secretary had spelt that out in specific terms when he made the appointment – the schedule for the Council meeting read – five o'clock. Their comprehensive agenda would probably take them late into the night, sometimes beyond midnight. Who moved the meeting forward? Why? My mind was in complete rout, asking questions haphazardly. Where was Chinua? And JP? Had they learnt of the disastrous end to our intervention? What part did Babangida play in all this? Was it all a game to him?

And then – horror of horrors! – could our intervention have accelerated the process that led to these executions?

Seyi had been standing in front of me, but I did not know when he left. I next saw him holding out the dead bird. I shook my head and waved him away, walked back to the house.

My sense of isolation was overwhelming. Too depressed to work or sleep, too depressed even to think, I dragged myself to Ìbàdàn the following day. It was the only spot on earth from which I could search for a sliver of light to relieve the doom of futility that appeared to lie in ambush for any endeavour in a humane cause. I developed an allergy towards the very sight of the military uniform for a long while after, including even photographs in the news media. I began to think that maybe I was on the wrong planet, certainly in the wrong part of it. This man *had given his word!* If it was all a game, then I really did not want to know these people. For another week, I considered leaving the country, going on voluntary exile for a year, maybe longer, maybe go away altogether and make my reasons public, returning only when the country had returned to democracy.

About two months later, I ran into the secretary, whose 'brother', or close relation had been among the casualties of that military justice. "Oh Prof., I had been hoping I would run into you. IBB wanted me to pass on a message."

"I don't wish to hear it." And I turned brusquely away.

"But you should, you should."

"No thank you, I do not know IBB. I do not wish to know him."

He smiled, somewhat ruefully. "I can understand. But then I also had a message of my own for you. In fact, I already asked JP to pass it on to the rest of you."

I stopped, and he continued. "That Council meeting - you should know what transpired at the meeting."

I shook my head. "It doesn't matter. I really am not interested."

"Prof., listen, you know I was affected. I lost a brother, he was virtually a brother to me. But I know you'll be interested in the truth. Babangida put up a fight, a really good fight for the lives of those men."

"Yeah?"

"He did, Prof. You see, these soldiers, they have their way of doing things. There was a point when the chairman of the judicial panel said to IBB - look òga, we are all agreed on what needs to be done. If you cannot put your hand to it, then please step aside."

"What do you mean? Were they asking him to resign?"

"Prof., all I can do is give you a report of how that meeting went. I think it's only fair that you know that IBB kept his word. He has been most anxious that you know it. He begged me to find you and let you know. And I swear, that decision really broke him up, it really did."

I emitted a sound that hopefully translated as a rasp of skepticism, indifference and disgust. Even as the man spoke, I had already made up my mind to use my own sources to check on the various roles played by the members of the death dealing Council. I wanted to know if these men of iron wore two faces or more. And then I checked myself in stride – what did it matter in the end whose voice steamrolled the accused into their graves anyway? Were they not all an indissoluble part of the collective machinery of killing? I recalled who cast the deciding vote that sent a General Ilya Bisalla to the stake for the 1976 'Dimka Coup' that saw the end of Murtala Mohammed, after the panel had deadlocked over a verdict. It was none other than my erstwhile military collaborator, adversary, and friend of sorts – General Obasanjo. And then again, the purported role of the affable General Ike Nwachukwu, who had also chaired a panel on yet another coup attempt that sent several soldiers to the execution stake. I did not know him then but, some years later, it would prove to be the same Nwachukwu, as Babangida's foreign minister, who would provide a support base when I came to engage in a secret diplomacy – an attempt to bring South Africa's Buthelezi and Mandela together in an effort to terminate an even more brutal cycle of revenge killings.

Predictably, the mood passed, even sooner than I anticipated. First, I believed the young functionaire whose brother was among the executed. Mostly however, there were causes to be pursued, a fellow being to be rescued, a screaming injustice to be redressed, lives that could be made more bearable, and even an insufferable limb of the same power structure that had to be restrained, punished or even amputated – cashiered from the army – using the same agents of destruction while they remained in power, and could not immediately be displaced.

Even without the rebuff by Vatsa's fate, the trio of literary 'elder statemen' knew that any intervention by them, after the next attempt to topple Babangida, in April 1990, was doomed from the start. Even by Nigerian standards, it had been exceptionally bloody. The mood of the military could be gauged in advance, and the reprisals that followed bore it out, evoking an image of the gutters of Lagos streets clogged with blood. No less than eighty officers and soldiers – mostly from the Middle Belt of the nation – had been led in batches to the execution stakes. It became known as the Orkar Coup, after one of its leaders, Gideon Orkar, and earned notoriety not merely from the bloodiness of the attempt, but from the unusual agenda of the coupmakers, outlined to the nation in their very first radio broadcast. No fewer than five states from the far North, identified as bastions of a feudal hegemony – were to be excised from the Nigerian national entity. They were to be cast in limbo, to find their fortunes as best as they could or else, to reform themselves along specified lines, and only then apply for reabsorption into the Nigerian state! The conditions for their re-admittance would be revealed in further announcements, the broadcast promised. It was a unique agenda in the history of coups d'etat.

Funded by a businessman, Great (his real name) Ogboru, an invading force successfully trained in secret, undetected for months, in the fenced compound of a fish depot in Ikòròdú, some thirty kilometers from Lagos. A section seized the national radio station in Ìkòyí while the other moved on Dodan Barracks, shot its way right into Babangida's bedroom with the single-minded purpose of eliminating him, together with his family. From all reports, Babangida seized a sub-machine gun and fought back but was stopped and spirited out by his bodyguards.

The machine gun mounted on the armoured car stationed for the protection of the seat of government had been spiked earlier by an insider, and the young aide-de-camp who rushed to man the gun for the defence of his master was easily mown down. The invaders decimated the sparse force that remained for the defence of Dodan Barracks while others sought out the senior officers of Babangida's government. The attempt would have succeeded – even if short-lived – but for an incredible act of neglect by the coup-plotters: their failure to disable the telephone lines. Mobile phones were a rarity in 1990, even within the military. Where they existed, they were so temperamental as to be mostly superfluous. This enabled a missed target, the Chief of Army Staff, who happened to have departed earlier from his anticipated location – quite a bodybag of glitches! – to make probing phone calls, determine the leaning and situation of his respondents, and mobilise loyalists. Suitably reinforced, that officer, Sani Abacha, launched a counter-attack while the coup-makers were already celebrating their presumed victory. The rest was a rout, and Babangida's government exacted a terrible vengeance on the losers.

The afternoon of that coup attempt, I had been present at the scene that would witness the fiercest battle – Dodan Barracks itself. It was symbolic of my relationships with power – that this bloody battle would erupt virtually on the heels of the only other tête-à-tête that I could count as a meaningful, extended discourse with that dictator. This time, it was a one-man 'coalition' undertaking a rescue mission, and not just for a fellow poet and his fellow accused, but for the endangered species – the entire nation entity called Nigeria.

The 'summit' had proved long in the setting-up, and the list that I took with me had built up over time, all items rehearsed in advance in meetings with my co-conspirator, Ojetunji Aboyade, the Chairman of his Presidential Advisory Committee. Our meetings invariably began with some frustrating, brain-beating that would then end in Oje's – *look, why don't you talk to him? Maybe if it came from you, from the outside... I think he's beginning to find me predictable.*   Some – not especially enthusiastic but not totally unwilling – moments later, we put through a phone call, attempting to set up an appointment. Usually accepted, and with vocal enthusiasm, it would suffer a postponement, then another, until the issues were perhaps overtaken by events. This time, it was different. Babangida had conscientiously reserved an afternoon when he was truly free of distractions.

The 22nd of April, 1990 was a public holiday, thus the seat of government on that afternoon was just as any day could be wished when one is impelled by serious matters that require a long discussion with the principal executive officer of a nation – unaccustomedly quiet, devoid of the routine officials and visitors, not forgetting the army of hangers-on. From my entry into the waiting room and, almost immediately, into his office, I encountered virtually no human being. Even the few plain-clothes security officers appeared to be in a state of suspended animation.

When one has strayed into an arena, only hours before a life-and-death drama has entered into its final rehearsals, it is not possible to forget, later, what one did or said within such a charged space. A creepy sensation intrudes – afterwards – insinuating that the outsider had somehow participated, albeit unwittingly, and disconnectedly, in setting the stage for the coming upheaval. It was afternoon, late, but far from dusk. For the first time, my encounter with Babangida was unhurried. The dictator had finally, with all serious intent, carved out the time I had insisted upon for an undisturbed, leisurely voyage through a turbulent list. Recalling the intense absorption on both sides, the thoroughgoing nature of our discussion, unhurried, an invisible observer might have wondered if the fate of a nation was being decided within those walls, that perhaps all the postponements had been orchestrated by some mystery force, simply to ensure that I was present that afternoon, an afternoon without the slightest distraction – just the dictator, myself, and the spectre of death.

Learning, a few days later, that the quiet young officer in mufti who had ushered me in and out had perished in the ensuing action only added to the mind's perturbation, imbuing an afternoon of straightforward exchanges, in retrospect, with a fatedness. That gentle, anything but warlike face of the young officer, Bello, haunted me for some time afterwards, as if it had hovered around the discussion, a silent moderator whose final act was to be the sacrificial lamb, an omen and surrogate for his master's close encounter with death. The invaders, after all, did hold Babangida by a sheer hair's breath away from the precipice of extinction. Indeed, the effect was still with him, months later, when we next met in Abuja. That was at a luncheon where Mandela, the guest of honour, sat between us. Babangida was haunted by memories of that night of close reckoning. He could not shake the topic free of his emotions at the time, as he yet again outlined the course of events to his sympathetic guest.

"There was no indication," he repeated again and again with a sense of wonder, so unlike what I expected from a soldier whose trade is dealing in and warding off death, "nothing at all, not a sign to indicate that anything was amiss. In fact" – and he leant across Mandela for the sixth or seventh time, as if I was the sole remaining source of reassurance or earthling device to the world of rationality – "the Professor was with me that afternoon. We were in my office, a long afternoon when we covered so much ground. Did you notice anything, Wole, any sign at all?"

I shook my head, negatively.

"I was mostly alone," he continued, settling back with his eyes still wide with the wonder of death, of death that came calling, very close, barely missed, "just a few security officers and my aide-de-camp, you know, the young officer" – again he leant across – "you remember him don't you, Prof. He was the one who was killed, did you know that?"

From deep within Babangida's eyes, as he recounted these events, shot the shafts of fear that must have assailed him when Orkar's men broke into his bedroom. Mandela appeared awestruck, turned to look at me in some amazement:

"You were present?"

I quickly corrected him. "No, that's not what he meant..."

Babangida looked lost. "But Prof., you were there. We spent over an hour, no, more than that, over an hour and a half in my office..."

"I meant, I left some hours before the invasion."

"Oh yes of course. But I mean, did you notice anything? Anything suspicious at all?"

"Nothing ominous," I affirmed. That there was no sign of a warning seemed to matter to the seasoned coup-maker – not that he worried about the issue as a practical security consideration, no. It was simply that it appeared to have acquired a kind of mystical relevance. Months after the event, Babangida sounded as if he remained entranced by this omission, found it weird, deeply unnatural that the coup-makers had sent no warning sign of their intentions.

"Prof. had come to see me on a number of national issues. You do remember what a wide range of topics we covered...?"

1. "Wild Christian"

2. "Essay"

3. In the late 1930s the Women of Aké, led by the author's aunt, the formidable Funmilayo Ransome-Kuti (*4th left, second row*), rose against unjust taxes and chased the feudal lord, the Aláke of Abéòkúta, from his throne.

4. A 1952 family portrait.
5. (*Inset*) "Wild Christian" on her 70th birthday with (*clockwise from left*): WS, Yeside, Kayode, Folabo and Tinu.

6. As "The Magician" in a school operetta at St. Peter's School, Aké, in 1943 (*middle, front row*).

7. First year at Government College, Ibadan, in 1946, with members of the Dramatic Club.

8. The Original Seven – founders of the first campus fraternity, the Pyrates, whose creed was anti-elitism and anti-colonial mentality – 1952.

9. As a first year student in Leeds in 1955: "Studying in England in the mid-1950s found most of us African students headed for London to earn some extra money, mostly as porters in railway stations, post offices and bars."

10. As Patrice Lumumba in Joan Littlewood's production of Conor Cruise O'Brien's *Les Anges Meurtriers* in Paris in 1970: "Joan knew that I did not speak French, yet she insisted on casting me in a play to be performed in la langue Française."

11. The author and his late friend Olufemi Babington Johnson: "a large presence in the 'extra-curricular' undertakings of my adult existence, whose meticulousness has always fascinated me … Perhaps what drew me to him was part recognition of that road not taken, the suppressed artist within a nattily suited businessman."

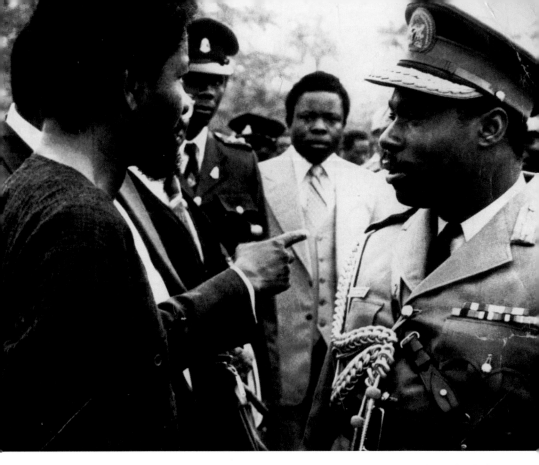

12. With Olusegun Obasanjo, as military ruler in 1978: "A bullish personality, calculating and devious, yet capable of a disarming spontaneity, affecting an exaggerated country yokel act to cover up the interior actuality of the same, occasionally self-deprecating, yet intolerant of criticism … "

13. "My perception of Ibrahim Babangida is that of a suave, calculating and persuasive listener, but with sheathed claws, ever ready to cultivate potential allies. He had a reputation for meticulous planning … "

Daily Times

THE INDEPENDENT NEWSPAPER

17,850 Monday, October 18, 1965 3d

Mr SOYINKA DECLARED A 'WANTED PERSON'

..to help cops in NBC blackout riddle

MR. Wole Soyinka, a lecturer at the University of Lagos, was yesterday declared a wanted person by the police.

He is wanted by the police in connection with an incident in which a man entered into the studio of the Nigerian Broadcasting Corporation and seized a recorded tape of the speech of the Western Nigeria Premier, Chief Samuel Ladoke Akintola, which was to have been broadcast at 7.15 p.m. last Friday.

The man was reported to have seized the tape at about 7.14 p.m. on the night of the incident. Consequently, instead of hearing the Premier's voice, listeners heard a "strange voice" shouting UPGA

14. "I was already underground before I was declared 'wanted'."

15. The prosecution had undone itself: "We had secured a verdict through a pure technicality that came from a crucial contradiction within the prosecution's elaborately presented case."

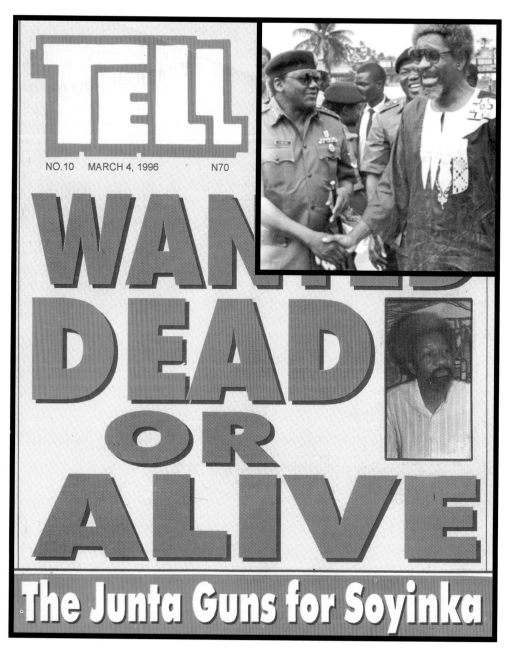

16. (*Inset*) One of two meetings with Sani Abacha who was Army Chief of Staff in 1989 when the author was Chairman of the Federal Road Safety Corps (FRSC). A few years later Abacha had seized power and started to muzzle all opposition; the author was "formerly declared a wanted man by the Abacha regime, quite a few colleagues paid a heavy price even for mere association that preceded the regime."

17. I finally presented myself at a press conference at the UNESCO headquarters in Paris towards the end of November, 1995; it was only then that my escape became known.

18. "Abiola was the elected president of a nation who never did preside over anything more than his home, his vast network of business and, finally, his place of detention. He was served the cup of tea that has now attained legendary status in the nation, for Abiola suffered a seizure minutes after that cup, collapsed and died."

19. At Dodan Barracks to plead for Mamman Vatsa: "JP's idea was that three of us, himself, Chinua Achebe and I ... should make a publicised personal appeal to Babangida and the Ruling Council for the lives of the accused."

20. A warm embrace with former leader, Yakubu Gowon, who kept the author in prison detention for twenty-eight months, twenty-two in solitary confinement.

21. In Bekuta: "a centuries-wide reunion with my own history sent a tingle down my vertebrae – an encounter with descendants from my own hometown, Abéòkúta, on a far-flung Caribbean island, in the hills of a once slave settlement called Jamaica."

22. With the "individual institution known as Archbishop Desmond Tutu".

23. Meeting Kofi Annan, secretary-general of the United Nations in Vienna, shortly before his trip to Nigeria where he would see Moshood Abiola in prison: "Warning of the death threat to Abiola was delivered into my hands only after Kofi Annan had left for Nigeria and had even held his meeting with the prisoner."

24, 25. "The house had been built almost entirely from the windfall of the Nobel Prize. I expanded it from its original design only because I wanted to create a space for periodic retreats for writers and artists, typical of fantasies of those who are suddenly bombarded with more money than family generations before them ever laid eyes on! Thus was born the notion of Essay Foundation, named after my father."

26. "My garage was home to my modest collection of mostly traditional artworks. I lavished all my spare resources in acquiring them … and this was where I spent most of my time, working among the ancestral masks, the Gods, their caryatids, shrine posts and votive vessels, basking in their aura … they provided relief for the mind when inspiration flagged and my fingers fluttered aimlessly over the typewriter…"

27. In 1987, honoured by Fidel Castro.

28. With former First Lady, now Senator Hillary Clinton.

29. South Africa, 2005, with "the sage Nelson Mandela".

30. With West Indian writer/philosopher, C. L. R. James
(*middle*) and Guinean poet, Tamsin Niane.

31. With Leopold Sedar Senghor, Negritude poet and former
president of Senegal, at Senghor's 60th birthday.

32. University of Leeds, April 2004: honorary award for Ngugi wa Thiong'o,
Kenyan novelist and fellow Leeds alumnus, and inauguration of the
Wole Soyinka Chair of Drama.

33. Stockholm, 1986: "As a laureate, you are expected to be different from whatever you were before. Others simply demand, even wordlessly, that one act different, eat different, talk different, dress different, walk different, abandon former haunts, former preoccupations, former idiosyncrasies, former likes and dislikes, and don, overnight, a totally fictitious persona that corresponds to their fantasies."

34. "Such sustained devotion to the cause of wine must have been mystically transmitted to the oenophile nobility of France and resulted in my most treasured recognition, to which even the Nobel takes second place."

Of course I remembered! And I remembered also thinking afterwards how lucky it was that the army traditionally opted for dawn or night time to stage its coups. Suppose the invading force had chosen to break with tradition – it was a public holiday, so there was not much movement about. In my view, that quiet, unprotected afternoon seemed perfect for such a venture – after all, surprise, springing the unexpected is part of military strategy.

The difference between Babangida and Obasanjo had struck me most forcibly yet that afternoon of the Orkar coup – both frustrating rulers in different ways. Babangida hardly ever argued in an oppositional manner, he listened, took notes, interjecting a comment from time to time or else giving an explanation why a policy was made in the first place, but always with a hint that it need not be so, that if the situation changed tomorrow, then the policy would change. Nothing ever appeared cast in stone when you spoke to Babangida who, either by temperament or practice, nearly always presented a *reasonable* persona. He did not hesitate to agree with you, then of course he proceeded later to do the opposite of what you thought he had agreed upon.

Only once, during the exchanges, did I see his face harden in an automatic, bunker rejection, and that was when we came to the sore subject of his intervention in the University of Ifè, where he had ordered the dismissal of some of the academic staff – all acknowledged leftists and radicals. It was as if I had bumped against a boil. He launched into a catalogue of the destabilising activities of which the dons had been accused. I asked him how he came by such information, and he kept fingering, casually but suggestively, a folder that he extracted smoothly from a drawer in his desk, as if that action fulfilled all the requirements of rebuttal that the subject demanded. Had he personally ordered the dismissal of the dons? No, he assured me, it was all the decision of his minister of education – only to trip himself up some moments later in a flash of anger that conceded that he had either given or approved the order.

And thus it went all afternoon, a relaxed but occasionally charged exchange, unconscious of armoured tanks being re-positioned around us, others being rendered useless by some undetected re-adjustments of their working parts, the final touches being put in place for the execution of what would go down as the messiest coup attempt in Nigerian history – a deadly broth of the arcane and the ruthless. Miles away, while we probed aspects of a national malaise, skirmished around factors and culpability for the blatant culture of corruption that had become synonymous with his government, an array of serving officers and ex-servicemen had begun to slip out from their training grounds in a fish depot in Ikòròdú twenty five kilometers away, infiltrate Lagos as passengers in public transport and private vehicles, regroup and take up positions, awaiting the descent of darkness.

Unusually, there had been no rumours. The nation – and Lagos – went about its business. Ọbálẹ́ndẹ́ – its usual hive of swarming humanity, of jostling '*danfo*' buses, touts and passengers hustling and querulous, steamy and grime-clotted, its night life gearing up to encroach upon, and eventually take over the daytime market life, one of the gateways to Dodan Barracks, was only slightly more subdued than usual, on account of the holiday. Quietly, in air-conditioned complacency, we continued our discussions. The nation was close to explosion unless a virtual U-turn in economic policies was effected soon – did he agree, and did he intend to act to provide relief or face the ire of Labour? Babangida appeared to be confident of having taken the measure of organised Labour, yet was willing to re-address the implications of the Structural Adjustment Programme.

From the sublime to the ridiculous, such as the overweening conduct of his wife, Maryam, who fantasised she was a Nigerian Eva Peron but was blatantly Imelda Marcos. I had already assailed that affliction, most stridently perhaps during a keynote address at the previous annual convention of the Association of Nigerian Authors where I formally pronounced the era of FirstLadyism and its attendant toadyism. To Babangida's credit, he had responded by curbing some of his wife's public excesses – but not by much. They crept, then galloped back, until the worthy lady was spoken of as running a parallel government. She plucked long-serving permanent secretaries from their duties to serve as ladies-in-waiting, bullied her husband's ministers at whim, and insulted them publicly, engineered one resignation here, a dismissal there. She took to ordering all radio and television stations to tune in to her endless stream of money-guzzling, self-promoting projects.

How much tact can one summon to impress on a dictator that his wife is considered a public pain in the neck? I like to flatter myself that I navigated those sensitive shoals as well as any untrained and reluctant diplomat could! The rebuked husband smiled wanly, gamely accepted that I was right and that he had begun to take steps, not only in his own household but with governors and senior officers. Outside, Dodan Barracks remained eerily silent.

And the elections in Jamaica? Could Nigeria aid the progressive candidate, Robert Manley to regain power. Oje and I had met the former Prime Minister, now opposition leader, during a lunch in his honour at Ọ̀tà Farm, the retirement place of Olusegun Obasanjo, then courting the role of elder statesman. Manley was visiting at the invitation of *The Guardian* newspapers for its annual lecture series. Tentatively but optimistically, he had expressed hopes that Nigeria might match the dollars that the United States was pouring into the campaign of his rival, tagged a creation of the CIA, Edward Seaga. His cause had been embraced, not only by Oje and me, but also by the former Head of State, Obasanjo, and *The Guardian* editors spearheaded by Yemi Ogunbiyi. There were hints that Babangida was already well disposed towards some help...

Outside, Dodan Barracks remained watchful and pensive – it was still so when I took my leave – as if it only waited for the departure of the notorious busybody to explode.

The àpárò survived. If the coup-makers had only taken the trouble to consult me, I would have advised them that his fate was already decried in those scattered feathers which were all that remained when the Artful Dodger fell to a dramatist's gun, but remained destined for the greatest escapist performance of his career.

Dinner With an Avatar

The most expensive dinner I ever ate in my life took place during a period of a great continental – indeed global – exultation. I did not choose the menu, the wines served were just about average, I have forgotten details of half the company that framed the large round table at the edge of the Parisian skyline but, I have never regretted nor grudged such unintended extravagance for one moment. I could not even write it off as tax deductibles. Even in 1990, I had yet much to learn from the world of taxation.

The individual at the heart of that dinner, the truly honoured guest that honoured that often dubious accolade, remains, till today, blissfully unaware of how he came to upset my monthly budget. No, he did not belong to the host of devils for whom the long spoon was invented; only those who gaoled him for most of his mature life perceived him as such. For that angelic host, a political progressive or liberation fighter, being only another expression for a communist, was the human clone of Satan, and they resolutely advertised that dinner guest as one.

Out of the blue, into my Abẹ́òkúta redoubt came an urgent message from the French embassy in Lagos. The chargé-d'affaires – the ambassador was away – wondered if I could travel to Paris the following day for a very important dinner being offered by

President Mitterrand. The embassy was standing by to do everything possible, anything at all to ensure that I was present.

I gave my *ha-ha* chuckle reserved for all outlandish proposals, sent the courier back with empty hands, and returned to whatever was then preoccupying me in my backwater township. Back came an even more intense plea from Lagos. The French President was insistent. My presence was considered vital, and now some further elaboration followed – it was not a state/official dinner but a private one. And it was not Francois Mitterrand who was offering this dinner but the foundation named for his wife – the Danielle Mitterrand Foundation. A private dinner, yes, but naturally the presidency was involved, thus the invitation had been routed through the embassy. The strange proposal began to attract my interest – fly into Paris for a dinner – this would be no ordinary dinner, since it could not possibly belong to the typical exhibitionist nature of a dinner-on-the-whim in which some of our Nigerian tycoons indulge – *àbí k'á tí ẹ ṣeré lo sí Paree, ka gbàgbé awón olòṣì tí wọ́n ńpe rá won l'óṣèlù...?*[1]

More details came tumbling through. The dinner transcended privacy – it was secrecy itself. It would take place at the roof garden restaurant of the Theatre National Populaire, in whose long-suffering bowels I had smothered *la langue francaise* in Joan Littlewood's quixotic production of Connor Cruise O'Brien's *Les Anges Meurtriers* in 1971. Then came the detail that should have preceded all others. Nelson Mandela was visiting Paris – one of his very earliest ports of call after his release – to consult privately with some French businesses and non-governmental institutions. The Danielle Mitterrand Foundation was 'sponsoring' the visit and had invited to this closed dinner in his honour some ten to twelve guests.

Nelson Mandela in Paris? And I invited to dine with him? If only that morsel of enticement had been served first, I would have been in Paris before the envoy arrived back at his station in Lagos!

The expected flight tickets had not arrived. The chargé-d'affaires implored me to buy my own tickets. Once I arrived in

---

[1] What do you say we take off for Paris for a quick spree and forget these ragamuffins who call themselves rulers?

Paris, I would be reimbursed and of course, hotel bills and other expenses taken care of. The scenario sounded familiar, it would happen again and again but, pity that individual – never mind Bertolt Brecht! – who has no one to call a hero. There was no way that I could miss an intimate dinner with Nelson Mandela, a first direct encounter since he was released from prison! Have passport, will travel. Visa was waiting. Off I flew two nights later, with nothing beyond the proverbial toothbrush. The refund never did materialise, but there was more chagrin to come – even the settlement of my hotel bill took on an embarrassing drama of its own: I had to pick this, of all visits to Paris, as the occasion on which to lose my wallet!

Mitterrand himself attended the dinner, stating demurely that it was his wife's event, not his – *I have only been invited as a husband.* Mandela's team consisted of his wife Winnie, Cyril Ramaphosa, strongly touted at the time as Mandela's successor, and Thabo Mbeki, who however ended up snagging that coveted position. Then there was Peter Brook the British director and an old friend – author of *The Empty Space, etc.* – and some others of the artistic/ political world whose names my brain failed to register. I was seated at the round table next to my favourite avatar, Nelson Mandela. All was resplendently well with the world, and especially the African world – well, almost!

It was one of those long dreamt-of evenings. Shortly after my collection of poems – *Mandela's Earth and Other Poems* – was published in the United States, I ran into a woman friend of an ANC official during a disinvestment rally at Cornell University where I was then teaching. When she informed me that she would be travelling soon to South Africa and had the channels to ensure that messages reached Nelson Mandela in prison, I gave her a copy of the poems. I added however that this was not the real copy I intended for him. That copy, I swore, would be delivered to him by my own hands, and I would read a verse or two to him as he sat in the full freedom of his living-room. The lady shook her head in pessimism, wondering if such a day would ever come about in her lifetime. I was brimful of optimism, pronounced a date beyond which, I swore, Apartheid would not last.

It was not the first time I had done that. At a lecture at the Polytechnic School of London in 1972 during the exile that followed my spell in Kaduna prison, attacked perhaps by some kind of mantic rage, I pronounced the year 1985 as the terminal year of Apartheid. No, not 'about', 'around', 'before', 'not long after', etc. but precisely – 1985! A few years later, as the magic date approached, I lost my nerve and extended the date by five years! When the cataclysmic event did materialise, it came with such suddenness that even this prophetic medium was caught completely off-guard. So now, seated by my very special prisoner at a round table in a restaurant that generously offered a panoramic view of the mother of the modern revolution, I felt deeply fulfilled – but also troubled.

As post-Apartheid elections for the governance of South Africa moved from mere speculations and negotiations to the hard realities of campaign rallies, electoral registers and ballot boxes, violence – especially between former victims, toned alike by decades of humiliation, disdain and denial – threatened to tear the emerging nation apart. Daily news from South Africa, and the commonest analysis of the array of forces that had brought down the Apartheid government, spoke of a brutal aftermath that would ensue from rival political claims of the ANC and the Inkatha movement of Chief Buthelezi, the traditional head of the Zulu. The extreme Afrikaner Right was well placed to exploit these differences, and it did. It was not sufficient to brand Buthelezi as a dyed-in-the-wool feudalist, reactionary and a stooge of the Boers. If he was, if that last especially was his entire political tendency, then the worse for the victory over Apartheid! What mattered was that he should not be thrown by default, fully kilted for war, into the enemy camp – like Jonas Savimbi of Angola in his turn – through the careful tending of his political *amour-propre* by a common enemy. Above all, Buthelezi was not without a fanatical following, even if not all of the KwaZulu nation favoured his politics. Perhaps a civil war in South Africa would be short-lived, all the same its consequences would be devastating for the continent.

Conversation turned inevitably, to this retrogressive phase that was already agitating the world, its grisly killings gleefully registered in some foreign media. Knowing heads wagged in smug satisfaction. It was still early in the blood letting rage. Figures had moved from single digits to double, and were now approaching triple. The question on the minds of the genuinely alarmed was predictable, and I turned to Mandela and asked, "Would you agree to meet with Buthelezi if he offered to meet you?"

Mandela did not pause one second. "Of course, I would. He was the first person I telephoned when I came out of prison. We have spoken on the phone several times and I have suggested to our party that we meet him and find out just what he wants. However, within the ANC, we try to do things in a democratic way, otherwise we would commit the same errors as the regime we are trying to replace. Unless the ANC authorises me, I cannot meet with him."

I saw both Thabo Mbeki and Ramaphosa prick up their ears. An unsmiling Mbeki said, "They are killing our people. Buthelezi is power mad, and he stops at nothing. He wants to create his own power enclave within South Africa. The ANC has not struggled for that. It is not possible to hold a dialogue with that kind of person."

Winnie Mandela's lips grew taut, a contrast to her matronly beauty that appeared to glow from the glossy skin of a newly bathed and oiled African child. She interjected, "The worst of it is that he actually allies with the National Party. They join forces to eliminate ANC cadres."

"We know where he's headed." Mbeki reaffirmed. "What he doesn't know is that we are waiting for him."

Ramaphosa gave me the impression of a businessman at a board meeting, measuring the opposition but very much in control, secure in the confidence of the majority of stakeholders whose interests are safeguarded by his reassuring presence. I could not help contrasting these battle-scarred men and woman with the delicate, near-fragile, soft-spoken Danielle Mitterrand. Equally arresting were the wax features of Mitterrand that had earned him the title of 'The Sphinx' from his national media – had he undergone a face-lift at some time that left his facial muscles seemingly paralysed? It was a thought that flitted through my mind as I succumbed to one of my accustomed flashbacks – my first ever encounter with the socialist president when, at the urging of Elie Wiesel, the Auswichtz survivor and Peace Laureate, he had hosted a meeting of Nobel laureates in the early spring of 1987.

That debut at the Elysse was not one of the most entrancing recollections. Francois Mitterrand received his guests with a near wooden, impassive face. Since he had taken the trouble of conferring me with the order of Chevalier de la Legion d'Honneur de la Republique Francaise some years earlier – instigated, I am convinced, by his minister of culture, Jack Lang – I felt that it behoved me to rehearse in advance a sentence or two of appreciation in French. As we shook hands, I delivered them in – surely – impeccable French. The man did not bat an eyelid. Did he even look me in the eye? No, he was a mummified presence that appeared to have been installed solely to gaze across my shoulder at some ancient history, visible to none but him! Yet the French Ambassador, who performed the award ceremony in Lagos, had assured me that Mitterrand had taken a personal interest in the conferment and would have preferred that I come to Paris to receive the medal directly from him – oh, those flattering diplomats! I was now convinced that the man could not have distinguished me from Mobutu Sese Seko, the terror of Zaire. It was rather unsettling. Not a tweak of a smile, only some murmur that I could not decipher, and a rather limp handshake. If I had not rehearsed those two sentences to perfection, I would have developed a permanent inhibition over any future attempt to communicate in that language – the only explanation that would make sense being that I had failed to make myself understood. Still, he proceeded to declare the conference open and left us to our devices.

An unscripted occurrence during the conference did however serve to compensate for my initial discomfiture – in a rather curious way. In the midst of solving all the world's problems in the elegant chamber, now festooned with cameras and microphones, one of the laureates collapsed and fell from his chair. I leapt up instinctively to go to his aid only to feel, the next moment, the restraining arm of an inner calm. I began to laugh at myself, silently of course, ordered that eager self to sit down and relax. Our colleague had collapsed among the cream of the world's medical brains and skills – at least so considered by the Nobel Academy – so what sort of aid did I imagine I was going to render?

I sank into an instantly apprehended but all too infrequently experienced state of detachment from the world of purpose, devoid of all anxiety. Something unsettling had taken place, yes, but there was nothing, absolutely nothing that was required of me. Others in that hall were superlatively equipped, a collective wealth of experience and familiarity with any ailment in the world. I distanced myself even further from my accustomed self in order to relish this generous isolation from all the furor, from the palpable concern that was evident in the others, wallowed in the unaccustomed condition of absolution that derived from the competence of others. I basked in my unsought enrolment in the world's unskilled and irrelevant population, immersed myself in the sheer luxury of revelation – *right now, at this very moment, you are useless, nobody needs you! Enjoy it while you can.* It was a paradoxical potency, to be able to sink oneself in inertia yet feel masterful – through others – for doing nothing, for being incapable of doing anything. My confidence was supreme – all would be well. An ambulance had been summoned, but I was not interested in details. *What do you think happened?* my next seat neighbour whispered, tortured by the thought that the first ever gathering of this nature – at least, that he was attending - might end in a tragedy. With the most limpid of offhand gestures eased naturally from my overabundant tranquility, I calmed him, assured him that it was nothing, that our colleague would be up in no time.

Was it a heart attack? An epileptic fit? A stroke? A diabetic crisis? It did not matter to me in my delicious apathy. *He's in excellent hands* – as if I had joined the doctors in diagnosing the cause of the man's collapse. He was assisted out and into the ambulance – perhaps from Mitterrand's official medical fleet – and the meeting continued. I was perhaps the most serene being in the halls and labyrinths of the Elysee all that day. It was a good thing that my faith was not misplaced. The patient recovered fully and rejoined us for the rest of the conference. Nothing however could match that moment when, for once, I understood what a gift it was to be at one with the superfluous population of the world.

It became obvious to me, some moments later, why the flashback had occurred. It was not the mere recollection of the bloodless face of Francois Mitterrand – which, in any case, proved quite capable of some animation and even occasional banter, mostly in the form of self-deprecatory remarks, as the evening progressed. More evocative was the contrast between that other gathering at the Elysee and the present. At the TNP restaurant, we were drawn into a tense discussion of life and death, the threatening collapse of a barely rising edifice on which millions of eyes were affixed in optimistic expectation. One was denied the luxury of indifference, even of detachment. To make matters worse, instead of an abundance of healers, I wondered – was this should-be celebratory dinner, in the tranquil air of a Paris night, a feast of undertakers?

I looked towards Ramaphosa, who had yet to speak. His message was similar, but his tone was more accommodating. All expressed grievances against the Inkatha, and against Buthelezi personally. Thabo Mbeki was obviously the main hardliner. He could hardly pronounce the name Buthelezi without his smallish, near triangular face expunging all expression, leaving only the hardness of his eyes. Mandela returned to the theme. He introduced a novel point of consideration by calling attention to Buthelezi's hurt feelings. He offered that perhaps Buthelezi had not been given sufficient credit for what he did achieve during the anti-Apartheid struggle. The problematic chief had, after all, remained steadfast to the cause.

"Why should we fight among ourselves?" Mandela asked, somewhat rhetorically. "If it were possible, I would go and meet Buthelezi tomorrow, even tonight. I know him. He respects me. If he and I were to sit down today and thrash it all out, all these unnecessary killings would stop."

Mbeki again interjected. His tone was stiff, it cut through the mellow ambiance like a party-line *diktat*. "His atrocities against our members are unforgivable. We cannot sit down and talk to such a man. There is nothing to be gained by it. For a dialogue to take place, there has to be a talking point. With Buthelezi there is none."

I thought Nelson Mandela looked rather sad and wistful. Obviously he did not share Mbeki's view. His smile was, however, not quite one of resignation. It could have been my hyperactive antennae but, I had the distinct impression that even Mandela's statement did not quite correspond to his inner intent, that he was biding his time. Certainly that surmise was contradicted when he said, "Well, you've heard our comrades. If the executive committee were to learn that I accidentally ran into Buthelezi and exchanged a 'Good Morning' with him, there will be a riot!"

I turned to Mbeki. "I hope you realise what you're saying. You are leaving yourself no choice but to kill him. You'll have to kill him. And you know where that might lead."

Mbeki gave a slight shrug, but said nothing further, at least, not on that subject.

By the following morning, the glow of an intimate evening with my favourite – and the world's – avatar had dissipated. It took no special political instinct or intelligence to understand the urge for reprisals. My recollection remained focussed on the sharp separation between Nelson Mandela's thinking and that of his 'young Turks'. Even the body languages of those two – Thabo Mbeki and Nelson Mandela – spoke volumes, and the contrast read out a stark warning. I returned to Nigeria far more uneasy than when I had set out for dinner – and had begun to consider if it was not time for another dinner with my reigning devil – the real one this time, but a pliable one!

The truth was – I realised – my student days' obsession with South Africa had merely gone into hibernation. Now it was bludgeoned awake as the figures of fatalities rose sharply by the day. No-go zones between Inkatha and ANC controlled areas in various cities – Johannesburg and suburbs most notoriously – had become battlegrounds, streets turned open spaces of death. The predicted was taking flesh, broken white power had regrouped and begun to exploit divisions between the fraternal enemies. It became difficult to understand – how was it possible that no influential

African nation had stepped in, brokered peace between the warring duo and left the Boer diehards stuck to the starting blocks of their devious plots? It was the looming taunt that haunted me – *see, we hand over power to them, negotiated power that is, and all they do is slaughter one another.* The suspicions, clashes and killings were not new, the jostling for political advantage and the fear of being overwhelmed by a more powerful partner in any struggle. It was not a situation that was peculiar to South Africa; liberation history has not been niggardly in its instructional scripts.

The continent needed a South African success! South Africa's task of recovery, black majority rule but in partnership with the rest of the nation, would be made less arduous – it seemed obvious – if, during its uncertain period of transition, she had a staunch shoulder within the black continent itself, to lean upon. The obvious candidate was Nigeria – her size, her resources, manpower. As so often happened, the motions began in Oje Aboyade's home. Could it... was it possible that we could play a role in this? Oje became caught up in the idea, activated his direct line to the Artful Dodger.

My first demand, in outlining a plan for a Mandela-Buthelezi encounter to Ibrahim Babangida, was absolute secrecy. Knowing the torrid ideological space that demarcated the ANC from Inkatha, the very idea of creating a bridge left one exposed. If the plans miscarried, we had to assure ourselves, in advance, of the means of a dignified withdrawal and a stout public denial of any attempt to intervene. Despite the substantial support it had received from successive Nigerian governments, the ANC leadership was especially jealous of its independence. The party was obsessed with its self-image of ideological purity, ostentatiously contemptuous of Nigeria as a nation that lacked political direction or a progressive ideology. The mood within that party hierarchy was not so different from that of the Bolsheviks towards their 'liberal' and 'bourgeois' allies after the success of the revolution – ANC considered theirs a disciplined, 'correct' struggle based on the class analysis of history. By contrast, Nigeria was a spoilt, rich brat, a crude succession of hotchpotch dictatorships and feudal conspiracies. That nation had done no more than its duty in offering diplomatic and material assistance to the South African liberation fighters – perhaps more than any other African country except Libya and the 'front-line' nations – Tanzania, Zambia, Angola, Namibia and Mozambique. It was no reason for any expression of gratitude or special recognition. The ANC was morbidly afraid of contamination by the directionless nature of Nigerian society. Once the Apartheid regime had fallen, it set out to distance itself from such an embarrassing benefactor.

This attitude would later cause vocal resentment in Nigerian leadership circles – the ANC (Mandela) was accused of pointedly travelling round the world immediately after his release but refusing to step into Nigeria en route to say 'Thank you!' Babangida nursed the same feelings of resentment – grumbled that the ANC leadership was made up of arrogant ingrates. No matter, he soon warmed up to the idea of doing this one thing – acting to stop the looming blood-bath. He had nothing to lose by a little investment – if it worked, his image would receive a free boost on the international scene.

Babangida agreed to send his Foreign Minister, General Ike Nwachukwu to talk to me. Nwachukwu, with his impressive 'soldierly' bearing, was one of those Nigerians who could claim to belong to any part of the country. Born of an Igbo father and Fulani mother, this General had grown up in the North where he also spent much of his military career. During the Civil War, he remained steadfast to the Federal cause. He spoke Yoruba with hardly a trace of an accent, while his English accent carried a faint upper-class tinge that was probably consciously cultivated from contacts with the British officer class during his military training in England. Hausa tripped effortlessly from his tongue. Nwachukwu was markedly urbane in manners – the result perhaps of his numerous sojourns in Lagos as well as his training spells and attachments in various countries. We met in Yemi Ogunbiyi's house, the rendezvous for many semi-official encounters that took place, of necessity, in Lagos. The General arrived in an excitable state, announced that Babangida had offered to make a plane from his official fleet available to Mandela and Buthelezi . They could fly secretly into Nigeria for a meeting, or indeed to any part of the world agreed between them. Then came Ike Nwachukwu's own proposal, one that virtually took my breath away.

Bubbling with enthusiasm, Nwachukwu outlined a plan for the Ọọni of Ifẹ, the historic ruler of Ilé-Ifẹ and acknowledged spiritual head of the Yoruba, to lead a full-fledged delegation of royal heads into South Africa! Chief Buthelezi, the amiable general reasoned, was a traditional chief in his own right. So was Nelson Mandela – the General had done some homework, I had to give him that! In his view, this shared background held the key to netting the two frisky fishes. The Ọọni of Ifẹ, accompanied by a galaxy of crowned Nigerian heads from all corners of the nation, would fly into South Africa in Babangida's private jet. The Ọọni would summon his two fellow (but junior) royalty to his presence. He would chide them for their belligerence – undoubtedly in the special language that traditional chiefs all over the continent use when they are among their own kind. He would say to them, presumably – *look here, fellows, it's time we crowned heads and chiefs sorted out this problem. We understand one another, we cannot afford to dent the prestige of our crowns in public* – not exactly Nwachukwu's words but definitely the spirit of his plan. The Ọọni of Ifẹ would load them into the presidential jet and waft them into a Nigerian seclusion where our local kings would act as arbiters. After which, the combatants would embrace, and the continent would live happily ever after. The world would see that we in Africa have time-tested ways of resolving our problems. I listened. Ike Nwachukwu was so carried away by the sheer originality of his plans that he failed to glimpse anything of my reaction, which was of plain, undisguised horror.

When I narrated the evening's encounter to Oje, we both conceded that the General meant well but that it would be best to leave the Ministry of Foreign Affairs out of the project, using that department strictly for logistical support. Thus did I come to embark on my initiation into the world of shuttle diplomacy – an activity that I clearly misunderstood until the first-hand experience taught me differently. The one-off Nigeria-Senegal FESTAC experience proved a most inadequate training ground – emphasis this time was on the word 'shuttle', not on the diplomacy. In any case, diplomacy of any kind still requires, above the necessary training or experience, a very special temperament.

Babangida agreed with our proposal to proceed step by step, making private contacts, rather than a royal blitz through the debris of Apartheid. I would first of all explore the mood within the ANC, very tentatively, discreetly, move next towards a tête-à-tête with Mandela, possibly involve the Archbishop Desmond Tutu, then track down Buthelezi. After that, we would consider how best to inveigle the two principals into a secret tryst in a place and at a time of their own choosing, a presidential jet always standing by to take off at a moment's notice. Babangida would send funds to the embassy in Washington to take care of my travelling expenses.

Thus came my saga of meetings – more accurately described as ambushes, of telephone calls from one end of the globe to another, wondering who had hypnotised, then brainwashed me into such an undertaking. Compelled to isolate the most defining of these encounters, I would list three. One was a long walk down Lisbon's avenue with an ANC communist, late into the night. Another was a telephone discussion with the Inkatha leader, Chief Buthelezi. The third was the last of my telephone exchanges with fellow writer and ANC, anti-Apartheid stalwart, Nadine Gordimer.

It had been a long day in Lisbon, a series of sessions – and receptions – at one of those encounters between 'North' and 'South', in 1991. I shared the podium with Mwalimu Julius Nyerere, then beginning to enjoy his honourable retirement from the presidency of Tanzania. We were interacting for the first time since the pan-African – resurrection – conference in Dar es Salaam, 1973, a year in which General Yakubu Gowon was consolidating his dictatorial rule on Nigeria. It was at this chaotic gathering that the original credentials of the pan-African movement as an all-comer, non-governmental forum were formally buried.

One after the other, suspect voices were censored, in response to pressure from their governments. Nyerere submitted to some diplomatic arm-twisting from Lagos, and I was successfully excluded from one speakers' list after another. Walter Rodney, author of the seminal work – *How Europe Underdeveloped Africa* – suffered a similar fate even though he was actually resident in Tanzania. He was 'invited' by the Tanzanian government to absent himself from Dar es Salaam during the conference. To pass the time, I did my best to demonstrate solidarity with a liquid product of that socialist nation, this being the most affordable accompaniment to Tanzanian cuisine: some Roman Catholic priests, fooled by the climate and soil of Dodoma region in Northern Tanzania, had engaged in a valiant effort to cultivate grapes and – table wines! Perhaps that product has improved since then but, like the experience of a gathering that was intended to breathe a new life into the pan-African movement, I was only rewarded with a sour taste in the mouth, and a prolonged sense of corrosion on the stomach lining.

Lisbon was of course a different setting, and a far more composed affair – a North-South dialogue. It seemed a perfect pointer. If North and South could dialogue, so could South and South or, in my immediate context, ANC and Inkatha. That a senior member of the ANC was also participating in the conference was a further signal that the stars of dialogue were in the ascendant. I had begun with brief but encouraging snatches of discussion with Nyerere as we sat on the podium, the coffee breaks and reception being hotly contested by far too many claimants. The ex-president was leaving Lisbon that very night, so I had to seize those few minutes in between the speeches of other members of the panel, and over interjections from the floor. I promised that I would get in touch with him through his secretary, call on him in Tanzania if necessary. It would be no exaggeration to claim that I had engaged his interest – or at least, that he was intrigued by the idea.

The ANC delegate was however the immediate target. As the conference ended, I asked him to take a walk with me towards my hotel, little suspecting that I was about to undergo a renewed induction into a troubling mind-set that bears so much responsibility for the deadly strains of revolutionary rhetoric. I had encountered it on numerous occasions, but perhaps it was the setting of the preceding exchanges of the day, an encouraging contact with that man of vision, Julius Nyerere, one of the least doctrinaire of progressive leadership on the continent, that left me so ill-prepared. For what the bespectacled, flaxen haired, fortyish, white militant responded to my plea that a solution be quickly found to the internecine killings was this: *The ANC was still at war. Nelson Mandela was like a general of an army. Generals cannot pause to take note of the loss, or potential loss of lives – it's all entered in advance into their calculations.*

Aghast, I looked at his pale face lit by the safe, street lamps of a safe Lisbon avenue. It was smug, self righteous, a composure that, paradoxically, approximated a Buddhist state of the resolution of all the seeming contradictions of a world of pain and strife. It required no thinking – I knew at once that this marked the end of that dialogue. I abandoned my plan to stop at a bar and engage him in a productive discussion, preferably over some Portuguese 'tapas' and *vinho verde.* Denial of my right to free speech by Nyerere – whom I deeply admired in any case – was one thing. Collaboration, indeed, rhetorical justification of internecine slaughter in the name of revolutionary theology was another. I turned abruptly. It was a most inauspicious beginning to the promise of a diplomatic career.

"Well, good night," I said. "Try and remember however that it is not people like you who are getting killed. And it is not your community that is being destroyed."

He looked shocked, perhaps the thought had not occurred to him till then. More likely, no one had ever uttered words in his hearing that conveyed this simple, stark truth. The following morning, he called me, promised to see what he could do within the ANC Executive Committee on his return to South Africa.

My hunt continued for a sympathetic and influential mind within the ANC – all that we sought, after all, was that both Mandela and Buthelezi should know that there was an avenue that could be used to meet discreetly – just meet, talk and hopefully discover that there was no forked tail hidden beneath either pair of trousers.

I encountered several dead ends and near-misses. Thanks to my former student, then a full-fledged professor at Cornell

University, Henry-Louis Gates Jr., I learnt that Winnie Mandela
was to attend an investiture at Duke University, where she would
also deliver a lecture. I headed for that beckoning rendezvous,
posting messages ahead. By the time I arrived in North Carolina,
Winnie had called off the event, owing to some emergency recall
from home, and travelled back to South Africa.

Buthelezi was also a near-miss. The chief had been tracked
down to Canada and was expected to remain there for some days
before travelling on, consumed with his mission of jettisoning the
'collaborationist' label that stubbornly stuck to him. I was then in
London. Based on his schedule, transmitted by the Nigerian
mission in Ottawa, I flew to Canada and found that our planes –
most probably – had passed each other in the ozone layer. This
was getting tiresome, but it was too late to complain. In addition,
blinded by the dazzle of the prize in view, the quarry always
seemed no further away than the arm could reach. There was a
fast connection to London to be made through New York and
thus, to that city did I head on the next available flight. This time
however, I had learnt not to place all reliance on the Intelligence
network of embassies, or be at the mercy of the sudden dispositions
of these moving targets. Armed with his phone number and hotel
address, I took the precaution of first calling Buthelezi from the
airport while awaiting the flight to London.

It was just as well. Buthelezi was packing his bags and would
shortly head for Gatwick airport en route for Johannesburg. All
party leaders appeared to be on the move, even the still ruling
National Party of de Klerk, preparing for the first post-Apartheid
elections, raising funds, seeking international recognition and/or
understanding of their policies. The ANC, for instance, had
mounted a campaign to overcome the general perception of being
a communist dominated organisation. De Klerk was propagating
his scheme for opening up the Nationalist Party to non-Boers, non-
whites. Buthelezi was contesting his 'collaborationist' label.

And so my dialogue with Buthelezi took place over the phone
– I have yet to encounter him physically. He spoke volubly, made
an obvious effort to sound reasonable, objective, but came through
as a man deeply aggrieved and hurt – Nelson Mandela was right.

Buthelezi forcefully reminded me that, despite acceding to the 'homeland' policies of the Apartheid government, he had stoutly refused to accept the offer of the status of an 'independent' nation – unlike other Bantustans – by which the regime had sought to consolidate the Apartheid ideology and weaken liberation thinking. A false sense of national sovereignty – the ruse was so transparent to the world, it remains a mystery till today that any prescient leader could pretend to have been taken in by its touted theology of mutual cultural and political respect: *separate but equal.*

"My big brother," said Buthelezi, "I am only too happy to do anything to bring me closer to my very own senior brother whom I have always considered my leader. You may enquire of the de Klerk government. Throughout, I insisted that I would not talk to any of them until Brother Mandela came out of prison. Unlike the others, I refused to accept this spurious self-government. What for? Our leader was still in prison. Brother, I am glad it is someone like you calling me, and if there is anything you are able to do to bring us both together – are you sure we cannot meet before my flight? Maybe if you flew into Gatwick, we can have some minutes together before I take off."

I assured Chief Buthelezi that I could not perform the magical feat of getting into London before he took off, not even if I took the Concorde. I heard his sigh of disappointment – whatever other impression I received of the KwaZulu chief, this much was certain – he was truly eager to seize any chance of mediation.

Buthelezi sounded a most embittered man. He felt that he had not been duly appreciated, that his strategy for confronting Apartheid had been misunderstood, unjustly misrepresented and villified. We spoke – or more accurately – he spoke for nearly an hour, and the burden of it all was that a wedge had been driven between him and Nelson Mandela by 'the hothead extremists' of the ANC. Those people hate me, he wailed. They want to destroy me!

As I admitted to Nadine Gordimer when I succeeded in contacting her in turn, I detected strains of paranoia even across the trans-Atlantic circuit. Chief Buthelezi accused the ANC of atrocities against his people; I reminded him, very gently, that the

ANC had accused his KwaZulu warriors of virtually the same crime. In the end I asked him once again – will you meet Nelson Mandela if such a meeting could be brought about? His response was a most grateful 'Yes'. There was no coyness, no playing hard-to-get. Buthelezi was ready for dialogue.

My last conversation with Nadine Gordimer administered, without doubt, the ultimate chagrin of my 'diplomatic' shuttle. I was now armed at least with Buthelezi's consent and could not wait to convey this to her. She had already warned me, just like Nelson Mandela, of the ANC's fervid democratic catechism – I encountered it so often, delivered like a creed of religious submission, that I would mentally recite it even as it was intoned by yet another ANC affiliate, including one or two of its writers. It went beyond liturgy however. Indeed, it affected, and was acted upon with such conformity, being virtually synonymous with 'party discipline', that it could be counted upon to prevent Nelson Mandela from taking any step without the full approval of the Executive Committee. Nadine was therefore hesitant, but agreed to lay THE PLAN before the ANC – Mandela and Buthelezi to Nigeria or wherever, secretly ferried thither in one of Babangida's presidential fleet.

Some days and several more post-Apartheid mass funerals later, I was off to Cairo to lay ambush for a heavyweight pair from within the ANC caucus, courtesy of information from my 'reformed' Marxist acquaintance of the Lisbon exchange – or was it in fact Nadine? I am no longer certain. Perhaps the unexpected softening up of the formerly doctrinaire revolutionary of the Lisbon encounter had imbued in me an inordinate optimism – no matter, I sought help from our embassy in Cairo, requesting specifically the young man who had rescued me from the near debacle of the All Africa Games. He had been posted away, but his replacement was more than ready to lend himself body and soul to the scheme. He succeeded in tracking down the elusive ANC voyagers who, it appeared, were on a fund-raising mission. The young diplomat also sent a message home in case there was need for a rapid follow-up from Babangida or his foreign minister. I was not over-anxious to meet the two travellers without an intermediary or at least, without some indication about their probable disposition. Nadine could help, and I was due to phone her anyway, since she had finally undertaken to lay the proposal – albeit without great enthusiasm – before the next meeting of the ANC Executive Committee. That meeting had now taken place.

It was indeed a most expectant one-man intervention force that made the call, joined by the embassy official who had also entered into the spirit of the chase. It was the briefest of my telephone exchanges with Nadine on the subject, but it had the effect – perhaps because of her own ambiguous position over the project – of transporting me vividly into the distant conference room where Nadine had tabled the initiative. I could almost swear that I saw each face seated around a table at the other end of the continent as the putative life expectancy of THE PLAN was summarily terminated. Nadine gave off a kind of throaty giggle – it was either a subconscious echo of the guffaws that rent the discussion room, or an embarrassed reaction of her own. Still, she eventually broke through her giggle:

"The meeting broke up," she announced, "in a bout of derisory laughter."

I think a spasm of shock must have surged across my face because the diplomat sitting across the hotel room half-rose from his chair, appearing more concerned with my well-being than with any message from a distant South Africa. He looked anxious as he asked me if I was all right. My reply was a revelation of my inner projections, even to me:

"She's just informed me that they are laughing all the way to the cemetery."

Of course, those were not Nadime Gordimer's words. They were however the words I used also when I telephoned Aboyade at home to signal the termination of my mission that very night. I asked him to be certain to transmit the message to Babangida just as I had phrased it, and let him know that I now considered the idea stillborn, and was returning my meddlesome self to more rational pursuits. I was not born for the diplomatic world.

The no-dialogue rhetoric continued for some months, escalating in intensity even as the sheer statistics of reprisals settled into a numbing spiral. Then one day, several select assassinations and indiscriminate massacres later, including the detonation of bombs at political gatherings, right on the heels of yet another fire-breathing ANC bulletin that promised to wipe out Inkatha, and Inkatha's like response, news emerged that Nelson Mandela had quietly shunted aside his executive and travelled out on his own to meet Buthelezi.

Not, I am certain, that Mandela ever accommodated the latter designation within his rich humanism but – the avatar had transcended the 'General'.

PART V

All the World...

Tonight, We Improvise

Usually one sees them in still photos – images of dying cattle in a land overtaken by drought, now landmarked by carcasses and skeletons, withered shrub and dry water holes. Occasionally however, the cine-camera takes charge, lingers over a calf that is reduced to nothing but skin stretched over a cage of ribs, and the final contractions of emaciated muscles. Flies settle and crawl over what remains of moisture on the prostrate beast, mostly around the eyes, ears, and nostrils. It makes a feeble attempt to lift itself, scuffing dirt with the sides of its hooves, then settles back on its side, immobile. Its enlarged eyes stare blankly into the lens. This disproportioned frame with extended ribs sinks slowly into immobility. At some point, you know the calf is doomed, its life slowly ebbing into the sands. The lens lifts towards the desiccated horizon, rises directly upwards to reveal a cloud of swooping vultures, suspended, circling, blotting out the pitiless sun.

What I have tried to convey here – complete with circling vultures – is exactly what a director sees as he watches his play die slowly on the stage – the convulsions, the evident lack of nutrition, but above all the ebbing away of any animating spirit. And the director-cowherd may turn away from the pathetic sight as often as he wants, or flee the theatre, the image remains branded on his retina to haunt him into the bar where he has taken refuge.

It hangs from the ceiling above the bed where he has flung himself in despair. He knows the vultures are circling. On the review pages, the corpse is exhumed, mocked, disembowelled and its tattered shrouds hung up as a warning to all foolhardy adventurers. This, in fact, is almost a deed of mercy, a kind of public therapy that dissipates the intensity of the agony of the previous night. Nor is one speaking of the malicious, or simply uninformed critic, the reveler in fascist power whose wife is probably bleeding him to death from alimony and must bleed someone else in revenge. No, when the playwright or director *knows* that a death has been enacted on stage, and not one that was called for by the script, he simply bleeds internally, and goes into hiding.

A death is of course vastly different from a disaster, that unscripted incident that inflicts on the director no worse consequence than the loss of a handful of hair or a temporary homicidal or manic fit. Most directors know them at first hand, especially those first-nights when everything appears to go wrong, lines are forgotten, the set collapses, a crucial technical effect is premature, or the lead actor has a seizure in mid-sentence. Such mishaps are gradually remedied, especially in a theatre culture where the critic understands his or her trade from within, as part of the creative totality of the dramatic occupation, and does not confuse his role with that of a feudal executioner whose only function is one of instant decapitation.

It goes without saying that from the commencing decision to stage a play – irrespective of the process that brings this about – through the casting of actors, to the end product, the director bears the ultimate responsibility – including even the choice of the play – for what appears on stage. He/she basks in the glow of a successful production and remains the architect of his own woes. However, the actual goings-on behind the scenes, which vary from the hilarious to the tragic, I am certain, often prove more riveting than the actual public product, having driven many a director close to suicide or onto the psychiatrist's couch. And yet again, many unorthodox, unsung and unacknowledged remedies have been known to rescue, if not the theatrical event itself, at least the actors and company spirit from collapse. Such efforts give 'improvisation' a totally new meaning, and may eventually lead to a new understanding of theatre sociology. But first, to put that elastic theatre routine in its place, a case against that very directorial equipment – improvisation.

Joan Littlewood and a Lumumba Fixation

In 1970 – but perhaps the notion had been gestating long before then – the erratic genius, Joan Littlewood, got it into her head that only one man of the entire black race could take on the role of Patrice Lumumba, the martyred leader of the newly independent Republic of Congo in Connor Cruise O'Brien's *Les Anges Meurtriers*. That man was none other than Wole Soyinka, recently emerged from prison detention in Nigeria. Perhaps some kind of parallelism was working on her mind – the nation of Congo just emerging from Belgium's colonial detention, and WS also regaining his liberty from a military power? So obsessed was Joan with the idea that she refused to fill that part while I was still struggling to regain my passport, rendering even my appearance in Paris somewhat precarious. For Joan, that was only a minor problem. She continued to rehearse other scenes, confident that the spirit of Lumumba would eventually descend on the Nigerian government.

It did. I travelled to Paris after the other actors had been at work for over three weeks, leaving me even less than that to master my role. The performance company was a mini-UNO. There were French film actors, used to playing detectives and/or romantic leads – like Jean-Pierre Aumont, with a record of pairing quite a number of glamorous stars. Others were straightforward stage actors. The black francophone actors – Senegalese, Congolese, Malians, etc. – were a mixture of professionals and amateur, the Congolese comprising of musicians who had never stepped on anything but a concert platform. Naturally, the director press-ganged the musicians into acting roles. The list was rounded out by British and Irish actors – Joan liked to have around her a sprinkling of tried and tested products of the Joan Littlewood method, based on the principle of inspired lunacy and a blithe disregard for the playwright's text, stage instructions, intentions, even language. Such a radical proceeding had transformed and invigorated British theatre of the sixties and seventies – Joan was now ready to destabilise French theatrical concepts with her unique style.

I was only a few days into rehearsals before I concluded that Joan Littlewood was indeed mad, stark raving mad, and that the only person who deserved to be institutionalised before her was myself. She knew that I did not speak French, yet she insisted on casting me in a play to be performed in *la langue francaise*. With nothing more than a proficiency in reading the language, but never having conversed in it, I agreed to act in that medium. At least I had an excuse. I had emerged from prison detention not long before, so it could be claimed that my mind was still somewhat scrambled. What excuse did Joan have?

The French – as the whole world knows only too well – are extremely language proud. They can forgive most things, including even watering down the wine, but they take strong exception to the murder of their language. The British complement in that company, on the other hand, spoke with an accent which, even to my untutored hearing was perhaps fractionally worse than mine. In addition however, I had the terrible disadvantage also of not being able to *hear* French at that stage, having never interacted with the francophone world for any meaningful period. In short, I never could understand what the actors were saying even after I had mastered my lines.

Now, regarding that little problem, learning one's lines, how did Joan Littlewood solve it? With a tape recorder, into which she had all Lumumba's lines recorded. And that tape-recorder – with ear-phones where necessary – played into my ears every waking moment – eating, drinking, walking, defecating, right up to the moment of falling asleep and first thing on waking up. A French-speaking Lebanese, 'Nadine', was attached to me as speech coach. This also helped, especially as we grew closer and closer and thus spent time in each other's company over and above the call of duty – an intense relationship which, but for my other marriage in Nigeria – national politics – would have resulted in elopement.

The lines were crammed, some intelligible delivery mastered. Instead of a correct French accent however, the language finicky audience would be treated to the experience of listening to their proud heritage passed through a Lebanese-Yoruba wringer. One problem still remained – how to ensure that Mr. Lumumba could understand what the others were saying in about ten different accents at any given moment. This was beyond even Joan Littlewood's genius, and it was left to me to find my own salvation.

The route to that salvation was however made near impassable by the very methodology of the director herself, Joan, the compulsive improviser. She encouraged her performers to play around with both text and act on stage, especially during performance, more than content to have the text altered from one show to the next. Well, improvisation is all very well when you can *understand* what the other person has just improvised. It's no good improvising 'Have they dined?', when your bodyguard has just informed you that mercenaries are blasting their way into your bedroom.

Seizing a moment when the company was assembled on stage, I pointed to them the marvelous example of the precision actor and French elocutionist Jean-Pierre Aumont who played the United Nations Secretary-General Dag Hammarskjold, shot down in his plane over the turbulent Congo. This actor was so precise, so coordinated that you could time his physical gestures and vocal gradations in advance, calculate the precise distance his fingers would travel as he moved to slide the handkerchief out of his breast pocket, pause at a dramatic angle, then raise his hand to mop, ever so gingerly, the sweat-beads on his forehead. John Wells – one of Joan's British imports – and I speculated that there were the exact number of sweat drops on Jean-Pierre Aumont's forehead at every performance. Certainly no one could fault the precision of his movements on stage – his deployment of the French language manifested the same daunting precision. His bloodless performance was of course a matter of taste.

Improvise your heads away – I warned them all – when you are interacting with one another, but not with me. You will get only the response I have crammed with such difficulty. I won't pick up what you've just said, and if by chance I do, I shall not attempt any French composition. Not only that, I know how long you should take to deliver your speech. If you exceed the time limit, I come in, whether you're done or not.

John Wells, the satirical writer/actor was the worst offender. He was the original *Èṣù*[1] behind the scenes, a totally irrepressible agent of mischief and with a horrible accent from which any music lover instinctively recoiled. That did not faze him one bit, and he remained incorrigible till the end of the run. Sometimes he would say, 'You've ballsed up things pretty badly here Mr. Lumumba, haven't you?', knowing very well that I would still follow with my response: 'Yes, we're very proud of the start we've made.' Fortunately, his accent was mostly incomprehensible to French audiences.

Now, that was where Jean-Pierre Aumont was a godsend. His lines never varied and were delivered to within a tenth of a second either way, night after night, and performance after performance. In return for the disdain with which he regarded the International Conglomerates of Accents however, the company spent most of the time sending up his undeniably robotic performance. I was the only one without that consolation – I needed every ounce of concentration – on and off-stage – in those terrible weeks that saw my politics of African liberation overcome all rational judgement, making me the fellow subversive of a madcap director in the demolition of the French linguistic heritage.

Years later, in 1987, President Francois Mitterrand conferred on me the prestigious title of the Chevalier de la Legion d'Honneur de la Republique Francaise. The ceremony was conducted by his Ambassador in Nigeria. Some years after, the earlier narrated conference of Nobelists, hosted by Monsieur Mitterrand took place, and I found myself at the Elysee Palace, my spoken French vastly improved, and a brief 'Thank you' speech, memorised, rippling off my tongue like an above average *vin courant*. I was taken aback by what appeared to be a set, inhospitable expression on his face as he offered me a limp handshake. For a long time, I could not understand what I had done to deserve such a rebuff.

---

[1] Yoruba god of mischief; the unpredictable factor.

I have formulated several theories but have finally settled on this possibility: the honour had been awarded to someone whom Mitterrand only knew by name. The day of our encounter at the Elysee however, there flashed through his mind the image of a young Nigerian actor who had stood on the historic stage in the very heart of Paris, and massacred his precious language.

No wonder – he froze!

A Festival Improvised

Who could resist the promise of Sienna? A theatre festival right in the midst of Chianti country, and timed for the 1992 wine harvest? I gathered together the old hands of my dormant theatre company, the Orísun Theatre, set aside all other work to complete a new play – *From Zia with Love* – and headed for the Italian vineyards. Alas, the festive context of the festival fell far short of the promised. Wine festival there was not. As we drove through vineyards from our billets to rehearsal spaces through picturesque Sienna – verge to horizon draped in grapes ready for harvesting, the air heady with the fragrance of imprisoned juice, imagination was set ablaze with processions of gaily costumed maidens with full baskets of grapes, drawn on ancient carts, mandolins and pipes in the hands of leather-kitted vignerons, kettle drums astride donkeys, a rain of wine drenching onlookers and a bride of Bacchus crowned on the doorstep of City Hall. Each day, we awaited notice of the festival, even some quaint rituals on the streets that would relieve the hours of hacking away at the unwieldy material of the dramatic text. No notice ever came, not even a drum signal.

We were lucky to make hay, near literally, while the sun shone. During that time of year, rain, we had been stoutly assured, was something unheard of – it was like Atlanta all over again, where snow had been unheard of for fifty years – until the arrival of WS! And so the performances were mostly billed for the open air, even though some makeshift arrangements had been made for alternative venues in Sienna in the absolutely unthinkable event that it rained. It *never* rained in summer – an article of faith to which a mostly reliable quality of the grape harvest had largely contributed. The festival venue comprised the sprawling, sloping

grounds of an ancient castle framed against the sky, so close to
the sky that one felt that the sky was simply the roof of a
performance dome. Acting spaces were dotted all over the open
grounds, usually with a renovated lodge as dressing and storage
rooms. Our production, like most others, was blocked and
rehearsed all five weeks on the open-air stage.

The presiding deity would prove to be not Dionysos, the
sunshine deity of the grapes. He kept away, probably sulking on
some distant mountain top on account of the cancellation of his
festival, thus creating a vacuum that was instantly filled by the dark,
brooding Ṣàngó, he of thunder and lightning, and torrential
downpour.

Even before his full-blown manifestation, the omens were all
around us. A third of the company took ill. Worse was to come
riding in on Ṣàngó's wind. The god of lightning, rage, and thunder
had also taken charge at home. A rain – of bullets – was beating
the walls and streets of Lagos. The people had risen against a hike
in the price of petroleum products and the police had responded
with fire. Now it was all anxiety for the company, uncertain how
their families were affected. They wore their apprehensions on
their faces and it played havoc with rehearsals.

They had been away from home for more than two weeks.
Reports filtered through to us of mounting casualties. These actors
spent most of their allowances on telephone bills calling families
and friends, but mostly obtaining no coherent, or else, contradictory
responses. Sometimes the line broke off in mid-sentence – the
Italian telephone exchange was every bit as rudimentary as the
Nigerian. There were rumours of a coup. Panic set in. Tunji
Oyelana, the resourceful musician, was able to get through to his
wife on an obliging line, his conversation crowded with messages
from the company to their families, followed by depression at the
thought that bad news was being kept from them.

Suddenly, I had an inspiration, probably quickened by my
own disquiet at being away from home at such a time. Certainly,
I could not deny that my concentration suffered from time to time,
however much I pretended not to be affected by the general mood.
I scheduled lengthier rehearsals for that week in order to increase,

by one day, the next weekend break. The company was to spend
that time resting and studying their lines. With an excursion into
Rome also organised for the interested, the company was fully
occupied one way or the other when I took off for Nigeria, armed
with letters and verbal messages from virtually every member for
their families. I was entrusted with the task of bringing back
truthful news of the situation.

Before late evening of my Friday afternoon arrival on an
Alitalia flight, I had accomplished my mission, spoken to members
of the artistes' families, assessed the current state of siege and
begun to prepare for my return on Saturday. And then I paused.
What else could I do to boost the morale of the company? Foremost
in my mind was how to relieve them of the tedium of the bland
diet – to the average Nigerian taste – that the catering department
was churning out. Personally, I was quite amenable to pasta but,
for most of the actors, pasta was a diet for the sick or convalescing
and, in any case, the portions were roundly damned as inadequate.

First candidate for the relief package was obvious – the
Nigerian farina – *gari* – a prolonged deprivation of which has
turned many a Nigerian to either crime or religion. To return
without even a token quantity, merely symbolic, would have
counted as an act of unconcern or worse – sadism. I was already
resigned to the fact that this had to be one of those exceptional
flights where I could boast of checked-in luggage. Next, hot
peppers, some dried fish, other seasoning items, some lightweight
delicacies around which the starving Nigerians could improvise
on the canteen cuisine.

And then I had yet another flash of inspiration! Or maybe it
was simply a burst of madness. At the bottom of my freezer, a
long, low-slung container of infinite capacity that preserved the
rewards of my hunting forays, was a member of the feral family,
the *ęta*. For months it had awaited the right occasion for
barbecuing, stuffing, smoking, and other forms of posthumous
torture. It was unskinned, frozen rock-solid, and thus could be
guaranteed to retain its edibility, even after thawing, for at least
forty-eight hours. I hesitated. It seemed an improbable idea but –
was it really? I did not know the Italian laws regarding importation

of live, cooked, or frozen venison. It seemed unwise to contact the Italian embassy for information in case it proved negative. In any case, I could always claim that it was a weekend and so the embassy was closed. Was it worth the risk?

I was already corrupted by my friend Femi Johnson, who would buy cheap, oil-proof suitcases specially for the importation of yards of strung-together salami, boulders of parmesan cheese and even entire haunches of cured ham from Italy to cater to his special cravings. I bugged him relentlessly over this embarrassing habit but had no qualms over assisting him at demolition time. However, in Femi's case, he loaded himself with foreign matter on his way home, not outwards when penetrating foreign borders. How would the natives take to such a potential health hazard – coming from Africa of course it had to be nothing less! The more I thought of it, the more appealing was the idea. A promised wine festival had failed to materialise, well, we would improvise! As a private bonus, I would be able to boast of beating my friend at his game, albeit with the trafficking direction reversed. Most compelling however was the picture that I conjured up of the faces of the troupe, as I delivered letters from their families, assured them that everyone was safe and the nation was not completely on fire. Then, pulling at the zip, I would slowly unveil the offering.

The decision taken, I dug out a respectable looking bag comfortably capacious for my uncomplaining travelling companion, padded its interior with foam and newspapers. Just before heading for the airport, I inserted the eta, crouched in full *rigor mortis*, and sealed up the bag. Saturday night, I was airborne for Rome, arriving on Sunday morning.

Then came the question. What would be my response if some over-assiduous customs officer chose to open that bag? That was soon resolved – he would be assailed by a factual but embroidered introduction to the ways of theatre culture. A theatre festival was taking place in Sienna for which the frozen animal was an essential stage prop. This was an event that involved a ritual for which no stuffed or symbolic substitute could serve. I would create a grandfather of all fusses, threaten an international incident, demand to call the embassy, lie that I had checked the beast's admissibility with an official at the Italian embassy, scream racism, invoke cosmic disasters – including a wretched wine harvest for all of Italy – if the ritually blessed and consecrated animal was not laid out on its appointed altar within the next twelve hours! In short, I was resolved not to leave Rome airport without that beast. If it came to that, I would even threaten to pull my company out of the festival. What would they do anyway? What could they do? What business was theirs with a frozen quadruped that was not after an immigration visa and would soon be cleansed and purified in ritual flames? It was clear, they had to let in the cadaver.

There was a conference attached to the festival and Bode Sowande, a playwright, lecturer and director, had travelled from London for that purpose. We found ourselves clearing Immigration at the same time. Good or bad augury, it was time for some rapid improvisation. I said to him, listen Bode, I am carrying *gari* and a few other items of consumption for the company. I don't know about the Italian Customs but they might try to be awkward. If we are pulled aside for luggage inspection, let me do all the talking. Bode was more than willing. As if the Customs were waiting specially for us, an official blocked our exit through the NOTHING passage and waved us both to the SOMETHING TO DECLARE.

Here we go, I sighed. Úgún, it is now your turn. You offered me this sacrificial beast on a previous outing, now it's your duty to ensure that it arrives at destination where it will do the maximum good. Am I selfish, Ògún? No. Did I leave that beast in my private refrigerator awaiting consumption by me alone, maybe with Femi Johnson who will surely raise hell when he learns that the *ęta* is gone? No. Do I smuggle drugs? Arms? Certainly not! Sex slaves? Diamonds? Am I a trafficker in any contraband? If you agree the answer to all the foregoing is 'No', then regard this animal as your companion dog, preserved for offering. Blind those customs officers to its presence, or cover them in illusions like Pentheus at the hands of your sibling, Dionysos, whose festival we had expected to celebrate but remains frustratingly elusive. Send these infidels dancing to ethereal music in honour of the tropical *ęta*, miraculously transformed into the watchwolves of Romulus, guardians at the Roman gates.

I unbuckled Bode's bag, chatting loudly with him about the festival and lamenting what a disappointment it had been that the wine part of the festival had been cancelled. I lauded Italian wines over and beyond their own claims, complained that the rehearsal facilities were inadequate, but that this disappointment was constantly tempered by the beauty of the Italian countryside and its unmatchable wines. If those officers understood that much English, they gave no sign. With a flourish, I opened Bode's two bags and let my hand hover absent-mindedly over the zip-end of the criminal one. The chill of the frozen meat had penetrated to the outside of the bag, with a film of moisture covering the outer skin. If the customs officer so much as laid a finger on the bag, even with the dismissive intent of pushing it aside, there was no way his curiosity would not be aroused. I tugged at the zip. The officer had become bored. He looked over the bags and waved us off.

Once safely ensconced in a car, heading towards Sienna, I revealed to Bode the nature of the bag's content, nearly causing him a heart attack. In Sienna, when the beast was unveiled, the delight on the faces of the company was, as I anticipated, an unquantifiable reward. Then, to cap it all, the Nigerian Ambassador in Rome, Rekya Attah, having learnt of the artistes' privations, arrived in her car with pots and deep bowls brimming with Nigerian food. By now, a rough fire had been built by the company in the field outside the Nigerian quarters, and the smell of singeing hair and burnt skin soon attracted the other troupes. In twos and threes they emerged from their rooms, incredulous eyes confronted by a roasting of ẹta – of a medium-sized sheep – at the edge of the rows of vines that dipped vertiginously from the artistes' row of houses.

What followed, three hours later, was a riot of a feast, with the ẹta as centrepiece. Music flowed, and a spontaneous festival began. That evening, there were no patrons for the festival cafeteria. The bus that came to take the actors for dinner was sent back empty, prompting even the organisers to jump in and return with it to investigate. Again, the bus returned empty; they opted to remain and partake of the festivities.

Pity, the opening night of the play was one of those events that recall the image of the dying calf. As the rain pelted down, one of the lead actors, Yomi, discharged from hospital just in time for performance, hobbled about on crutches, in deep pain from a sciatic nerve. Playing opposite him – there were just the pair of them on stage – the other actor, perhaps empathetically afflicted! – blacked out on his lines, totally and irremediably, leaving the stage entombed in one of those silences that all directors dread. To ensure that he could not extricate himself from the marshland of silence, a bunch of children burst onto the stage wing, led by an Italian mamma, a schoolteacher, who could not understand what the company was still doing on stage – the hall had been booked for her pupils' end-of-school concert, following *Zia*, and she had come to take possession. Struggling to find his place, the actor returned to a point that had been played over forty minutes before. The Italian sound manager, totally lost, put on the next music cue anyway, judging that it was about time it came on....

We lost the play that night. Still, the spirit of the impromptu festival of *ẹta* appeared to take over, and redeemed the remaining performances.

A Digression on the Purpose of 'Accidents'

Few cultures exist where the beginnings of drama have not been traced to the rituals of the society. It goes without saying therefore, that the fortunes of a play may depend on a respect or disrespect for ritual observance, especially in those instances when ritual comes knocking on the stage door, unbidden, and is either welcomed or denied entry. My 1981 production of *The Road* at the Goodman Theatre in Chicago proved to be, beyond a doubt, yet another of those instances of a clear correlation between a ritual/festival denied, and the consequences for a production.

My assistant in that production, Malcolm, was uncharacteristically late for rehearsals one Sunday night. He had driven home for the weekend break and, on his way back, racing to return in time for the Monday resumption of rehearsals, a deer ran onto the highway and attacked his motor car, getting the worst of the encounter. Thereupon Malcolm proceeded to wait until the state patrol arrived!

The story was so surreal that at first I thought he had been hallucinating. Are you sure you were struck by a deer? I persisted. No, the deer ran across the highway, he tried to quibble. I was having none of that. Did the deer collide with your car or not? He admitted the incident and even offered to show me the dent on his car.

Then I thought it all had to do with insurance. Was a police on-the-scene report essential to ensuring that his car was repaired on his policy? Apparently not. Then I proposed – well, maybe the animal was not dead and you were awaiting an ambulance? – the Euramerican world is filled with animal lovers of the decidedly lunatic fringe, and maybe it would be considered cruel if he put the animal in the boot of his car, even for the purpose of taking it to the nearest veterinary clinic. That would still appear a ridiculous proceeding but, I was willing to make allowances. But no, the animal was quite dead, he assured me, dead as warm venison. So what was the problem?

It was the law, he explained. He was not permitted to take the game away. In the United States of America, when game decides to commit suicide by car, it is only the police who can remove it! Malcolm plummeted in my estimation, from that moment, to a level from which it took quite a while for him to recover. The law? What did the law want of a dead deer – perform a post-mortem? Was Malcolm a closet vegetarian? I projected myself onto those moments of involuntary deerslaughter and the tame surrender of legitimate kill – Scene: *commuters rushing to and fro, minding their own business. Self-sacrificial deer jumps onto the road, hits oncoming car with violence (also damaging the vehicle!). Victim driver has been working on* The Road, *a play about the god Úgún, sacrifice, ritual and a mystic quest, knows very well that the director would gladly relieve him of any burden of guilt – if any is felt – organise an after-rehearsal convention on the mythological symbolism of a stricken deer, even if it required motoring to some wasteland where a bonfire would attract little attention...* Malcolm, in short, had a ritual responsibility to have thrown that deer in the boot of his car and reported to the director of this production, who could not be bound by any impious American law, where policemen took charge of such carcasses which then totally disappeared from sight.

Till today, no one has offered me a credible answer to the question: what happens to those mammals that are carted away by the state patrol? Incinerated? Sold as dog food? Sent to veterinary teaching hospitals for dissection? Ha! And my assistant tamely hands over a warm blooded wild game to the police – it was a most cowardly conduct, an act of betrayal and repudiation of every new knowledge I had imparted to the company. It was unacceptable conduct in a close collaborator. I refused to speak to him outside professional contact for days, and viewed him with deep suspicion for at least a week afterwards.

It would be my fate to be present at such deviant conduct in later years – once, in Cornell University, this time with my former student Skip Gates, then a professor, and a visiting collaborator from the days of Orísun Theatre, Femi Euba. Skip was at the wheel of his car where we came upon a freshly slain deer, still warm to the touch, victim of a hit-and-run driver perhaps no more than ten seconds ahead of our vehicle. Our duty to the world of rationality and ritual was to pick up that deer, repair to Skip's ample garden and commence proceedings. I had no cooperation. On the contrary, Skip moved his car far from the carcass to ensure that I did not heave it myself into the car. I was becoming schooled in the peculiarity of Americans, and so I contented myself with letting him know that he had inflicted a mortal wound on our friendship. The Chicago experience remained my introduction to the wastrel habit of American drivers after they have been victims of assault by rampaging game. A little more education and such drivers would know that there was only one explanation for such 'accidents' – they are a gift from Úgún, and should be honoured as such – atop a funeral pyre with the accompanying music of popping corks and roasting peppers.

It was that play, *The Road*, appropriately, that commenced the formulation of the image of the dying calf for any disasters I would later incur on stage. The contribution to that dismal experience by the lead actor was of such a nature and dimension that he became known as The Black Hole, so resolutely did he suck the energies and vitality of the rest of the company into the anti-matter of his stage presence. The play should have been retitled, for that production – *The Eclipse*. As for the director – hidden in a corner seat, having long abandoned the pointless exercise of note taking, I had only one wish left in the world – to sink into the theatre vomitorium and be deposited directly into the underworld. Since that vanishing trick refused to oblige, I considered myself guilty of a double dereliction of duty by failing to step onto the stage in the middle of the ongoing performance, apologising to the audience for having abused their evening out, and would they please leave now and collect their entry fees at the box office – with a glass of champagne plus canapés, compliments of the establishment, and free theatre seats for the rest of the season. And if anyone felt that this was not sufficient to assuage their assaulted dignity, they were invited to remain behind and witness an impeccable demonstration of a classic *Exit*, to be performed by the director, in that terminal idiom known as *seppuku*...

When that evening is contrasted with another in the same theatre, the production of *Death and the King's Horseman*, the difference is instructive. This was a production that was bedeviled by more than the usual production problems, giving off the feeling, sometimes, that the entire project was under a severe psychic attack, threatening the very survival of the actors. Despite such malevolence however, this production – in Chicago and the JF Kennedy Centre in Washington, DC – not its post-Nobel revival at the Lincoln Centre, New York! – proved to be an aesthetic and critical success, a rare combination. It earned the *New York Times* accolade as one of the best twelve productions of that year.

In Chicago however, where it received its American premiere, accidents of a physical nature threatened its very emergence on stage – accidents on the highways, within the city and within the theatre. Unlike *The Road*, no divine signal in the form of a productive accident came our way, only debilitating ones, such as that of 'Mrs. Pilkings', the wife of the district officer in that play, whose leg remained in plaster cast till only a few days to performance, duplicating the cast-in-plaster-cast spectacle of Sienna. No equivalent of Abraham's ram was spied entangled in the rigging, pointing us in the direction of what the gods demanded – instead, it was a stage hand who did his best to substitute. He landed barely one inch from the concrete flooring and the certainty of a shattered spine. Another day, giving directions from beside a plush curtain that covered an exit in the auditorium, I escaped, literally by sheer whiskers, the certain pulverisation of my chin. I felt my goatee swept violently aside by an offensive weapon that was inadvertently launched by one of the actors awaiting his entry – of course it had to be the actor who was also a fanatical body builder! My beard was swept aside, and such was the gale force that followed in the wake of that truncheon that I finally understood the origin of that expression – a close shave. I was astonished to find my beard still intact. And then, the illnesses – in so many ways, the seeds of serene Sienna appeared to have been sown in the wilds of Chicago.

There was a clear demand by invisible forces for some rites of exorcism. The black actors were of the same mind, but the management, fully in agreement that some kind of psychic remedy was called for, balked at the proposed format. The Chicago state by-laws, I was made to understand, forbade the slaughtering of a ram within city limits. And what of a cockerel? I enquired. It made no difference – the Chicago city fathers definitely frowned on the conversion of public buildings to private butcheries. The accidents continued. The management let it be known that their position had not changed, but noted that they were not equipped to prevent any illegal act that was committed without their knowledge. It was thus left to the company to let management know roughly between what hours the company might commit any purely conjectural, illegal act.

After the theatre had closed on the appointed night, which was to be during a week of the theatrical run of another play, the entire company – black and white – plus the technical director, assembled under the stage, gathered around a white, outsize cockerel, smuggled in by one of the actors. Kolanut was offered, libation – moonshine, for lack of palm wine in its distilled form – *ogogoro* – was poured. The bird was put out of its misery. I improvised a ritual, sprinkled blood in hidden corners beneath the stage and smeared some more on the spots of the major near-

accidents. The cockerel was then prepared in the apartment of
one of the actors and consumed, each member of the cast eating a
piece, however small.

Miraculously, the accidents ceased. Not one more actor so
much as stubbed a toe in the darkened theatre, tripped over wiring
or suffered food poisoning, neither during the rest of the rehearsals
nor through the lengthy run. Not even when the production left
the scene of the sacrificial cockerel and transferred to the Kennedy
Centre in Washington, DC. If the spate of accidents had continued,
I had my defence: substituting a cockerel for a ram, and other
forms of improvisation on stage are all very well for humans, but
the deities reserve the right of a final, critical approval, or rejection.

From Ghetto to Garrison

Of course, it feels grand and comparatively stress-free to work occasionally in theatres where everything is predictable – the stage mechanics work, actors are paid, there is a set division of labour etc. – but, I confess that such ventures still leave me hankering for the more precarious existence that characterises much of theatre culture on the African continent. There, theatre is not so much a noun as it is a verb – theatre is where theatre *happens.*

Unlike my first, semi-professional theatre company, the *1960 Masks*, I created the *Orísun Theatre* principally as a political vehicle. Its first home, the *Mbari* Writers and Artists Club, Ìbàdàn, was its nurturing place, and that environment became a formative factor in the distinct characteristics of the Orísun Theatre. Mbari was located right at the base of the Dùgbẹ̀ market hub in the chaotic city of Ìbàdàn, a crossroads of beggars and touts, pickpockets and gangsters, improvised motor parks, open urinals, lunatics, street vendors and itinerant preachers, beer parlours that were recruitment centres and haunts of freelance thugs high on marijuana, local gin and the guarantee of protection from their political masters, no matter what mayhem they caused. Often it struck me that the daily street theatre – to which most people remained oblivious – was far superior to anything that we could mount on the stage, but of course, while that demanded no entrance fee, payment could be exacted in rather unpleasant ways. Certainly, the drama of the very environment contributed markedly to the development of the character of the Orísun artiste, an existence on the thin edge of survival and the ability, not just to identify with, but to merge, chameleon-like, with the colours, sounds and pulses of its habituees.

It was only just, therefore, that *The Beatification of Area Boy*, a play evolved from the Nigerian slums, in Lagos, and from the improvisational working method of Orísun – it actually began as a series of sketches – would prove, fortuitously, the vessel on which the Orísun impulse would travel – and along the same route that African slaves had taken - to the 'New World'. It certainly provided me one of the most unforgettable – frustrating but infinitely rewarding – theatrical ventures I ever engaged upon, and at a time when I desperately required some form of relief – its production took place during the high season of the anti-Abacha struggle.

Firstly, however, *Beatification* received its – unexpectedly poignant – premiere at the West Yorkshire Playhouse in Leeds, England, under a British director, Jude Kelly. On the eve of its premiere came news of the hanging, by Sani Abacha, of the writer and environmental champion of the Ogoni – Ken Saro-Wiwa – and his eight comrades. I was not present at the opening, but the news predictably cast a pall over the theatre and created a quandary for the artistes – to cancel the event as a gesture of protest and respect, or dedicate the performance to their memory. They decided on the latter.

Six members from the Orísun workshop in Nigeria – called the *Sisi Clara* Workshop – including three pioneers of that company, travelled to England to participate. I was involved in the production, unusually, as I prefer to leave a director of any of my plays to his or her own devices, but Jude Kelly was no less determined to block all my escape routes! As I lent a hand to her efforts, I returned wistfully again and again to that play's interrupted naturation in its own spawning ground, and wondered whether the Yorkshire production would ever be seen by its intended audiences in Ìsàlẹ̀-èkó (Lagos), in Dùgbẹ̀ (Ìbàdàn), the original Orísun home, or indeed in other main Nigerian cities – Kaduna, Enugu, Benin, Jos or Port Harcourt. The production toured Europe, the United States (Brooklyn), Australia, always to uplifting reviews and reception, but it remained, for me, just another successful production. Not even its transfer to the violent environment of Brooklyn, New York, came close as a substitute for Dùgbẹ̀ or Ìsàlẹ̀-èkó.

And then, a Jamaican producer, Sheila Graham, ran into the play in a drama bookshop, read it and said to herself – but this is Jamaica! This is Kingston, Jamaica, even if it did set out from Lagos! Sheila sought me out in Atlanta where I taught at Emory University. A few months later, I was in Jamaica on a reconnoitring visit. I visited the various performing spaces and, among the choices, never was a decision made well in advance by the very social topography of a place!

As I confessed in my programme notes, the easiest part of the production turned out to be the very choice of a theatre. Among all the contenders, including the far more modern Little Theatre, it was quite straightforwardly a case of – No Contest! I settled for the Ward Theatre the moment I was driven through a pulsating community to confront this antique looking structure from the Victorian age. It was as if I had been transported to Broad Street or Yaba in Nigeria's Lagos! Groundnut sellers, cigarette hawkers, rickety stalls with the usual knick-knacks were all on display, layabouts lolled on broken walls, tree stumps and pavements, in various stages of boredom and alert opportunism. Present and vacantly ambulatory was the regulation quota of an indulged street lunatic or two, probably high on *ganja*... *summatively*, an exterior of dust and noise and vitality but also – an efficient sound-insulated interior! It was a most unusual combination. Much as, confessedly, I feel at home in street theatres, I also prefer major productions without unscripted 'noises off'. The environment of Ward Theatre was unbelievably the identical environment of Glover Hall in Lagos, whose boards had often played host to Orísun Theatre and its parent company, The 1960 Masks.

The *process* however proved to be no such easy walkover! Never before has that eve-of-performance greeting, 'Break a leg!' held such resonance as during the entire preparation of *Beatification*. Over the project, more than a mere leg was broken – literally this time – for better or worse: social mythologies, insularity, professional attitudes, aptitude limitations, conventions, performance concepts, taboos, etc. etc., not to mention my own stoical ceiling and personal endurance record! The very violent context of the *Area Boy* project in Kingston also provided a powerful antidote to the pessimism that daily threatened my existence from the stubborn tenacity of a dictator's hold on my own political space, the daily reports of new atrocities on the populace, accompanied by news of capitulation and collaboration by much of the political class.

Focussing on *youth, youth, youth!* – that all too familiar marginalised, disadvantaged, frustrated, exploited, under-utilised, straining-at-the-leash-of-opportunity, but also often dangerously romanticised *youth* – proved most efficacious as a restorative agent. There was also Tunji Oyelana, my dogged collaborator around, as a constant reminder of an unending mission. He was, after all, a founding member of Orísun. Now, as co-musical director of the production, he was a figure of continuity – thirty-plus years of collaboration, the product of a rather stubborn social-artistic impulse that began even before the nation's Independence. All the same, when one embarks on a creative adventure in an environment that is paradoxically both familiar and estranged, it is always wiser to prepare for the roadblocks of the latter, girding oneself for a barefoot journey into unknown territory.

It was a welcome break – the first and only sustained break – from working to topple Abacha's regime and being hunted in turn by his goons – that is, I was insulated even from news about Nigeria. The long reach of the menace was however accorded due place, and I was assigned a police 'minder' by the government for most of my stay in Jamaica. I felt reasonably safe however; Jamaica was itself such a violent place that I felt that Abacha's agents would have met their match locally before they came within a stone's throw of their quarry.

I found myself thrust into a bubbling, undirected ferment of uneven talent, a dubious mix of professionals, semi-professionals and rank amateurs, several of them unaccustomed to the discipline that is basic to the theatre profession. It helped that Tunji Oyelana was also available to take some of the strain. Tunji, with his wispy goatee and avuncular manner, never set out directly to be accounted a political dissident, but a consistent and stubborn streak of conviction, even when strictly engaged in an artistic pursuit would invariably result in his being marked down for negative attention by successive regimes.

After the Yorkshire Playhouse production, he had been unable to return to Nigeria, having been singled out for reprisals by the Abacha regime for his prominent role in that project. He had further compounded his pariah status by comments in interviews on the BBC, and in a documentary that was made of the production and screened on Nigerian television. By now, I had been formally declared a WANTED man by the regime, and quite a few colleagues paid a heavy price even for mere association that had preceded the regime. As frequently happened, warnings from highly placed contacts reached us in time, and the other actors could take due precautions in their mode of re-entry into the country. Until the death of Sani Abacha, Tunji's home and office in Ìbàdàn remained under constant surveillance.

It was not simply a play project intended solely for rehearsals, performances, and dispersal. The Kingston venture was approached by Sheila Graham, from the very beginning, as one that would not merely rehabilitate the disadvantaged youths of Jamaica but transform the degraded 'inner city' environment. Would-be artistes were invited through advertisements and media promotion to apply for places in what was dubbed 'The Area Boy Project'. They underwent auditions and a final selection process – hundreds, apparently, had applied! They differed from Orísun in the quality of their background, much of which sometimes made the Nigerian sixties' environments of Ìsàlè-èkó or Dùgbè seem like boarding schools in comparison. They were young – the youngest was ten, the 'grand-daddy' twenty-two, with a deep baritone operatic voice – but mostly they were all still at school, yet already adult and life-stressed in various ways.

'Mamma' for instance, a battle scarred sixteen-year old, was living alone and taking care of her younger sister. Her father had long abandoned the family and later, the mother died. She took in washing and did other odd jobs to survive, and ensure that her sister went to school. 'Clipper' – no one appeared to be without a nickname, and I wondered if this was another survival strategy, creating a deflective personality – 'Clipper' was a boy cadet who was clearly enamoured of the glamour and discipline of the military while 'Chicken', perhaps one of the handful without a notable background of trauma, attended rehearsals under the ambiguous shadow of her stepfather. His principles were against his stepdaughter appearing on stage, but he found all the attention paid to Chicken's evident talents irresistible.

'Molewa', by contrast, had a Rastafarian father, also remarried, who proudly appeared at rehearsals, sought every opportunity to discuss world politics with me, and to appear in photographs. 'Sally' – fourteen – had lost an eye in mysterious circumstances. The widely accepted story was that she had been battered by a drunken father, but she persisted in her own tale of a mysterious bird which flew in through the window of her home one day and – smack into her eye! She claimed that the seemingly blind eye was not truly blind but was her eye into another world with whose denizens she could commune. And for this reason she would not agree to visit an eye specialist. 'Aston' had lost his brother in a shootout, then, during rehearsals, his father would also die, victim of another shootout. And Tanya would lose her life, at fourteen, a few weeks after the close of *Beatification*. She walked out of her home one normal morning and straight into a bullet from the cross-fire of a gang war...

Jamaica *was* a space of violence. I knew that already. I had received my education on that island years before, during CARIFESTA, the Caribbean Festival of the Arts when, ignorant of the turf wars that were waged between the 'garrisons', two colleagues – Kole Omotoso and Abiola Irele – both university lecturers – and I, had come close to a messy end with a taxi driver on a lonely road. Now I was thrust amidst the products of those hard beginnings, amidst youths who grew up forbidden to cross the lines of close neighbourhoods. Enemy lines were clearly demarcated. Touching in their idealism and innocence, plaintive, yet messianic were the voices of our young recruits:

My dream is to see the world come together and live as one in peace and love and stop the killing....

I have learnt that you cannot categorise everyone as the same, each person has their own feelings, you need to know how to deal differently with each person...

If we don't pull the 'turfs' together, Kingston is not going to survive...

I believe that we as young people can make a difference in the community...

Those were the voices of the garrison children, seeking liberation into a world of creativity and fulfilment, into which they also sought to liberate their community. At least half of them had emerged from broken homes. Most had known violence at first-hand, or indirectly, in one form or the other. In the worst of the 'war zones' – as they are actually described! – residents often slept beneath, not on their beds, for fear of being killed before morning by stray bullets crashing through their thin walls at night. 'Theatre' was a strange concept to many. They grew up learning to know their own turfs and accepting that it was dangerous to stray across certain streets, or cross border lines.

It was the politicians who created these garrisons. In order to guarantee and seal tight their political fiefdoms, they built schools in them, clinics and recreation centres of sorts, created jobs – usually in construction – for their supporters and their dependants, some of whom doubled the job of foremen and supervisors with the more powerful positions of being or serving the 'dons' of the garrisons, controlling lives from infancy to death, which for many was sudden and violent. The marijuana trade sustained many, so did trafficking in harder drugs.

The garrisons, polarised in deadly destructiveness, went by exotic names – Tel Aviv, Barbican, Tivoli Gardens, Trenchtown, etc. A full generation had been raised, gone to school, married, raised their own families and sometimes died without stepping across the street that separated them from the next garrison. Even schooling was uneven, since sometimes the 'wars' prevented pupils from emerging from their homes for long periods at a time. During our rehearsals, it was not unusual to receive frantic messages for help that were somehow smuggled out from a youth – a stripling of upwards of eighteen years – who had been locked up by his mother to prevent him leaving home for fear of his getting killed. She would mount guard over the door and swear that he would only leave home over her dead body. Public transport traversed these streets, moving through one garrison into the next, but you simply did not get down from the bus until you were safely in your own neighbourhood.

I was pursued, I sometimes felt, by the violence from which I had sought to escape, if only for a while. I had an early taste of it one afternoon when I toured the garrisons to obtain a flavour of this Lagos live-alike, stopping in a bar from time to time for a beer and conversation. I was accompanied – a condition to which I was learning to adjust – by an assigned security officer in mufti, but mostly to validate my presence in suspicious neighbourhood. Less than two hours after we left Trechville, a shoot-out occured, right outside the bar where we had sat. The female bartender, a buxom wit of immense vitality with whom we had passed an enjoyable half hour or so, caught a stray bullet and was killed. For some moments, I wondered, could Abacha's roving squads have successfully tracked me down, hit the right place but mistimed their operation? But no, it was indeed nothing more than the daily dose of local garrison violence.

That violence constantly intruded, but violence had become part of their lives. After each rehearsal, it was a quasi-military operation to ensure that these youthful enthusiasts got home safely, and there were times when the police came to rehearsals or radioed my minder to pass on a message – either we let the kids return home early on account of information of an impending gang war, or else the gang war had commenced and we should keep the affected members with us for the night. Every constraint only made them more resolved to break free, and this theatre activity was their personal and collective instrument.

It was thus, the Orísun experience raised several levels, an intense, life-and-death Kingstonian strain. Brief, occasional theatre sketches outside rehearsals for *Beatification* served as outlet for long repressed experiences and emotions. Gradually, tentatively, they moved towards the creation of their own ensemble within the production company. Stringing together their sketches with songs, they designed their own very special show, all boundless energy and exuberance. For their first outing as an independent ensemble, they settled, poignantly, on the title *Border Connections* – for most of them, they were crossing borders for the very first time in their lives. Creative borders, obviously, but also violent, artificial borders that had been deliberately erected by the absentee political kingpins. Their obsessive theme was thus – political manipulation, the exploitation and division of their communities. They decried the violence that ruled and ruined their lives and depicted the agonies of mothers constantly obliged to bury their children. The titles of the sketches reflected a touching crusading zeal: *Youth Oppressed; Mi Son Dead; Mi Hungry, Mi Angry; Isn't There Another Way? Put Down de Gun!* They were apostles of change and hope.

It seemed a forlorn cry, doomed from its very utterance but, incredibly, the 'dons' who had either heard of the show, watched it on television or on other neutral ground, embraced it as a revelation. They negotiated 'command performances' on their turfs, over which they proudly presided and played host. These were men who would end a twenty-year friendship in a burst of gunfire, for no other cause than a suspicion by one that he had been 'dissed' – disrespected – by his lifelong friend. Rape was a way of life for most. Beneath the bravado of the warlords however was an infinite war-weariness, for which the 'message' of the youths offered prospects of eventual relief and a change in social sensibilities. The proof was not long in coming – the 'dons' passed the word among rival gangs that it was time for a cessation of random violence! Was flirtatious eighteen-year old Patrine being proved right? – in her mission statement, the formal declaration that each participant made of his or her assessment of the *Area*

Youth programme as it was renamed – she declared – *the youth have displayed the power to change and the will to conquer and eradicate violence from our society.* The dons appeared to have subscribed to that. They sent out the word: *Bring out the guns, or bury them.*

Of course, it was by no means over. The emergence of a band of evangelists does not transform any community overnight, not where there are those who feel threatened, who see their domination of society through the tactics of fractionalisation being eroded by a youthful gospel of oneness. A performance of *Border Connections* for the 23rd of November in 2000, in one of the inner-city community centres had to be cancelled, owing to what was publicly acknowledged as 'war in the community', and the waste of young Tanya Thomas at the unfulfilled age of fourteen remained a harrowing reminder of the enormity of their task. However, the area youths operated on a different kind of battlefront, where the conquering band remained undeterred. *What we captured,* proclaimed Theresa Whyte, one of the older members of the group, *was something we can't let go. We'll never let it go.*

They did not. What started out as a movement of youthful idealism became the Area Youth Foundation, touring the world, acclaimed everywhere. I receive the occasional postcard, email, even newsletter.

Beatification was, by no means, an easy exercise. Undertaken as a collaboration with Sheila Graham's quaintly named 'The Company', by the University of West Indies and Emory University, Atlanta, where I was teaching at the time, it was supposed to mark the beginning of a special relation between the two universities. That sisterly bonding nearly foundered before it began. I was obliged to walk off the production once, agreeing to return only when the company had persuaded itself and its recruited members that it wanted a serious, professional production. The situation had become *impossible!* Before the show was finally over, from first casting to performance – I had rehearsed for *each* role in a large cast an average of two and a half actors – surely an unprecedented turn-over rate in the history of most theatres!

The Orísun experience may prepare a director for the unexpected, but it was not in the running for an entry in the

Guinness Book of Records in directorial self-flagellation! I let loose on the assembled cast, production team and took off, laying out conditions for my return. We did not succeed in re-grouping for another two and a half weeks. By the time I returned however, the company had succeeded, among other creative insurmountables, in filling the role of one of the two principal characters in the play. The 'professionals' also appeared to have finally imbibed the dedication of the younger, rawer elements in the troupe – *they* were the professionals, at least in commitment!

The lighting director however continued his existence in his accustomed, invisible and unique time zone. I began to wonder if he was a phantom of The Company's creation, perhaps one of the famed West Indian zombies, for his capacity for sustained evaporation. He remained so despite the efforts of Rex Nettleford, the university rector, to trap him in the world of the living. Zombie or not, he barely escaped a truly terminal, irreversible death from a beckoning stage prop on the very day of the premiere! After disappearing throughout the crucial countdown days, Mr. Lighting Tech. turned up only five hours before opening, blithely announced that he had under two hours to work to my direction as he had yet another performance to light that same evening! Then, sticking to that time concession as if he had swallowed an alarm clock, he left the control booth, sauntered across the stage and headed towards the exit, his tongue cheerfully tripping off the traditional theatre greeting, *Break a leg.* I succeeded in keeping my hands off that iron rod only by retorting – *Break your neck!* – but he was already halfway to his next engagement – no doubt in a rummery – and I doubt if he heard or cared.

Vinnie Murphy, from Emory Theatre arrived that morning for the premiere with a university delegation. Like most directors who worked in conditions that approximated the norm, he was accustomed to technicals that took a steady, meticulous week. They found me in an empty theatre, awaiting the levitation of the lighting director. I was still waiting there till late afternoon, occupying the time in brief spurts of activity with individual actors and other crew members. They helped in preserving my outward calm.

The opening performance was thus, as in many such

productions, a Technical-cum-Dress Rehearsal. In addition however, it took the record by being the first complete run-through of that play ever to take place – that is, its first uninterrupted performance in the correct order of scenes – thanks to the rotating absence of the principal actors. When Murphy returned to Atlanta, he took to regaling his students with the account of how he had actually witnessed a full-length production lit in an hour and forty-five minutes, but I doubt if any of them believed that it was anything but a ploy to work them like slaves in future Emory productions.

To watch the company leaping up and down on stage like a family of long-restrained, high-spirited monkeys the moment the curtain closed to sustained applause, they *knowing,* with their newly honed theatrical sensibilities that they had indeed brought off a singular, near-impossible theatrical feat – despite flawed moments here and there – savouring the vindication of unaccustomed days of discipline, self-privation, creative exploration – engulfed by bodies as I emerged from backstage and they screamed the roof down, turning somersaults, broke into spontaneous snatches from their *Connections* – was a most affecting moment. I rescued 'Chicken' from her self-pitying corner – she had forgotten to make a costume change in one scene – and I made her join the others. I told her, consider this – but for the Lighting Zombie, you would have had a lighting cue. Soon, she was feeling less suicidal.

They basked in the adulation of families and friends who swarmed backstage, responded to the slightly more formal felicitations and suggestions of Rex Nettleford, his colleagues from Emory – Rudolph Byrd and Vinnie Murphy, then Sheila Graham and the city worthies. What they did not know was that – again on so many levels, since theatre has no parallel in this territory of largesse (and denial!) – despite frequent bouts of despondency, theirs was easily the most valued single gift that I received throughout the four dark years of the struggle against the tyranny of General Sani Abacha.

PART VI

Bernard Shaw
Was Right!

How the News
Came to Me

George Bernard Shaw is reputed to have said: I find it easy to forgive the man who invented a devilish instrument like dynamite, but how can one ever forgive the diabolical mind that invented the Nobel Prize for Literature?

Yes, the Nobel was born of dynamite, but should that mean that it must transmit the shock waves of dynamite, and for so long afterwards? It is not my business to account for how it came to take such a hold on the imagination of the world, to the extent that when I find myself in a number of countries, the Asian especially, the first question asked me is nearly always: what must we do to bring the Nobel Prize to this country? It is a question that never ceases to astonish, even shock me – why should anyone worry their heads over a prize whose mode of attribution you can in no way influence? Indeed, why should one *strain* for a prize? If it comes, fine, if it doesn't, what was one before the prize? Why should one notice the existence of a prize for anything?

Acknowledged competitions, I understand. At least, one knows what the rules are. In my youth, I sent in my poems and short stories to the Arts Festivals in colonial Nigeria, won a bronze medal or two – it was always bronze medals, for some reason – and I was highly elated. My competitiveness was restricted to such adventures. It retained its keenness, perhaps until I had returned home from my studies in the United Kingdom and created my theatre company. From then on, I turned increasingly indifferent to the very notion of competition, which can only mean that, somewhere deep down, I was persuaded that competitions in the world of creativity are meant for the young, or early adulthood, not for the mature, self-cognising being. Contradicted though I am by the existence of numerous prizes of great prestige, much sought after, and their undoubted enhancements of one creative enterprise or another, I have experienced no urge to revise my visceral conditioning.

The third hardest part of the Nobel is to be found in the expectations of others – in the main. As a Laureate, you are expected to be different from whatever you were before. So confident and self-fulfilling is that expectation that, in some cases, a difference is noticed – with marked approval or resentment - even by those who encounter their Nobelist for the first time! Others simply demand, even wordlessly, that one act different, eat different, talk different, dress different, walk different, abandon former haunts, former preoccupations, former idiosyncracies, former likes and dislikes, and don, overnight, a totally fictitious persona that corresponds to their fantasies. Certain chores become too commonplace for the Nobelist, and the poor sod is faced – thank goodness! – with desertion if he fails to deliver on their expectation.

Second place – nearly in dead heat with the first – goes to the loss of the final shred of anonymity, especially hard for those who carry around with them a landmark of luxuriant moss that goes for a head of hair. This, however, can be ameliorated by a good stock of hats. Such disguises are not perfect, but at least they give one a running start. The prime place, however belongs to one's overnight transformation – in the conception of most in your own community – into the drinking buddy of Bill Gates.

There are compensations however, and mine came right at the beginning. Not too many of the laureates, I am certain, could have relished coming into knowledge of their award the way it occurred in my case. Let me recall, first of all, the previous year, 1985, in which all kinds of speculators had been deservedly chastised for their premature celebrations, the Nigerian media most especially. It is a pity that no one can take a comprehensive copyright on his being, so that public speculations about any individual prospects in any field become actionable infringement on one's privacy. How the rumours began, only the gods can tell but, there they were, and I at the distasteful centre of it all. Confronted by confident predictions, plastered all over the pages of the Nigerian newspapers, pursued by journalists in the weeks leading up to the announcement in October 1985, then pursued after the deflation of *their* prophetic presumptions, just to be asked what I felt, my answer oscillated between: 'let that be a lesson to you all', 'serve you all right', 'no comment', 'can I now get on with my writing?' etc. etc.

However, the media had learnt its lesson, so all was silent in 1986. Indeed I did not even recall that the time of the Nobel was at hand as I took leave of Cornell University where I was then teaching, boarded a plane and headed for Paris to chair the executive meeting of the International Theatre Institute (ITI). I was to stay with my cousin, Yemi Lijadu, north of Paris where he had an apartment. I arrived early in the morning. I hated those flights from the East coast of America to Europe – they are what I call the overnight neither-nors – not long enough to permit a decent sleep, and too long to prevent one from dozing off. My routine after such flights is to crawl into bed, close all the blinds, put on my eye-shade and sleep for between two to three hours. Getting into Paris at an early hour, Yemi would normally leave the keys with a neighbour or in an agreed hiding-place and take himself off to work. This time, he was home. I found him in a state of barely suppressed excitement, his slight goatee bobbing up and down, his dark cheeks dancing with the well-being of French wines and lunches, not to speak of the results of his own kitchen prowess. Before I could set down my bags, my cousin had commenced his 'dramatiser-routine', one that had become second nature. If Yemi had exciting news to deliver, he would never do it straight – the more exciting, the greater the garnishing. This time, he surpassed himself with so many peripherals, incidentals and parentheses that I finally had to interrupt.

"Yemi, who is dead?"

"Dead? No! Oh no, just wait, I am trying to..."

"Yemi, what's the bad news?"

"Bad news? No, exciting news. But wait, of course you couldn't have heard..."

Finally at some point, he ran out of delaying prefaces and side commentaries and came to the point. When he did, I sighed and shook my head. "You too! You mean you failed to learn from last year?"

He shook his head vigorously. "No, no, this time, it looks like it. Solidly. The press have been all over UNESCO"

"Yemi, I am tired. I need to sleep." And I went off to the toilet. He followed.

"You have to start thinking what to tell them. How are you going to handle it? And there's a journalist from Stockholm who is coming here any moment."

I screamed. "You invited him here?"

That was the ultimate betrayal. Yemi, the normally protective Yemi, had allowed a journalist to invade my (his) sanctuary.

"I haven't had any rest myself since yesterday. You'll find out when you get to UNESCO..."

I disappeared into the bedroom. I heard the phone ringing incessantly. I indignantly refused to take any calls and crawled into bed. Finally there was one I had to take – it was Anne-Marie, the Secretary to the ITI. She wanted to know when I was arriving at the meeting because, she said, the press was going mad.

"Did you invite them?" I asked.

"No".

"Then ignore them."

"I can't do that. You're the only one who can send them away. We can't function here. They've taken over the entire frontage of rue Miollis. No one can do anything."

"Anne-Marie, I am going to sleep. And then I shall turn up for the meeting two hours late, as already agreed. Goodnight – or Good morning if you prefer."

"You'll have to go and face the press sooner or later", Yemi offered.

"Yemi, aren't you supposed to go to work?"

He shrugged. "All right, I'm off. But look er... I promised that journalist. His newspaper sent him all the way from Stockholm so, it's a serious matter you know. He explained to me – as soon as the decision is made, the committee starts tracking you all over the world. Please, when he comes, let him in."

"Yemi, I don't live on speculations. I came to Paris for the ITI meeting, and that's all I have on my mind."

The bell rang. "Aha, I think that's him."

"He's your guest. You do what you want with him."

I pushed deeper into bed while his voice pursued me. "I made him promise he won't even attempt an interview. All his newspaper wants is for him to be with you when the news is made official. That's all."

Now, at this stage, surely, something must have begun to give. I have gone over and over those moments, trying to discover when it was that my wall of disbelief and/or indifference began to crumble, the moment when I said to myself, suppose it is true after all? I'm afraid I have never recovered that moment. I think the slamming of the door as Yemi let in the journalist could have been it – I cannot swear to it. I was sure of only one thing – I wanted, needed my two-hour sleep before confronting the Executive of the International Theatre Institute, where I presided over a group of genuine theatre artistes, researchers, theatre historians as well as – ideological apparachiks from the Soviet bloc, for whom even administrative choices had to be entered into a party-line framework. The Wall was not yet down. One required, ideally, a solid night's sleep before dancing on such a trampoline. Deprived of that, nothing should disturb a measly two hour preparatory sleep, duly fortified after by a double espresso. Through the sheets I heard Yemi say good-bye as he left for work, assuring me that he had extracted from the correspondent a promise that I was not to be disturbed, that he was prepared to wait, all he wanted was to be the first to see me after the news was formally announced.

I ignored him and pulled the blanket closer round my head, heard the door slam as Yemi left for work. About two minutes passed in the marvellous, soothing silence of his apartment, so high up that the demented noise of traffic below arrived through bales of cotton fluff, and all the neighbours had gone to work. I sank effortlessly into the first stage of sleep. Any moment, and I would be wholly gone when suddenly, there were voices in the apartment. Who else now? Who else had this sole journalist let into the apartment? Camera men? I threw myself out of bed and marched into the living room. Well, there he was, and all alone, this Nordic figure humped over the television set and twiddling the buttons! I watched him for some time and then he turned round and saw me.

"Oh, I am sorry if I disturbed you. You are of course Wole Soyinka."

I stared at him through bloodshot eyes. He continued, "Your cousin let me in. I was trying to tune into Bernard Pivot's culture programme. That is where the announcement will be made."
At which point, I surrendered all further thoughts of sleep. I shut the door and went into the bathroom to take a shower. It was better going to the ITI meeting than staying cooped up with this journalist.

I took my time, dressed, and got ready for UNESCO. I brewed some coffee, and then, realising I wasn't really being gracious to my cousin's guest, decided to offer him some. He accepted gratefully and we both sat in the living-room for what I expected would be only until we finished our coffees. Then I would leave him to his own devices. If he chose to follow me to UNESCO, that was his business. But he soon put paid to all that.

"Everybody is waiting for you at UNESCO" he said, as if he had read my thoughts.

"So I'm told. There must be a back way of getting in for my meeting."

He smiled. "I don't think you'll be having much of a meeting. I don't think there is much work going on at the UNESCO Annexe right now. When I left, the excitement was really high."

I decided to take him on. "You know something? This nonsense happened last year also, only it happened at home, in Nigeria. The press there behaved exactly the same way as the ones here appear to be doing. It came to nothing. I was just as far from taking them serious then as I am now. I don't believe in speculations."

He shook his head. "Oh, I think this is more than mere speculation Mr. Soyinka. My newspaper specially sent me to track you down and..."

"Oh yes, that's right. To do what exactly? I warned my cousin that I am not giving any interviews."

"No, I don't want an interview. Although of course, if you do wish to say anything..."

"Nothing."

"That's fine, that's absolutely fine. All I need is that you simply allow me to be with you until the announcement is made. That's all. We're not asking too much."

I shrugged.

Then he saw the radio and dashed towards it. "I'd better put this on too. The radio may broadcast it before Pivot."

So the man began fiddling with the tuning knobs of the radio, seeking to lock in on the Arts Programme. Then he would dash across the room again, tune the television set to another programme, then return it to Bernard Pivot. Across the room again he dashed – always at a crouch – to try another radio channel. I saw his face becoming anxious and, quite frankly, I began to enjoy his discomfiture. There was I, a candidate for this much-envied prize, ensconced in a room with a journalist who was waiting on tenterhooks for the announcement, and all I was thinking was, 'Serve you right; this will teach you not to indulge in idle speculations.' I think I must have a sadistic streak somewhere in me after all, because I really was enjoying the creases of anxiety that began to form on the man's face. He kept muttering to himself – *but it's eleven o'clock now, well almost.* A few minutes later: *but now it's actually past eleven. The announcement was to have been made at eleven.* And he actually looked at, then shook his watch. He made the occasional check on me, as if I had agreed to be his fellow news monitor – *you didn't hear anything did you? Do you think I missed it on the radio?*

The Norwegian, or Swede, was interrogating the radio when a man walked into Bernard Pivot's programme and handed him a piece of paper. Pivot excused himself, adjusted his glasses and read it, then faced the discussion panel while the camera focussed on him. *Breaking News,* as the Americans call it, as Pivot smoothed out his piece of paper and made his statement. The Academy had announced the winner of the Nobel Prize for Literature for 1986, and the winner was – the writer from Nigeria... and he managed to garble my name. Across the room, the Nordic journalist continued his frantic struggle with radio static.

I suppose it is time to attend – as honestly as one can – to some personal dissection. The first admission I must make, and truthfully is – I did not sense any quickening of my pulse. Did I know this writer? I was not sure. Was I asking, did I hear aright? No, I did not ask such a silly question. My French was sufficiently competent, the man had referred to the Nobel Prize for Literature, and he had coupled my name with it. So, there it was. The trouble was that the announcement was made in the most ordinary fashion, quite routinely, so it did not really tie up with all the excitement with which I had been confronted from the moment I stepped into my cousin's apartment, beginning with his long rigmarole. Nor was it linked to the Scandinavian gentleman still fiddling with the radio controls and wearing a lengthening frown on his face.

I continued to sip my coffee, watched him return to his chair from where he proceeded to give his undivided attention to the Bernard Pivot programme. It ended some twenty minutes later, and now the man really looked defeated, totally baffled.

"But that's the end of the programme," he announced piteously.

I nodded agreement. "But what happened? The official announcement should have been made. It was supposed to be on Pivot's programme."

"Do you mean, the Nobel Prize for Literature?"

Irritated, he snapped, "Of course. At eleven o'clock."

I told him, matter-of-factly, "But it was announced."

He looked thunderstruck and I saw immediately what was going on in his mind – he had been chasing the wrong quarry. But I wasn't being mischievous in prolonging his agony. I think that, in taking my time, I was also passing the news to myself. I did not feel I owed the intruder any special treatment, so there was no reason why we should not both learn of it at the same time, my absorption rate having been slowed down, probably, by the transatlantic flight.

"Well, well, what...? Who? Tell me."

I shrugged, I think. "You were right. It was me."

Now he really was staring wide-eyed. "You? But when? What happened?"

"You were fiddling with the radio. Someone walked up to Pivot and handed him a piece of paper. He looked at it, and he made the announcement."

"It was you? Well? Well?" Now his voice was accusing. "But why didn't you call me? That's what I was waiting for?"

I was not sure how to answer him, how to explain it, so I simply reminded him, "You didn't ask me to". I picked up the coffee cups, took them to the kitchen.

"But you are saying nothing" the man protested, following me. "What are your reactions? What do you feel?"

Did he expect me to fall down in a faint? Or burst into a Yoruba ululation? I did not understand the man's question. Just what did he want? What was the entire idea of coming to trap me in my cousin's apartment so he could report on my reactions? It seemed to me that the world – or his section of the world – was quite mad. Immediately of course, the phone had to ring, and it was Anne-Marie on the line. "You have to come here at once. You simply have to come. Nobody can move or get past the press corps. This place is a madhouse."

"I did not invite them. Get whoever invited them to get rid of them."

"You're not being reasonable. Please try and be reasonable. They know already you're in Paris. There is no way they'll leave here unless you come."

"I am not coming," I insisted, and I meant it. Suddenly, all I wanted was the accustomed peace and quiet of my cousin's apartment, or something better. My next course of action, I felt, what I really wanted for myself, was to throw out the journalist and resume my interrupted sleep. I shook my head ruefully as I rinsed the coffee cups, realising that that prospect was too late, what with the lethal stuff I had just swallowed.

"Well," snapped Anne-Marie, "Don't complain if they invade your hiding-place."

I hadn't thought of that, but Yemi evidently had, because a few moments later, he was charging into the apartment, ready to drag me to UNESCO with the aid of the French gendarmes if necessary. I decided to go quietly. I saw the face of the journalist, intently reading my own, looking for what exactly, I still had no idea. He followed us to UNESCO, and disappeared among the crowd.

As Yemi drove towards the frontage of No.1, rue Miollis, I regretted my decision. I suddenly realised that there was an option that was available, one that I should have taken and that was – head in the opposite direction, towards Charles de Gaulle Airport, and disappear from sight. But then I would have needed the cooperation of my cousin. For what struck me was that there were no more microphones, no more cameras, no more tripods, flash-bulbs or notepads left anywhere in the world. All had been miraculously and aggressively assembled at Number 1, rue Miollis. I was attacked – there is no other way of describing it - attacked by a bristling, rearing, snarling pack of hunting hounds straining at the leash, blotting out the world of reality. For the first time, I understood how the metaphor 'news hounds' came about. I tried to duck back into the car but Yemi, all cousinly responsibilities abandoned, had pulled off, leaving me at the mercy of the rampaging horde. Questions ripped through the air like tracer bullets. I mumbled inaudibly, mostly to myself, asking where I thought I was heading when I first set pen to paper, found that someone had managed to take charge and was imposing some kind of order, so that I could at last make sense of a few questions and provide some coherent but uninspiring answers, was then dragged through the mêlée and hustled into the office where the ITI Executive had assembled. A bottle of champagne appeared miraculously, and now I was feeling safe among my ITI colleagues – never before had I appreciated what a lovable, harmonious family this was, until I had run the gauntlet of the press.

The press would not leave so soon, and we decided to adjourn an impossible meeting. Already I had made up my mind: I had to escape from UNESCO, then flee Paris on the next available flight, whenever that was. I never wanted to see a news camera, flash-bulb or microphone for as long as I lived. All I could think of was the two point six hectares of bushland that I had acquired and on which I had already laid the foundations of a modest cottage, and the vista that opened up before my eyes was WS thrashing through the dense forest to that patch of absolute tranquility, forsaking the world forever. I had not taken the full measure of what I had got myself into, but if it was anything like what confronted me at the UNESCO Annexe, beginning with what should have been a routine arrival in my cousin's apartment, I wanted no part of it. Abẹ̀òkúta, here I come – was all I could think as I gulped down the champagne, looked around the conference room at the faces of my colleagues and apologised silently for the abandonment that was coming to them – if only they knew it! I had made up my mind to retire from the world, simply – disappear!

Thorns in the Crown

And then calamity struck, and from a totally unexpected direction. I arrived in Nigeria on October 14th, to what came close to being a national mood of euphoria, formally abetted by the wily IBB, who sent his Minister of Culture, Tony Momoh, to spring an ambush as I arrived at the airport. Accompanied by carefully selected colleagues, among them JP Clark, Tony Momoh brought with him a letter that conferred me with national honours. It was a carefully executed *fait accompli*, but one that was not especially difficult for me to accommodate. By October 1986, Babangida had been in office only a year and, at that time – a fact that many Nigerians find most convenient to forget – could still lay claim to the approval of much of the nation, in whose mind the terror reign of Buhari and Idiagbon was still fresh.

That Nobel-induced festive mood came to an abrupt, and bloody ending. It had not lasted even a week, and the nation was plunged into mourning, relieved only by a surge of outrage. An unprecedented event had taken place in Nigeria – assassination by a letter bomb. The victim was an investigative journalist whose biting columns had disturbed the peace of many complacent crooks in government.

Dele Giwa was seated at a table in his study, breakfasting with a London-based colleague, Kayode Soyinka – no relation –

when he opened a parcel that had just been delivered to him by a motor-cycle courier. He took the full brunt of the explosion on his lap. His guest was blown across the room, with permanent damage to his ear-drums. Nothing remained of Dele's thighs and legs but pulp.

Only a few weeks before, Dele Giwa, a co-publisher and editor of *Newswatch*, Nigeria's earliest version of news magazines in the format of *Time* and *Newsweek*, had been summoned by the head of Babangida's national security, Colonel Halilu Akilu, where he had undergone an encounter that shook him to his heels. He confided in his solicitor, Gani Fawehinmi, that he was afraid for his life and additionally raised a public outcry. Dele Giwa claimed that Akilu had accused him of gun-running, or of possessing knowledge of gun-runners and dissident groups who wanted to overthrow, or destabilise Babangida's government. The charges were so preposterous that Dele Giwa had only one conjecture: this was a red herring, designed to prepare the grounds for his already decided elimination.

A few days after his public outcry, Halilu Akilu telephoned to assure him that all was well, that the charges had been thoroughly investigated and there was nothing to worry about. To reassure him even further, Akilu informed Dele that President Babangida wished to speak to him to allay his fears. Later still, the security chief again telephoned Dele Giwa to ask him for directions to his house, informing him that Babangida wished to send him some documents. This was the background to the well-publicised remark that Dele Giwa made on receiving the package. As he proceeded to open it, he observed to his guest, Kayode Soyinka:

"This must be from the President."

Immediately after, the murderous explosion.

I saw Dele Giwa on the very night of my arrival in Lagos. After the impromptu official reception at the Airport, I fled to the home of my junior sister, Yeside, in Súrùlérè, a partially developed part of the suburb and thus, reasonably quiet, where I had decided to spend the night. Fooled again! A handful of friends knew that I sometimes stayed with her and were lying in wait – Deji Akintilo, the budding entrepreneur, Yemi Ogunbiyi, then an editor of *The*

Guardian, Vera Ifudu the broadcaster, Sunmi Smart-Cole the photographer and a handful of others. The determined celebrants were committed to making an evening, even a night of it. Vera Ifudu and Deji Akintilo lived only a few blocks from Yeside's and, after a brief tussle, we transferred to Ifudu's.

It was about an hour before midnight when Dele arrived, looking very casual but rumpled in a loose shirt and equally loose, Bermuda shorts, looking like an American on vacation. In his hand was a bottle of his favourite XO cognac. He had already gone to bed when someone – Yemi Ogunbiyi undoubtedly - rang and informed him of my arrival, also that an impromptu party had commenced at Vera Ifudu's. Dele promptly shook himself out of bed, grabbed a bottle he had earmarked for some other event and drove over to join the group. He left, like most of the others in the early hours of the morning, by which time I had long retired.

Dawn found me on my way to Abẹòkúta, the only place from which I could mount effective defences against any further encroachment. I needed time to sort out my thoughts, the enormity of the award having finally begun to percolate through to my mind. The media assault in Paris had merely impressed on me the monstrosity of the event, it was the palpable fervour with which the nation had embraced the award that finally imbued it with an exceptional value. I could not believe that even total strangers whom I encountered as I left the airport, and since, had taken it so *personally*, that they saw in the award something that was individually, and collectively theirs. It was not possible to underestimate the sense of triumph, of vindication that rode on their responses, a disposition, if they could, to slaughter all the goats, cows, chickens and milk all the palm trees within reach, in celebration. I realised now that I had to do some stocktaking, start studying how to cope with this avalanche of attention.

It was in Abẹòkúta that the news slammed into my mundane planning through the telephone. Given the background to the murder, one thought flashed instantly through my mind – the national award! I could not accept anything at the hands of the government. Not unless it could demonstrate, quite openly, that its hands were clean of the murder.

The following day, I called my friend, Oje Aboyade, Babangida's right hand man. "Your Boss' hands are covered in blood," I told him. "I cannot accept any honours from those hands. Neither will I accept any government representation at the Stockholm ceremony." The appointment agreed upon earlier with Aboyade over the telephone – to meet the dictator and discuss the modalities for a special ceremony for the national award – should be regarded as cancelled.

Aboyade fell in with my position. We agreed to meet a few days later to discuss it, perhaps to agree on the wording of my letter of rejection, about which Oje was apprehensive – quite unnecessarily, in fact. Sending out a downright accusing or abrasive letter without a hard basis in fact, even of plausible deductions, was not an option.

First, a visit to the bereaved family, then prolonged discussions with his immediate associates, friends, other journalists, and a calm review of details of the events that preceded and surrounded the murder, and I felt ready to embark on my own plans for looking into the case. At the heart of it, as usual, was the Pyrates Confraternity, with its information network. We were, still are – *everywhere* – within the army, the police, customs, SSS, the media, etc. Every member was schoolmate of, married or related to, professionally or otherwise connected with some listening source. I was not particularly close to the murdered man but, like many, had long admired his investigative verve and identified with his political attitudes – they were progressive and fearless.

Some, it was true, and from quite respectable quarters, considered his relationship with the government rather ambiguous – for no discernible reason. Some of his own close associates, even within *Newswatch,* were not long in beginning to rationalise his murder. One, and a close friend of his to boot, accused him of having been caught in a web of his own spinning, trapped in some power play in Babangida's court. There were even insinuations, and from his own colleagues in the media, that Dele had been silenced because he had uncovered some hard facts about drug dealing in high quarters and had been blackmailing the racketeers. Nigeria, alas, is the original rumour mill of the world and, the more untoward the event, the more creative and bizarre are the theories and concoctions that are bruited about as fact! Rumours however can provide useful leads, though not in the direction that the rumour purveyors intend, and this was where a loose network of information gatherers can best pursue the most disconnected clues. Nothing justified such a callous murder, nor the manner of his death that could have equally eliminated any of his household – wife, children, relations, any visitors. At my urging, the Pyrates Confraternity posted a financial reward in the media – in hard currency – for any useful information.

Now I could concentrate on the President of the nation who had been mentioned by the slain man as the supposed author of the deadly parcel. After hours of debate – Aboyade, Yemi Ogunbiyi and I – we agreed that I would go ahead and keep the appointment, as if nothing had happened to affect the agenda. It would then be my turn to spring an ambush, ambush because Oje gave his word not to warn Babangida in advance that I now had negative thoughts about the national conferment. I would simply arrive with a formal letter, then set out my conditions for reinstating the honour.

'You can say what you like to him.' Oje reiterated, 'I'll back you up. The nation needs to get to the bottom of the crime, and if I find the situation untenable, I shall also hand in my resignation.'

We met in IBB's office, the dictator all set to finalise details of the participation of the Nigerian government in the Swedish event. Oje also came along, as did Yemi Ogunbiyi. No sooner were courtesies over and we were seated in front of the vast presidential desk than he brought out a slim file from a drawer and carefully opened it, began to turn over some papers. It was Oje who stopped him.

"Mr. President, I think we've run into a snag. Maybe it would be better if you heard it directly from the horse's mouth."

Still unsuspecting, Babangida turned to me. "Oh, Professor, I am sure we can sort out whatever difficulties there are. Is the Stockholm date clashing with ours?"

I studied him very carefully, eyes glued to every gesture and motion of his hands and face. This was perhaps the most absurd test I ever set myself, attempting to decide, even within those first seconds, whether I was seated before an unconscionable killer, or simply an innocent drawn into some fatal survival struggle that had been engineered by his subordinates. This was a soldier to whom killing was no stranger, a schemer who had had a hand in several coups d'état. I knew all about the rumours that surrounded him. Even his coup against Buhari was strongly rumoured to have been a pre-emptive coup for his own survival in the military, that Buhari was about to move against him and push him out of the Army.

Among the rumours that floated round the murder mystery was that the dead man had been working on the mysterious death of one Gloria Okon, caught red-handed with hard drugs, and said to be a 'mule' of one of Ibrahim Babangida's close relations. Was her death under arrest and hospitalisation 'natural'? Was she dead at all? Had she been spirited abroad, another corpse interred and a coroner's report fabricated? Dele Giwa was credited with having penetrated the seamy intrigues, then become snared within them – the Nigerian rumour mill is fecund, each story spun for a purpose that might divert attention away from, neutralise or anticipate the rumours of others.

"Yes, Professor? Is there anything we can do from here to sort out the problem?"

I kept my eyes on him, my voice dispassionate (I hoped) as I said, "I'm afraid things have gone beyond any solution. Dele Giwa's death has put a stop to everything. I cannot see myself accepting this national honour. In fact, I don't think I can accept government participation in the Stockholm event. I would prefer that government stayed out of it entirely."

A chill descended on the room, and a silence that held for ages. I only felt, not recognised the presence of the other two. At that moment, it seemed that Babangida and I were the only beings in the sound-proofed chamber. What I read in Babangida's face went beyond ceremonies and national honours. It was this: the dictator felt that he was about to be confronted with a new enemy where he had been led to believe that he might cultivate a potential ally. The initial expansive, amiable confidence had vanished. So be it, I thought to myself. I watched him slowly close the file, then slide it, almost imperceptibly into the drawer. Then he asked:

"Do you believe I, or the government had a hand in Dele's death?"

"I have no idea. But I am amazed that up till now, your government has failed to set up a judicial enquiry into the bizarre murder."

Slowly, he slid shut the drawer, taking time to regain his composure. "Professor, I give you my word of honour" he began, very calmly. "I have never indulged in or encouraged any act of murder in my entire career. I am a soldier, and I've taken part in coups, but I do not plan murders. If I decided that Dele Giwa needed to be eliminated, I would put on my uniform, put a gun in my holster, drive up to his house, enter and shoot him. But I will not for one moment engage in a sneak killing. I give you my word."

I scanned his face. Truthful? Or a suave, practised actor? It was, we both knew, a decisive moment. Oje said nothing. Neither did Yemi. They left us two alone, watchful.

"In that case," I said, finally, "do you agree to set up an independent judicial commission of enquiry? Transparently independent?"

"Of course" he said, without hesitation. "In fact, it is something we're discussing right now. We've nearly finalised the composition and I'll be giving them a time-limit within which they must make a report. I want this matter cleared up as much as you, maybe even more. And we'll put someone in charge in whom the nation will have full confidence – I promise you that. Within the next month, the commission will begin sitting."

No, I did not thereby believe in Babangida's guilt or innocence. I suspended belief, one way or the other. What I did believe was that a commission would sit, and in public. And I was confident that the offer of a reward from our side - hopefully augmented from other sources, Dele Giwa's own journal for instance - would loosen a tongue or two, however indirectly. It is never easy to keep secrets in Nigeria, it is just that secrets, when divulged, are tied up in many distractions. But hardly any crime has been committed in the nation whose perpetrators are not known at least to twenty other people. It was all a question of finding which one of them would speak under inducement, guaranteed protection, or from a falling-out among conspirators. A judicial commission, sitting in public, would serve as our starting point.

The investiture was a near official disaster. I went to the wrong venue, itself a giveaway about my enthusiasm or concentration on, or attention to details. I had not studied the invitation card particularly well, and so when my brother stopped to see me the previous night to the day, I readily bought into his thinking that the venue was not Lagos State House, as I thought, but Dodan Barracks, the seat of government. Lateness is a self-indulgent habit that I deplore, and I had positioned myself to take care of all traffic hazards and arrive at the venue at least fifteen minutes beforehand.

My consternation is best imagined when, as I turned into the final avenue that led directly into the gates of Dodan Barracks, I encountered a motorcade belting out of the government seat with outriders and sirens blaring. It could only have been Babangida but I checked with the driver anyway – had he seen and recognised the occupant of the protected vehicle? Well, he had not seen the face, but that was the usual security detail of Ibrahim Babangida. Even then, so thoroughly had I ingested the last information – my brother's choice of venue! – that it never crossed my mind that I could have been right all along. Otherwise, I would have ordered the driver to spin around and tail-ride the convoy. I persuaded myself that maybe it was Aikhomu, Babangida's deputy, off to represent his boss at some other event, or a visiting dignitary being whisked to the airport, etc. So we proceeded to the gate, where the expression on the face of the security official who recognised who I was, told the entire story even before he opened his mouth – yes, that was indeed the head of state speeding to Lagos House to pin a medal on my chest.

We changed direction, pursued the convoy, breaking every traffic rule on the way. Of course, the streets had been sealed off round the security perimeter of State House. They were opened for the president's convoy to pass through, and were immediately closed off after him by trigger-ready soldiers and patrolling SSS agents with walkie-talkies and bulging armpits. All other vehicles were diverted onto a different approach. I leapt out of the car, dashed up to the nearest soldier whose face fell apart on seeing who it was. He found my gasped explanations superfluous and broke into a run. I jumped back in the car and he led the way screaming for the roadblocks to be moved – which was how I arrived only ten minutes late, having nonetheless broken the golden rule of protocol.

Thoroughly flustered as I was, I had time to notice, among the select crowd, even more desperately flustered faces. Among them was one that clearly scowled its displeasure, muttering something about how typical this was of WS. It had the predictable effect of ending my fluster abruptly, then getting me riled, angry and aggressive. It was the wrong moment for a voice to be raised in protest at my unintended discourtesy – keeping a Head of State waiting. I turned to snap back at that voice but was forcefully steered into the place of conferment. All I wanted at that moment was simply to turn around and tell them all to forget the ceremony.

The ceremony over, I learnt that – as usual – some of the panic had been caused by the usual quota of *ab'ọbakū*[1] who voiced loud, indignant opinions that I had deliberately set up Babangida in order to humiliate him publicly, that I never had the slightest intention of showing up or accepting the honour. This, despite the fact that my brother 'Jamani', had patiently explained that he had himself discovered his error at the eleventh hour, had misled me and that I was now busy finding my way to the State House!

No, there had never been any thought of my reneging on a clear understanding: the ceremony would go forward as planned, and the commission on Dele Giwa's death would be inaugurated. I intended to keep to my side of the bargain, and I expected Babangida to keep to his.

Weeks passed. The national conferment had nearly been forgotten, yet no further word on the commission emerged from Dodan Barracks. I set up another meeting with Babangida, determined to obtain some answers. What stage had it reached? Why had its

---

[1] Literally – one who dies with the king. Unregistered power courtier.

composition not been announced, nor its terms of reference publicised? Why were no dates set as yet for its commencement, or its duration? Babangida again brought out his file, spread out his hands and pleaded for a fair hearing.

"What was I supposed to do? You see it here," – and he isolated a piece of paper and some news clippings – "your friend, your fellow activist, Gani Fawehinmi, has filed a criminal action in court accusing two highly placed security agents of committing the murder – Halilu Akilu, my National Security Adviser, and Colonel Togun of Military Intelligence. Still, we went ahead with our publicised moves to set up the commission, and what does Gani do? He continues to breathe down our necks, threatens fire and brimstone in further court proceedings that would stop the commission from being sworn in and beginning its work. He claims that the matter is now *sub judice* in the criminal courts. Of course, it stopped us in our tracks. We have no choice but to let the criminal charges run their course."

Gani! Brilliant and erratic, a great humanist and compulsive loner, more than deserving of his Bruno Kreisky Award for Human Rights, yet nearly every colleague, collaborator or beneficiary of Gani, virtually without exception, has gone through a phase of temporary derangement when they wondered whether it would not be much better, for the sake of the very cause that he advocated, if Gani were to be heavily sedated, kidnapped and hidden away, then revived and released only when the challenge had been resolved. Commissions of enquiry, even when cynically instituted, are productive exercises, guaranteed to reveal much outside the official 'terms of reference'. In short, commissions provide the very opportunity to expose even what they attempt to conceal, thus throwing the issue back onto the court of public judgement and sometimes, future reckoning. The one-judge commission set up under Obasanjo's regime to investigate the 1977 burning down of *Kalakuta Republic,* the commune of the musician Fela Anikulapo Kuti, cynical though its formal conclusions, did succeed in removing all ambiguities in the public mind over the zone of guilt. The role of Obasanjo's military regime was laid bare beyond all doubt, and the exercise gave birth to what became a public refrain for all suspected state crimes thereafter – *Unknown Soldier*.

Dele Giwa's murder predictably aroused public outrage at its most intense, a passion for truth and justice at all costs, and Gani had placed himself, as always, at the forefront. It was during this heated period that Gani encountered one of the accused, Colonel Togun, at the airport, and the defiant manner of that officer produced the expected reaction in the volatile advocate – he not only openly accused the colonel, and his superior Halilu Akilu, of Giwa's murder, he also proceeded to seek leave of the courts to file a private criminal suit against the two officers. Gani had set himself a trap. His request was granted and he sued. In the media, Gani, never averse to publicity, also continued his campaign of open accusation, naming names.

Their acquittal was predictable. Emboldened by the judgement, the two men sued their tormentor for defamation and won substantial damages. The immediate damage was more far reaching, however. Babangida – willing or unwilling in the first place – could take shelter behind a threatened legal interdiction, and he did. All we had left was the assertion of his innocence, and the hope of a leakage from within the evident conspiracy at the very highest level of Babangida's security organisation. The independent commission was stillborn. It was left to the rest of the nation to continue the search for the truth – with one hand tied behind, and a leg amputated.

To Stockholm and Back

Only two years before the Nobel, I had received the Enrico Mattei Award for the Humanities, and the Mattei Foundation basked in the satisfaction that it had recognised my work before the Nobel Academy did. Now, on the way to Stockholm, I received an invitation from the Foundation to pass through Italy as a guest. I accepted with alacrity. I find Italy and Italians congenial in the main, and I was ready to leave Nigeria for a while, with its recent memory of the murder of a friend who had roused himself from his bed to celebrate my award.

Basically irreligious – certainly in the sense of not being a worshipper at any shrine – sacrifice, or sàárà, the notion of the surrogate, is one that I share with most faiths, christianity included. Certainly sàárà, in the Yoruba traditional mode, was routine even in the christian household into which I was born. Childbirths, funerals, supplication to ward off danger, be it from childbirth or voyaging – all the way down from the pastor himself, the head of the Anglican church, to his catechist or lay-readers, the bookseller, organist and the extended neighbourhood of christians, moslems and òrìṣà devotees - hardly any household did not respond to such milestones or occasions with the sàárà, when food was cooked and taken round to neighbours, and children were invited to the celebrant's household to eat, drink and play with other children. To me, sàárà has always been instinct.

No, I was not in fact making sàárà for myself. I have, I like to think, a very personal, intuitive understanding with my protector demiurges. They take when they please. When I lose money, or any valuable, I tell myself that the insatiable daemons have been at it again. I once lost – in 1962 – my only manuscript of *The Strong Breed,* a play that deals – interestingly – with the notion of sacrifice! Such a loss, for a writer yet pubescent in his career, was not easy to absorb. After the shock, I consoled myself by saying that the gods of creativity were really out for their tithe. When, a year later, nearly to the day, I felt a sudden surge of total recollection, sat down and tapped out the one-act play non-stop, I merely groused at the invisible light-fingered deity – what took you so long?!

Sacrifice, preferably as a voluntary act, is part of communion. Once, every new year, it was *de rigueur* that I sacrifice a ram for my family – or, to be specific – for my children. At least, it was them I thought about. Sàárà is simply a way of life. A powerful attachment to this function was thus responsible for my first act after I had left for Rome, thinking of all I had done or left undone. Foremost on my mind was the large Nigerian contingent – half a Boeing 707 was taken up – that would be attending the ceremony. I sent a message to my sister Yeside to ensure that, before the plane took off, she would get hold of a hefty white or black ram, slaughter it and distribute the meat to neighbours and family.

I also hold the view that there should be no beggars in society, that it is the responsibility of the state, the community to look after its less fortunate, either create a means of livelihood for them, or else house and feed them in some kind of commune, not leave them on the streets, dependent on the uncertain generosity of others. Mostly, I do not offer money to beggars. My visit to Italy – en route Stockholm – proved to be one of those occasions when I contradicted myself yet again.

What happened was this: I found myself on the receiving end of further generosity from the Enrico Mattei Foundation – the ENI (Agip) people. I was set up in a luxurious hotel where, if I chanced to sneeze, the management came running. I was not allowed to pay for anything. I was provided with an escort who was extremely pleasant and charming but talked my head into a coma. She was entrusted with a budget for shopping – outfitting me for the cold of Stockholm. I picked a modish coat that looked as if it would withstand the promised day of the apocalypse when hell itself freezes over. It took me a whole half hour to decide on that coat – I who normally whisk in and out of a shop with two shirts, two undershirts, four underpants and two pairs of trousers while the average shopper is still spinning with the revolving door. In the end I did not even buy the coat at the shop where I first saw it but only on encountering it again, after I had purchased a pair of fur-lined dress boots whose soles were guaranteed not to slip on ice. What else? The budget was not yet exhausted, so off we went again – didn't I need some handkerchiefs? Socks? Shaving set? Anything else I would like to do?

Well, it so happened that the restored Sistine Chapel was just being opened to the public, amidst great controversy. Was it aesthetically enhanced by the clean-up, or was it banalised by the face-lift, in tonalities rendered garish and bereft of emotional appeal? The controversy had raged throughout the European (artistic) world. I remarked off-hand that it would have been interesting to view the frescoes I had last seen as a student. However, the queue that we drove past had put paid to such thoughts. It wound itself endlessly round and round the Vatican walls, then disappeared into some sloping tunnel in distant neighbourhood. I shook my head.

The following morning, I received a call. An hour later, we were walking into the chapel through a side entrance where a curator's assistant was waiting for us. He made his apologies – the notice was short and he had earlier commitments – and left us alone. Thus began a private, exquisitely privileged viewing of the ceiling and other murals, before the chapel was open to lesser mortals. If there is one aesthetic thrill over and above what is engendered in contemplating works of art, it is the internal dialogue with such works in a space of unabashed selfishness, a discovery that I made through attempts to address the strange phenomenon of millionaire collectors who pay fortunes for 'hot' works of art that they cannot publicly display, share with others, or acknowledge openly as being a member of their extended family. To the question: why do they do it? What do they derive from it? I came to the conclusion that the essence of art induces a certain communicant dimension that is best apprehended in a space of private solace, even when the object of contemplation is of a criminal origin. It thus becomes easy to picture – and understand – these high heist millionaires in their secret bunkers, contemplating their possessions with the morning espresso before going out into the phillistinic world of Mammon that, paradoxically, also provides the means to this very private, aesthetically charged space.

Not having the means to engage whatever local mafia happened to be art inclined, in transporting the Sistine Chapel, or indeed any individual canvas or sculpture from across the globe to Abẹ̀òkúta, I luxuriated in the unanticipated viewing space of the Sistine Chapel, emptied of virtually all humanity. The only trouble was my charming escort who would not stop talking, insisted on giving me a guided tour even though I continually reminded her that I had visited the chapel years before it was closed down for restoration. When she began to gush over what she referred to as the 'contact point' of creation - the finger of God animating the prone figure of Adam – or something along those lines – I reached the end of my tether and was ready to explode. Fortunately for both, I recalled that this again was the donor deity at the game of exactions – operating through Èṣù, the mischievous one – taking his own share of my pleasure by inflicting such unnecessary agonies on me. It was hard though, very hard. I left the Sistine Chapel persuaded – what with my escort's Italo-American accent still rattling in my ears – that the Nobel had condemned me to a life where the savouring of unalloyed pleasure no longer existed. One way or the other, I would always encounter a fly in the froth of my palm wine.

Considering the foregoing, I should seek no self-excusing for breaking my rules later that night. Ordering a sacrificial ram for the home front was one thing but this other – what came next – was, truly out of character. However, I appeared to have been receiving, receiving, receiving! And so, walking down the Spanish steps where Rome's beggars of every national origin congregate, suitably rid of my escort, I began to experience an unusual urge. I walked around for a while, stopped at a bar to prime myself, left the piazza with my hands clutching fistfuls of lira but stuck firmly in my pockets. After some dithering, I turned round by a circuitous route and returned shamefacedly to another bar. I knew I needed to, was deeply impelled to, would have no peace unless I did, but was equally resolved not to submit to the unusual urge. Finally, I had had enough of my shilly-shallying. I selected a quiet gypsy woman with an infant, one of the non-aggressive kind, rather than the intrusive, even truculent breed. I am preternaturally immune against the other kind – those who thrust their stumps in your face in front of hotels or at traffic hold-ups, or bare their bodies to expose acid-eaten flesh that looked like some nightmare creation of Frankenheimer Studios.

I emptied the lira into her hands and fled. Even so, my urge to make sàárà locally remained unassuaged. I took a few more turns around the piazza, dodging from time to time into the side streets, doused my – totally paranoid – sense of embarrassment with a shot of *grappa* in a bar, then surged out again. And suddenly there he was, the scruffy bearded twentieth century Michaelangelo of indeterminate origin. I dashed across the road, transferred the other fistful of notes, the rest of my Enrico Mattei shopping bursary, into his unbelieving hand and vanished round the nearest street corner. Out of his sight line, I waited a few moments, then walked back to peek around the wall. The incredulous, then rapturous expression on his face was worth the Nobel Prize a hundred times over. I was now free to proceed to the main business of the evening: seek out a small, secluded, no-frills trattoria with an instantly recognisable ambiance of the single-minded *Eat* as in *Eatalian*, far from the maddening world of tourists. I embarked on a very private celebration of my unexpected award, a simple ritual that I had imbibed from my friend, Femi Johnson: I ordered a sumptuous dinner.

It was meant to be a solitary act of celebration but, in fact, I was not completely alone. I had never met any of the other Nobelists but, going through the list of my designated classmates for that year, I had been struck most pleasantly by the name of the Laureate in Medicine who, to round off good auguries, was a native of the very country that was playing pre-Stockholm host to me; that name was – Rita Montalcini. I ordered a bottle of Brunello de Montalcino!

Stockholm. The elegant Grand Hotel overlooking a canal, sleek yachts, cruise ships and well-lit piers. My obligatory event – acceptance speech before the Academy – appeared to have gone down well. The Nigerian contingent was enlivening the staid streets with colours, textures and exotic sounds. In short, all was well with the world and only one dread hung over my ease – would I escape before the descent of snow?

Now it was the night before the award ceremony itself, virtually midnight. I had settled down to sleep and was awakened by the phone. The voice was extremely querulous.

"I wish to speak to Professor Soyinka."

"Who is this?"

"Who is this? It is a man looking for his wife everywhere. Tell Wole Soyinka to send down my wife."

"Excuse me, but who is this speaking?"

"Who? Why do you ask me who it is speaking? Who are *you* in any case? I said I wanted to speak to Wole Soyinka, isn't that his room?"

"I am Wole Soyinka and this is my room. Now who are you and what do you want?"

"You're Wole Soyinka? You *are* Wole Soyinka? And you ask me what I want? I am telling you to send down my wife right now. Or bring her to the phone. I know she's in there with you."

The last mists of sleepiness were shredded from my eyes, leaving me not merely wide awake but fully alert. And now the man began to unburden himself, lumbering back and forth in tones that were successively belligerent, maudlin, coarse and deferential. "Why should you be having a party in there with other people's wives?"

"First of all, Mister Whoever-you-are, I am not having a party..."

"Don't lie to me. You are a famous man and you shouldn't be lying. Do you think I can't hear noises in the background and music being played?"

"...secondly, I do not know your wife. And now I am going back to sleep."

And I put down the telephone, angry that the hotel staff had put a call through to my room when, as of habit, I had instructed that all incoming calls should be blocked. The entire stay had been organised so far with impeccable efficiency and I couldn't understand how there could have been such a serious slip-up. I took the precaution of going to the doors and double-checking all the locks. It was a sumptuous, sprawling suite, with doors leading to the kitchenette, another to the balcony. This bizarre awakening could spring further surprises.

Again the phone rang. I picked it up and, before I could even say a word, the same voice was ranting at me. "Mr. Soyinka, will you please tell your boys to give me back my wife?"

My boys! Now what was this new development in the mystery of the missing wife? I became rather intrigued. Numerous speculations flew through my mind. Who was this man? Could there have been a case of mistaken identity or was it a thorough-going set-up gone wrong?

By now it was well past one o'clock at night.

"So now it's my boys who took your wife? Listen, I'll give you one minute to make sense," I warned, "and then I shall call the police."

The words came tumbling out. "Call the police! Call Interpol if you like, and then you'll have to explain if you had been brought to Stockholm to abduct other people's wives. You all came to my night-club. You danced with my wife and then you took her to your hotel to continue partying. I want her back and now you're pretending she's not there. You may think you're world famous, I don't care if the world thinks you're famous but that doesn't give you the right to go round breaking up my marriage... Hey, talk to me Mr. Famous! Answer me will you? ...Hallo... hallo... are you there? If you think you can hang up on me..."

At last something rang a bell. Earlier that evening, some of 'the boys' had indeed invited me to accompany them to a nightclub.

They had been at the club the previous night and had been effusively welcomed by the lady proprietor. She invited them to return the following night – indeed, make her club their late night haunt throughout their stay – but also sent a special invitation to me to accompany them. She was a 'collector' of sorts, and in addition to the nightclub, she ran an African Arts gallery. Her 'husband' was from one of the East African countries. The 'boys' painted a glowing picture of the nightclub, all decorated with African motifs, served African snacks and played African music. I asked them to convey my regrets to the lady however, having taken the decision to avoid any spot of potential 'incidents', to which even the most staid boozerie is always prone. I began to picture what happened. The 'boys' must have gone there and left with the hostess to continue partying elsewhere.

As gently as I could, I tried to explain to him where he might find his wife – not at the Grand Hotel where all the Nobelists were lodged, but at one of the other two hotels where the Nigerian contingent was staying. He repaid me with an earful.

"Oh, are you still there? Why do you continue to talk to me from upstairs. You're too big to come down and talk to me? I am standing here in this cold lobby while you're enjoying yourself in the warmth of your room. You can't do the polite thing and come down to talk to me, is that it?"

For the first time since that telephone intrusion, I found something that interjected a light note into the proceedings. The thought of me going down to this enraged and basically incoherent stranger, already smarting from the loss of his wife's companionship, maybe with lurid thoughts in his head of a gang of randy Nigerians taking turns to warm up her Swedish or whatever blood, was so idiotic that I laughed out aloud. That only sent him into a new bout of rage.

"You may laugh at me, sir. Because you're a big man and I am a nobody. But let me tell you I have my rights. I am also a human being and won't be trampled on by you."

I cut short my merriment. "I am laughing at you because you dare take me for a moron. You actually expect me to leave the safety of my room to come and confront you, a total stranger in a strange hotel in the middle of the night? Now listen, I am going to put down the phone, and if you dare call back again, I guarantee you'll sleep in a police cell tonight."

I put down the phone and dialled the operator. Our hosts had not even left it to us to take the initiative of instructing the operator about calls. From the moment we arrived, we were consulted about how we wanted calls and other forms of intrusions to be fielded. Any caller whose name was not on the list simply did not get through, and of course a 'Block' message was sacrosanct. So how...!

The operator explained that the man must have been calling from within the hotel, probably from the lobby, thus by-passing the switchbox. He could only do that if he had my room number however, although how he managed to do that was a mystery. So I asked him to connect me quickly to the hotel's security detail. There's a lunatic in the hotel lobby I informed him. You'll find him at one of the house phones, still trying to dial my room. Moments later, the security officer phoned back. Yes, indeed, there had been a man, an African, at the phones, but he left just some moments before. The guard looked outside and he thought it was the same man he had seen getting into a car.

My official 'aide-de-camp' from the Foreign Ministry was given the report the moment he arrived the following morning, and of course it became quite a moderate-sized scandal. The response of the Nigerian squad was to set up their own round-the-clock protection unit. During the day, they moved physically into the lobby of the Grand Hotel and would not depart until I was safely locked up in my room. First thing in the morning, they were back.

The woman in question was interrogated. She admitted that she had in fact booked a room at the Grand Hotel before the arrival of the laureates so as to be able to hand me a present, personally – a commissioned painting. So the 'husband' was indeed right in some of his suspicions. Was it all an innocent jape? The lady had taken the trouble to book a room well in advance so as to have easy movement in and out of the hotel occupied by the laureates, never mind that she lived in the suburbs of Stockholm.

I received a note from her afterwards. She was very upset that she was now obliged to move out, having earned herself a hostile interrogation by the hotel security – and some discreet checks by the police – all undeserved, she protested. I was bombarded by messages sent through every Nigerian she met. She even attended, quite legitimately, a party organised by our embassy – she was on the regular embassy guest list, it seemed, or at least had acquired a genuine invitation. However, by then, the 'boys' – Olu Agunloye, Deji Akintilo, Yemi Ogunbiyi and others had formed a *cordon sanitaire* around me and would not let her get within spitting distance. Each time she attempted to move in my direction during the party, she was physically blocked – all this I was not aware of at the time, though I did notice some deft footwork, some strange concerted movements and signals going on around me.

Not that she gave up, so desperate was she to explain her side of the story and hand over the present. Her 'husband' was not a husband as such but a business partner with whom she once lived, but that affair was long over, even while they still maintained their business relations, including running the night-club. She desperately wanted me to visit her gallery, wrote a letter asking for a face-to-face meeting. I replied, thanking her for the present and her hospitality to my compatriots, sympathised with her for her ordeal from her business partner and the police. I did not consider a meeting necessary however, and regretted that it would not be possible.

Swiftly pushed to the forefront of my mind, from the moment that the 'irate' husband uttered his first accusation, was the scandal – also involving a woman – in which Martin Luther King was very nearly embroiled in Oslo when he received the Nobel Peace Prize. The CIA was alleged to have engineered that incident.

The Nobel appears to be a bug whose bite is craved, sometimes without a sense of discrimination or inhibition. The best organised siege that was laid to my newly acquired sponsorship clout – as perceived by the outsider – was a whirlwind 'courtship' by the wife of a former European minister who had established a quite impressive philanthropic foothold in East Africa, especially with children. Hers was a bold, direct, and quite impressive semi-official campaign. At first, I did not know what she wanted.

I received a message that the lady had flown in by private plane the morning of the ceremony. She could only be present in Stockholm for the day as the plane was taking her somewhere else for another engagement, and she had to be back at her African station some time later. My recollections are somewhat imprecise over this high-powered encounter, as so many encounters took place at the same time. If she did indeed arrive that morning, an advance party must have preceded her because, when I came down to the lobby, an impressive section had been devoted to literature by her and about her. Coffee table publications, expensively produced, jostled with brochures, photographic displays, citations, a few artifacts from the regions where she had worked with children. There was a huge tome of a register for visitors to the mini-exhibition to sign, and it was not enough just to sign it. Visitors were urged to write their impressions – in effect, testimonials to the humanitarian work being done by the lady.

The Madam had an able assistant – a suave, lanky, government official – whose duty appeared to be to prepare visitors in advance for the phenomenon they were about to encounter, enumerate her virtues, her selfless dedication to The Cause, and ensure – or perhaps this service was performed only for myself? – that they were not fooled by her reticent and inhibited nature. He owed it to her mission to place her achievements in perspective, lamenting how the world had so far failed to appreciate them sufficiently, but confident that I, as a discerning person, would see how this kind of work needed to be catapulted onto world attention. She had met numerous African leaders, I would see the glowing testimonials they had written when we arrived at the exposition. As for her journeys by boat - her favourite mode of transportation, it seemed, and one that enabled her to penetrate the continent with tons and tons of supplies for undernourished and sick children – they were epics in themselves. First, the boat had to be cajoled from their owners or sponsors, then – I believe he explained – she sailed round the world obtaining supplies and medicines from governments, companies and other donors. She then sailed around African ports from where commenced yet other gruelling journeys into the interior – jeeps, camels and any other form of transportation, breaking through into neglected areas where no one trod before.

At some point we finally came upon the lady, waiting dutifully by her exposition. She piloted me through the eloquent photographic essays on the table – she fending off African heat in a safari outfit all complete with pith helmet, with supplies in the boat, with one prime minister after another, then masses of photographs of her with African babies in her arms, crawling all over her, scrawny babies, plump babies – before, and after – and the testimonies galore, and the heavy photo publications – Voyage I, II, and III, and now preparations for IV. The 'reticent' lady went over the grounds already covered by her able spokesman, filled in more gaps, presented copies of these back-breaking tomes, then wondered how best to package the books for convenient transportation. No sooner was the thought spoken than she seized her wine-red Henri Cartier briefcase, flung its contents on the table, then began to stuff it with books, photographs, brochures... and of course I was to keep this expensive designer briefcase and, while I was at it, did I smoke? I was mumbling that I did smoke the odd cigar now and then when from nowhere an elegant Cartier lighter, still in its case. And then there was a third item that was pressed into my hands, and of course I was not to worry – it would all be sent up to my room since she appreciated that I did not have much time and we should really go now and have that coffee together. It was kind of me to spare her that much time but she just wanted to draw my attention to the children's book especially, the ones that contained the children's spontaneous songs to her, expressions of their childlike faith in her works, much more important than any tribute a head of state might pay or any state decoration she might receive. "Mr. Soyinka, what you could do for this cause..."

"Ah yes, Madame, what would you like me to do?"

"I am preparing a new book, and how wonderful it would be if you could write the foreword, endorsing our efforts and – yes – wouldn't it be wonderful if you could compose a poem on this work for the children of Africa, and it would be a poem both in your own language and in English, and we would translate it into other languages. I think it is something those children would understand. Did I tell you that they call me the White African Mother? It's in one of those children's tributes. So if you wrote a poem..."

"I have to warn you, I do not find it that easy to simply sit down and scribble a poem to order. Not even the simplest looking poem."

"Well, it needn't be a poem, Mr. Soyinka. It could be simply something from your own tribe – are you Ibo? That would be Biafran, not so?"

"I am Yoruba."

"A-ah, of course, Yoruba. I know about the Yoruba, very rich culture. So, some kind of children's Yoruba poem which you would translate for us. Something that has to do with a mother's care for her children. The relation between mothers and their children is something that struck me so forcefully as I travelled all over the place. We are like that in my country, you know. So do you think you could do this for the cause? It would be like a kind of dedication to the work of the White African Mother...."

"White African Mother," I said. "You'd like a poem to the White African Mother?"

"Or some Yoruba saying that could be adapted, something to do with the mother. I am sure you still retain some songs, something from your own childhood."

I nodded full comprehension. "Well, you'll have to give me some time to think about it. This hectic atmosphere does not exactly facilitate regressions into childhood, you realise."

She was fully understanding, but abundantly prepared. "Actually, my aide and I were thinking about that, and we found what might be the solution. An original poem can come later if you feel like it, a traditional song, or saying. But we brought along this poem and it's already translated into English, ready to go into the new book. So, what is needed is for you to translate it back into your own language Yoruba, and then dedicate it to these children's White African Mother. Anything else you care to send later on, that will be more than kind, Mr. Soyinka. Do you think the translation is something you can do in the next few days. I have to be gone – my government was very kind to lend me a plane but now it must take me back. But my assistant – there he is, you've met already – will be staying around with the exhibition. You can copy your translation directly into the large book I showed you, and then, with the dedication, it will appear in this new publication."

It would be easier dealing with the gentleman assistant, I decided. I stood up, feeling battered and bruised. I had actually dared to imagine that all she sought was the use of my newly augmented profile for promoting her work on the continent, obtaining more support from African governments especially, and calling attention to the plight of the children. Well, maybe that was the ultimate goal. The enthronement of a White African Mother might just open up the sluice-gates of the milk of human kindness. She kindly let me off to prepare for my morning's engagements and I took my leave, unsure whether I should kiss her hand or give her a filial embrace. Her assistant dutifully followed with the spoils of the encounter, determined to see me to my room.

"Did she mention the other matter?" He asked.

"You have more than one project? Apart from the boat campaign?" I was most impressed. Being a White African Mother, I would have thought, was already a full-time job.

He rolled his eyes, shook his head in despair. "I say it all the time, she is a very reticent lady. Too reticent for her own good. She said nothing about the nomination?"

"Nomination? You mean as the White African Mother?"

"No, Mr. Soyinka, that is only to show how she is perceived in Africa. How she is loved and respected, like a mother. We feel that with that kind of acknowledgment, if you Mr. Soyinka can give support to the idea, she will definitely win the Nobel Peace Prize. I have to tell you Mr. Soyinka, that the lady is too reticent, which is why the government gives her some staff to help her. She has been nominated before but did not win. We feel that, against next year, she has a hundred percent chance with your support. This is a work that is done in Africa, for Africans, for the

African children, and you are now the African Voice. This is why we came to see you, we need your support for it to take place".

I gave myself a few seconds for the idea to sink in, then scrambled for a solution. "I'll tell you how we proceed. Our ambassador here happens to be a woman, very cultured, very sophisticated and most caring. I have known her for nearly twenty years. I shall speak to her – I assure you, she'll be most happy to take this on – I mean, continue where I leave off. Maybe you can leave a set of these publications with her?"

His eyes lit up. "Certainly. Certainly Mr. Soyinka. We'll be delighted to do that."

It was a very happy man who deposited my 'gifts' on a convenient spot in my room, bowed in gratitude, and took the good news back to the White African Mother. On my part, I cast my eyes in the direction of the gods of restitution in whatever corner of my suite they were chuckling and asked, "Is this a mere foretaste? Do you have more exactions riding on the Nobel?"

Three Lost Years

*A*fter a few months of resistance, I surrendered. There was clearly a price to be paid by Nobel Prize winners, most especially by someone from the African continent. No one had prepared me for it, but I soon found that I had embarked on the rites of restitution – I handed over 1987 to the implacable Swedish deity of dynamite and fulfilled my duties, swearing silently that the moment the next beauty queen was crowned had better be recognised as my hour of liberation. I had been stretched to the limit. My constituency was always wide – in the creative industry, in home politics and those of the continent, issues of Human Rights – which, for me, includes the right to life, a commitment that led to my creation of a national Road Safety Corps, and the unglamorous labour of hounding homicidal maniacs off the Nigerian highways, and educating them the hard way.

This constituency had swollen beyond all rational projection. Still, I consoled myself, perhaps a full year was not too heavy a price to pay. I found myself compelled to acknowledge that, in the Third World especially, my presence at a number of events appeared to induce so much plain, undisguised pleasure, generated such a sense of collective vindication for a variety of causes – and in the least expected places – that some of the satisfaction bounced back to me. I could even persuade myself, sometimes, that I had got the better part of the bargain. There is pleasure in giving pleasure – even as one feels that a portion of one's self is constantly shed in the effort, that one is being, literally, eaten piecemeal. No matter, one year, and that was it! 1987 proved indeed to be a dry year for creativity, not even so much as an occasional poem that I can recall. I envisaged 1988 waiting in the wings, when the frustrated mind would slide back gradually into a creative normality.

I could not have been more mistaken. Too late, I recalled Garcia Marquez's warning when we met in Cuba the year after my 'nobelisation'. Marquez asked me how I was bearing up and I replied, "Well, it is rather hard, but that's all right. In a few months, another beauty queen will be crowned and this queen can turn himself into a Sleeping Beauty.'

Garcia smiled wryly and warned, "It never ends, my friend. It never ends."

1988 followed the path of '87 but only much, much worse. So did most of the following year, and then 1990 began to look like following the example of the others. It took a while for me to realise that my increasing unease went beyond the non-event of *not* writing – that had never been a problem. I have never felt under a compulsion to write. If I felt non-creative, for months, for a year, I underwent no pressure, no sense of a dereliction of duty. There are always other things to do with one's time.

This time however, I did not merely *not* write, I did not *wish* to write, did not wish to think creatively in any direction, to be involved in any creative project. I was indifferent to any artistic activities around me. Abroad, I rarely visited the theatre. No concerts, no opera, no jazz clubs. My short list of books marked down for reading expanded beyond the normal growth rate – oh, I still browsed through the review pages of journals, I could somehow manage that, but it was more an accustomed drug on which my system had grown dependent, not an act of pleasure, curiosity or enlightenment. I jotted down titles because I feared that the phase might pass suddenly, and I could not rely on my memory. Mostly, I simply did not care. I was overwhelmed by the futility of everything I had ever done or known in the realm of literature and the arts. Even during normal times, this was always a question I deplored, but if that intrusive brigade with the perennial question *'what are you working on now?'* only knew what leapt to the tip of my tongue during this period, they would have recoiled at the furnace that raged within me, and regretted their unintended temerity. They were not to know of course, but a huge void had settled into my life, usurping the habitat of a vital presence.

I remained in thrall to this absence whose memory still haunts me, as it does so many others in varying degrees – from Ìbàdàn and Lagos to London, Beirut, Cannes, Cairo, or Bergamo – a now disembodied life force that pops up in the midst of festivities, not dampening the spirit but resurrecting bereavement, a throbbing amputation, but – mostly evoking the presence of an enlivening guest, bringing with his recollection a sense of wonder at the unimaginable plenitude that we had all shared in the sheer being of this individual.

Why did his family choose to abandon his body in an obscure German village called Wiesbaden? Was it envy? Hate? And why, when I finally brought him home, did they frustrate the anticipation of so many to bid him adieu, to pay simple tribute to him as friends, acquaintances, business partners, even business rivals who respected him for his remarkable enterprise and flair? Why? And then, unavoidably my own nagging sense of guilt – seven months of total rupture – had it been truly necessary? Really unavoidable.

I have tried to imagine my attendance at the Nobel Prize conferment without Femi, that instinctive embodiment of pleasure and celebration – it would have been such a hollow event. The Nobel was made for O.B. Johnson! He had to be there for the ceremony to have any meaning, for any rite of celebration to become a rounded experience – once one has incurred a life sentence for the crime of knowing OBJ even for one day. And so I felt profoundly grateful to the ancestors that they had intervened to ensure that I was not deprived the attendance of one who was capable of *enjoying* and enlarging the occasion in ways in which I never could, right there in the flesh, absorbing the panoply of it, ingesting and exuding it through his own larger-than-life persona, as a shared acquisition over which he exercised the major right of possession.

Mí ò r'íkú l'ójú ẹ – no, I read no death in his eyes. Neither did any of his insurance colleagues in Cairo where, according to reports, he performed his accustomed gastronomic feats and enlivened the gathering of brokers. We parted company in London, his plaints pursuing me into my taxi because I would not change my flight, return to Nigeria via Cairo, and share with him the excitement of his induction into the marvels of Egypt.

A week after London, working in my study in Abẹ́òkúta, a car drew up. I recognised it from the window and went to open the door. It was Gboyega, Femi's personal chauffeur.

"I've been asked to come for you sir."

"When did he return?"

"Just two days ago sir."

"And he's been working non-stop in his office as usual, I bet."

I thought I detected a faint hesitation, but he still said, "Y-yes sir."

"Well, tell him – me too, I'm still tied to my desk. When I've cleared it – maybe by the weekend – I'll see him."

His next words came out in a rush. "Please, come sir. It was Madam who sent me, not him. He's been taken ill and rushed to hospital. It is quite serious sir."

"Femi. In hospital?"

"It happened in his office. They sent for Dr. Soyanwo. He ordered an ambulance, but it did not arrive in time, so a car took him to hospital."

I broke loose from the spell, dashed back into the house. An hour and a half later, I was by his bedside at Ìbàdàn University Teaching Hospital. Femi had begun the fight for his life.

It was a stroke. Two seizures, it would seem. When the first happened, Femi thought he merely had a fainting spell. He came to, found himself on the floor, and somehow succeeded in pulling himself back to his desk, then he was smitten a second time. One of his secretaries looked in and found him on the floor.

His wife, who now sat beside him, visibly distraught, had taken the call at home, but she was merely informed that her husband was feeling poorly and a doctor had been summoned. Next she learnt that Femi had been taken to hospital. Her first thought was to send a driver to go and find 'Prof.', bring him over from wherever he was and whatever he was doing. Now she sat with her head bowed, wringing her hands. As soon as she saw me, she was convulsed afresh with sobs.

I sat by his bedside, looking at my friend, a drip through his arm and a tube up a nostril. His discomfort was near palpable, he tossed about and unconsciously tried to rip the tube from his body, so his other arm had been tied to the bed. Some time later, Femi opened his eyes, rolled them towards me and tried to speak. I gestured to him to be quiet – there would be time enough for that. He appeared to fall asleep again but was mostly tossing around in a state of half-consciousness. A doctor entered, an acquaintance. He patted me on the shoulders and tried to convey his sympathy. His examination over, I followed him outside and we discussed Femi's condition.

Two to three hours later, I said to Folake, "You can go home now. Go and pack his things and send them over, then get some rest yourself while you can. There is nothing more you can do here." It took the doctors and I a long while for her to be moved. Femi's condition did not improve. The decision became unavoidable – fly him abroad for specialised treatment. Inevitably, and with a sense of belatedness, I remembered how Femi had tried to interest some doctors to start a home-based diagnostic hospital. It was an idea that came from his annual check-up in the favourite health spot of the nation's politicians, top military and other well-heeled of society. Once, Femi found himself in a queue behind the then Prime Minister, Tafawa Balewa, ruler and ruled equalised by the bleached hospital smock that covered their otherwise naked bodies, by the urine and excremental samples and diagnostic cards that they carried as they moved from one room, cubicle or window to the next. It was typical of Femi's creative mind to seek remedies at home – *if I must carry my own shit in my hand, why should I do it abroad rather than here?* He tried to interest a few doctors in the idea – my own brother, his namesake, among them. He asked them to prepare estimates, and offered to put down the working capital. Whatever stage his efforts had reached at the time of his illness, they were clearly too late to help him. The premier teaching hospital in the nation lacked even the drugs required to stabilise his condition before he could be flown abroad.

And so – a familiar scenario for a teaching hospital – an all-out search! In all of Ìbàdàn, the drugs could not be found. Throughout Lagos also – once the nation's capital, and still its commercial centre – this critical drug was equally unavailable! Finally news came that a pharmacy in a most unlikely town, Ilorin, had a small stock in store. A driver was dispatched. In anticipation, the air ambulance was alerted, perhaps even the same plane that had once flown his brother, Bolus, to Germany after a horrifying motor accident. It would take off from Germany as soon as the word was given, fully equipped for any emergency. The news grew graver by the day. A blood-clot had been discovered in Femi's brain, and now we were looking at what, for us laymen, was going to be a critical brain surgery. Suddenly, time was ranged against us. In the meantime, Femi tossed between full consciousness and partial incapacitation. He understood all that was going on around him, was lucid enough to mutter one of his favourite mantras from time to time: *Ikú ló m'éja kákò.*[1]

It was a familiar self-mocking lament for a moment of frustration, for any form of constraint, no different, for instance, from an inability to embark on, or expand a business venture, owing to a lack of opening or capital. Only after the event, re-winding the reel of our last moments together in all their detail, did its prophetic pertinence strike me, or anyone else. In any case, I was preoccupied with some practical concerns – how quickly could I wind up my affairs, re-schedule appointments, etc., and prepare to join Femi in Germany?

Femi was brought out from the ambulance, his stretcher laid on the tarmac for some fresh air, awaiting his transfer into the

---

[1] It was death that curled up the supple fish.

ambulance plane. The clearance papers for the plane's departure were being processed. I stood some distance away, to let him and his wife have some moments alone before his departure – she had just been told that there would be no room for her in the plane. My eyes swept over trees, horizon, tarmac and parked planes, contemplated the slim craft that would bear Femi away, then came to rest on the stretcher. In obedience to some strange pull, I walked slowly back towards the couple. Femi must have heard my footsteps because he tried to move his head and see behind him, but he only succeeded in rolling his eyes skywards, then tried to extend his scope of vision to embrace whatever it was that approached.

As I looked down on the stretcher, I received a jolt, rather like an electric shock, a crude intimation of finality. Nothing had prepared me for the plea for help that I encountered when my eyes looked into my friend's. His, glassy and mud brown, rolled upwards to encounter mine, eloquent in their depth of bewilderment. *What is happening to me? they pleaded. Help me up out of this pit, just help me emerge from this darkness.* Femi's eyes appeared to dissolve and sink into a deep, endless tunnel, fathomless. I stood above these opaque windows and stared into their roiling recesses, encountering nothing but space, just space, infinite space into which I was violently pulled, so that I felt weightless. I came to, and found that I had leant over and encased his free hand in both of mine.

I withdrew slowly, chilled to the bone, acknowledging that he had withdrawn himself from the world, even as my hands left his. For I knew, in that moment, that I had left Femi at the very end of the tunnel, within that fathomless space, that the friend who lay on that stretcher would not return home in the form we knew, and cherished.

Despite that moment, I was unprepared when the news came. I had permitted myself to banish the sad, eloquent glimpse that I had received of Femi's certain destination, and restored him in my mind to his familiar surrounds. That dark presentiment, I decided, had been nothing but the product of my own fears. The doctors, the omniscient ones, had sent word back that we could banish all anxiety. From being extremely grave, there had been an upward swing in his condition, said the experts. I telephoned the hospital and received their reassurance – the pressure on his brain had eased, his condition had stabilised to such an extent that the surgeons were now prepared to operate on him. He was alert, could speak, and was fully aware of his surroundings and of the preparations for the operation. He had even shown signs of recovering his habit of self-deprecation. What stupid fears! It was a buoyant mood in which I prepared to ensure my arrival in Frankfurt in time for his operation, or as soon as possible afterwards, taking as much work as I could with me. Every moment I could spare would be spent with him during the period of his convalescence.

I was on my building site, when the news came. The workers had left for home and I had gone there to look at the progress they had made and, as always, marvel at my temerity in expanding the scope of the house I had planned originally - just a cottage with plenty of grounds. The Nobel Prize had however engendered grandiose ideas – a writers' annex, no less, to play host to three or four writers, artistes or researchers for a few months every year. It was an ambitious concept, one that was still within my means at the time, but of course it played havoc with the original, quite modest architectural plans. Once modified, they dragged in their wake further modifications as the building progressed. Femi's words constantly rang in my ears in absent complaint – *I want to be involved in the project, you hear, make sure I am involved in it right from the beginning.* The hell, I thought, you built that golden pillar, Broking House, from scratch, keeping me out. You'll see this only after it has been roofed and ready for occupation!

It was typical of the irrationalities that sometimes marked our skirmishes. After all, the funds that enabled me to make a start had come from Femi in the first place. On the advice of my bank manager, I had placed a substantial chunk of my Nobel Prize money in a fixed deposit for the first six months, where, if it conformed to habit, it was supposed to earn me some interest. I had not realised that this deposit would again be re-invested, automatically, for the next six months and so on and on, unless I gave instructions to the contrary.

Blithely, a month or two after the first half-year, I attempted to withdraw what was needed to shore up my grand project with the material of gravel, clay blocks, cement, steel rods and labour. Nothing doing, said the bank manager, your money will not be available till the end of the year. Femi, amazed as usual at my naiveté in money matters, immediately wrote the cheque for what was needed to break the grounds, purchase material and rescue my building schedule.

Now I stood alone on a mound of gravel, surveying my domain wistfully, wondering how soon I might see it finally materialise into the edifice I could picture so clearly in my mind. Motunde, my young ward and grounds manager drove up in my jeep. She had long finished her own work and normally would have had no cause to return to the building site. I wondered what determined visitor had penetrated my rented home and sent her racing to warn me. Young enough to be taken for my daughter, I would often wonder if the roles were not really reversed – she, the patient, indulgent guardian and I, a precocious but unpredictable ward – it was the way she had resolved to relate to me, to my frequent amusement.

I watched her take her time descending from the Jeep, then walk slowly towards me. To her normal expression of an ambiguous, often unsettling affection was now added the quiet but determined air of one who had come to take command of a crisis situation – this change in her bearing was familiar, and I simply waited for her to reveal the cause. When she came close, she stood still, looked wordlessly at me for some moments. Then, abruptly, she shook her head as if to rid it of some unbearable pressure, turned her gaze away, as if she wanted me to follow that gaze beyond the twilight gathering over the rim of the surrounding hills, and see what I feared to know. I understood, instantly. I think I let out a deep sigh, walked away from her and stared into space.

She walked back to stand facing me, her large eyes bathing me in compassion. I asked her to leave, that I wanted to be alone. She did not argue. I wandered off the building grounds, walking along the red laterite tracks that passed for roads. I did not feel bereaved, or sad. I felt nothing but rage, rage at myself for permitting hope, having seen what I had in the dark glassy tunnel of my friend's eyes. How could I have permitted myself to be so blinded by the pronouncements of mere doctors when I had glimpsed the truth and bidden him goodbye. For it was that moment on the tarmac that returned to rebuke me, the definitiveness of my gaze into an opaque tunnel and my encounter with the abyss of emptiness. If I had kept faith with that unambiguous intimation, I would by now have ceased grieving, and could turn my foreknowledge into a source of strength from which others, more needful, could draw solace.

Involved or not in the planning, designing or the laying of brick on brick, Femi was integrated into this house yet struggling to take shape, his laughter and interminable stories formed part of the foundations, echoed in advance of the raising of the walls. It was impossible not to see him striding from his bedroom – assigned to him right from the designing – to the dining room, groaning with fatigue as he took off his boots on a return from a hunt in my own locality, reminiscing on the highs and lows of the day, looking forward already to the next outing. It seemed incredible there was nothing physical left of Femi to inhabit the grand undertaking, nothing but a yet elusive shadow that I vaguely grasped as an impossible absence.

It is only when a house has been lived in, when its walls have been pawed, its doorstep scraped by feet and its humanity defined by the blend of human sweat, waste, and cooking that it may earn the right, through some accident of abandonment, to become a ghost house. Without having once leaked at the roof however, without having squeaked at the doors, echoed with music, eavesdropped on a domestic quarrel or played voyeur at the rites of love, this mere statement of intent, criss-crossed only by foundation channels, pocked by excavated mounds of sand and stacked clay bricks - my home to be, my long dreamt sanctuary had suddenly become a ghost dwelling.

PART VII

Nation and Exile

The Road to Exile

*I never feel I have arrived, though
I journey home. I took the road
That loses crest to questions...*

I brahim Badamasi Babangida, the genial dictator, had taken the nation for a long and twisted election ride that lasted nearly five years. From his first proclaimed date for handing over power, to his ousting in 1993 when he 'stepped aside', Babangida set up commissions for the 'return to civilian rule' and took his time studying their reports. He decided on election dates, postponed them, banned and unbanned politicians at will, detained some and released them, set down rules and impossible conditions for the registration of parties, set the same rules aside, promulgated two ideologies – *a little to the left and a little to the right* – created two political parties that would supposedly reflect both, wrote the party constitutions, built two identical headquarters in the capital of each state of the federation, subsidised individual contenders simply to engender false hopes, changed the balloting system, the registration system, the primaries system, etc. etc., then began all over again. Finally, in May 1993, bowing to pressure from the international community, the dictator permitted the elections to take place.

Voting was completed, over two thirds of the results released into the public domain by the Electoral Commission, with a clear indication that Bashorun Abiola was headed for a victory, when Babangida annulled the entire process. His response to the avalanche of cautionary articles, satirical cartoons, public rumblings, threats, reasoned advice even from within the military, and passionate denunciations that inundated private and public spaces and the media, was to remain holed up in his fortress, silent. By now I had given up on all hope of reformation for a fumbling, yet manipulative mind. I resisted all appeals to resort to the telephone, call the dictator and remonstrate with him. Indeed, I contributed only one published tract – *There is Life After Power, IBB* – and that, only after much persuasion from multiple directions, including within the military.   Not for the first time, I felt that words had reached the limit of their effectiveness. In the adage of the Yoruba, the dog that is fated to lose its way in the bush will remain deaf to the hunter's whistle.

It was the final insult, a contemptuous thwarting of popular will. There was a lull, a period of utter disbelief, then civic movements commenced plans for contesting such brazen arrogance. I travelled to Europe to wind up overseas commitments in readiness for what promised to be a protracted struggle when, on June 26, 1993, the people took to the streets. A graduated strategy of protests and street demonstrations was swept aside by public impatience – or even, possibly, by the regime's *agents provocateurs,* the government's massive counter-measures being already primed for pre-emptive action. I had been part of the planning, so I really did not have much of a choice – I prepared to return to Nigeria. It turned out to be that kind of a journey which, in calmer moments after the event, I would come to regard as a mirror reflection of the nation's journey towards democracy – every bit as laborious, twisted and unpredictable, an obsctacle race devised and overseen by the wily manipulator to whom Nigerians had given the name of Maradona.

I was frankly annoyed that yet another crisis was devouring my life, making me shortchange other constituencies – the creative, principally. Once again, a part of myself was being placed on 'Hold', and it was clear that this was going to be a long 'Hold'. I wound up my affairs as fast as I could, then braced myself for yet another period of turmoil.

The main uprising was in Lagos. Lagos has always tended to

be volatile and, additionally, Lagos was the base of the dispossessed president, even though he was an indigene of Abẹ́òkúta. On the morning of June 27th, I was at Charles de Gaulle Airport, ready to board my plane. So were dozens of other passengers bound for Nigeria. Then the announcement that all passengers dread, at least those who have anxious ones awaiting their arrival, business to attend to at the end of the flight, or who simply want to get home, shake the dust of alien lands off their feet and sleep in long abandoned beds. No, the flight was not postponed, delayed or cancelled. It simply was not touching down in Lagos. Owing to unrest in Nigeria, and in Lagos especially, the airline had been advised not to fly into Lagos. It would only go as far as Cotonou. Dissatisfied, I spoke directly to a flight officer. The report that his airline had received was that rioters had taken over Lagos, traffic was halted everywhere and the entire city was paralysed. Fatalities had occurred in double digits. There was mention of a curfew.

There was an ominous incident at the French airport that morning, and perhaps it played a role in the airline's decision not to land in Lagos – unlike others flying from other European airports. At the beginning, it did look as if it was simply another false alarm – an absent-minded passenger had left a shopping bag on a bench, and the area was cordoned off. The French 'Swat' machinery went into action and eventually, the package was blown up in a mild, controlled explosion. It was sufficiently near our departure gate for my curiosity to be aroused, so I spoke to one of the police officers who had been left to guard the debris. The bag, it turned out, had contained a small radio. After poking through, the bomb squad had determined that the radio was packed with some timers, detonators and other bomb related material, though it contained no real explosives. The owner of the bag could not be traced, but everything pointed to him or her being one of the Lagos-bound passengers. It was not a comfortable prelude to returning home. I could not help surmising that the owner had panicked for some reason – perhaps at the sight of an approaching officer – and decided to abandon the compromising baggage. Was this linked in some way to the confrontation that was building up in the nation over the aborted elections?

Knowing the volatility of Lagosians especially, a delay of even a day or two might mean that it would become impossible to enter Lagos at all. It was not a pleasant prospect, having to wait out the protests in Europe – how would I explain this to others? How would I explain it even to myself who, after all, bore the responsibility for travelling out just before the planned eruptions? The airline staff proposed that the next day's flight might be able to enter Lagos and offered to put up passengers for the night. That was not only dangerously late for me, there was no guarantee that the next flight would not undergo the same fate. There was only one solution – fly into neighbouring Cotonou with Air France, then travel overland into Lagos the following morning, by taxi if necessary. I had friends in Cotonou from whom I might be able to borrow a car and a driver – I would play it by ear. This was one instance when I definitely lacked prescience, but my passage into exile was about to begin – only, I was journeying in the wrong direction.

Paulin Houtounji was Minister of Culture in the Republic of Benin at the time, a feisty academic philosopher with a small compact frame, now tending towards a slightly comic rotundity, who never allowed his stammering impediment to prevent him saying whatever he had in his head. On arrival, I decided, I would check into a hotel, then contact him. Air France may have exaggerated the Lagos situation – other flights did land without any problem in Lagos, we found out later, but then, many passengers also found themselves compelled to pass the night at the airport and all of the following day, and the next. The streets were impassable. Still, if I wanted any confirmation about the grimness of the situation in Lagos, Paulin soon settled that for me when I appeared in his office the following morning. He snorted his disbelief, struggled with his stammering for even longer than usual, then exploded.

Lagos? He declared to everyone within earshot that I was mad. He had no problem providing a car to take me to the Seme border but, after that, I was on my own. Both car and driver, as well as his secretary were at my disposal for as long as I needed them, but I would discover, he assured me, that Seme was as far as either could go, no matter how willing they were. No vehicles had been able to cross the border for the past thirty-six hours. Official, diplomatic vehicles, commercial transport or whatever – everything was being turned back. Paulin insisted that his secretary accompany me in the hope that, along the way, she might talk some sense into me and bring me back in time for a reunion lunch in the sane environment of Cotonou.

I must confess here, to an irrational presumption in my ability to penetrate any space, however hostile. It has to do, I suspect, with a deeply lodged rejection of restriction to my movements, be it on the authority of state, of an individual or circumstance, or of some material impediment, directed at me personally or generally. Perhaps it is not so much irrational as it is non-rational, that is, I tend not to subject such challenges to the process of reasoning. If the space is obviously unbreachable, then of course, it simply never occurs to me to want to go there. It poses no challenge whatsoever since it has placed itself beyond my human interest. Need also has to do with it – do I *need* to go from Apanla to Oponlo? I do? Good! I need, therefore I shall. Obstacles are supposed to disappear, simply because ọ̀gá[1] needs to go. It is one of the mysteries of my existence – looking back that is, oh yes, only on looking back after the event, after several such instances. Only then does it strike me that I have conducted myself in a non-rational manner – at the time however, the situation is outside the province of reasoning. *Have need, will travel.* End of doubts and beginning of motion.

The approach to the Nigeria-Cotonou border told the story at first glance. For miles we cruised past a long line of vehicles, parked along the road, right up to the border, unable or unwilling to cross. On the Benin side of the border, a few quickly conducted interviews with motorists painted an even bleaker picture.

I crossed over to the Nigerian side of the Immigration post. There I met those who had earlier risked penetrating the Nigerian space beyond the safety of the border post. They returned within

---

[1] Boss. Master.

an hour into their venture either with damaged vehicles or with depleted pockets, having been forced to pay a toll for even coming as far as the first roadblock mounted by demonstrators. Checkmate? Well, at least I was now standing on Nigerian soil. I sent back Paulin's car, his secretary's voice still ringing in my ears till the last moment, urging me to return with them and take up the lunch offer in the affable company of Paulin.

The taxi drivers on the Nigerian side were mostly strolling aimlessly around the border post, an accustomed beehive now unnervingly emptied of any noticeable motion. They lolled under the tree shades or hung around the exits with their eyes strained in the direction of Lagos, determined perhaps to be the first to catch any bit of news emerging from there through some luckless traveller. I stood with my all-purpose bag in front of the Immigration office. Resting against a window-sill was an easily identifiable Secret Service agent – the notorious SSS - perhaps in charge of that sector. He recognised me, looked astonished but was instantly alert. I told him that I needed to get into Lagos.

"Prof.", he said, "I don't think it is wise to go into Lagos today. In fact, I don't think you'll be able to get in at all." He waved his hand in the direction of the idle groups of men and abandoned vehicles. "None of them will risk it. Some tried, and they've brought back sad stories."

"And you? What kind of stories have you got?"

"Stories? That's what I have just told you."

"Intelligence reports" I said, bluntly.

He laughed. "*Haba*, Prof.!"

We went among the taxi drivers, and the response was uniform, and firm. Even as we approached, a number of them had scrambled up and were waiting, expectantly. I wasted no time in disappointing them.

"I am in no position to tell you anything," I said. "I've been away nearly a week, so you know more than I do. I flew in only last night from Paris, through Cotonou. That's because the captain refused to fly us into Lagos. Now, which of you is taking me into Lagos?"

Almost in concert, their gazes fell away, some to the ground, others to overhead wires or some distant spaces above my head. Their feet scuffed the dust and a few shoulders drooped. These were fervent admirers who, in different circumstances, would have fought each other for the delight of dropping me off wherever I chose. This was different. Finally one said, simply:

"Ọ̀gá Wole, Èkó ó da o."[2]

Yes, I already accepted that Lagos had gone sour. And I understood that it was simple logic not to wish to venture into Lagos. The taxi was their sole livelihood and it made no sense to drive it into an inferno. And even risk their lives in the process. The only problem was that I needed to get into Lagos. Surely somebody had to understand that!

Another proposed that I wait another day, and then we would see how the situation developed. One came forward, pointed needlessly to his bandaged head with a bandaged hand. He proceeded to narrate the hot reception he had encountered, the bloodthirsty gang that still pursued him even as he drove his car in reverse gear at full speed until he found a safe place to turn around. He nodded his head in the direction of his clutch of stranded passengers seated in a shade some distance away.

"Ọ̀gá, dose na my passengers. You fit go ask dem if you like. Dose rioters break my windshield even as I dey already reversing back. Na God save me self. Hn-hn. Èkó ti dàrú."[3]

"Babangida done spoil everything. Àfí kí ẹ bá wa le lọ!"[4]

Heatedly I replied, "And how do you expect us to chase him out if you won't even take me into Lagos?"

One of them spoke decisively. "Prof., you won't be able to do much if you run into one of those gangs of wild ruffians and get killed."

SSS interjected at this point: "What are you talking about? Nobody is going to touch Prof., you all know that."

"A-ah, you haven't seen these ones. Wọn ò m'ojú.[5] Many of them are high on drugs. They'd have done their damage before they even recognise who it is."

---

[2] Master Wole, Lagos is not good.
[3] Lagos is in chaos.
[4] You have to chase him out for us.
[5] They recognise no one.

"No, they won't touch Prof.," someone else conceded.

I quickly pressed the advantage. "I tell you what – each time we approach a roadblock, I shall come out of the car so they'll see me clearly. I guarantee they'll let us through. If I fail, we'll simply turn back."

"Prof., there is something else you haven't thought of," offered yet another. "Let's say we get you into Lagos. How do *we* get back?"

They all looked up in anticipation - let's see how he deals with that. I had no response of course. I tried to lighten the atmosphere: "I could provide you with a *laissez-passer*. Special passport. We'll have it signed on the way in, by the leader of each roadblock." Only the SSS man joined me in a brief chuckle. The general mood remained sombre, the silence was thick with fear.

"Come with me, Prof.," said SSS abruptly.

He led the way to where a solitary driver had remained in his taxi, doors wide open and the seat flattened out as far as it would go, fast asleep. "Hey, wake up!" The driver sat up, rubbing his eyes. "I have a passenger for you," said SSS.

"Where to?" The man demanded.

"Where to? Where you dey take your taxi go? Lagos of course."

The driver giggled and began to sink back to sleep. "Ọ̀gá, I beg. Make you let man sleep." Just then his eyes caught sight of me and he snapped fully awake. "Hey, na Prof.! Prof., na you wanting to go Lagos?"

I nodded.

"The road is ba-a-ad. Very bad. This ọ̀gá no tell you?"

"I know. But we'll get there, don't you worry. I'm in the car with you, don't forget."

Have need, will travel. As we approached that lone driver, I just *knew.* Right from the preliminaries, I had deposited my bag on the back seat of the vehicle – this was one fish that would not get away. The same arguments ensued. Yes, maybe they know you, but the first rock that is hurled at the taxi won't know who you are. And even if we make it, how will I get back? But by now I had thought up a solution to that one. Abẹ́òkúta was my ultimate destination, I said to him, but if passage to Abẹ́òkúta proved truly impossible, I would remain in Lagos. He would stay at my place, no matter what, and only leave when the rioting was over. Someone else would drive me into Abẹòkúta. He thought deeply about this as I stood over him, vulnerably crouched in the space of the front seat, and mentally bullied him. It was not clear if the SSS man had some hold on him that he subtly exerted, or it could be that the man was anxious to rejoin his family who, he told us, were all based in Òtà, halfway between Lagos and Abẹòkúta. There was the factor also – I felt this instinctively as we made our way towards him – that he had unwittingly rendered himself susceptible by isolating himself from the others. This placed him outside the protection of a collective rationality. No matter what, he finally agreed, comic in his dolefulness, with an air of one who felt he was being led to a place of no return. And thus began the most nightmarish journey of my existence – well, one of the most nightmarish.

The roadblocks were made up of empty petroleum barrels, discarded tyres, wheel hubs, vending kiosks, blocks of wood and tree trunks, huge stones... anything at all that could form a barrier for any moving vehicle. The strategy for that day was 'Stay home. No movement on the roads', its purpose being to shut down the cities in a national campaign of civil disobedience. This was where all semblance of uniformity ended. The methods of enforcing the strategy varied from roadblock to roadblock, as did the levels of interpretation.

The freelance hoodlums had taken over. Else they had been conceded place through plain *force majeure* by the authorised monitors of the stay-at-home campaign. At some roadblocks there was a going fee, you paid it and were allowed to pass – but that safe conduct lasted only until the next barrier. Sometimes the fee was a gallon or more of fuel siphoned from your car, and then you were permitted to proceed – until the next barrier. The rows of parked vehicles at various roadblocks, with disconsolate passengers taking shelter under the shades of trees, milling aimlessly about, told the stories of those who had managed to navigate a few roadblocks only to meet their Waterloo at the next. Some vehicles had clearly run a gauntlet of missiles, cudgels and even fists, others could have arrived directly from the film set of *Jurassic Park* – one could swear there were abnormal teeth marks in the bodywork. The stories had only slight variations – some drivers had been obstinate, tried to force their way through the vigilantes, or had attempted to point out – logically, they thought – that they had paid 'tolls' at earlier roadblocks, and were they not part of the same army fighting for the same cause?

Hadn't I been here before? I seemed doomed to find myself in a seeming replay, with even the violent faces taking on familiar features. It was 1965 all over again, after the rigging of elections in the 'Wild, Wild West'. There we were, driving to Lagos in my friend Bola Ige's car, on the old Ikòròdú road, heading for Lagos. The same crowds, the same passion or desperation, the same opportunism all wrapped in violence, so often gratuitous. Between Ṣàgámù and Lagos, a distance of some forty kilometres, we had encountered no less than three dozen roadblocks. Several were within clear view of one another, and the guardians of each barrier clearly saw a vehicle being 'cleared' just a few yards away, yet the new set stopped the same vehicle, extorted what money they could before letting it through. The occasional dead body lay on the verge of the road, usually burnt to death, some unfortunate political figure who had been recognised and whose crimes, in that mindless moment, were considered to merit instant justice. Faces are either passports or death warrants – depending on circumstances. Fortunately ours were the former, and constantly validated. Again and again we were let through to shouts of solidarity. Some ran ahead and cleared our passage.

Inevitably however, there would be the totally unimpressionable stalwart who did not give a damn whether it was Bola Ige, Wole Soyinka, Jesus Christ, Mohammed or even Obafemi Awolowo in person... *who cares who the hell it is? We are suffering* – the face becomes one extended snarl, its bloodshot eyes incinerate the air.... *Who cares? They're all the same. None of them knows what suffering is. If they want to pass here they must pay something.* Others to the rescue – *Are you mad? Don't you know who these are?* But the leveller is unmoved, if anything he becomes more truculent, interposes his body between the car and the barrier.... *To hell with all of them! They have to pay, otherwise no way!* And the sudden, brittle sound of a bottle smashing against the car, and its neck miraculously in the hand of this implacable toll-collector, its jagged end pushed virtually in Bola's face since his was the nearer, mere inches away. *You want I put this for your face? Put your hand for pocket and pull out money my friend!* I am frightened for Bola but, inside? Mad, raging mad! But there is nothing to do except play for time, play for those extra seconds until the others can leap on him from behind, pin his arms behind him and yank him away. The scene repeats itself, with variations. Mostly any such extortionist hold-up is apologetic, even ingratiating... *ọgá, we never chop since morning, leave us something make we put for mouth...* we do not have to wonder what it must be like for other motorists, since we are sometimes obliged to go to their rescue, vouch for their political *bona fides*. Finally someone with overriding authority plonks himself down on the bonnet of the car and we drive steadily through until we have cleared all the barriers around Ikòròdú. Our last sight of this sergeant-major of the vigilantes is of him commandeering another vehicle going in the opposite direction to take him back to his post – that vehicle is the envy of other motorists.

Thirty years later, and here I am undergoing these identical rites of passage. As we approach each barrier, I poke out my head and, most of the time, this is more than sufficient to clear the way. In between such blissful passages I spend my time trying to guess how soon we would come upon the drug-crazed exception with burning eyes, one who would refuse to countenance any exception. Before long, we begin to encounter the barracks lawyer.... *You people gave the orders that everyone should stay at home, now you're breaking your own rules.* I wonder how much more gleeful he would have been if he had known that I had initiated the stay-home strategy, selling it to the campaign as a variant on continuous street demonstrations with their often numbing fatalities... a few days on the streets, then the next few within doors. That way, the army and police would not know exactly what to expect from day to day. *Stock up on food and drinks, close down the towns and cities, turn the streets into ghost spaces and let Babangida rule over emptiness!*

I round on my interlocutor in mock aggression – *and is this your home? I don't see your kitchen. Where is your shit-house?* He gives a half-ashamed smile while others laugh at his discomfiture. The barrier is lifted. But finally, the inevitable occurs, and we encounter the no-exemptions type, albeit somewhat diffident and uncertain. At the very least, he insists, we must supply a bottle of petrol - the forces of resistance must be sustained by taxation of the rich, in cash or kind. Thin and wispy, he is probably still in school, but has already established himself as the ideological guru of the barricade. I tell him to get lost, and engage the obvious leaders in a discussion on the prospects of the resistance. Then, through the corner of my eye, I observe a suspicious movement. The sly revolutionary has only pretended to slink away; now he is actually engaged in prising open the cover of the petrol tank and, obviously well practised at the task, has a rubber tube already snaking down into the tank. I dash out of the car and snatch the tube away, warning him that if he tried it again I would make him drink the petrol, then throw a lighted match down his throat.

Profiting from the 1965 experience, I take to picking up a guard at one barrier, dropping him at the next and picking up a new one. One or two ask for money to get back to their station – never more than half a mile distant – but I remind them that taxis are not running. Then the impudent grin – *Oh ọ̀gá, you sef, you know say na for take buy something for chop!* That's better, I grin back, just come clean with me and we'll get along. A handful of small denomination Naira changes hands - at least they did earn their pay. The backup plan remained the same – if we encountered a truly unbreachable roadblock, we would simply remain there until a more influential stalwart came along. It never did happen, but progress remained excruciatingly slow. I started out from Cotonou at about eight o'clock in the morning. Normally the journey into the heart of Lagos would take two hours. Now it was already five hours later and we had only covered some fifty kilometres. I became increasingly anxious.

The taxi driver was beginning to enjoy himself. Even the faint smallpox dents in his jet-black, fleshy face appeared to glow with delight at our progress. From a timorous beginning, his palms sweaty and lips mumbling prayers as we approached the early roadblocks, he had gradually convinced himself that I exercised absolute control over even the most dangerous ruffian or situation.... *Ah ọ̀gá, na you alone, for all of Nigeria, unless for say someone like Gani Fawehinmi or Doctor Beko, or say Femi Falana fit pass this road as we dey pass through today.* I watched him grow more and more confident, then bold and aggressive. The very back of his neck was quite expressive – if I was dissolving roadblocks as if magically, then he too had become the ultimate miracle worker. He began to ignore our rule – *slow down, wait for me to be recognised and let me do the talking. Above all, do not open your mouth.* Not any more.

He took offence at having to slow down at all – *Whas the matter with you? You no get eyes? You no see who I dey carry for inside car?* He took umbrage at any delay in removing a tyre rim or log of wood, at having to negotiate broken bottles – *You people, you no think how all this broken bottle fit begin cause tyre puncture?* He became personally affronted by any query from the vigilantes – *Thas the way with our people, is the person trying to help common man that they no respect.* I became tired of rebuking him, simply resigned myself to undoing his braggadocio by popping out my head, getting down and turning on the lubrication tap, gesturing that he be ignored. Underneath his bluster however, was simple anxiety – he wanted to be out of the string of roadblocks and back in the calm security of his home.

Of all the taxi drivers, why had I landed this one? Well, the answer to that was straightforward enough, I reminded myself – he was the only one stupid enough to take on the trip. When admonitions failed to work, I resorted to threats. If he were not so obviously a pious, abstemious type, full of instant homilies and prayerful thanks to Jesus, I would have suspected him of sneaking a drink when I was not attentive. He was certainly high on something – was it some slow-fuse marijuana he had been smoking before I came upon him? Finally I grew weary and half-threatened – *at the next roadblock I shall tell the vigilantes to detain you. I'll take over your taxi, and then you can pick it up tomorrow.* The bloodshot eyes in his round face looked as if he believed me. Anyway, it held him in check, but worse was to come – the bravado began to peel off. I watched it physically vaporise as we approached the outskirts of Lagos.

Fifty, maybe sixty kilometers in five hours? It finally got to me, and I became anxious. The tension in the air became palpable as we moved nearer Lagos. The roadblocks became more frequent, so did the sight of damaged vehicles, and worst of all, corpses. At the sight of the first corpse, my driver simply disintegrated as a human being. We encountered abandoned roadblocks and one could see that they had been violently dismantled, smashed through by forces that were clearly not of the popular resistance. Lurking around the peripheries of such posts were the temporarily destabilised vigilantes. They had changed tactics and become mobile forces, swooping out from hiding places to enforce the implacable *No Movement* order, inflict what damage they could on the erring motorist, and then retreat before the forces of law and order came into sight. The frequency of corpses increased, but with a marked difference - these were not victims of immolation but of neat, clinical bullets. Danger was thick in the air, accompanied by an acrid sting on the nostrils, it penetrated through to, and invested the taxi, and I finally understood that I had been watching a rare case of hysteria. All that bravado? The man was undergoing a long-drawn attack of hysteria. It was a strange experience, watching a human being disintegrate before one's very eyes, and so rapidly.

There is a turn off, a few miles before the junction known as Mile 12, that offers a direct route to Òtà, on the way to Abéòkúta. I decided that it might be best for us to use that route. It would take us to yet another possible route into Lagos, a hardly used road, and therefore certain to be less patrolled by the vigilantes. The driver was falling to pieces, and was no longer capable of thought. I offered to take over the driving several times but the steering wheel had become a crutch. It was an object of familiarity, it offered the last crumbs of friendship and security that were left to him in a situation into which he had been tricked – I could read that accusation forming itself slowly on his face – tricked! Everything else had been taken from him. The steering wheel was his last hold on any personal reality, and he was not about to give it up. Suburbia turned gradually to greenery as we took to the diversion through rural land, lined by cassava bushes, okra and vegetable farms.

The roadblocks diminished and, where encountered, were far less aggressive but no less dangerous. On those deserted stretches through mostly farmland, a car and its passengers could simply disappear forever. The personnel at these non-urban barriers were far less frenzied, less overtly menacing. They watched you approach with lazy, indifferent eyes, watched you approach the barrier with total unconcern, remained inhumanly still as they waited for you to make the first move. I leant out of the car, spoke to them in Yoruba. These were mostly farmers and villagers. They moved slowly. I could read on their faces their difficulty in accepting that someone like 'Prof.' would be on such roads at that hour, but then, moments later, I would read again that they had decided that this was the most natural thing in the world. The lethargy disappeared, to be replaced by concern for my safety and an evident boost for their morale. The barrier was pushed aside, warnings were given about other barriers further on – *tell them you've just been through Agbára village and that you met Yekini.*

And then the skies opened up and a deluge began. I tapped my driver on the shoulder and told him to cheer up. The rains would at least send the vigilantes seeking shelter, so we would have easier passage from then on. He was beyond consoling. We finally came to decision point – the fork in the road where one led to Ọ̀tà, then on to Abẹ́òkúta. The other led to Ìpájà – and Lagos. At first he badly wanted to go to Ọ̀tà, where he would rejoin his family the soonest. Ọ̀tà suited me also, since this was closer to Abẹ́òkúta. Suddenly however, he no longer wanted to go to Ọ̀tà. The road was much too abandoned. He saw armed robbers everywhere – they would have taken over the deserted roads by now, he swore. They were not interested in any revolution, all they did was take advantage of the uprising and rob people of their vehicles. On that lonely stretch, he whimpered, we did not stand a chance – much better to take our chances where the Lagos people were out in force. *At least people there get sense, ọ̀gá.* Yes, suddenly, his earlier tormentors were the more rational.

And so we turned towards Lagos. Several more roadblocks and we were on the main dual carriageway that links Lagos through Agége to Abẹ́òkúta. He knew some short cuts, according to him, which meant of course that, in a short while, we were totally lost. This was a part of outer Lagos where I had never been, and this same driver, who had earlier boasted that all of this sector was his regular beat, became thoroughly befuddled. Moreover, the rain now took on an intensity – like a third force intervening in the confrontation. Visibility approached zero. We came into a fairly populated suburb and found that we had only come upon a recent battleground. The streets were mostly deserted. A few stragglers moved cautiously from time to time, first peeking out from a door or window barely cracked open, then stepping out. We stopped one and asked for directions into Agége. He pointed, then warned – but you musn't go that way. Soldiers? I asked. No, but it all came to the same thing. These were the Mobile Police, the *Kill-and-Go*, also known as 'MOPOL'. They had just shot six people in that area – if you go past that side street, he said, you will see the bodies. They came in, shooting wildly. And they've just chased some of the demonstrators in the direction of Agége, so I advise you not to go there. Was there another route? Oh yes, we could go back the way we had just come, then take the first right at the roundabout...

At the roundabout, we came on the remains of what had been the best constructed barrier yet. The hulks of long discarded vehicles, nothing left of them but the skeletal frame and rust, lay across the approaches. Heavy wooden logs had been inserted between the eye sockets – once side windows – as reinforcements. It was possible to find a passage, but only by weaving through, slowly, sometimes with one set of wheels on the broken kerb. We succeeded, and without getting down to move any obstacles aside, only to come to yet another barrier, this time more makeshift than before. This was where we heard the first shots, followed almost immediately by the sound of a heavy engine at full speed, and it was clear that the vehicle was heading our way. The driver hesitated, stalled the car right in the middle of the road. I screamed at him – *Hurry up, pull over, pull over!* – only to bite my tongue as I realised that I had only made him more nervous. Miraculously he succeeded in restarting the engine, pulled onto the grass verge just as a Peugeot station-wagon roared round the corner, virtually on two wheels, and loaded with at least eight Mobile Police – the MOPOL – bristling with arms. In what was obviously a well-practised manoeuvre, the two front doors were flung open at the same time with booted legs that held the doors stiff, turning the entire vehicle into a battering ram. The barrels went flying off the road as the motor vehicle crashed through. Two policemen from the rear seats then leapt out, guns at the ready, raced round the barrier in an obvious attempt to find whoever had been manning the barrier and cut them down. The vehicle roared off, leaving the two policemen behind, presumably to sweep the environment clean of any rebels. I guessed that the patrol car was engaged in dropping more of those killers at various stops at top speed, and would return the same way to pick them up.

By now, the rains had eased off though the clouds were regrouping in readiness for a new discharge. We watched the MOPOL manoeuvres for a while, and then I asked the driver to pull back onto the road. Driver? No. I no longer had a driver. The creature that attempted to restart the taxi and operate the steering wheel was some kind of animated jelly whose lips moved and uttered some half-human gibberish. From time to time I could make out Yoruba words that suggested that he was thinking about his wife and children, and the home that he last saw nearly a week before. Gone was the last shred of that earlier bravado that had sustained him as our passage continued its near magical course from Ìdí-ìrókò. But he had not yet touched the nadir of his collapse.

I directed him towards one of the policemen, who had clearly got weary of his sweeping operations and was now resting under a tree, presumably awaiting the return of the van. All I wanted to do was to ask for directions – we needed to get ourselves out of that embattled zone, and the policeman seemed to me the most obvious person to ask. We parked some distance away, so as not to make him jumpy, then I came down and approached him in the most non-threatening manner I could muster. If I had had a white flag, I probably would have held it aloft, intoning – *Peace, brother man, I come in peace.*

His jaw dropped and his eyes opened wide as I approached. "Wait, wait, wait, am I seeing... wait, is this not the Professor...?"

His eyes were bloodshot and he stank of alcohol, unquestionably a particularly lethal brand of *ogogoro*. When he stood up unsteadily to salute, he had forgotten that the gun was resting on his lap. It clattered down, but he ignored it.

I waved my hand around the deserted space. "You appear to have been having some trouble."

"But Professor, you are here? In this place? Sir, this place is very dangerous."

"We drove in from Ìdí-ìrókò. As a matter of fact, we took this route to avoid the battle zones around Lagos – at least, so I thought - but it seems to be all over the place."

"Where you want to go sah?"

I hesitated. "Well, right now, if I could get to Allen Avenue or as close by as possible. My house is in that area."

"The ground is bad, oga. Too many killings today. The ground is very bad. What you see here is not the worst. My advice sir is, don't try to go into Lagos."

For a while I stood thoughtfully. The clouds had grown dark, inky dark, there were rumblings that appeared to warn that the earlier downfall would be child's play. Only four in the afternoon and it felt more like midnight. The more I reviewed the situation, the more distant appeared even my now adjusted goal of reaching the heart of Lagos. I asked the policeman if there was any kind of hotel, motel or lodging rooms in that area. He proceeded to describe one, so I waved to the driver to bring his car nearer so he could take on the directions himself. I had committed one of my many errors of that day. The *Kill-and-Go* did indeed begin by trying to give directions but his words were slurred and his arms waved so imprecisely that neither my companion nor myself could tell in what direction he pointed – in any case, on backtracking to repeat his last direction, he contradicted everything he had said before.

The sooner we extricated ourselves from him, I thought... so, I thanked him, assured him that we were now fully enlightened. I asked the driver to move on. The next moment however, this drunk had opened the front door and was thrusting himself into the empty seat.

"No, no, there's no need to come with us. We can find the hotel perfectly from your instructions – thank you so much."

But he was struggling to bring his body, then his gun into the car. "Ọgá, this place is dangerous, very dangerous."

"I know. That's why we've decided to stay in a hotel for the night."

"Yes, and that's why I must accompany you. Sir, I can't let anything happen to you. How will the papers carry it, enh? That something happened to Professor Wole Soyinka in our juri...juri...jurisidintion? God forbid bad ting!"

"Nothing will happen, I promise you. We've managed so far from Seme. I assure you, we're quite capable on our own."

"Sir, you don't understand. I must make a report when I get back to the station. I have to tell my ọgá that I find Professor Soyinka on the road, trying to get to Lagos. And do you know what he will ask me? Sir, he will say, did you escort him? And when I tell him that I left you on the road, first he will give me a dirty slap? Sir, I swear to you, he will give me a dirty slap, then he will lock me in the guardroom."

"I'll give you a note if you like..."

But he was no longer listening. His gun, which he had somehow persuaded to enter the car before him, was now wedged between him and the driver who, by now, had no more will power, no form of volition visible on his face or discernible in his limbs. And no wonder, since he was now staring, riveted, at the gun whose slanted muzzle was pointing directly at his head. I leant forward and pushed it away from him and towards the unwanted passenger who gratefully assumed temporary control of his weapon.

"Thank you sir. Ah, you don't understand, we all done see fire for eye today, and yesterday. But yesterday na child's play compare with today. As we break down one barricade, these people build it up again. Nothing anybody can do to them, they just won't give up. Too many people killed. So you see sir, I just can't leave you like that, the streets are not safe and my ọgá will kill me if 'e hear say I abandon you. But I can bring you safe to the hotel, and I stay with you until things cool down..."

I felt my patience slipping away. Then I had an idea. "Where is your police station?"

"Not far from here. Is just round that corner."

"Good. We go there first. Then we go to the hotel."

His gin-glazed eyes took on a manic gleam, but it was all delight. "You mean... you want go first to our station?"

I nodded. He beamed as if he had won a lottery.

"You say sir? I mean, you say you want come and greet our ọgá?" Beginning with an overwhelmed tremulo, his voice waxed ecstatic. "You mean, you will... oh my God, when I enter police station with you sir, nobody will believe my luck. Nobody sir! That is me get the luck to bring you to introduce you to the station..."

We got to the station and I told the driver to stop at the gate. He protested immediately: "No, no, it's all right to go in. Go inside, driver."

I stopped the driver. "No. This is as far as we go. We'll drop you here. Listen, you're very kind and I appreciate your concern. What you don't seem to understand is that your being in the car is the greatest danger to me. Do you think you can manage to understand that? All the people you've been fighting since yesterday, you think they want to see your uniform right now?"

He appeared to mull that over. I thought I detected a tiny light of comprehension in his eyes. Then he grew sad. "But ọgá, we're all fighting for the same thing. Only we have no choice. We have to carry out orders. But Prof., make I tell you, even as we discuss this matter in the barracks, everybody, all of us, we want these soldiers to go. I am an Abiola man myself, first and to last. The whole country know say he win this election, so why Babangida refuse to go?"

I patted him on the shoulder, pushed the snout of the gun away from my driver's face for the last time, and opened the door for him. "We shall win, don't you worry. And tell your ọgá it was

I who refused your protection. Explain to him what I said, that anyone in uniform is a danger to me right now – he'll understand."

I watched him walk up the driveway towards the main block of the police complex, his uniform sticking to him from the soaking he had had, more a bedraggled chicken than a *Kill-and-Go* Swat machine. Since he was also thoroughly soaked on the inside, my mind flew to an item on Chinese menus that I had never sampled, but often wondered about – *Druncken* Chicken, as it was spelt – and I used to wonder if the chicken was first made drunk before being dispatched or was alcoholised after the terminal event. Still, I hoped he would arrive in one piece, which seemed very much open to question, since he chose to drag his gun along the ground. The rain continued to pelt down but this did not appear to bother him one bit. At that moment, he struck me as perhaps the unhappiest being in the universe

A teeming crowd of humanity is an awe-inspiring phenomenon. As an objective spectacle, that is all it is, a spectacle, but when you are within it, when you are one of the bits and pieces that make up the tumult, you become one with it, you share in the force that it represents and you endure a loss of identity, except as a compressed lump within the crowd. I confess that I have never *experienced* being fully melted into the pack, so I can only approximate. When I am caught in one, I cannot wait to find a way out of the swarming promiscuity. The safest crowds are those that are made up of a majority of individuals who know *why* they have coalesced into one, why they have chosen to jettison their individual identities to form a new substantive, a *mass*. One can talk to such a crowd. One can reason with it, one can even modify its purpose and direction. Above all however, one can recreate such a crowd, transform the solidified mass of humanity, and turn it, at its most violent, towards pacifism or, from its most pacific condition, make it heave, a mountain in convulsion. I had lots of tutelage in mob characteristics on that day of my foolhardy plunge into Lagos – not for the first time, but never in such heavy and sustained doses.

When we had found a hotel – in reality a suburban brothel and general congregation bar for night-lifers and day drifters in shadowy rooms – I set down my bags and devoured a long beer. I discharged my long-suffering driver, paid him generously above the agreed fare. I offered him a room for the night but he was under some kind of spell. Nothing would make him share my comparative safety – to him I spelt danger, deadly peril, and his instincts warned him that he could recover his damaged self only by extricating himself from my presence. Had he also come to *hate* me? I wondered.

The rain had stopped but darkness was approaching as I set off for my Lagos home on the pillion of a motorcycle taxi, known as the *okada*, one form of transportation that could at least manoeuvre its way effectively through obstacles that now sprouted up virtually every few yards. The stoppages and interrogatories by vigilantes did not diminish, but they were brief and apologetic. The motorcycle aroused less of the instinctive hostility of a motor car, and the shock of recognition easily did the rest. If only I had known it at the time, it was a practice ride for a future escape through the forest that lay between Ṣhàkì and the border with Benin. Instead of lashing branches however, this was a forest of arms and limbs that tugged at my body and threatened to unseat both the driver and me. At their stubborn insistence I addressed a batch of my captors – before a few sentences, others poured out of crevices like soldier ants from hidden warrens. All sought a reassuring voice, craved some knowledgable view of the future. I had nothing to offer but hope.

I appeared to have entered a warzone, the scene of recent battles, mostly one-sided. Corpses littered the streets, casualties with horrifying wounds, patches of caked blood that discoloured the tar and sometimes the grey concrete divider on the motorway. Those smears often suggested that a wounded man had tried to climb the barrier, perhaps to seek vain cover on the other side, failed, but left his trail on the winding slab of cement. I began to reassess my progress, finally gave up all hope of reaching Abẹ́òkúta. I adopted, purely by default, this improvised set of insurgents that multiplied by the hour. Too many groups had lost contact with their leaders and simply did not know what to do next – stay put, or disband and resume the protests the following day? Was the stay-home order intended for two, three or four days, or was it to last a full week? What would happen afterwards? Was there a change of tactics that they knew nothing of? *Prof., what are we doing here? Why are we not training? Prof., I'm volunteering. Take me, take me with you, I know you have an army in the bush, just take me along.* Clutches here and there surrounded their radios, hoping to obtain some direction, some news of what was happening elsewhere. Darkness approached and some groups began to prepare bonfires, resolved to spend the night at barricades. Students had commandeered station-wagons and tipper lorries. They wore white T-shirts marked with the Red Cross emblem and ferried bodies and the wounded to first-aid centres and hospitals. That day was one of the finest in the mottled career of university students, and I could only wish that the lessons of their conduct would inform their lives, collectively, forever.

I was warned against military and MOPOL drive-past snipers, the hit-and-run specialists, it seemed that many casualties had been sustained that way and, on the motor bike, I was a recognisable target. Eventually I was prevailed upon to transfer to another car with a volunteer driver wearing the Red Cross T-shirt and cap. It was not long before I ran into a new source of anxiety. At a recent killing ground that had been personally supervised by a military commander identified as Sani Abacha – he arrived with a truckload of soldiers, the soldiers poured out and Abacha gave the order to open fire – a policeman stopped me and pulled me aside. The deaths that had taken place, he warned, were nothing compared to what would come at night, yes, that very night. He implored me to ensure that the demonstrators did not stay out of doors overnight. He had overheard an officer give orders to another to mobilise soldiers for a night operation. They were to clear out any remaining barricades, and take care of any sleeping protesters that were encountered.

I headed back to Ìpájà where I had earlier woven through barricades and back streets on the motor bike. This time, we drove on the main road, snail speed. In no time at all, I was engulfed by a teeming humanity that stretched miles and miles on both sides of the Ìpájà junction between Ọ̀tà and Lagos. I was awed by this phenomenon. It felt as if hundreds of bodies were sitting on the car, on the bonnet, hanging from the windows, clearing a route that only drew more and more people until there was not a visible patch of that road, only heads and bodies, all threatening to crush the life out of the steel body of this misused vehicle. A man in a track suit, one of those who appeared *not* to be of the crowd yet exerted some confident authority, pushed his way forward. Through the window, I told him what I had heard and asked him if he could disperse the crowd with the fall of darkness. No, he said, you had better do it, in fact, I don't think they will let you through unless you address them.

After a joint effort, we succeeded in pushing the door against bodies to provide just sufficient space for me to emerge. Before I knew what was happening, arms had raised me onto the concrete divider, and next, I was standing on the roof of the car. The vehicle vanished, instantly swallowed by a human throng. If I thought before that I had obtained an unforgettable sense of the massed impact of a crowd density, I now discovered that I had sensed nothing yet. The sight from my new vantage point reduced my sense of individuality to a mere speck. The world appeared to have been emptied into a sky-line of heads and torsos pressed into immobility, yet seething with life.

Somehow, silence fell over the crowd. Then a roar and then silence, a roar again that rose and fell, and that vibrant silence that sucked the neigbourhood into a tense expectancy. I shook my brain awake from stupefaction, succeeded in locating my voice. There was nothing to say except to commend their steadfastness, assure them of the certainty of victory. *But now, you must disperse. Don't be fooled by pretenders. You know your leaders, they will reach you by radio. Do not stay out on the streets tonight. Go home and return in the morning when you can see from which direction the enemy is coming in to strike. You've taken enough casualties. Don't let them slaughter you under cover of darkness. Go to your beds, but be back at your posts in the morning.*

Lying in my own bed late that night, my mind running through the reel of the day's events from departure point at the Seme border, I found myself compulsively trying to occupy the skin of some luckless stray from the enemy camp, who found himself entombed within the inhospitable pulse of such humanity.

By the Waters of Babylon

Between the conclusion of the June 12, 1993 elections, and June 26 that year – three days to the date on which the military should have handed over power to the victorious candidate – the nation stood still. One felt that sense of congealment, of eerie immobility near palpably, as if a hundred million people were massed in an outsize stadium, compelled to hold their breath. In only one section, raised like a press or adjudicators' box, did there appear to be a semblance of life –this was the law courts where the noise and frenzy seemed resolved to make up for the loss of vitality elsewhere. There, case counter case was filed between Babangida's surrogates on the one hand, and the president-elect on the other. The former wanted to legitimise the obliteration of the results of a concluded contest, turning it into a non-event, while the other fought the travesty of a reality in which millions had participated. The frenzy of litigations only warned about how deceptive was the lethargy that had descended on the rest of the arena, filling it with an ominous expectancy.

During that month, the military regime launched one of its crudest, most cynical assaults on the already battered independence of the judiciary. It imported a rookie state magistrate from distant Edo state to hold court in the federal territory, Abuja, on a case that was clearly a federal matter. She was flown in by a presidential jet alone, sat at midnight, and found in favour of the regime – the elections, she declared, were illegal. The aggrieved parties took their hint, filed for redress in other state courts – of higher jurisdiction. Those judges ordered the regime to release the remaining results immediately, and install the winner in power, one such judgement adding: 'even if the heavens fall!' The heavens did not fall, but a self-outmaneouvred despot did.

I.B. Babangida had defied the courts and dug in, but his ousting was only a matter of time. Within a month after the elections, his formidable array of armoured cars, guns, bribes and wiles, tear gas and batons notwithstanding, Ibrahim Babangida was forced out of office. There was nothing soldierly or dignified about his departure. The Yoruba – as always! – have a malodorous but apt expression for the manner in which colonial powers, forced to grant independence to their colonies, invariably made their exit – *òyìnbó ṣu s'ága* – before leaving, the white man defecated on the throne. Even thus did Babangida take his bow. The dictator attempted to cushion his departure – or was it to pave the way for his anointed? – by appointing a civilian surrogate to rule the nation. That poisoned mantle fell on a Chief Ernest Shonekan, a gangling business executive, formerly of the British United Africa Company (UAC), with a history of obliging figurehead or pointman for Babangida's creative transitional ploys. Shonekan's appearance as a recycled tool of despotic machinations was a renewed affront to the nation. His official title, this time, was Head of the Interim National Government, which quickly prompted his more popular sobriquet – the King of ING.

That Babangida was casting about within the ethnic group and hometown of the nationally elected president, Bashorun M.K.O. Abiola, merely added insult to injury – *here, suck on this. Sure, I took your gúrúdì[1] but here's gúgúrú.[2]* Much of the nation felt affronted by this patronising gesture, but none more than the elected president's immediate constituency – the Yoruba West. As a fellow Yoruba and partial townsman – the other part being Ijebu – of Abiola and Shonekan, I took the insult personally. Was this

---

[1] A flat corn-and-coconut candy.
[2] local popcorn.

how low Babangida estimated the pride, and sense of justice of
that part of the nation to which I belonged? At great material and
human sacrifice, the entire nation, not just a section, had made a
choice, and here was one individual usurping the will of a hundred
million people, reducing a national voice to a gesture of sectarian
appeasement.

Came June 27, and the *gúgúrú* was spat out, spat upon, and
the days of rage began. With the dictator's departure – 'stepped
aside', in his own words – and the installation of the substitute,
the direct violence of three days subsided into a campaign of
attrition – shifting levels of civil disobedience. An already tried
strategy of citizen stay-at-home was revived. Trade unions went
on strike, citing one grievance or the other – underlying it was the
real cause, a rejection of illegitimate power. Centres of commerce,
Lagos most prominently, were turned into ghost towns. Shonekan
became a prisoner, ostracised by his own people, isolated in his
Aso Rock fortress but playing at being a Head of State. Real power
lay with his Chief of Army Staff, Sani Abacha, who watched him
with amused contempt, awaiting the right moment to make his
move.

The stalemate exacted its price however. It took a strange toll
on the fighting spirit of some of our noted civil rights leaders, as
well as the supportive media – they grew impatient, even
desperate. They began to utter the once unthinkable, called on
the army to step in, dethrone Shonekan and install the truly elected
man in the presidency. At the forefront of the choir was my
unpredictable ally, Gani Fawehinmi who, with increasing
stridency, abandoned the forensic for the mystical. Gani added
and subtracted, analysed and synthesised dates, signs, portents
and some other arcane ingredients to arrive at a clairvoyant
conclusion: destiny, he declared, had laid its hand on the head of
the chief of staff for this solemn duty – to oust the civilian usurper
and install the choice of the people. He identified the date by
which the stars would align for the inevitable event. I was
nonplussed. Hadn't the nation learnt, from bitter experience, that
you do not entrust a hyena with even the mere whiff of meat,
however rotten?

I could not help thinking how little this differed – in methodology – from the invocational motions of the women of Abẹ̀òkúta when the cup of power was dashed from the lips of their own son. Their response was to resurrect an ancient rite of anathemisation. They made the ritual *àkàrà* – the fried bean cake – devoid of all condiments but impregnated with deep, ancient curses. They stripped to the waist and surged out in silent procession to place the *àkàrà* at crossroads and other spots of ancestral significance. It was a fearful ritual, its potency stamped on the grim-faced procession.

If not provably felled by the women's necromancy, Babangida had at least fallen to the accompaniment of other civic chants of rejection. His surrogate, Ernest Shonekan, would in turn be swept away on the tide of cabalistic numerology invoked from the legal redoubt of my friend, Gani – with some assistance, undoubtedly, from the inordinate ambitions of a little man called Sani Abacha.

Shonekan continued to twitch within other invisible webs spun by forces he little understood. It also appeared that Babangida – or perhaps it was simply his loyalists acting independently – became concerned at the tenacity of popular resistance. Prompted or not by the master schemer himself, these loyalists moved to seek ways of neutralising the problematic load their boss had deposited on the seat of power as his parting gift.

First came a visit from a young ambassador to South Africa, Tunji Olagunju, who pretended that he was just passing by, learnt that I was staying in Lagos with my usual host, Yemi Ogunbiyi, and stopped to pay his respects. It was transparent that he had been sent to discuss the political impasse, to test the grounds, as it were. Olagunju proposed plans that would involve the abandonment of the presidential elections, perhaps leading to a repeat of the exercise, the setting up of a government of national unity, etc., Abiola would also be free to participate in both. I quickly let him know that the 'abandonment' clause was a non-starter. The nation had chosen, and that choice must be respected.

Olagunju's visit indeed turned out to be preparatory for another, and at a higher level. The next caller was another Babangida affiliate, General Mohammed Gusau, National Security

Adviser to the Babangida regime, now continuing his chief bodyguard role to the King of ING. He tried to break through an initial awkwardness of the meeting by a comment on what I knew already – that the filing cabinet in the State Security Services dedicated to the subject of Wole Soyinka was not a cabinet at all but an entire room, filled from floor to ceiling with surveillance reports, news clippings, photographs, tapes from tapped conversations, departmental assessments, etc., but – 'believe me Prof., the summative view is that you act on principle, and everyone in the service has a great respect for you.' I assured him that I also believed that 'the service' acted equally on its own principles but what a pity its principles were constantly at variance with the people's. Further mutual assessment banter for a little while longer and then, very strangely, came the question – *why had I requested to see him?*

At first taken aback, I proceeded to correct him gently – Olagunju, I said, had asked me if it might help if some individuals, high up in government, intervened in the crisis, and would I agree to meet one or two of them? Yes, I did agree. I had however never met him, did not know who he was – so why should I have asked to see him? Gusau feigned surprise but, that gambit over – whatever he hoped to gain by it remained a mystery – we got down to business, how to break the political deadlock.

I proposed an unannounced mini-summit in next-door Republic of Benin – between Ernest Shonekan the usurper, Bashorun Abiola, the President-elect, his defeated opponent, Bashir Tofa, the chairmen of their political parties, with a few arbitrators-cum-moderators from either side. They would meet away from public pressure, and work out a formula for the transfer of power. I insisted however – *there would be absolutely no military participation.* The military was out, discredited, unwanted and mistrusted. Elections had been held and now the elected candidate must take over the reins of government. Agreement would be reached on a government of national unity – to restore trust and confidence – but, Abiola must occupy the driving seat. Gusau demurred on the total exclusion of the military, set out the advantages of their presence. I agreed in part but insisted: *strictly as observers.* They would not participate in the discussions or try to influence them in any way. Their role would be to listen, bear witness and return to report to their constituency. Gusau accepted the amendment. We agreed that a resolution was urgent, indeed that it must take place within the month. The nation was breaking down, it had become ungovernable and would remain so as long as Shonekan remained in power.

The following day found me at the embassy doorstep of our neighbours – the Republic of Benin. The Ambassador was away in Cotonou, the capital – which could not have worked better in our favour. A signal was sent to him by his deputy, so he could immediately begin consultations with his minister of foreign affairs, obtain the blessing of the Béninois president, etc. etc. Word came back as expected – the meeting was more than welcome and all was prepared – a weekend dash across the border by all the principals – no publicity, no fanfare. If all went well, the nation would wake up the following Monday to learn that civil society had seized the initiative and resolved the crisis its own way. It all struck me as déjà vu, but this was easier territory than my earlier foray into peace brokering. I began to wonder if there wasn't a diplomatic career waiting for me whenever the dramatist's stream of inspiration ran dry.

Contacts with the principals were immediately initiated. Was Gusau sincere, or was the purpose of these visits merely to test through me how resolute the opposition remained, and how mobilised? We never did find out. The termination of that undertaking came from Aso Rock – Shonekan, we were informed, was developing other ideas that would shortly be made public. Was he indeed? Were they his? Come to think of it, was the King of ING ever possessed of any idea beyond the delusion of power? Or did he simply take orders from his handlers, that is, Sani Abacha and his power hungry hyenas – it was impossible to tell. Abiola and his advisers were more than prepared for the Benin summit when, suddenly, all was scuttled.

The bets on Chief Ernest Shonekan's tenure were now placed, not on whether he would survive, but on how brief his tenure would be. He was probably the only individual in all of Nigeria who did not know this. In November 1993, Sani Abacha decided that the comedy had run long enough and moved to bring down the curtain. Surrounded by his praetorian guards, he presented Shonekan with a letter of resignation and ordered him to sign it. Shonekan, we learnt, actually made some kind of protest, which must have generated some barracks merriment among the putschists.

I was horrified at the jubilations even among the die-hard democratic combatants in the nation. The media, for once, lost its habitual watchfulness and some proceeded to censor my articles, on the grounds that they were too strong. Abacha, many believed, actually meant well, and would shortly fulfil their democratic expectations. Sani Abacha! Was this not the officer who had commanded the detachment that opened fire on unarmed protesters at the Ìpájà sector on June 28? Sani Abacha was single-handedly responsible for some two hundred dead, shot in cold blood, within Lagos state alone! He had given orders for a severe crackdown nationwide, deployed specially selected troops to ensure that his orders were carried out. During the same public protestations, he once appeared on television, a puffed-up officer bristling with arrogance, to threaten the Lagos state governor with unilateral action if that politician failed to put down the unrest in his state. The elderly governor shrugged, told him that he might as well take over his state that very moment, since he lacked the means to effect any cessation of popular protest. Abacha did not take over the state, but he did his best to decimate its population. In any case, while the continent has known an exception or two, military caretakers who actually handed over power to a civilian unfairly dispossessed of power, you simply do not employ an alcoholic as security guard in a distillery.

A pall had descended on the nation, but not many were yet willing to acknowledge that we were approaching Arthur Koestler's darkness at noon – not even Moshood Abiola the President-elect, who accepted to deal with Sani Abacha on the face value of his protestations. With Yemi Ogunbiyi in tow, I called on my friend, Ibrahim Alfa, the Air Vice Marshal, whom we had involved in the Benin scheme. We found him in like mood, sunk deep in dolefulness, cradling a glass of his favourite German Riesling.

"Sani came to see me the night before the coup," he admitted, "told me that he was taking over – to bring stability to the nation! I was horrified. I asked him why he would want to do such a thing and he replied that the people wanted it. They felt he was the only one who could put an end to the anarchy." 'All right,' I told him finally, 'but be sure you don't stay longer than three months, just enough time to install the elected president.' Of course I said that only because he was going to take over anyway. Everything was already prepared. Inwardly, I shook like a leaf and began to think seriously of plans for relocating. Abacha in charge of Nigeria? The man has the brain of a lizard!"

It proved impossible not to feel and express outright contempt for the lizard's promulgation of his own unending programme of a transition to civilian rule. The process of self-entrenchment was blatant enough, but most depressing of all was its lack of originality – Abacha had decided that any scheme of deception employed by Babangida was worthy of emulation, simply multiply the brazenness of it twice or thrice over, and it would become palatable to the public. If it proved not to be, the obvious remedy was force-feeding, and with as much brutality as could be mustered.

At first, the new dictator permitted the civilian state governors and legislatures, elected under the interim arrangements of Babangida's gradualist ruses, to remain in office. Suddenly, with a Cromwellian flourish, he sent them packing – *the political class had not learnt its lesson, the legislators were unserious, corruption reigned unbridled, etc. etc.* The public crowed approval – serve the bickering moneybags right!' Emboldened, he began to toy with the captive populace. Inauguration of yet another constitution writing body, one-third of which would be his own nominees. A new timetable for civilian restoration, then another. Arrests. Detentions. Constitutional Assembly sent on enforced vacation, returned sober and compliant. Mysterious assassinations, generally attributed to armed robbers. Abrupt retirements of the more professional soldiers. Deployment of suspect military units to the civil war front in Liberia. Flights of targeted individuals – including the dictator's earlier collaborators. Phantom coup plots against the regime – it only took a moment to make up an attempted coup d'etat, then weave a net elastic enough to contain the entire population if necessary.

Now increasingly suspicious of the dictator's true intent, the Press found itself under siege as it fought back. Under Ibrahim Babangida, when the journalists began to feel the cutting edge of the affable dictator's smiling teeth, Babangida's sadistic agents would simply wait until the daily or weekly print run had been completed, then swoop down on the editorial houses and cart off their irreplacable haul. At a lecture at the University of Lagos, I challenged them – *why do you let Babangida's police raid your offices, your printing presses, cart of copies of your journals without a fight? Have you never heard of underground publishing? Set up more than one editorial office and divide up your pages among various presses. Use fronts. Scatter your editors and let your journalists link up with them by telephone, fax, or carrier pigeon if it comes to that!*

When, two or three years afterwards, Abacha came into power, their guerilla tactics appeared to have been readied and honed overnight. The garage behind my Abẹ́òkúta office on Lalubu street was perhaps the earliest office of the *samizdat*. It was already used for clandestine meetings by a youthful group working out their own plans for making Abẹ́òkúta a no-go area for Abacha's forces of occupation. There they prepared torrid pamphlets and organised their distribution. The journalists among them put their training to good use. I left the gates to my office compound open when I went home. They came at night and left by morning, leaving the garage clean of any evidence of their nocturnal presence or activities.

The ascendancy of raw, naked power was rapid. Abacha's police had graduated from merely seizing editions and setting fires to media houses, they now took to seizing journalists, then taking their relations hostage – including wives and children – to force a wanted journalist or suspected dissident to turn himself in. A notorious episode, photographed by another journalist, showed a

State Security Services agent – the SSS – pressing his pistol to the head of a six-year old boy screaming, "Where is your father?" even as his mother was bundled into a waiting vehicle. Not long after occurred, albeit in a muted key, the curious incident around my son.

A botched kidnap? Or just a clumsy attempt to identify and enter him, even at that age of four – into the album of surveillance? Whatever their purpose, the agents were clearly handicapped by the fact that, as they skulked behind some flower shrubs at his school in Ikeja, a Lagos suburb, they were uncertain which of the pupils was who. So they called out the name 'Tunlewa' in the direction of a bunch of children going by. Their aim was to see which of the children would turn round. David, my nephew, who shared the same car pool was already walking towards the car. He heard the name and turned round instinctively, wondering who was hailing his cousin, expecting to see him coming towards the car that would take them home. But strange men pointed urgently towards him, all friendly smiles – *yes, you, you are young Soyinka, aren't you?* David shook his head in the negative, turned and quickened his steps towards the safety of the car. Once home, he spoke to his mother about it, guardedly, such was the impression of some impending danger that the incident had left even on his youthful senses.

That event took place against the background of over a year's round-the-clock, hardly subtle surveillance on our rented bungalow in Ikeja, as well as my private office in Abẹòkúta, where I gave most of my press conferences, the offices of the Úgùn State chapter of the National Union of Journalists being just round the corner, and always eager for a political statement.

Curiously, the same journalists worried more about the safety of their contributor than about themselves, sometimes censoring something I had written for fear that it would prove the last straw for Abacha. It took weeks of angry pressure from me before *The News* finally published what was probably my defining prediction, an article written soon after Abacha's takeover, and a year before my flight. There I warned that the new ruler was a killer, that 'this man would gaol, torture, kidnap, maim and kill at will simply in order to remain in power'. I knew him. I had studied him. I made it my business to follow the careers of a number of the military players on the Nigerian political field. Sani Abacha was a psychopath, certifiably so.

Now Head of State and Commander of the most celebrated armed forces in West Africa, his security machinery translated into action his paranoid assessment of individuals opposed to his rule. Around my office, the attempt by Abacha's agents at invisibility was so laughable that a foreign visitor, a Swiss producer and cultural animator, Niggi Popp, could not contain himself. Long after I had opened the door to let him in, he remained on the doorstep, surveying the street. Then, in a loud, provocative tone, as if he wanted to make absolutely certain that he was overheard by the furtive presences, he demanded to know what I had done to deserve a horde of snoopers attempting to merge with the local colour.

Of the constant faces that came to check on my 'state of health', the most wryly bewildered was perhaps Kunle Ajibade, one of the younger generation of investigative journalists. Kunle was correspondent for *The News* magazine, in Abẹ́òkúta, and was one of the pioneers of the *samizdat* publication, towards which I had nudged his profession some years before he would himself undergo the experience of a mock trial and incarceration – without ever losing his sense of the absurd. Kunle came almost ritualistically to my office, sat opposite my desk and, with a mixture of amazement and expectancy on his face, demanded to know:

"But, Prof., why haven't they come for you?"

"Why? Do you want them to?"

"No, but it doesn't make sense. By now they should have taken you in."

"Well, they haven't. So, what's your problem?"

"Well, I simply don't understand what you're still doing here," he persisted. "It's either you should be heading out of the country, or they should be pulling you in."

It was such a persistent puzzle for him that I teased him, insisting that he was hoping for a scoop, making sure that he was on the spot when Abacha's men did come for me. The opposite was true of course, especially as Kunle sometimes took it on himself to censor the odd article or an interview that I granted him, having resolved to protect me against myself! *But Prof.* – he would protest in his high-pitched voice – *if we had published that article as you wrote it, we would have lost you to Abacha right away! And then where would I obtain my exclusive interviews?*

This much one must say for police surveillance – its helicopters certainly provided the nation some rich moments of comic relief, for which, I insist on claiming credit. In the early months of 1995, unable to find their way to my house – the nearby villagers always misled uninvited visitors, sent them in all directions and left them going round in circles – the police resorted to scouting the terrain from the air. Thereafter they buzzed the house whenever they wanted some diversion or relaxation. Finally tired of their game, I summoned a press conference, issued a tongue-in-cheek warning, sounded the war drums in the hyperbolic accents of a famous *cri de coeur* that was once wrung out of one of Abacha's predecessors in office, my dangerous friend and antagonist – Olusegun Obasanjo.

Then retired and turned statesman at the time of his famous outburst, Obasanjo was a member of the Commonwealth's Eminent Persons Delegation that was set up to negotiate the end of Apartheid, and became the first African leader to breach the prison confines of Robben Island and actually meet Nelson Mandela. Deeply incensed by the intransigence of the Boers, frustrated by the slow progress of the liberation struggle, the general forgot his role as negotiator and let forth a most unusual rallying cry: *where are our famed metaphysical powers? Is it not possible to call on our ancient spiritual forces to smash the Apartheid system? Where is our juju force? Where is our much vaunted èpè* [3] *potency?*

And so, in response to the aerial aggression against my domestic peace, I belted out an extended war chant modelled on Obasanjo's bellow of rage... *but for my humanity, and the compassion that I feel for the innocent officers in that craft, I would have taken traditional measures against this noisome intruder. If the police boss Coomasie doubts me, I dare him to return alone, or with that cowardly torturer, Ismail Gwarzo. I shall teach them that there are powers beyond*

---

[3] curses.

the white man's machine-guns, rockets and missiles. I shall stand outside
my house and recite some potent ọfọ̀, incantations from antiquity that
will bring the craft spiralling down into my cassava fields!

The journals made a feast of it! Playing along, they churned
out caricatures of this Ìjègbá warrior, matted hair and beard, with
cowrie shells strung round my neck, a belligerent conch or horn
in hand, pens and pencils vying with quills and amulets in my
hair, one arm raised towards the intruder in the sky. More than a
few were witty and hilarious. I framed my favourite and hung it
behind my living-room bar. In exile, my mind easily reverted to
that cartoon when I learnt that my house had been smashed up
on the pretext of seeking the opposition radio, making me wonder
if it was still hanging there, had caught the eye of one of the
invaders with a sense of humour and ended up in his pocket, or if
I would still find it lying among a heap of smashed furniture.

It all helped to ease a people's tension, dispersing a real aura
of menace with ridicule. I did not fool myself however. Even at
that stage, it had become clear to me that the space for such mock-
heroics was rapidly contracting, and that comic turns were
becoming indistinguishable, literally, from gallows humour. Such
moments became rarer and rarer. Civil society was knuckling
under. There never is a shortage of willing collaborators within
civil society, and the roll of recruits lengthened by the day. The
prospect of a slave plantation, over a hundred million at the last
census, subject to the whim of one man, stared me in the face. It
was time to revitalise public sensitivity to what was happening,
where it was all headed, and incite its will toward self-recovery.
Wearily, I acknowledged that it was time for some drastic initiative.

In August 1994, surrounded and menaced by fully armed and
kitted Mobile Police who pressed their faces against windows and
a metal grill that surrounded the open assembly hall, I nevertheless
held a press conference at the Mayflower School, Ìkénné, run by
that late school master and social reformer, Tai Solarin. There,
with a detailed map, I outlined plans to expand an exercise we
had undertaken during the sit-tight season of Ibrahim Babangida.
Then, we had embarked on a walk from the Labour headquarters

in Ojúẹ́lẹ́gba, on Lagos outskirts, to the Race Course in Ọbálẹ́ndẹ́ – it was on that exercise, prevented by the police from entering the Race Course where the march would end with speeches, that I flung down my national award and stamped on it. I had brought it with me for that very purpose, just in case we were prevented from carrying out the march. This time we would advance to the scope of Martin Luther King's march on Washington and confront the lizard in its hole – mobilise the people and embark on a Million Man March on Abuja! We would converge from all four compass points of the nation, march on Abuja and invest the seat of government until the tyrant was dislodged.

The planning was well advanced when, a few weeks later, I returned from a light hunt in the surrounds of my Abẹ́òkúta home one morning and came upon three obvious security agents. They had been waiting for me since very early in the morning, early enough to have found me if I had not gone into the bush. The 'State Annexe' – the demure name for the offices of the State Security Services throughout the country – had just earned itself a rocket from Aso Rock, the seat of government. It appeared that the director's predecessor in office had received an earlier memo to pull me in and interrogate me about my public statements and activities. That luckless official had failed to track me down for weeks when, lo and behold, I appeared on the front pages of the media yet again, not only spouting off, but organising a march that would converge on Aso Rock from all corners of the nation. A sizzling signal scorched the desk of his successor – the commander-in-chief demanded instant explanation – how could I be at once untraceable, yet conspicuously present in the national media, even to the extent of holding a press conference in that very town. The new director did not await a renewed warning. He dispatched three of his men with orders to stake my house night and day and bring me in the moment I appeared.

They could not very well take me into their station carrying a firearm, albeit a simple shotgun, so they let me into my house. I deposited armoury and feathered victims, showered and changed my clothes. I followed them in my car to their office, which was in fact in the same neighbourhood – albeit tucked away – as was my personal office, in Lalubu. As I was not sure if I was heading straight for detention, I scribbled a note and left it with my househelp: *If I am not back by a certain time...* it had become routine, even second nature to many, and my househelp knew where to deliver the note.

I entered to strained smiles. The director brought out a bulging file, extracted and pushed towards me the memo from Aso Rock. His office had gone to incredible lengths to track me down – Lagos, Ìbàdàn, Abéòkúta...his voice was tinged with irrational rebuke... *but where were you, Prof.?* I waited until he had rid himself of the umbrage from high up into which I had plunged his office by my elusiveness – of which I knew nothing! At the time, I had not begun any attempt at subterfuge – the trouble was that I was in perpetual motion, since we were mobilising at all hours of the day and night. Methodically, he reviewed my recent activities, implored me to understand that the government was not trying to curtail my freedom of expression or right to legitimate activities. Then he moved straight to the point.

"Professor Soyinka, this Million Man March of yours, how do you propose to carry it out?"

"The details were spelt out at my press conference." I pointed out.

"Well, you realise, I am new on this case. I've just been transferred from Benin – you know, I was the one in charge of that armed robbery case – you know, the notorious Anini - which implicated one of our officers. I didn't really have much time left to follow much else of what was going on in the country."

I obliged, first pointing that the stated theme – *ONE STEP FOR FREEDOM* – itself summarised the overall strategy. "Obviously, we are not going to march all the way to the capital, Abuja – if you take Lagos alone, we're speaking of over a thousand miles to the capital. Maiduguri in the far North is at least two thousand five hundred. The idea is to create a relay of marchers. Some will accompany the main column no more than a few steps and return to their homes. Others will merely walk from one end of the city to another. The main column will take off from wherever they are based and proceed along designated routes. Their places will be taken by others while they are transported in vehicles to the next stage – you may call it a massed exercise in leapfrogging. Of course those who are capable of it are free to walk all the way. But the climax will be the convergence at the outskirts of Abuja, when we'll march en masse on Aso Rock."

The man had begun to shake his head: "Professor Soyinka, do you think you can achieve all this?"

"Why not? It's all being very carefully coordinated. Schools, mosques and churches, private clinics, market women, students, factory workers, etc. etc. – they're all going to be involved. Several schools have already offered their premises as stops on the way. Give or take a day or two, we'll all be in Abuja in a week."

"But this is a massive undertaking!"

I agreed with him, pointing out however that the people were more than willing.

"Professor Soyinka, let me be candid with you. Only one organisation has the capability and the resources to mount a vast operation like the one you're telling me about, and that's the military. I want you to understand that this is the thinking in Aso Rock, and frankly, I agree with them."

"You couldn't be more wrong. And we're going to prove you all wrong."

"Oh, I don't think so, sir. I think that, surely, you will not be allowed to prove anything."

"Why? If the government thinks the March will fail, then what is it worrying about? All you have to do is watch us fall flat on our faces."

"Ah, but Prof., that's the point. The government thinks that you can succeed."

I expressed puzzlement. "You're contradicting yourself."

"No – *you, you,* sir, you Professor Soyinka. The government is convinced that if there is anyone who can pull it off in the country, it's you."

I confessed to being flattered but assured him that there were thousands of others with even better organisational skills and resources – the trade unions, farmers and market women's organisations, student movements...

"But the international connections, Professor! Your 'shopping list'! All those items for which you solicited at your press conference – camp beds, sleeping bags, first aid kits, iron rations, banners, boots and backpacks, a hundred thousand balloons – even walkie-talkies! And of course you will need money. This kind of operation requires money. Taken together with all those costly items, it is certain that you are relying on outside sources."

"Both inside and outside," I conceded.

He pounced. "So you agree that foreign bodies are involved in this."

I demurred. "Well, I don't know that we can call them foreign bodies. We have lots of Nigerians living outside who are just as determined to take the nation back to democracy."

He sighed, brought out another folder, much slimmer. His demeanour changed, turned primly official. "Sir, it is now my duty to pass on to you, formally, the message from the government. If you don't mind, I must ask my immediate assistants to be present. I am required to read you this message in the presence of witnesses, after which I shall report back to Aso Rock."

He pressed the bell, two assistants entered and took their seats. It was clear that they had been awaiting the summons. He cleared his throat.

"I am about to pass on the message from Aso Rock," he said, and his colleagues nodded. "Professor Soyinka, the government has been disturbed by the announcement of your intention to march on Aso Rock with over a million people. While it is not the intention of this regime to clamp down on anybody's freedom of movement, the government is of the opinion that this may lead to a serious breach of peace. Your group may encounter other groups who disagree with you and may try to stop you. This would lead to a breakdown of law and order. It is therefore the firm intention of the government – in fact the government considers it its duty – to prevent your march at all costs. This government will act in the best interest of national security."

The riot act had been read. He tucked the piece of paper back in its file, then extracted another and pushed it towards me. "And now please, Mr. Soyinka, you have to write a statement."

Now I was baffled. "A statement?"

"Yes. Those are my instructions. From headquarters."

"A statement about what?"

"About everything that has taken place here. The...er...conversation I've had with you, the fact that I have read out this directive of government – everything in fact that has transpired here. I would strongly advise that you include a sentence stating that you have called off the march."

"Oh no, I cannot do that."

"Professor Soyinka, the government has decided that this March cannot take place."

"Sure, I understand the position of the government. You've made that abundantly clear."

"And the message says clearly that the government will do everything within its power to prevent your march."

"That's plain enough but I have no authority to call off the march. I have to consult with others."

A pause. Clearly this was unexpected. Then, "How soon can we have a response?"

"As soon as possible."

The director sighed. "Professor, I wish you could find your way to calling off that March."

"I've told you, a decision cannot be taken by me alone. In any case, what's the hurry? The March is still months away. We are only at the beginning of organising."

"Well, I'm afraid you will have to put that also in your statement. You have to say something in reference to the government position that I have just read to you. Those are my instructions. Please..." And he pushed the statement form to me again and offered me a pen.

I offered him a compromise. I was tired, I sighed, and in any case, I would rather type out a statement at home. I needed time to digest everything he had said, reflect on it, and provide a well thought-out response.

"My officer can follow you home and bring it back?"

"What of tomorrow?"

"Tomorrow? I have to report back to headquarters."

"Maybe by tomorrow I would have succeeded in contacting some of my colleagues. You do want an early response, you said. So? Why don't we simply make it one statement instead of two or three? If I gave you an answer tomorrow and the others rejected it..."

He pounced eagerly on this. "All right. Tomorrow morning then. In the meantime, I shall send a message to reassure them at headquarters that we found you at last and that we've had an amicable meeting. But please sign here, on the government's letter, that you've seen this. That way I can send a signal right away that we've had a frank and amicable meeting."

"Yes, you may do that. It has been an amicable meeting." I signed the document.

I was amicably accompanied with all amicableness to my car. We agreed on noon the following day for collection of the 'statement', to allow more time for contacts to be made. I returned home, typed out a brief statement acknowledging that we had had a frank but cordial meeting, that the message of the government had been conveyed to me, and that I would make a due response after consultations with my colleagues.

Noon the following day, and the assigned officer was at my house to collect the statement. He read it, chuckled, shook his head and proceeded to place it in the folder he had brought with him. I asked him what he found so funny.

"Prof., there is nothing here to indicate that you're calling off the March."

"No. I've tried all morning and I still haven't reached any of my collaborators."

"Prof., there is no phone in this house. And you haven't left the house all day."

"How do you know? Do you know this neighbourhood better than I?"

The smile never left his face even as he cast a casual look around him, ensuring that there was no one within earshot. "Prof., you don't know me. You saw me for the first time yesterday but, please believe what I am about to tell you, and take my advice."

"Yes?"

"Don't go on that March."

"I've told your boss. It's not my decision alone."

"Don't go on that March, Prof. And leave the country. Please sir, as soon as possible. And don't even tell anyone before you leave."

A few nights later, other pursuers would catch up with me, expressing agreement with the man from the State Annexe – but the motivations could not be more different. Among them, the most passionate was the old man, Pa Ajasin, a constant in the democratic struggle, now in his eighties, one of the recipients of the brutality of another dictator, General Buhari. He had sent over a dozen emissaries to track me down, but it was Olu Agunloye who knew where to find me and deliver the same message, the same passionate plea: *Do not go on that March. Do not take anyone on any march. Abacha will mow them down in their thousands without losing a wink of sleep – remember June 93.*

From danger to safety, the river crossing had taken less than ten minutes. In real time however, it had lasted days, weeks, even months. Half a dozen times at least, I had prepared to leave the country, only to draw back at the last moment. Hours before dawn, I pulled on my boots and sat on the doorstep, ready to take off as if on a routine hunt, knowing however that this step would end only when I had crossed the national border. The sun rose and I withdrew into the house, exchanged the shotgun for my laptop, and sat down to work. From within Abacha's camp, our sympathisers came close to despair. A fishing boat had been readied in Lagos, stood down, summoned again, earning me the imprecations of its owner, Chief B.A., a normally cautious businessman, who threatened that if I ever commandeered his craft again and failed to board it, he would personally hand me over to Abacha. A colleague accused me of seeking martyrdom. Others wavered, uncertain of the hazards – and outcome – of any choice. A handful felt that it might be a good thing for the cause – *if that madman made the mistake of arresting you!* Oh yes, they argued, then the world would have to ask what was the fate of lesser beings, and Abacha would learn just what it meant to fly that far in the face of international censure. Even in Ọ̀yọ́ town, halfway to the border, my friend Francis Oladele, pioneer of the Nigerian film industry, urged me to remain - Abacha would not dare, he insisted. Deep within the cells of my marrow, I already knew better. I tried to make light of the dilemma, justified another day's delay by going for a final hunt. We would read the entrails of any bird or mammal that fell, I proposed, then take a decision. No one laughed.

I dawdled, not because I underestimated the complexed despot, but because of a deep resentment that, at sixty years, I was again about to be dislodged from home - and by a being I truly despised. I knew his record from the Civil War, so did the Army. Abacha was a prime player on the killing fields of the MidWest Region - men, women, even children - after the Biafran forces had been routed. The future maximum ruler did not discriminate. It was sufficient for him to be spurned by a woman or lose her to a rival, and a killing was guaranteed. Shehu Yar'Adua, then Chief of Army Staff, had recommended his dismissal from the Army - not that I knew this at the time, any more than I knew that - irony of ironies - the man who overruled this recommendation was none other than General Olusegun Obasanjo, then Commander-in-Chief and Head of State. Years later, Obasanjo would come within mere whiskers of death by firing squad under the machinations of this same psychopath, while Yar'Adua perished in his prisons, his arms tied behind him as he was forcibly injected with poison. Not for a moment did I believe that the Nobel had conferred a charmed life on me - *he wouldn't dare touch you!* Not touch me? This man, I knew, would gladly flavour his *tuwo*[4] with the *ngwam-gwam*[5] of my head. No, it was simply that often fatal contradictory state of mind - I knew that it was time to leave, but did not want to.

I had developed a lethargy whose primary cause I continued to refuse to admit to myself: this exile could only be an embattled one from which there would be no retreat. That prospect made my return an uncertainty, and I had grown deeply attached to the tranquility of my private environment. Despite frequent forays

---

[4] A corn mealie, popular in Northern Nigeria.
[5] Eastern Nigeria delicacy, made from chopped-up head of sheep or goat.

into the cauldron of the nation's politics, indeed, perhaps on account of those very eruptions, the quiet rhythm of my Abẹ́òkúta retreat had become essential to a desperate need for an inner equilibrium. It had nothing to do with a 'creative environment' – it was an interweave of tactility, smells, the muted sounds and silences that compensated for often resented public impositions. I knew of nowhere else in the world where I would rather be, at any moment, and for any stretch of time. At sixty, the thought of an indefinite separation from my Ajẹ́bọ̀ sanctuary was intolerable. My preference was to go underground, become truly 'elusive' but – within reach of my cactus patch.

Objectively however, I had no answer to the insistence of my embattled colleagues – we needed an opposition radio, and I was the one, they felt, who could bring it about. The wife of the imprisoned president-elect, the combative Kudirat Abiola, to be later felled by an assassin's bullets in a busy Lagos street, would wring her hands, lamenting whenever we met: *Prof., radio tí a ò ní yi, ó njẹ́ wa ń'yà.*[6] I promised her that she would have her radio – this was one contribution I had decided that I must make, from the outset. In my hunting expeditions, miles from human habitation and even lost in a forest fastness, I had frequently come upon the incongruous sounds that could only have come from a radio. Following the direction of the sound, I would come upon cattle drovers with their transistors, their only connection to the outside world.

There were however other pressures from every side, an unfair imposition, I sometimes felt, from a collective undertaking – only WS could mount a successful overseas campaign for the democratic front, or mobilise resources if, as seemed increasingly likely, we had no choice but to engage in armed resistance. Much mythology surrounded these expectations. Still, I could not deny that I did possess some advantages that others lacked. Nothing approaching the magical potency that they all imagined but, what did it matter anyway? It was one of the factors that went into reinforcing the nation's morale. Till today, many believe that I raised millions that

---

[6] Prof., this radio that we lack, it is causing us much grief.

sustained the democratic cause, and that Charles de Gaulle's commandos during the French Resistance were mere Boy Scouts beside the warriors I had infiltrated through the Nigerian borders, awaiting only my signal for the final liberation of the nation!

The irony of my night ride through the Nigerian forests would remain lost on me until much later – that is, I did not even recollect at the time that, only a year and a half before, I had been forcing my way *into* Nigeria in a near equally outlandish manner, through a series of man-made obstacles that were no less determined than Nature's slip soil, gullies, boulders and tree branches that sometimes threatened to decapitate my driver and me. Even a mild equivalence of the police role had not been lacking – a tense moment at embarkation, when I clearly identified a man as a border agent, but one who was cold sober and intense, and I wondered if I had not left my departure till too late after all. The precautions we took had been thorough enough – only a handful were involved – so I had full confidence that our security had not been breached.

The arrangements had been in place for months, and only awaited my decision to activate them – false trails, improvised exits, the familiar hunting expeditions that were so well known to the SSS – the State Security Services – that its code name for me was *Antelope*. As a matter of fact, I did find that rather troubling, if not downright unflattering. Was this all they thought of me? As game to be hunted down and eaten? Not that I was after anything glamorous, I did not aspire to any of the more lordly species – assuming that the SSS had been generous enough to have offered me a choice. After all, the name I had chosen for myself during the 1983 fight in Ọyọ State against an earlier fascism, that of the National Party of Nigeria, was the modest *Tracker*. Still, I consoled myself that perhaps *Antelope* was a concession to my supposed elusiveness, or my passion for hunting. If I hoped, however, that my namesakes in the bush would learn that we were now bound together in these unsolicited naming rites, and lose their suspicious attitude towards me during my incursions, I was mistaken. They continued to make our encounters as meager and as frustrating as possible.

For the urban denizens, I had loudly announced plans for rehearsals of *The Beatification of Area Boy*, to keep the SSS reassured of my continued presence in the country all through December. We tied down the obvious government spy squad around my office by having my car driven there with regularity even when I was nowhere near the office, maintained a semblance of normal activity through the usual stream of callers, some of whom had been given appointments that I never meant to keep – they would understand everything in due course! That ruse must have worked well enough, since the SSS detail along Lalubu street continued to haunt my office dutifully for a full week after my escape, when I finally presented myself at the UNESCO headquarters in Paris, for a press conference. Sani Abacha went berserk, dismissed the top echelon of the Immigration Officers at the Ìdí-ìrókò border through which he naively presumed that I had made my escape.

Yet, at departure point, an unmistakable agent had surfaced who pretended to be just one of the nocturnal crowd. While we waited for the canoe to arrive, he hung around, avidly scanning my features whenever he thought I was not looking, quickly taking off his eyes when I turned my gaze on him. When a rough meal of watery beans and *gari* [7] was prepared for my escorts and me, famished as I was, I took one look at it and my expression showed that I would prefer to fast until we reached the Benin side. This volunteer minder could not wait to offer to dash over to a not too distant goods shack where he could obtain some bread and tinned sardines, and even a bottle of stout. I told him, factually, that I did not drink stout, but lied that I was not hungry. If he had insisted, I would have accompanied him, as I had also resolved not to let him out of my sight until we left.

The tensest moments came as we began to board the canoe, after the loading of goods was done. This helpful figure of indeterminate functions took out his torch and began – quite unnecessarily but acceptably – to beam the torch against the floor of the craft, guiding the feet of the passengers. When it came to my turn however, he shot the beam straight in my face and kept it there. I pushed his hand away. Even with his eyes hidden behind his torch, behind all his unctuous concern for my safety, I could see a pair of fevered eyes fastened on my face, feverishly attempting

---

[7] Farina from cassava.

to recollect its features - or was it memorise them? I hoped it was the latter but, prepared for the worst, my hand closed around the Glock pistol I still had strapped to my waist. After that gruelling ride that had brought me just one river's width to safety, I firmly decided, I was not about to become an actor in any weepy movie of last-minute reversals, where the fugitive, with one foot virtually on the soil of freedom, is dragged back into captivity to the gnashing and wailing of violins!

The sudden roar of the canoe's outboard motor drowned the sounds of any tragic mood orchestra waiting in the wings, and the facial inspector leapt back on shore. It took no more than five minutes, and we crossed the innocent stream that demarcated the formal spaces of two nations. The 'wharf' on the Benin side was a broad, flat slab of rock on which the reverse track contraband was already waiting, laid out in neat rows. A few minutes to wait while the motorcycles, then the bales of merchandise were off-loaded, I stood apart from the jostling bodies, staring across the stream, this moment of separation branding itself onto a template of infinite sadness.

For one who had sworn to himself that no tyrant would ever again chase him off the bounds of his nation, it was a moment of bitter defeat. Even when the choice is willingly made, exile sinks into one as a palpable space of bereavement. At that moment, I believe I died a little.

What I tasted in my mouth was worse than ashes, I distinctly felt the crunch of cold cinders between my teeth, and they set them on edge. The river bank was spare of cover on the Benin side, so now that we had parted company from dense, overhanging foliage, the clouds also parted to bare the landing of all subterfuge in a wash of moonlight, as if to ensure that this place of leave-taking was deeply etched on my mind – every detail of that moment, the stolid slab of rock basalt, the bales of smuggled goods, the practised motions of the passengers as they emptied the canoe of jute bags, outsize cartons, cylindrical portmanteaux that I thought had disappeared with the advent of cheap, infinitely expandable plastic suitcases, *Ghana-must-go*[8] bags, sealed baskets and tied-up bundles. With the casualness of practised hands, the

---

[8] Local name for an all-purpose Jute bag, with a later notoriety for underhand dealings.

canoe operators piled rolls and boxes in improbable shapes across the carriers of the now off-loaded motorcycles, or hauled them onto the heads of waiting porters. Already the canoe was spluttering towards that opposite bank and the question that came to mind was – when again? In that moment of self-pity, the line that sprang to my mind came straight from childhood, when I made a habit of appropriating to myself those lyrical lines that the bible could offer. I tried to recollect – was this from Songs of Solomon or the Psalms of David? *By the waters of Babylon, we lay down and wept...*

...except that I did not feel in the least like weeping. A huge wave of rage swept through and engulfed me, voiding all other emotions. Would he triumph in the end, the tyrant who had brought this upon me? Just how much was required of any individual in his lifetime? Was my life now bound together with a killer, albeit in absolute power, in a struggle to the death? How long would it take before a savaged people woke up, recovered their sense of worth and knocked him off his pedestal into a hole so deep that generations to come would seek his remains in vain? What role would I play in this, for how long and at what cost? The rest of my life? Would I perish in the attempt? Mercifully, there was not much time for further self-pity. All too soon, it was time to climb back on the pillion and resume the journey, riding at a more humane pace through the Benin forest.

The insides of my thighs ached. These were muscles that had never been subjected to an endurance test, and I marvelled yet again how the body so easily takes for granted every strand of muscle or ligament that makes it function, forgetting that some simply never come up for use in years, or decades. Even if I had been a chronic jogger, it would never have occurred to me to prepare the inner thighs for a ten-hour journey on a motor-cycle pillion. Three times I was compelled to ask my pilot to stop while I walked up and down, improvised exercises to regain circulation and loosen up the muscles as they were repeatedly assailed by severe cramps. They ached so badly that I began to fear that I might have done permanent damage to myself, some calamity such as uncontrollable muscle spasms in the future. As a hapless passenger, with nothing to do except stay glued to the seat of the motor-cycle, the night passage was fertile ground for the direst imagining. In addition to three stops, I was thankful when we came to streams that had to be forded, or when we stopped to refuel the tank from the spare jerry-cans with which we were amply supplied. I was even thankful for spills in sudden marshes or loose soil. As we rode deeper into the forest, my face was steadily lashed by branches. My driver did his best to sound a warning as a branch loomed up round a corner and he ducked but, it was mostly pointless. I took vicious slashes, began to wonder if the branches were exacting vengeance for the nocturnal disturbance of the peace of the forest. I could hardly complain; my companion took far more whipping than I did.

Occasionally, we ran into night caravans of smugglers, strung out in a line, loads of every form of merchandise on their heads – but mostly of cloth and plastic vessels – plates, bowls and other utensils, flasks. They had obviously come up from the Lagos factories and had a ready market in Benin and Togo, neither of which, I presumed, had any such factories. Using the clandestine routes meant that they could avoid payment of duties, but also escape harassment by rapacious customs officers whose exactions could prove even more onerous than the legal customs duties. Not too far off, muffled by dense vegetation, came the sound of a lorry engine, retreating. I guessed that the driver had taken his passengers as far as he could on a barely motorable route, disgorged them, and was returning to collection point for the next group. It struck me again and again as absurd, this separation of peoples into artificial nations, peoples who, despite their occasional wars, nevertheless regarded one another as one of a racial kind. Now they had to brave the forests and unpredictable border patrols in order to ply their time-ordered trade, gather at feasts of reunion and celebrate their ancestral bonds.

I thought then of the people of Bobo-Dioulaso in Burkina Faso to the north-west of Nigeria, of whose annual homecoming for the obsequies of the departed I had learnt during my research days. That custom was only a focus for a much larger purpose however. At this annual festival, all the people came together, both from the nation's metropolis and from beyond the borders of the nation that was once known as Upper Volta, bringing news, retrieving relationships and – 'burying' those who had died outside the community, but now with appropriate rites that involved weeks, even months of preparation. I wondered if I would one day be brought home, even symbolically, to rest among my own people.

It was then, I now believe, as the motor-cycle plunged southwards into the Republic of Benin, placing a stamp on my exile, that I formulated the last wishes on my remains, one that became an obsessive catechism: *if I should die outside my own borders, bury me in whatever alien land I expired – as long as Sani Abacha still bestrides the nation at the time of my death!* The thought of Bobo-Dioulaso set off the fear, and I recoiled in horror at the prospect – that the gloating feet of such a ruler should trample over the same soil that held my remains. It would later become an all-consuming dread, perhaps the only visceral fear that I nurtured throughout my years of exile. I imparted strict instructions to my family – let no well-meaning relation even think of bringing my body home as long as that monstrosity holds sway over the portion of earth that I consider my own! Lost on me was the irony that, only seven years before, I was incapable of one moment of tranquility until I had brought home the remains of my friend, Femi Johnson, and re-interred him in the earth of Ìbàdàn.

We had set out from Ọ̀yọ́ just before daybreak in order to hole out at Ìsẹ́yìn until the motorcyclists joined us for a ride that would begin before the onset of darkness. It was a routine safety precaution, but in fact, I needed a final ramble in the woods, if only as a token farewell. Two birds fell, and I sent them back to Francis with my escorts. Now I wished I had kept one – a small fire, a rushed barbecue – bliss. Instead, nothing had passed between my lips since morning. I thought briefly of the streams we had forded and dismissed them – they were not the answer to my thirst. With the prolonged privation, my mood had hardened, my concerns had undergone a drastic change! Democracy, Sani Abacha, the SSS and the rest of the impositions of the world faded into irrelevance. The moment the motor cycle wheels began to churn deeper into the Republic of Benin, with the bush track yielding to motorable, though still untarred road, all my worldly and spiritual desires took on a marvellous simplicity, a reduction to the barest essentials that were projected onto two events and two events only. They shimmered behind eyelids that were caked with squashed moths and other winged life of the night, wracking me in anticipation.

One was a long, cold shower. Next, a long, cold beer. For both, at that moment, I was prepared to barter even my cactus patch. My throat was caked with dust, I felt I could taste pollen, bugs and grime all the way down into the remotest coils of my intestines. The prospect of the materialisation of those two events took on an agonising intensity. After a ride of another two hours, the lights of human habitation replaced the swarms of fireflies that sometimes turned the bushes into fantasy groves, suggesting possible sources of inspiration for Fagunwa's *Ògbójú Ọdẹ Nínú Igbó Irúnmalẹ̀.*[9] I felt my tongue rattle in the dried gulch that passed for the cavern of my mouth and I swallowed hard in agony of expectation. The sparse lines of electric poles meant only one thing - beer, and refrigerated! I began to look out for familiar signs that would indicate the watering hole of the inhabitants of that region of Benin.

The lamps on the tubular poles were virtually transformed into advertising beacons for that single commodity – a supremely chilled beer. I understood, for the first time, the essence of mirages since, from time to time, I could swear that I saw a sweaty beer bottle thrust itself out of a billboard and reach towards me, cold to the touch, only to melt away again into the dark surround of the pool of illumination provided by the motorcycle lamp. Then, in a reversal of normal expectations, instead of the lighted road lamps becoming more frequent as we approached the first township, they stopped abruptly, even though the poles retained their precisely spaced levitations from the dark, and their lamps, unlit, were visible in the moonlight. When we entered Tchaourou, the nearest border town to our point of incursion, only the moon provided any glimmering of light. Then I observed that there were no lights visible in the houses, not even the town centre which, to

---

[9] The Forest of a Thousand Daemons, trans. WS.

make matters worse, appeared completely deserted. It was not long past midnight, so what kind of town was this, clearly not a rural habitation, yet the inhabitants appeared to have retired with the poultry?

It turned out that, most inopportunely, we had timed our arrival for the *Orò* [10] festival of Tchaourou. No one was permitted in the streets, all lights were extinguished – not even a cigarette could be lit out of doors – and women in particular could not be seen. It meant of course that the late night bars were closed.

My guide could not have been more disconsolate as he returned from conversing with a cluster of men who sat on their porch, speaking in low voices. He soon grew cheerful however and assured me that the situation would be remedied somehow, once we were safely within the compound of his 'uncle'. It meant also having to find his uncle's home with his lamp switched off. This was no simple task. Our destination proved to be a kind of way station for travellers of both night and day who had good reason to evade encounters with customs officers and the police. The house was just outside the township itself and could only be approached by two-wheelers such as ours. Threading our way towards it between the warren of houses was no different, it struck me, from swerving around natural obstacles in the forest, except that here, it was recumbent goats and sheep, upturned cooking pots and pails, stacks of firewood, open hearths, pestles and mortars propped against walls in narrow passages, even water wells – all had to be carefully navigated. Fortunately, the moonlight was generous. We made it safely, my pilot stopping to speak to two or three of the locals and deliver messages.

Arrived at the household of his 'uncle', welcome was spontaneous but also instinctively wary, marked by curiosity. Even in my dishevelled condition I stood out conspicuously, an obvious stranger. Eyes followed me but no questions were asked. Perhaps my pilot operated by telepathy, or the whispered conversation he had held earlier had involved couriers racing ahead through hidden passages, for, unknown to me, a miracle lay in wait. I had barely time to note that the uncle, in whose home I had been

---

[10] A masquerade of the male secret cult.

billeted, had his radio tuned to news from Nigeria when, courtesies over, he pointed to a seat, then waved towards a low table.

Seated in splendour on that table was that which I had spotted from the moment I entered the room, but from which I stolidly turned my gaze, fearful that a sudden visual assault might make it vanish but – yes – it was indeed a bottle of beer, moist and cold to the touch, the loveliest object that fugitive humanity could ever hope to set eyes upon. In a moment, its existential mission was fulfilled. It sat depleted but transfigured in the effusiveness of my gratitude. Next came the other half of the unspoken covenant. A crude shed in the open yard, with only a token cover to shield its user from passing eyes – within it stood a bucket of water. I threw all inhibition to the winds, peeled off my clothes and began to scrub the dust, grime and squashed flies off my body. And my hair received a rare soapy cleansing; it had become a haven for every species of bug and moth that ever coursed the night paths of the tropical forest, my hat having flown off early on the ride. Hardly done, my ears picked up a long forgotten sound that suddenly violated the calm of the night.

Orò festival! It said it all. I could have been in Ìṣárà, my paternal village, within an identical warren of mud houses that are so familiar in a typical Yoruba town. Even the red baked earth, with its mild contortions and undulations mimicked Ìṣárà. When the masquerade arrived, it went from house to house, decanting blessings and receiving tokens of the people's gratitude. I remained outside, beside the door, in the shadow cast by the roof of the house in that strong moon, watching this denizen of the spirit world flit from house to house, vanish within and emerge a few moments later with his retinue. Around us, retreating and advancing, the whine of the bullroarer. Seated on the ground, my legs stretched full length, I rested my strained back against the wall of my dwelling for the night, shirtless, basking in the night of Orò that the firmament appeared to honour with such a vast, luminous sky. Or perhaps it was the other-worldly orò that chose to call human attention to the splendour of that night by ordering all terrestrial lights extinguished. Certainly – and how could it appear otherwise to a voyager who had just survived the hostility of the night forest? – it seemed to me that I had never known a night so deep, so eternal and serene. All rage was gone, all physical pain subsided. I chuckled to myself as I recalled that moment of panic, now remote and unreal, when I thought that the busybody at the departure wharf had no other mission in life but to haul me back to Abacha's insatiable dungeons. My sense of peace was like a velvet cape that floated down to cover my semi nudity. I could not stem a wave of nostalgia for what I had known, longing for what could be, lamenting how simple life really was – a cold shower, a cold beer and then, an ancestral presence that roamed the night to touch a people deep down, within that secretive space where their communal soul resides.

The *Orò* spirit mask whirled gradually in my direction. It was a most unnerving moment because, a micro-second before, I happened to look down to my right side, my eye caught by a twin spot that was boldly reflected in the moonlight, glowing so brightly that I thought a pair of fireflies had settled on my skin. I saw what it was and was deeply embarrassed – had I broken the taboo? For they turned out to be the luminous bead of the Glock. I had retained this incongruous object next to my skin throughout the journey for self-defence. It had become such a part of my attire for so many months past that I came to feel undressed without it. Thus, after my shower, even here, I had routinely restored it to its place, beneath the waistband. I snatched at it, yanked it out and stuck it under my buttocks. I was in the shade of the roof however and no one appeared to have observed anything unusual. The masquerade procession moved to accept me into a community into whose bosom I had been thrust so unceremoniously. *Orò* spun round and round before me while I watched listlessly. One of his attendants offered me a kolanut over which *Orò* had whispered some incantation. It was all so familiar, albeit an infrequent manifestation. With only a variation here and there, this was a scene that tended to insinuate itself, unbidden, into telling moments of my existence. I took the kolanut and bit into it. *Orò* chanted what were clearly prayers in a low tone as one who communed with intimate forces. Silently, spontaneously, I muttered mine alongside his own. It was a deep, heartfelt, impossible craving – I prayed that the peace of this night, this pool of infinite solace, might endure for ever.

Dawn ended the magic of the night, ushering in a harsh pronouncement on my future existence. I stayed yet another night on the way to Cotonou, in Ouesse, in a hotel, to be alone, and to ease myself, body and soul, into that future. I had need also to shop for mundane items – a pair of casual sandals, a shirt, but most importantly, a new hat to hide my give-away head of hair. Abacha's agents, we knew, had already infested Cotonou, thick as flies. I kept, as the expression goes, total 'radio silence', even towards my family. My companions to the edge of the forest would have returned with news that my departure had been without any untoward event, and that there had been no sign of pursuit.

Fifty hours after my departure from Abẹ́òkúta, I was in Cotonou, announcing myself at the reception booth of the French Embassy. The French ambassador in Lagos had sent word ahead – he was one of the few in the secret, and indeed a willing contributor to one of my other optional escape plans. On my way to the embassy, I stopped at a cafe. As I fortified myself with an espresso, it struck me as a wryly defining moment of transition. Kolanut and coffee, both courted for their caffeine, yet culturally divergent in their essential natures – the ritual apprehension, cultural significances, social symbolism of one, and the straightforward, consumerist absence of complication of the other – I needed no further reminder that the brief idyll of the night of Orò was indeed a blissful culmination to the violence of exodus. The world of the espresso was worlds apart from that of the ritual kolanut of which I had so unexpectedly partaken. If I had any inclination to return to my cactus patch, it was now too late. I had submitted myself to an unalterable rite of leavetaking, and the prediction that lingered in my mouth was that of the kolanut, bitter and gritty.

Diplomatic Recruit

There was an old enemy awaiting me in exile. Often, my outside engagements had been conditioned by his real or projected presence in the environment. Invitations to conferences, workshops, lectures, etc., were subjected to a selective process based on avoidance of this implacable foe as the first principle of well-being, or indeed survival. Alas, the first casualty of my new state of exile, I soon realised, was – Volition. I had lost the right to choose my engagements. I was also precluded from taking refuge in hibernation like some of the most sensible mammals on earth, as obligations forced me into that enemy territory again and again. After a few days' grace, Old Man Frost – to give him his *nom de guerre* – arrived in all his malevolent majesty to welcome me formally into exile, his 'keen tooth' – thus certified by the non-tropical blooded Bard himself – only a fraction less dread worthy than Abacha's vampiric fangs. My talismanic adoption, since student days, of Shakespeare's *Blow, blow thou winter wind... thy tooth is not so keen...* hummed through tenderised nostrils, was sheer bluff, lacking in true defiant conviction, as invisible icicles scythed through successive layers of padding.

Freeze, freeze, thou winter sky... My re-induction took place on my way to Harvard University, Cambridge, after a short stay in Paris and London, weighing options. One winter blast sliced through my trousers as I stood outside Boston airport, awaiting transportation. No one had informed me that my sentence of exile would be served in the Arctic wastes. How could I have forgotten that this climatic zone shared the same latitude as Cornell University, whose topography – so reminiscent of my own university at Ifẹ – had actually succeeded in holding me down in the years between 1984 and 87! That was a record three years in succession, but then I was still imbued with the masochistic recklessness of a borderline middle age. Even so, I found more reasons to travel back to Nigeria than were warranted by necessity, especially during the winter months and, in the end, offers of a tenured association fell on frozen ears.

Now, ten years later, one visitation of the northern wind from the Great Lakes activated my rights to limited choice. Ahead of the next winter, I bade adieu to my disconsolate academic host, Henry-Louis (Skip) Gates, and fled southwards to Emory University in Atlanta, much closer to the tropics. A surprise lay in wait. Old Man Frost had leap-frogged ahead of me and I actually arrived in the infamous 1995 blizzard, Atlanta's first since the thirties, I was told! I did not believe one word of that, and felt like suing the university for deception over my working environment.

Still, the treachery was not repeated the following year, nor the next, and I settled in – a sarcastic expression if ever there was one – to be joined by my now intolerably menaced family, whose exit was also another cloak-and-dagger episode. Preparations were aided and abetted by the French Ambassador in Lagos, Pierre Garriguere-Guyonnaud, while my younger friends, Yemi Ogunbiyi, Olu Agunloye and others carried out the physical part of decoys, espionage, disinformation, and the eventual passage of the fugitives to safety. From friendly Cotonou, I monitored progress, and we travelled back to Atlanta together via Paris, where the American Embassy awaited them with the necessary papers. It was a huge weight taken off my concerns. The surveillance over their residence in Ikeja had reached a pitch of intensity that signalled the likelihood of some imminent development of a sinister kind. Additionally, our man in Abuja, *Longa Throat*, had urged on their evacuation, and that settled all further equivocation.

The U.S. Embassy in Paris also had a message for me – at least, one of its diplomats did. I was given a draft letter being prepared to protest the action of one Arpad Bosch, a highly placed official of the World Intellectual Property Organisation, an affiliate of the United Nations. This international civil servant had chosen to award WIPO's highest recognition, a medal for the defence of intellectual property, to one Sani Abacha – for his championing of intellectual rights. Arpad had even travelled to Nigeria for the honour of decorating the dictator in person. Such an act was typical of the grotesque gestures that would surface from time to time from the international community, and they never ceased to baffle me. Are you sure, I asked? It was true enough. Could it be, I suggested, that Abacha had undertaken to pursue foreign book royalties for Nigerian authors under the illusion that they meant oil royalties? The transit through Paris took a little longer than we had planned but, in the end, the action was formally repudiated and the official forced to leave the organisation.

This was symptomatic of my new role within the exiled opposition and I took it in stride as additional compensation for the stress I had undergone in extracting my family from danger. Similar battles were already being fought elsewhere as the foreign handlers of the Nigerian dictator sought to buy him respectability in the outside world, including attempts to name professorial chairs and fellowships after him in some American universities. The luckier of these institutions were those about which we had pre-knowledge – they could at least withdraw before the opposition publicly intervened and the scandal blew wide open. The others – two or three at least – were forced to make painful and embarrassing withdrawals, returning funds that they had already added to their coffers.

Hardly had my family begun to adjust to Atlanta when Winter's unconscious ally, Sani Abacha, won the fight to set up a consulate in Atlanta, now rated as the major bastion of opposition in his estimation – higher than New York and Washington – once it came to his ears that WS was hibernating there. Abacha's millions triumphed over the scruples of the City Council, and his killers were brought to nest right on my doorstep.

Obliged to travel extensively, the family was left vulnerable. The sinister addition to Atlanta's residents left me with no choice but to move them as far from Atlanta as I could – first to Rancho Cucamonga, then Upland, always on the other side of the American land mass and – *southwards* – in California. Peace of mind reasonably secured, I was free to extend myself as much as duty required. Only my head of department, his secretary, and the university president, William Chace, knew that I no longer lived in Atlanta. My activities were organised on an *ad hoc* basis, while I stayed at the Conference Centre Hotel. Student lectures, seminars, public interventions – including a memorable public dialogue with Archbishop Desmond Tutu – and other engagements took place en route other parts of the world or the US.

When Abacha declared me a Wanted Man in 1996, and placed me – with a number of others – on trial for treason, William Chace, a most astute political being, and former anti-segregation activist, immediately read all the implications and placed me under police protection. When the dictator's specially-created smear brigade began its offensive through the publication of an obscenely libellous journal under the cynical name of *Conscience International*, circulated world-wide, with a special complimentary copy to Emory's president, he promptly raised the level of protection. The university police – usually in mufti – met and escorted me through the airport and kept a watch on my safety, until I learnt to 'forget' to notify them of my movements. Not all the protestations of the even more solicitous Rudolph Byrd, my head of department, could persuade me to change my seemingly careless disposition. It was not that I underestimated the risks, but by then, we had an effective organisation. I simply preferred the less obvious measures that our membership in Atlanta and environs– including a strong presence of Nigerian taxi drivers – willingly provided.

I had not left Nigeria the hazardous route just to imbibe the air of foreign climes, and soon set about gathering a number of exiles – students and workers – together to create the National Liberation Council of Nigeria – NALICON. There was already an opposition movement, the National Democratic Coalition – NADECO – in existence, formed within Nigeria by a combination of former military officers and political veterans who had finally resolved to challenge Sani Abacha's dictatorship.

In late 1995, NADECO issued a number of ultimatums to Sani Abacha, the most crucial of which was a deadline by which to quit office. Abacha responded in a way that should have been predictable to those seasoned politicians and men of war – he came down heavily on them and scattered them to the four winds. Using brute force – arrests, fire-bombing and bullets, and economic blackmail – forcing banks to call in their loans, pauperising their businesses, etc. – he quickly brought some to their knees, while the more resolute fled into exile. They regrouped and resumed activities outside. To the intense resentment of several of its members, I did not even consider for one moment being part of NADECO, but was more than ready to collaborate with them in every way. With the exception of two or three members, I was temperamentally ill-suited to that company. One of their principal spokesmen had already compromised himself badly with Abacha, having canvassed for a business contract, and on terms that provided the dictator some of his earliest propaganda coups against the opposition – he simply published the outrageous terms of the proposal.

It went beyond business compromises however. The first *getting-to-know-you* meetings with NADECO made it clear that this was a ponderous organisation, top heavy, and with competitive egos. Singly, its membership boasted experience and dedication, collectively however, they tended to indulge in peripheral contests that consumed time and eroded their political credibility. There was a civil service approach to the taking of tactical decisions for the overthrow of a tyranny. NADECO became an even more difficult working partner, with the arrival of my favourite political maverick, Chief Tony Enahoro who, paradoxically, thrived on endless meetings, copious minutes, points of order, standing orders and the moving and seconding of motions, counter-motions and amendments to motions. Worse still, his very arrival appeared – without his intending it – to galvanise the already simmering rivalries within the movement, causing them to burst open. It was difficult to associate the committee man with the same activist who had challenged Sani Abacha in the streets of Lagos and barely escaped with his life. I began to avoid meetings that should normally enhance our collective efforts, since they led nowhere and only ate up time and scant resources – flying across the Atlantic ocean or the American landmass deserved some concrete justification in planning and results! Bickering was tearing that group apart, intrigues and the politics of ranking – little did I know that NALICON, especially when it moved to expand its membership, would come close to foundering on the same boulders of petty ambitions.

Actual undertakings were a different matter, and there, collaboration was not too difficult, especially on the diplomatic front. The case for the Nigerian people against a despotic regime had to be placed before the world, the international community challenged to come to the aid of the people. This was one activity into which I was immediately co-opted both through expectations and my own objective recognition of an 'international profile' that placed me at an advantage. It did not take long however for a long-held suspicion to harden into absolute certitude – if I was destined for a late-life change of career, it was not meant to be the diplomatic profession. I could turn myself into a *yo-yo* like the famous Middle-East Shuttle Diplomat, I was still no Kissinger. Still, willy-nilly, this became my primary field of assignment.

The average human composition – the range in which I group myself – has ensured that there is a limit to how many heads of states the body is built to encounter; how many ignorant – wilfully or genuinely so – foreign affairs ministers it can educate, how many cause-famished pressure groups it can co-opt, under how much solidarity by Human Rights organisations it can bask, how many meetings of the EU/UNESCO/UNO/OAU caucuses, etc. etc., it can attend, into how many diplomatic gatherings it can be escorted like Dresden china or else gatecrash, how many 'working' lunches, dinners, etc. it can absorb, how many congressmen and women, parliamentarians – feisty, outraged or impotently sympathetic – it could lobby, how many bureaucracies it can infiltrate, how much mealy-mouthing it can stand, how many compromises it can withstand, how many promises are left to believe in, how many immigration officers it can mentally eviscerate, how much debt – both moral and material – it can accumulate, how many slanderous counter-campaigns it can endure, how many safety measures it can tolerate, how many distractions it can overcome, how many betrayals it must anticipate... every day, it seemed as if I had reached the end of my tether, and yet, one dared not give up.

Indeed, when it was all over, I proceeded to dedicate the thousands of unused mileage benefits to the creation of a Frequent Flyer Family Foundation (FFFF) – the only salve that came the way of the resentful souls of my immediate and extended family for the disruption of their existence, and other forms of collateral damage incurred from the patriarch's political activities. Any aspiring beneficiary was obliged to fulfill a number of stringent conditions, my favourite being the applicant belting down the telephone some lines from the soul preacher, James Brown, as amended by my cineaste friend, Francis Oladele, whose home was my last stop before the midnight ride into exile, and commencement of a precarious life of economic brinkmanship:

Say it loud, I'm black and broke.

Any singing off-key, or insufficient infusion of soul feeling, meant instant rejection.

I accosted uncertain prospects, not even always within the targeted nations themselves, but in their embassies, sometimes in a hotel suite in a country where a head of state, a foreign or defence minister or simply an influential politician was visiting, and an ambush could be hastily organised, especially for leaders from the African continent. Great Britain, after the ascendancy of the Labour Party, a willing Canada, a sometimes ambiguous France, a consistent European Union, and the United States – at least at the beginning – were the most sustained recipients of such diplomatic importunings, sometimes undertaken by our collaborators, NADECO, and sometimes jointly. But at least NADECO had two experienced hands in this field, perhaps even more – one had been a minister of foreign affairs, the other a career ambassador.

Always with a succession of tightened jaws, grimaces, silent imprecations, moments of deflation, elation, imprisoned laughter... well, one could always chuckle afterwards, but at the time... hardly a laughing matter.

The Germans were a mixed bag. The junior minister of home affairs, with the attitude of an undertaker deprived of a corpse, had been unbearably curt – my visit was not even so much on behalf of our own struggle as in solidarity with our German chapter – NALICON had begun to sprout chapters in several countries. The chapter had joined cause with a group of Nigerians who had fled – or claimed to have fled – Abacha's persecution, and had entered Germany illegally. They sought sanctuary in a church, backed by its servants of God and their followers, but the earthly ministry was determined to evict and deport them. Our reception by this thin-faced undertaker hovered between diplomatic incivility and downright rudeness, the ultimate and unpardonable expression of which was – according to our German domiciled Nigerian liaison – his failure to offer us coffee and biscuits! Knowing nothing of these protocols, I was fortunately still left with his vocal nuance and body language – and were these eloquent?!

I responded by signalling an end to the meeting. I summoned my best Humphrey Bogart lop-sided smile, got up with my 'entourage' from our now clearly confrontational side of the table – the setting appeared to be always: government on one side, delegation on the other, (missing) line of coffee/tea/sparkling water and biscuits in the middle – and announced that there appeared to be no point in continuing with the session. My relief was unbounded on discovering that our Nigerian facilitator was even less of a diplomat than I – the missing coffee and biscuits, he insisted, demanded a stronger response, a total diplomatic rupture, maybe a challenge to a duel at dawn, sabers drawn on the banks of the Rhine.

Germany did make up for the boorish undertaker however. The first opposition radio – *Radio Freedom* – enabled by the dissident General Alani Akinrinade, had been set up in early 1995, and was functioning inside Nigeria. Its range was limited however, but it nettled the regime sufficiently for it to secure the expertise of the German Dornier company in the effort to track down the source of transmission. I flew to Germany. The Foreign Minister himself, Herr Kinkel, was more than generous and affable when I again invaded Rhineland – protocol of coffee/tea/biscuits being anything but lacking. Kinkel, whose grasp of profound issues was rather disparaged, we learnt, by his compatriots, displayed an appreciable sense of humour when I reassured him that I had not come to deprive the German company of legitimate business. However, forget that biblical promise – *Seek, and ye shall find* – I urged. This is a time to *seek, but not to find. Take Abacha's money and contribute a small percentage to our movement.* The minister chuckled loud and long, guaranteed the former, but declared that it was beyond his ministerial powers to make a business enterprise part with hard-earned money. Still, through Kinkel's influence – or at least with a nod in that direction, I am persuaded – two of Germany's foremost foundations made contributions to some of our logistical requirements, in addition to their own efforts at assisting some of our younger, imperiled writers.

Contradictions in the actions of some foreign governments remained baffling. An especially aggravating instance was the plight of Cornelius Adebayo, a former Governor of Kwara State in North-Western Nigeria. Having barely eluded a hit squad from Abacha, he headed for Ivory Coast from where he applied to enter Canada. But he found himself stuck for over a year while both exiled groups made strenuous representations, plied pressure on the Canadian government to allow him into their country, assuring its officials of Adebayo's *bona fides*. For an otherwise supportive government, this was a game of impenetrable ambiguity and cruelty that left a fugitive stranded in a place that was meant to be a temporary stop. It was incomprehensible, since the same Canadian government had shown itself so uncompromisingly hostile to the Abacha regime that it was forced to close its embassy in Nigeria!

In so many ways, the diplomatic field remained indeed part of the battlefront, and once, an eruption of that battle took place in a rather odd way. Long after the event, echoes of a day of – what else could have been responsible? – a paranormal attack would assail my ears, a day when turbines of a hydro-electric power churned uncontrollably, pursued me from meeting to meeting with commissions of the European parliament, vindicating my instinctive designation of water as an unruly tenant of the human intestines, especially its aerated version, and when taken on an empty stomach! Never had a delegation's leader felt so mortified, as a swallowed concertina or Scottish bagpipes insisted on participating in serious exchanges. All stomachs do rumble occasionally, but this was a marathon! In vain did I contract the stomach muscles, change seating positions, cough energetically, punch the offending guts surreptitiously under the table – all it provoked was a subversive will of its own, while my hosts did their best to pretend that a seismic event was not taking place right there, across the table. And it was not one of those one-off days when the work is done at one meeting, two or three, all humanely spaced out – no – it had to be the day of the serial killer rounds, when one was ferried from room to room, from building to building, with little recovery time in between. Nothing, not even a quick lunch could silence that wind bag until after the last of the day's engagements. I was left to wonder if Abacha's long arm had finally caught up with me, since we knew that he engaged a round-the-clock squad of marabouts both to guarantee his survival and pursue his enemies across the waters. No other explanation was possible – since the purpose was to undermine the talks – and this was evidently a stomach in demonic possession!

Even before the return of Abiola to the country in 1994, to be followed by his arrest, the United States had been a primary target of the opposition's diplomatic push. Less than a year into my exile, and soon after the birth of NALICON, I requested the US government to assist us in dismantling the Korean-trained killer squad set up by Sani Abacha, and placed under the command of the notorious Major Al' Mustapha. Our contact in Abuja – the one code-named *Longa Throat* – had supplied details of their secret location – a nondescript hotel in a crummy section of Abuja – their methods of operation, and a draft list of their targets. An overseas section was also being assembled – hence the resolve of the regime to establish consulates in Atlanta, where I was teaching, and also Houston which had also been identified as a den of

Nigerian dissidents. I passed the details on to Susan Rice, then at the Africa desk of the state department, urging, at the very least help in destabilising the killers' operations. Not long after, the squad struck down Alfred Rewane, a close associate and backer of Abiola, right in his bedroom, shot him through a pillow placed over his head. They had gained entry into the protected home by using a fake delivery van that claimed to have come from Rewane's own factory. Kudirat, the combative wife of that ill-fated tycoon politician, Abiola, was another prominent victim, shot in a busy Lagos street. A number of other assassinations and disappearances have since been traced to this sinister force, including the failed attempt on the life of the proprietor of *The Guardian* newspapers, Alex Ibru. He survived, but lost an eye and some fingers, and remained badly traumatised for years.

Susan Rice, together with a fortyish, serious-faced colleague, DeShaezer, had been part of a triumvirate with whom NALICON maintained direct contact in the White House, in addition to Anthony Lake, Clinton's National Security Adviser. A thoughtful, intellectual-looking type, he would wander into his subordinate's office occasionally, as if by accident, listening intently to the discussion for some moments. Later, we met privately in his office. Rice and DeShaezer leant significantly to the anti-Abacha cause, while the third, whose name my mind stubbornly refused to retain, was insecure, pugnacious, and a miserable listener. I distrusted him on instinct, even before we had a sharp exchange. With no attempt to disguise his resentment, he groused that everyone expected the United States to pull out their chestnuts out of the fires. I reminded him that most of the world's raging infernoes had leapt from US and European campfires. As the US policy appeared to begin to shift towards accommodation with our enemy, I fantasised my invisible self slipping into his stuffy little office to catch him working on sneaky memos that advised against us, slipping them in the dead of night under the office door of his boss.

Rice exhibited a quiet intelligence and a deceptive guilelessness that could easily throw one off guard. Once, when the spate of bombings began at home and we met in her office, she looked me in the eye and asked, without any preliminaries, if I was behind the campaign. The directness was unexpected, but I returned the look and told her 'No'. The subject of violence having been broached however, I asked her in turn – emphasising that it was a purely hypothetical question – what would be the position of her government if the opposition found that it had no choice but to take up armed struggle. Not to plant bombs all over the place but – suppose we asked the government to open up some abandoned facilities in the US for the training of volunteers – such mothballed facilities were scattered all over the American landscape – what would be the likely response? She appeared to mull over that for some moments but in fact, the answer was already obvious on her face – after the Iran-Contra affair, the US was not over-anxious to support any acts of insurgency, real or hypothetical. I imagined not, I replied, and there the matter ended.

It was, most ironically, South Africa that handed us our bitterest defeat. Civil society – the Labour Union, literary groups, Chamber of Commerce, the individual institution known as Archbishop Desmond Tutu, and other public leaders remained staunch, but the attitude of the government slid from lukewarm to the level – in one instance at least – of sabotage. This took place during efforts to weld all outside based opposition groups into one. Towards that end, a congress was organised in Johannesburg in 1996, on the invitation of civil society. Kayode Fayemi, Olaokun Soyinka – my son – shuttled between London and South Africa, consulting with the civic leaders, government officials and representatives of the ruling party, the ANC. The go-ahead was given by the South African government and, at the beginning, all proceeded smoothly. Passports were gathered, sent in a bunch to embassies in London and Washington for visas.

Then, with no explanations, only that 'instructions had been received', the London embassy not only stopped issuing further visas but became passionately attached to the passports when we moved to retrieve them. The timing was near fatal. Delegates had taken leave of absence, wound up their affairs and geared themselves for the journey. Some had purchased their own cut-price tickets, non-refundable. We could not change the dates. I turned to Norway for help, specifically to Jan Egeland, the Secretary for Foreign Affairs with whom I was already acquainted. The spontaneity of the Norwegian government counted easily as one of the very high moments of our embattled existence. Visas were issued in record time, a number of flight tickets donated to the effort. Our friends in South Africa would not accept a shift of venue, however, and refused to accept a subjection of *their* democratic rights to the political whims of their government. It was a matter of principle, they said, and insisted that the conference be held as planned.

South African visas being already in possession of half the delegates, there was only one solution – we ended up holding the conference simultaneously at two venues. I presided over the South African group in Johannesburg on the first day while a colleague, Professor Sekoni, held the fort in Oslo. I then flew overnight to Norway, and chaired the final session. A two-way flow of faxes and telephone lines united the two groups, making it possible to take joint decisions. When it was all over, I was left wondering whether it had all been a merely imagined event or one that had actually taken place. The minutes, resolutions, plan of action and lists of participants fortunately testified that it had. Over and above mere records however, was the testimony of the human body in silent protest – on the flight back to the United States, I remained without recollection of time passing, without any awareness of the plane taking off, or landing.

I had hardly recovered from that exercise when, thanks to a meeting with the South African poet, Breyten Breytenbach, former prisoner of Apartheid, we found an opening through which we could advance the newly unified organisation from the beginnings made at the Johannesburg/Oslo meetings. The George Soros sponsored Goree Institute in Dakar, of which Breyten was a board member, agreed to facilitate the second meeting of the umbrella group, now going by the name of the United Democratic Front of Nigeria (UDFN). That gathering took place over strong diplomatic representations by the Abacha regime. The Senegalese government replied that it did not make a habit of intervening in a 'cultural' meeting which, to the best of its knowledge, this was meant to be, since it was sponsored by the Goree Institute.

It was a moment to be savoured, the solidarity of the Senegalese government with the democratic cause, and the coming together of twenty-seven organisations spread all over the globe – from Australia to Canada. Alas, the affliction I sought to escape in NADECO travelled with the luggage of a handful – a mere quartet, American-based – of the delegates. It served to increase my bewilderment at the craving for position and power in human disposition, one that seemed especially absurd where an intervention in the fate of millions is initiated from the position of a weak challenger. It proved to be a near death at nativity, a movement that was formed to liberate a nation from the very bane of power found itself enmeshed in a tawdry tussle for position.

I had declined any formal position within the new body. This however signaled a contest for what the ambitious quartet read as an opportunity for self-promotion into a vacuum, and the complete take-over of the organisation. The plot had been hatched well in advance. It began from the moment that the liaison officer for Boston discerned that I really meant what I said – I would not run for office and would remain content with my function as an informal ambassador to the movement. The irony of such jostling was totally lost on the conspirators – one, a self-hating Igbira – a minority tribe from the Nigerian hinterland – whose yearning to be mistaken for a Fulani aristocratic scion resulted in his changing his name from Daniyan to Dan'Iyan. Partnering him was an ambitious youth from Swathmore College, Jude Uzowanne, a Walter Mitty character. The third member was a labour unionist from Edo in Southern Nigeria, Tunde Okorodudu, an activist in his own right who fell under the spell of the fourth member and centre of intrigue, the liaison officer for the US, Boston chapter, Maureen Idehen, a pharmacist, who had worked closely with me and was central to the coordination of activities for much of the United States. Together, this Gang of Four – the accolade was spontaneously bestowed – succeeded in serving a timely lesson of the power lust even among a yet inchoate formation that sought to curb power at its most virulent and malignant.

It was a low point in the career of the anti-Abacha movement, suddenly compelled to confront the banal distractions of trite intrigues and personal ambitions. Expelling the miscreants took its toll. The liaison officer, the Boston based Maureen Idehen, made off with our scant funds, leaving behind a trail of bad checks. I should have been warned by the extra-long talons, garishly decorated, that she affected in place of fingernails, but this highly efficient intriguer was the daughter of an old school-friend and classmate. His visits to his daughter in Boston had even served as an updating source for much of what was happening on the ground at home, and his support of the cause was quite vocal. As it turned out, he had also immersed himself in position grabbing on behalf of his daughter, even to the extent of poring through the minutes of the Dakar meeting and placing transatlantic calls to argue with son – elected secretary-general – to champion the position of his daughter in the movement. To say that the entire episode constituted a personal embarrassment would be understating an experience of intense chagrin. I had the unpleasant duty of reminding the doting father that he was not a member of the movement and would he kindly keep sons and daughters outside an already draining undertaking.

Ironically, it was the 'vengeance' of one of the subversives that raised the profile of the opposition in the mind of the Abacha regime, far above its own ambitions or capabilities. A 'confession' appeared in a northern-based newspaper run by the brother of the Inspector-General of police, Alhaji Commassie, contributed by Jude Uzowanne. In it, the writer claimed that he had been involved in the recruitment and training of a secret army, that he was in fact, chief of staff of this force under my military command. In the meantime, naturally, he had had second thoughts, was now opposed to violence, had voluntarily quit the organisation for this reason, and was doing his patriotic duty by revealing these terrorist plans.

Of all the fabrications put out by Abacha's men about our activities, this was by no means the wildest – in any case, armed struggle, even from the start, was a subject that was openly introduced into discussions. This young man's claims, self-ingratiating concoctions though they were, did have one decidedly negative effect. They had, after all, emerged from one whose earlier membership could not be denied, albeit now expelled and turned a 'born again' pacifist. He had come into the UDFN through an affiliating group, and was assigned the role of mobilising the youth wing of the movement. If young Uzowanne's claim had been true, it would have been his second conversion within a year. Revelations came tumbling in, confirming earlier rumours of his instability. He was confronted with a position paper he had sent to Sani Abacha, outlining how the dictator could turn himself into the Pinochet of Nigeria. His intellectual prowess, of which he had no modest estimation, was humbly offered to Abacha for the historic transformation. A small, ambitious Walter Mitty character, emotionally unstable, Uzowanne would indeed have been a most unusual choice for a military assignment, being additionally short-sighted, virtually blind behind his inch thick lenses, and of such physical insubstantiality that the slightest wind from the heat of New York streets threatened to blow him right off the sidewalk on to summary execution by the traffic.

Alas, some of our supportive foreign embassies in Nigeria did swallow this 'revelation' without any qualification, reported to their governments which began to distance themselves from the opposition movement. This would have been a minor nuisance, on balance, since we were also positively served in other ways by this egregious piece of fiction. Certainly it played havoc on Abacha's peace of mind; all reports indicated that it contributed to imbuing in him a holy terror at the very mention of the name of WS or NALICON.

Such fears were further bolstered on a daily basis by a formidable weapon in our armoury – the Radio Kudirat, sponsored by Sweden and Norway, with some help also from the Westminster Foundation of the U.K. I had made the acquisition of the radio, formerly named Radio Democrat, my obsessive priority from the moment I stepped into exile and embarked on my diplomatic shuttle. Alani Akinrinade's Radio Freedom had played its part, but it was limited in coverage, vulnerable and intermittent. Much too soon, it fell silent altogether. With the powerful and secure transmitters of Radio Kudirat however, the entire nation was covered. Tens of millions tuned in to its two-hour transmissions every evening – our clandestine studies revealed – including soldiers in their barracks. Prisoners behind walls looked forward to this daily treat, huddled around transistor radios brought in by their warders. No single event boosted the morale of the opposition as reports of its corrosive effect on Abacha's equilibrium filtered back to us. The regime struck back in a number of ways, employing the same instrumentation of propaganda. One of its most sinister plots was to circulate rumours in the prison where the former Head of State, Olusegun Obasanjo was held that a Wole Soyinka squad was on its way to storm his prison and rescue the inmates. In the confusion of course, the former Head of State would be gunned down.

Generally, I preferred working quietly, and individually. Indeed it would be an understatement to state that I am more than allergic to being a part – especially as leader – of a delegation. However, a scouting mission undertaken by Kayode Fayemi with his long-standing colleague, the ebullient, irrepressible Tajudeen Abdulraheem and a roving new generation pan-Africanist, resulted in our most sustained, structured diplomatic offensive in Africa, with generous help from the Canadian government. The UDFN divided the continent in two, after identifying those governments that might be persuaded to pay attention to what was happening to us in Nigeria. Two delegations took off, not particularly bubbling with optimism, but at least we would leave no room for later excuses – *why didn't they come to us? We would have helped.*

It proved a productive recommendation. A number of the government leaders that we visited either feigned ignorance or were genuinely uninformed about the degree of repression in Nigeria. If the latter was true, one could only wonder what their diplomatic representatives were doing to earn their salaries and privileges, what kind of reports even a mentally retarded, but innately honest observer could possibly relay home except that the most populous nation in Africa was rapidly sinking into a state of power insanity that shamed a continent to whose aid nearly the entire world had rallied – however belatedly – when it was confronted by the humiliation of Apartheid. If my remarks to the bosses of those diplomats resulted in only one of them being deprived of his sinecure, those mostly frustrating visits, undertaken as an unavoidable duty, would have been worth it.

The tour was not a total loss. There were at least two noteworthy encounters with African leaders, though drastically divergent in the impressions they made on me. One was the Ugandan President Yoweri Museveni, who, as it happened, occupied a very special position in relation to our struggle. None other than Moshood Abiola, the elected Nigerian President, still in prison, had funded Museveni's revolt against the tyrannical misrule of Milton Obote, the former Ugandan President who was dethroned by the homicidal buffoon Idi Amin, restored by the idealistic Julius Nyerere of Tanzania, yet proceeded to surpass, it is arguably estimated, the atrocities unleashed on that nation by Idi Amin Dada, the 'Conqueror of the British Empire'. I was on my best diplomatic behaviour and resisted a strong impulse to remind Museveni that our fight was also that of his benefactor, especially when he took time off our urgent concerns to pontificate about the 'grammar spewing intellectual elite' who should be held responsible for the woes of the African continent.

I had not known that this was a familiar Museveni line of peroration, or I would have spared myself the irritation. Still flushed with the victory of his guerilla movement, he received our delegation late into the night. It was difficult to envisage him as a guerilla fighter, since he proved to be a poor listener – a guerrilla in the bush simply must *listen*, common-sense dictates, even to the language of the leaves! The Ugandan leader struck me as being more suited to his former profession as a schoolteacher, and an opinionated one at that, with an often embarrassing notion of the profundity of some of his most commonplace notions or comments. Still, once we succeeded in dismounting him from his hobby horse, he proved quite positive. Abdulrahaman, then resident in Uganda, ensured that our host and I ended up in an inner room where we spoke with greater confidentially. Contact continued for some time afterwards, through a specially assigned minister. Nothing material emerged from this supportive direction however, though we were able to ensure that Abacha's regime received no comfort from Uganda, especially within the Commonwealth. Proposed meetings with our contact minister each time he was due in Europe had a way of being called off at the last moment. Still, I had to accept the fact that Alice Lakwena's Lord's Resistance Army was stretching the headmaster's attention to the limit in the northern part of the country.

A year or so after our meeting, while our struggle was still on, we did meet again, this time in Davos, at the World Economic Forum, where we shared a podium. I was still appreciative of the attention he had paid us in Uganda and so, was able to react indulgently when he resumed his patchy pronouncements on African history, half-baked theories of African social development and whatever else, all delivered magisterially and with a bland indifference to the thematic assignment of the panel. Afterwards, I ran into some of his aides and implored them: *Look, you people must really try and place your man under some kind of restraint, or one day soon, he'll be taken to task on a public platform and ridiculed.* They broke into laughter and one replied, "Professor Soyinka, why are you complaining? You only had him for an hour and then you're gone, we undergo this every day. We can't escape him."

Impossible to imagine a greater contrast than Paul Kagame, then only the Vice-President of a nation that had undergone a near unspeakable horror, the like of which the African continent had never experienced in oral or recorded history. No visit that I undertook, either on my own or in delegation, could have been more poignant, and yet more bracing than that to Rwanda, where Kagame's liberation forces had routed the *genocidaires* and were pursuing them into neighbouring countries, but mostly into the central African jungles. At the same time, a government of restoration was being positioned, confronted with the 'impossible' task of suturing the mangled nerve-ends of Rwanda's nation being, restoring confidence in its corporate existence. Kagame, seven foot plus, every inch exuding intelligence and discipline, was a formidable force to encounter, and without any effort on his part to appear one. Even when he said, 'I am a fighting man. I love fighting', it was a statement that spoke of a disciplined vocation, delivered without a trace of bravado. It was a considered summation of a personal temperament that was also validated by the Rwandan circumstances. The same objective assessment informed his accounts of some of the horrors perpetrated by the Hutus on both Tutsi and Hutu objectors, his accusation of French complicity, and justified his decision to terminate the place of French as an official language of the nation. It made his confidence credible when he stated that, despite the seeming terminal sentence on national unity, his mission of reunification was already pre-determined.

With the same grounding in reality, Kagame went on to explain that it was necessary for him, the victorious Tutsi, to cede the top position of president to a member of the Hutu tribe while contenting himself with being the political second-in-command. A number of Hutus had also been victims, or else had been coerced into collaborating with the murderers. It was essential for the purposes of rehabilitation that one of the majority Hutu be seen as occupying the top prominent position. We had however built up an intimacy so quickly and effortlessly that he admitted – with a slight, apologetic smile that lit up a wafer thin face, sculpted like a wedge of the àbàtà kolanut – that yes, it was a temporary arrangement. When the fighting part was over, it was indeed likely that he would take over the political reins but – 'Right now, the arrangement suits me. I'm a fighting man. I love fighting.'

One of the continent's extremely rare breed of leaders, I thought, and if there ever was a moment in our search when I felt, yes, we could confidently entrust our volunteers into the hands of one man, it was there, in Rwanda. Indeed, recalling my brief student flirtation with soldiering, I could not help thinking how fortunate it was that Her Majesty's government had been unable to call on such a talent in its recruitment exercise. Kagame belongs to that uncommon leadership order beside whom one would willingly march into battle, and indeed relish the moment of confrontation with an overwhelmingly superior force.

The morning after our meeting was one that I awaited with dread, but it was a solemn obligation, not one that could be evaded.

One should *see*, even if one had already imagined. We were driven round to see two or more of the 'museums' that had been created to document the killing rage of Rwanda, testaments yet again to the unfathomable propensity of man that leads him to butcher and mutilate his own kind. Among such memorials was the optimistically named Mandela's Park. There were others that were simply plain fields, with rows upon rows of white crosses. We visited a hut stacked high with skulls, hundreds and hundreds of skulls, several with bullet holes, others with the unmistakable gash of the machete. A curator walked between the shelves, calmly dusting exhumed skulls and skeletons. The most poignant was a church into which the victims had fled, several deliberately lured with the promise of sanctuary, before the Hutu army, assisted by the vigilante killers – the *interhamwe* – were summoned. The bodies, now skeletons, were left exactly where they had fallen – these were the clothed skeletons, and the stories of their deaths were superfluous... the most enduring image of all – a baby's skull with a panga still embedded in it.

These were not of course victims of war, but of organised butchery, nevertheless the lessons remained sobering, and apposite, reinforcing a constant openness on the part of our opposition groups to dialogue at every turn. Neither NALICON nor UDFN ever made direct overtures to the Abacha regime – any such initiative, we knew, would only have provided material for hilarious propaganda. To every leader that we did meet however, we took pains to stress that same message – the Nigerian crisis could still be resolved by dialogue, and we ensured that we did not turn our backs on any such opportunity.

Abacha's first reach towards us came early – towards mid-1995 – through Air Vice Marshal, Ibrahim Alfa, my beanpole friend who had revealed details of Abachas's visit to him on the eve of the 1993 coup. Alfa's message was direct – *Abacha wants to negotiate. He says, choose your time and place, send your representatives and he'll send his.* Ibrahim took back my answer – *first, free all your prisoners.* For months I heard nothing further. Then came an apologetic message from Ibrahim, advising me to ignore any further invitations, not just from him, but from any other direction. *The man is not serious, he said, he has other plans, and I hate being used for a charade. He's only pandering to public opinion, wants to be able to claim that he's made overtures to the opposition.* Ibrahim resigned his commission as go-between and ambassador extraordinary, returned the use of the jet plane assigned to him from Abacha's fleet.

There was a falling out. Abacha had Ibrahim's bank – Alpha Bank – listed among 'distressed banks' and imposed impossible conditions for its re-certification. He attacked Ibrahim's other businesses and sought to pauperise him for his refusal to openly endorse the dictator's regime. They had a confrontation, during which Ibrahim protested – *Sani, why are you doing this to me? You know my bank is solvent.* Abacha feigned surprise, swore that he had nothing to do with the harassments and would look into the mistake. Ibrahim read the signs, withdrew from his normal Lagos/Abuja beat and retired to the safety of his village in the North. He died not long after. It was impossible to determine if his death came naturally, or was assisted.

The second and final overture, several months later, was the very stuff of melodrama. It involved a famous 'seer' who had warned the superstitious leader that his salvation lay in finding a common ground with the opposition, and specifically with WS who, he declared, was protected by 'a certain aura'. Abacha must be credited with an even-handedness in this respect: he dealt with both moslem marabouts and christian prophets, plus a sprinkling of indeterminate psychic consultants whose gory prescriptions provided some of the content of my play – *King Baabu*. So hush-hush was the operation with the 'seer' that the religious leader was persuaded to host some kind of church convention. Abacha's secret service personnel then dressed up as reverend delegates, went into secret sessions with the 'seer' to decide on the best approaches to the arch-dissident. They reported back to their boss, and the search then began for an emissary that could be trusted by the designated opposition leader. Someone remembered that my son-in-law, Tola Onijala was a diplomat in Foreign Service – and that was how Tola became the dictator's emissary to me in Washington.

He brought the same message as Ibrahim Alfa – a meeting at a venue of our own choosing, and without preconditions. Again I made the obvious response – before I would even table the proposal before the UDFN and NADECO, there had to be one precondition, and that was the release of all prisoners. Tola argued that my purpose was being defeated by such insistence. I warned him – in confidence – of Ibrahim Alfa's assessment of these overtures, an assessment that I fully shared. We had no time for cosmetic meetings that would then be presented to the world as serious attempts at a resolution.

Tola held on to his conviction – Abacha's proposed meeting offered the best venue to present such demands. If we insisted on that pre-condition and the meeting was aborted, the nation – and the world - would blame the opposition, and the prisoners would remain Abacha's hostages. Finally I said, all right, we'll make it a test. He's merely attempting to buy time to consolidate his rule but – take back the message that we've agreed to meet without pre-conditions. Our representatives will be ready whenever he is.

And that was the last we ever heard of Abacha's accommodative intent. No one in the opposition lost a second's sleep or let down his or her guard in deference to Abacha's approaches. On his part, at some moment that was difficult to determine but was definitely after these overtures, Sani Abacha raised the stakes in his assault on all opposition. Officers whose loyalties were deemed suspect fell victim to attacks by 'armed robbers' while others, like the luckless Customs Officer, Omitola, a cousin of the fugitive general, Alani Akinrinade, were disposed of in bomb explosions. After the death of Alani's cousin, his office was then raided and, naturally, bomb making equipment was 'discovered' in all its sophisticated glory. Originality was given scant consideration, since a cheque with Akinrinade's signature was also found within the car – just as a copy of Wole Soyinka's *The Man Died* had lain beside the body of the journalist Bagauda Kaltho in the toilet of Kaduna Hotel. It was a season of maximum saturation of every known elimination device, including, as would later be discovered, poisoning, which in all likelihood, was the fate of a number of sudden, mysterious deaths, especially within the military.

No one was excessively surprised when, after what he must have deemed a decent interval from the day of Sani Abacha's ascension to power, Idiagbon's former accomplice, the no-nonsense, 'incorruptible' General Buhari accepted to serve the all-conquering dictator, manning the so-called Petroleum Trust Fund with a free hand to dispense millions as he pleased. At home and abroad, the spectre of assassination hovered over every mind. Plots were manufactured to resolve the nightmare of resistance through the route of judicial lynching and opposition figures were rounded up, cynically accused of responsibility for the assassination *of their own colleagues!*

As for the outside opposition who continued to elude his roving assassins, Abacha unleashed a novel weapon – not original, but certainly unprecedented in its unprincipled inventiveness and its venomous intensity – he resorted to the weapon of slander.

A Digression on the Power of Slander

The spate of assassinations was indeed sustained, but assassinations were not only of one kind. Protecting ourselves against the obvious, we had overlooked the other kind – that of character. Not that it mattered – that is one assault weapon against which no individual or organisation has ever invented adequate means of prevention – something in the nature of a bullet-proof jacket. The Sani Abacha propaganda unit went into action and commenced its toxic rampage with the launching of the most virulent publication in the history of propaganda, the cynically titled *Conscience International*.

My son, Ilemakin, was the first to alert me to the existence of the journal – he had seen it on sale in a London magazine store which specialised in off-mainstream and foreign journals. My picture decorated the cover, which of course was designed to attract the curiosity of Nigerian, and indeed African readers. Within Nigeria itself, it was not on sale but was distributed free. Once, at a high society wedding in Ìbàdàn, a few dozen copies were unloaded on unsuspecting guests who eagerly grabbed their copies and took them home, only to discover the putrid contents.

Each issue was devoted, near-exclusively, to one prominent opposition figure at a time. I had the dubious honour of launching the series – Vol.1, No.1. At the very first glance, my mind leapt in the direction of the anti-Semantic product of the Czarist era that was later absorbed into the armoury of Nazi propaganda – *The Secret Protocols of the Learned Elders of Zion.* That feeling of empathy with an ancient, visceral violation did little to lift, in moments when I recollected its contents, the mottled cloud that would suddenly envelop my innermost space, even in the midst of the most energetic public activities. *Protocols* were directed at an entire race of millions; this was dedicated to the single individual, meant to be absorbed by just one human psyche without a dissipation in numbers.

The journal was produced under the direction of a Chief Abiola Ogundokun, an infamous politician who had served under Shehu Shagari, President of the nation between 1979 and 1983. Ogundokun's real claim to history was that he jumped bail in the United States after being charged with rape in a Baltimore hotel. He returned home, a fugitive in disgrace, but not in the eyes of Shehu Shagari who promptly made him a director of a government-owned chain of newspapers. Thereafter, he was allocated one hatchet job after another, a series of dirty undertakings that even some of the notorious enforcers of his political party, the NPN, would not touch. Year after year, regime after regime, Ogundokun's career underwent the usual ups and downs until Abacha's talent scouts spotted him in a condition of abject penury. He was clothed, fed, set up in an office in Abuja and generously supplied with funds. His assignment: to publish a journal of unprecedented grossness in the history of the Nigerian yellow press, as an offensive against all real and imagined threats to Abacha's regime.

Collaborating with Abacha's point man was the similarly qualified Major R.O.A. Salawu, who had been drummed out of a state organ that owed its existence to my initiative – the first Road Safety Corps in Nigeria, probably in all of the African continent. The Corps constituted my 'citizen response' to the insensate slaughter on Nigerian roads, especially between Ìbàdàn and Ilé-Ifẹ̀ where I lectured, a veritable 'slaughter slab' that devoured my colleagues and students and made a mockery of one's efforts to fill the latters' brains with knowledge. Major Salawu, alas, proved to have been more preoccupied in the non-humanitarian aspects of the undertaking, and eventually found himself, at my insistence, charged to court on over thirty counts of stealing, forgery, conspiracy, etc. Then came the Abacha coup and the trial was stalled, and stalled, and eventually hiccupped to a stop. The thieving major was mysteriously reabsorbed into the same organisation which, being the brainchild of the now exiled dissident, had become a nest of subversion in the dictator's mind. The Corps was undermined, its autonomy and public integrity badly compromised. It was only a matter of time before Salawu teamed up with his soul-mate, Chief Abiola Ogundokun, in the service of the greatest reprobate of them all, General Sani Abacha.

In a lighter mood, I sometimes speak of the earth-shaking achievements of fellow Nobel Laureates, whose discoveries bestow palpable lustre to the Nobel directory of recognition. Some have solved the riddle of the DNA, others have transformed communication technology, yet others have found the cure for hitherto incurable diseases and so on and on. None of them however, except this writer, I boast, has ever waxed a musical record. (For all I know, this may be an unfounded claim, but it makes a good story!) That record, an LP, was titled *Unlimited Liability Company*. It was made in 1983, at the height of the profligate rule of the National Party of Nigeria. One solitary verse in the lyrics – in the vernacular pidgin English – was devoted to the US escapade of Ogundokun:

> *Another Director is a Wanted Man*
> *He commit rape for Washington, DC*
> *He run come home, you give am bigger post*
> *As Director of a chain of newspapers*

The randy chief had never forgotten nor forgiven.

The least putrid ingredient in this toxic broth – from which the rest can be imagined – was the attribution of a daughter, then twenty-seven years old, whom WS was supposed to have fathered on one of his students. So thorough was the propaganda work that a physical daughter was launched – albeit furtively – on society. A most garrulous young lady, she visited members of my family, circle of friends and colleagues, an ex-governor or two, etc., to advertise her parentage. Obviously not so well coached however, or perhaps weaned on pulp novelettes, she volunteered a slight embellishment: she was the daughter of a housemaid in my family employ, and knowledge of her true paternity had come through a death-bed revelation by her mother. While we battled Abacha from abroad, the young lady, named Yinka – to rhyme with Soyinka perhaps? – was welcomed among the well-to-do, ate free in restaurants, partied in discos and night-clubs – all expenses on the house – and generally lived off a land that was mostly peopled by Sani Abacha's opponents. Her claims did not alarm me as much as the dangers posed by her infiltration of my family and circle of colleagues. I took action as soon as I learnt of this new family member, caused a letter to be circulated through her known haunts, though this did little to stem her free-loading career.

It was not an original ploy. 'Unacknowledged' children, already long in the tooth, do have a habit of turning up after the death of a prominent figure – the variant here was that the confectioners of the sob story did not even wait for my passing away! Equally unoriginal, but of mind-numbing diabolism, was the squalid catalogue of attributed crimes which were indeed based on actualities – only they belonged, right down to the most sordid detail – to Major R.O.A. Salawu, even as set out in the police charges against him.

Beneath the outward *insouciance* – this truth must be admitted – the contents of that journal drilled a corrosive hole into the most secretive core of my being. I had to improvise, go through processes of trial and error – from immersion in overwhelming symphonic music that drowned out the voices in my head, to spells of meditation, those exercises that stood me in such good stead in prison solitary – in order to counter the threatened erosion of my combative consciousness. My outer shrug was a lie; we had work to do, and others needed the impervious confidence of my leadership. For the sake of the opposition – as well as for my family – I had to hide a suppurating wound that ate into my vital organs.

Several nights I lay awake, wondering if any human psyche was really equipped with an internal armour, strong enough to protect the essence of his being against a seepage of such venomous intensity.

Yes, those publications did succeed in depriving me of several nights of my accustomed sleep, and even ate into my waking preoccupations. My concentration would trail off occasionally in the midst of a discussion, as a phrase in a tract of irredeemable vileness flashed across my mind. Reading a book, minutes swept by – five, ten, maybe fifteen or more – and I would find myself still on the same page, unable to recall what lines I had read, what the book itself was that I held in my hand. Over and over again this would happen until I gave up after hours of zero absorption.

I was not unaccustomed to gossip, defamation and slander – I doubt very much if any people in the world can match the conglomeration called Nigeria in the propensity of its inhabitants towards the game of character denigration – it is all part of a justly remarked creative energy, unfortunately much of it of a negative, even self-destructive temper. This brand of the abuse of inventive energy has driven many valuable individuals away from any form of civic commitment, or public service. In this publication however, the most tenuous restraints had been jettisoned. A total stranger, a *doppelgänger* with an odious smirk, was being invented between the lurid pages, and I was swamped by this illicit being, this fake persona who dispensed spores of corruption guaranteed to percolate through the most protective layers of society.

Group therapy sessions, so favoured in the United States, represent for me the ultimate in the abject abandonment of human dignity, self-respect and the human will, a negation of that very private space within which, declares my temperament, the deepest wounds are healed. But then, it must be understood that I have a deep contempt for much that goes under psychiatric practice, especially in the United States. *I have an appointment with my therapist* – and off he/she goes for a weekly, twice, thrice weekly session with a shrink. Obviously, these remarks do not apply to the genuinely in need, victims of diagonised mental illnesses and disturbances. Among my acquaintances, alas, are several who make a fashionable pastime, or simply a consumption habit, very chic – like attending wine-tasting sessions – out of viable modes of treatment for psychiatric disorders. So how come it that I have caught myself wondering why no psychiatrist appears to have considered a particular area in which I have felt that I could do with some serious counselling myself – and of the groupie variety? For this is the stark truth, during that dark period, I sometimes felt that perhaps I could have done with a group session over this one experience – slander! Forget the dismissive shrug of the shoulder, the snarl of genuine contempt for the purveyors of degrading fantasies – something sticks to the soul, and succeeds in dragging down the spirit, intermittently, and sometimes for prolonged spells.

I understand why the word 'smear' is such a preferred expression – yes, one feels smeared, dirtied, polluted. Feeling pure and uncontaminated within is all very well, but anyone who has ever accidentally stepped in dog excrement – a guaranteed event in some neighbourhoods of New York - knows that you can scrape your shoes as much as you like against the pavement, step deliberately in puddles and then rub the soles against tarmac, gravel, patches of grass, even mud – that peculiar, nauseous odour of *dog shit* simply never disappears - or what really matters – you feel it never does! The smell hangs around you or - again this is what matters – you are convinced that it does. Even after you have finally reached home, taken off and left your shoes outside, the sense of a foul stench continues to dog you. And of course as you walk alongside or share public spaces with others, the question surfaces – can they *smell* you?

Slander is very much in that vein. Even among colleagues and acquaintances professing the usual trust and respect - well, they have heard of course but, do they believe? When they say, 'oh, no one believes a word of that', are they really thinking, *Hm. The dirty hypocrite. Exposed at last*? Maybe, after all, a few sessions among those thera-groupies would have helped. With this particular affliction, I believe that there is need for a forum where one can compare notes. No holding of hands in a circle, no group meditation, none of that 'confessional' attitude, no passivity roles in face of simulated assaults – no, none of that! Simply an orgy of music and poetry, lots of wine – the very robust – the favourite food of each participant, video clips of libellers undergoing mild forms of social censure – such as flaying alive, slow roast over an open fire, hot tar and feathering, public castration or simply splayed over an anthill from dawn to dusk under an unblinking sun, while the more energetic among the victims are provided air-guns, darts, for target practice on the effigies and photographs of such vile social malcontents. Brushes, pots of paint and broad canvases for some action painting should of course be provided for the more artistically minded...

Within the opposition, a few voices did propose a campaign of retaliation, targeting some of the more notorious props of the regime, such as Tom Ikimi, the Foreign Minister, or Ofonagoro, the Information Minister. It was pointless going after the principal himself – no mind was equipped with the fiendish imagination that could invent crimes to beggar the reality of atrocities committed by the innermost core of the Abacha regime. I shot down the idea however. The mental and practical energies that would be expended on such sterile activities were best reserved for psyching ourselves for the irreversible moment when – or if – we actually committed to armed struggle. We never did reach that moment but – as the Bard said – *the readiness is all!*

Requiem for an 'Eco' Warrior

The calls upon that state of readiness were not slow in coming, but none that equaled the brutal clamour of the event of November 10, 1995, an event that addressed the world in the most lacerating accent yet, even by the savage register of General Sani Abacha's rule. Primarily, the event was designed for the Nigerian populace – it warned, very simply, that a new force had come into its midst, a force that admitted of no constraints, no scruples, was contemptuous of world opinion, and would remain deaf to the counsel of the most revered. That event was therefore timed to make the maximum impact on global awareness, to serve notice on political watchers, Amnesty International, Human Rights organisations and other busybodies that the threshold for the impunity of power had been lowered beyond their meddlesome projections. The United Nations felt sufficiently exercised to send a commission of enquiry after the event – its members were treated with derision by Abacha's government, most directly and publicly by the Foreign Minister, Chief Tom Ikimi, who proceeded to lecture them on the limits of their mission. For most of us in the opposition – certainly for me - the state murder of Ken Saro-Wiwa and his eight companions signalled the futility, indeed the death of dialogue.

The trial of the Ogoni Nine, right from the beginning, was a proceeding that would be farcical but for its lethal implications. The defence lawyers, led by Gani Fawehinmi, had been openly taunted, subjected to indignities – on orders – harassed, and even rough-handled, as they arrived for each day's hearing. Stricken by remorse, one of the state witnesses had confessed on videotape that he and others had been offered lavish inducements to perjure themselves and were coached in what evidence to give – most especially against Ken Saro-Wiwa. The hanging judge, Justice Ibrahim Auta, dismissed this damning rebuttal of the state's case as irrelevant. Frustrated and unwilling to continue to be counted part of a deadly charade, the defence lawyers withdrew – albeit controversially – leaving the accused to conduct their own defence. A travesty of justice could now proceed, unimpeded by, and indifferent to the presence of international observers, a number of whom were, in their turn, barred from future proceedings. Every form of protest or intervention merely served to feed the arrogance of power. The spectacle played out its tragicomic script, right on to the designated end.

The verdict – Guilty – was fully expected. Very few individuals however believed that the sentence – death by hanging – would ever be carried out. I was not among the optimists. Power had mounted the head of the dictator; it needed its periodic nourishment in blood.

Ken had sought me out years before in Abẹ̀òkúta – perhaps in 1989 - to seek support for his Ogoni Bill of Rights – the inception of a structured struggle by the people of a devastated, oil-soaked land. The Ogoni remain one of those minority people in the Delta region to the South, with a distinct history, language and culture. Oil prospecting and extraction had doomed their land and impoverished their peoples, but conferred – still confer! - on the rest of the nation, the military especially and their business conduits, limitless wealth from the proceeds of the very agent of their misery. The Bill was a manifesto for Ogoni social, cultural and economic justice. Seeking my voice on behalf of that cause, Ken came accompanied by a small delegation that included his son, Ken Junior. Intense, committed and organised, they were demanding reparations for past abuse, neglect and state robbery, as well as a degree of political autonomy.

I needed no persuasion. How many times had I flown over the Niger Delta – the main oil prospecting part of the nation – and seen the landscape dotted with flues that burnt night and day, several of them for decades! Even before Ken's visit, I had contributed to a special feature in *The Guardian* (Nigerian) on the destruction of Ogoni land by the oil companies, the degradation of ancient farmlands, pollution of fishing ponds, and the poisoning of the very air. Saro-Wiwa's struggle was thus joined to mine within that most fundamental condition of social being that I summarise quite simply as – justice.

In the process of that struggle and its factional degeneration, four Ogoni chiefs had been murdered, denounced as collaborators with the military government and the oil companies. These were brutal, horrendous killings, totally indefensible. To the extent that the murders had been committed by Ogoni youth militants, members of MOSOP – the Movement for the Survival of the Ogoni Peoples – who owed loyalty to Ken Saro-Wiwa their leader, and that he failed to condemn the murders in the most rigorous language, Ken could be assailed with a measure of *moral* responsibility. But to accuse him of complicity, direct or indirect, was an act of cynical opportunism. To try him and his companions in a 'special tribunal, a military contrivance albeit with a civilian judge as its figurehead chairman, then convict them on the 'evidence' placed before the nation, was an act of minds totally devoid of all conscience, perhaps steeped in a diabolism that required human sacrifice. Finally, to proceed to hang those victims, before they had exhausted all channels of appeal that were open to them, even within the provisions of the decree that established the 'judicial process', was a step that no sensate person ever thought possible – from the Ogoni infant in his village to the sage Nelson Mandela. Mandela arrived at Auckland airport exuding with confidence and dismissing the anxious questions of journalists with a jovial wave of the hand. Had Abacha not personally assured him, in a telephone exchange, that he would not execute those men? After the deed, Mandela would give vent to his outrage in those unforgettable words: *General Sani Abacha is sitting on a volcano and I am going to make sure that it blows up under him.*

I was due in Japan, but not for a number of days. I left early, detoured to Auckland where the Commonwealth Heads of States were gathering for their biannual summit, and it was clear that they alone, at that stage, still commanded the weight of voices that might save nine innocent men from the gallows. My message was insistent, desperate and even strident: *only strong threats will save these lives, strong threats backed by unmistakable indications that such threats will be enforced if the sentence is carried out!* Occasionally, very exceptionally I encountered a member of the governmental delegations who listened and thought hard and deep, as if resolved to influence attitudes within his delegation or the routine caucuses. I would then walk back into Auckland's sunlit streets, desperately plucking courage from such meagre signs.

Today, even after the tragic *denouement,* I am mildly surprised to find, it is not anger or bitterness that I feel as my mind traverses the few years, only sadness, tinged, of course, with renewed pain, as I recall the responses of those leaders. In the main, very few of these Heads of Commonwealth States – former colonies of Great Britain from Canada through Asia and Africa to Australia – few, despite their varied experiences of humanity, had ever encountered, except in history books, the likes of Sani Abacha. Maybe even now, they still believe that Hitler, Stalin, Pol Pot and others were all mutants, created perhaps by undetected spores that spilled out of some secret Chernobyl, or the singular gas seepage from our neighbouring Cameroons' Lake Nyos that killed, in the eighties, hundreds of sleeping victims between night and dawn. These leaders conveniently forgot the lesson of Idi Amin Dada within their own club of nations. The majority of their foreign ministers, ambassadors, advisers, political analysts and others were versed in bloodless briefings, attuned to cynical lobbies, cocktail and diplomatic reception circuits where the formal attire is camouflage for both viper and dove, and the garb of atrocities is shed at the door, with a crested visiting card. The rest, like the rulers they served, were potential clones of the Abacha breed, and simply wondered what the fuss was all about.

I *knew* Sani Abacha – no, not personally, though we had met twice. It was simply his type that I knew intimately, a species that I had studied closely, lectured and written about. I did not share the confidence of the others, but I was hopeful – at least, at the start. And that was just as well. We were all doomed to be eviscerated by an invisible blade wielded by a psychopath from a place called Abuja. My only saving grace was that I had already felt its thrust, long before the noose tightened around Kenule's neck.

Even now, I still relive those moments of intense isolation, leaving one truly 'spaced out' – spaced out as in spinning in outer space - an alien among supportive, courteous mortals, with a feeling that clung to you, that, among the teeming population of that island, you were one of the mere handful of creatures – no more than two or three, one of whom was Ken's son – who knew, with absolute certainty, that a mass murder was about to be committed, yet you were powerless to stop it or persuade anyone to believe you. My final moment of certitude came from a chance crossing of paths.

On the streets of Auckland, where I exorcised my restlessnes and frustration with incessant walking, between appointments, a car drew up with young Ken, the son of the condemned man, with some workers from the Body Shop and other NGOs who were looking after him. Ken leapt out, holding out a cyclostyled statement from the Shell company. If ever there was a scripted form of Pontius Pilate washing his hands before handing Christ over to his executioners, this would be its very corporate equivalent! *If anything untoward happened to the Ogoni Nine,* the statement declared, *others were to blame – the agitators whose aggressive tactics only hardened the mood of the military regime and undid all the careful work of silent diplomacy being undertaken by their company, and well-meaning others.*

Yes, *we* were to blame, not Shell! Not the oil exploration companies. Not the military regime, its corporate allies, its kangaroo courts, but we! I handed back this tract of self-exoneration, of company unctuousness, and – it seemed clear to me – accessory knowledge. In my distraction, I thought I had spoken aloud, and flagellated myself long afterwards for an outburst that lacked consideration for the son's presence. But he assured me, much later, that I had the sequence of events all wrong. For what I thought I had blurted out without thinking was, *He's dead. They've decided to hang them. This statement - Shell knows of the decision already.* Even today however, the words still ring in my head as I thought I heard them, clear as the tolling of a funeral bell.

Walking myself into a state of total exhaustion from a sweaty pace around the humid streets of Auckland, mostly along the harbour, beginning to feel somewhat dizzy, and recognising why – I had had only my usual morning espresso that day - I entered a restaurant off the beaten track where I attempted to stuff my insides but again, mostly drank. Then, instead of returning to my hotel, I went to the improvised office of the Body Shop NGO – it was abandoned, the volunteers were between hotels, waylaying and canvassing whatever delegates they could. I knew why I remained there, in that abandoned office – it was to await the news. I did not wish to be found, did not wish to be invited to join in canvassing one more statesman or delegate. I returned to my hotel room only when it was late, and news of the confirmation of sentence by Abacha's military ruling council had been formally announced.

Now I had only one thought – to get out of New Zealand! I had an engagement in Japan – a gathering of Nobel Laureates – but we were not expected for two more days. That was just too bad. I sent a message, but did not really care whether or not I was met, or if I upset the protocols that appear to be encoded in the national genes of the Japanese. I had only one goal in mind – to escape the island that would shortly host a wake for complacent heads of states, their political advisers and their pundits. They would fashion statements of indignation and perform other accustomed rites of assaulted dignity – that would be their problem, it was no longer mine. The statement from Shell may not have been a death warrant, it was so clearly a death certificate that I no longer thought of Ken as being in the world of the living, and I had no wish to encounter politicians and statesmen after the event. Above all, I most certainly did not wish to speak to the press... *so what is your view on these executions, Mr. Soyinka?* Finally, I did not wish to witness the agony of a son when the now inevitable hole in his life yawned before him. All these sent me looking for the next plane out of Auckland, heading in the direction of Tokyo where I knew I would have a clear two days alone before I was again obliged to face the world.

I obtained relief from this irrational dread of pursuit only when the plane was airborne and out of New Zealand air space. Arrived in Tokyo, ensconced in a temporary suite by my polite hosts, I awaited the expected.

It came in the morning, in the form of a young journalist, ushered into my suite by a geisha-attired woman who had been specially assigned to look after me, sitting just outside my room at all times – I later discovered – as if my hosts from the *Shinbum*, the publishing house, feared that I might go into depression, do some kind of harm to myself. Ken Saro-Wiwa, and his eight companions, the young man said, had been hanged in Port Harcourt prisons, shortly after the rejection of their appeal by the Supreme Military Council of Sani Abacha.

Never were hosts more gentle, more sensitive, self-retiring yet solicitous. The editor of the newspaper house, sponsors of the conference, called on me. His brief stay was virtually soundless. In the most delicate manner, he indicated that the contents of the envelope that he was leaving on the table were for me to use in any way I wanted, that it was a gift of sympathy from his fellow executives who wished to ensure that I lacked nothing, yet were conscious of my likely preference to be alone. If I wished to look round the city however, I need only inform the lady by the door and she would get in touch with his office. Even the choice of the young journalist who broke the news could not have been more deft. He looked more like a medical intern with practised bedside manners, tried to hide his astonishment (and relief) that I took the news so well. How was he to know that I had prepared myself, that I had left Auckland wondering only how soon the killing would be carried out! He tiptoed his way out, saying that he knew I would wish to be alone. Not that he forgot his calling - he left his card on the table by the door - if at any time I wished to make a statement, he would remain on call.

Being prepared for the worst is always one thing; confronting its stark actualisation is another. There is a point at which the mind threatens to fold up, succumbing to its own destructive power of evocation... how does one erase the image of a friend and comrade, suspended in the immense loneliness of a prison yard! This was worse than mere depletion. My human landscape appeared to me irremediably desecrated.

The laureates, when we finally gathered, were founts of humanity. Mikhail Gorbachev, architect of *glasnost* and *perestroika* - we were meeting for the first time - seemed awkward in his anxiety to offer solace. Mostly, he shook his head in bewilderment. How could such a thing happen, he repeated over and over. Was it really possible? Could a regime act with such brutality? And then, businesslike - what should other governments, individuals and organisations do? On that he was specific - boycotts, sanctions, expulsion from world organisations - anything but platitudes! Gorbachev's horror was palpable. He was first to sign the document of condemnation and call to action that I prepared and proposed to my colleagues as a collective reaction. All the laureates signed it, joined by our Japanese counterparts from various disciplines. One of the many posthumous resonances for Ken and his cause, it was I who benefited from the therapy of having it vociferously adopted at the plenary gathering.

How ironic it seeemed - here was a product of the Soviet Union that was once defined by - and still is sometimes inconceivable without - a Stalinist mentality. A product - perhaps even a sometime participant - in the operations of that most brutal era, the era of mock-trials, banishments to arid wastes, tortures, forced psychiatric 'medications', executions that saw the end of so many artists, writers, thinkers, workers and peasants - yet here he was, actually shaking his head in disbelief at the crime of a dictator in some distant land called Nigeria? Gorbachev with the unusual signature patch of a red birth mark on his forehead, hamming it up with the Japanese, donning and strutting around in the 'peace jacket' – or was it 'love jacket'? – that was presented to each of us. And his ebullient wife Raisa, basking in the approbation of a world that had faced down a totalitarian monstrosity, whose internal collapse owed so much to the resolve and planning of her husband and his fellow conspirators. I spent most of my stay observing Gorbachev, a once powerful lord of a wide swathe of the globe, for all the world at peace with himself, oblivious, to all appearances, or maybe simply reconciled, to the ironic fate of 'the prophet that has no honour in his own land'. For by then, Mikhail Gorbachev's own people had turned on him. He was now fair game for every woe that had befallen the once all-powerful nation, most especially its economic collapse. Greatly reduced in public reckoning, I thought, he had become the great gift of liberty. The euphoria of freedom had all but evaporated within the Soviet Union.

The absurdities – albeit deadly – of ideological somersaults in the play of nations, the cruelties and absurdities of individual fates, all joined forces with personal self-revelations of that timely company – solemn, comic, self-mocking, an inter-cultural *potpourri* of experiences and futuristic schemes – to act as gradual restoratives to a battered psyche, contest its debilitation by ghosts of a horrific bereavement. I turned my mind to practical duties. The most efficacious antidote for grief – this I learnt from the death of my friend Femi Johnson – comes in a practical conscription of the mind, its re-direction at some practical task, however distanced, but related. In Femi's case it had been quite simply the single-minded task of bringing his body home. I pursued his exhumation, accompanied him home from Frankfurt, and re-interred him in the cemetery of the Chapel of the Resurrection, University of Ibadan. For Ken, not even knowledge of his remains was permitted – it was all classified secret, held close to the triumphalist chests of a predatory class – the military rulers. But his cause remained intact; one that, I quietly swore, we would some day bring to fruition.

Ken Saro-Wiwa's death also served as a well-earned rebuke to my fatalism in exile. At least I enjoyed the freedom to go in search of a resting place, in case Abacha did succeed in fulfilling his plans for me. Saro-Wiwa's relations were not even permitted access to his body. Some reports claim that it took four attempts to hang him, others that it took more. What is undisputed is that the initial attempts failed, that he was taken down from the scaffold while his companions were executed, so that he witnessed it all, and then took his turn.

I was left with the sense of a compulsive burden of debt to Ken, his companions and their cause. Not even my long poem – *Calling Josef Brodsky for Ken Saro-Wiwa* that I failed twice to read to the end in public, overcome by emotion – at Emory University, and in Purcell Room, London – written nearly a year after his death, seemed to discharge that burden. Indeed, both the title and subterfuge – fastening on Josef Brodsky, the Russian dissident poet as a courier between Ken and me – was self-revealing...

> I play
> The simple messenger, dared thus far
> To link two kindred souls from worlds apart
> In passage to the other world

I had tried and failed to write to, for, in memory of, in homage to, in posthumous dialogue with Ken after his death, yet I needed to, needed to purge my psyche of yet another failure, one that, unlike the death of Moshood Abiola – the president-elect who was murdered in prison – had involved a desperate effort from the moment that I knew, with absolute certainty, that Abacha was resolved on Saro-Wiwa's death. Dirging his end through another combative soul was the formula that finally worked.

The dismal proceedings of Kenule's murder in a Port Harcourt prison were video-taped on orders of the dictator who held viewing sessions afterwards with some of his officers, not all of whom knew, in advance, to what macabre feast they had been summoned. A witness has since revealed that one of the dictator's young aides fainted during a viewing. Abacha turned round and laughed – *look at him,* he mocked, *and he calls himself a soldier.*

I am persuaded that I have always known that human aberrations such as Sani Abacha exist, I have learnt to identify them since childhood, although of course, mostly by intuition at that age. It is sufficient, a modest life mission, to ensure that such monsters do not enjoy the last laugh, do not rob individual beings of the fundamental right to a dignified life and a dignified exit, afflicting one's living thoughts with echoes of the brutal laughter of power over the courageous, farewell words of a fighter, or the tread of triumphal boots that desecrate the peace of that rightful bequest from the cradle – the cactus patch.

Lord receive my soul - Kenule Saro-Wiwa shouted as he stepped on the scaffold - *but the struggle continues.*

Within such a commitment, I believe, is captured the essential teaching of that paradox, the Yoruba god of the restless road and creative solitude, of the call of the lyric and the battle cry – *Ogun.*

Arms and the Man

Now we come to the question: would we have resorted to armed struggle to rid the nation of the dictatorship of Sani Abacha? How does one come to terms with issues of pacifism and violence, make peace with their moral questions? Did we actually begin preparations for armed struggle?

The question of a willingness to take up arms against a cruel despot was not one with which I found myself suddenly confronted – I had once resolved it in a minor mode during the Western Nigeria uprising of 1964/65, which had necessitated the takeover of the broadcasting station in Ìbàdàn. Several within the opposition movement however found themselves faced with what, for me, was familiar, though not fully settled territory. I have pondered numerous times over the many faces of violence, its limpet attachment – it would seem – to the very genes of humanity. I could not deny its existence in some accommodating space within mine. I felt no especial urge to prise it off and exclude it absolutely from the means of retrieval of a people's violated dignity, a community that defined my own existence as a human being. A monster had reduced us, collectively, to a plantation of slaves, and the word 'liberation' could not be restricted to being a mere rhetorical device.

I was burdened with a special responsibility – beyond mere leadership. Not many within the movement could claim to have been thrust, as I was, with an uncanny predilection, into situations that straddled the divide between peace and violence, compelling a constant review of the imperatives of both, each circumstance a unique instruction on its own. I had not escaped even the Irish 'troubles'. During my stint as a Fellow in Churchill College, Cambridge, in 1970, I was invited to lecture in Belfast at the very height of the violence. Our lodgings were situated on a street whose entry points were heavily sandbagged positions – once a normal, cosy neighbourhood. I arrived at night, thus missing out on the sight of fortifications, woke up early the following morning – a Sunday – and sauntered out in all lordliness, little dreaming that eyes watched me from behind curtains, taking note, passing on news of an intruder through the local bush telegraph. The streets were eerily empty, a sensation that eventually percolated through to me, even though I felt no particular alarm. I had however set up a panic among my hosts – a black face in the streets of Ireland, at that time in 1970 – meant only one thing – a serving soldier in the British forces, and thus fair game for the IRA. Search parties were immediately sent out and, later, we were formally informed that an IRA cell had been alerted.

A year or so later, I would find myself setting up a meeting between the Irish Provos and the 'Regulars'. Only one and a third names have stuck to my memory from that experience – Seamus Towney, and, the one-third – Mac-something. One side wanted a return to the violent days, the other was for a political solution. The two factions had just begun to tear each other apart, and an effort was being initiated, before the conflict became irreversible, to come to a resolution. During the run of *Les Anges Meurtriers* in Paris, Joan Littlewood, in whose Blackheath home I would sometimes meet not only the literary but the violent compatriots of the playwright Brendan Behan, asked me one day if I could find a safe house in Paris for the two factions. They had agreed to meet in secrecy and resolve their differences.

Through Nadia, the secretary to my Lumumba in Connor Cruise O'Brien's play, I secured an apartment just off Boulevard St. Michel, owned by the daughter of the proprietor of one of the huge brasseries in that arrondissement, Titi C. It was all appropriately cloak-and-dagger. The Irish billigerents slipped away from under the nervous eyes of British agents, travelled on a channel ferry. The address had been sent to them in Ireland. On landing, they were informed in which letter-box – that of an untenanted apartment – the key was hidden. Their meeting lasted nearly all night – by morning, they had boarded the ferry, headed for the Irish seas.

As I complained to Mary Robinson, then Irish Prime Minister when we met in Davos, Switzerland, two decades later, that intrusion of WS into Irish contemporary history sank into the Irish seas without a ripple, I had looked forward to the outcome as others might the result of a World Cup final, and to the private celebration of my unsung triumph – together with Nadia and Titi C. – in the cause of peace. Fortunately, I had no active consciousness, at the time, of the existence of a Nobel Peace Prize, or I would have felt very badly done by when, not long after, the peace effort succumbed to the superior lure of bombs and guns. Unable to fire a public salvo at those fratricidal let-downs, I moped around for some days afterwards, and boycotted Irish literature and music for some weeks longer. Fortunately, I never did take to Irish whisky.

To concede genuine revulsion at the phenomenon of violence does not however contradict an acceptance of its sometime necessity and even – justice. There are those who *relish* violence – there is no other word for it. They are juiced up at the prospect of its eruption, and some even consciously seek it out. Others merely *reconcile* themselves to violence but, having done so, direct it in as practical, minimalist and humane a way as is compatible with the objectives, propelling it towards that moment when one may look back with relief at the jettisoning of such a phase that violates one's loftiest ideals, celebrate its termination, and hope – *never again?*

I have recognised and accepted my membership of this latter group since I became conscious of injustice and the tendency to domination as ingrained aspects of the conduct of society and individuals. I have always found it abnormal that violence should be offered as a normal commodity of exchange between individuals, or that nations should conduct their diplomacy through the pulverisation of one another's cities and the decimation of their populations. To gauge the greatness of nations – as my earliest history texts would have it – by their capacity and cunning for destruction, and award the title of 'Great' to successful warmongers in a confused context with nation-building and social enhancement, has always struck me – well, as far back as I can recollect – as a perversion of human values. To respond to terror with violence, or attempt to defeat violence with its own instrumentality is, however, unblameworthy. I admire the saints – the Ghandis, the Martin Luther Kings, the Dalai Lamas, the Aung San Suu Kyis, Gautamas and all, but I cannot aspire to companionship with them.

Many were the encounters I had with loving apologists of rabid power during the Abacha era, those who tried their supine best *not* to know of the violence that was meted out daily to their fellow citizens, often right before their eyes. The more daring made efforts to reassure me that the dictator was a much misunderstood man who cared very deeply about the potholes in the roads – *Prof., one is not saying he's perfect, but you should see how he's been rehabilitating the roads* – or else lauded his commitment to sanitising the banking system – *those mushroom banks Prof., he's really putting an end to their activities* – and so on, and on, and on! Such encounters, often at airports or hotel lobbies during my exile, never failed to call to mind one occasion in which I was physically caught up in the web of absurdity that is sometimes spun by violence. A common enough occurrence in domestic settings, this was acted out in the public arena. I have thought often of my interlocutors, the Abacha apologists while he lived, as actors in that street scene – they on the receiving end, our dictator as the natty young man who doled out violence in the full confidence that he had a submissive partner – and a tolerant environment. That scene remains my favoured morality tale, both as a moment of self-revelation – in addition to its cautionary lesson – and of my contempt for a tendency towards 'reasoned' submissiveness or its partner – the psychologically induced – a probable masochistic streak.

An evening – yes, I admit it – of egregious folly! New York, Upper Manhattan, 1970s. I was returning from some function or the other in the company of my host, Joseph Okpaku, a trained engineer turned publisher, literary critic and business adventurer from Benin, then domiciled in the United States. Joe was driving. A taxi overtook us, then swung sharply to the kerbside, screeched to a stop just a few yards to one of those apartment blocks with an awning and sidewalk carpet running from street to door, presided over by a stolid commissionaire in uniform, fully braided, at least an ex-boxer or wrestler – in short, well able to take care of himself and any disturber of the peace. Before the taxi had rolled to a complete stop, the kerbside door flew open and a woman leapt out, screaming at the top of her lungs and running – obviously – towards the protective presence of the commissionaire. After her leapt a man, caught up with her in a couple of strides, and pinned her against the wall. The taxi drove alongside the pair – perhaps, we thought, he still had his fare to collect. Joe had also pulled up, and together we watched.

"Get back in the car," the man screamed at her. "No, no!" she screamed back. "Leave me alone. Help!"

The next sound that we heard was a crunch of her head against the wall as the man took her face in his hands and – *bang, bang, bang* – against the wall. Over and over again went that head against that wall, as if the neck would snap. The man would stop briefly, step back, point and order the woman once again to get back in the taxi. We watched in anticipation – that is, anticipation of help from the commissionaire. Nothing. He simply watched, stolidly.

The man grabbed her again, ready to resume his pounding but the woman broke loose, fled screaming along the sidewalk, the man in pursuit. The taxi crawled alongside, we crawled behind it, still expecting the commissionaire to intervene. When her companion caught up with her again and resumed the same process, with such increased violence that I felt I could hear those bangs reverberate against the wall of my stomach, some unseen force must have lifted me out of the car and catapulted me forwards because, the next thing I knew, I was standing over the man. I could only assume that I had knocked him down – from behind!

Well now, what next? Having knocked him down, what was I supposed to do? Had I got myself into a fight? Was Joe calling the police? Would the commissionaire at last act as a decent citizen and come to my aid? I dared not take my eyes off the fallen bully, dared not turn my back on him. I had no thought of doing anything to incapacitate him before he turned his fury on me, and I certainly could not leave him lying there while I regained the sanity and protection of Okpaku's vehicle. In short, I felt stuck, and I now began to feel stupid into the bargain. Not for long, however, since matters were taken out of my hands by a staccato of blows on my shoulders from behind. Reinforcements? From within the taxi? But no, the ownership of those tiny fists was soon established when I heard that earlier screaming voice now whining.

"Don't you dare hurt him. I love him! I love him!"

My jaws began to loose their tautness. I felt my mouth distinctly slacken, opening slowly in silent questioning of my hearing. Now thoroughly scared, I hoped that the footsteps that I heard running up were Joe's, which indeed they were. The tattoo persisted, accompanied by increasing protestations of love. I dared not turn round, dared not take my eyes off the prostrate figure. I simply wished that the wind would whisk me away from that spot and deposit me in my Ìṣarà village, where human beings still conduct themselves with some measure of normality.

Recovering some volition, I bent over the man, all red lights flashing as my mind resumed functioning in the mode of extreme caution. There were passersby, quickening their pace as they skirted our group, and I believe that it was at that moment that I first became conscious that the surrounding humanity, including the three central figures – assailant, victim and commissionaire spectator – were white. Solid pink-white upper-class Manhattan. That is, I finally came down from the clouds of righteous and impulsive fellow feeling, landed plumb in the heart of habitual violence, the US Alien land. Strange people! Until that moment, I had only seen three human beings, devoid of racial identity, one whose head was about to be reduced to squashed melon. So, I bent downwards, apologetic. My sole concern was now, very simply, self-preservation, and the instant question on my mind was – was Lover Boy carrying a knife? Or better still, a gun?

I helped him up, tenderly, cooing contritely, my arms hooked under his armpits. Each hand took turns to dust him down so that he remained constantly half-pinioned in a helpful manner. I felt no weapons. All the time, I uttered purring, conciliatory noises.

"My mistake sir, you're not hurt are you? Obvious misunderstanding. We were far away, misjudged the situation, you understand? Very, very clumsy of me..."

Lover Boy – straight from a tailor's fitting session, it seemed – ignored me, adjusted and smoothed down his jacket, and ordered his consort:

"Get in the taxi!"

"That's it," I eagerly concurred, ushering them both towards the taxi. Once they were inside, the door slammed against them, I took a giant step backwards. "Take her home please, and sir, beat her shitless. I mean, beat her to a shitty pulp."

The words sounded somewhat familiar and I recalled that I had used similar lines in *The Trials of Brother Jero*. It only made me wax more creative. I retreated even further, backwards ever, keeping my eye on the taxi whose occupants had fallen silent. Joe was now closer to me and I grew more confident. "That's right sir, please love each other to death but, I implore you, first beat the living shit out of the lady. She needs it, she deserves it, and you'll be fulfilling both a lover's and a civic duty."

As we came past the commissionaire, he now appeared to have woken up, ready to advertise his role as a concerned citizen and spectator. I could not believe my ears at his fatuous enquiry.

"What happened there? What did he say to her?"

At which point, I did not care that he still struck me as a cross between Mike Power the Nigerian wrestler and Sonny Liston at the height of his reign of demolition. I stopped, fixed him a glare full of naked Ìjẹ̀gbá hatred, then ejected onto him a brief, semi-coherent but pithy summary of my assessment of him, his race and his sick society. There was so much violence stored up in me that I think I secretly wished he would take a swing at me and connect, if only to remind me forcefully that there are societies where the norm is to remain uninvolved, even if murder is being committed right under one's foreign nose.

Thank goodness, my compatriots who refused to 'get in that taxi' far outnumbered those who were not only content to go for the ride, but narrated to the outside world the idyllic vistas through which their purring limousine was being driven, and its utopian destination. The majority of Nigerians were being forced, not even into taxis but into Black Marias, straight from domestic haven or workplace, and sometimes directly into hearses. Their screams for help did not come from them alone, or reverberate against our gut linings as exiles, but rose from within ourselves. The only question that was left to us was: what form should such self-help take? If we were compelled to embrace violence, we had to analyse the conditions of violence, mediate its unpredictable nature with a controlling, discriminating philosophy of violence.

One evolves specific rules of engagement, simply from habit, even if only as a theoretical framework from within which one can endure, morally, a violent world. Combatants in war know the nature of the terrain into which they are thrust – an unambiguous arena of violence. However, even within the conceded space of violence, codes of restraint must exist – for instance I have always considered the taking of innocents as hostages a despicable form of struggle, a pathetic mimicry of the renegade state that takes its entire people hostage. I always took my leave, thankfully and painlessly, of rhetoricians of sweeping, non-discriminating violence, especially during those heady days of Marxist and Troskyite arrogation, now supplanted by a *jihadist* competitiveness of all religious colours. *There are no innocents:* thus is the slaughter and kidnapping of innocents justified in the name of the Higher Cause – secular or religious. The right word is – *megalomania* – a presumptuousness of a divine right of the random appropriation of lives. It has always struck me as merely blasphemous, no matter how just one may find the fundamental causes to which such catechisms attach themselves.

In the solitude of moral conscience, there is a genuine dilemma when one is confronted by the spectre of actually generating violence. Such a dilemma is a natural product of reflection. It is a recollection of one's humanity, bringing to the forefront of one's thoughts the invisible future, the potential transformation – for better – of the social entity that must pay the price of bloodshed and social disruption. When it is glaring that power has gone rabid in society and the reality of daily existence is that of ongoing terror, cruelty and repression, there is really little room for hand-wringing or agonising. The choice is made, and then the mind is set free to address the management of such an unwanted commodity, to set limits to its deployment in the cause of redress, and restitution. The schooling of the individual participant is crucial; a keen and constant assessment of the ultimate goal and, an awareness of the danger that such a goal can be corrupted by divergences from a code of conduct that must be set beforehand, and subscribed to collectively.

After the first Gulf War and the release of prisoners, I was riveted by a programme of interviews with some of the former prisoners of war. A pair of infiltrators from the anti-Saddam coalition force, two Britishers from the Special Unit - those adepts of derring-do who preceeded the invasion and established tactical vectors in the empty dunes behind enemy lines – had been surprised by a mere child of some six or seven years. He had wandered far from his home and stumbled on their hideout. For several moments, the invaders stood staring at the seeming apparition, moments during which they could have shot, knived or smothered him.

Said the Special Unit man – *my training was really to have killed him but, I couldn't do it.* The child was allowed to run off. He reported the presence of the intruders to his parents who alerted their local army unit. The capture of the intruders and their imprisonment followed swiftly. I have often compared that moment to the *'there are no innocents'* combatants of Ireland – both the Ulster Union Defence psychopaths and their soulmates within the IRA who think nothing of tossing a bomb into a pub, or blowing up a crowded shopping mall. Nor do I find any enlightenment in suicide bombers – never mind the sobering thought that some do it out of total, terminal conviction, their entire consciousness consumed by the indignity of what to them is an existential negation – i.e. life is not living when lived as such, but may be validated, indeed purified when sacrificed in avenging its indignity – I die, therefore, I *am;* or better still, *I die, and thus – become.* And yet others immolate themselves in this manner out of expectation of an eventual, eternal reward – the guarantee of resurrection in the eternity of a sybaritic paradise. They *believe* in this recompense, and that is the true inducement towards their surrender to self-immolation.

The accidental casualty that is inflicted on the innocents in the course of a conflict – I detest the expression *collateral damage* when applied to human lives – occupies a different level of responsibility and censure, to be judged on the discernable efforts made by participants in the conflict to avoid such violations of innocence or neutrality. But that disingenuous mantra – *violence is violence* – requires repudiation as an abdication of all moral responsibility, an attempt to justify any level of criminality, under the untenable, indeed obnoxious argument that when consequences are the same, the causes acquire a moral equivalence. The glorification of random violence in particular leaves no room for moral ambiguity, that conditioning of the mind that declares all of humanity culpable, and deserving of random punishment, for being whole while others are mutilated, or satiated while others are starving, or sleeping soundly because others are insomniacs – indeed for being alive while others are dead!

One more instructive encounter, this time with the thrill-seeker, the vicarious collaborator in indiscriminate violence. Travelling between London and the USA in summer 1971, I found myself an object of attention by a young eager face from Egypt, a member of a group on its way to attend some kind of youth event, sponsored by the United Nations. I was working at my portable typewriter, and he could not resist coming over to ask me if I was a writer. I confessed to the crime. Where was I from? Nigeria, I said. He was clearly dying to engage me in conversation, perhaps because there were just the two black faces in the plane – my female companion and I. The youthful interloper – he could not have been more than nineteen – plunged straight into the politics of colonialism but did not really take too long to ask the question on his mind – how did we, in Nigeria, view the Palestinian problem?

"With support for the displaced Palestinians," I responded. "They deserve their own homeland."

We discussed the plight of the refugees, the ambiguous role of the United Nations and the likelihood (or unlikelihood) of peace in the Middle-East in our lifetime. He was then unaware that the Nigerian government – and most African nations – had broken off relations with Israel after the Six-Day War with Egypt: Israel had been warned not to advance into any portion of the African continent, but had ignored the warning. So the OAU exhorted all its members to break off relations. Several did. When I revealed that Nigeria was indeed one of the first to do so, it was all he could do to refrain from throwing his arms around me. Our love-feast underwent a sudden hiccup however when, with a confident, even gloating smile on his face, he said:

"A-ah, my friend, so what do you think of the blow struck by the liberation movement against Switzerland?"

I thought I was sure what he meant but I asked anyway, "A blow against Switzerland? When was this?"

"But you must have heard. The plane – *boom!*"

I studied him with some keenness, put my work aside and said carefully. "If you have any friends in the P.L.O., I suggest you tell them that that kind of outrage is certain to lose them the support they enjoy right now among most African governments – and peoples."

He stopped dead. My companion, an African-American, gave a quizzical smile, as if to say, well, end of in-flight romance.

"And you?" asked this young man of righteous intensity. "What do you think?"

"Sickening," I said.

Slowly, he sank down on his knees beside me, the intent, would-be tutor of a backward child. "But you see, the Swiss government had been supporting the Zionist cause. And Swiss business – they pour millions and millions into Jewish business, and that money is used in turn to suppress the Palestinian movement."

"I don't know about your facts," I told him, still in the same comradely mode. "You probably have information that I do not but, even if that were true, does it justify the murder of the innocents." His face was wreathed in that understanding smile – the patient, dedicated teacher accommodating a retarded pupil. "A-h, my Nigerian friend, you have to understand that the Swiss government is guilty of the deaths of many innocent Palestinians at the hands of the Israelis. This was a plane owned by the Swiss government. The profits find their way sooner or later into the hands of the enemies of the Palestinians."

I decided to change tack. "For how long have the North Vietnamese engaged, first the French, and then the Americans in a bloody war of liberation?"

He looked puzzled. I spoke as gently as I could. "Well, at least two decades taken together, wouldn't you say?" He nodded agreement.

"Well then," I continued, and with self-conscious gentleness, "would you claim that their cause is any less just than others? Than the Palestinians' for instance? For nearly twenty years they've fought superior forces armed with the most sophisticated weaponry, defeated one and brought the other to a virtual standstill. Explain to me why they haven't chosen to go around blowing innocent people out of the air. Do you think they are mentally retarded? Trapped in antiquated notions?" – The effort to keep my voice even was becoming frayed – "Do you think it possible there may be some valid principles – even pragmatic reasoning – behind such restraint? Some careful political calculations? Well tell me, whose choice strikes you as being more politically rational, and/or morally superior to the other? Which one do you find arrogant and insulting?"

At the time, enquiries had not uncovered the source and details of the Swissair attack, simply that the plane had exploded in the skies – the work of an altimeter bomb. Yet to come was revelation of the callousness with which the perpetrators had set out to gain the affection of two females, invited them home on holiday, then made excuses that prevented them from travelling at the last moment. They would join their women later. An engagement had been concluded with one, a marriage was to follow shortly afterwards. What was more natural than that the bride-to-be should agree to take her fiancee's suitcase with her? In short, in addition to the total strangers aboard, there were two beings with whom they had broken bread, drunk wine, whom they had fondled and to whom they had made love – then sent to their deaths, making them the very instruments of their annihilation. The cynical details were yet to be uncovered, one could still approach the outrage clinically, devoid even of that personalised dimension. My liberation warrior continued to stare at me with an expression that I could not immediately decipher, and I decided to restrict our scope of discussion to overall strategic choices, even within the brutal parameter of armed struggle.

"Any liberation war," I pressed on, "involves more than mutual destruction. It is also a war of opinion, a contest for support, for solidarity. In other words, all action should be guided by considerations of a long-term advantage. So when one side acts with a brutal contempt for innocent lives, it alienates potential support – doesn't that stand to reason?"

"But first we have to defend ourselves," he insisted. "And we defend ourselves by attacking the profit machine of our enemies or all who support our enemies."

"Wait a minute." I said, "You don't believe that travellers would start avoiding Swissair, do you?"

He shrugged. "At least, it may make them think twice. Certainly the profits of Swissair will be cut, and that will affect their policies."

I smiled at him. "Permanently? That is, even if at all?"

"At least Switzerland will experience some commercial insecurity. A blow has been struck at the Swiss industrial machine."

The homicidal thrill of the vicarious killer – oh yes, I have been here before, I said to myself, heard it all too often. In a moment, he would begin to drool, openly. It was time to encourage the young man to return to his seat so I could resume my work.

"Oh, undoubtedly," I reassured him. "The blow was heard all round the world. However, with your permission, I intend to retain my moral outrage. That was a thrill killing, nothing to do with a liberation war. It is even impious – you assume the power of life and death over *all* of humanity. I find that arrogant. Offensive. I come from a culture that despises such tactics. It's an assault on my humanity."

And that was when I received what I still consider a prime candidate for the most profound insult of my life. It grates, it rankles till this very day, whenever I recall it. This youth – at least a decade below my age – this weasely, pampered, pimply, unripe specimen of humanity, who had earlier bubbled with the effervescence of an anticipated week or fortnight vacation at a youth jamboree, courtesy of the United Nations in the very heartland of 'Zionist apologists and supporters' – arranged his face into a sweet, understanding smile, appropriating to himself a power of absolution that normally resides in the voice of one who has witnessed much, suffered much but understood and transcended it all. Looking up at me from his bended knees, he let me know, in effect, that I had his full sympathy, that the only mission that he now had left in the world was to comfort and exonerate me from the implications of utterances that, presumably, would have been a capital crime from the lips of other mortals.

"A-ah but, I understand," he said. "You are a writer, a poet."

I was terribly conscious of the mischievous smile on the face of my companion. We had been together long enough since my release from prison for her to grasp what my fingers itched to do at that moment. My strangulated voice, stressed even beyond the very endurance limits of the metal skin of a contraption that did not permit such responses, one that was also headed for a destination where such impulses, if given rein, would have to be sternly answered on landing, miraculously succeeded in forcing from me a response in a non-manic mode.

"Perhaps I should let you know this," I said – and the calmness of voice was deserving of a medal for composure under enemy fire – "I have just emerged from prison detention in my own country." It gained his attention, but this only knotted up my insides even more violently. "I am sorry I have to bring it up, I don't like talking about it, especially to a total stranger, but you should know that I did not earn that prison spell from being a poet. We recently concluded a civil war – I was imprisoned on account of my role in that war. Wait." – I saw his face undergoing yet another instant plastic surgery – I was about to be insulted with comradely sympathy. "That was not my first brush with the law – the first time, I was on trial for armed robbery."

I do not recall any further exchanges after that, since I returned immediately to my typewriter. He did say something, but it was lost on me. Indeed I do not recall when or how he left and returned to his seat, only that he could not have prolonged his stay, since he was still intact when I saw him seated among his companions an hour or so later on my way to the toilet, and there was no sense of any bruising on my knuckles. I had decided to ignore him altogether, but the sight of this commander of life and death, this fount of understanding of the lofty, idealistic but pitiably innocent world of the poet, a youth seated among his friends, all of them so full of life, so fired up with anticipated thrills and new experiences in the despised but accommodating USA, proved unbearable. My imagination projected youths like him and his companions in that ill-fated plane, or another like it, with a doomsday parcel tucked in one of their rucksacks. I stopped and looked at him, at his companions, then back at him. He returned the look with something of fear and uncertainty. I confess that I rather enjoyed that look.

"By the way, I knew no one on that plane," I said to him, "but I easily could have done. Maybe a friend, a relation, or even a comrade from our own very modest struggle, not so earth-shaking as yours. If I had... well, just be careful where you're going – I mean, to whom you say such things. Some of us – poets – are not exactly – poets. We live sometimes – beyond the word."

My ethical code on violence evolved through such numerous encounters, but not only from them. One is after all, an assiduous student of history, and a product of a world still in thrall to the mandates of violence. I did not really sit down to ask questions of my temperament but listened to its responses to non-pacific situations, both real-life and as articulated by others. As the century began to close upon the struggle against Abacha, so did our choices contract.

It was indeed approaching a time to prepare, having clarified in our minds what we would and would not do, how to preserve our humanity even in the midst of violence. There were zones of potential help that we meticulously avoided. For instance, contacts were made on behalf of the movement with some warlords in Liberia – we turned down the idea. And once, I received a personal invitation from a rebel leader in Sierra Leone who felt that we should make common cause. It was not until much later, indeed after my return home, that I came to uncover how the contact ever came to be made.

In the ranks of that rebel leader was a former journalist and radio broadcaster – we had done programmes together on the BBC – indeed, he had interviewed me more than once on Nigerian arts and politics. The timing of this reaching out to us was in fact, well judged. The Nigerian army under Sani Abacha was considered an army of occupation by quite a sizable section within Sierra Leone, thus this rebel leader was persuaded that he was involved in a genuine war of liberation. We were equally resolved to unseat a dictator in Nigeria – that made us natural allies, thus went his reasoning. He would confront the Nigerian war machine on Sierra Leonean soil while we eroded its base within Nigeria.

His calculations did not lack affirmation within the military itself. By 1996, many Nigerian soldiers, even units, had begun to fraternise with rebel forces. They saw no reason why they should be in Sierra Leone, fighting for democracy while that commodity was denied them and their families at home, and under the most brutal conditions. And there was massive discontent and suspicion among the officers and rank. Some southern officers had become convinced that Abacha was using the war in Liberia and Sierra Leone either to keep them from intervening at home, or to decimate their ranks, while simultaneously installing his own regional minions in cushy political positions at home, turning the war into a money-spinning industry over their body count. I once encountered a former US Ambassador to Nigeria, Thomas Pickering, in Washington, DC. In the course of reviewing his desk duty on Nigeria, he revealed how Sani Abacha, while Chief of Staff, had brought him an invoice for the hiring of transport planes for ECOMOG troops, a cost that the US government had promised to underwrite. One look at the figures and the Ambassador screamed. More calmly, he reminded Abacha that the United States had a very long experience in air lifting troops all over the world – Abacha, he said, quietly withdrew the invoice and he never brought it back – he had simply added two zeros to the invoice.

Disillusionment was therefore at its highest, and morale at its lowest, especially after the costly 1996 attempt by the Nigerian army to install President Tedjan Kabbah in office in that country. That effort had resulted in the rebel forces marching on the capital, Freetown, penetrating close to the very heart of the city and nearly routing the Nigerian forces. The Nigerian soldiers – in the main – simply did not want to fight. There was an instance – one of many – when a commander actually arranged for his unit to be 'captured' by a rebel force. After some weeks of fraternising, they arranged similarly to be 'released – as a gesture of good-will' – by their captors. The charade was so transparent that the commander was later court-martialled and, I was informed – shot. The rebel commander was therefore not so illogical in thinking that we could have something in common with his cause – and at that stage, the war in Sierra Leone had not truly degenerated into a state of mindless atrocities in which a young generation of recruits – sometimes as young as six or seven – were turned into drug-crazed killers, agents of defilement and torture. The frenzy of amputations, thrill killings, rapes and arson had not begun. Scattered incidents, yes, but they had not attained the status of a competitive policy of near indiscriminate dehumanisation. We decided to keep our distance, but it would be false to say that the offer was not objectively considered.

We did seek help elsewhere – in Ethiopia, Eritrea, South Africa, Rwanda, Uganda, Burkina Faso – and these were not all necessarily from their governments. Responses were, as expected, varied. Some assisted with logistics, others with mobility, some were generous with sweet words, and yet others lent us expertise. Burkina Faso was especially liberal with travel documents and the President, Blaise Campaore, spontaneous and sympathetic. His ambassador in France kept in constant touch, let me know when his leader was likely to pass through Paris, in case I wished to arrange a further meeting. However, the war scenario in the West African sub-region, in which Campaore was clearly playing a controversial role, made us somewhat chary. We withdrew further and further from someone who was clearly disposed to be a keen ally, one whose nation harboured a large Nigerian population, and was strategically positioned in relation to Nigeria. Through General David Mark, another dissident general who escaped Abacha's net quite early in the game, we learnt that our abandonment of that resource did not stop Abacha's Intelligence Service from reporting that I had a trained army of infiltrators already positioned in that country.

We prepared shopping lists, followed leads that took us to both dubious and idealistic corners. We allied with the rump of the ill-fated Ogboru-Orkar warriors who had tried and failed to topple the regime of Ibrahim Babangida. (Most were war weary) A Vietnam veteran who had once been a business associate of the imprisoned President, Moshood Abiola, a voluble, boastful and ultimately unproductive ally appeared to have a recurrent boatload of arms anchored somewhere on the high seas, ready for delivery but requiring a down payment that our combined lifetime resources must have found hilarious. In the end, all that we gained from him was the privilege of being used! Ron smuggled himself into a photo opportunity from my encounter with President Clinton, set up for a university commencement. He then took the photographs into a bankruptcy court hearing as proof that he had used his resources to back a democratic struggle – headed of course by none other than the Nobel Laureate in the photograph. He presented a folder of news clippings of my denunciations of the regime and its human rights abuses. Clinton's presence was proof that he had the tacit approval of the US government, thus his 'contributions' should be declared tax deductible.

If only we had a fraction of Ron's business adroitness! Still, we did set up a financial unit, tried out the most arcane routes to generate funds. Our allied financial wizards prepared plates for Liberation Bonds in readiness for D-Day. Others set up small ventures, specifically for the cause – one, Bola Tinubu, who had escaped from Abacha's dragnet through a hospital window, and would later become the elected governor of Lagos State – set up a trade in rice with Taiwan! Lacking even the most rudimentary sense of trade, I stuck to my own narrow groove for generating funds – I accepted lecture engagements anywhere, any time, for virtually any fee or none at all. Propagating the cause was itself an essential resource on which we could draw.

Numerous factors continued to push us beyond the line of mere readiness. Indeed, less than a year before Abacha's death, we found ourselves, within NALICON, compelled to reassess the state of the struggle. It was not difficult to confront the truth – the route that the democratic movement had travelled so far – albeit creatively and sometimes courageously – was close to a dead end. Every moment saw Abacha consolidate himself deeper in power and terror. More and more opposition voices were being silenced while the political figures were falling like ninepins under the spell of power. If you cannot beat them, they shrugged, join them. There was no question about it, the so-called masses were losing hope.

Thus, for us on the outside, it was time to re-examine our level of commitment.

A new impetus was needed. One by one, the opposition movements at home were being emasculated. The Campaign for Democracy was barely functioning. Most of the internal leaders – Beko Ransome-Kuti, Femi Falana, Shehu Sani, etc. – were either in gaol without charge, sentenced in kangaroo tribunals, awaiting trial on treason charges or otherwise incapacitated. Gani Fawehinmi, the Civil Rights lawyer continued to shuttle in and out of gaol, perpetually harassed, his chambers shot up as an occasional warning, his nightwatch leaving a blood-trail that dragged over a paved courtyard and a gate – for all the world like a film sequence – as he tried to clamber to safety. That Gani had won the Bruno Kreisky Award for Human Rights only appeared to incense Abacha all the more, making him an even more desirable target for persecution and indeed, elimination. Our NADECO partners within the country, constantly exposed, lived under the sudden visitation of the assassin's bullets. In plain daylight, at a petrol station in a busy intersection of Lagos, the elderly but vigorous Abraham Adesanya, former senator, unbelievably escaped death as his car was drilled through and through by the sub-machine guns of Abacha's killer squad. The combative wife of the imprisoned president, Kudirat Abiola, was not so lucky. She was waylaid in full traffic flow, in the morning rush-hour, stopped, and shot through the head. Not until after Sani Abacha's death and the dismantling of his murder organisation would it be discovered that one of her closest confidants and political advisers was an agent of Sani Abacha, and had indeed provided details of her movements on that day to the assassins.

Sani Abacha appeared to have it all his own way, even as the nation hoped, futilely, that he would soon overreach himself – at least, through his over assiduous servitors. His confidence and impunity further bloated by capitulations and defections from the ranks of well-known political figures, Sani Abacha moved to announce – yet again – new plans for a return to civilian rule, but this time, with a difference. A new electoral body was set up – armed with that now routine Nigerian democratic variant – the powers to approve the formation of new parties. Five such consortiums were eventually approved, three of them being instantly recognisable as the personal property of Sani Abacha. Even before their formal registration, all three had announced the name of their flag-bearer for the presidency – none other than the incumbent, General Sani Abacha. The 'independence' of a fourth, funded and owned single-handedly by Abacha's former minister of petroleum, Dr. Etiebet, was short-lived. Its existence degenerated into farce when its founder, owner and presidential candidate, emerged from several days seclusion in his home to renounce his presidential ambitions and defect, with all appropriate apologies, to one of Sani Abacha's parties. That seclusion, it turned out, was a spell of house arrest, broken only by visits from Abacha's man of all purpose, officially his security adviser – the sinister Major Al' Mustapha.

This left only one party. It put up a determined fight, led by Alhaji M.D.Yusuf, a former Head of the Secret Service of an unusual liberal cast of mine, and of Fulani extraction. The nation did not hold its breath while it awaited the outcome. Even so, all bets were wrong. What most people had imagined was that this last party would be allowed free play in order to give the elections a semblance of choice – after all, the electoral machine was firmly under Abacha's control, and any results could be announced even before the completion of voting. Abacha's handlers were taking no chances however. At a meeting held in Kaduna to select and anoint that party's own presidential candidate, Abacha's stormtroopers, headed by the same Major Al' Mustapha, made an unscheduled appearance with a 'goodwill message' from the Head of State. The authentic leaders of the party walked out of their own meeting in protest against the intrusion. The rump that remained behind had no difficulty in concluding the meeting with a formal adoption of Sani Abacha as the presidential candidate. Thereafter, all five parties became known – in the coinage of my late friend, Bola Ige – as the five fingers of one leprous hand.

After which, it was the turn of traditional rulers – the *obas, obis, emirs, chiefs* and other titled heads. One after the other, they visited Aso Rock to endorse their new king – a coy heir-apparent to his own crown – who continued to deny that he had any ambitions to transform himself into a civilian president but would submit, albeit reluctantly, to the wishes of the people. The 'people' soon made their wishes known, most vociferously, through the antics of a flamboyant impessario with an eye on the main chance. The young man appeared from nowhere, launched an amorphous body with the rousing title of YEAA – *Youths Earnestly Ask for Abacha* – and proceeded to launch what he billed as a 'Million-Man March' on Aso Rock. My aborted 1994 march on Abuja to demand the exit of Abacha from Aso Rock had been cynically turned on its head – this time, the March was to plead with the dictator to remain in power as a civilian Head of State! Armed with a bottomless campaign chest from a treasury that was flung wide open to any such ventures, this upstart, Daniel Kanu – who also swore that he would commit suicide if Abacha failed to heed their plea – organised a musical extravaganza in Abuja, at which political office seekers – men and women – former military officers, ex- and aspiring governors and a sprinkling of traditional rulers gyrated to rousing rhythms from prodigally renumerated musical groups. It was an awe-inspiring performance, one that plumbed the very abyss of self-degradation, a veritable wallowing in sycophantic sludge that, it would appear, some people accumulate in their passage towards self-definition and nation-becoming.

For the musicians, the repercussions were instant. As they returned to their home towns, their erstwhile fans were waiting, but not with the welcome banners to which they were accustomed. Many went into hiding, issued statements that claimed how they had been duped into performing. In some cases, this was true. The campaign for self-succession took place during the build-up period towards the global soccer madness known as the World Cup, and some bands had been taken in by the tale that this was a fund-raising event for the Super Eagles, as the Nigerian national team is known. Most knew the truth, but could not resist the mouth-watering inducements. The response of the erstwhile fans, among others, was one cheering note, but a challenge also – it was a crop whose harvesting could not be long delayed, or it would shrivel in the heat of a tyrant's desperation. There were other responses that were no less encouraging, all indicative of a mood that needed to be reinforced and structured before it dissipated from battle weariness.

Abacha's campaign moved with increasing boldness and impudence. It was now the turn of the most palpable bastions of resistance, the physical, peopled arena, to be subdued. A well-known Abacha crony of Yoruba stock, a commodity supplier for the operations of ECOMOG – West African peace-keeping forces – in Liberia and Sierra Leone during Abacha's tenure as the Nigerian Army Chief of Staff, suddenly appeared as point man for his benefactor. This was another 'Triple A' – Alhaji Alao Arisekola – a long-standing shadow player in Ìbàdàn politics. He proceeded to organise a public rally at the Ìbàdàn Sports Stadium at which his now adopted political protégé, Sani Abacha, would be presented as presidential candidate to the Ìbàdàn people.

A reedy, normally self-retiring specimen, more given to sneaky, behind-the-scene activities and intrigues than overt confrontations, the Yoruba 'Triple A' astonishingly discovered a hidden promotional verve in his psyche and became a public promoter of the Abacha regime. Indeed, the obsession of this trader, possessed of the messianic destiny of Abacha, was matched only by his contempt for his own people, the Yoruba who, by contrast, mostly held his protégé, Abacha, in deep abhorrence since the imprisonment of Moshood Abiola, the elected president of the Nigerian nation.

The Alhaji's performances on radio and television on a single-minded mission of imposing Sani Abacha on the Nigerian people was quite complex. It went beyond gratitude to a business benefactor and revealed astonishing depths of self-loathing. Once, on television, he chastised his fellow Yoruba in the most scabrous language, denigrating whatever qualities he held responsible for their hatred of domination.

"The Yoruba people are too clever for their own good. Because they are educated, they think they know everything and so never recognise where their true interests lie. That makes them act stupidly. If the Yoruba had any sense in their heads, they would have long realised that it is not the portion of the Yoruba race to rule this nation. God has given the Northerners that mandate. The sensible position therefore would be to adopt Sani Abacha as a divinely chosen leader and cooperate with him. That way, their interests would be well protected..."

The Northern scion and original propagator of the divine right to rule, Alhaji Maitama Sule, a former Nigerian representative to the United nations, could not have preached it with greater conviction.

Now, it was time to present the divinely anointed to the Yoruba, and Ìbàdàn, his home town, was Triple A's logical launching pad. The entire forces of the Police and Army were placed at the business mogul's disposal. A moderate rent-a-crowd had already taken up positions within and around the stadium with YEAA caps, T-Shirts and a few flags. Motorcades and delegations trickled into the stadium, the demeanour of that last, for all the world, like chain-gangs being led to roadside labour.

The governor's motorcade would invade the stadium at any moment. Triple A himself arrived in his distinctive armour plated Mercedes stretch limousine, with police escorts, screeching sirens and – promptly ran into an ambush. Unknown to him, a fair portion of the rent-a-crowd were infiltrators from the camp of Comrade Ola Oni, a Marxist agitator from time immemorial who, with a handful of resisters, had plotted all night in a small lecture room at the University of Ìbàdàn campus. They moved at an amazing pace through the warrens of Ìbàdàn to mobilise the populace and set them up at strategic positions. Triple A take Ìbàdàn for Abacha? Never, they swore!

There were running battles. Lives were lost, prisoners taken, but the Alhaji's forces were routed. He took refuge in an outside broadcasting van of the television station, sat upon for his own safety by policemen as the opposition combed the nooks and corners of Liberty Stadium, searching for him. Triple A emerged after dark, then, with a handful of his reconstituted bodyguards, moved to exact revenge for his public humiliation by combing the hospitals in turn, looking for the wounded. At a General Hospital, he and his men dragged out the wounded – anyone who looked as if he had been in a fracas and was not one of his followers – and shot them in cold blood, shot the doctor who was operating on them, routed the remaining medical attendants and left other patients without aid.

The swollen face of Olisa Agbakoba, with one eye closed and blackened – an image that was splayed all over the Nigerian media – told the entire story of a similar contestation in Lagos. Olisa, an Igbo living in Lagos, was a Human Rights lawyer who had immediately responded to Kanu's YEAA by threatening a Two-Million counter rally of his own within Lagos. He re-charged the flagging mood of the opposition and the people responded, coming out in defiance of the cynical orders of the police – the peace-keepers who continued to ban all public gatherings, pronounced them illegal, but were always at the protective service of the YEAAs and AAAs and allied groupings.

Although, like Comrade Ola Oni, Agbakoba's defiant public

rally was to ensure that Abacha did not claim the city of Lagos as conquered territory, it was also a part response to the wavering that had become apparent in the attitude of some foreign governments – they had begun sliding towards a policy of accommodation. Their diplomatic representatives were telling us bluntly, both outside and within the country – *the opposition appears to have faded away. There is no real action on the ground.* It was an outrageous sentiment. No real action? It was not the opposition that placed its own people in prison dungeons, subjected them to torture. Those victims had not voluntarily submitted themselves to their gaolers but had been arrested for *doing something!* And their innocent relations and dependants were being held hostage, even children but – *there is no real action!* The sad truth was that most of these governments were eager to return to business as usual. Abacha looked more and more impregnable every day and they feared that their business interests were being jeopardised through a principled policy of denying a tyrant their recognition.

In the same breath however, the same governments repudiated any notion of armed resistance! The few bombs that went off – attributed at the time to the opposition – were vigorously condemned by these governments. One government – again our friends the Canadians – demanded from me an unambiguous pledge to refrain from violent tactics. I refused. The nation was subjected to a sustained regimen of state violence yet here we were, hamstrung in every way, being asked for a pledge to eschew violence – it struck me as absurd. So did it Chief Tony Enahoro, the Chairman of NADECO abroad. Indignantly he refused to make any such pledge. We both realised that this cost us much financial assistance both from the Canadian and other governments, but it was not a pledge that we could make honourably.

It was an ironic situation since, even at that stage, we continued to explore strategies for avoidance of a dreaded resolution in an unpredictable armed struggle.

Not surprisingly, the basic handicap of the opposition groups remained – funds. Not even funds for what those governments imagined – explosives, arms and ammunition – but funds for basic engagements in the most peaceful activities, such as public demonstrations – just enough to print posters, leaflets, pay for transportation, fuel, first-aid and medical bills. Both NADECO and UDFN received urgent appeals from Olisa Agbakoba – he had grasped the full foreign implications of Abacha's expanding campaigns for 'popular approval' and recognised the need to thwart or counter them. His desperate appeal to us on the outside for his Lagos campaign was one of the lowest moments for me personally, since I understood the critical nature of his undertaking. The public face of resistance had to be bolstered, else, other governments would join Bill Clinton in what – in our view – surely ranked as the most execrable pronouncement of his career. Asked, as he stopped in Senegal on his 1998 African tour, what would be his reaction towards Abacha's now apparent bid for self-succession, the leader of the world's most populous democratic nation replied, in obvious reference to the fifteen-year old self-transformation of Flight-Lieutenant Jerry Rawlings of Ghana into a civilian president:

"Well, it is not unknown where a military dictator has taken that route, shed the military uniform for the civilian, and thereby saved his country from the edge of chaos. As long as he is able to win the people's mandate...!"

Words to that effect were of such devastating potential for numerous other nations in Nigeria's shoes that Susan Rice, Clinton's Under-Secretary of State for Africa, threw herself into damage control. She issued an immediate disclaimer, insisting that her president's words had been taken out of context or distorted, assured the world that America's policy towards unelected rulers remained the same, etc. etc. Too late. The damage had been done, and it was extensive. Abacha no longer awaited the steamrolled affirmation of the people's will. The words had hardly rolled off Bill Clinton's tongue than Abacha shed all further coyness and declared himself a possible presidential candidate. The appeal for material help from the home front attained a truly frantic intensity.

Was armed struggle still avoidable?

By now, the opposition groups were financially drained. It was a pitiable sum that we succeeded in transmitting to

Olisa Agbakoba from NALICON – a thousand dollars! Sadder still, it was the only contribution, as we later discovered, that Olisa received from outside. YEAA's Kanu spent that much at one sitting in a bar with his cronies. Nonetheless, with even more meagre contributions from other sources from within, but mostly relying on volunteer work, Olisa and his colleagues succeeded in flooding the streets of Lagos with demonstrators, breaking up and regrouping under the weight of police attacks. Banners were raised, leaflets distributed, and a jubilant media boosted a remarkably courageous outing, against all conceivable odds, that was equalled only by that of Ola Oni's doughty warriors of Ìbàdàn.

Both Abacha's ploys and the responses by the internal opposition – tenacious but weakened by increasing casualties – indicated only one course of action: a new 'front' to keep the momentum of struggle alive, and keep the evil day – armed struggle – at bay for as long as possible. It did not have to be anything dramatic; all that mattered was that the war be taken to the Abacha regime, on Nigerian soil, relying on the people themselves to provide a network of protection for identified but elusive organisers. Psychological warfare appeared to be a pre-requisite – panicking, eroding the confidence of an oppressive regime and, by the same token, boosting the morale of the active opposition and the prostrate populace.

I could not deny the logic of this step any longer, nor evade the fact that I was the obvious choice to spearhead the new initiative. After all, there had been so many sightings of WS by Abacha's agents, leading to police and troop movements on a massive scale, high-alerts at airports, ostentatious surveillance of known WS haunts and hosts, inflicting unpleasant experiences for a handful of travellers who happened to bear the slightest resemblance to the fugitive – at least in the eyes of over-zealous security agents of a paranoid. We were aware that these sightings – nearly all of which were mythical – were a constant source of strength to the opposition – indeed, we would later discover that some of these sightings had been deliberate inventions, not by Abacha's security agents and propagandists, but by opposition plants who fed them to the agents! It was time to flesh out this apparition and earth it within Nigeria. The move would resuscitate a flagging resolve, structure sporadic acts of defiance into a sustained campaign of civil disobedience – more accurately, a resumption of the civil disobedience campaign of June 1993 when the elections were annulled, and the follow-up of November, when a spirited effort was made to remove Ernest Shonekan, the parting gift of the outsted dictator, Ibrahim Babangida. The ground needed to be softened up, made accommodative, if the ultimate weapon of resistance – armed struggle – could not be avoided.

At the third full meeting of the new opposition grouping – the UDFN – in Pittsburgh in March 1998, I announced that our gathering would be the last outside Nigerian soil, and that the next meeting would be in Abuja, the nation's capital. The elation and raucous applause were expected, but only a handful were aware that this was a formal annunciation of a new phase in the struggle, not simply a morale booster. Sola, our bearded Secretary-General with the bearing of a bantam cock, now a member of the House of Representatives, was one of the few. Taken into confidence, he promptly swore that I would not re-enter Nigeria without him. I felt guilty that I could not inform my deputy, Julius Ihonvbere, then Programme Officer at Ford Foundation, or other key members such as Kayode Fayemi, the fusslessly methodical organiser who had made a detailed study of military mentality – I feared that they would strenuously object and probably summon a meeting of the Governing Council of UDFN to overrule the decision. It would not have changed my mind, I had completed my own analysis of our situation, and was in no mood for arguments to which I had no intention of contributing.

My family, safely ensconced in California, had to be treated on individual basis. The most troubling decision concerned my wife, Folake. Her reaction was predictable, and it was no time for emotional entreaties. I briefed my two sons – Olaokun and Ilemakin, both operating from England. I thought the eldest, Olaokun, a medical doctor, would be ruled by a pragmatic approach and accept the supportive but crucial role that I was entrusting to him – from the outside. He shocked me by his adamant response – if I was going in, so was he – and as advance guard! His brother

Ilemakin made matters even worse by declaring that he would not be left behind. Over my dead body, I decided, even as I agreed to include them in the infiltration team – they would learn soon enough that they had been ditched when I made my first broadcast from within Nigeria!

Only three non-Nigerians had either knowledge of, or were involved in the planning of my return. One was a German quasi-diplomat who worked for a foundation – he agreed to organise a noisy cultural event as decoy on the day of our entry into Nigeria. Now that was a brief alliance with a most unsettling termination, for the man would back off shortly after, denying even the generous sum he had contributed, unsolicited, as well as his offer to take up all further travel expenses. So fervent was his dissociation that it was with some anxiety that I called up my young companion on that visit, Kayode Fayemi, seeking assurance that I had not suffered a brainstorm in Hanover, where the meeting took place. The crucial exchange had been necessarily private but, fortunately, on emerging from his office, I had transferred the donated sum, all in hard currency, to Fayemi, so I now wanted to know if it had been phantom notes that I shoved into his hands, evaporating perhaps as soon as we had left Germany!

Of more durable matter was the second ally whose name it does no harm to mention – this was Gerry Feil, a long-standing collaborator in a medley of projects – artistic and political - who would become a friend and support in myriad ways since my earliest brush with renegade regimes. Gerry's cluttered studio in downtown New York, known as The Village, was virtually surrendered to me whenever I required its use and for whatever. It was either the venue for meetings that required the highest security, for leaving and retrieving messages, or simply for dossing down. It was just as well for us that an FBI operative's recommendations for 'taking care of Mr. Gerry Feil', on suspicion of aiding the revolutionary 'Weathermen' in the seventies had not been implemented. As revealed in a book[1] by another operative, now retired, Gerry was to have been locked in a car, suspended

---

[1] M.Wesley Swearingen: *FBI Secrets – An Agent's Expose* (South End Press, Boston, 1995).

on the edge of a cliff and 'made to sweat until the bastard reveals all he knows'. Gerry, alas for him, had had the misfortune, some years earlier, of leaving his car in the custody of a documentary film maker on the violent, revolutionary 'Weathermen'.

That FBI agent has since been exposed for the lunatic he was but, I would have stayed miles distant from Gerry had I known at the time how dangerous a revolutionary he had been regarded in some FBI circles! Not that this would have prevented me from making use of the professional make-up skills of his colleagues in the film industry. Those practical aids were essential not only for a successful re-entry, but for the ability to move openly, yet remain undetected.

The voice, introduced in zones infiltrated by the police, would be a problem, but this was not one that an amateur actor, keeping a low profile, could fail to overcome, even without voice distorting gadgets. The problem did not arise for the formal broadcasts, and I had prepared the speech that would be transmitted over Radio Kudirat the moment our small team set foot again on Nigerian soil. After that, any UDFN statements would issue first from within the nation's boundaries, and only then be re-broadcast by Radio Kudirat from its Scandinavian base. Thanks to *Reporters sans Frontières*, we still laid claim to ownership of an idle mobile FM radio transmitter, stored in a basement of an apartment building, in the very heart of Paris - the short-wave Radio Kudirat had rendered it temporarily redundant by successfully covering the entire space of the Nigerian nation on its own.

The third was our man in Paris – still an international civil servant in UNESCO, Nigerian born but of French nationality – whom I asked to prepare to take possession of the transmitter and travel with it to Cotonou in the Republic of Benin. From there it would travel into Lagos, a repeat exercise of the first incursion of any opposition radio into Nigerian airwaves in 1996 - *Radio Freedom*. That venture had been made possible by the dissident general, Alani Akinrinade. His Lagos home had been firebombed by Abacha's men, but by then he had already escaped from the country. To Alani also belonged the professional assignment of preparing for a worst case scenario, if that came to pass. Early in 1996, the first mobile sets had been secretly tested in the Republic of Benin, dismantled, smuggled piecemeal into Nigeria by women traders and other volunteers, then re-assembled within the country. Among such volunteers were the mild-looking Dapo Olorunyomi, a journalist, Kayode Fayemi, who from writing doctorals on military domination had become an agent for its reversal, and the self-effacing 'Lemi'. Like Olorunyomi, Lemi had once enjoyed Abacha's hospitality but lived to tell the tale. My private nickname for Lemi was 'The Gecko' – he had a natural gift for blending with walls, and this perhaps had helped his survival and eventual 'ransom' from Abacha's dungeons. The impact of that radio on the Nigerian populace, the first time that the monopoly of state broadcasting had ever been breached, had been nothing short of galvanising. It could only cover a few square miles at a time, but its mobility made it appear far more extensive in its coverage. A search for that transmitter also provided the pretext for the invasion of my Abeokuta home by the military, the real purpose of course being to destroy whatever could be destroyed. The new radio, our gift from *Reporters sans Frontières*, and more powerful than Radio Freedom, would follow the same route and operate in the same way, only, this time, its broadcasts would be picked up and rebroadcast all over the country by Radio Kudirat.

At the lagoon village of Ganvie in Cotonou, in next door Republic of Benin, a canoe with outboard motor, and two escorts, were placed on stand-by, ready to take me into Nigerian waters. They were provided by a Nigerian businessman who, despite his careful cultivation of a low profile, enjoyed seemingly unlimited reaches into the Béninois police and customs commands. This entrepreneur had already assigned us isolated, mostly disused warehouses in which we were free to store whatever we wished. If our incursion into the Nigerian borders had its desired effect, a psychological front would be effectively established, and the nation might be spared a war of insurrection. If not, the people would be primed for resistance.

A Farewell Mission

I had one more 'diplomatic offensive' to execute before departure, and that was to Israel, a state I had never before visited. Among the preliminaries for venturing into the lion's den in that year, 1998, one that UDFN had designated the Year of Liberation, was the fullest possible penetration, and hopeful disruption of Sani Abacha's security apparatus. He had inherited it from his predecessor, Ibrahim Babangida, and it was largely run by the Israeli. Even before my flight from Nigeria, a notorious, irrepressible multiple agent of successive governments, Godwin Daboh, once offered to draw me into a plot to topple Sani Abacha. Among his – largely improbable – boasts was that he had a direct connection with the Israeli-run security operations as well as intimate links to the Israeli government. If we could come to an agreement about the composition of the civilian succession, he would simply contact the Israeli government who would then authorise its nationals to do whatever was necessary. The Army, he assured me, was ready to move and install the winner of the 1993 presidential elections in Aso Rock.

Daboh was most specific, even down to technical details. One switch, he said, controlled the entire security gadgetry of Aso Rock – communication, lights, signals, etc. etc. Without it, Abacha would be stripped naked, suddenly bereft of protection. Daboh claimed to know the Israeli engineering firm that had set up the entire circuit. He swore that he had the blueprints in his possession, or at least that he had access to them at any time of his choosing. If I had tarried long enough, I have no doubt that he would have claimed that he had the remote control button right in his pocket and might even have offered to demonstrate a fraction of its efficacy!

It was an embarrassment to have Godwin Daboh screaming all this at me virtually at the top of his voice in the courtyard premises of the Lagos Magistrate Court, where I had gone to institute a civil suit against Abacha's usurpation of power. That was a purely symbolic gesture – we knew in advance which way the judge, a well-known AGIP (Any Government in Power) would make his ruling. Daboh was nothing if not consistent – *Stop wasting time on a case with a predictable judicial outcome. Let's get to work on something practical.* Hurriedly, to shut him up, I agreed to a fictitious rendezvous and fled!

The Israeli security connection was real, however, and it was one of the first targets of the opposition groups, once we moved into exile. NADECO had already taken the initiative and written to the Israeli government to protest the technical support still provided to a brutal dictator in the area of security. Questions were raised in the Knesset, and NADECO received a letter of assurance that all Israeli had been told to withdraw from any activities that implicated a direct or indirect collaboration with the Abacha regime. My visit was a follow-up. It was no longer sufficient for the Israeli to have withdrawn; we now required active support from the government, especially in their Intelligence section.

This had to be the last such engagement! Each moment carried the same thought – I was freeing myself of the mind-numbing itinerant diplomacy, leaving the field to the NADECO stalwarts to whom this was meat and drink, but also on our side, NALICON, to Kayode Fayemi whom I had watched navigating those shoals with increasing self-assurance.

The chauffeur arrived. I attended a Knesset meeting, then met with individual members of that House, including the female representative who had tabled the original motion that barred any further collaboration with the Abacha regime. They all gave reassurances of strict compliance by Israeli citizens with the directives. Brief meetings with small committees, representatives of the various coalitions that made up the government, the opposition, a politician or two who had been in Nigeria and wanted a few minutes, just to ask about old friends...

Then followed a quiet lunch with Shimon Peres, and an abrupt change of mood. The secluded restaurant, clearly not open to the public, aided the transition, more like a private, discreet clubhouse where members of the government might take visitors for confidential exchanges, and my host hinted as much, though he added that he enjoyed dining there by himself, since it was one place that he knew his thoughts would not be interrupted. Peres was no longer prime minister. His party was in opposition, but Israeli politics were such that he still wielded a great amount of influence in government. Shimon Peres – we had interacted before on a few occasions – always struck me as one of those rare species: a politician of principle, even in the heated combat zone that his nation had become. We engaged the Palestinian issue only towards the end – I had not travelled to Israel for a conference on Middle-East politics but of course, how could that eye of a global storm be completely avoided? When I began to outline developments in the Nigerian predicament, he nodded in familiarity with the subject. Israel, he responded, was committed to democracy, and he gave me his solemn assurance that, even though he was no longer in government, he could and would ensure that his nation did not overtly or covertly act in any way that would give joy to the Abacha regime.

I continued, more cautiously, as I went on to explain that my visit was exploratory, and I would be followed shortly by a team that would be led by someone by the name Alani Akinrinade, a former general in the Nigerian army – I wrote down the name for him. How soon could they visit, and could he facilitate their visas? As soon as they wish, he said, just give me a few days' notice. He would also give a call to the relevant consulate. I provided indications of the new thinking of the opposition – that we had to begin operating from within, preparing for any eventuality. I watched his reaction as I stressed that we were not thinking yet of armed conflict but could no longer rule out any measure, that the situation was deteriorating so rapidly that we expected more than mere neutrality, or diplomatic niceties from the Israeli government. What we needed above all was help to penetrate Abacha's security network – we could do, for a start, with some sophisticated technological gadgets.

Shimon Peres listened, expressed himself as one who was already working on a problem and could be relied upon not to take refuge in evasion. The afternoon passed quietly, we spoke like old friends, an older man whose life had encompassed much, the other, younger, but infected with his presence, so that he began to feel prematurely aged, deep inside. Peres introduced the Palestinian situation, as if to draw parallels – not of politics, but of the frustrations of conflict – running lightly over the numerous and abortive attempts at peace. His voice, a deep rumble as if emerging from deep caverns of thought, was a mixture of quiet resolve, tinged with some regret that logical policies – in his reckoning – had failed to result in his vision, conceding a barely disguised anxiety for the future. Only during this part of our exchanges did his measured rhythm change character, revealing a deep anger and contempt for his predecessor, Benjamin Netanyahu, whose imported brand of Zionism he found depressingly barren. Regardless of my view of Israeli policies towards the Palestinians, responding to Peres just as a human being and a leader of people made one marvel all over again how it ever came about that the Abachas of the world could actually dare aspire to any ranks of leadership, even of a pack of hyenas. I felt quite contented. Even if we obtained nothing from the resources within Peres' scope of influence, his wistful gaze left me feeling that this was a friend who shared similar ideals, and who wished with all his heart that the world were different from the one we both inhabited.

It was one of those balmy afternoons when a glow settles over one, inexplicably, although in this case I could attribute it to the serene atmosphere of our meeting place, the fussless attention of the waiters, the calm exchanges and the quiet attentiveness displayed by a host towards the concerns that had brought one thousands of miles across the globe. In addition, I was already feeling the sense of satisfaction that comes with knowing that one was shutting down a particular line of duty, and freeing oneself for the next. It struck me as a fitting end to shuttling around on foreign lands, attempting to assess what others might or might not give, urging on the former and adjusting to the latter, mentally casting about, even within an encounter, for where one might turn next in the rounds of exploration. I never really felt cut out for this role, and it was an added bonus to be about to end it on an altruistic, though powerless note – altruistic, because I was concluding an unwanted career on a land upon which I truly wished I could bestow something in turn – a just resolution of its own travails. Perhaps my visit to the Holocaust Museum that morning also had something to do with this feeling. The measured, modulated voice that read out the list of victims in that somber, yet riveting space still echoed in my head, albeit muted, even sepulchral, coursing round the retentive skull.

There was some time before my final engagement – an informal one, just a reception in the home of Professor Zvi of the University of Jerusalem, whose invitation to lecture had served as cover for my visit. It was a long-standing invitation, one that I had warned him I might wish to take up with only a few days' notice. I decided on some sight-seeing. My chauffeur, every bit of whom smelt MOSSAD, the Israeli Secret Service, took me to Old Jerusalem.

At the foot of Temple Mount, known also as the Noble Sanctuary, I excused my minder, since I prefer to explore new places by myself, without a guide or running commentary, even without map or guide-book. I descended into the crypts, the grottoes, the temples and mosques, the reliquaries and the mythologies of the spirit. It was not difficult to decipher the architectural rivalries inscribed on walls, the altered passages, sealed-up niches and alcoves, sealed up archways and altars as one faith supplanted the other, temple turned to church, to mosque, to church and then temple or mosque again, each attempting to eradicate the manifest presences of the last, but with the signatures of each faith still visible, if only vestigially, but sometimes cohabiting the same space as if in an optimistic testament to the potential accommodativeness of the human spirit. There was no doubt about it – a communion of sheer spirit, elevated above theology, sect or creed pervaded every niche, perfumed the air with the rich distillation of numinous presences. My path crossed those of other tourists – they were not many – and would be more truthfully described as pilgrims, since their faces, even bodies radiated that awareness of being in a place of history, hallowed by the passage of prophets and seers. It was approaching dusk when I emerged, and stood looking down over the plains.

The next moment, I was hailed by name, and by voices whose accents were distinctly familiar. They turned out to be from a busload of Ghanaian soldiers, a detachment from the United Nations peacekeeping force in Lebanon who had motored to Jerusalem to visit the holy sites. I waved to them. Encountering them so far from home within this foreign space, bound on a mission of peace, immediately moved me in a strange way, as if it was some kind of message from the distant coast of a continent where my cactus patch was eternally lodged, and from within which my obsessive mission acquired its enigmatic endorsement. Within the mandates of peace and strife, this encounter struck me, quite inexplicably, as a gracious, indeed benign portent.

The bus was already pulling off when some of them recognised my head of hair – always the giveaway! – and excitedly stopped the driver. I was mobbed. They insisted on taking souvenir pictures and obtaining autographs. One of them was reading an anthology of African writing. He proudly opened a well-thumbed page – he had been reading the section of my poems! That was unusual. Most of the time when I catch one of our own reading any work of mine, it's *The Lion and the Jewel*, or *The Trials of Brother Jero*. Most frequently however, they are reading Chinua Achebe's *Things Fall Apart!* It was one of those rare times that I was devoid of any sense of resented duty in that sometimes exasperating labour of signing autographs and posing for photographs – I signed these most willingly and gratified the insatiable cameras. Finally, they departed, and with the dwindling of the bus into a speck in the distance, came a sudden silence that enveloped the dusk, as if that busload of peaceful warriors was the last intrusive object, of either noise or motion, into a contemplation of timelessness. I resumed my gaze outwards, but with a marked difference in response.

Not even the passage of a shy straggle of youthful, visitors, wordless and reverential appeared to disturb the silence that had descended. One moment, I watched them pause at the Garden of Olives, stand still for several moments, then, as noiselessly as they had appeared, they were gone, seemingly swallowed up by the earth as they vanished down stone steps that led into the chambers, grottoes and galleries of the Mount. With their passage, it seemed as if, finally, the last human presence in the world had been sucked into the underworld. I slipped gradually into a consciousness that merged totally with my surrounding, the arid slopes that swept into an endless horizon from the splayed feet of Temple Mount, slipped into one of my inexplicable, flotation experiences, those moments when a part of one's self appears to separate from the body, and moves to inhabit a pure realm of sensations that have drifted in from all sides, emanating from nowhere, never defining themselves for what they are, what they portend, why they have chosen to assail that detached portion of the self within a neutral, elusive territory. Perhaps the self becomes more receptive in those moments when one has truly shed the encumbrances of options, and submits only to a straightforward choice of action, or none at all. Certainly, the only identified thought that my mind had retained for the past hours had been – going home. The rest was up to others, and I felt supremely light-hearted and light-headed, readied only towards one direction, one uncomplicated goal, regaining my own terrain and moving anonymously on familiar earth. An end to the frenzy of 'ambassadorial' hustling, leaving only the task of infiltrating, settling in, watching and waiting, preparing. I felt supremely at peace.

It crept gradually on me – the strange, yet familiar, and always mystifying experience. I found myself entranced by a dusk that would remain memorable in its surreality, elusive to the grasp, impossible to apprehend. There is a most eloquent spirituality about that much fought over land – I, an adherent of none of the three principal faiths that inhabit it, testify to this.

I remained with a vast silence at the confluence of embattled slopes, bathed however in a protective calm, a now placid crossroads of multiple civilisations and faiths. Sunset had descended. My gaze swept over centuries of history – strife, trade and spirituality. It brought with it a slow wave of melancholy, settling imperceptibly on the pores of the skin. Then I felt I could sense the seepage of incense, spices and unguents from ancient times, a sensation unprecedented on any foreign soil that ever attempted to entice me into a shedding of my discrete sense of being. Unresisting, I submitted to the experience, hovered above aeons of time, surrounded by a sough of winds in a dusk of absolute stillness.

Restored to my immediate surrounds, I wondered, why? Why was this generous mat of peace so deeply soaked in hate? For I felt nothing but a protective cloak that opened into an endless vista to dissolve rocks, groves and monuments, lifting from an air of peace from that patch of earth, one which, in those ineradicable moments, percolated through the soles of my feet, affirming the essence of that earth as the spiritual navel of the world. And I felt a gift had been passed to me. It was without definition but it was, clearly, a much sought-after bequest. It left me uplifted, endowed with infinite certitude of a resolution of all things. I felt, somehow, that the future was resolved and its truth transmitted to me – not revealed, since I had no idea what it was – only that I was already a secret confidant of the end of discord. And I knew it had to do with the nature of the mission that brought me to this place. Temple Mount to some, Noble Sanctuary to others, I left this space subdued, yet buoyant, curiously at peace with myself. I was no longer seeking, I had found. I had not known that condition of equanimity, an interior accommodation with the outer world in many years – certainly not since my departure from home. There was no expectation of anything. But I felt no more anxiety, only a quiet trust in that moment, a serenity that transcended questions and uncertainties, as a pilgrim might be who finds the mundane substance of his quest subsumed in a vision of eternity.

Outside the borders of my own land, this kind of intimation was rare. I once experienced a kindred sensation on a visit to the rockhills of Ìdànrè, in Úndó, the Western part of Nigeria, and a more contrasting landscape would be difficult to imagine, a rockhill that I elsewhere described as 'a god-suffused grazing of primal giants and mastodons, petrified through some strange history, suckled by mists and clouds!' Yet there also, something similar had occurred, a silent intrusion of presences that would be conjured up – or more accurately, would levitate and dissolve – into a walk in the dead of night through the woods of a yet virgin part of Mòlété, just outside Ìbàdàn, over two hundred miles from that originating experience, and all of two years later. That took place in 1965 and it gave birth to the long poem, Ìdànrè. And occasionally I would undergo spells of quiescent self-dissolution in the moist, densely wooded grove of Òṣun, the goddess that presides over the city of Oṣhógbó, an hour's drive from Ìbàdàn. But never before in a strange land, not entwined in a few moments of twilight communion with whatever deity or more presided over this land of such austere beauty, sibilant with ancestral whispers, so remote from the rancorous sermonising of its intemperate clerics of separation and hate. It would take a year – a standard pause, I have come to recognise – before I would revisit that scene in the lines:

> Pondering war, I trod the sandal-paved stones
> Senses lulled in light incense, brushed by hems
> Of robes from distant sages, pilgrims of all faiths.
> And the dark hour beckoned to me in hope.
> From that seared land that I had sworn
> I would not leave with empty hands, came a gift...

I went straight from Temple Mount to the reception in the home of my host and there, a persistent journalist finally trapped and interviewed me on the usual themes, of which the immediate politics of Nigeria were prominent. He was actually a pleasant young man who impressed me with his unusually intimate knowledge of our situation, and I was content to speak to him quite extensively. On his way home, he turned on his car radio as usual and – could not believe the news that was emerging! He spun round immediately and raced to catch me before I left the reception, ran up the stairs and attempted to drag me into another room where there was a television set. I resisted a little, mumbling protests about the improbability of the news he was repeating so excitedly. He turned on the box.

It seemed unreal, but I knew it was true. Sani Abacha, the cause of all my incessant peregrinations all over the world, had quit the scene, terminally. The journalist wanted my immediate reaction, had raced back at breakneck speed to obtain a scoop, hardly believing his luck. From him and a handful of the guests who had followed us into the television room, I shut off the exulting – no, not exulting, not euphoric, not even vindicated but simply accepting, grateful and fulfilled – part of me and said, repressing a smile:

Have they carried out a post-morten? Has the man been cut in little pieces? Taken out his brain? Understand this – Sani Abacha has a feudal mentality. He may have faked his death simply to see who is mourning and who is dancing. Come back when the doctors have chopped him up to determine the cause of death.

But it was true. Deep within me, I knew that this time, it was no wish-fulfilling rumour, of which there had been no shortage in the past.

It was as if an opaque glass was shattered and I was confronted with the reality that lay hidden behind it, straining to be released. The element of doubt was not altogether absent, but it was more a distrust in the rapidity with which such intimations that assailed me on the Noble Sanctuary were now clarified. The sudden opening of long-sought possibilities was the certain part; a lingering mistrust, within my inner reality remained. Nonetheless, time was fractured – suddenly everything was in the past!

Was I truly about to be relieved of four years of body-and-soul-sapping itinerancy? Years of disappointments, of reverses and the ambitions of little monstrosities lurking in corners of the abruptly vacated citadel of terror kept one in check, preached hard caution. Still, one could not but savour this prospect – the prospect of an end to a clandestine existence, of planning, scheming, organising, bullying, cajoling – heads of states, defence ministers, dissident caucuses within Abacha-contented governments – sessions with military strategists and veterans of guerilla struggle, retired or still active, sometimes actual combatants on furlough – East, West, Africa, South Africa... but now, a rescue? Suddenly, the sheering away of a crushing, life altering burden?

Forty matured years distanced from the first reprieve of this nature – my volunteer flirtation with the Hungarian uprising – mentally dressed again for an outing that was cancelled at the eleventh hour, I wondered what my collaborators were feeling at that very moment. Profoundly relieved as I was, I hoped, but perhaps some of them would be caught also in that ambiguous zone of deflation that appears to surround such moments. All I experienced, once I had gained the peace and quiet of my hotel room, was an overwhelming urge to *be* home at that hour, undetected – maybe even wearing the grotesque disguise that would have been perfected by Gerry Feil's colleagues, but grinning to myself underneath it – stroll through my cactus patch, let the mood of the people percolate to me while it still flowed jubilantly, indifferent to tomorrow's uncertainties, and be part of their sense of vindication.

I longed to see those especially from whom it had been necessary – for their own health – to steer a clear path, those with whom I was known to have a close relationship. No attempt to make contact, no telephone calls, only the occasional verbal message through accidental meetings with mutual acquaintances at airports, or in a hotel lobby – tell so-and-so we are alive, and keeping safe. And often the careful, anxious messages from within: *please keep your head down, we are all praying for you.* The world of friendship or closeness was split in two: those who were directly involved, at some level or the other, in the single-minded mission of ousting a tyrant, accepting all attendant risks, and those who were at one with the cause but could not be seen to be involved, however remotely. For the former, one lived by the rules of comradeship and a respect for their chosen level of participation and risk-taking. For the latter, one emptied all emotional storage tanks and hoped that maybe, some day, you would meet again.

Most burdensome of all, you also packed the anguish of a nation with you everywhere, as familiar as your toilet kit, poring over reports, moving from high-level, highly publicised meetings to clandestine encounters, worrying about the insiders with a purely clinical, practical concern. Who are the latest arrivals in gaol? How do you penetrate the walls to reach them, to let them know they are not forgotten? Who is left outside the walls, and how tightly is their existence now circumscribed? How do you get support to them? To their families? Is *Radio Kudirat,* the opposition voice that was driving Sani Abacha frantic, reaching everyone? Often enough? Effectively enough? And sometimes, warnings from our listening posts, even from deep within Abacha's security system – those warnings were more safely delivered to us on the outside than to those inside; it removed the danger of a direct linkage and exposed such supportive sources to lesser risk. We then became the roundabout conduit to those who remained on the ground: *it's time for you to move – Move out – Now!!!* Or else *– change your routine – drastically.* Or *vanish under, dig deep underground and remain there.*

Move! Move some more and then – Move again! And again and again! The sheer physicality of so many years had usurped the norm, overwhelming the rightful claims of spaces of serenity, creativity, the elusive space of resolution, even of contrary things. Was this about to end, and so suddenly? It was difficult to surrender to such an enticing, desperately craved prospect, one that translated simply as – *going home.* Not a sentimental homecoming, but *simply going where one should never have left.*

When my chauffeur came to take me to the airport for departure, he, like the young journalist, had been unable to contain his excitement. He rushed at me, and the words came tumbling out in a cascade.

"It's him! It's him! I know him!"

"Know whom?"

"Your new Head of State, General Abdulsalami. At first, when I heard the name, I wasn't sure. But his picture was on the television screen this morning."

Well, should I have been surprised? What was more natural than that MOSSAD should know every one of our top military brass, and indeed lower ranking officers? What, among other reasons, had brought me to Israel?

"Did you meet him in Nigeria?' I asked.

"No, here, in Israel! Every year. Some of his colleagues too. But he has a bad back and came for treatment. Every year I took him to the private clinic. Same clinic. Very nice person. He would stay – maybe, two or three weeks. Unfailingly. While he received treatment, I would take his wife shopping. They were a very nice couple."

I did not need to pump him for information about the new face in Aso Rock. All the way to the airport, he spoke incessantly, "I can't believe it. I simply cannot believe it. Here am I driving you, and all these years I have been driving the general, and he turns out to be your new head of state."

"Well, you never know who you get to meet – especially in this profession of yours."

He blinked, did a double take – my imagination? – but certainly took another look at me through the rear-view mirror.

"Oh yes, running this car-hire service, one gets to meet so many people. The government likes to use our firm for important visitors." He drove thoughtfully for a while, then shook his head yet again.

"Still, it's a miracle. Maybe you also become the next head of state?"

I had to smile at that, and comforted him with a pat on the shoulder. "Miracles were never intended to stretch that far."

PART VIII

Homecoming

An Interim Welcome - Official!

Perhaps after all, I am a secret junkie for a measure of the unpredictable, for a slight tinge of risk. Even a closet masochist? I am reluctant, indeed embarrassed to admit to a vague discontent over my prospective return but, it is there, even palpable. Something is about to end, and I already experience a feeling akin to amputation. I know that at sixty-five, I should be grateful to glimpse the end of a nomadic imposition and the precariousness of certain forms of contestations but, there is this old man still nursing a twinge of deprivation, rather than overt, wine-cork popping gratitude.

It seemed unreal but, all that was over. I could actually contemplate, then discuss with others the ideal moment for our return, yet I found myself compelled to acknowledge a sneaky sense of disappointment scuffing the hairs on the old man's skin, one who was already several years a pensioner (albeit without a pension), already old enough to profit from the subsidised fares on California's railways and some airlines for a 'senior citizen' status – another irritating coinage of the *pseudo-language* of American 'political correctitude' – just what is wrong with the tried and tested 'elder', 'elderly', etc.? Still, what a weird feeling it was to exercise that gerontocratic privilege for the first time – on a San Bernadino Metroliner! Mentally, I poured a libation for my

admission to the new age-grade – a call, surely, to cease from
further strife.

My momentous age-grade induction, ignored by all the world
except the automatic ticket machine, preceded the moment of
liberation by a clear two years. Perhaps, whenever I made the
voyage home, I thought, I should be made to submit to a painful
age-grade ritual since, on looking inwards, I continually caught
my elderly *alter ego* furtively drawing a dry tongue over his own
teeth of discontent at a moment when I should be salivating with
satisfaction, savouring my own portion of a collective vindication,
the true essence of the approaching homecoming.

Then the messages began to pour in or, more accurately, the
same message from multiple directions – the successor, General
Abubakar Abdulsalami, himself former Chief of Defence Staff to
the monster I had dubbed 'Triple D' – the diminutive, demented
dictator – wanted us to meet. Was this a replay of the never-never
Abacharian dialogue. I consulted with both NALICON, and key
members of NADECO. The feeling was unanimous – go and listen
to what he has to say.

As if in a beggarly compensation for the now expunged thrill of a
sneak return, we prepared for our meeting with Abdulsalami the
way we had operated for nearly four years – only, this time, our
cautionary moves were not to thwart any danger to ourselves,
but to avoid contamination by the new political hangers-on.
Nothing that we had enquired into remotely suggested that
Abdulsalami was planning an Abacha-style act of treachery on
American soil – on the contrary, this general appeared to have
read the national (and international) mood aright. He accepted
that he was permitted just the one mission – to return the nation
to apparent civilian rule, and make a graceful exit. How thorough-
going would be the transfer, how faithfully distanced from a mere
surface change of baton, became the primary concern of the
organised opposition.

As soon as he took over after Sani Abacha, Abdulsalami
blithely announced that all exiles were free to return home. We
found this extremely hilarious. There we were, subjects of

WANTED posters all over the country offering rewards for our capture – the posters were mostly torn off or defaced as a matter of fact – but the reality was that charges of treason, a capital crime, still hung over our heads. Abacha's men were still on the loose. Any policeman or soldier could arrest us on sight, or shoot us 'for resisting arrest'. In what kind of a world, we asked, was this former associate of Abacha living? Did he understand how deeply the Abacha machinery had burrowed into normal safeguards against arbitrariness? Had we survived Abacha's roving death squads all over Europe and America only to walk into a trap at home?

Cautiously however, we had to admit the possibility that the new man might be serious. He had the treason charges against us formally withdrawn and their cancellation widely publicised. What was even more remarkable was that as soon as he began to plan his first overseas trip a few weeks after taking office, he was already instructing ambassadors to the nations on his itinerary to track me down and arrange a meeting. The democratic movement decided that we had nothing to lose. And so, we met, at the New York Palace Hotel in Manhattan, New York. We set down unambiguous terms for meeting - this was strictly political business, not a courtesy visit. Next, to avoid that latter colouring, ensure that we did not find ourselves trapped among the usual train of appendages who had trailed him from Nigeria to Europe where their ranks had been swollen at every stop, and were now virtually swarming round him in New York – we insisted that the meeting should be set for a time when he had rid himself of his train. Most emphatically, I did not wish to run into the man who became known as the King of ING – Ernest Shonekan – former head of the Interim National Government.

When the elections of June 1993 were abruptly annulled by Ibrahim Babangida, the nation became too hot even for that survivalist to juggle in his nimble hands. Violent demonstrations especially in the West where the winner, Moshood Abiola came from – compelled him to 'step aside', but not so far aside as to disinterestedly do the right thing, which was to hand over power to the elected president. He prepared a cushion to break his fall – the Interim National Government – then named a pliant fall-guy to head a nation of a hundred million restless souls. Babangida often deluded himself in presuming to understand the psychology of Nigeria's peoples. In nominating Shonekan to the position of Head of State, he assumed that the Yoruba would be content with the swap – one Yoruba, any Yoruba, as long as it was one Yoruba for another! This crude gesture of appeasement only incensed the Yoruba. On the one hand, there was a president elected by the entire nation; on the other, a puppet nominated by a disgraced dictator who was bent on clinging to the last shreds of authority. Shonekan became a pariah among his own people.

Ninety days after his illegal occupation of Aso Rock, he was unceremoniously tossed out by Abacha, but even one hour in office would have sufficed the company servant. It was still something to place in his curriculum vitae. Till today, this Ègbá 'king' is probably the sole mind in our shared hometown, Abéòkúta, that harbours the notion that he was ever a functional chief executive of the Nigerian nation.

It is one thing for a dog to cringe under the lash of a sadistic master, it stretches the pathology of cravenness to watch the whipped creature follow the same master around, licking his hand, whimpering for scraps, jumping to 'fetch it' when a training stick is tossed, then racing to ingratiate itself with that master's replacement in competition with a hundred attendant curs in a roving kennel. After serving Sani Abacha in various menial roles, the presence of Ernest Shonekan in Abdulsalami's entourage, even before the new dictator was a month old at the head of affairs was a truly unsavoury sight. We singled him out as one individual whom we absolutely did not wish to encounter in our meeting. It went beyond the one individual objection however. We had to take measures to ensure that our visit was perceived for what it was – not a courtesy visit but a formal encounter with the new man at the helm of power, without any encumbrances.

And so we went into a relaxed version of the kind of security routine to which we had become accustomed when Abacha's agents roamed the world at will. Getting to the rendezvous, for once, the restraining kennel insultingly known as a New York taxi, came in useful in more ways than one – within it, one was truly invisible from the outside. Cooped in the constricted space with one's nose against the armoured divider between driver and passenger, the fare is rendered incognito since the knees are drawn up to the face and the body sunk in the most uncomfortable seats ever designed for public transportation. It was a measure of my new-found liberation that I proceeded to vent, with two companions as captive audience but in full agreement, my long pent-up aggression against this New York model of the taxi – also proliferating throughout the nation. No other word for it, those vehicles are rude, downright rude! That a driver deserves his protection from armed, usually drug-crazed urban bandits is one thing, that a modern nation, famed for space-age designs, one that had known the humane and commodious 'checker' cabs could fail to design taxis that are considerate and respectful, yet protective of the driver, had always struck me as typical of an attitude of contempt for fare-paying humanity, an indictment also of the supineness of passengers from all over the world, or a testimony to their forbearance. What, I now proposed, prevented a one-day universal boycott by tourists as well as natives against such insolent conveyances? Or a blockade of the streets against them through civic action... it made a pleasant change to be able to launch a vitriolic outburst against a long-resented necessity that could not answer back. With a sense of relief, I knew I was already recovering my taste for earth-shaking issues!

We had decided, as base, on an Italian bar-cum-restaurant opposite the hotel where we kept a lengthy watch on the premises to see who went in and came out. Sola Adeyeye, the mercurial Secretary-General of the umbrella organisation, the UDFN, had taken on the task of inspecting the locality and securing our vantage point. I would wait in the bar until he, and the third member of the team, my Vice-Chairman Julius Ihonvbere, were absolutely certain that all unwanted visitors had disappeared. Only then was I to enter the hotel and join the others. Wearing one of my lighter disguises, I shot out of the taxi trap – though clambered would be a more accurate word for the contortions for exiting that mobile pit! – dived into the bar and ensconced myself in the left corner by a window from where I could view the street without being seen. Adeyeye went into the hotel to negotiate my movements with Dr. Ibrahim Gambari, the Ambassador to the United Nations who was in charge of Abdulsalami's visit – it was he who had finally tracked me down and arranged the encounter. So anxious was Gambari to ensure that 'you do not suddenly decide on one of your vanishing acts', that he came over to the bar to assure me that all was clear, and would I now follow him so as to avoid the wastage of even one minute? I asked, where is Sola? Sola came charging through a moment later to insist that I stay put. The hotel lobby was still filled with all the unwanted and undesirable, he said. Julius followed shortly and confirmed it. I was quite contented with my position; the bar appeared to be sufficiently stocked for a prolonged siege.

Eventually Gambari prevailed on us to transfer into the hotel. The environment was not yet fully sanitised but he proposed – quite reasonably – that we wait in his own room. That way, he could take us up to Abdulsalami's suite at a moment's notice, once the last visitor had departed. How he must have regretted his quite practical proposal – but that would come later. For now, the regret was all ours – we could not have chosen a worse moment. A lift was just disgorging the last set of stragglers as we stepped into the lobby and we were obliged to run the gauntlet. Several handshakes, hugs and backslaps later with the not-so-leprous among them – even so, it seemed an eternity – we fled into the sanctuary of Gambari's room where a few ladies – wives to some of the accompanying officials – appeared also to have found a haven. Among them was Gambari's wife who, to my now recurrent chagrin – considering that she had hosted me to sumptuous meals in calmer days, as she reminded me – I did not recognise! Gambari left us to our devices while he went up and down on his protocol duties.

On the coffee table were some publications – a picture on the cover stood out conspicuously – the photograph of the deceased dictator – mentally, I re-titled him the Quadruple 'D' – diminutive, demented, now deceased dictator. But why was it so conspicuously displayed? Worse was to be revealed. On the cover of this lavishly produced volume of selected speeches, was the rubric, 'With a Fore*ward* by General Abdulsalami, Head of State'!

It was an inauspicious beginning. What message was this meant to convey? That the new military regime wished to enshrine the legacy of Sani Abacha? I browsed rapidly through Abdulsalami's introduction, then passed the book to Julius. He flashed through it, sighed, and passed it to Adeyeye. Adeyeye took one look at the cover and instantly exploded. His reaction was most telling of our individual states of mind, since it was not much different – I later reflected – from my earlier tirade against the insolence of New York taxis.

"Look at this! This is a book printed at great expense to be distributed to the whole world, and those illiterate officials can't even spell."

His outburst took us by surprise. "What? Spell what? What has spelling to do with it?"

"Didn't you notice? Don't you see how they've spelt 'Foreword'?"

I hadn't noticed, but now I did. I sighed. "Is the spelling something to bother about?"

"It's a disgrace. Look. This is supposed to be our window on the world. Everything that comes out of an embassy represents the image of the nation. It should be meticulously prepared, every dash and dot!"

Between Julius and me, we succeeded in bringing the discussion back into focus. "Two things strike me as sinister," I observed. "You can tell that this collection was in preparation while Abacha was alive. No doubt it was part of the campaign to turn him into a world statesman – remember Nigeria has been trying to win a seat in the Security Council? The publication was clearly not ready by the time Abacha died, but did they pulp the copies or hide them away in some warehouse? No, they actually hold off the final production until they can co-opt the new Head of State into writing a foreword."

"I bet Abdulsalami did not write that foreword himself." Julius observed.

"I bet he didn't even bother to read it," I agreed, and proceeded to share the picture I had formed of what was clearly a typical con operation.

"Some bureaucrat – special adviser or whatever – goes to the new Boss and says 'Sir, we need some kind of continuity. It would look good in the eyes of the world if you paid a tribute to your predecessor. Here is a prepared text, sir. We are close to grabbing a seat in the Security Council, and this publication will clinch it. Once you've done your part in just this foreword sir – you can put Abacha's regime behind you and carry on with your own programme, etc.etc.' That's one possible scenario."

Both Julius and Sola nodded agreement.

"The second is – a million dollars or two have been voted and cornered by someone for this publication and a number of other Abacha sanitisation projects. With Abacha dead, the lucky ministry in charge – information or foreign affairs, very likely the latter – knows that there is no point going ahead with it. But are they about to give up that loot? No way. In all likelihood they've pocketed the bulk of it. So they rush through the publication, get Abdulsalami to endorse it. They print maybe two hundred copies – just enough to decorate the reading desks of a few of our embassies all over the world and send to foreign embassies in Nigeria. They tag several zeroes onto the end of the number they're supposed to have printed and distributed – all in the name of campaigning for a seat in the Security Council. And that's it! Who's going to bother about that particular budgetary item once Abacha is gone? It has fallen in the crack between two regimes."

"Could be a combination of both scenarios," Julius nodded.

"But the least they could do is spell *Foreword* correctly...!

And there was nothing I could do to suppress Sola's spelling-bee in the bonnet. Unconsciously, we had all transferred to a vastly reduced territory of rights and wrongs, competence and improprieties, all non-lethal, on which the built-up passions of the past years were being gradually expended – from spelling mistakes to insolent taxis!

During welcoming pleasantries, that is, as each side keenly summed up the other, I was tempted to transmit to our host greetings from his regular Israeli chauffeur and watch his reaction. Then I decided against it – who could tell if we would have to renew opposition against this new man, and what form it might take? Instead, as soon as we were settled into our seats, I offered him the publication.

"What signal is this publication supposed to send? Is it an endorsement of the Abacha regime? Is it a message, a warning to the nation that this regime intends to walk in Abacha's steps or what?"

Abdulsalami looked baffled, turned the booklet over in his hands and turned to his ambassador for clarification. Gambari spluttered and launched a most curious counter-attack.

"But Prof., what does this mean? You mean you were rifling through my private papers?"

All three of us responded almost at the same moment. "Private papers? A publication on your coffee table, displayed with other magazines? What are you talking about! Was this not meant for distribution?"

A sweaty Gambari then went into some long-winded explanation. He had received the publications from the ministry, he said, but they had been prepared a long time before and were designed – our guess had been right – to promote Nigeria's campaign for a seat on the Security Council. Obviously they couldn't be discarded, Gambari claimed, a lot of money had gone into the publication and so, to make it current, the Head of State had been invited to provide a foreword...

Bang on cue came our Secretary-General's explosion. "And these people couldn't even spell *Foreword* correctly!"

"Sola, could you...?"

The new Head of State appeared intrigued, insisted that Sola should have his say – "no, no, I think it's an important observation. I really want to hear about this."

Our Secretary-General needed no further prompting. Adeyeye, a smallish, disproportionately dynamic scientist, whose movements sometimes suggest to me what a tree-sprite must be if it existed in real life, is propelled by an inner force that feeds on the nearest anomaly in the way that life or humanity expresses itself, with a blithe unconcern for its immediate context. Then his eyes distend, his arms stiffen into lightning rods as he irradiates the object of attention with instant passion! I often suspect that it has to do with his occupation – that of a biologist – where the minutest specimen must be subjected to an expository procedure that more or less renders all items equal under the microscope. He launched into a tirade on the general sloppiness of our embassies abroad, pummelled the bureaucracy, excoriated the level of decay in public service that could possibly result in the disgraceful misspelling of such an important word. Abdulsalami clearly felt – or had decided that he should be seen to be – seriously concerned with this distraction. Inwardly, I fumed, wished I could leave the two of them alone to thrash out the finer points of spelling, diplomacy, Nigerian image abroad, etc., while I awaited their conclusions in the Italian bar across the street. Julius struck the posture of the urbane international executive that he was – an intellectual who happened to be working for a foreign foundation at the time, but who had not hesitated to throw himself into a political fray that now approached some form of conclusion – or respite. I looked to my deputy – he was nearer – to kick Sola surreptitiously on the ankle, but he seemed to be totally oblivious or indifferent to my impatience. It seemed ages but, finally, we did get back to substantive issues. Our guess was right however – Abdulsalami had not seen the finished product. Now he wanted to know everything about the publication.

It was a relief when Sola Adeyeye's background as a preacher, rather than as a grammarian, took over some moments later – he was a Baptist who sometimes took to the pulpit in his church. Without a break in rhythm, he now launched a fiery and robust sermon directly at Abdulsalami – whatever god the soldier believed in, thundered our Secretary-General, that god stood over him at this crucial moment of Nigerian history. Such a god would call him to strict accounting if he failed to toe the path of rectitude! A short span of time had been allotted him, Abdulsalami, for rescuing the nation from the morass into which it had been plunged by Abacha's regime. Adeyeye's eyes bored into the startled general, his beard was stiffly pointed like a painting of one of prophets of the Old Testament... *if you believe in any god sir, if you believe that Allah is waiting for all of us on the Day of Judgement, you will ensure that you do not fail the nation at this crictical moment...* Abdulsalami's face appeared to weather the onslaught like a trained soldier who finds himself unexpectedly under fire, nodding from time to time in subdued agreement.

Julius followed, albeit in a different mode. Methodically, he outlined the position of the joint opposition movements over the period of transition. From his briefcase, he extracted copies of the memorandum from the conference of both internal and external groups that had been rapidly organised after Sani Abacha's death, by the Centre for Development and Democracy, headed by Kayode Fayemi, one of the few structures that had emerged and survived from the democratic struggle. That meeting was marked by a vastly different atmosphere from earlier encounters – for the first time, participants were not obliged to sneak out through secret routes and return the same way, every step fearful, and anonymity rigorously maintained. Now all was in the open, and while apprehensions remained about the intentions of the new regime, it was impossible not to be infected by the euphoria that clearly enveloped the gathering.

Julius handed over the document. Its conclusion could be summarised in two central demands, and read as the defining statement of the opposition: a transitional government of national unity to take over from the military and, simultaneously, the summoning of a sovereign national conference to debate and decide the future of the nation – its structure, if it must continue as a federation, and its constitution.

Abdulsalami listened carefully but, it would appear that he had far more modest pursuits on his mind.

When are you coming home? We responded that certain conditions still needed to be fulfilled – we enumerated these. Abdulsalami took notes, promised to look into them. He played the role, not only of a good listener, but of one who enjoyed listening to others talk – or maybe simply enjoyed letting others provide some earnest sounding noises as background to his private thoughts – and already decided intentions. I obtained the impression that nothing in the world could ruffle this man. We had spent nearly an hour already. All had been said that we came to say, and the encounter was now over, at least from our side.

Each had sized up the other beneath the courteous exchanges. The General had kept his part of the bargain – he had received us alone, except for his ambassador and someone who appeared to be his secretary. He appeared to have no secret agenda, nothing outside his main commitment to supervise the transition to a new government and embark on whatever retirement plans he had worked out for himself. He did not divulge any hint of what path he and his military colleagues would take to achieve that goal, nor was there any glimmering on his placid face of his reaction to *our* proposals for taking the nation back to democratic rule. In the little that he said, he *appeared* convincing, but we had not come this far to take any politician or 'militrician' at face value. Sola Adeyeye summed up our response to him in the same preacher accents, his keen-edged trowel of a beard aimed, it seemed, at Abdulsalami's heart: *you will be judged by your actions, not by your declarations.*

Abdulsalami did not seem anxious to bring the meeting to a close. It was evidently his last engagement of the day, and I suspect that he was fascinated by the small group. I wondered if his thoughts strayed to the publication of our Walter Mitty – Jude Uzowanne. As the top soldier under Abacha, he must have been compelled to address contingency plans in case of the genuineness of the alleged guerrilla threat. Whatever the rest of the military thought about our effectiveness, all sources – from visiting ambassadors to domestic servants – testified, both during and after Abacha's reign, that the dictator believed that we commanded the forces of hell, all of which had joined hands with hitherto unheard-of monsters of outer space to destroy him! Abacha's exceptional interview, perhaps the only one with a foreign newspaper – *The Washington Post* – was marked by an obsessive devotion to his favourite monster: *that Wole Soyinka, he is supposed to be a poet, to be writing poetry, but what he does is throw bombs all over the place, is that the function of a poet?* – all rattled off in his reedy voice. As Sani Abacha's military right-hand man, Abdulsalami must have been occasional witness to Abacha's famed paroxysms that had the latest act or statement of the opposition –and WS especially – as their trigger.

There were thus moments during our meeting when I felt that this soldier was sizing us up, wondering if this trio represented the forces that he must contend with if he succumbed to the temptation to cling to power. A quizzical look would pass over his face and then he seemed to engage in a keener inspection of the team than was warranted by the subject under discussion. He had one of those faces that did not readily smile, simply because it was so relaxed that the entire head constituted itself into one simple, understated smile. It broke its mould only when we came to the subject of those victims – both military and civilian – who had been framed by Sani Abacha and were still held in gaol, a full month after Abdulsalami had taken office.

Why, I demanded, had General Olusegun Obasanjo been released from prison, but not General Diya, Adisa, Gwadabe and others? Abdulsalami replied that their cases were being closely studied. That was clearly evasive, and I insisted that the continued denial of their freedom was illogical, an unwarranted endorsement of the process that landed them in prison in the first place.

General Oladipo Diya, Abacha's former second-in-command whom Abdulsalami had replaced, was widely believed to have been framed, just like Olusegun Obasanjo. However, the conduct of some of these soldiers during trial had been far less than soldierly. The nation was treated to video clips of the whimpering generals, secretly filmed by Al' Mustapha, Abacha's Chief Security Officer. Confronted with evidence of their alleged complicity in the coup attempt, a number of them had fallen on their knees, sobbing and pleading for forgiveness. In one scene, Abacha contemptuously hands his former Chief of Staff his handkerchief and gestures that he should wipe off his tears.

"Look, General," I protested, "there is no justifiable reason for their continued detention. What I propose is this: set them free immediately and re-absorb them into the Army. Then you can legitimately court-martial them for cowardice under fire, and then – shoot them if you like. I won't complain."

Abdulsalami nearly fell off his chair as, for the first time, his placid mask cracked and he doubled up with laughter.

I had a personal matter that I had left to the last. "I think I should serve you notice," I warned. "I am going to sue your government."

"What for, Prof.?"

"For gross defamation. I am going to sue your government, and your ambassadors are going to be summoned as witnesses."

Gambari was visibly startled and I wondered if he already guessed that I was referring to the lurid invention of Abacha's propaganda machinery, the glossy product of the fugitive rapist, Abiola Ogundokun – *Conscience International.*

"This packaged bundle of obscenities", I continued, "was sent to key Nigerian embassies throughout the world, several of which in turn distributed them to institutions, human rights organisations and even the international media. The president of my university was sent a copy" – and here I turned to Gambari – "directly from the information department of our United Nations mission, with a complimentary slip signed by one E. Agbehir."

Again, Abdulsalami turned wordlessly to Gambari. The ambassador sighed, probably relieved that this publication at least had not been encountered by our delegation as a companion piece to the eulogy of Abacha as world statesman.

"All I know sir," he stammered, "was that this box of magazines was sitting in the office of Agbehir, the information officer – I saw it one day when I entered the office, and I was attracted by Prof.'s photo on the cover. So I took a copy and opened it. Almost immediately I realised what was inside, I dropped it, I remember saying, 'Ngh-ngh, I don't want any part of this. I don't want anything to do with this.' Later on, I found that the information officer had already sent me my own copy. I don't think I've even read it till today – it must be sitting somewhere in my office."

"I am going to sue the government," I repeated quietly. "That's my first duty whenever I return to Nigeria. I'm serving you notice, so that you don't complain that, after all, we had an amicable meeting and so on. It's nothing personal, but I have to take you to court."

The man smiled his broadest yet, spread out his surprisingly soft hands and said. "Prof., everybody is suing me. Obasanjo himself has threatened to sue for wrongful imprisonment. What am I supposed to do? So many people are going to sue this government – I am not saying you're not justified but, where are we going to get the money to pay all these damages?"

"Well, that's for you to worry about. I'm suing. It's a duty imposed on me. Anyway, that's the one item I have on my personal agenda – I needed to get it off my chest. We really should leave you now – I'm sure you have other people to see."

The photographer was summoned for the inevitable photographs. "But when are you coming home?" As we were set up, positioned and re-positioned for the satisfaction of the photographer, Abdulsalami continued to insist, "Next week? Next month? Everybody wants you back, you know. What am I to tell them when I return home?"

"Soon, soon," I kept responding. "Soon. I can't simply pull up roots and return just like that, you know. I have acquired quite a few responsibilities here."

"Well, at least a visit. Come home for a week or so, you can manage that. I'll give you my phone numbers. If you'd just let us know when you're coming..."

"I will. That's a promise."

In the vestibule, an official rushed in. "Your Excellency, I wonder if the Prof. can delay a few moments. Madam is just coming in, and I'm sure the Prof. would like to meet her."

"Where's she?"

"They're coming up the lift. They should be here in a moment."

"Ah, please wait Prof. My wife won't forgive me if she knew you were here and I didn't hold you long enough for both of you to meet."

Mrs. Abdulsalami came in a short while later, accompanied by four women. It was a remarkable change. In the heydays of the two M's – Mariam Babangida and Maryam Abacha – there would have been no less than a caravanserai of women – at least two dozen, if not thirty to forty over-dressed, over-painted, simpering satellites. Abdulsalami's wife was dressed very simply and, I soon discovered, had spent nearly the entire day observing the proceedings of the Supreme Court, being herself a judge. I spoke to her briefly, could not help observing that she was somewhat ill at ease with me. Not conspicuously, but she did seem a little short on spontaneity. I wondered which of my many reputations she had swallowed that created that air of discomfort, or if my entire surmise had been misplaced. Perhaps it was nothing but a cultivated judicial mien.

Later I was informed by a childhood friend of Abdulsalami that, during the Abacha period, she had been very critical of the language of contempt that I employed towards Sani Abacha. She was in agreement with the content, but belonged to that school of thought, quite prevalent among a substantial portion of our educated elite, which holds that a head of state was still a head of state, no matter what else he might be. This meant that he was entitled to the fullest respect from the nation's citizens. No matter what he did, you simply did not refer to him as a 'murderous imbecile', 'cretin' and other standard epithets that I found objectively descriptive of the man. Approval for the role I was playing in the struggle – yes – but it was wrong to be so abusive. A head of state was still His Excellency.

As further knowledge was obtained of Abacha's plots to get rid of all probable or imaginary obstacles in his bid for self-perpetuation, it emerged that Abdulsalami was himself next for the jump. During interrogation, which routinely involved torture, some of the accused coup-plotters had been offered the chance to shorten their agony and even purchase their freedom or survival, by implicating Abdulsalami in one of the phantom plots against the Abacha regime. This attempt had commenced, it turned out, right from the interrogations that preceded the trials and convictions of General Diya and others. A Colonel Lawan Gwadabe in particular, once one of Abacha's most trusted collaborators, had undergone horrendous torture in the effort to make him implicate his boss. He was hung upside down, flogged, electrically shocked, had buckets of excrement poured over him.

Unfortunately for that colonel, he was, like his master, a devoted client of *marabouts,* one of whom sealed Gwadabe's fate by divining that he would one day become Nigeria's head of state. The prophecy came to Abacha's ears, and he promptly took preventive action. Perhaps the *marabout* also predicted a like elevation for Abdulsalami – those *marabouts* loved to please! Speculations were pointless with Sani Abacha however. For whatever reasons in the murky recesses of what passed for his mind – and with steady prodding from his hatchet man, Al' Mustapha – Abacha had begun the process of removing Abdulsalami from office and trying him for treason, with predictable results. Gwadabe was to be the prime witness but, that loyal soldier, notoriously of Abacha's cast of mind in many other ways, refused to break. I wondered if, after learning that truth, Mrs. Abdulsalami would still be of the opinion that Abacha's anointed 'Number One Enemy' was too extreme in his choice of language.

The past began to recede in the mind, ceased to influence daily habits, instincts, or govern practical choices. Finally, I accepted my papers of release from the custody of fear and sent prudence on indefinite sabbatical. I could begin to act on the spur of the moment, plonk myself down at a table on the open pavement of a café or restaurant, walk the streets and enter recreation spaces with greater spontaneity, constrained only by my craving for anonymity. It was in this new mood that, headed for London, I accepted an offer of two tickets to Wimbledon from a Nigerian tennis coach, Jacob Akindele, who had been one of my volunteer marshals in the heydays of the Road Safety Corps. Jacob had a more impressive distinction however – he could boast of having coached John McEnroe in his rookie days! In my mood of liberation, I prepared to venture into Wimbledon's hallowed precincts – my first such visit in over forty years.

Not that I have ever been one for blood sports, least of all lawn tennis, whose genteel setting – most especially in England's Wimbledon, I have always considered a contradiction, the game itself being no more than a sublimation of the blood instinct that has stuck, with such tenacity, to every rung in the ladder of human evolution. Boxing is another matter entirely – it does not pretend to be anything else – thus, I have never been averse to watching the occasional round in a boxing match, almost exclusively on television.

It was only natural that my mind should travel back to my last visit to Wimbledon as a fresh graduate, in the company of Barbara, my first wife, perhaps even then pregnant with Olaokun, my first son. Everything fell in place – Olaokun was bound to be in London and I had two tickets. He also, I thought, must be feeling the pangs of withdrawal, having thrown himself into the fray body and soul, served as secretary to the UDFN, neglected the small computer publication business that had developed from his medical publishing enterprise, until it went bankrupt in the service of democracy. He was compelled to return to his first profession, a part-time doctor on call. I pictured him wondering what to do with himself, now that he was deprived of preparations for preceding me into Abacha's lair, tried to gauge his reaction when I informed him that I never had the slightest intention of gratifying his wish! I called him up – did he wish to come with the old man? He was more than ready.

A summery day, the kind that Wimbledon aficionados pray for, and sometimes get. Whatever was going on in Olaokun's mind, I did not know, and I wondered if his mother ever told him that we used to bus and walk to Wimbledon during my stint at the Royal Court Theatre in 1958/59, when we lived in Maida Vale, Willesden and Putney, the last being nearest to Wimbledon. What went through the old man's mind however was the sheer air of freedom. I was walking among crowds, without sprouting eyes all round my head, or accompanied by a volunteer bodyguard or two, inconspicuous but close by. All I dreaded was to be recognised by any one – *just make them leave me alone,* I pleaded with the unseen gods.

Those deities are however practised in turning a deaf ear. As we walked past the gates and began to drift through the crowd, the familiar sound shot through the air:

"Prof! Prof! Professor Soyinka."

I always know when I cannot bluff my way, pretending to be someone else. This was no voice of uncertainty and, whoever it was, we were going to be ensconced within that place for the next few hours, when she would have lots of time to scrutinise me closely if I tried the gambit of self-denial. It is always an embarrassment when a 'senior citizen' finds himself caught in a bald lie, especially by a mere juvenile.

I turned. She was petite, light complexioned, and could easily have passed for an Indian. But it was not she who really caught my interest but her companion. Darker, and of a somewhat more substantial build, she remained rooted by the entrance gate while the one who had called out ran forward excitedly. Not one probing step did she take in our direction. Her face read horror, unrelieved horror, her body – total petrification. She shrank progressively into her distant self, staring at the scene with wide-eyed apprehension.

The girl came up to me, her excitement bubbling over. "Yes, I knew it was you. I recognised you in spite of the hat." She continued breathlessly. "I've read your books, I admire them a lot."

"Thank you. And you? What's your name? Are you studying here?"

"Zainab, and I'm reading law."

I nodded, gestured towards Olaokun. "My son, Olaokun."

They shook hands. The congealed companion appeared to have thawed sufficiently to drag closer to our group on heavy limbs, but remained several strides away. Her expression distinctly read, "Zainab is mad. She's stark raving mad. What's going to happen now."

"When do you finish schooling?" I enquired.

"Oh, I've finished. I've qualified but now I'm serving my attachment."

"Congratulations. So you're on holidays? You enjoy tennis?"

"I love it. But I'm not on vacation. I live in London."

I gave my self-deprecatory gesture. "I'm afraid I'm not very fond of tennis, but I wanted to see if I could recover my former taste for it, especially with the Williams sisters playing. When it comes to sports, I'm a racist. Are you also heading for Centre Court?"

"No", she sighed. And she mentioned the names of the players she had come to see.

"Well, I hope you enjoy your match." I made one more effort to include her shrinking companion in the exchange, nodded briefly towards her. And then, intrigued by this retiring girl, I decided on a little more time with both, wondering if there was a history that could be dredged up from my lamentable memory. Keeping my eyes, not on the forward one called Zainab but on this other, I asked, "You did not tell me the rest of your name. Zainab what?

The girl leant forward, raised herself on her toes and whispered in my ear: "Abacha", and quickly drew back, still smiling, to watch my reaction.

I have, I have been told, a most expressive face, but I do wear, I have also been told, a companion mask that comes down even faster and hides the expression. This time, neither alternative was on call – there was certainly no need for the mask. I was neither startled nor alarmed, I took it all in stride. Neither internally nor by any outward gesture did I sense any instinct towards recoil. Difficult to explain, but it seemed to me that the most natural encounter in the world had just taken place, it fitted into the pattern of so much that had happened over the past five years. Yes, within that mannered, manicured setting, to be accosted by, and come face to face with the daughter of the man who had done his uttermost to terminate my existence, and on a day that I was relishing my release from her father's custody – it all fitted in. If I had any emotion at all, it was delight. After dropping her 'bombshell' she had moved quickly back to watch my reaction and I could see she was a little disappointed. She saw me smiling, and it was not faked. I admire *chutzpah*.

"Ah," I nodded, "of course. So you're not coming back soon?"

She nodded, somewhat wistfully. I had of course recalled her being named in investigations into accounts that were suspected to hold her father's stolen billions. The Abdulsalami regime had set their recovery as a priority agenda – at least from all appearances – for his one year in office.

"You think you will sort out your problems with the regime?" I asked.

"Yes," she said, "we are talking with them."

I looked at the other girl, still immobilised, and dumbfounded. I shook Zainab's hand once more, nodded to both. "Good luck. We must go and find our seats."

She flashed a smile at us, and we parted.

The games began. It was as I expected. At the end of the first set, I turned to Olaokun and announced that I was leaving, but that he should feel free to remain and watch the game to the end. We would arrange a rendezvous.

"You're not enjoying the game?" he asked.

"Not really. It's the atmosphere. Stilted. I may still come back for the last game, but I have something more interesting I would rather be doing."

"All right, I'll come with you."

We went out, giving out our tickets to a couple among the loitering hopefuls. They could not believe our refusal to take their money. Only after we were out in open air did I reveal my objective to the puzzled son. "I didn't feel right." I said. I think maybe I was too abrupt. Let's find them. I want to buy that girl a drink."

"Who? The Abacha girl?"

"I may have left her thinking I hated her, just because I detested her father. We should have offered to buy them a drink. There was still time."

Olaokun nodded agreement. We set out to look for them in the other courts, in the pavilions, the bars, everywhere. No luck.

I felt strangely sad. My outing would have been perfect if I had been able to offer a drink to the pert, daring girl, and her petrified companion, with words that could be something like - "Here is to your generation. Try and wean yourself from the past."

The king is dead; long live the king! Or, more accurately, the usurper's dead; long live the heir presumptive?

Moscow Road, London, housed an apartment - 20, Alexander Court - whose ready hospitality I had scrupulously denied myself during the usurper years. It belonged to a young friend, Deji Akintilo. A businessman - in the oil sector - he would have qualified for Abacha's instant reprisals if that dictator's 'international observers' had reported any signs of him fraternising with the enemy. The air of liberation had also touched this den of potential subversion, and it became the trysting ground for a high-level contact, with its owner acting as intermediary for yet another emissary from Nigeria, armed with a confidential message.

I was myself setting out for Europe, so I agreed to meet the mystery man in the London apartment. He turned out to be one of the young generation of quietly aggressive entrepreneurs, a former medical doctor who had turned to business. Dr. Tunde Soleye's not so open background was that of a close confidant of General Abdulsalami, with whom he had grown up in Kwara State.

The doctor came straight to the point. His mission was on behalf of a powerful political consortium which was in the process of deciding the future of the nation. The transition programme was a reality, Soleye assured me, and this group needed to take an immediate decision. They wanted Wole Soyinka to run for President.

I was not taken aback. It was not the first of such offers of the crown, among which, on the scale of ego vitamin, my favourite remained that of General Joseph Garba, once the commander of the national Brigade of Guards that had toppled General Yakubu Gowon in 1975, and then served as Foreign Minister in the ensuing regime. On retirement from the army, he became a 'mature student' of the Harvard School of Law, where he graduated, later venturing into politics. In 1995, he decided to run for the presidency under Sani Abacha's own transition charade. To this end, he revisited Harvard where I was then teaching, booked himself into a hotel for two nights to acquaint me with his ambition, discuss his chances, outline his vision, only to undermine it all by declaring:

'There is only one person in Nigeria for whom I am prepared to sink my own ambition and that's you. You should run. My real preference – I'll be sincere with you – is to have you run.' And he proceeded, with some passion, to set out the reasons for his conviction.

I reminded him that there had been an election. Someone had won that election and that person was in prison. Joe's view was that the nation had to move beyond that election. We remained divided on that, but I sincerely wished him luck. Joe Garba and I had become very good friends. He was an honourable man and I truly wished that the political field were not polluted by the immorality of Abiola's predicament. Joe would have made a very good president.

Now, once again, the crown was up for grabs, and a 'powerful consortium' had gone head-hunting, settling on mine. I could read the reasoning behind it. The dispossessed, and now dead president-elect was from my own part of the nation, a Yoruba, indeed from the same town as I - Abẹ́òkúta. A section of the nation had been wronged, and some pragmatic politicians thought it expedient to make amends – or at least appear to do so. It was a replay of the 'King of ING' scenario, albeit under a democratic 'legitimation'.

With Akintilo offering vigorous support, Soleye urged, "You should take it. They want you and, any way you look at it, you are entitled to it. You've paid your dues. It will cost you nothing, and the nation needs you."

My immediate objection was that I would not make a unifying president. An influential caucus in the North viewed me with great suspicion – a feudal elite whom I had never spared, and who in turn had indoctrinated their constituency with the convenient notion that I hated the North in entirety. To make the ideal president, I would first have to dismantle that lie, and that, I knew, would require making undeserved concessions.

The doctor shook his head – those misconceptions had vanished with the five-year taste of Abacha. The consortium, he assured me, included powerful figures from that very part of the nation – it was a pity, but he could not mention names.

So I sought refuge in my lack of resources. I could not fund myself even for a local government election. What little money I had left from the Nobel, even bolstered by intensive lecture rounds, had gone on the struggle. Dr. Soleye smiled indulgently. "That is the least of your worries. Your campaign budget is guaranteed. You will not spend a penny of your own money."

Over dinner and late into the night, the exchanges continued, but it was mostly a one-sided affair. I could not subscribe to Abdulsalami's rushed transition programme, I reminded both, any more than I believed that I was temperamentally suited to managing a nation such as Nigeria. If the proposal had been to act as a short-term interim president in keeping with the opposition's manifesto, there would have been a viable basis for consideration. Possibly. This nomination however smelt distinctly of manipulation by the very forces I had often publicly castigated. I had no inclination for the rigours, the ordeal of a campaign, yet it was clear that the election would be 'won' for me anyway. One could read the blueprint of authority that would emerge - a head of state with inbuilt obligations to undemocratic forces. A hostage.

"The position is yours." Dr. Soleye repeatedly urged. 'Take it. It has to be now. This chance will never come your way again."

Wearying of the pressure, I conceded one or two days to think it over but that was only to end the long night. I had just won my liberty and could not contemplate its abandonment so soon, and in such a questionable manner. The transition from plain Mr. Citizen to heir presumptive simply stalled, even at the thought of it. I deeply craved a personal space, and it beckoned from the surrounds of my cactus patch. A disappointed Soleye took back my message, leaving behind the even more disconsolate proprietor of 20, Alexander Court.

When the Earth Says - WELCOME!

Business Class seat, courtesy of Lufthansa Airlines which had donated the ticket for my return, my journey is pampered, not one that requires slipping in through one secret route or the other to supervise plans for a war of attrition. The air of unreality continues to taunt, pervades the soothing interior of the plane as the events and plans of the past five years course through my mind, wreathed in a whiff of discontent. It was an impossible hope, that months of planning would end so tamely, on a routine passenger flight, treated like some privileged species both by the staff and other passengers! I had schooled myself differently, existed within a totally contrasting reality. The word was – deflation! While not seeking to be a victim, I had been primed to return to claim quite simply – if need be – my cactus patch. Everything about this palpable present therefore feels as contrived as the sudden, sordid death of the dictator, Sani Abacha in the arms of Asian prostitutes flown into Abuja for one of his periodic orgies. For five years, the existence of this man had dominated my own – it was still difficult to believe that he would vacate that space of power with barely a whimper. The prospect of a peaceful resolution of the Nigerian crisis through the mediation of a successor, the choice of dialogue over confrontation, probably with violence, was a luxury we had begun to deny ourselves.

That which I had thought of as being unnaturally absent – emotion – still does not return as I actually step down from the plane into the airport. Clinically, I observe a difference in the Murtala Mohammed airport of my last recollection. This new airport appears – disciplined. Restrained. It is immediately apparent that security is tight. The last time I arrived in Lagos airport with such advance preparations had been on the occasion of the Nobel Prize, whose announcement had caught me in Paris. Protocol this time is just as efficient, but less rambunctious. The airport commandant leads the way. Only a few voices punctuate the unnaturally empty passages. *Welcome! Welcome back! Prof., you are most welcome! Welcome back to Nigeria, sir!* As I watch the starched back of the airport commandant, I wonder on whose side he was during the struggle to remove his erstwhile boss. Certainly he would have shot me out of hand had he succeeded in laying his hand on me during those years when his boss held sway over the nation.

Our plane has arrived early. It overflew Lome, a scheduled stop, for one reason or the other – it would return there afterwards – and so we have landed an hour and a half before the scheduled time. The protocol officer is full of apologies – I would have to wait in the VIP lounge for a while. He has a list of those who have been given passes – Pa Adesanya, Arthur Nwankwo, Bola Tinubu, Ayo Adebanjo and a host of NADECO stalwarts – and they have yet to show up. But Arthur Nwankwo is already there, he informs me – Arthur Nwankwo, one of the foolhardy ones who sneaked out of the country to attend a meeting of the allied democratic resistance in London. Olu Agunloye – my co-victim in the libellous assault of *Conscience International* – had wangled his way in somehow. Yet even those who had passed through the security zone were disappointed – they had planned to join the formal welcoming group right up to the door of the aircraft, but we have arrived impossibly early.

A grin breaks through my face as I recall a flight from Paris to Cotonou, quite early into the fight against Abacha. Already Cotonou was heavily infiltrated by Nigerian undercover agents, but we had our own people there too, and they knew everyone of

Abacha's spies. Both sides kept watch on each other and sometimes even fraternised. Early in the game, I would walk up to a group – usually of two or three – in the lobby of a hotel, cheerfully identified them to themselves, and bought them drinks. Going to Cotonou, just an arm's throw from Lagos was risky, but not as foolhardy as it might sound – at least, not then. Ghana, much further away, was more dangerous. Its leader, Flight-Lieutenant Jerry Rawlings, was well-known as an Abacha ally and was even on his payroll, as would be later revealed by Abacha's Chief Security Adviser, Ismail Gwarzo. We had a dependable base in Benin. I openly addressed Nigerian groups in Cotonou, and in the ancient harbour town of Porto Novo, a visit that was sponsored by Professor Albert Tedjevore, my elder collaborator in more than a few African causes. At one stage, the Abacha regime had threatened Matthieu Kerekou, the Béninois Head of State with serious consequences for harbouring 'enemies of Nigeria'. Himself a former, but now reformed dictator, he refused to be intimidated, though he did pay a 'brotherly visit' to Abuja to reassure the paranoid ruler. After his visit, we received a message of reassurance, but one that urged us to please conduct our activities with greater discretion. The loss was Abacha's 'agents'; we could no longer buy them drinks.

That roundabout flight into Cotonou had made a transit stop at Ougadougou, Burkina Faso. I stood in the doorway, at the top of the stairs, as the plane was re-fuelled. The pilot also came out to stretch his legs.

I turned to him and asked – *suppose, for any reason, we are unable to land in Cotonou – due to weather conditions or whatever – what would be your alternative airport?* Without any hesitation, he replied – *Lome, in Togo*. Well, I continued, *suppose the weather was also bad in Lome, or there was a coup and the airport was closed. Which would be the next choice? Abidjan*, was the response. *What of Lagos?* I asked. *No*, he replied, and shook his head very firmly, *we don't go to Lagos. For one thing, we couldn't even guarantee aviation fuel.* So, I thanked him and then added, *please, if for any reason you find yourself compelled to head for Lagos, just find me a parachute, open the door so I can jump out.*

The hostesses, standing by, laughed aloud but the pilot did not. He nodded quite seriously and said, *I understand. Don't worry. We won't land you in Lagos.*

Looking at the back of the airport commandant who turned round from time to time to grin his welcome at me, I wonder what role he would have enjoyed playing during the Abacha period if my plane had taxied down Lagos tarmac in an unscheduled stop. It was a permanent nightmare that all our dissident exiles underwent, and one of our NADECO associates, a minister under a former regime, had actually undergone that undesired experience, landing unscheduled in Lagos. The security officers boarded the plane – this had become a routine security measure – looked over all the passengers to search for fugitives. It seemed that they did recognise him but pretended not to. And yet another fugitive, within our own organisation, UDFN, found himself trapped in a plane that had been similarly diverted to Lagos. He succeeded in overcoming his initial paralysis when he realised that he was about to descend into the lion's jaws, signalled to a waitress and confided his plight to her. The captain gave him his jacket and cap, kept him in the cockpit until the plane took off again.

The emptiness of the airport is most striking – at four-thirty in the afternoon, it is abnormal. Later, I would learn that even essential workers had been cleared from the arrival section of the airport – all in the name of security! Do they plan to keep this up for every arrival? I enter the VIP lounge to encounters with individual beaming faces, emotional embraces and crisp, military salutes. Later, I observe that the protocol officer is hovering around uncertainly, so finally I ask him what he wants. He whispers near inaudibly: your passport sir. But I have no passport, I inform him. The commandant has overheard the exchange and bellows: are you asking for his passport? Take yourself out of here! But the tone is lighthearted. Again, I would later discover that orders had been given that if any Immigration Officer so much as dared to ask me for any papers, he was to lose his job on the spot – obviously the protocol officer was not aware of this. I have my United Nations laissez-passer on me, and I also have a courtesy diplomatic passport from a friendly African government but, my position over this is straightforward: it was the Nigerian government that seized my national passport, and I have no intention of using any other passport to enter my own country.

The cat-and-mouse games that resulted in the seizure of my passports had taken place at this very airport, on the Nigerian side of the immigration post. The first round ended with the seizure of my national passport, on my way to attend a meeting in UNESCO. The second time, I was headed for the inaugural meeting of the International Parliament of Writers in Paris. Neither setback was unexpected; indeed, I routinely told my Lagos hosts, the Ogunbiyi couple, to keep my dinner waiting.

I had become adept in the rites of travel restriction and its manifold forms – one anticipates, but one never really becomes inured to its destabilising impact. Movement is the palpable essence of freedom. That seems obvious enough, since restraint is its negation, but it needs to be stated and re-stated. Freedom expresses itself in many ways, but its real essence is movement – that is, the right to exercise the choice to move or not to move. Even thought, that is so marvellously secured from the encroachment of chains and walls, thought, we learnt in school, is made possible only through the motion of electrical charges in the brain.

The first time it happened to me – it was some time in 1965, at the time of the Western Region insurrection. I was stunned. It seemed that the world itself suddenly stood still, so that I experienced a distinct vertigo. *You are telling me I cannot travel? That I cannot leave the country?* And the unbelievably matter-of-fact but quaintly officialese response – *That's right sir. We have instructions that you are not to be allowed to proceed out of the country.* The bloodless, expressionless face behind the desk, calmly tucking your passport into a drawer! And sometimes the elaborate deception, a charade with a foregone conclusion – *Will you step this way, sir? Which way? What for? Just follow me please.* And so into an office, where a higher personnel is waiting. *Is that all your luggage? No, I've checked a suitcase. In that case, could you go with the officer and bring it here?* And so these strange hands invade your luggage, piece by piece, item by item, pore through your papers, turn the suitcase upside down looking for heaven-knows-what else. Sometimes, long enough to ensure that you missed your flight. Or else simply kept you waiting, speaking into the telephone to some unseen powers beyond, glancing at you from time to time, fingering the passport like a strange, lethal disease, toing and froing, then at the end – *Sorry sir, you are not allowed to travel*. And so you learn, bit by bit. You learn never to check in any luggage, and you either send whatever papers you need ahead of you, or find a friendly passenger to take them for you, because it is papers that enslave them most of all. They want to understand what is in the papers, why even a scrap of paper should be part of your luggage, what it says, what it hides, what subversive magic it performs... so you ensure that you have no papers with you but your passport. And above all, no address book. How do they cope these days, I wonder, with the world of computers and near-impregnable passwords?

The last bout had been tense, very tense. When my national passport was seized at the earlier attempt to travel to Paris for a meeting at UNESCO, Federico Mayor, the Director-General of UNESCO had been outraged. He immediately ordered that a UNESCO passport be sent to me. Within days, his Lagos office had contacted me and handed me the new passport. Armed with the UNESCO document, I resumed my attempt to breach the immigration barrier. We knew the results beforehand; the only question that remained was – would they stop at merely preventing my travel, or would I end up at an unwanted destination? Within the informal circle of our inchoate democratic movement, the debate was tense. At the time, we had not yet arrived at the option of exile, only at a choice of remaining above or underground. One assertive view was that it was better not to tempt fate at all by going to the airport, that it was best to take the plunge once and for all and disappear from sight.

Things came to a head when I began to organise the Million Man March on Abuja in May 1994. The State Security Services, the SSS invited me for an interview and gave me a clear message from Aso Rock – abandon the March or you will be held responsible for the consequences. But it was also from within the same SSS that the warning came to me - keep away from the airports!

It might be difficult to understand - sometimes it does puzzle even me a little - but I was obliged to engage in that final proof at the airport, nevertheless. Brinkmanship perhaps, but quite within rational limits, since we knew enough to be fairly certain that a clear decision had not been taken over my fate. Moreover, the political capital to be made from the failure of Abacha government to respect a United Nations passport was not one that we could lightly discard. Within the Abacha camp, the situation was fluid. Various options were being considered about how to silence me - the Minister of Foreign Affairs, the unctuous Tom Ikimi, one of Nigeria's breed of Uriah Heeps, had proposed that I be given an 'enhanced' Aung Sang Suu Kyi treatment - confined to my house, allowed access to visitors, etc., and then, after a decent interval - whisked off to a distant prison. Others proffered even more drastic, immediate ideas. Still, it was those early days when international opinion counted for something with Abacha and his advisers; they were not yet so firmly entrenched that they could afford to alienate that community altogether.

The moment I arrived at the airport - virtually with no luggage - and presented my passport at the Immigration, I knew that I was not going to leave the country. The pit of my stomach also informed me, very clearly, that I had taken a near unpardonable risk in coming to the airport at all. After a while, you simply *know*. It is inexplicable. A man is seated at the desk, he takes your passport. He is the Immigration Officer. Standing over him is a man in mufti, a superfluous presence in that booth, except of course that he is there to scrutinise passengers, even those whose names have not shown up in the computer that is located, and slyly consulted, beneath the desk. The Immigration Officers and the SSS are clearly not on the best of terms. The latter are usually arrogant, filled with an inordinate sense of power. They consider not just the Immigration Officers but all other officials - and passengers, including visitors - inferior beings. And yet - thank goodness - there are the exceptions to be found among them!

It is only natural that a bond should exist among 'inferior' beings, a silent but palpable hostility towards over-weening superbeings. It has to be this current of sympathy that transmits itself to the potential victim and, the greater the danger, the stronger the current. It is not so much that they speak directly to you, it is a language in their body, eloquent, effortlessly communicated to others with whom they share a bond of this imposed 'inferior' status. Since they know what is happening, or what is about to happen, they emit a silent wave of despair or anguish, a deep resentment and a sense of impotence. It flashes past you and your antenna picks it up – I think that is all there is to it. And so, when you arrive at the Immigration counter and hand over your passport, there is a way in which the officer does *not* look at you that is beyond verbal expression. You sigh inwardly – o-oh, here we go again! Then follows the immediate question – where, in the course of this night, shall it all end?

The SSS of course stands there as if indifferent to your presence. He is just passing the time of day, has no interest whatever in the immigration process. He does not care that the Immigration Officer and you are engaged in a defining moment – *Sorry Mr. Soyinka, I'm afraid you cannot travel. Oh, really? And why not? I have no idea sir, but you cannot travel. In that case, can I have my passport back?* The SSS man is obviously bored by this uninteresting exchange, he knows it all beforehand and he knows how it will end, so he steps backwards, maybe to see something more worthy of his attention at the customs or security check, which is just behind the line of immigration booths, or else to pick his nose more comfortably. As for you, you have to make a clear statement, so you insist on having the passport back, but the response is just as clear as it is expected. *I have instructions to detain your passport... Detain my passport? Do you see what passport that is? That is a United Nations passport. It is not the property of the Nigerian government so you have no right to it! I'm sorry sir, I have instructions to detain it.* And so of course I demand it back once more, just for the record. *I don't think you understand – that passport is the property of the United Nations, not of the Nigerian government. I want it back! Well sir, all I can do is give you the address where you can go and claim it! When? Tomorrow morning if you like! In that case, I want a receipt for it! I'm just preparing it, sir. The address is on the receipt – that's where you go to reclaim the passport. I suggest you telephone in advance to make an appointment – this is the telephone number.*

Work has slowed virtually to a stop at the other booths. The officers are still flicking through pages of passports, looking over immigration forms and stamping them, but their minds are elsewhere, their minds are within this one booth, and their motions have become heavy with apprehension. It weighs on the air and percolates through to you. The SSS man has become less and less interested in what is going on, his covert eyes having taken in what is on the form to ensure that no secret information is being passed from one lesser being to another. Now he is merely sight-seeing, taking the air, and refuses to have his equanimity disturbed by any unseemly row. Yet even if he had retained his earlier attentive position, virtually looking over the shoulder of the Immigration Officer, he would have missed the tense whisper that issued from the closed lips of the latter: *Please, Mr. Soyinka, go now. Please go. Leave the airport.*

That Immigration Officer does not look up, not even with the sparest of glances. He busies himself pushing my passport into an envelope, then into a drawer, pulling up a file or whatever. And then once more – *Go now, Please!*

Hardly the time to compliment him on his impressive ventriloquist skill, I permit myself a departing tirade against fascism, the abuse of my human rights, the commencing rape of the nation etc.etc. *You can tell Abacha I said that he only thinks he owns this country, but he does not. And we'll reclaim it even if he fills all the airports with his goons and his mimic Gestapo...* noises of support and sympathy reach me from the other travellers as I snatch my carry-on and move towards the exit with a set face. Anyone would think I was about to commence a one-man march right there and then to go and yank Abacha off his seat! I rage past incoming travellers – *Prof., what happened? Have they stopped you again?* But I only increase my pace, snarling invectives as my eyes search for my escorts whom I had warned not to leave the departure hall until the plane was actually airborne and a friendly ground staff had assured them, as pre-arranged, that I was actually inside the plane.

And now I am back to these same stressing grounds, five years later, within the same airport, the circumstances much closer to 1986 when a reception committee awaited me after the announcement of the Nobel Prize for that year. But I feel far less harried than on that occasion, when I had not expected an exultant intervention of the Nigerian government – and a military dictatorship at that – in a foreign award, thinking, very foolishly in hindsight, that I was returning home to a haven of peace, away from the European journalists who appeared bent on rending me limb by limb. The contrasting sense of peace on this occasion is further augmented by the flushed figure of the army commandant who has just re-entered the VIP lounge, sweating, hot and bothered.

"Professor, the crowd is becoming impossible to control!"

I find this puzzling. The airport had seemed quite empty to me. Arthur Nwankwo interjects, "There is quite a crowd outside. We could enter only because we had passes."

I ask him, "When are the others coming?"

"Any moment from now," Arthur replies. "The plane arrived early..."

"I know, I know," the commandant wails. "It overflew Lome. But what do I do about the crowd? "

I make a proposal. "Do you think I should go and show my face."

"I don't know, I don't know. If anything goes wrong... I'm worried. But they say we must wait for the rest of the delegation before escorting you out."

Before we can assess the situation any further, a breathless inspector of police – or some officer of such ranking – rushes in and informs the commandant that the situation is getting out of hand. The crowd is threatening to break through the security cordon.

"You see what I mean? Oh God, I just want this night to be over so I can go home to my family and sleep." And he rushes out with the inspector.

Ten minutes later he is back, and this time his immaculately pressed uniform is rumpled, his cap askew and his swagger-stick flailing wildly.

"Professor, we have to do something about the situation. They think we're holding you here against your will and they're threatening to break down the barriers and force their way in. The security forces are going to be overwhelmed any moment."

"In that case..."

"There is one man in particular. Most uncooperative. I warned him I would arrest him and he dared me to go ahead. He wanted to come in and I said, 'No', he had no permit. We have strict instructions that only those with passes can come in. We are in charge of your safety and we can't afford to take any chances."

"Who is the man?"

"I don't know him. The man sounds quite educated, so I was very disappointed. I expected someone like him to understand the situation but he's the worst, the very worst of them. Very bad-tempered. They all call him Doctor..."

"Doctor?" That wouldn't be Agunloye, who was already inside. "Is the man short, tall, thin, fat or what?"

"Stocky. Dark complexion. He's throwing his weight all over the place, inciting the crowd."

I laugh. "I think I know who that is. My advice is, let him in."

"But the crowd will just follow him in."

"No, you let just him through. Announce that he's coming in to see things for himself. Once he comes in and sees I'm all right, he will go back and calm down the others."

The commandant only looks more confused and uncertain. "I don't know, Professor..."

Suddenly it becomes clear that he simply does not wish to face the crowd another second without me, so I get up. "Let's go. It's too bad about the rest of the welcoming delegation but I'd better go and show my face."

The relief on the commandant's face confirms my suspicion. "Thank you Professor, thank you. I think that's the best thing to do right now. Let's go, sir."

We have barely reached the hall containing the duty-free shops when we encounter 'Dr. Trouble-maker' himself in golfing shorts, a *Welcome Home* T-shirt and a *Welcome Kongi* cap, accompanied by some half a dozen others, all of whom had been sensibly let in by the next in command after the harried departure of the commandant. They had been mandated to go and investigate what was happening and report back to the crowd. The commandant points a shaking swagger stick at Yemi Ogunbiyi.

"That's the man! He's got in! You see what I mean – he has forced his way in."

"Look at this *yeye*-man," Ogunbiyi retorted. "You've been creating unnecessary tension for the crowd."

The rest is lost as the cause of all the commotion is himself smothered in hugs. The next moment both the Trouble-maker and the commandant are engaged in friendly insults as we double-quick-march our way through the corridors. I am escorted through the departure, not the arrival section, so we march through the line of security and scanning equipment and approach the immigration kiosks where an officer had warned me off five years before with his ventriloquist performance. A blur of salutes, beaming faces and shy *Welcomes* from passing airport staff, very restrained, as if yet under watchful eyes. Still I feel no particular excitement. Now we are right at the infamous line at which so many Nigerians lose their passports, vanish into interrogation rooms and from there are rendered invisible for long spells. Officers leap to attention, salute follows salute. It is all a very correct welcome, near emotionless, as if they are adhering to some strict textbook of protocols. But I *know* them. These are long time conspirators in furtive transmissions and I know what is really going on inside their minds so, after passing through, I stop, turn round slowly and summoning a deadpan face, I demand:

"Which of you last seized my passport?"

A moment of double take, and the tension is dissolved. Now their laughter roars out loud, their uniforms vanish and their stiffened bodies explode in a gamut of emotions. In turn, I distinctly feel myself thawing – not much, but definitely responding to the human warmth.

Twilight has descended outside. The vast departure hall is virtually empty – it strikes me yet again as strange – there had been no passengers milling around on the departure side of immigration, in the lounges or around the duty-free shops, and now, none at the entrance to Immigration – and this is about six o'clock in the evening. I find it extraordinary that the airport should be so free of teeming humanity at this hour. To complete the unusual feeling of a deserted hub, hardly any of the varied uniforms of airlines staff is visible – none since the occasional stragglers we had met on our way from the VIP lounge.

And then, something makes me turn round, and – there they all are, choking the long balcony that runs above the departure hall where they must have been herded, just to empty the floor. Whose idea of security was this, in heaven's name! I wave, and that is when the gods of vocal decibels turn loose. The pent-up torrents of *Welcome* cascade in my direction, and at that very moment a wave of humanity, from the opposite side, comes crashing through the shut gates of the main entrance, and then it becomes a matter of struggling to keep my feet on the ground or be crushed. The Pyrates – that fraternity of unending controversy – are on hand and form a protective phalanx to clear a path to the waiting vehicles. Their tactics are not working quite as well as they might, and threaten to create further tension. Bola Ige, friend and political ally since student days, has joined up and together we succeed in shouting instructions over the crowd noise. The Pyrates change tactics and we move more easily through the crowd, but the arms that reach out for a handshake, a grab, even a touch are like a forest of bamboos – slashing and whipping. A fear that my arm might be torn out of its socket – *haven't I been here before?* – is soon submerged under the greater fear that some of the crowd might get knocked down and be trampled upon. The scene seems primed for inevitable disaster and it is now only a question of what form of injuries many would sustain. And then again I find myself compelled to direct my concerns to myself – it has become obvious that it is this very idiot, fast losing his balance while worrying over others, who would prove the likeliest casualty. The loss of balance changes to a sensation of being choked, and I hear the police officer shouting in a panic:

"They're going to kill him. They're going to kill him."
I realise that the 'him' is none other than me. I had earlier felt a

hand on my throat, desperately clutching at my windpipe and attempting to choke me. It has happened twice already and I peeled off the hand, not even thinking that it was the same hand, but of different people trying to save themselves from falling or being crushed. But I had felt the choke-hold, so when I feel the hand again, I grasp it and turn to look for its owner. The next moment the hand is torn from mine and I catch a faint glimpse of its owner being borne halfway down – no, not deliberately, simply from the sheer weight of the crowd. The grey 'French-suit' looks familiar – I last saw it in the VIP lounge but the chaos is so overwhelming that I cannot recall who was wearing it. Suddenly a voice rises in a song, strongly, taming the din:

> Kaàbọ̀ o, ku àbọ̀
> Kaàbọ̀ o, ku àbọ̀
> Ọmọ à b'ílẹ̀ sọ̀rọ̀, ọmọ à b'ílẹ̀ sọ̀rọ̀
> K'ílẹ̀ y'anu, ka à bò [1]

And something gets through to me at last. It is a song I last heard in my paternal hometown, Ìṣarà, the song with which I was received at the entrance to the town and led in procession to the ọba's palace where the ọba and his chiefs and priests had laid on a triumphal gathering for the returning 'son of the soil'. At that unforgettable welcome by the town, even the highest of the chieftaincy hierarchy had been caught unprepared for a unique moment, very rare in occurrence. This was when the potent egúngún, the most numinous and dreaded of the ancestral guardian spirits of the town emerged. As it whirled around, it made a sudden leap towards the table of honour and, in one swirling movement, enveloped me in its garments so that I vanished completely from the sight of mortals. For what seemed an eternity, I was shrouded, sucked into the dark abode of ancestors. One moment I was watching, a spectator like the rest, and suddenly I was no one, drained of all palpability, transported from plain daylight into the immensity of an eclipse, from within which the voice of the egúngún rose in spells and incantations, invoking blessings from

---

[1] Welcome, welcome
You who speak and the earth
Opens its mouth in wonder. Welcome

the living, the dead and the unborn. This face, whose features I could not discern in that total darkness of the charged tent, chewed on a kolanut and squirted its grainy juice in my face, unhitched a gourd from within the recesses of its linings, sloshed the contents into its mouth and spat it on my face, then unleashed a stream of invocations that seemed to emerge from the very bowels of earth. And then the voluminous tent was lifted, the *egúngún* rose to its height and raced out of this charged circle, headed towards its sanctuary, acknowledging no one else, not even the *ọba*, his handlers in hot pursuit, clearing the way to ensure that he did not touch any other being until he had completely melted from human sight. It was a sudden, breathless emanation, and it left the gathering paralysed with awe.

This song, now filtered through the enveloping twilight, was one that I would permanently associate with my reception, living, into the bosom of the ancestors. Its accent differed in the mundane setting of an airport, but it swept me back to that day when, without being an initiate, with no warning and no self-preparation, I partook of communion with the deepest mysteries of earth, and the munificence of the ancestors.

> *Ọmọ à b'ílẹ̀ sòrò, ọmọ à b'ílẹ̀ sòrò*
> *K'ílẹ̀ y'anu, ka à bò...*

Oh yes, finally, at this homecoming, I feel deeply stirred, but the tangle of arms and bodies bring me back to the present, struggling not to be dragged down and probably inducted – literally this time – into the realm of the departed as we battle our way to the waiting vehicles. Finding some hidden energy from nowhere I succeed in forcing a stop even as I am borne onwards, my feet now barely touching the ground. I find my voice and take back some control of the situation.

A despairing appeal for order – "Listen, please! All of you, listen to me! I want nobody to get hurt. No one must get hurt today, not at this homecoming. So please, stand aside and let's move towards the car." Someone loudly demands that I should address them.

I belt out a few sentences above the din, and somehow, we make it to the line of cars. In front of the four-wheel drive, I see the wearer of the grey French suit being resuscitated. It is

Arthur Nwankwo, it was he whose hand had been at my throat, clutching for support as he was overcome by waves of dizziness. Finally, he had collapsed and fainted, fortunately being rescued before he was trampled upon by the crowd. I am hustled into Olu Agunloye's jeep but still the crowd will not let go. There are hands banging on the windows, clinging to fenders and bodies splayed on the bonnet. Again, the feeling of *déjà vu*, recollecting the nightmare drive from Ìdí-ìrókò to Ìpájà during the demonstrations to terminate Babangida's rule. The police are frustrated. I open my window, thinking to shake a hand or two – a kind of symbolic good-bye for now. A great mistake and I curse myself for failing to learn from the earlier grabs at my arm – this time, I come really close to dispensing with a ligament or socket – I am not sure which, but something definitely feels as if it has given. Then the arm is somehow extricated and the vehicle takes off. I sink back into the obscurity of the jeep with relief.

No, there is no question about it this time – at long last, my viscera yields and concedes – *I am back where I never should have left.*

Appendix

National Liberation Council of Nigeria
Att: Dr. Wole Soyinka

Stockholm 96 08 14

Dear Dr. Soyinka

the Olof Palme International Center will support the project we talked about on the phone. I will contact Nalicon in London to obtain more information on the total budget etc.

All the best,

Mats Elovsson

program manager

46 - 8 - 791 77 18

Wole Soyinka

African American Studies, Emory University
201B Candler Library Building, Atlanta, GA. 30322, U.S.A.
Tel. (1) 404 727 6847 Fax. (1) 404 256 3992

April 2, 96

Pierre Schori, Minister of Foreign Affairs, Stockholm.

Dear Pierre,

Needless to say, my mind flew to our last telephone discussion after reading the Reuter report of the Press Luncheon in Johannesburg.

Well, here is how the London Times reported the discussions - same meeting, as it happens, the only Press occasion I had time for in Jo'burg. I don't know what Reuters has been using for ears, but the London Times was obviously listening!

Both meetings went very well. We managed to overcome the nasty snags created by South African government's eleventh-hour coyness, thanks to Jan Egeland in Norway. The Norwegian Council for Africa pulled off a miracle - no less.

All the best for Easter. I suppose you'll be heading up the ski slopes like the Norwegians!

Wole

Peter Donatus;
Germany

Ola Soyinka
London
per Fax

Hi Ola,

1.Dr. Kinkel's statement

like I told you earlier, Dr Kinkel, the Foreign Minister of Germany was reported as saying that Germany is withdrawing her earlier demand for the imposition of sanctions against the Nigerian military junta. Reason: "There are clear indications that the junta are serious and sincere about their transition to civil rule programme." A lot of German parliamentarian have criticised this new move. I spoke with the Permanent Secretary today on phone and he claimed that the said press reports were not true and that the press misquoted him. According to him: "The German position as regards sanctions against Nigeria still remain unchanged" Although he denounced the press reports, I still think that the UDFN should write a letter of protest to the Minister and issue a press statement to this effect. I shall translate the press release into German for the German press and media.

2. The Visit of Prof. Wole Soyinka to Germany
Here is the tentative programme for his visit:
11. November 1996
* Before 9.30 AM: Arrival at the Cologne/Bonn Airport. He will met on arrival by two German MPS.
* 9.30 - 10.30 AM: Breakfast with some MPS
* 10.45 - 11.30 AM: Meeting with the Deputy Speaker of the German Parliament
* 11.30 - 12.15 PM: Press Conference with the deputy Speaker and some other MPS
* 12.30 - 13.45 PM: Lunch with MPS
* 14.00 - 15.00 PM: Meeting with MPS from the Green Party
* 15.15 - 16.15 PM: Meeting with MPS from the Social Democratic Party
* 16.30 - 17.30 PM: Meeting with MPS from the Christain Democratic Party (the Party of Helmut Kohl, the German Chancellor)
12. November 1996
The exact programme is still on the making, but he shall be meeting the following persons and institutions:
* Dr. Kinkel, Foreign Minister
* MPs from the Party of Socialists
* Friedrich-Ebert-Foundation - 15.00PM
* A Foundation of the evangelical Church 16.30 PM
* The Press and Media
* Symposium: 19.30 - 21.30 PM and a small party
13. November 1996
9.00 - 10.00 AM: Meeting with the Heinrich Böll Foundation
10.15AM - 12.00 Noon: Press meetings
12.30 PM: Departure

*** Pl. don not mind some mistakes in this letter, it was written in a hurry!

You can reach me on Fax through this no. in the next few days. I will call you tomorrow.

Fax:
0049-221-739
2071

Greetings from Germany!

OFFICE OF THE PRESIDENT

26 August 1994

To: His Excellency General Sani Abacha
       President and Commander-in-Chief
       Federal Republic of Nigeria

My dear brother Sam Abacha,

I hereby wish to express my profound gratitude to you for attending my inauguration ceremony in Pretoria. Our discussions on that occasion confirmed the close relations between our two nations. In particular, it laid the basis for our co-operation in the development efforts both in our countries and in the continent.

I am writing to you personally and confidentially to express my concern over recent developments in Nigeria. I have noted with keen interest your serious attempts to resolve these problems; and I am confident that you will find a lasting solution in the best interest of the Nigerian people and continent as a whole.

We share your own views that a stable and developing Nigeria will always be of utmost importance in Africa's renaissance, as well as in dispelling perceptions abroad about Africa as a continent in political and economic decline.

Nigeria has been and will always be an inspiration to the continent and to me personally. I am therefore concerned that these developments should not tarnish Nigeria's image.

I have been closely following your efforts to find a solution to the crisis, and wish to commend you most sincerely for this.

In this regard, I have noted that you have taken many initiatives to seek the release of Chief Moshood Abiola. I concur with you, my dear brother, that his release will pave the way for constructive discussions, and undermine attempts aimed at ruining Nigeria's political stability and development. I urge you most humbly to ensure that Chief Abiola's release is expedited.

Accept once more my brotherly greetings and assurances of your highest esteem. I look forward to the pleasure of once again meeting you personally as soon as possible.

Yours sincerely,

Nelson Mandela

*En confidence
_le 4/10/94_*

C-IN-C/26

State House
Abuja

/G²October, 1994

His Excellency
Dr Nelson R Mandela
President of the Republic of
South Africa
Office of the President
Pretoria

République du Bénin
Présidence de la République
Courier   SP/PR
Enrégistré S/No....2.1.12.....

Dear Mr President and Brother,

1.   I write to thank you for your kind and thoughtful letter on relations between our two countries and the political situation in my country. We discussed these matters in Pretoria when I was there last May in the course of your impressive inauguration.

2.   I note, with admiration, that you have already begun the process, along with other leaders of Southern Africa, of giving a new purpose and direction to the integration and development of the region. As you know, Mr President and Dear Brother, we in West Afrcia have been engaged in similar efforts over the years. It has not been easy. I am confident that, in the end, we shall all succeed.

3.   As regards the political situation in Nigeria, the Constitutional Conference continues to make steady progress towards resolving the underlying problems which brought about the crisis.

4.   I am, however, not unmindful of the useful role which MKO Abiola can play to help along the process. This is why I was encouraged when a Federal High Court in Abuja decided to release him on bail on the condition that he would not engage in activities that would destabilise the country so that all hands should be put on the deck to assure the success of the Constitutional Conference. However, Chief MKO Abiola did not feel able to accept the decision of the Court.

5.   I am confident that in the renewed effort in the Federal High Court to secure the release of Chief MKO Abiola on bail, a just decision would be reached. You will agree with me, Mr President and Dear Brother, that in the interest of the independence of the Judiciary and of Justice in Nigeria, and the need to maintain law and order the question of the release of Chief MKO Abiola should be determined in the course of the judicial process.

6.   Let me assure you that I understand your genuine concern over the situation in our country as a true friend of Nigeria. In the same breath, I should also thank you for your fraternal interest in our efforts to bring about peace and stability and to establish an enduring democracy that meets the aspirations of all Nigerians through the Constitutional Conference.

7.   Accordingly, I would appreciate your continued support for our efforts, and seek your co-operation in explaining the Nigerian situation to the international community particularly the United States of America, Britain, France and the European Union.

8.   May I renew to you Mr President and my Dear Brother my best wishes for your continued good health and for the prosperity of your great country.

SANI ABACHA
General
Head of State, Commander-in-Chief
of the Armed Forces of the
Federal Republic of Nigeria

NALICON			
PITTSBURGH FUND-RAISING - DR ADEYEYE			
DONORS	**AMOUNT**		
Leonard Plotnicov	$ 50.00		
Karen Kanell/Conrad Koch	$ 25.00		
Patricia Callahan	$ 50.00		
Paul Johnson	$ 50.00		
Dr. Christianah Adeyeye	$ 75.00		
Dr. Sunday Adekunle	$ 20.00		
Ernest Miller	$ 125.00		
Janice Gallagher	$ 150.00		
Elmira Lloyd	$ 20.00		
Ben Ugbajah	$ 25.00		
Michael & Elisa Labriola	$ 100.00		
Velma Scantlebury	$ 50.00		
Adeola Oyeola	$ 50.00		
Alafia	$ 50.00		
Delorese Ambrose	$ 50.00		
Martin Akpo-Esambe	$ 100.00		
Soga Ewedemi	$ 100.00		
Athena Beldecos	$ 50.00		
Stephen Jolayemi	$ 50.00		
Edward & Mei Hwang	$ 100.00		
Willis & Anne Ludlow	$ 100.00		
Emmanuel Anise	$ 700.00		
Patrick Tobin	$ 50.00		
Lekan Adisa	$ 50.00		
Raphael & Gladys Kollah	$ 50.00		
Dr. Rujani Chuensumran	$ 50.00		
John Pollock	$ 100.00		
Javier Lopez & Marie Robles	$ 100.00		
Douglas & Dorothy Kay	$ 25.00		

Jampole Communications	$ 50.00			
Olusola Akindele	$ 150.00			
Olu Sangodeyi	$ 100.00			
Dabney Smith Associates	$ 100.00			
Sandra Murray	$ 50.00			
Saar Caborith	$ 50.00			
Duquesne University	$ 500.00			
Edwin Fischl	$ 100.00			
Cash Donation / Prof's Cheque	$ 1,354.00			
Total #38 checks	**$ 4,969.00**			
EXPENSES				
Prof's Ticket	$ 752.00			
200 plates at $11.80	$ 2,380.00			
20% Gratuity	$ 476.00			
500 stamps at $0.32	$ 160.00			
Invitation cards	$ 400.00			
RSVP Cards	$ 38.00			
Umoja	$ 500.00			
Hotel for Kongi	$ 191.00			
Airfare for Kongi	$ 168.00			
Total	**$ 5,065.00**			

Wole Soyinka

African American Studies, Emory University
201B Candler Library Building, Atlanta, GA. 30322, U.S.A.
Tel. (1) 404 727 6847 Fax. (1) 404 256 3992

Mar. 20, 96

Reporters SansFrontieres, 5 rue Geoffroy Marie, 75009 Paris Fax: 33 1 45 23 11 51
attn. Herve Deguine

Dear friends,

Further to our recent telephone conversation, and my earlier visit on the occasion of the
Chris Anyawu Award Ceremony, I am now in a position to appeal to your formally for
assistance with equipment for our opposition broadcasting in Nigeria.

You will have learnt by now that we succeeded in launching Freedom Frequency nearly a
year ago to challenge the total monopoly of the airwaves by the Sani Abacha regime. It
operated with considerable success for some six months before it was silenced by a series
of technical problems. I should mention that the transmitter was built by one of our
technicians. It was kept mobile throughout and, despite the desperate efforts of the
regime, it was never discovered.

With the increasing ruthlessness of repression against the media in Nigeria, we need to
get back urgently on the air. Already we have some promise of short-wave facilities from
some friendly countries, but that is still in the formative stages. A loan of FM equipment
in the meantime would be a great asset in countering the propaganda of the regime and
raising public morale in the ongoing struggle.

I leave for Johannesburg on Mar. 27 for a meeting of the various pro-democracy groups -
both from within and outside Nigeria, and plan to return through Paris during the first
week of April. Would it be possible for a decision to have been taken in time for my
arrival?

All the best,

Wole Soyinka

27 March 1996

Mr Wole Soyinka
Organising Committee
Nigerian Pro-democracy Summit
P.O. Box 9663
LONDON SE1
United Kingdom

Dear Mr Soyinka

NIGERIAN PRO-DEMOCRACY SUMMIT IN SOUTH AFRICA

President Mandela has received your letter dated 26 February 1996 in regard to the above matter.

The concern of President Mandela and the South African government for the speedy restoration of democracy in Nigeria is well known, as are the various steps taken to assist in achieving this. The major feature of the South African government's approach to this matter is to work within the framework of the Commonwealth and the resolutions adopted at the recent Commonwealth Summit. You will be aware that South Africa is part of the Commonwealth of Eight Member States designated by the Commonwealth to deal with the matter.

it is therefore not for the President or the South African government to grant approval for the proposed summit. The President and the government will within the multilateral context described continue with their efforts to assist the process of democratisation in Nigeria.

Yours sincerely

**G J GERWEL
DIRECTOR-GENERAL**

ROYAL MINISTRY OF FOREIGN AFFAIRS, OSLO

Telefax:	+47 22 24 95 80/81
Telex:	+71004
Telephone:	+47 22 24 36 00

PRIORITY:	URGENT
CLASSIFICATION:	
DATE:	16.01.96

TO:	MR. WOLE SOYINKA
	NALICON
	FAX NO. 1-909-987-6741

47-22
833 9394

COPY TO:	MR. JAN EGELAND
RESPONSIBLE DIV.:	AFRICA DESK
OUR REF.:	FHN/-
YOUR REF.:	TELEFAX DATED JAN 15, 1996

SUBJECT:	TRAVEL EXPENSES FOR 10 DELEGATES TO SOUTH AFRICA - NIGERIA PRO-DEMOCRACY AID COMMITTEE MINI-SUMMIT IN JOHANNESBURG

Dear Mr. Soyinka,

I refer to your telefax of January 15, addressed to Mr. Egeland.

The Ministry would like to help in providing up to 10 tickets for the delegates. The Ministry's travel agency, Bennett Reisebureau, will handle the practical side of it, by issuing so-called "pre-paid tickets".

In order for Bennett to proceed we need the following information for each ticket holder:

1. Full name (and if available: telephone/fax where he/she can be reached)
2. Travel route (i.e. airport of departure, destination (Johannesburg?) and return)
3. Dates for travel (departure and return)

Page 1 of 2 page(s)

If pages are missing, call:
+47 22 24 39 50

Wole Soyinka

African American Studies, Emory University
201B Candler Library Building, Atlanta, GA. 30322, U.S.A.
Tel. (1) 404 727 6847 Fax. (1) 404 256 3992

Mar. 9, 96

Tony Wohlfarth, CAW, Toronto, Canada.

Fax: 416 495 6559

Dear Tony Wohlfarth,

Michael Fleshman will have spoken to you before you receive this. We are still hunting for some eight tickets for prospective delegates to the Johannesburg pro-democracy summit - five from the U.S. and three from Nigeria. We have received some assistance from various bodies (including the Canadian government), but we still need those extra fares. Can your organisation assist?

The meeting is being hosted by the recently formed South Africa-Nigeria Democracy Support group, non-governmental, and made up of Human Rights organisations, COSATU, COSAW, lawyers and some other professional bodies. It will last from Jan 29 to Jan 30. The delegates from Nigeria, needless to say, will be making their way across the border to Benin or Ghana and will fly from there.

I can be reached at the above address. Any assistance, however little, will be most welcome.

Best Wishes,

Wole Soyinka
for National Liberation Council of Nigeria (NALICON)

Royal Ministry of Foreign Affairs
The State Secretary   Oslo, 4 June 1996

Dear Mr. Soyinka,

On behalf of the Norwegian Government I have earlier expressed to you the willingness and intention of Norway to support democratic organizations in your country and thus contribute to promote the fundamental human rights of the Nigerian people. On this background the Norwegian government have, through different channels, granted financial assistance to a number of pro-democracy and human rights activities in Nigeria. I also have the pleasure to confirm to you that Norway will contribute, provided that other donors contribute to the same end, up to the amount of USD 200.000 to a pro-democracy radio for Nigeria.

The Norwegian Government will transfer funds to this activity as soon as you can present written confirmation from other donors of their similar commitment within a revised budget for the operations. Worldview International will be the formal recipient and channel for the Norwegian financial assistance, which will be subject to normal accounting and reporting procedures as decided by the Ministry of Foreign Affairs.

I hope this confirmation will help enable you to start the broadcasting as soon as possible to the benefit of the struggle for democracy in Nigeria and I look forward to hear from you in the near future on this issue.

Yours sincerely,

Jan Egeland

Wole Soyinka

African American Studies, Emory University
201B Candler Library Building, Atlanta, GA. 30322, U.S.A.
Tel. (1) 404 727 6847 Fax. (1) 404 256 3992

Maarch 9, 96

His Excellency the Ambassador,
South African Republic
Washington, D.C.

Attention: The Consular Officers, South African Consulates, U.S.A.

Your Excellency,

I have the honour to refer to the forthcoming meeting of Nigerian pro-democracy groups, in Johannesburg on March 29-30, being hosted by the South Africa-Nigeria Democracy Support Group. Archbishop Desmond Tutu has kindly consented to open the conference, subject to the constraints of his duties on the South African Truth Commission.

I attach a list of *bona fide* delegates to this conference in support of their applications for visas at your consulates. Your kind assistance in facilitating their requests will be greatly appreciated. A supplementary list may follow, as we do have a wait list of delegates still seeking sponsorship.

Please accept my sincere fraternal good wishes, and our gratitude once again to the South African government for its solidarity with the democratic struggle of the Nigerian people.

Wole Soyinka
Political Spokesman, NALICON.

Department of Foreign Affairs and International Trade

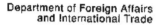

Ministère des Affaires étrangères et du Commerce international

Ottawa, Canada K1A 0G2

Secretary of State
(Latin America and Africa)

Secrétaire d'État
(Amérique latine et Afrique)

March 7, 1996

GAF-0278

Dr. Wole Soyinka
African-American Studies
Emory University
201-B Candler Library Bldg.
Atlanta, Georgia 30322
USA

Dear Dr. Soyinka, *Wole*

Thank you for your letter of February 22. It was good to see you again in Ottawa a month earlier.

As regards the Nigeria Democracy Summit in Johannesburg at the end of March, I am pleased to confirm that CIDA will be assisting two participants from Canada (Democratic Alliance for Nigeria in Canada). Our High Commission in Lagos is also assisting at least three participants from Nigeria to attend.

I wish you well in the further preparations for the Summit, and hope that our favourable decisions will help you attract the support you need for participants from the USA.

Since some of the work of the Summit is addressed to the international community and some sessions appear open to observers, we would like, if you agree, to have our High Commission in Pretoria cover it for Canada.

Yours sincerely,

Christine Stewart

[handwritten:] ~~Establishes~~ ~~Nigeria as~~ Nigeria as a threat to regional security in Africa and ~~the~~ ~~its~~ democratic governments on the continent.

The future, rebuilding
  Think tanks and policy units
  Research units

Afternoon Session

This will be devoted to a discussion of the role of the international community in the liberation struggle, focussing on sanctions, the use of International Legal Instruments, the role of the International Trade Unions etc. *[handwritten: shipping and]*

[handwritten:] A call on the world's Trade Unions to refuse to handle ~~oil~~ *[various]* products, especially oil.
Clear, consistent and repeated statements of what the prodemocracy movement regards as an acceptable minimum from this regime, ie (Release June 12th results, Immediate departure, Govt of National Unity headed by Abiola, release of all political prisoners.)

Outline the steps of escalation that we wish the international community to take to put pressure on the regime to leave; preventative diplomacy etc (Diplomatic, business and sporting isolation, asset freeze, travel limitations, sanctions, etc).

Engage in a diplomatic offensive aimed at uniting the countries who have taken a strong stand so far. This will bolster Mandela's current stand and provide new links and support for countries who are currently subject to blackmail by the junta.It will hopefully give the international organizations a lead to follow *[handwritten: Demand for a United Nations Commissioner of Human Rights]*
Assistance with the legal offensive based around human rights abuses and corruption
The role that international trade union solidarity can ~~assist in strengthening the genuine~~ *[handwritten: play in restoring the autonomy of]* indigenous labour movement, and in implementing actions against the regime and major supporters such as Shell.

~~Advice and~~ Assistance from delveloping countries ~~who~~ *[handwritten: which]* have transitioned democratic rule.
[handwritten:] The question of a government in exile,

Morning Session of February 3rd

This session will focus on the role of the pro-democracy movement, aid and support for the pro-democracy movement.

The role of the Pro democracy movement
  Improving our effectiveness and efficiency
  Uniting the movement, and creating an alternative "Focus" for international diplomacy.
  (Alternative Governance)
  Improving performance: (Infrastructure, administration, communication, professionalism).

Improving Aid and support
  (See Nigerian Pro democracy Aid Committee proposal)

Afternoon Session

Adoption of consensus statement and Charter of Democracy.

[handwritten in right margin: dictators]

[handwritten:] Invitation to foreign business interests: look to long-term advantages ~~begin~~ ~~of~~ support for the enthronement of a democratic ~~respectable~~ acceptable open government ~~as opposed to~~ the short-term gains from collaboration with a discredited, corrupt and inhumane regime.

We will meet tomorrow to finalise the agenda and then I'll send it to Dele. Please give me your comments so I can pass them on tommorrow.

This is what I wrote to Dele, it summarises what I understand so far:

Dear Dele

[handwritten:] A ~~call to~~ call to governments to publicise details of funds ~~settle~~ lodged within their banking systems by military ~~officers~~ rulers and their civilian collaborators

Nadeco have expanded it into a programme as below (normal type). In italics are my
suggestions for Nalicon positions or points for discussion for each agenda item.

Draft Programme For The Nigerian Summit

February 1st: Opening Session

Welcome address by Chairman of Conference - NADECO
Opening address by President N. Mandela or his representative
Keynote address by Professor Wole Soyinka - NALICON
Solidarity messages from ANC, COSATU, Council of Churches and other invited guests.
Tea break to allow President Mandela to depart
~~Speeches~~ by leaders of delegations

[handwritten left margin: brief Statements]

Break for lunch

Afternoon session: Debate on ~~alternative to Military~~ *terminating military rule and outlining* ~~the~~ *the structure of its replacement.*
This will be a free discussion on how to force the departure of the military and implement a democratic
structure based on June 12 mandate.

Removal of the junta
Encourage Civil disobedience / Mass mobilisation (Education mass communication)
~~Promote and Sustain~~
~~Sustain and encourage~~ *International pressure.*
Refuse to negotiate or dialogue with the military; they leave on our terms.
Refuse to recognise and participate in any part of the transition programme.
Create problems by AMN.   ✓

Implementing democratic structure (based on Chief Enahoros address)
Immediate release of Chief M.K.O.
Government of National Unity and Reconciliation led by him
Release all political detainees and convene a Sovereign National Conference to: Re-negotiate
the basis and structure of the Nigerian Federation and Frame a new constitution for the country.   ✓
A Policy on Minorities ~~and Issue~~ *and the Devolution of Revenue*

February 2nd: Morning Session

This will focus on how to foster democracy and good government in post military Nigeria, deterring
military return to the Nigerian political scene, and planning for a democratic future, and the rebuilding
of Nigeria.

Fostering good government
Expose the misdeeds of the junta/civilian members of regime. *Set* ~~Setting~~ *up machinery for* *restitution*
Education / mass communication
~~Sovereign National conference~~
A Permanent Commission on Corruption and Abuse of office.

Deterring Military return
~~Forcing~~ *recognition of June 12th* *election results* ~~order~~ *essential to upholding this*
~~Disgrace them out of office~~ *Sanctity of popular will in the choice of leadership*
Embark on an legal offensive ~~based around~~ *against human rights abuses and corruption*
Educate both the military and civilian population in the role of the military in developing
country
Restructure the military — *decentralisation and redefinition of role.*
Creation of civilian militia.
A Commission on Civilian-Military Relations

Wole Soyinka

African American Studies, Emory University
201B Candler Library Building, Atlanta, GA. 30322, U.S.A.
Tel. (1) 404 727 6847 Fax. (1) 404 256 3992

May 23, 96

Barbara Hendricks, Corsier, Switzerland   41 21 964 76 27

Hallo Barbara,

I knew I had a very slim chance of catching you while I was in Solothurn/Zurich for a just concluded Literary Festival. If I had, I would have briefed you directly on developments regarding the Democracy Conference. The enclosed letters explain the present position.

As you will observe, the venue is prepared for us; all we have to do is assist the delegates to get there. Towards that end however, the immediate task is to get our three contact agents into Nigeria - in short, an immediate need for three tickets to Lagos. Could your organisation assist us tackle that, firstly? They are all three in London - the contact is Dr. Kayode Fayemi: Phone: 44 171 403 8599, Fax: 44 171 403 6985.

You are probably still in Tokyo, but I hope this catches up with you wherever. I leave for Italy on Monday 27th, moving towards Stockholm for the 12th June meeting. I shall brief you fully on the various projects going on, and the assistance we are receiving in some friendly quarters. That way, you will always know what areas require help.

We are eager to set a date for Dakar, but can only do that after these emissaries return from their mission. **Do remember that we must continue to maintain confidentiality about the venue.**

See you in Stockholm, but let me hear from you before then if possible.

**National Liberation Council
of Nigeria**

URGENT.

Jan Egeland, Secretary of State, Oslo, Norway   Fax: 47 22 833 934

from: Wole Soyinka, Ca. USA. Phone/Fax 1 - 909 - 987 - 6741

Dear Jan Egeland,

Last week, we were contacted by a newly formed South Africa-Nigeria pro-Democracy Aid Committee - made up of Human Rights Lawyers, ANC, and Trade Unions - who wish to sponsor a mini-summit of the various Nigerian Human Rights and pro-democracy groups in Johannesburg. The initiative was taken when the group learnt of my impending visit to South Africa (Jan 27 - 30), and the meeting has been scheduled for Feb. 1- 3. Already the organisers have contacted groups within Nigeria and invitations have been sent out.

Their resources appear to be limited and, while accomodation and hospitality have been guaranteed, we are expected to raise the travel costs for most of the participants travelling from Europe and the United States. Some of these have already signalled their ability to pay for their own delegates but we are still short of about ten tickets - four from Europe and six from the United States. There is also the likelihood that the Campaign for Democracy (CD) in Nigeria will seek assistance from your embassy in Lagos.

Any assistance can be routed through NALICON's U.S. office. I can also be reached directly through the phone/fax number given above.

Once again, my profound thanks for the moral and practical support of your government.

Wole Soyinka

Tel: 171 403 8599; Fax: 171 403 6985
UK: NALICON, Hiteck House, Suite 58, 18 Beresford Ave, Wembley, Mddx HA0 IAY
USA: Tel:(617) 364 4455, Fax: (617) 364 7362

INDEX